Organic Chemistry Lab II

CHEM 30476

Kent State University

WILEY *Custom*
LEARNING SOLUTIONS

To order books or for customer service, please call 1(800)-CALL-WILEY (225-5945).

Printed in the United States of America.

ISBN 978-1-118-44014-8

Printed and bound by EPAC.

SKY38CC05E8-CDB9-40B2-A52D-FB68D2F38ECF_120623

CONTENTS

Chapter 1	Safety in the Chemical Laboratory	3
Chapter 2	Glassware and Equipment in the Laboratory	15
Chapter 3	Organic Reactions: from Starting Materials to Pure Organic Product	69
Chapter 4	Qualitative Analysis of Organic Compounds	204
Chapter 5	Spectroscopic Analysis of Organic Compounds	276
Chapter 6	Keeping Records: the Laboratory Notebook and Chemical Literature	397
Experiment 60	Diels–Alder preparation of *cis*-cyclohex-4-ene-1,2-Dicarboxylic acid	591
Experiment 16	Preparation of 4-bromomethylbenzoic acid by radical substitution and conversion to 4-methoxymethylbenzoic acid by nucleophilic substitution	468
Experiment 51	Preparation of 4-vinylbenzoic acid by a Wittig reaction in aqueous medium	563
Experiment 6	Preparation of 4-bromoaniline (*p*-bromoaniline)	439
Appendix 1	Hazardous Properties of Chemicals	669
Appendix 2	Organic Solvents	677
Appendix 3	Spectroscopic Correlation Tables	683
Index of Chemicals		699
General Index		705

EXPERIMENTAL ORGANIC CHEMISTRY

Standard and Microscale

LAURENCE M. HARWOOD
BSc, MSc, PhD (Manch), MA (Oxon), CChem, FRSC
Department of Chemistry, University of Reading

CHRISTOPHER J. MOODY
BSc (Lond), PhD (L'pool), DSc (Lond), CChem, FRSC
School of Chemistry, University of Exeter

JONATHAN M. PERCY
BSc (Lond), PhD (Cantab)
School of Chemistry, University of Birmingham

Second Edition

Blackwell
Science

Harwood – Experimental Organic Chemistry

© 1989, 1999 by Blackwell Science Ltd, a Blackwell Publishing company

Editorial Offices:
Blackwell Science Ltd, 9600 Garsington Road, Oxford OX4 2DQ, UK
  Tel: +44 (0)1865 776868
Blackwell Publishing Inc., 350 Main Street, Malden, MA 02148-5020, USA
  Tel: +1 781 388 8250
Blackwell Science Asia Pty, 550 Swanston Street, Carlton, Victoria 3053, Australia
  Tel: +61 (0)3 8359 1011

First published 1989
Reprinted 1990, 1992, 1994, 1995, 1996 (twice)
Second edition published 1999
11   2012

ISBN: 978-0-6320-4819-9

Library of Congress Cataloging-in-Publication Data

Harwood, Laurence M.
    Experimental organic chemistry:
standard and microscale. –2nd ed. / Laurence M. Harwood, Christopher J. Moody,
Jonathan M. Percy.
      p.   cm.
    Includes bibliographical references and indexes.
      ISBN 978-0-6320-4819-9 PBK
      ISBN 978-0-6320-5246-2 HBK
      1. Chemistry, Organic – Laboratory
manuals. I. Moody, Christopher
J. II. Percy, Jonathan M. III. Title
    QD261.H265   1998
    547'.0028–dc21   98-13113
                                                          CIP

A catalogue record for this title is available from the British Library

Set by Excel Typesetters, Hong Kong
Printed and bound in Malaysia by Vivar Printing Sdn Bhd

Contents

Preface to the Second Edition, vii

Part 1: Laboratory Practice

1   Safety in the Chemical Laboratory, 3

2   Glassware and Equipment in the Laboratory, 15

3   Organic Reactions: from Starting Materials to Pure Organic
    Product, 69

4   Qualitative Analysis of Organic Compounds, 204

5   Spectroscopic Analysis of Organic Compounds, 276

6   Keeping Records: the Laboratory Notebook and Chemical
    Literature, 397

Part 2: Experimental Procedures

Introduction, 421

List of Experiments, 424

Experiments which can be Taken in Sequence, 427

Experiments which Illustrate Particular Techniques, 428

7   Functional Group Interconversions, 429

8   Carbon–Carbon Bond-Forming Reactions, 522

9   Projects, 612

Appendices, 667

Index of Chemicals, 699

General Index, 705

Preface to the Second Edition

This book grew out of our conviction that highly developed practical skills, as well as a thorough grasp of theory, are the hallmark of an organic chemist and that chemistry is illustrated more vividly by experiment than from a book or lecture course, when the facts can seem abstract and sterile. Our aim therefore, was to produce a book containing safe, interesting experiments of varying complexity, together with all the associated technical instruction, which could be used in a variety of courses from the elementary to the advanced.

With the goal of enthusing people we have attempted to design experiments which are more than just recipes for preparing a particular compound, or manipulative exercises. Rather, we have attempted to wrap each experiment around some important reaction, an interesting mechanism, or an underlying principle; without forgetting the practical skills to be acquired along the way. Within the constant and overriding demands for safety, the range of experiments has been chosen to illustrate as many techniques and cover as much organic chemistry as possible, in order to link up with lecture courses, and provide depth and relevance to the whole teaching programme.

As with most practical texts, the book is divided into two main sections; the former surveying aspects of safety, apparatus, purification and analytical techniques, and the recording and retrieval of data; the latter containing the experimental procedures and appendices. In keeping with our aim of covering a range of procedures commonly used in the research laboratory, the first section involves a progression, from the basic apparatus and techniques required in the initial stages of a teaching course to the level of sophistication demanded at research level work. For instance, along with the more traditional descriptions, such as setting up a reduced pressure distillation or using a vacuum desiccator, are directions for analysis by gas chromatography, transferral of air-sensitive liquids by syringe, and the handling of pressurized gases. In line with current trends, the second edition contains additional sections covering the specific apparatus and techniques associated with microscale manipulations, which have found favour in many teaching laboratories due to the economy of working at reduced scale and the concomitant reduction in associated hazards and disposal of waste. Selected experiments in the second section have been chosen to exemplify this approach and are presented as both 'standard' and 'microscale' procedures. For this reason, Jonathan Percy has joined the team and has been responsible for preparing these aspects of the second edition.

As this is a practical book, greater emphasis has usually been placed on describing the practical aspects of the techniques, with any theoretical treatment being supported by cross-referencing to other works. However, space has been devoted to both the theoretical and practical aspects of spectroscopic analysis, and we make no apologies for this in light of the crucial role played by such analytical techniques. We have retained the contribution on NMR spectroscopy made by Dr Andy Derome but are deeply saddened to record his tragic and untimely death in 1991, aged 33.

Despite the emphasis on spectroscopy, the book does not ignore the more traditional elements of qualitative analysis as, although such methods have now been largely superseded by spectroscopic methods of analysis, they are invaluable for developing small-scale manipulation techniques as well as fostering an appreciation of physical and chemical properties of different classes of compound.

The second section of the book, containing the experimental procedures, has been further subdivided into chapters covering functional group interconversions, carbon–carbon bond-forming reactions, and projects. Within the first two subdivisions, we have attempted to include examples of most of the important reaction types at varying levels of experimental difficulty, so that a concerted series of experiments might be designed that is tailored to the specific teaching needs of a class or an individual student. Thus, for example, in the chapter on functional group interconversions, there is a series of experiments on reduction reactions and these range in difficulty from a simple ketone reduction with sodium borohydride to an advanced level experiment that uses an alkali metal in liquid ammonia. Likewise, in the chapter on carbon–carbon bond-forming reactions, you will find experiments involving simple carbonyl condensation reactions, progressing through to examples of modern enolate chemistry. Indeed, it is our hope that the experiments in these two chapters will come to be recognized as 'standard procedures' for carrying out, say, a lithium aluminium hydride reduction, a chromium (VI) oxidation, or a Wittig reaction. The final chapter contains experiments which are loosely described as projects. These experiments include natural product extractions, multi-stage syntheses, and physical organic investigations. We particularly wanted this chapter to reflect not only synthetic work, but also fundamental investigative work on the properties of organic compounds and on the mechanisms of organic reactions. As well as duplicating selected procedures in microscale in the second edition, several experiments from the first edition which have been judged to be less easily repeated or unduly duplicative have been deleted, while other new procedures have been included to reflect recent developments in organic chemistry.

Safety in the laboratory was always the paramount consideration when choosing an experiment, and we have attempted to minimize potential hazards by avoiding toxic materials wherever possible and by highlighting in the text any possible hazards at appropriate points of the procedure. In addition, the scale of each standard experimental procedure has been kept as small as is commensurate with the level of difficulty, to minimize any adverse consequences of an accident, in addition to lessening disposal problems and cost.

Within this consideration, the experiments have been chosen for their reproducibility and educational content. To this end the experiments have been independently assessed by chemists from around the world. Each experiment is preceded by a general discussion, outlining the aims and salient features of the investigation, and is followed by a series of problems designed to emphasize the points raised in the experiment. To make the greatest use of time available in the teaching laboratory and encourage forward planning, apparatus, instruments and chemicals required in the experiment are listed at the beginning of the procedure; together with an estimation of the amount of time necessary to complete the experiment. Wherever possible, extended periods of reflux or stirring have been avoided and long experiments have been designed so that they have clear break points at roughly 3 h intervals, indicated as margin notes in the procedure. The degree of difficulty of each experiment is also indicated:

1 = introductory level experiments requiring little previous experience;
2 = longer experiments with the emphasis on developing basic experimental techniques;
3 = experiments using more complex techniques and spectroscopic analysis;
4 = research level.

However, it must be remembered that the time and level assessments are only subjective guidelines and should not be taken as absolute. The use of spectroscopic analysis in level 3 and 4 experiments for characterization of materials reflects the overwhelming importance of these techniques in organic chemistry. However, it is not necessary to have access to spectrometers to carry out these experiments, as IR and NMR spectra of most of the compounds prepared are contained in the Aldrich Libraries of IR and NMR data. References to these, together with data on yields and melting points, useful hints and checkers' comments for each experiment, and guidelines for answers to all of the problems, are contained in an accompanying manual which is available to instructors from the publisher, free of charge.

It was not our intention to provide an exhaustive series of tables of these data in this book, as we felt it desirable to encourage the use of the chemical literature and other sources of data instead of providing all information necessary. Nevertheless, we have brought together some data in appendices at the back of the book (hazards, purification and properties of solvents, spectroscopic data) which we felt were liable to be of greatest use both to students working for their first degree as well as research chemists.

Finally we would like to acknowledge certain individuals whose help has been fundamental in the production of this book. Special thanks go to Dr Neil Isaacs of the University of Reading who provided us with a series of experiments for inclusion, particularly those having a physical organic slant, and the late Dr Andy Derome for the section on NMR spectroscopy. We would like to thank Professor Charles Rees of Imperial College for his involvement with the project from the beginning and his encouragement to take it on in the first place. Mr Peter Heath and Dr Simon Tyler kindly recorded the NMR and IR spectra which are reproduced in the experimental section of the book. Dr Jeffrey Seeman, Philip Morris Research, and Dr Jeremy Evans and Dr Guy Casy, University of Oxford, spent much spare time on the first edition and provided us with many valuable comments. We also reiterate our gratitude to those who checked the original experimental procedures or who subsequently suggested valuable modifications. In addition, we thank members of our research groups who checked the new procedures and the microscale variants in the second edition—these are the sort of enthusiastic organic chemists we hope this book will be instrumental in producing.

On the book production side we would like to thank Anne Stanford for her help and efforts in making this second edition a reality, and Nick Parsons, whose hard work on the first edition made the second edition so much easier to produce.

Laurence Harwood
Department of Chemistry
University of Reading
Whiteknights
Reading RG6 6AD

Jonathan Percy
School of Chemistry
University of Birmingham
Edgbaston
Birmingham B15 2TT

Chris Moody
School of Chemistry
University of Exeter
Stocker Road
Exeter EX4 4QD

PART 1
LABORATORY
PRACTICE

1   Safety in the Chemical Laboratory, 3

2   Glassware and Equipment in the Laboratory, 15

3   Organic Reactions: from Starting Materials to Pure Organic
    Product, 69

4   Qualitative Analysis of Organic Compounds, 204

5   Spectroscopic Analysis of Organic Compounds, 276

6   Keeping Records: the Laboratory Notebook and Chemical
    Literature, 397

Chapter 1 Safety in the Chemical Laboratory

The chemistry laboratory is a dangerous environment in which to work. The dangers are often unavoidable since chemists regularly have to use hazardous materials. However, with sensible precautions the laboratory is probably no more dangerous than your home, be it house or apartment, which, if you stop to think about it, also abounds with hazardous materials and equipment—household bleach, pharmaceutical products, herbicides and insecticides, natural or bottled gas, kitchen knives, diverse electrical equipment, the list goes on and on—all of which are taken for granted. In the same way that you learn to cope with the hazards of everyday life, so you learn good laboratory practice, which goes a long way to minimize the dangers of organic chemistry.

The experiments in this book have been carefully chosen to exclude or restrict the use of exceptionally hazardous materials, whilst still highlighting and exemplifying the major reactions and transformations of organic chemistry. However, most chemicals are harmful in some respect, and the particular hazards associated with the materials for each experiment are clearly stated; **these warnings should not be ignored**. Unfortunately it has not been possible to exclude totally the use of some chemicals, such as chloroform, which are described as 'cancer suspect agents', but if handled correctly with proper regard for the potential hazard, there is no reason why such compounds cannot be used in the organic laboratory. Ultimately, laboratory safety lies with the individual; *you* are responsible for carrying out the experiment in a safe manner without endangering yourself or other people, and therefore it is *your* responsibility to learn and observe the essential safety rules of the chemical laboratory.

1.1 Essential rules for laboratory safety

The essential rules for laboratory safety can be expressed under two simple headings: ALWAYS and NEVER.

Most of these rules are common sense and need no further explanation. Indeed if asked to name the single most important factor which contributes towards safety in the laboratory, the answer is simple: common sense.

ALWAYS
- familiarize yourself with the laboratory safety procedures
- wear eye protection
- dress sensibly
- wash your hands before leaving the laboratory
- read the instructions carefully before starting any experiment
- check that the apparatus is assembled correctly
- handle all chemicals with great care
- keep your working area tidy
- attend to spills immediately
- ask your instructor if in doubt

NEVER
- eat or drink in the laboratory
- smoke in the laboratory
- inhale, taste or sniff chemicals
- fool around or distract your neighbours
- run in the laboratory
- work alone
- carry out unauthorized experiments

Laboratory safety procedures

Your laboratory will have certain safety procedures with which you must be familiar. Some of these procedures are legal requirements; others will have been laid down by the department. Make sure you know where all the exits to the laboratory are, in the event of an evacuation because of fire or other incident. Make sure that you know the precise location of fire extinguishers, fire blankets, sand buckets, safety showers, and eye-wash stations. Make sure you know what type the fire extinguishers are, and how to operate them, especially how to remove the safety pin.

Eye protection

You must wear eye protection at all times in the laboratory. Even if you are just writing in your notebook, your neighbour may be handling corrosive chemicals. Eyes are particularly vulnerable to damage from sharp objects such as broken glass, and from chemicals, and therefore must always be protected to prevent permanent damage. Protection should be in the form of approved safety goggles or safety glasses. Ordinary prescription glasses do not provide adequate protection, since they do not have side shields, and may not have shatter-proof lenses. If you are going to do a lot of laboratory work, it is probably worth getting a pair of safety glasses fitted with prescription lenses. Alternatively, wear goggles over your normal glasses for full protection.

Contact lenses

Contact lenses are often forbidden in chemical laboratories, because in the event of an accident, chemicals can get under the lens and damage the eye before the lens can be removed. Even if contact lenses are permitted, then you must wear well-fitting goggles for protection. Inform your instructor, the laboratory staff and your neighbours that you are wearing contact lenses so that they know what to do in case of accident. Although no experiments in this book require them, full face shields should be worn for particularly hazardous operations. If a chemical does get into the eye, you must take swift action. The appropriate action is discussed on p. 13.

Dress

Dress sensibly in the laboratory. The laboratory is no place to wear your best clothes, since however careful you are, small splashes of organic chemicals or acids are inevitable. For this reason, shorts or short skirts are unsuitable for laboratory work and are forbidden in many institutions. A laboratory coat should always be worn, and loose fitting sleeves which might catch on flasks, etc. should be rolled back. Long hair is an additional hazard, and should always be tied back. Proper shoes should be worn; there may be pieces of broken glass on the laboratory floor, and sandals do not provide adequate protection from glass or from chemical spills.

Equipment and apparatus

Never attempt to use any equipment or apparatus unless you fully understand its function. This is particularly true of items such as vacuum pumps, rotary evaporators and cylinders of compressed gas, where misuse can lead to the damage of expensive equipment, your experiment being ruined or, most serious of all, an accident. Remember the golden rule:

If in doubt, ask.

Before assembling the apparatus for your experiment, check that the glassware is free from cracks and 'stars'. Always check the apparatus is properly clamped and supported and correctly assembled *before* adding any chemicals. Again, if in any doubt as to how to assemble the apparatus, ask.

Handling chemicals

Chemicals are hazardous because of their toxic, corrosive, flammable or explosive properties. Examples of the various categories of hazardous chemicals are given in the next section, but all chemicals should always be handled with great care. The major hazard in the organic laboratory is fire. Most organic compounds will burn when exposed to an open flame, and many, particularly solvents, which are often present in large quantities in the laboratory, are highly flammable. A serious solvent fire can raise the temperature of the laboratory to well over 100°C within minutes of it starting. Good laboratory practice really demands that there should be no open flames in the organic laboratory. Steam baths, heating mantles and hotplates should be used wherever possible to heat reaction mixtures and solvents. In many laboratories, the Bunsen burner is still the main source of heat, and therefore a strict code of practice is needed to prevent serious fires. **Never** light a burner before checking that there are no flammable liquids in open containers in the vicinity. Conversely **never** transfer a flammable liquid without checking that there are no open flames in the vicinity. The correct use of burners is discussed in more detail in Chapter 2. Remember that solvent vapour is heavier than air and will therefore travel along bench tops and down into sinks and drains; never pour flammable solvents down the sink.

Always check for flammable solvents before lighting a burner

Never pour flammable solvents down the sink

Avoid inhaling the vapours from organic compounds at all times and whenever possible use a reliable fume hood. The use of a good fume hood is essential for operations involving particularly toxic materials and for reactions that evolve irritating or toxic vapours.

Wear gloves when handling corrosive chemicals

Avoid skin contact with chemicals at all times. This is particularly important when handling corrosive acids and chemicals that are easily absorbed through the skin. It is best to wear disposable plastic gloves for routine laboratory operations; this minimizes the risk of chemicals coming into contact with the skin, but you must always be alert to the risk of seepage under the glove which will exacerbate the dangers due to the material being held in close contact with the skin. The risk is also reduced by good housekeeping, ensuring that your bench and areas around the balance are kept clean and tidy. When highly corrosive or toxic chemicals are being handled, thin disposable gloves are inadequate and thick protective gloves must be worn. However, remember to remove gloves before leaving the laboratory; do not contaminate door handles and other surfaces with soiled gloves.

Spills

All chemical spills should be cleared up immediately. Always wear gloves when dealing with a spill. Solids can be swept up and put in an appropriate waste container. Liquids are more difficult to deal with. Spilled acids must be neutralized with solid sodium bicarbonate or sodium carbonate, and alkalis must be neutralized with sodium bisulfate. Neutral liquids can be absorbed with sand or paper towels, although the use of sand is strongly advised, since paper towels are not appropriate for certain spills. If the spilled liquid is very volatile, it is often best to clear the area, extinguish all lighted burners and let the liquid evaporate. When highly toxic chemicals are spilt, alert your neighbours, inform your instructor, ventilate and clear the area immediately.

1.2   Hazardous chemicals

One of the fundamental rules of laboratory safety requires you to read the instructions before starting any experiment. The experimental procedures in this book contain clear warnings about the hazards associated with any particular material or operation. The properties of chemicals are given as a simple one word hazard warning—**flammable**, **explosive**, **oxidizer**, **corrosive**, **toxic**, **cancer suspect agent**, **irritant**, **lachrymator**—although some chemicals may fall into more than one hazard category. These warnings are similar to the warnings that are given on reagent bottles, although these are often accompanied by a symbol or sign. These symbols are usually the standard hazard signs required by the regulatory authorities. For instance, in the United States, the Department of Transportation is the responsible body, and in Europe there is an EU directive about warning signs. The hazard labels are usually square or diamond shaped, and consist of a pictorial warning together with appropriate words. Some examples of the commonly used symbols are shown in Fig. 1.1, and examples of each type of hazardous chemical are given below. In addition, Appendix 1 (p. 670) lists about 100 commonly encountered laboratory solvents, chemicals and reagents with a summary of their hazardous properties.

Flammable reagents

Always follow the general guidelines (pp. 5–6) when handling flammable reagents, **continually checking that there are no open flames in the vicinity**.

Solvents constitute the major flammable material in the organic laboratory. The following organic solvents are all commonly used and are highly flammable: hydrocarbons such as *hexane, light petroleum (petroleum ether), benzene, toluene*; alcohols such as *ethanol* and *methanol*; esters such as *ethyl acetate*; ketones such as *acetone*.

Ethers require a special mention because of their tendency to form explosive peroxides on exposure to air and light. *Diethyl ether* and *tetrahydrofuran* are particularly prone to this and should be handled with great care. In addi-

Fig. 1.1 Common hazard warning signs.

tion, diethyl ether has a very low flash point and has a considerable narcotic effect.

Carbon disulfide is so flammable that even the heat from a steam bath can ignite it. The use of this solvent should be avoided at all times.

Additionally some gases, notably *hydrogen*, are highly flammable, as are some solids, particularly finely divided metals such as *magnesium* and *transition-metal catalysts*. Some solids such as *sodium* and *lithium aluminium hydride* are described as flammable because they liberate hydrogen on reaction with water.

Explosive reagents

Some chemicals constitute explosion hazards because they undergo explosive reactions with water or other common substances. The alkali metals are common examples: *sodium metal* reacts violently with water; *potassium metal* reacts explosively with water.

Other compounds contain the seeds of their own destruction. This usually means that the molecule contains a lot of oxygen and/or nitrogen atoms, and can therefore undergo internal redox reactions, or eliminate a stable molecule such as N_2. Such compounds are often highly shock sensitive and constitute a considerable explosion hazard particularly when dry. Examples include *polynitro compounds*, *picric acid*, *metal acetylides*, *azides*, *diazo compounds*, *peroxides* and *perchlorate salts*. These are avoided in procedures described in this book.

If you have to use potentially explosive reagents, wear a face mask, work on the smallest scale possible and work behind a shatter-proof screen. Never do so without consulting an instructor and alert others before commencing the procedure.

Oxidizers

Oxidizers are an additional hazard in the chemical laboratory, since they can cause fires simply by coming into contact with combustible material such as paper.

Nitric and *sulfuric acids*, as well as being highly corrosive, are both powerful oxidizers.

Reagents such as *bleach*, *ozone*, *hydrogen peroxide*, *peracids*, *chromium (VI) oxide* and *potassium permanganate* are all powerful oxidizers.

Corrosive reagents

Always wear appropriate protective gloves when handling corrosive reagents. Spills on the skin should be washed off immediately with copious amounts of water.

The following acids are particularly corrosive: *sulfuric*, *hydrochloric*, *hydrobromic*, *phosphoric* and *nitric*, as are organic acids such as *carboxylic acids* and *sulfonic acids*.

Phenol is a particularly hazardous chemical and causes severe burns, as well as being extremely toxic and rapidly absorbed through the skin.

Alkalis such as *sodium hydroxide*, *potassium hydroxide* and, to a lesser extent, *sodium carbonate* are also extremely corrosive as are *ammonia*, *ammonium hydroxide* and organic bases such as *triethylamine* and *pyrrolidine*.

Bromine is an extremely unpleasant chemical. It causes severe burns to the skin and eyes, and must be handled in a hood. In addition, its high density and volatility make it almost impossible to transfer with a pipette without spills.

Thionyl chloride, *oxalyl chloride*, *aluminium chloride* and other reagents which can generate HCl by reaction with water are also corrosive and cause severe irritation to the respiratory system.

Harmful and toxic reagents

Always handle toxic chemicals in the hood

The distinction between *harmful* and *toxic* is one of degree; most organic compounds can be loosely described as harmful, but many are much worse than that, and are therefore classified as toxic. Commonly encountered compounds that are particularly toxic and therefore must always be handled in a hood include: *aniline*, *benzene*, *bromine*, *dimethyl sulfate*, *chloroform*, *hexane*, *hydrogen sulfide*, *iodomethane*, *mercury salts*, *methanol*, *nitrobenzene*, *phenol*, *phenylhydrazine*, *potassium cyanide* and *sodium cyanide*. You must always be aware of the difference between *acute* and *chronic* toxicity. The effects of acute toxicity are usually recognizable more-or-less immediately (for example, inhalation of ammonia) and appropriate remedial action can be taken promptly. Chronic effects are much more pernicious, exerting their influence during long periods of exposure and generally only manifesting their effects when irrecoverable long-term damage has been caused. Many compounds are classed as *cancer suspect agents* for instance. This need not negate their use in the laboratory but does require particularly stringent precautions to avoid exposure and these compounds must always be handled in an efficient hood.

When using the fume hood, make sure that the glass front is pulled well down. This ensures sufficient air flow to prevent the escape of toxic fumes. As a general rule, never start any experiment involving a highly toxic chemical until you have read and understood the instructions and safety information, fully appreciate the nature of the hazard, and know what to do in the event of an accident.

Cancer suspect agents

The exposure of healthy cells to certain chemicals (carcinogens) is known to result in tumour formation. The period between the exposure and the appearance of tumours in people can be several years, and therefore the dangers are not immediately apparent. The utmost care is required when handling such chemicals. In this book we follow the current practice of labelling such reagents as **cancer suspect agents**. This means that the chemical is either known to cause tumours in people or in animals, or is strongly suspected of doing so.

The following compounds or compound types should be treated as cancer suspect agents: biological alkylating agents such as *iodomethane*, *epoxides* and *dimethyl sulfate*; *formaldehyde*; *hexane*; *benzene*; aromatic amines such as *2-naphthylamine* and *benzidine*; polynuclear aromatic hydrocarbons (PAHs) such as *benzpyrene*; hydrazines in general, *hydrazine* itself and *phenylhydrazine*; *nitrosamines*; *azo compounds*; *chromium (VI) compounds*; chlorinated hydrocarbons such as carbon tetrachloride; *chloroform* and *vinyl chloride*; *thiourea* and *semicarbazide hydrochloride*.

Irritants and lachrymators

Many organic compounds are extremely irritating to the eyes, skin and respiratory system. To minimize the chance of exposure to the reagent or its vapours, the following chemicals should always be handled in a hood: *benzylic* and *allylic halides*, α-halocarbonyl compounds such as *ethyl bromoacetate*, *isocyanates*, *thionyl chloride* and *acid chlorides*.

Some organic compounds, as well as being irritants, also have a particularly penetrating or unpleasant odour. These are usually indicated by the word **stench**, and examples include *pyridine*, *phenylacetic acid*, *dimethyl sulfide* and many other sulfur-containing compounds, *butyric acid* and *indole*. Again these chemicals should be confined to a well-ventilated hood.

1.3   Disposal of hazardous waste

Waste disposal is one of the major environmental problems of modern society and the safe disposal of potentially hazardous chemical waste places a great burden of responsibility on those in charge of laboratories. It is important that everyone who works in the organic laboratory appreciates the problems and exercises their individual responsibility to their fellow citizens and to the environment by not disposing of chemical waste in a thoughtless manner. In addition to statutory legal requirements, each laboratory will have its own rules and procedures for the disposal of chemical waste; we can only offer general advice and suggest some guidelines. More information about disposal methods can be found in the works mentioned at the end of this chapter.

Think before disposing of any chemical waste

Solid waste

Solid waste from a typical organic laboratory comprises such things as spent drying agents and chromatographic supports, used filter papers, discarded capillaries from the melting point apparatus and broken glass. Common sense is the guiding principle in deciding how to dispose of such waste. Unless the solid is toxic or finely divided (e.g. chromatographic silica, see p. 179) it can be placed in an appropriate container for non-hazardous waste. Filter papers can be disposed of in this way unless of course they are contaminated with toxic chemicals. Toxic waste should be placed in special appropriately labelled containers. It is the responsibility of your laboratory staff and your instructor to provide these containers and see that they are clearly labelled: it is *your* responsibility to use them. Some toxic chemicals need special treatment to render them less toxic before disposal. This often involves oxidation, but your instructor will advise you when this is necessary.

Broken glass, discarded capillaries and other 'sharp' items should be kept separate from general waste and should be placed in an appropriately labelled glass or sharps bin. Chromatography silica should be transferred to polythene bags in a fume hood after removal of excess solvent, moistened with water and the bags sealed for later disposal.

Water-soluble waste

It is very tempting to pour water-soluble laboratory waste down the sink and into the public sewer system. It then becomes a problem for someone else, namely the water authority. This is bad practice. The only waste that can safely be poured down the sink is non-toxic, neutral, non-odorous, water-soluble material such as discarded water layers from aqueous–organic extractions. The waste should be washed down with plenty of water, and strongly acidic or alkaline solutions should be neutralized before disposal. Any chemical that might react even with dilute acid or alkali should never be disposed of down *Never pour solvents down the* the sink. For safety's sake, if there is any doubt, do not dispose of material *sink* down the sink.

Organic solvents

Organic solvents are the major disposal problem in the organic laboratory. They are usually water immiscible and highly flammable, and often accumulate very quickly in a busy laboratory. Waste solvent should be poured into appropriately labelled containers, never down the sink. The containers are then removed from the laboratory for subsequent disposal of the solvents by burning. There should be two waste solvent containers—one for hydrocarbons and other non-chlorinated solvents and one for chlorinated solvents. Chlorinated solvents have to be handled differently during the combustion process since they generate hydrogen chloride. It is therefore very important *Never mix chlorinated and* that you do not mix the two types of waste solvent. If the waste container is *non-chlorinated solvents* full, ask the laboratory staff or your instructor for an empty one; do not be tempted to use the sink as an easily available receptacle.

1.4 Accident procedures

In the event of a laboratory accident, it is important that you know what to do. Prompt action is always necessary, whatever the incident. **Tell your instructor immediately**, or if you are incapacitated or otherwise occupied in dealing with the incident, ensure that someone else informs the instructor. It is the instructor's responsibility to organize and coordinate any action required.

Fire

For anything but the smallest fire, the laboratory should be cleared. Do not panic, but shout loudly to your colleagues to leave the laboratory. If you hear the order, do not become inquisitive: **get out**.

Burning chemicals

The most likely contenders for chemical fires are organic solvents. If the fire is confined to a small vessel such as a beaker, it can usually be contained by simply placing a large gauze or a bigger beaker over the vessel. Sand is also very useful for extinguishing small fires, and laboratories are often equipped with sand buckets for this purpose. Remove all other flammable chemicals from the vicinity, and extinguish any burners. Since most flammable solvents are less dense than water, **water must never be used to try to extinguish a solvent fire**; it will have the effect of spreading the fire rather than putting it out. For larger fires, a fire extinguisher is needed; a carbon dioxide or dry chemical type should be used. However, the use of fire extinguishers is best left to your instructor or other experienced person; incorrect use can cause the fire to spread. If the fire cannot be quickly brought under control using extinguishers, a general fire alarm should be sounded, the fire services summoned and the building evacuated.

Burning clothing

If your clothes are on fire, shout for help. Lie down on the floor and roll over to attempt to extinguish the flames. Do not attempt to get to the safety shower unless it is very near.

If a colleague's clothes catch fire, your prompt action may save his or her life. Prevent the person from running towards the shower; running increases the air supply to the fire and fans the flames. Wrap the person in a fire blanket or make them roll on the floor. Knock them over if necessary; a few bruises are better than burns. If a fire blanket is not immediately to hand, use towels or wet paper towels, or douse the victim with water. **Never use a fire extinguisher on a person**. If the safety shower is nearby then use it. Once you are sure the fire is out, make the person lie still, keep them warm and **send for qualified medical assistance**. Do not attempt to remove clothing from anyone who has suffered burns unless it is obstructing airways.

Burns

Minor heat burns from hot flasks, steam baths and the like are fairly common events in the organic laboratory. Usually the only treatment such minor burns require is to be held under cold running water for 10–15 min. Persons with more extensive heat burns need immediate medical attention.

Any chemical that is spilled on the skin should be washed off immediately with copious amounts of running water; the affected area should be flushed for at least 15 min. If chemicals are spilled over a large area of the body, use the safety shower. It is important to get to the shower quickly, and wash yourself or the affected person with large volumes of water. Any contaminated clothing should be removed, so that the skin can be thoroughly washed. **Obtain immediate medical attention.**

Chemicals in the eye

If chemicals get into the eye, time is of the essence, since the sooner the chemical is washed out, the less the damage. The eye must be flushed with copious amounts of water for at least 15 min using an eye-wash fountain or eye-wash bottle, or by holding the injured person on the floor and pouring water into the eye. You will have to hold the eye open with your fingers to wash behind the lids. **Always obtain prompt medical attention, no matter how slight the injury might seem.**

Cuts

Minor cuts from broken glass are a constant potential hazard when working in the chemistry laboratory. The cut should be flushed thoroughly with running water for at least 10 min to ensure that any chemicals or tiny pieces of glass are removed. Minor cuts should stop bleeding very quickly and can be covered with an appropriate bandage or sticking plaster. If the bleeding does not stop, obtain medical attention.

Major cuts, that is when blood is actually spurting from the wound, are much more serious. The injured person must be kept quiet and made to lie down with the wounded area raised slightly. A pad should be placed directly over the wound and firm pressure should be applied. **Do not apply a tourniquet.** The person should be kept warm. **Prompt medical assistance is essential;** an ambulance and doctor should be summoned immediately.

Poisoning

No simple general advice can be offered. **Obtain medical attention immediately.**

Further reading

Appendix 1 (p. 670) deals with the hazardous properties of some commonly encountered laboratory chemicals. However, there are a number of texts which deal with laboratory safety practices in general and with the specific properties of, and disposal of, hazardous chemicals. These texts are written by safety experts and give far more detail than is possible in this book. If in doubt, consult the experts.

Prudent Practices in the Laboratory for Handling and Disposal of Chemicals, National Research Council, National Academy Press, Washington DC, 1995.

L. Bretherick, *Bretherick's Handbook of Reactive Chemical Hazards*, Butterworth, London, 1990.

A.J. Collins and S.G. Luxon (eds) *Safe Use of Solvents*, Academic Press, New York, 1982.

M.J. Lefevre, *First Aid Manual for Chemical Accidents*, Dowden, Hutchinson & Ross, Stroudsberg, PA, 1980.

R.E. Lenga (ed.) *Sigma-Aldrich Library of Chemical Safety Data*, 2nd edn, 1988.

R.J. Lewis, *Hazardous Chemicals Desk Reference*, 4th edn, Van Nostrand Reinhold, New York, 1997.

G. Lunn and E.B. Sansone, *Destruction of Hazardous Chemicals in the Laboratory*, 2nd edn, Wiley & Sons, New York, 1994.

D.A. Pipitone, *Safe Storage of Laboratory Chemicals*, 2nd edn, Wiley & Sons, New York, 1991.

N.I. Sax and R.J. Lewis, *Sax's Dangerous Properties of Industrial Materials*, 9th edn, Van Nostrand Reinhold, New York, 1996.

Chapter 2   Glassware and Equipment in the Laboratory

In this chapter we will consider some of the standard pieces of glassware and equipment that you will use in the laboratory. The emphasis will be on descriptive detail (Chapter 3 is largely concerned with experimental techniques and assembly of apparatus), although the operation of equipment such as oil immersion rotary pumps will be dealt with here.

Broadly speaking, equipment can be divided into two categories—that which is communal and that which is personal. Cost is usually the factor which decides the category into which an item falls, although no hard and fast rules apply and any distinction is purely arbitrary. A further arbitrary division within each category might be made by dividing equipment into that which is glassware and that which is non-glassware. Glassware is fragile and so there is much more potential for breakage within this subdivision—particularly with personal glassware. Communal glass apparatus, such as rotary evaporators, tend to be built fairly ruggedly.

Adhering to the procedures described in this and the next chapter will result in safe working and should help to minimize breakages which are costly, not only in financial terms, but also in popularity.

Remember the golden rule for working in a laboratory:

If in doubt, ask.

Never plunge headlong into a strange procedure without first verifying the safe and correct way of carrying it out. Breaking a piece of apparatus is bad enough; injuring yourself—or somebody else—is a far worse consequence of carrying on regardless. *Never* rely simply on the advice of your neighbour; you must always get instruction from a qualified individual. *Never* be frightened of pestering and upsetting instructors; that is the job for which they are paid. In any event, the surest way to annoy an instructor is to break an expensive piece of equipment or cause an injury!

On entering the organic laboratory for the first time, the first job, of course, is to familiarize yourself with the laboratory safety procedures and with the location of fire extinguishers, safety showers, fire exits and so on. The second job, however, is to check out the equipment, both personal equipment stored in your bench or locker and communal equipment. Personal equipment can be divided into glass and non-glass (hardware), and your locker will contain a set of such items. Obviously there is no such thing as a standard set of equipment, since each laboratory provides what is deemed necessary for the courses that are taught therein, but our set (see Figs 2.1–2.4) is fairly typical for classes dealing with standard-scale laboratory procedures. Apparatus specifically designed for use in microscale experiments will be dealt with in the corresponding sections.

2.1 Glass equipment

Glass equipment can be divided into that with ground glass joints and that without. For convenience and ease of use, standard-taper ground glass joint equipment is strongly recommended. Apparatus for a range of organic experiments can be quickly and easily assembled from relatively few basic items. Standard-taper joints ($) are designated by numbers which refer to the diameter and length of the joint (in mm): for example, 14/20, 14/23, 19/22, 19/26 and 24/29. As the name implies, standard-taper joints are fully interchangeable with those of the same size.

Standard-taper ground glass joint equipment is expensive, but with careful handling is no more fragile than any other glassware. The only problem is with the joints themselves, and when assembling the apparatus it is usually better not to use grease. The only laboratory operations which require the use of grease on the ground glass joints of the apparatus are vacuum distillations using oil pumps for pressures lower than about 5 mmHg, and reactions involving hot sodium or potassium hydroxide solutions which will attack the glass. If grease is used it should be applied sparingly; a very thin smear around the joint is all that is required. Hydrocarbon-based greases are easier to remove from glassware than silicone greases. The misuse of grease can cause ground glass joints to become stuck or 'frozen'. Occasionally this happens anyway, and, of course, unless the joint can be unfrozen and the pieces of apparatus separated, the equipment becomes useless. As with many things, prevention is better than cure, and the best way to prevent frozen ground glass joints is to disassemble the apparatus as soon as it is finished with. Wipe the joints clean, checking that they are completely free of chemicals. Never leave assembled dirty apparatus lying around the laboratory. If, despite precautions, ground glass joints do become tightly frozen, it may be possible to loosen them by squirting a few drops of acetone (or other solvent) around the top of the joint. Capillary action may be enough to suck some solvent into the joint and loosen it. If this simple trick does not work, the joint may be loosened by gentle tapping, or failing that, by heating it in a flame. However, these techniques must be left to an expert. If you are unfortunate enough to break a piece of equipment that has a standard-taper ground glass joint, do not throw all the broken glass in the glass bin, but keep the ground glass joint (the expensive bit!) since your glass-blower may be able to utilize it. Some items of equip-

Care! Flammable solvent

ment, such as addition and separatory funnels, possess stopcocks. These may be ground glass or Teflon® and should be handled carefully to prevent the stopcock 'freezing' in the barrel. The correct use of separatory funnels is discussed in more detail on pp. 110–117.

A typical set of standard-taper glassware is shown in Fig. 2.1, and consists of:

- *round-bottomed flasks* for reactions, distillations;
- *three-neck flasks* for more complicated reaction set-ups (two-neck flasks are also available);
- *addition funnel* for adding liquids to reaction mixtures (may be cylindrical or pear-shaped);
- *separatory funnel* for extractions and reaction work-up;
- *condenser* for refluxing reaction mixtures, distillations;
- *air condenser* for high boiling liquids (can also be packed and used as a fractionating column);
- *drying tube* for filling with a drying agent and attaching to the apparatus to reduce the ingress of water;
- *stoppers*;
- *reduction/expansion adapters* for connecting equipment with different-sized joints;
- *still head* for distillation;
- *Claisen adapter* for distillation or converting a simple round-bottomed flask to a two-neck flask;
- *distillation adapter* for distillation;
- *vacuum distillation adapter* for distillation under reduced pressure;
- *take off adapter* for attaching to tubing;
- *thermometer/tubing adapter* for inserting thermometer or glass tube into apparatus.

Glass equipment with and without ground glass joints is available in small sizes. However, there are certain drawbacks in simply using small-scale versions of equipment with standard-taper ground glass joints, because the joint size becomes large with respect to the volume of the reaction and vapour path lengths increase proportionally. One obvious solution is to use the hemispherical ground glass joints which usually involve a smaller area of surface contact between male and female components, but most commercial microscale kits solve this problem by either replacing the male/female glass joint with a polytetrafluoroethylene (PTFE) ferrule, or alternatively, by securing the joint with a threaded closure and a *greaseless* 'O'-ring compression seal. An extensive range of the latter type of glassware is offered by several commercial suppliers. The equipment is robust and offers reasonable resistance to corrosion while resembling closely in appearance the more familiar macroscale ground glass equipment (Claisen adapters, reflux condensers, vacuum distillation adapters, etc.). The fragility of small reaction flasks is offset by the use of

Fig. 2.1 Glass equipment with standard-taper ground glass joints.

thick-based tapered reaction vials (Fig. 2.2). Special microscale distillation equipment is also available (see pp. 154–159).

A typical set of microscale glassware would include:

- *reaction vials and round-bottomed flasks* for reactions, distillations;
- *jacketed condenser* for refluxing mixtures, distillations;

microscale reaction vessels: thick- and thin-walled
reaction vials and round bottomed flask

air and jacketed condensers   Hickman and Hickman–Hinkle stills

drying tube   vacuum distillation adapter   Claisen adapter   threaded adapter

Fig. 2.2 Microscale glass equipment.

- *air condenser* for high boiling liquids;
- *Hickman and Hickman–Hinkle* stills for distillation;
- *drying tube* for filling with a drying agent and attaching to the apparatus to reduce ingress of water;
- *vacuum distillation adapter* for distillation under reduced pressure;
- *Claisen adapter* for converting a single-neck reaction vial to a two-neck reaction vessel;
- *threaded adapter* for attaching a tubing connection to a reaction vial.

Non-graduated standard scale glassware without ground glass joints is much less expensive. A typical set might contain some of the items shown in Fig. 2.3:

- *beakers* for temporary storage or transfer of materials, reactions;
- *Erlenmeyer flasks* for recrystallization, collecting solutions after extraction (versions with ground glass joints are also available);
- *funnel* for transfer of liquids, filtration;
- *powder funnel* for transfer of solids;
- *stemless funnel* for hot filtration;
- *filter flask* (Büchner flask) for suction filtration;
- *Büchner funnel* for suction filtration;
- *Hirsch funnel* for suction filtration of small quantities;
- *Pasteur pipette* for transfer of smaller quantities of liquid;
- *graduated cylinders* for measuring liquids by volume;
- *graduated pipettes* for accurate measurement of liquids.

Check for cracks and 'stars'

When checking out the glassware in your bench, examine each piece carefully for cracks and 'star-cracks'. Star-cracks are often caused by two round-bottomed flasks impacting on each other, for example if a drawer full of flasks is opened too rapidly, so care should be taken to ensure round-bottomed flasks are not touching when stored. Any damaged equipment should be replaced from the stockroom. Try and get into the habit of checking glass equipment each time you use it. This is especially important for flasks; you certainly want to avoid a cracked flask breaking half-way through a reaction or distillation.

Cleaning and drying glassware

Good laboratory practice requires that organic reactions are carried out in clean glassware. Unless the reaction is being carried out in aqueous solution, the glassware should also be dry, since many organic chemistry experiments are ruined by the presence of water.

Glassware can usually be cleaned with water and either industrial detergent or a mild scouring powder using an appropriate brush. Make sure that you clean all the inside of the piece, and that you rinse it thoroughly with water afterwards. The final rinse should be with distilled or deionized water, and the glassware should be left upside down on a drying rack or on absorbent paper to dry. The glassware can be dried more quickly by placing it in a drying

beakers

Erlenmeyer flasks

funnel

powder funnel

stemless funnel

Büchner flask

Büchner funnel

Hirsch funnel

Pasteur pipette

graduated cylinders

graduated pipette

Fig. 2.3 Other glass equipment.

oven, and this is essential if it is to be used for a reaction involving air- or moisture-sensitive reagents. For *complete* drying, glass should be left in an oven at 125°C for at least 12 h (see also p. 81).

The drying process can also be speeded up by rinsing the wet glassware with acetone. Acetone is freely miscible with water, and rinsing a wet flask with 5–10 mL of washing acetone (*not* reagent grade acetone) removes the water. The acetone should be drained into the waste acetone bottle, not thrown down the sink. The remaining acetone in the flask evaporates quickly in the air, but the drying can be speeded up by drawing a stream of air through the flask. To do this, connect a *clean* piece of glass tube to the water aspirator via thick-walled tubing, turn on the suction and place the tube in the flask. Never use the compressed air line to dry equipment; the line is usually contaminated with dirt and oil from the compressor, and this will be transferred to your glassware. Alternatively the flask can be dried with hot air using a hot-air blower of the 'hair dryer' type (pp. 30–32), but **remember that acetone is flammable**. Indeed many laboratories do not permit the use of acetone for cleaning purposes because of the additional fire hazard, possible toxicity problems associated with long-term exposure and, of course, expense.

Glassware that is heavily contaminated with 'black tars' or other polymeric deposits will not normally respond to washing with water and detergent as the organic polymer is insoluble in water. Large amounts of tar material can often be scraped out with a spatula, but the remaining material usually has to be dissolved out with an organic solvent. Acetone is usually used since it is a good solvent for most organic materials, although vigorous scrubbing and/or prolonged soaking may be necessary in stubborn cases. The dirty acetone should be poured into the waste container; many laboratories attempt to segregate washing acetone that has only been used to rinse water from a flask, and therefore can be reused, from dirty acetone that has been used to wash out tars. Always check that you are draining your acetone into the correct waste container.

Some books recommend the use of powerful oxidizing mixtures, such as sulfuric/nitric acids and chromic acid, as a last resort technique for cleaning dirty glassware. **This practice should be strongly discouraged from the safety point of view as the mixtures used are all highly corrosive and some are potentially explosive.**

Cleaning and drying glassware is an unavoidable chore in the organic laboratory, but it is part of the job. However, it can be made much easier by following one simple rule: *clean up as you go along*. By cleaning glassware as soon as you have finished with it, you know exactly what was in it and how to deal with it, and freshly dirtied glass is much easier to clean than dried out tars and gums. There are plenty of periods during the laboratory class when you are waiting for a reaction to warm up or cool down, for a crystallization to finish and so on. Make use of such times to clean, rinse and dry your freshly dirtied glassware. It is thoroughly bad practice to put dirty glassware back into

Use acetone sparingly for cleaning flasks. Check for flames in the vicinity. Acetone is flammable

Do not use compressed air line to dry glassware

Clean up as you go

your locker at the end of the day, and it will certainly waste a lot more of your time in the subsequent laboratory period. Deposits are much more difficult to remove once they have dried onto the glassware.

Hardware

Your locker will also contain non-glass equipment such as that shown in Fig. 2.4. Many of these items, often known as hardware, are indispensable to experimental organic chemistry. A typical set will contain:
- *metal stands* for supporting apparatus;
- *clamps and holders* for supporting apparatus (the clamp jaws should be covered with a strip of cork or with a small piece of flexible tubing to prevent metal–glass contact);
- *metal rings* for supporting separatory funnels;
- *cork rings* for round-bottomed flasks;

Fig. 2.4 Laboratory hardware.

- *spatulas* for the transfer of solids;
- *wash bottle* for dispensing water or wash acetone;
- *Neoprene® adapters* for suction filtration;
- *pinch/screw clamps* for restricting flexible tubing.

The items which require special mention are stands, clamps and clamp holders, which are essential items for supporting your glass apparatus during reactions, as well as safety screens for protection during reduced pressure distillations and other potentially hazardous laboratory operations.

Chemical apparatus should always be securely clamped and fixed to a stable support.

The metal stand is the most commonly used form of stable support since it is freely movable, but its heavy base ensures that in proper use it is sufficiently stable. The only practical alternative to such stands is the purpose-built laboratory frame, a square or rectangular network of horizontal and vertical rods firmly fixed to the bench and/or wall, but this is usually only found in research laboratories. The correct use of support stands requires that the clamped apparatus is always directly over the base of the stand as shown in Fig. 2.5(a). The alternative arrangement is highly unstable and potentially dangerous. Similarly there are right and wrong ways of using clamp holders and clamps with only one movable jaw. Clamp holders should be arranged so that the open slot for the clamp faces upwards (Fig. 2.5b), and when in the horizontal position, clamps should be fixed so that the fixed non-moving jaw is underneath (Fig. 2.5c).

Most complete microscale assemblies are very light; minimal clamping is required, usually at the neck of the main reaction vial. Additional clamping of condensers and adaptors is neither necessary nor recommended. Small clamps, compatible in jaw gape with the microscale reaction vials, are readily available and most effective.

Safety screens made of toughened glass or plastic should be used whenever you are carrying out reduced pressure distillations or experiments in which there is some risk of an explosion. If in doubt, ask an instructor. In addition, any operations in the hood should always be carried out with the toughened glass front pulled down, leaving just sufficient space at the bottom to permit access to the apparatus. This serves the dual purpose of protecting the face and top half of the body in the event of an explosion and permitting the hood extraction system to work most efficiently. The front of the hood should never be pushed all the way up as, in this position, it is not possible for the extractor fan to maintain the inrush of air necessary to contain noxious vapours. With the front pulled down, you will also get into the habit of not leaning over the apparatus when working. Leaning into the hood is very bad practice, negating all of the reasons for operating in the hood in the first place. It is attention to details like these which make for good laboratory practice and characterize the good experimentalist.

Do not lean into the hood

(a)   WRONG

(b)   WRONG

movable jaw on TOP

fixed jaw underneath to
support, e.g. a condenser
(c)   WRONG

Fig. 2.5 Right and wrong ways of using support stands, clamp holders and clamps.

2.3 Heating

Working in the laboratory, it will not be long before it will be necessary to heat a reaction mixture or distil a product. Several methods of heating are commonly encountered in the laboratory, but the ready flammability of a wide range of organic solvents, coupled with their volatility, always requires vigilance when heating. Open flames pose an obvious hazard in this respect, but the hot metal surfaces of hotplates and the possibility of sparking with electrical apparatus can also give rise to dangerous situations. Whilst flames are visible, it is impossible to gauge the temperature of a metal surface simply by looking at it, so take particular care when working with hotplates.

Burners

Although the most straightforward means of applying heat, burners should normally only be used for heating aqueous solutions in open vessels. They are also useful for distillation and reflux procedures involving high boiling point materials, but in these instances care must be taken to ensure that no flammable vapours come into contact with the flame.

Never use a burner to heat flammable solvents in an open container, or if flammable solvents are being used in the vicinity.

Always check for flammable solvents before lighting a burner

Burners come in two basic forms, both of which are variants on the same design. The *Bunsen burner* (Fig. 2.6a) is useful for heating aqueous solutions in flat-bottomed vessels supported on a wire gauze. The size of the flame is usually too large to permit good control during distillation and, for such procedures, it is preferable to use a *microburner* (Fig. 2.6b) which produces a smaller flame. Various designs of these burners burn natural gas or coal gas and produce a hot (blue) flame by allowing the introduction of air at the base of the barrel. The air supply is controlled by moving an adjustable collar around the inlet hole and some designs permit control of the gas supply by use of a needle valve. When not in use burners must be extinguished but, if heating is interrupted temporarily, the air inlet should be closed to give a slightly luminous, more visible flame.

Always use a wire gauze between the glass vessel and the burner flame

When heating flat-bottomed vessels or round-bottomed flasks with a burner, a wire gauze should be placed between the vessel and the flame, with the vessel resting on it. This serves both as a support and as a means of dispersing the heat. This lowers the risk of cracking the container and stops the formation of 'hot spots' and the ever attendant 'bumping' when localized overheating occurs.

Fig. 2.6 (a) Bunsen burner; (b) microburner.

Pear-shaped distilling flasks may be heated directly without the need for a gauze, but it is recommended that microburners be used for such distillations. The burner should always be held in the hand and moved continuously over the surface of the flask below the level of the liquid in order to avoid hot-spot formation. It makes much more sense to move the burner to the apparatus than vice versa. When commencing the distillation, it is a good idea to start heating around the top edge of the liquid, moving the flame all of the time, and slowly work down the body of the flask. Heating at the bottom initially seems to be more liable to produce bumping, even when boiling stones have been added.

Keep the flame moving over the flask

Heating baths

Water and steam baths

Electrically heated water baths and steam baths are convenient means of heating liquids up to 100°C, although water condensing on and running into the vessel being heated can be a problem. This is particularly true if it is necessary to ensure anhydrous conditions within the reaction. Although the risk of fire is lowest with steam baths, you should be aware that carbon disulfide, which possesses an autoignition temperature of around 100°C, is still a potential fire hazard. In fact, carbon disulfide is so toxic and such a fire hazard that its use in the laboratory as a solvent should be avoided at all costs.

Heating with steam can be accomplished by suspending the vessel above the surface of a boiling water bath, or the laboratory may be equipped with a supply of superheated steam. With piped steam it will take a few minutes after turning on the steam source before the system clears itself of water and produces live steam. Set up your apparatus before turning on the system as everything will be too hot to handle afterwards.

Be careful with steam

You must always respect steam which, due to its high latent heat of condensation, can inflict rather nasty burns.

Steam and water baths are the heating methods of choice for carrying out recrystallizations with volatile solvents. The baths are normally equipped with a series of overlapping concentric rings, which can be removed to give the right size of support for the particular vessel being heated. Flat-bottomed vessels should sit firmly on the bath without any wobbling (Fig. 2.7a). Round-bottomed flasks should have between one-third and one-half of the surface of the flask immersed in the bath with a minimal gap between the flask and the support ring (Fig. 2.7b).

Oil baths and their relatives

Electrically heated baths are frequently used in the laboratory due to the wide temperature ranges possible with different heat-transmitting media (for example, polyethylene glycol, silicone oil, Wood's metal; see Table 3.1, p. 106).

Fig. 2.7 (a) Heating an Erlenmeyer flask on a steam bath; (b) heating a reflux set-up on a steam bath.

The bath can be heated on a hotplate (see Fig. 2.10) and determination of the bath temperature is possible using a thermometer. Alternatively some hotplates are equipped with thermostatic temperature control.

Although particularly amenable to a wide range of heating demands in the laboratory, oil baths do possess several drawbacks. One disadvantage is the thermal inertia of the oil bath, which can cause temperature overshoot, although this can be minimized by choosing an oil bath that is not excessively large compared with the flask being heated. The container cannot be made of ferrous material if it is desired to stir the mixture magnetically, but at the same time it is advisable to avoid glass containers such as beakers or crystallizing dishes due to the danger of breaking a glass vessel full of hot oil. Another minor irritation associated with oil baths stems from the mess and cleaning problems that result with flasks that have been suspended in silicone oil. This can be overcome by using polyethylene glycol for the heat-transmitting medium, as this is water soluble, but this has the drawback of a limited heating range before decomposition commences. Alternatively, it is possible to use sand baths or powdered graphite baths to overcome this problem although it is less easy to control temperature gradients within the heating medium. Wood's metal baths pose their own particular problems as the alloy is solid at room temperature and thermometers and flasks must always

Use an oil bath size compatible with the size of the vessel to be heated

Remove flasks and thermometers from Wood's metal baths whilst hot—care!

Use oil baths in the hood

be removed before the bath is allowed to solidify. Heating the baths to a temperature higher than the decomposition temperature of the fluid will result in evolution of vapours which at the least are unpleasant, but are also likely to be toxic. Oil baths should always be used in the hood for this reason. Silicone oil has the greatest thermal stability and is preferable to paraffin-based oils although it is much more expensive. Proprietary oils used for culinary purposes must not be used in the laboratory (see Table 3.1, p. 106). By far the biggest problem with oil baths is the danger of spattering if an oil bath becomes contaminated with water and is then heated over 100°C. This is extremely dangerous and any oil bath which is suspected of containing water should be changed immediately. Heating baths must be examined before use and the fluid should be changed regularly, disposing of the old oil in containers specifically available for such waste.

Never use oil baths which have been contaminated with water

Electric heating mantles

Heating mantles provide a convenient means of heating mixtures under reflux although their use for distillations is to be discouraged.

Mantles are designed only for heating round-bottomed flasks and must never be used for heating any other type of vessel.

Never use a mantle which is too small or too large for the flask being heated

The mantle consists of an electrical resistance wire wound within a hemispherical woven glass jacket. Each mantle is designed specifically to accept a flask of a particular size which should sit snugly in the cavity, touching the jacket at all points with no exposed heating areas. The mantle may be housed in a casing for greater protection, but all designs are particularly vulnerable to spillages of liquids. The construction of mantles can lead to the surface being abraded with constant use and this can lay bare the wires within the heating element. Any mantle suspected of having been damaged must first be verified and, if necessary, repaired by a qualified electrician before use.

Never use any mantle which you suspect to have had any liquid spilled on it or which has a frayed appearance

Most new mantles have their own heating control, but, if not, the mantle should be connected to a variable heating controller and never directly into the mains power supply. Owing to their high heat capacity, mantles tend to heat up rather slowly and are particularly prone to overshoot the desired temperature substantially. Always allow for the possibility of removing the heating quickly if it appears that a reaction is getting out of hand due to overheating. The best way to achieve this is to clamp the apparatus at such a height that the mantle can be brought up to it or removed from it on a laboratory jack (Fig. 2.8).

Use a laboratory jack to support heating mantles

Stirrer hotplates

Stirrer hotplates are designed for heating flat-bottomed vessels, such as Erlenmeyer flasks or beakers, for which they are ideal as long as the liquid being heated is not flammable (Fig. 2.9). The built-in magnetic stirrer permits

apparatus clamped
immobile

clamp

mantle raised
and lowered

adjustable
laboratory
jack

to electrical supply

Fig. 2.8 Assembly for reflux using a mantle.

efficient agitation of non-viscous solvents by adding an appropriately sized magnetic stirrer bar to the liquid in the container (see Fig. 2.9, p. 31).

Although round-bottomed flasks cannot be heated using a hotplate alone, due to the very small contact surface between flask and hotplate, this problem can be overcome by immersing the flask in a flat-bottomed oil bath. With such an arrangement, stirrer hotplates are very useful for heating under reflux with simultaneous stirring (Fig. 2.10).

The flat exposed surface of the hotplate, designed for transferring heat rapidly, makes it extremely dangerous when hot. It is good practice whenever you have finished using a hotplate to place a beaker of cold water onto the hot surface. This will have the dual effect of cooling down the surface and alerting others to the potential danger—a hot hotplate seems very much like a cold hotplate until someone puts a hand on it.

Always check that a hotplate is cool before attempting to move it

The hot-air gun

Hot-air guns are particularly useful as a source of heat that can be directed fairly precisely in much the same manner as a burner flame. Commercial hot-air guns (Fig. 2.11a) are capable of achieving high temperatures near to the nozzle and can be useful alternatives to Bunsen burners for distillations.

The guns are able to produce a stream of heated air, usually at two rates of heat output, as well as cold air. After the gun has been used, it should not be

Fig. 2.9 A stirrer hotplate.

Fig. 2.10 Using a stirrer hotplate with an oil bath to heat a round-bottomed flask.

placed directly onto the bench, as the nozzle remains very hot for some period of time. It is recommended that the gun be placed in a support ring 'holster' with the cold air stream passing for a few minutes before switching it off completely (Fig. 2.11b). Do not forget that the hot nozzle can ignite solvents as well as causing nasty burns.

Heat guns are particularly useful for rapid removal of moisture from apparatus for reactions in which dry, but not absolutely anhydrous, conditions are required. Another use is for heating thin layer chromatography (TLC) plates to visualize the components when using visualizing agents which require heat as part of the development procedure (see pp. 169–170).

variable speed motor unit

cold air in

hot air out

heating elements

(a)

(b)

Fig. 2.11 (a) A commercial hot-air gun; (b) after use the hot-air gun should be allowed to cool in a support ring.

In all instances, it must be remembered that any form of hot-air gun poses the usual fire hazards associated with any piece of electrical equipment which may cause sparks on making or breaking contact.

Heating microscale reactions

Thermal transfer is rapid in microscale glassware and sand baths can be used for reflux and distillation. Sand is easy to clean up if spilled and cannot be splashed, and neither can it be caused to smoke or ignite. A glass crystallizing dish containing sand can be reused many times with no deterioration, though regular checking for chemical contamination is recommended. Aluminium blocks which can be used on top of conventional stirrer hotplates are also available; the blocks are bored with holes which match the external diameters of the tapered reaction vials (Fig. 2.12). Thermal transfer is efficient and stirring occurs as normal.

Fig. 2.12 Aluminium heating block, drilled to accommodate thick-walled reaction vials and thermometer.

When rapid heating is required, the use of an electric hot-air gun may be advantageous.

2.4 Stirring

The methods for stirring reactions are described on pp. 92–95 and so in this section it is sufficient to describe the main types of equipment. There are three main ways that mixtures can be agitated—by hand, with a magnetic stirrer, and with a mechanical stirrer; only the last two require any particularly sophisticated equipment! Remember that homogeneous solutions do not in general require any stirring after the initial mixing. The exceptions to this rule are reactions which are carried out at low temperatures (for instance, reactions involving alkyl lithium reagents or diisobutylaluminium hydride) and, in such cases, agitation is required for heat dispersal rather than for mixing of reagents.

Magnetic stirrers

Magnetic stirring (see Fig. 3.20a, p. 93) is the method of choice if an extended period of continuous agitation is required, since it is easy to set up the apparatus, particularly for small-scale set-ups or closed systems. The main drawback to the technique is that it cannot cope with viscous solutions or reactions which contain a lot of suspended solid. In addition, volumes of liquid much greater than 1 L are not stirred efficiently throughout their whole bulk. The magnetic stirrer may also be equipped with a hotplate, and these combined stirrer hotplates are particularly versatile pieces of apparatus. In general, the larger the volume of material to be stirred, the more powerful the motor needed and the longer the magnetic stirrer bar required.

Stirrer bars come in various designs and dimensions; a selection of bars, approximately 10, 20 and 30 mm (or 0.5 and 1 inch) long, of the variety which possesses a collar around the mid-section (Fig. 2.13a), will be suitable for most occasions. For reactions in the larger volume round-bottomed flasks, heavy duty football-shaped (American or rugby—depending upon which side of the Atlantic you live!) bar magnets (Fig. 2.13b) are excellent, but these can be liable to break any delicate pieces of glassware that get in their way.

Fig. 2.13 Useful shapes of Teflon®-coated bar magnet.

Although bar magnets can be obtained with all sorts of different coatings, only Teflon®-coated stirrers are universally useful—and even these go black when used for stirring reactions involving alkali metals in liquid ammonia. This discolouration does not affect the efficiency of the stirrer, at least in the short term.

Mechanical stirrers

Larger scale reactions or viscous mixtures require the greater power of an external motor unit turning a stirrer blade. It is highly advantageous for the motor to possess a variable speed control and a typical model is shown in Fig. 2.14. These units are rather heavy and so it is necessary to support them firmly.

Mechanical stirrers need firm support

The stirrer is most simply attached to the motor by a flexible connection made out of a short length of pressure tubing. However, when stirring open vessels (see Fig. 3.20b, p. 93), the flexibility of this connection necessitates the use of a stirrer guide (such as a partially closed clamp) half-way down the stirrer shaft to prevent undue lateral motion ('whip'). With closed systems, such as when stirring refluxing reaction mixtures, a solvent- and air-tight adapter is required. A simple adapter, sometimes called a *Kyrides seal*, can be constructed from a tubing adapter fitted with a short length of flexible tubing which forms a sleeve around the shaft of the stirrer (Fig. 2.15a). The point of contact between the stirrer and the flexible tube is lubricated with a little sili-

Use a stirrer guide

Fig. 2.14 Typical mechanical stirrer.

Fig. 2.15 Stirrer guides for closed systems: (a) Kyrides seal; (b) screw-cap adapter (exploded view); (c) fluid-sealed stirrer.

cone grease, and a carefully prepared seal of this type will permit stirring under water aspirator vacuum (*ca.* 20 mm). A screw-cap adapter, commonly used to hold thermometers, can also be used to good effect if a little lubrication is applied to the silicone sealing ring and the plastic screw-cap is not tightened to its fullest extent (Fig. 2.15b). Mercury-sealed stirrer guides (Fig. 2.15c) have lost favour due to their tendency to splash highly toxic mercury metal everywhere when used at high speeds. In addition, although the arrangement does permit a good air-tight seal, it cannot be used with systems under vacuum. If such an adapter is used, it is preferable to use silicone oil in the place of mercury.

The stirrer rods may be made of glass, metal or Teflon® and the paddle or blade arrangements come in a bewildering array of forms. Teflon® is the material of choice for construction of the whole stirrer as this will not break when placed under stress (when dropped on the floor for instance), and neither is it likely to break the flask in which it is being used. Normally, however, the propeller-type stirrer (Fig. 2.16a), which is useful for stirring open containers with wide mouths, is commercially available constructed from metal. A glass or Teflon® stirrer, possessing a movable Teflon® blade (Fig. 2.16b), is a very simple and robust design that is suitable for use with vessels possessing restricted openings. In addition, the Teflon® blade possesses a curved edge, making it ideal for efficient stirring in round-bottomed flasks.

Stirring on the microscale

Magnetic stirrer bars (also known as beads, fleas or followers) are available in very small sizes in a number of patterns; spherical stirrers can be used in the smallest tubes, while the more usual parallel or bullet forms are suitable for

Fig. 2.16 Two useful types of stirrer: (a) propeller design for use in open vessels; (b) movable Teflon® blade for use with tapered-joint glassware.

Fig. 2.17 Triangular spin vane for magnetic stirring in conical reaction vials.

use in small round-bottomed flasks or test tubes. Triangular spin vanes (Fig. 2.17) can be obtained to fit the the tapered portion of the conical reaction vials sold in most of the commercial microscale kits; when using this combination of glassware and stirrer bead, it is important to centre the apparatus accurately on the magnetic stirrer or stirrer hotplate or the vane will not revolve smoothly. High torque stirring is very difficult on the microscale; manual stirring using a glass rod probably represents the most cost-effective solution to stirring very viscous media.

2.5   Vacuum pumps

The common procedures which call for reduced pressure in the organic chemistry laboratory are filtration with suction (pp. 77–79) and reduced pressure distillation (pp. 152–155). The former technique, which simply requires a source of suction, is adequately served by use of a water aspirator, although the reduced pressures which can be achieved with this simple apparatus (*ca.* 10–20 mmHg) are frequently sufficient for use with reduced pressure distillations. Alternatively, reduced pressures of this magnitude can be attained using a diaphragm pump. However, very high boiling materials, or purifications involving sublimations, require recourse to a vacuum of 0.1–1.0 mmHg which is provided by an oil immersion rotary vacuum pump. An even higher vacuum is achieved by using a mercury vapour diffusion pump in series with a double

Fig. 2.18 Schematic diagram of a water aspirator.

action rotary oil pump, but such conditions are required only rarely in the laboratory and will not be discussed here. It should not be forgotten, however, that mass-spectrometric analysis would be impossible without the ability to achieve reduced pressures in the region of 10^{-6} mmHg.

Water aspirators

Water aspirators are made of glass, metal or plastic (Fig. 2.18) and operate on the Venturi effect in which the pressure in a rapidly moving gas is lower than that in a stationary one. The aspirator is designed such that the water rushing through the aspirator drags air along with it and thus generates the region of low pressure.

The theoretical maximum vacuum attainable with such an apparatus is equal to the vapour pressure of the water passing through it and is therefore dependent on the temperature of the water source. In practice, the working pressure is usually some 5–10 mmHg higher than the minimum due to leaks. Anything lower than about 30 mmHg should be acceptable in a teaching laboratory. Unfortunately, water aspirators do not work efficiently at high altitudes and alternative methods have to be found in these circumstances.

The major disadvantage with a water aspirator is that the pressure generated depends on the speed with which the water passes through it and that, in turn, is directly affected by the water pressure. In a busy teaching laboratory, the use of a large number of water aspirators at the same time places great demands upon the water supply and may be too much for it to cope with efficiently. The result is that the pressure generated by aspirators around the laboratory is liable to be variable depending on their position in the line. The tendency for the vacuum generated by any individual aspirator to vary over a period of time as the water pressure changes can have deleterious effects in reduced pressure distillations where boiling points are very sensitive to pressure variations within the system. The worst situation occurs with an abrupt drop in the water pressure (for instance when your neighbour turns on his aspirator) as this leads to 'suck-back'. In this case the vacuum generated by the aspirator suddenly cannot cope and water floods into the apparatus—a very sad sight indeed, but one which can be avoided by interposing a trap between the aspirator and apparatus (Fig. 2.19).

Using a water aspirator

Always use aspirators with the water full on

Whereas the flow of water passing through a condenser does not need to be more than a gentle trickle, *water aspirators must never be used with the water at less than full blast*. (Why do students always seem to get this one the wrong way round?) With the water turned on full, check that the air bleed screw on the side arm is open (as these little screws have a tendency to become stuck or get lost from communal apparatus, some aspirators do not have them, but an

Fig. 2.19 Typical examples of water traps suitable for use with water aspirators.

additional stopcock attached to the water trap will serve the same purpose) and then attach the pressure tubing to the apparatus to be evacuated. Close the air bleed (or stopcock on the water trap) and observe the pressure drop on the manometer. For vacuum filtrations, the actual quality of the vacuum is largely unimportant but, of course, it will be necessary to note and regulate this pressure if you are carrying out a vacuum distillation.

The critical stage in working with water aspirators comes when the vacuum is to be released. It is imperative that the water supply to the aspirator *remains on until the pressure within the system has been allowed to return to that of the atmosphere.* If you do not observe this simple procedure, the inevitable result will be a suck-back of water into the apparatus.

Never turn off the water aspirator before releasing the vacuum

With suction filtration it is frequently sufficient simply to remove the pressure tubing from the side arm of the receiving vessel before turning off the tap, although this lazy practice runs the risk of spillage when the tubing is suddenly removed and air rushes into the receiver. The correct procedure for both reduced pressure filtration and distillation involves the unscrewing of the air bleed on the side arm of the aspirator (or opening the stopcock on the water trap) until the manometer registers a steady increase in pressure within the system, or the tone of the water rushing through the aspirator changes abruptly. Do not continue to unscrew the air bleed, otherwise the screw will drop out and be lost for ever down the sink. It is always good practice when carrying out reduced pressure distillations to allow the residue in the distilling flask to cool down to near room temperature before admitting air, particularly if the flask has been heated strongly during distillation.

Water traps

The danger of water sucking back into the apparatus when a sudden drop in water pressure occurs, is a constant problem when working with water aspirators. To safeguard against this, a water trap must always be included between the aspirator and the apparatus. Two simple examples are shown in Fig. 2.19; the optional modifications might include the attachment of a manometer or a means of introducing air into the system. The latter is necessary when the aspirator does not possess an air bleed, but even when one is present, using the stopcock on the water trap avoids leaning over the bench to the sink or losing the air bleed screw. As the trap simply acts as a dead space between the apparatus and the aspirator, which fills up with water on suck-back, it must be large enough to cope with this and should be no less than 1 L in volume.

Always use a water trap between the aspirator and your apparatus

Oil immersion rotary vacuum pumps

Frequently, vacuum distillations demand a better vacuum than that which can be achieved using a water aspirator, either because a lower pressure is needed, or because that produced by the aspirator is too erratic. In these instances an oil immersion rotary pump is ideal. Unfortunately, with the lower pressures comes increased complexity of operation of the pump and there are several extremely important rules that must be observed when using such equipment. Whilst the instructions given here should be generally applicable, always check the precise operation of your particular piece of apparatus with an instructor before use.

As well as the pump itself, the set-up will have a series of important pieces of ancillary equipment essential for the protection of the pump, achievement of the highest vacuum possible and measurement of the pressure within the system. All of these accessories will be connected by a rather complicated set of glass and flexible tubing, but the general arrangement will look something like that depicted in Fig. 2.20.

The pump is mounted firmly on its base on the bench top, or more conveniently, on a trolley which can be moved to wherever it is desired to carry out the distillation (such as in the hood). It is supplied with two connecting tubes made of thick-walled tubing. One (the 'downstream' side) is the exhaust tube and should always be led into a hood, whilst the 'upstream' tube leads eventually to the apparatus to be evacuated. It is what occurs on the upstream side of the pump which is crucially important.

The basic construction of the pump involves a rotor which is concentric with the motor drive shaft but which is mounted eccentrically within a cylinder (Fig. 2.21). In the commonly encountered 'internal vane' design, the rotor is fitted with one ('single action') or two ('double action') pairs of blades which bear tightly against the walls of the cylinder. Double action pumps are

Fig. 2.20 Schematic diagram representing the typical arrangement of a rotary vacuum pump.

capable of attaining a higher vacuum and the internal vane design is preferred because of its quiet operation.

On turning, the rotor blades cut off pockets of gas and sweep them through the pump to be exhausted via an oil-sealed non-return valve. A thin film of oil within the cylinder maintains a seal between the blades and the cylinder wall. The very close tolerances between the rotor blades and the cylinder mean that the pumps are very susceptible to damage by solid particles or corrosive gases.

Never draw air through a rotary vacuum pump

Under normal circumstances, the pump must never be allowed to work whilst open to the atmosphere for two very important reasons. Firstly, drawing air continuously through the oil in the pump will cause water vapour to be trapped in the oil. This reduces the vacuum that can be achieved due to the vapour pressure of the contaminating water and might cause the pump to seize. Abuse of the pump in this way will necessitate frequent oil changes and other more extensive repairs. However, a second more important reason is the possibility of condensing liquid oxygen in the cold traps if liquid nitrogen is being used as the coolant.

The potentially lethal consequences of combining liquid oxygen and organic material cannot be overemphasized and this situation must be avoided at all costs.

One of the authors (LMH) clearly remembers the sensation he experienced when, after carrying out a reduced pressure distillation in his first week of postgraduate research, he succeeded in half filling a cold trap with liquid oxygen by forgetting to remove the nitrogen Dewar flask for 25 min after opening up the apparatus to the atmosphere. Do not learn this particular lesson the hard way. Unlike the author, you may never get a second chance to get things right.

Pressure measurement

Whilst the order of attachment of the accessories may vary, in Fig. 2.20 the

Fig. 2.21 The 'internal vane' double action oil immersion rotary pump.

nearest attachment to the pump is the manometer (A), attached by a three-way stopcock (B). The design of manometer usually found on most rotary vacuum pumps is a compact variant of a McLeod gauge which allows accurate measurement of pressures between 0.05 and 10 mmHg. Its correct use is described more fully in p. 48. but it must always be kept in the horizontal position when not being used to measure pressure. The three-way stopcock is designed to permit isolation of either the pump, the manometer or the distillation apparatus at any one time, or to allow all three to be interconnected. One design for such a stopcock is shown in Fig. 2.22.

Air-leak stopcocks

The next attachment, which should be found between the pump and the cold traps, is a two-way stopcock (Fig. 2.20 [C]). This allows for both isolation of the pump from the apparatus and also entry of air. Its positioning here is important for safety reasons, as the system must never be arranged such that the pump can draw air through the cold traps if it is left switched on with this stop-

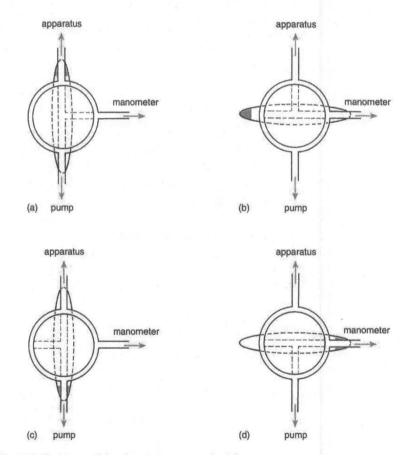

Fig. 2.22 Positions of the three-way stopcock: (a) pump, manometer and apparatus connected; (b) pump isolated; (c) manometer isolated; (d) apparatus isolated.

cock open to the atmosphere. A typical design uses a double-bored key as shown in Figure 2.23.

Cold traps

Cold traps must always be used to protect the pump

Organic vapours must not be allowed to pass through the oil of the pump as these will be trapped in the oil and will very rapidly reduce the capacity of the pump to produce a vacuum. To protect the pump, it is necessary to place two cold traps between the distillation apparatus and the pump to condense out any vapours which pass through the receiver flask. Two forms of trap are commonly found on such systems and are used for cooling with a solid CO_2–acetone slush bath (*ca.* −78°C) or liquid nitrogen (−196°C). However, neither cooling system is really ideal and care must be taken when using either of them to avoid splashes on the skin as unpleasant cold burns can result. The apparatus shown in Fig. 2.24(a) is particularly suited for use with a slush bath as fresh pieces of solid CO_2 can be added easily. That shown in Fig. 2.24(b) is better used with liquid nitrogen, as the Dewar flask containing the coolant can be removed before permitting air into the system at the completion of distillation. The drawback to the use of the slush bath is its relatively low condensing efficiency compared with liquid nitrogen. Nonetheless, its use is recommended, at least for the type of pump found in the teaching laboratory, as there is a very significant hazard associated with the use of liquid nitrogen which will cause liquid oxygen (bp −183°C) to condense in the cold traps if air is allowed into them.

Never, never draw air through a liquid nitrogen cold trap!

All mixtures of liquid oxygen and organic materials are dangerously explosive. If using liquid nitrogen as the coolant in the cold traps, NEVER permit air to enter the system. The Dewar vessel containing the liquid nitrogen must not be placed around the trap until immediately before turning on the pump and must be removed before releasing the vacuum in the system. Always wear insulating gloves when handling liquid nitrogen.

apparatus ← → pump apparatus ← → pump

atmosphere atmosphere

Fig. 2.23 A double-bored key two-way stopcock.

Fig. 2.24 (a) Solid CO_2–acetone trap; (b) liquid nitrogen trap.

Isolation stopcocks

The system should be equipped with a standard stopcock (Fig. 2.20 [D]) at its extremity in order to isolate the pump unit from either the atmosphere or the distillation apparatus.

Operation of the rotary vacuum pump

The procedures detailed below attempt to cover the general points and potential hazards associated with the use of rotary vacuum pumps. Nonetheless, it is imperative to consult an instructor before commencing to use the apparatus, particularly for the first time. It is quite possible that accepted procedures in your laboratory may differ from those outlined here, which are for general guidance only. In such circumstances, you must always follow the rules laid down by your laboratory.

Evacuating the system

Before using a rotary pump to evacuate the distillation apparatus, it is essential to have ensured that only minimal quantities of volatiles are present in the sample by connecting the system to a water aspirator for several minutes. The cold traps on the rotary pump will condense out small amounts of volatile materials, but it is unsafe to permit quantities of material to accumulate as there is a potential risk of explosion when reintroducing air into the traps at the end of the distillation.

Isolate the pump from the distilling apparatus by closing stopcock D, from the atmosphere by closing stopcock C and from the manometer by closing stopcock B, with the stopcock positions such as to allow the cold traps to be evacuated (refer to Fig. 2.20). Do not add any coolant at this stage, but if using solid CO_2–acetone, the traps may be one-third filled with acetone (Fig. 2.24a). Turn on the pump and immediately add the solid CO_2 or liquid nitrogen to the trap, being careful to avoid splashing the coolant onto yourself. The few seconds of pumping without coolant in the isolated traps will do the pump no harm, but will ensure that the air-filled traps are not surrounded by liquid nitrogen. (Although this is irrelevant with solid CO_2–acetone, it is a good idea to develop the habit of doing things this way whatever the coolant.) After about 1 min, check the quality of the vacuum using the manometer, returning the manometer to its horizontal position after obtaining the reading. If the pump is pulling a satisfactory vacuum (at least 1.0 mmHg and probably better), *slowly* open stopcock D to evacuate the apparatus (**safety screen!**). Allow several minutes for residual volatile solvents in the sample to be removed and for the system to stabilize, then recheck the vacuum with the manometer. When satisfied that an acceptable stable vacuum has been established, the distillation may be commenced. Remember to check the pressure periodically during the distillation and make sure that the traps do not need additional coolant (generally unnecessary unless the distillation is protracted).

Releasing the vacuum

At the end of the distillation, close stopcock D to isolate the apparatus from the pump and wait until the distilling flask has cooled down. Ensure the manometer is in its horizontal position and then turn stopcock C such that the traps are isolated but the pump is open to the atmosphere. You will hear the air rushing in through the outlet. Turn off the pump without delay, as drawing air through the oil in the pump for extended periods of time will cause a degradation of its performance. However, you must never switch off the pump when the line is still under vacuum, as oil from the pump will be sucked back into the line ruining the whole unit. If liquid nitrogen is being used as the coolant, the Dewar flasks should be removed without delay. Turn the two-way tap to allow air into the traps and dismantle them carefully (**wear gloves—they are very cold**). Place the collecting tubes or flasks in a hood ready for disposal of any condensed material (some of which may be toxic— consult an instructor) at a later stage. Finally, *slowly* open stopcock D to allow air to enter the apparatus. Always make sure that the traps have been cleaned, dried and any coolant removed after use.

Ballasting the pump

A common cause of poor performance with rotary vacuum pumps is the presence of occluded gases and solvent vapour within the sealant oil. Even with careful use, this cannot be totally avoided and it is usually necessary to carry out an oil change at regular intervals of 6 months to a year depending on the treatment the pump has had. The life of the oil and the performance of the pump can be increased by degassing the oil at regular periods; a process referred to as *gas ballasting*. The ballast valve is designed to protect the oil from condensation of liquids by allowing a small amount of air to bleed continuously into the pump. This obviously reduces the performance of the pump, and it is more common practice to use the pump with the ballast valve closed and compensate for this by ballasting for an equivalent period of time after the experiment. In the laboratory it is convenient to ballast a pump overnight after every 8 h of use.

To ballast a pump, isolate the vacuum side of the pump from the atmosphere and open the ballast valve fully—no cold traps are necessary. Lead the exhaust pipe into the hood to remove any potentially toxic fumes and turn on the pump. If this procedure is carried out regularly, the pump will continue to operate satisfactorily for long periods of time, perhaps requiring topping up with a little fresh oil occasionally.

2.6 Manometers

The type of manometer used depends on the vacuum being generated and hence on whether a water aspirator or a rotary oil immersion pump is being used. Manometers for use with water aspirators need to be able to measure pressures in the range 5–200 mmHg to an accuracy of ±1 mmHg, whereas the type of manometer used with oil pumps normally has a range of 0.01–10 mmHg.

Manometers for use with water aspirators

The simplest form of manometer consists of a glass U-tube with one arm about 1 m long and one somewhat shorter. The long arm is mounted vertically against a 1 m ruler with the open end dipping into a mercury reservoir. The other arm is attached to a water trap (Fig. 2.25a). The height of the mercury column in the tube is subtracted from the prevailing atmospheric pressure. The scale may be movable so that the zero can be placed in line with the reservoir liquid level, enabling the height of mercury to be measured directly. Owing to the necessary length of the glass tube, this type of manometer has a tendency to be both unstable and fragile and also requires rather a large mercury reservoir. Breakages and spillages of highly toxic mercury metal are a common occurrence with such apparatus. Despite this, the simplicity of construction means that these unsatisfactory and inaccurate manometers are frequently found in laboratories.

Far more robust and accurate manometers work on the principle of a short U-tube sealed at one end and filled with mercury. This arrangement has the additional advantages of requiring less mercury and permitting easier reading

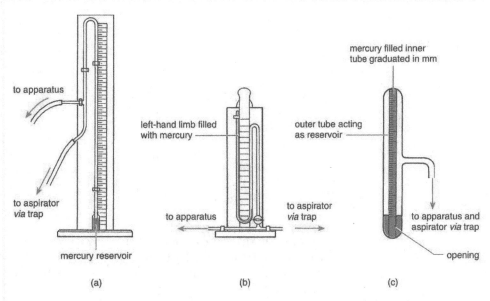

Fig. 2.25 Simple manometers for use with water aspirators (not to scale).

of the reduced pressure. The vacuum range covered is usually 0–100 mmHg with an accuracy of ±0.5 mmHg, and this is adequate for just about all requirements when distilling using a water aspirator vacuum. There are two common designs of manometer which work on this principle. The simple U-tube (Fig. 2.25b) has a tendency to accumulate air in the closed end of the tube over a period of time and is slightly less compact than the design using two concentric tubes (Fig. 2.25c). This latter piece of apparatus has an inner graduated tube filled with mercury which possesses a small outlet at its lower end. The outer tube acts as the mercury reservoir as well as the second arm of the U-tube.

With either arrangement the reduced pressure within the system is obtained by reading the difference in the mercury levels between the two halves of the manometer.

Do not release the vacuum too abruptly

A serious disadvantage common to both designs is the danger of breakage if air is allowed to re-enter the system too quickly. This allows the mercury to rush back into the tube where it may strike the sealed end with such force that it breaks the glass. All manometers should be used in conjunction with a water trap to avoid contamination with water in the event of a suck-back.

Manometers for use with rotary vacuum pumps

There is one design of manometer which is particularly suitable for the accurate measurement of pressures in the range 0.1–10 mmHg. This is a variant of the McLeod gauge. When not being used for pressure measurement it is held horizontally and the mercury is kept in the reservoir (Fig. 2.26a). To read

Keep the gauge horizontal unless taking pressure readings

Fig. 2.26 The McLeod gauge for measuring pressures accurately below 10 mmHg: (a) apparatus horizontal when not in use; (b) apparatus vertical when taking pressure readings. (Adapted and redrawn by kind permission of W. Edwards & Co. Ltd, Crawley, UK.)

the pressure within the system, the gauge is rotated to the vertical when the mercury enters the two arms. The gauge is tilted such that the meniscus of the mercury in the right-hand arm touches the zero and the pressure is read off from the left-hand arm (Fig. 2.26b). The gauge must always be returned to the horizontal after use and the mercury allowed to drain into the reservoir. If this is not done, there is the danger of mercury rushing forcefully to the sealed end of the tube, on release of the vacuum, and breaking the glass.

2.7 Pressure regulation

More often than not, you will find that the boiling-point information that is available is quoted for a pressure different to that produced by your equipment. There is little you can do if the quoted pressure is lower than that which can be achieved in your case, although it is worth checking for leaks and examining the thickness of the capillary if one is being used. If the pressure cannot be reduced any further by these means, you will need to estimate the likely boiling point with the help of a pressure–temperature nomograph (see Fig. 3.52, p. 153). If the quoted pressure is higher, then you have the option of regulating the internal pressure within your system to correspond. The various devices to do this in conjunction with rotary vacuum pumps are rather complicated and beyond the scope of this book. However, a simple needle valve with a fine control dial (Fig. 2.27) can be used in conjunction with a water aspirator to provide steady pressures higher than those being produced by the aspirator.

Fig. 2.27 Needle valve for controlling pressure in conjunction with a water aspirator.

2.8 The rotary evaporator

This piece of apparatus, usually communal in the teaching laboratory, is designed for the rapid removal of large quantities of volatile solvent at reduced pressure from solutions, leaving behind a relatively involatile component. Rotary evaporation finds greatest use for removing extraction and chromatography solvents used in the isolation and purification of reaction products. The principle of operation which distinguishes the apparatus from that used for ordinary reduced pressure distillation is the fact that the distillation flask is rotated during the removal of solvent. This performs the two important functions of reducing the risk of bumping (which accompanies all reduced pressure distillations), and increasing the rate of removal of solvent by spreading the contents around the walls of the flask in a thin film, with a consequent increase in the ratio of surface area to volume of solution.

A wide range of designs is available commercially for a variety of specific uses, but a basic model most commonly encountered in the teaching laboratory is depicted in Fig. 2.28.

The apparatus

The *evaporating flask*, which may be pear-shaped or any round-bottomed flask possessing a standard-taper joint, is connected to a glass sleeve (*vapour duct*) which passes through a seal permitting a vacuum to be maintained, but at the same time allowing rotation. The vapour duct leads solvent vapour from the flask onto a spiral condenser and the condensed solvent is collected in a round-bottomed *receiver flask*, connected by means of a hemispherical glass joint. The motor unit for rotating the flask is housed above the point of the seal and the rate of rotation may be varied. The water aspirator is attached through the condenser outer jacket and the application and removal of the vacuum is

Fig. 2.28 (a) Typical example of a rotary evaporator; (b) exploded view of glassware showing vapour duct.

controlled by using the stopcock at the end of the condenser. This stopcock may be fitted with a long flexible tube which passes the length of the condenser into the evaporating flask to permit introduction of additional solution without releasing the vacuum and interrupting the evaporation.

The whole unit is mounted on a stand, of which several models exist, all designed to permit easy vertical movement of the rotary evaporator for introduction of the evaporating flask into a heating bath. The clamping system also provides for adjustment of the inclination of the rotary evaporator. The most convenient angle is somewhere around 45° from the vertical but this should not normally require adjustment.

Report poor rotary evaporator pressures immediately to the person responsible

Regular maintenance of the rotating seal is necessary to produce a reliable vacuum. Failure of this seal will result in poor and variable pressures, but any corrective work should be left to others after first ensuring that it is the seal and not the water aspirator which is the cause of the trouble. To do this, isolate the rotary evaporator and examine the pressure developed by the water aspirator. The only components which you will need to remove in the ordinary course of events are the evaporating and receiving flasks, for filling and emptying.

Always use clips to hold flasks on the rotary evaporator

During evaporation, the reduced pressure within the system will tend to hold the distilling flask firmly in place. However, **never rely on a combination of friction and vacuum to hold the evaporating flask onto the rotary evaporator**—the additional precaution of using a clip for the flask must be followed (the hemispherical joint on the receiver flask makes such a clip an absolute necessity). The sight of a flask bobbing upside-down in a hot water bath is only too common in the teaching laboratory where water pressure

Fig. 2.29 A typical splash trap for use with a rotary evaporator.

fluctuations (and hence the quality of the water aspirator vacuum) are liable to occur.

If a standard round-bottomed flask is being used as the evaporating flask, it is likely that an expansion adapter will be necessary to attach the flask to the cone of the vapour duct. A very useful piece of apparatus for use with rotary evaporators—particularly communal ones—is a splash adapter which is placed between the evaporating flask and the vapour duct (Fig. 2.29). This acts as an expansion adapter, and at the same time prevents your sample contaminating the vapour duct by bumping up into it and also stops refluxing solvent or a bumping solution washing down somebody else's prior contamination into your sample. You should get into the habit of cleaning the splash trap before and after use with acetone from a wash bottle.

Splash traps reduce the risk of contamination

Correct use of the rotary evaporator

Ensure that the receiving flask is empty of solvent and that water is passing through the condenser coils at a slow but steady rate. Turn on the water aspirator to its fullest extent and then attach the evaporating flask (with adapter if required) to the vapour duct, using a clip to ensure that the flask stays in place. Support the flask lightly with the hand, commence slow rotation and then close the stopcock at the end of the condenser. When the manometer indicates a significant reduction of pressure within the system (if no manometer is attached to the apparatus, listen for a marked change in tone of the sound made by the water rushing from the aspirator) it is safe to remove your hand and regulate the speed of rotation to spread the solvent out around the flask without causing it to splash. If the mixture commences to boil uncontrollably, *temporarily* open the stopcock at the top of the condenser to allow entry of air and then reclose the stopcock. Once the evaporation from the solution has stabilized, the evaporating flask may be introduced into a bath of warm water if desired. However, be ready to remove the flask immediately there is any

Keep the flask supported until the system is under vacuum

Heat cautiously

indication that the mixture is beginning to boil too vigorously. The majority of common solvents such as ether or light petroleum have boiling points well below room temperature at the reduced pressures possible using this system, so you must exercise great care when heating the evaporating flask. With the more volatile solvents it is advisable to place the flask in a cold water bath at the outset and then allow the bath to warm up slowly during the course of solvent removal. The last traces of solvent are difficult to remove from samples, particularly the kinds of gummy materials which are often isolated from reactions, and so it is necessary to leave the residue on the rotary evaporator for at least 5 min after the last of any solvent has been seen running into the receiver.

Continuous evaporation of large quantities of solution

If the volume of solvent you wish to remove is inconveniently large for the size of the evaporating flask you are using (which should never be filled to more than about one-quarter of its volume), it is possible to introduce additional solution if the stopcock at the top of the condenser is fitted with a length of tubing which reaches into the evaporating flask. Simply attach a length of glass tubing to the external connector on the stopcock and dip this into the extra solution you wish to add (Fig. 2.30). Opening the stopcock carefully will cause solution to be drawn into the evaporating flask by the reduced pressure within the rotary evaporator and the solvent removal can continue after closure of the stopcock.

Do not leave your solvent in the receiver flask and check that the vapour duct is clean

When you are satisfied that all of the solvent has been removed from your sample, stop the flask rotating and raise it from the heating bath. If you reverse the order of these operations you will get wet with spray from the flask! Open the stopcock to allow air into the system, **supporting the flask with your hand**, remove the flask and turn off the aspirator and condenser water. Empty the contents of the receiver flask into the container designated for used solvents **(not down the sink!)** and check that you have left no material adhering to the

Fig. 2.30 The procedure for continuous solvent removal using a rotary evaporator.

inside of the vapour duct as this will not only reduce your yield, but also contaminate the next user's sample.

Sample concentration on the microscale

Sample concentration can be achieved with containment. For small (*ca.* 1 mL or less) volumes of solution, the solvent can be simply blown off by allowing a fine stream of nitrogen gas to pass over the surface of the solution in a hood (Fig. 2.31a). The tube containing the solution should not be allowed to cool, or condensation will occur in the tube, wetting the sample. Clamping the tube in a bath of warm water or in a warm sand bath will prevent this. This method should not be used in the open laboratory—this technique is unsuitable there because of the release of solvent vapour. Instead, the use of a water aspirator or vacuum pump is recommended (Fig. 2.31b). For small volumes, attach a Pasteur pipette via flexible tubing to the water pump and position the pipette tip close to (but not under) the surface of the solution. Warming the tube will volatilize the solvent and the aspirator will draw the vapour away, at the same time avoiding condensation of atmospheric moisture. The same technique can

Fig. 2.31 Small quantities of solvent can be removed by blowing a stream of air or nitrogen over the surface of the solution with gentle warming, or using an aspirator, in which case the solution is stirred to prevent bumping.

be used if water aspirators have been replaced by mechanical vacuum pumps, though these should be protected by placing traps between the experiment and the pump (see p. 43–44). If a solid product (and subsequent recrystallization) is anticipated, concentration into a Craig tube directly will minimize losses.

see p. 43–44

2.9 Catalytic hydrogenation

Catalytic hydrogenation is a particularly useful means of reducing alkenes and alkynes (see Experiments 25 and 26). Frequently it is necessary to avoid over-reduction, for instance in the Lindlar catalyzed reduction of alkynes to alkenes, or if it is desired to reduce selectively only one unsaturated site within the molecule as in Experiment 26. In such instances it is necessary to use a gas burette system which enables the volume of gas taken up to be measured at atmospheric pressure and at the same time permits a certain amount of over-pressure (up to about 0.5 atm) to be applied to the reaction mixture. An example of such an arrangement is shown schematically in Fig. 2.32.

Hydrogenations at higher pressures (2–400 atm) require very specialized apparatus to enable safe working due to the highly explosive nature of hydrogen, especially when under pressure. These are beyond the scope of this book but, whatever the pressure and whatever the quantity of hydrogen being used, all naked flames must be extinguished.

Fig. 2.32 Schematic of low pressure hydrogenation apparatus.

Whenever working with hydrogen, there must be no naked flames in the laboratory. Any electrical apparatus in the vicinity must be spark-proof.

The hydrogenation burette

The essential features of the apparatus are the hydrogenation flask (Fig. 2.32A), linked by a flexible connection to a gas burette (B) and reservoir (C). The size of the burette, usually between 2 L and 100 mL, depends on the scale of the reaction to be carried out and whether the liquid used to fill the system is water or mercury. The hydrogen pressure over the reaction mixture is controlled by adjusting the height of the reservoir. Higher internal pressures are possible using mercury in the reservoir, but this becomes impractical for larger burette volumes due to the weight of mercury necessary. If water is used, it is common practice to dissolve a few crystals of copper(II) sulfate in it to discourage algal growth and to help visualize the meniscus. Attached to the system is a manometer (D) and a pressure release safety trap (E). Hydrogen is obtained at about 1 atm pressure via a regulator valve from a pressurized cylinder (F) (see pp. 64–68). All flexible tubing used to carry hydrogen must be impermeable and is best composed of clear PVC. It should be tightly wired onto the apparatus.

Hydrogenation procedure

In carrying out any procedure involving hydrogen, two rules must be observed at all times.

Never allow naked flames in the vicinity when hydrogen is being used. Avoid the formation of air–hydrogen mixtures.

The warning about flames and hydrogen cannot be repeated too often and this is particularly important if the experiment is being carried out in a busy teaching laboratory with lots of people all doing different things. It is far better for the apparatus to be kept in a separate room specifically designed for hydrogenations.

Fill the burette with water or mercury by opening stopcock X and raising the reservoir C until the liquid level in the burette reaches the stopcock; then close stopcock X and lower the reservoir to its former level. Place the sample to be hydrogenated in flask A, with a magnetic stirrer bar, and dissolve it in the specified volume of reaction solvent. Add the catalyst to the mixture, ensuring that none adheres to the sides of the flask by washing the walls with a little solvent from a pipette. Connect the flask to the system and secure the tubing adapter to the flask with metal springs or elastic bands. Turn the two-way stopcock Y to connect the system to the water aspirator and evacuate until no further movement registers on the manometer. Open the hydrogen supply at the cylinder and regulate the reduction valve on the cylinder adapter to give a working pressure of 2–3 psi (about 0.2 atm—see pp. 67–68). Turn the cylinder stopcock Z carefully and observe the gas bubbling through the pressure

Care! Some catalysts are pyrophoric

No flames when hydrogen is being used!

55

release trap E. Connect the evacuated system to the hydrogen cylinder, turning stopcock Y slowly, and observe the fall in the mercury level of the manometer as hydrogen is drawn in. Once again, connect the system to the aspirator, evacuate until the manometer shows a steady vacuum, and then reintroduce hydrogen. Repeat this cycle of charging and evacuation at least three more times to ensure that all of the air originally in the system has been flushed out.

Air–hydrogen mixtures are very likely to inflame if they come into contact with the catalyst.

After the fifth cycle, open the burette stopcock X and allow it to fill with hydrogen to the desired level, lowering the reservoir if necessary. Turn stopcock Y to isolate the system and shut off the aspirator and hydrogen cylinder. To obtain the initial volume reading, place the system at atmospheric pressure by moving the reservoir up or down to equalize the mercury levels in the manometer, and read off the volume in the burette. Knowing the amount of sample to be hydrogenated, the prevailing atmospheric pressure and room temperature, the amount of hydrogen uptake desired can be calculated. Raise the reservoir to develop an over-pressure of hydrogen within the system (registered on the manometer), stirring the contents of the reaction flask. Frequently, hydrogenation reactions are agitated by shaking which also serves to increase the contact area of the reaction mixture with the hydrogen atmosphere. If shaking instead of stirring, you must use a long-necked hydrogenation flask in order to avoid solution entering the PVC tubing. Periodically lower the reservoir to bring the system back to atmospheric pressure and measure the amount of hydrogen taken up on the burette. This is usually fairly rapid initially but slows down as the reaction reaches completion. The apparent uptake is often slightly greater than that calculated and may never quite stop as it is very difficult to eliminate all leaks of hydrogen within the apparatus. In addition, even small amounts of catalyst can adsorb appreciable amounts of hydrogen and, for accurate small-scale work, it is necessary to presaturate the catalyst with hydrogen. This is a rather tricky procedure, however, and should only be carried out by those with experience of hydrogenations. Certainly there will be no need to do this in the hydrogenation experiments within this book.

When the hydrogenation is complete the system must be evacuated again and the excess hydrogen must be removed before permitting re-entry of air to avoid spontaneous combustion of the air–hydrogen mixture on the catalyst surface. After assiduously filling the apparatus, many people forget this part of the procedure, with dangerously spectacular results. The reaction mixture may then be filtered with suction to remove the catalyst and the catalyst placed in the residues bottle for recycling. This filtration must always be carried out using a glass sinter funnel and care should be taken not to draw air through the dry catalyst as many are pyrophoric.

All electrical apparatus must be spark-proof

Do not draw air over the catalyst

Hydrogenation on the microscale

For microscale use, generation of hydrogen gas becomes practicable; remember that 1 mmol of gas will occupy 22.4 mL at standard temperature and pressure. The gas can be generated in a small flask or tube by the action of sulfuric acid on zinc metal, conveyed through fine polypropylene tubing and collected in an inverted measuring cylinder or microscale burette and used subsequently. The advantage of this type of procedure is the availability of equipment for multiple use; clearly the hazard associated with the use of a flammable gas still exists and utmost care must be taken to avoid contact between the gas and naked flames. The Brown procedure represents a useful *in situ* alternative. Platinum(IV) chloride is reduced by sodium borohydride in the presence of decolourizing charcoal to generate a reactive supported catalyst. Hydrogen gas is generated *in situ* by exposure of sodium borohydride to acid, and retained in the reaction by a pipette bulb, wired on to the reaction vessel.

Further reading

H.C. Brown and C.A. Brown, *J. Am. Chem. Soc.*, 1962, **84**, 1495.

P.N. Rylander, *Hydrogenation Methods*, Academic Press. Orlando, FL, 1985.

2.10 Ozonolysis

The cleavage of double bonds using ozone, followed by either a reductive or oxidative work-up to yield carbonyl-containing fragments is an important procedure in synthetic work (see Experiment 73), as well as in structure-determination studies when characterization of the fragments may be easier than the original alkene. The great advantage of ozone is its selectivity; hydroxyl groups, for instance, remain untouched by this reagent.

Ozone (O_3) is obtained by passing oxygen between two electrodes which have a high voltage electrical discharge between them. Commercial ozonizers can provide oxygen enriched with up to about 10% ozone by regulation of the operating voltage and the oxygen throughput, and yield around 0.1 mol h^{-1} of ozone. It is possible to estimate the production rate of the ozonizer by passing the ozone stream through a solution of potassium iodide in 50% aqueous acetic acid for a measured period and then determining the liberated iodine titrimetrically. However, many commercial instruments have reliable calibration charts and, in any case, it is usually sufficient to monitor the progress of the reaction by TLC and adjust the ozone production rate accordingly.

The operation simply involves passing dry oxygen over the charged plates at a predetermined rate, although the exact procedural details vary with each instrument and you must consult an instructor before attempting to use the ozonizer.

Remember that the instrument contains a very high voltage (7000–10 000 V) when in operation. Ozone is highly toxic and experiments must always be carried out in the hood. In addition, the intermediate ozonides must never be isolated as they are potentially explosive compounds. An appropriate work-up must always be carried out before attempting to isolate your product.

The apparatus

Ozone is toxic—HOOD!

A typical arrangement is shown in Fig. 2.33 and essentially consists of an oxygen supply, the ozonizer, a trap and the reaction vessel. Some means of testing the effluent gas for the presence of ozone may also be used to check for completion of reaction. The oxygen supply comes from a cylinder and that part of the apparatus which delivers or contains ozone (from the ozonizer outlet onwards) must be contained in an efficient hood.

Ozonolysis procedure

The substrate is dissolved in an inert solvent, commonly dichloromethane or cyclohexane, in a flask arranged for stirring at reduced temperature (Fig. 2.33) and fitted with a sintered inlet tube and a means of venting the ozone. The sintered inlet tube disperses the incoming stream of gas, increasing its surface area and hence the rate of absorption of the ozone. The ozonolysis is carried

Fig. 2.33 Typical arrangement of apparatus for ozonolysis.

out with external cooling of the reaction mixture using an ice bath or a solid CO_2–acetone bath ($-78°C$). The progress of the reaction may be monitored by TLC, observing the disappearance of starting material, or the effluent gas may be checked for ozone using moist starch-iodide paper which turns blue-black if ozone is present in the effluent gas. Simple observation of the reaction mixture should give a good indication when excess ozone is present, as solutions of ozone are pale blue. If the passage of gas is too rapid for all of the ozone to be absorbed, a positive blue-black colouration may be obtained with the starch-iodide paper before the reaction is complete and so it is always a good idea to check by TLC before moving to the next stage of the experiment.

Ozone is highly toxic and irritates the lungs. Extreme care must be exercised when removing samples from the reaction flask for TLC analysis.

The ozonide contained in solution must be decomposed either by reduction or oxidation before any isolation work can be carried out.

Ozonides are potentially explosive and must never be isolated.

A particularly convenient reductive work-up procedure involves treating the reaction mixture with excess dimethyl sulfide which is immediately oxidized to dimethyl sulfoxide. However, dimethyl sulfide possesses a repulsive odour of rotten cabbage and its use in a crowded teaching laboratory might not be very popular! Reduction with zinc in acetic acid or triphenylphosphine present slightly more involved, but much more socially acceptable, alternatives. Use of sodium borohydride permits reductive decomposition of the ozonide with further reduction of the carbonyl fragments to alcohols. Alternatively the ozonide may be hydrolyzed, but in this instance the hydrogen peroxide produced oxidizes aldehyde groups to carboxylic acids. To ensure complete oxidation, excess hydrogen peroxide should be added to the reaction mixture in such instances. Details of these procedures may be found in the publications listed below.

Further reading

For a procedure for reductive work-up of ozonolysis reactions using catalytic hydrogenation, see: B.S. Furniss, A.J. Hannaford, P.W.G. Smith and A.R. Tatchell, *Vogel's Textbook of Practical Organic Chemistry*, 5th edn, Longman, London, 1989, p. 106.

J. March, *Advanced Organic Chemistry*, 4th edn, Wiley & Sons, New York, 1992, p. 1177.

V.N. Odinokov and G.A. Tolstikov, *Ozonolysis—a Modern Method in the Chemistry of Olefins* [*Russ. Chem. Rev.* (Engl. trans.), 1981, **50**, 636] and references cited therein.

2.11   Irradiation

The commonest way of increasing the rate of chemical reactions is to supply additional energy in the form of heat. Electromagnetic radiation in the ultraviolet (UV) region is also useful in synthetic organic chemistry, and serves not only as an energy source, but may also alter the course of the chemical reaction ('thermally forbidden–photochemically allowed' processes). The only requirement is for the incident light to possess a wavelength which can be absorbed either by the substrate (*direct photolysis*) or by an added molecule which can transfer its energy to the substrate molecule (*sensitized photolysis*).

In favourable climates, sunlight is a convenient source of radiant energy with wavelengths down to 320 nm suitable for carrying out a wide range of chemical reactions. However, this option is not open to all laboratories and, additionally, a wide range of photochemical transformations require higher energy light with wavelengths down to 220 nm. Mercury arc lamps are the most convenient sources of radiant energy in the organic chemistry laboratory. There are three types available—*low, medium* and *high pressure* mercury arc lamps, which differ in the range of wavelengths and intensity of the light they produce. The low and medium pressure types are those most commonly used in photochemical synthetic work. Commonly, low pressure lamps, operating at roughly 10^{-3} mmHg, emit light particularly rich in the 254 nm wavelength, together with some at 184 nm which can be filtered out. However, other low pressure lamps are available which emit at 300 nm and 350 nm. Medium pressure lamps, with internal vapour pressures of 1–10 atm, produce a range of wavelengths between 200 and 1400 nm with intensity maxima at 313, 366, 436 and 546 nm. High pressure lamps effectively give an intense continuum between 220 and 1400 nm, being particularly rich in the visible region. Both medium and high pressure lamps produce a great deal of heat during use and so relatively elaborate cooling arrangements are necessary when using these.

Low pressure lamps give out minimal heat and the main requirement of the apparatus is containment and focusing of the light onto the sample. Attention must be paid to the container in which the sample is held, as Pyrex® glass—the usual medium for laboratory glassware—is opaque to light below 300 nm. Reactions requiring shorter wavelength light must be carried out in quartz vessels and these are very expensive items. Great care must be taken when using them, not only against breakage, but also against touching with the hands as this leaves UV opaque deposits.

The light may come from an external source shining onto the reaction vessel or the apparatus may be designed such that the lamp is totally surrounded by solution. A Rayonet® reactor is frequently used with low pressure lamps for external irradiation. The silvered interior, together with rotation of the reaction vessels on a 'carousel', permits efficient and even irradiation of samples, whilst the low level of heat generated is removed by a fan. Medium pressure lamps are usually used as internal irradiation sources. In this arrangement, efficient heat removal is assured by enclosing the light source in a water jacket.

Both the intensity and the wavelengths of the emissions from all mercury vapour lamps make the light produced intensely hazardous to eyesight as well as having deleterious effects on the skin. Special eye protection against UV light and gloves must be worn at all times when working with mercury lamps. All photochemical reactors must be thoroughly covered in order not to permit the escape of light and, wherever possible, experiments should be carried out in a specifically designated blacked-out hood. Never commence a photochemical reaction in the teaching laboratory without first consulting an instructor to check the apparatus.

The Rayonet® photochemical reactor

The reactor container consists of an enamelled housing which contains the reaction chamber, together with the ancillary equipment for supplying power to the lamps, the fan and the carousel (Fig. 2.34). All electrical controls are on an external console to permit control of operation without the necessity for access to the interior. The internal walls of the reaction chamber are silvered and the lamps are aligned vertically around the outside walls. The sample tubes are held in a rotating holder (the carousel), and the combination of sample rotation together with the internal silvering, permits even illumination of a series of sample tubes in the same reactor.

Use of the reactor is straightforward, but special eye protection must be worn at all times during the operation. Switch on the cooling fan and load the samples into the carousel which is then set in motion. Close the apparatus, using aluminium foil to block off any small gaps which may permit leakage of

Fig. 2.34 Schematic diagram of a Rayonet® photochemical reactor.

UV light, and turn on the lamps. The reaction progress may be monitored by TLC but the whole power supply to the machine must be disconnected before opening the reaction chamber to avoid any chance of accidental exposure to UV light when the protective covers are removed.

To prepare the sample, dissolve the substrate in an appropriate solvent and place the solution in quartz tubes. Take care not to contaminate the walls of the tubes with grease from the hands and fill each tube no more than two-thirds full. Stopper the tubes with serum caps and degas the solution. Do this by connecting a long needle to a nitrogen supply and pass this to the bottom of the solution. Pierce the septum with a second short needle, making sure that this does not touch the liquid in the tube, and pass nitrogen through the solution for 10 min (Fig. 2.35).

Degas samples before irradiation

Internal irradiation with a medium pressure mercury vapour lamp

The apparatus used is shown schematically in Fig. 2.36. It consists of the lamp, which is fitted into a sleeve made up of two quartz jackets. These are fitted with inlet and outlet tubes to permit the passage of coolant water. The areas of the jackets surrounding the region of the lamp which emits the light are made of particularly optically pure quartz. The same arrangement can be made of

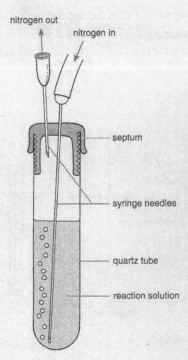

Fig. 2.35 Arrangement for degassing a sample before irradiation in a Rayonet® reactor.

Pyrex® in place of quartz when all wavelengths below 300 nm are filtered out before reaching the reaction solution. The lamp and jacket assembly is then fitted into the reaction vessel which may be a 1 L three-necked flask or a smaller two-necked vessel depending on the volume of the solution being irradiated.

Eye protection — UV light is hazardous

Before irradiation commences, the solution should be degassed by bubbling nitrogen through it in a vigorous stream for at least 20 min — longer with larger solution volumes. The whole apparatus must be encased in a light-proof container and special eye protection must be worn before illuminating the lamp. Any leakage of light from the container must be blocked using aluminium foil. Depending on the reaction being carried out, reaction times vary from a few hours to several days and monitoring by TLC, observing all of the necessary precautions, is recommended.

Microscale apparatus suitable for immersion photochemistry, which accomodates a low pressure mercury lamp and allows the photo-irradiation of 5 to 15 mL of solution, is available.

Fig. 2.36 Apparatus for internal medium pressure irradiation: (a) set-up with 1 L reaction vessel; (b) container for smaller quantities of reaction solution.

Further reading
J.D. Coyle, *Introduction to Organic Photochemistry*, Wiley, New York, 1986.
J.H. Penn and R.D. Orr, *J. Chem. Ed.*, 1989, **66**, 86–88.

2.12

Compressed gases

Whilst procedures do exist for generating some gases such as hydrogen chloride in the laboratory, it is always preferable to use gas from a cylinder. It is much more convenient to obtain the gas directly from a cylinder; the purity is more assured and the dangers associated with intermittent supply are removed. Nevertheless, pressurized gas cylinders introduce their own particular hazards and correct handling procedures must be observed at all times. The main areas of concern stem from the high pressure of the gas contained within the cylinder and the weight of the cylinder, although many gases are available in small 'lecture bottle' cylinders which are much easier to handle. It is also imperative to use the correct design of pressure regulator for the particular gas being delivered. All cylinders require a pressure-regulating device to permit controlled release of gas, but certain gases—for instance oxygen, flammable gases or corrosive gases—require a special design of pressure regulator. To minimize this problem, each specialized regulator is fitted using an adapter which is only suitable for use with the specified cylinder type.

Safe handling of gas cylinders

Gas pressure

Cylinders of gases such as hydrogen, nitrogen, oxygen and argon, which are commonly used by organic chemists, are usually supplied in cylinders at up to 200 atm pressure. The cylinders are designed to withstand rough treatment and it is extremely unlikely that any damage will be done to them in the normal course of events. Nonetheless, the cylinders should be treated with respect and, wherever possible, the valve assembly of the cylinder should be protected with a cap. This is the most vulnerable part of the cylinder and if it is broken off, for instance if the cylinder is dropped, the cylinder will be propelled with extreme force by the escaping gas and will destroy anything in its path. Any cylinder which is suspected to have been damaged, particularly around the valve, by an impact, fire or exposure to corrosive materials, must be reported immediately to the supplier.

The very real danger presented by the possibility of cylinders exploding in a fire has led to legislation in many countries banning the storage of pressurized cylinders inside laboratories. This arrangement should be followed whenever possible even where it is not mandatory.

Size and weight of cylinders

Whilst very variable, a common size for laboratory cylinders is about 1.6 m in height with a gross weight of anything between 70 and 85 kg. Consequently, these are heavy and unwieldy objects which are easy to topple over if left free-standing. A cylinder of these dimensions can easily break or crush limbs and cause severe internal injury to anyone caught in the path of its fall. This very real danger must be minimized by attaching the cylinders securely to a wall or a laboratory bench with a chain or stout canvas belt (Fig. 2.37). This procedure *must* be followed for any storage even if the period is only temporary.

Cylinders must always be secured to a firm support and not left free-standing

Cylinders must always be transported using an appropriate trolley: a two-wheeled trolley designed for this, including chains to secure the cylinder during transport, as shown in Fig. 2.38. Cylinders should not be moved by rolling along the ground or by tilting at an angle and rolling along one end whilst gripping the valve. Both procedures leave too much room for personal injury.

On transferral, the trolley should be moved as close as possible to the cylinder. Unchain the cylinder from its wall support and carefully edge it into

Fig. 2.37 Cylinders must always be strapped to a wall or a sturdy bench.

chains for securing
cylinder during transport

Fig. 2.38 A suitable trolley for transferring cylinders.

the trolley using both hands. Immediately rechain the cylinder to the trolley and transfer the cylinder to the desired place. Unload the cylinder from the trolley and fix it securely in its new position. This procedure is awkward and heavy work, and it is recommended that even the strongest people work in pairs. One should hold the trolley steady during the transfer and the other should move the cylinder. If the cylinder begins to topple out of control it should be allowed to fall, as severe injury can result from attempting to halt its fall.

Identification of contents

It is, of course, essential that the contents of all cylinders be correctly identified. All cylinders have labels bearing the names of the contents and details about hazards and degree of purity connected with the contents. However, labels can be lost or destroyed, so, as an additional precaution, the cylinders are painted with a colour code to indicate the gas contained within. Unfortunately, what seems to be an excellent idea in principle has led to a very confused situation as different countries have adopted different codes. In the USA no standard coding system has been adopted, although the EU has now addressed this issue and EU-approved colour codes are described in European Standard EN1089-3: 1997. However, even within Europe, code variations remain in some member states. In case of doubt, the relevant supplier's catalogue should be consulted and any further queries about identification should be addressed directly to the supplier.

Cylinders containing liquefied gas

Some cylinders containing liquefied gas are designed to deliver either the liquid or the gas as desired. This is usually the case for ammonia and chlorine which are fitted with *goose neck* withdrawal tubes capable of removing gas when the cylinder is held vertically and liquid when it is held horizontally (Fig. 2.39). Such cylinders should be supported in a specially designed cradle and must be chained in the vertical position when not in use. When using liquid ammonia for dissolving metal reductions such as the Birch reduction (see Experiment 27) it is recommended that the ammonia be obtained as a gas with the cylinder vertical and condensed into the receiver flask using a dry-ice acetone condenser (see Fig. 3.30, p. 104). Otherwise particles of ferrous material may be carried into the reaction and catalyze the formation of sodamide.

Wear protection against splashes of cold liquid

Quite apart from the corrosive and toxic nature of these gases, severe burns will result from splashing the cold liquid on the skin and suitable protective clothing must be worn when dispensing any liquid from a cylinder. Needless to say, the receiving vessel must be in an efficient hood and the correct type of respirator should also be readily to hand in case of spillage in the open laboratory or the valve jamming open.

Keep a respirator to hand

Fig. 2.39 Systems for delivery of liquid or gas from cylinders using a gooseneck adapter arrangement: (a) cylinder vertical, gas delivered; (b) cylinder tilted, liquid delivered.

The diaphragm regulator

The controlled release of gas from within the cylinder requires a pressure reduction regulator to deliver the highly compressed gas at steady flow rates and pressures which may be varied from about 0.1 to 2 atm. The regulator is attached to the cylinder by a threaded bullet adapter which fits tightly into the socket of the cylinder valve (Fig. 2.40). Regulators for use with cylinders containing flammable gases are equipped with flash arrestors to stop any combustion entering the cylinder. These regulators have fittings with left-hand threads and this is indicated by a groove cut into the edges of the hexagonal nut.

The pressure drop is achieved using a diaphragm regulator and this may be a single- or double-stage arrangement. Single-stage regulators are less expensive, but do not maintain as steady an outlet pressure as double-stage regulators. In systems where it is necessary to have a very stable gas delivery, such as in vapour phase chromatography carrier gas supplies, the double-stage regulator is necessary, but for the majority of operations requiring an inert atmosphere, a single-stage regulator is adequate. The regulator is equipped with two pressure gauges, one to indicate the cylinder pressure (A) and one to indicate the pressure on the outlet side (B) (Fig. 2.40). The outlet pressure is controlled by turning the large screw controller (C). Clockwise movement causes an increase in outlet pressure and anticlockwise movement a corresponding decrease. The regulator is also fitted with an outlet tap (D) and a bursting valve (E) as an emergency pressure release valve.

low pressure gauge

high pressure gauge (cylinder)

bursting valve

outlet tap

threaded bullet adapter to fit into cylinder

diaphragm regulator control

increase outlet pressure

Fig. 2.40 The diaphragm pressure regulator.

Attaching the pressure regulator to the cylinder

All traces of dust and grease must be removed from the socket to permit a gas-tight seal between the cylinder valve and regulator. However, this is particularly important in the case of oxygen cylinders because oil residues are liable to explode on contact with compressed oxygen. Fitting requires firm tightening to achieve a gas-tight seal and care should be taken to ensure that the adapter is firmly in place before opening the cylinder valve, otherwise the escaping gas may eject the regulator with great force.

The outlet valve should be closed and the diaphragm regulator should be turned fully anticlockwise in order to close the valve completely. On opening the cylinder valve with a square-shaped key, the cylinder pressure should register immediately on the high pressure gauge, whilst the low pressure gauge should show no movement. Slight leaks can be detected by listening for escaping gas and by applying a weak soap solution around the joints. If all appears sound, the outlet pressure may be adjusted by turning the diaphragm regulator clockwise until the desired pressure registers on the outlet pressure gauge and opening the outlet valve permits delivery of the gas.

Check for leaks at the regulator–cylinder connection

Further reading

For full details on safe working practice with compressed gases, see: *Handbook of Compressed Gases*, 3rd edn, Van Nostrand Reinhold, New York, 1990; W. Braker and A.L. Mossman, *Compressed Gas Association, Matheson Gas Data Book*, 6th edn, Matheson, Lyndhurst, 1980; *Safe under Pressure*, BOC, 1997; European Standard EN1089-3, 1997.

Chapter 3

Organic Reactions: from Starting Materials to Pure Organic Product

Experimental organic chemistry is all about carrying out organic reactions, converting one compound into another in a safe and efficient manner. The route from starting materials to pure organic products involves a number of discrete operations which can be summarized as follows:

- Assembling suitable apparatus in which to carry out the reaction.
- Dispensing, measuring and transferring the correct quantities of starting materials, reagents and solvents for the reaction.
- Running the reaction under defined conditions, controlling, as appropriate, rates of addition of reagents, rate of stirring and, importantly, the reaction temperature. In addition, it is often necessary to follow the progress of the reaction by some means.
- Isolation of your product or products from the reaction mixture at the end of the reaction. This isolation procedure is often referred to as the reaction *work-up*.
- Purification of the product.
- Analysis of the product (Chapters 4 and 5).

This chapter explains how the first five steps of these processes can be safely and efficiently carried out, for standard and microscale processes, and ideally should be read and understood before attempting any of the experiments in Part 2 of this book. All of the basic techniques of the organic laboratory are included here, and this chapter serves as a reference for the experimental procedures that are encountered in Part 2.

3.1   Handling chemicals

Safe handling of chemicals

When handling any chemical, safety is of paramount importance. Before starting any experiment in organic chemistry, you should familiarize yourself with the properties of the chemicals and solvents that you will be using. As explained in Chapter 1, the general properties of a chemical are usually indicated on the container by a written warning or by use of standard hazard warning symbols. Get into the habit of looking at the labels on reagent bottles, and take note of any warnings given. So, before setting up any organic

Check labels for hazard warnings

69

experiment, check the experimental procedure for warnings about chemicals, and **think**!! The mental check-list goes something like this:

- Are any of the reagents or solvents particularly corrosive? If so, wear adequate hand protection.

Always check for lighted burners before using flammable materials

- Are any of the reagents or solvents particularly flammable with very low flash points? If so, check that there are no naked flames in the vicinity.
- Are any of the reagents or solvents particularly toxic or unpleasant smelling? If so, they will need to be dispensed and used in a fume hood.
- Are any of the reagents or solvents highly air or moisture sensitive? If so, special handling techniques will be required (pp. 83–89).

Always take the utmost care when transporting chemicals around the laboratory from the stockroom or storage shelves to your bench or hood. Remember to check that the top of the reagent container is securely fastened before moving it. Large (2.5 L) solvent bottles are most safely transported in wire or basket bottle carriers.

Use bottle carriers!

Remember, if in any doubt about how to handle a given compound, ask!!

Measuring and transferring chemicals

For a successful organic chemistry experiment it is important to use defined amounts of starting materials and reagents. It is very rare that you can get away with using approximate quantities. Therefore, unless your instructor suggests that the *scale* of an experiment be changed, the amounts of chemicals given in the experimental procedures in Part 2 should be strictly adhered to. If the experimental protocol requires the use of 1.2 g of reagent, **do not** use 2.4 g in the assumption that the reaction will take half the time or give twice the yield. This is a mistaken and possibly dangerous assumption.

Do not alter the scale of a reaction without consulting an instructor

Solids

The correct amount of solid for a chemical reaction is always given by weight. Therefore, setting up your experiment requires the weighing of one or more reagents, and, or course, the final product. Careful weighing is a time-consuming process because widely differing densities of solid materials make estimation of weight very difficult. Even with experience, 'weighing by eye' is notoriously inaccurate. The accuracy of weighing required depends on the *scale* of the reaction; if the reaction is being carried out on a millimolar scale, typically 100–300 mg, then weighing to the nearest milligram is required. On the other hand, for most of the larger scale reactions described in this book, weighing to the nearest 0.1 g will usually suffice, and in cases where the amount of reagent is not critical, to the nearest 1 g. Therefore you should always use a balance that is appropriate for the accuracy of weighing required.

Use the right balance

There are a vast number of balances on the market, ranging from analytical balances that weigh to the nearest 0.01 mg, requiring totally draught- and vibration-free conditions, to simple scale pan balances. Some typical examples are shown in Fig. 3.1. Modern electronic single pan balances are by far the most convenient to use, since they have digital read-out and electronic zero facilities, making preweighing of containers unnecessary. Whichever type of balance is available in your laboratory or balance room, the first thing to do is to familiarize yourself with its operation.

For convenience it is often better, although not essential, to weigh chemicals into a suitable container, and subsequently transfer the chemical to the reaction flask or addition funnel. However, it is important to use an appropriate container for weighing out your sample. For example, do not use a large flask or beaker weighing more than 200 g to weigh out 0.1 g of solid. Even with modern electronic balances, this is bad practice, since you are dealing with small differences between large numbers. Rather use a small sample vial (which can be capped if necessary), or, if the solid is not air or moisture sensitive, or hygroscopic, it may be weighed out onto special weighing paper which has a smooth glossy surface. Use a micro-spatula, normal spatula or lab spoon—the choice depends on the amount of solid—to transfer the chemical from its bottle or container to the weighing vessel, although utmost care should be taken to avoid spills during the transfer. It is particularly important when using accurate balances (the type with doors as in Fig. 3.1a), that no transfers are made *inside* the weighing compartment. Spills of chemicals may seriously damage the balance mechanism.

Use a small container to weigh small quantities

Wipe up spills immediately

Occasionally it may be necessary, because of the properties of the chemical, for the weighing operation to be carried out inside a hood. Laboratories with plenty of hood space often have a balance permanently located in a hood for such occasions, otherwise a balance will have to be transported. However, accurate weighing on an open pan balance is difficult in a hood because the balance is adversely affected by the hood draught.

Unless you have weighed your solid starting material or reagent directly into the reaction vessel, the chemical has to be transferred from the weighing

(a)   (b)   (c)

Fig. 3.1 Some typical examples of modern balances (not to scale): (a) electronic four-figure balance (weighs to nearest 0.1 mg with maximum of *ca.* 100 g); (b) single pan electronic balance (weighs to nearest 0.01 g with maximum of *ca.* 300 g); (c) scale pan type balance (weighs to nearest 1 g with a maximum of *ca.* 2000 g).

paper or container to the reaction vessel. A convenient way to do this is to use a creased filter paper or weighing paper as shown in Fig. 3.2. Place the solid on the paper, hold the paper over the vessel, and carefully scrape the solid into the vessel using a spatula. With care, this is a quick and easy technique. For transferring larger amounts of solids it is much better to use a wide bore (>2 cm) funnel (often called a powder funnel, see Fig. 2.3). These are available with standard-tapered glass joints so that they can fit directly into the reaction flask.

Treat low melting solids as liquids

Transferring and weighing low melting (<30°C) solids can present special difficulties, since they have a great tendency to become liquid during the operation. If the chemical persists in melting, it is often best to treat it as a liquid, although you may have to warm it gently. However, do not attempt such transfers using narrow bore Pasteur pipettes, since the substance is sure to re-solidify in the pipette!

Liquids

Measure liquids by volume

Liquids can be measured by weight or by volume, but it is usually easier to measure by volume. The main exceptions to this are liquid products from reactions which have to be weighed to determine the yield of the reaction. Many experimental procedures give the quantities of liquid reagents required as a volume in millilitres. If, however, the quantity is given by weight in grams, then the required volume can easily be calculated, provided that you know the density of the liquid (often quoted on the reagent bottle or in the supplier's catalogue), using the formula:

$$\text{Volume (in mL)} = \frac{\text{Weight (in g)}}{\text{Density (in g mL}^{-1})}$$

Fig. 3.2 Transferring solids with the aid of a creased paper.

There are various vessels available for measuring the volume of liquids: beakers and Erlenmeyer flasks, which have approximate volumes marked on their sides, graduated cylinders, graduated pipettes, and syringes, all of which can be obtained in several standard sizes. Again the choice of equipment depends very much on the accuracy of measurement required. For rough work, for example when *ca.* 60 mL of a solvent is required for an extraction, then a graduated beaker or Erlenmeyer flask will suffice. When a little more accuracy is needed, it is better to use a graduated cylinder. Always choose one of appropriate size; do not attempt to measure 7 mL in a 100 mL cylinder, use a 10 mL or 25 mL cylinder. If care is taken it is possible to pour liquids from a reagent bottle into a measuring cylinder, but always use a funnel to minimize the chance of spills. However, never attempt to pour a small amount of liquid, say 5 mL, from a wide-necked 2.5 L bottle into a 10 mL cylinder. Use a Pasteur pipette to transfer the liquid, although always ensure that the pipette is clean, otherwise you run the risk of contaminating the entire reagent/solvent bottle. This is particularly important when transferring deuterated nuclear magnetic resonance (NMR) solvents, as contamination from other hydrogen-containing solvents must be rigorously avoided (see Chapter 5). Smaller volumes of liquids are best measured in a graduated pipette. These are available in a range of sizes, typically from 0.1 to 10 mL, and if used carefully are very accurate. Always use a pipette filler; smaller pipettes can be filled with a simple PVC teat (as used for a Pasteur pipette), but larger ones require a special filler. Whatever the liquid, never be tempted to suck it into the pipette by mouth; even if the liquid is non-toxic, you risk ingesting chemicals from a dirty pipette. Syringes are also useful for measuring small quantities of liquids quickly and accurately, and for certain air- and moisture-sensitive liquids, the use of a syringe is essential. This technique is dealt with specifically on pp. 83–89.

Having measured out your liquid reagent or starting material it needs to be transferred from the measuring vessel to the reaction flask or addition funnel. Liquids measured in a graduated pipette or syringe can simply be run in; the last drop must not be forced out because such apparatus is calibrated to take account of the 'dead space'. Slightly larger volumes of liquid may be poured from a small cylinder or transferred by Pasteur pipette. In the latter case it is probably worth rinsing out the pipette with a small amount of the same solvent that is being used for the reaction. Large volumes of liquid are simply poured, but remember it is always better to use a funnel to avoid spills. One technique which also helps to prevent spills is to pour the liquid down a glass rod as shown in Fig. 3.3.

Mechanical losses of material are extremely undesirable on the standard scale; however, on the microscale, where very small (sub-millimolar) quantities are involved, they are disastrous. The unnecessary spreading of material over the glass surface should therefore be avoided wherever possible. Liquids are rarely poured and transfers should be made using pipettes or syringes.

Do not contaminate the reagent bottle. Use a clean Pasteur pipette

Never pipette by mouth

Always use a funnel

Fig. 3.3 The use of a glass rod to help in pouring liquids.

Pasteur pipettes are useful for transferring larger quantities of solutions or reagents (*ca.* 0.5 mL); drawing out the pipette in a hot flame reduces the cross-section of the aperture and makes the transfer of smaller quantities of material easier to control. Small graduated pipettes can be useful but adjustable pipettes which use disposable polypropylene tips can be used accurately and rapidly for transferring volumes from $10\,\mu L$ to 1 mL. Syringes can also be used for this range of volumes though the smaller (microlitre) syringes are expensive and block easily. Disposable syringes which are available with $10\,\mu L$ graduations are useful; they can be weighed accurately before and after reagent transfer to a reaction so the amount of material delivered is known precisely. Some caution is necessary because the material of the syringe may be softened or dissolved by certain solvents; testing before use is recommended.

Filtration

There are few experiments in organic chemistry that do not involve at least one filtration step. Filtration of a suspension to remove insoluble solids is a fundamental technique of preparative chemistry and is achieved by allowing the liquid to pass through a porous barrier, such as filter paper or sintered glass, whereby the solid remains on the barrier. In many cases, gravity alone is sufficient force for the liquid to pass through the porous barrier; this is referred to as *gravity filtration*. However, many organic solids are bulky, and filter slowly under gravity alone. In these cases the process is speeded up considerably by using the *suction* or *vacuum filtration* technique, in which a partial vacuum is applied to the filter flask (which must be thick-walled), and hence air pressure on the surface of the liquid in the filter funnel forces it through the porous barrier.

The choice of which filtration technique to use depends on what you are trying to achieve, but, *in general*, the following rule applies:

If you want the filtered liquid (filtrate) use gravity filtration.

If you want the solid material use suction filtration.

Gravity or suction for filtration?

Thus, if you are trying to remove small amounts of unwanted insoluble impurities, say, from a solution, gravity filtration using a folded (fluted) filter paper is often better. This is particularly so for *hot filtration*. If you need to remove larger amounts of unwanted solids, such as a spent drying agent for example, then you can still filter by gravity, although it may be considerably faster to filter by suction. In cases where you want to collect a solid material, such as a precipitated or recrystallized product, it is much better to use suction filtration.

The filtration of very small volumes of solution and the collection of small quantities of solid by filtration present special problems. These are discussed on pp. 79 and 137–138.

Gravity filtration

Gravity filtration is a simple technique only requiring a filter funnel, a piece of filter paper and a vessel, usually an Erlenmeyer, for collecting the filtrate. Glass funnels are available in several sizes, and may or may not have a stem; stemless funnels are particularly useful for hot filtration. Always use the correct size of filter paper for the filter funnel; after folding, the filter paper should always be below the rim of the glass funnel. As a rough guide, use the size of filter paper whose diameter is about 1 cm less than twice the diameter of the funnel. For example, for a funnel with a diameter of 6 cm use a filter paper with a diameter of 11 cm.

Use the right size of filter paper

The purpose of folding or fluting the filter paper is to speed the filtration by decreasing the area of contact between the paper and the funnel. Everyone develops their own way of fluting a filter paper, but one way is shown in Fig. 3.4. Start by folding the paper in half, then in half again, and then crease each

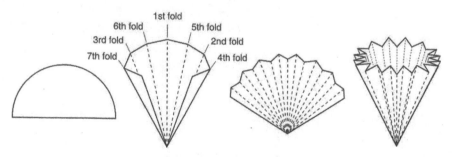

Fig. 3.4 How to flute a filter paper.

quarter into four more sections with alternate folds in opposite directions. Pull the paper into a half circle and arrange it into a pleated fan, ensuring that each fold is in the opposite direction to the previous one. Pull the sides apart and place the paper into the funnel.

Always support the glassware

Always support the filter funnel in a metal ring or clamp (Fig. 3.5). It is very tempting to place the funnel directly into the filter flask with no additional support; this is bad practice since the whole assembly is top heavy and is easily knocked over. The solution to be filtered is then simply poured into the filter paper cone, and the filtrate is collected.

Hot filtration

A useful variation on gravity filtration is *hot filtration*. This is particularly important when carrying out crystallizations (pp. 131–140), when having dissolved the material in a suitable hot solvent, you need to filter it to remove insoluble impurities. The filtration has to be carried out whilst the solution is *hot*, before the material crystallizes out of the cooling solution, and has to be conducted under gravity. Attempting to filter hot solutions by suction will

ring clamp
supported
on stand

Fig. 3.5 Gravity filtration.

result in the hot filtrate boiling under the reduced pressure and in possible loss of material due to frothing. The aim of hot filtration is to complete the operation before the material starts to crystallize. For this reason, always use a stemless funnel to prevent crystallization occurring in the stem and the consequent blocking of the filter. It often helps to pre-heat the glass filter funnel before commencing the filtration and to keep the bulk of the solution to be filtered hot by pouring only small amounts of it into the filter at once. When pouring hot solutions, always use adequate hand protection; wear heat-resistant gloves or hold the hot flask in a towel.

One useful technique that considerably aids the filtration of hot solutions by keeping the funnel hot is shown in Fig. 3.6. Before commencing the filtration add a few millilitres of the same solvent to the Erlenmeyer filter flask and then heat the flask on a hotplate or steam bath. **A steam bath must be used if the solvent is flammable.** Allow the solvent to boil gently. The hot vapour will keep the funnel hot and prevent crystallization occurring in the filter. The technique necessarily generates solvent vapour, which may, of course, be flammable or toxic. In this case use a hood.

Suction filtration

Carrying out a filtration using suction is faster than using gravity alone, but requires some additional equipment. Since the technique relies on producing a partial vacuum in the receiving flask, a thick-walled filter flask with a side arm, often called a Büchner flask, must be used, although smaller quantities can be filtered using a Hirsch tube. The flask should be securely clamped and attached to the source of the vacuum by thick-walled, flexible pressure tubing. Such tubing is heavy and will almost certainly cause unsupported flasks to topple over. The source of vacuum in the organic laboratory is almost invariably the water aspirator and the filter flask should be protected against suck-

Always support the filter flask

Fig. 3.6 Filtration of a hot solution.

Use the right size of filter paper with Büchner and Hirsch funnels

back of water by a suitable trap (see p. 38). The most useful design of trap incorporates a valve for controlling and releasing the vacuum (see Figs 2.19 and 3.7). Different types of funnel are also used in suction filtration; the usual types are the so-called Büchner and Hirsch funnels. The Hirsch funnel with its sloping sides is particularly suited to the collection of smaller amounts of solids. Both funnels contain a flat perforated plate or filter disk at the bottom, which is covered with a piece of filter paper. Always use a filter paper of the correct diameter. Never attempt to use a larger piece and turn up the edges; if the paper is too large, trim it to size with scissors. Finally, in order to ensure an adequate seal between the filter funnel and the flask, the funnel is placed on top of the flask through a Neoprene® filter adapter. The completed assembly for suction filtration using a Büchner or Hirsch funnel is shown in Fig. 3.7.

Wet filter paper with solvent first

Before starting the filtration, wet the filter paper with a little solvent—the same solvent as that used in the solution that is about to be filtered. Turn on the water aspirator *gently*, and ensure that the dampened paper is sucked down flat over the perforated filter disk. Pour the mixture to be filtered onto the centre of the filter paper, and slowly increase the suction. The partial vacuum in the filter flask results in rapid filtration. With very volatile solvents, do not apply too strong a vacuum, otherwise the filtrate will boil under the reduced pressure.

When all the liquid has been sucked through, release the vacuum. Wash the collected solid with a little cold clean solvent and re-apply gentle suction. Do not wash solids under strong suction because the solvent passes through too quickly. Another advantage of suction filtration is that continuation of the suction for a few extra minutes results in fairly effective drying of the solid. To make this drying as effective as possible, press the solid flat onto the filter plate

Fig. 3.7 Suction filtration using (a) a Büchner funnel or (b) a Hirsch funnel for smaller quantities.

Suck solid as dry as possible

using a clean glass stopper, and then maintain the suction to remove the last traces of solvent, sucking the solid as dry as possible. This process, which involves drawing large volumes of air through the solid, is a quick way of drying solids, although it should not be used for compounds which are air or moisture sensitive. More rigorous ways of drying solids are discussed on pp. 140–143. After completion of the suction filtration, always release the vacuum and disconnect the flexible tubing from the filter flask **before** turning off the water aspirator.

Release vacuum before turning off aspirator

An alternative to filter paper as a porous barrier is sintered glass. A variety of filter funnels containing sintered glass disks of varying size and porosity is commercially available (Fig. 3.8). These make excellent, although more expensive, alternatives to a Büchner funnel plus filter paper. In the simplest form, a sintered glass filter funnel has a stem for use with a Neoprene® adapter and filter flask as above. More sophisticated versions have a standard-tapered ground glass joint with a built-in side arm for attaching to the aspirator. These can be used for filtering directly into a standard-tapered joint round-bottomed flask, ready for subsequent evaporation or reaction.

Filtration on the microscale

Losses are incurred easily during the collection of small quantities of solids by filtration. Craig tubes are ideal (see pp. 137–138) and Hirsch funnels are available in very small sizes (5–10 mm bed size). When the filtrate is required, columns of filter agent (Celite®, Hyflo® or silica gel) can be packed into short (1 cm) columns in Pasteur pipettes (Fig. 3.9) or small chromatography columns or syringe barrels and the suspension can be forced through under pressure applied using the pipette teat. It is usually necessary to wet the filter bed with solvent to ensure that the filtrate is not held up and lost. Subsequent washing of the filter bed with small (*ca.* 0.1 mL) portions of solvent is also recommended.

Air- and moisture-sensitive compounds: syringe techniques

When working in the organic laboratory, you will eventually come across a

Fig. 3.8 Some typical sintered glass filter funnels.

Fig. 3.9 A filtration column can be made in a Pasteur pipette plugged with glass or cotton wool, covered with a thin layer of sand which supports the filter agent (Celite®, Hyflo® or silica gel).

reagent which is described as moisture sensitive or air sensitive. Depending on the degree of this sensitivity, the reagent will need special handling, which may just simply involve bubbling dry nitrogen through the reaction mixture to maintain an inert atmosphere. At the other extreme, it may be necessary to work in a purpose-built 'dry box' under conditions which rigorously exclude air and moisture down to the last traces. However, for the experiments encountered in this book, this very specialized handling is not necessary. Rather, we attempt to describe briefly how conventional tapered glass joint apparatus, with a few additional items, can be used to handle moderately air- and moisture-sensitive reagents. A detailed treatment of such techniques is outside the scope of this book, but for those who want more details, various specialist texts are available (references on p. 91).

Air-sensitive materials are compounds which decompose on reaction with atmospheric oxygen, water or carbon dioxide. Other compounds are *pyrophoric*, that is they catch fire in air. Provided that the decomposition is *stoichiometric*, handling these compounds presents no special problems. Compounds which decompose on exposure to *catalytic* amounts of oxygen, etc. are much more difficult to deal with, and are very much the province of specialist research laboratories. The sort of reagents that you will encounter which might, depending on their precise reactivity, require some special handling are:

- alkali metals, e.g. Li, Na, K;
- metal hydrides, e.g. NaH, CaH$_2$;
- hydride reducing agents, e.g. LiAlH$_4$, diborane (tetrahydrofuran solution);
- organometallics, e.g. Grignards, BuLi (hexane solution);
- strong bases, e.g. NaNH$_2$;
- Lewis acids, e.g. BF$_3$·Et$_2$O, TiCl$_4$;
- powerful electrophiles, e.g. acid chlorides, anhydrides.

Reactions involving air-sensitive reagents can be carried out in thoroughly dried conventional glass apparatus, but do require some extra equipment, the most important of which is a source of an inert atmosphere. In addition, a supply of syringes, needles and septa will be needed. However, when working with air-sensitive reagents, several essential points have to be borne in mind, and many quite basic operations—measuring and transferring for example—have to be carried out much more carefully than usual. The essential ingredients for success are:

- drying the apparatus thoroughly;
- drying the solvents thoroughly;
- providing an inert atmosphere;
- dispensing and transferring the reagents carefully;
- running and working-up the reaction carefully.

Drying the apparatus

Dry glassware thoroughly

It is important to ensure that your glassware is properly dry. Although glass may look completely dry, there is usually an invisible film of moisture on it, which must be driven off. This is best achieved by heating the apparatus in a drying oven, but thorough drying takes longer than most people think. For example, if the oven temperature is 125°C, then the apparatus should be left in the oven overnight. At the higher temperature of 140°C, thorough drying still takes at least 4 h. Any Teflon® (PTFE) parts such as stopcocks should be removed prior to drying, since Teflon® softens at these temperatures. After drying, the apparatus should be rapidly assembled whilst still hot (**use heat-resistant gloves**) and should be allowed to cool under an inert atmosphere. Alternatively, glass apparatus may be assembled cold and dried by flaming the outside with a Bunsen burner whilst passing a stream of inert gas through the

Check for flammable solvents before lighting a burner

apparatus. Do check, however, that flames are allowed in your laboratory before using this technique and take care if you have any Teflon® stopcocks or polypropylene septa in the apparatus.

Drying the solvents

Pure, dry and deoxygenated solvents are essential when working with air-sensitive reagents. The purification and drying of organic solvents is discussed in detail in several texts (references on p. 91), and methods for the more common solvents are given in Appendix 2 (p. 677). Solvents are best when freshly distilled, and although your laboratory may keep a supply of distilled

Rigorously dry solvents must be prepared immediately before use

Solvents stills must be supervised

solvents, when solvent dryness is essential for the success of a reaction, there is no substitute for distilling it yourself immediately before it is required; then you *know* how good it is (or is not). If there is a regular need for a particular solvent in your working area, then it is possible that a special solvent still will have been set up. Provided that this is regularly supervised, it can be left running, so that aliquots of pure, dry solvent can be withdrawn as required. When absolute dryness is less crucial, bottles of solvent which have been pre-dried by standing over an appropriate drying agent are often available. For example, diethyl ether is often dried by standing it in its bottle over sodium wire ('sodium-dried ether'). However, although this may well be dry enough for many purposes such as standard Grignard reactions, it should not be considered as rigorously dry.

Providing an inert atmosphere

The single major difference between working with air-sensitive reagents and 'normal' reagents is the need for an inert atmosphere. The source of this inert atmosphere is a gas cylinder which, depending on the arrangement in your laboratory, may be fixed to the bench or on a mobile trolley (see pp. 64–68). Alternatively your bench or hood may be equipped with a purpose-built inert gas line, although this is only likely in research laboratories. The most commonly used inert gas is nitrogen, which is relatively cheap, and is available in a range of purities. For most purposes, high purity grades of nitrogen, which contain no more than *ca.* 5 ppm of water and oxygen, are adequate. In cases where nitrogen is insufficiently inert, for example with reactions involving lithium metal, argon should be used. Although argon is more expensive than nitrogen, it does have advantages in that, as well as being more inert, it gives better 'blanket' protection than nitrogen since it is heavier than air and diffuses more slowly. Provided that there is no severe air turbulence, an argon-filled flask can be opened briefly and the inert atmosphere maintained if you are careful.

Do not attempt further purification of inert gases

Use shortest possible tubing

It is always better to use higher grade gases, and not to carry out further purification. Invariably, attempts to remove water or oxygen by passing the gas through various potions in a 'drying train' introduces *more* contamination than it removes, through the extra glassware, joints and tubing involved. On the question of tubing, always use the shortest possible length of flexible tubing between the inert gas supply and your apparatus. Ensure that the tubing is dry, although do not attempt to dry it in an oven!

The exit from the apparatus should be protected by a gas bubbler filled with a little mineral oil. The bubbler serves both to monitor the flow of inert gas through your apparatus and to prevent back diffusion of air. Common types of bubbler are shown in Fig. 3.10, and should always be used for reactions involving highly air-sensitive reagents. Guard tubes containing a drying agent such as calcium chloride remove little water and no oxygen, and hence should not be used in situations where exclusion of moisture is essential. Some

Fig. 3.10 Some typical gas bubblers for use with inert gases.

sort of bubbler should also be used in the gas supply line itself to act as a monitoring device and, more importantly, a safety device so that the system is not completely sealed (Fig. 3.10c).

If an inert atmosphere is only needed for a short time, say less than 20–30 min, a balloon inflated with the inert gas may be used. The most convenient way of using a balloon is with a two-way stopcock (Fig. 3.11), which allows for evacuation of the apparatus and the filling of the balloon with inert gas. However, be warned: atmospheric oxygen, water or carbon dioxide can diffuse through a balloon skin at a surprising rate, even against a pressure of inert gas. Therefore do not think that the comforting sight of a nitrogen balloon atop your apparatus provides total protection from the atmosphere. Nevertheless, it is a quick and easy way to provide a relatively inert atmosphere for a short time, and is considerably better than nothing at all.

Balloons only provide a temporary inert atmosphere

Dispensing and transferring air-sensitive reagents

Liquid air-sensitive reagents are best dispensed and transferred by syringe, and therefore a discussion of basic syringe techniques is called for. Syringes are ideally suited for the transfer of up to *ca*. 20 mL of liquid, and are available in a range of sizes with different needle lengths. Gas-tight syringes with 'locked' (Luer lock) type needles are the best (Fig. 3.12). As with other glassware used for air-sensitive reagents, syringes and needles should be thoroughly dried in an oven before use; but take care always to remove the needle and plunger from the syringe assembly before drying. After drying, allow the syringe to cool in a desiccator, where dry syringes can also be stored.

Fig. 3.11 Use of a balloon to provide a temporary inert atmosphere.

Fig. 3.12 Flushing a syringe with inert gas from the line.

Air-sensitive reagents are often sold as stock solutions in an inert solvent; butyl-lithium, for example, is sold in hexane solution in a range of concentrations. Nowadays, these solutions are sold in bottles which have special tops, to make the subsequent transfer of reagent much easier. An example of such a bottle is shown in Fig. 3.13, and is based on the Sure/Seal® system of the Aldrich Chemical Company. The metal crown cap has a small hole which allows a syringe to be inserted through it. After withdrawing the syringe needle, the hole in the crown cap liner often self-seals, but even if it does not, the lined plastic cap, when screwed down, will ensure that the bottle remains air tight.

If your air-sensitive reagent has been supplied in a normal bottle with a simple screw cap, then it must be fitted with a septum so that the reagent can be withdrawn by syringe. A quick and easy way to do this is to open the bottle under an inverted funnel attached to the inert gas supply (Fig. 3.14a). This provides a 'blanket' of inert gas to protect the reagent whilst the cap is **quickly** removed and a septum inserted. Check that you have the correct sized septum to hand **before** opening the bottle. Better protection for an open reagent bottle is provided by a polythene bag attached to the inert gas supply

Fig. 3.13 Air-sensitive reagent bottle fitted with special seal and cap (adapted from the Aldrich Sure/Seal® system).

Fig. 3.14 Two ways to open a reagent bottle under an inert atmosphere.

(Fig. 3.14b). The septum should be tight fitting, and after puncturing with a needle, can be sealed by covering with paraffin wax sealing film.

When withdrawing air-sensitive reagents from stock bottles by syringe, the following general procedure should be used.

Fig. 3.15 (a) Withdrawing an air-sensitive reagent by syringe; (b) transferring the reagent to an addition funnel (see also Fig. 3.22).

1   Make sure your apparatus is clean, dry and assembled correctly for carrying out the reaction under an inert atmosphere. The neck of the vessel (reaction flask or addition funnel) that is to receive the air-sensitive reagent should be equipped with a septum. Some typical assemblies are shown in Figs 3.15(b), 3.16 and 3.22.

Always support the reagent bottle

2   Support the bottle of air-sensitive reagent in a ring clamp (Fig. 3.15a). This is very important; knocking over such a bottle would be potentially disastrous.

3   Insert a needle attached to an inert gas line through the seal or septum on the reagent bottle, and ensure a slight positive pressure of gas. This is to maintain an inert atmosphere in the bottle during and after the withdrawal of reagent. To prevent over-pressurizing the bottle, you must have a bubbler device in the inert gas line.

4   Flush your syringe with inert gas (Fig. 3.12).

5   Insert the syringe needle through the bottle seal, and fill the syringe to the desired level by slowly withdrawing the plunger, or **better**, by allowing the positive pressure of inert gas to push the plunger back (Fig. 3.15a).

6   Withdraw the syringe, and complete the transfer of reagent to reaction vessel or addition funnel as quickly as possible by puncturing the septum as shown in Fig. 3.15(b).

When larger volumes (greater than 20 mL) of air-sensitive reagents have to be transferred, syringes become unwieldy, and it is much better to use the

Fig. 3.16 Transfer of air-sensitive reagents using the double-ended needle technique.

Use a double-ended needle to transfer larger amounts of air-sensitive liquids

double-ended needle (or cannula) technique (Fig. 3.16). Support the reagent bottle, and as before insert a needle attached to the inert gas line through the bottle seal. Insert a pre-dried, long, flexible double-ended needle through the bottle seal **into the head space above the liquid**. This causes the inert gas to flush through the needle. Insert the other end of the needle through a septum into the receiving vessel or flask and, finally, push the end in the reagent bottle below the surface of the liquid. The positive pressure of inert gas forces the reagent from the bottle, through the needle, and into your vessel. When using this technique, the volume of liquid transferred has to be measured by using a pre-calibrated receiving vessel. When the required volume has been transferred, immediately withdraw the needle from the liquid in the reagent bottle to the head space. Remove the other end of the needle from the reaction vessel before removing the needle from the reagent bottle completely.

Clean syringes immediately

All syringes and needles must be cleaned **immediately** after use. If this is not done, needles will become blocked and plungers will stick in the syringe barrel because of oxidation and/or hydrolysis of the reagent. The cleaning should be carried out carefully; do not simply wash with water in the sink since many air-sensitive reagents react vigorously with water. The complete syringe

Fig. 3.17 Transferring solids under an inert gas blanket.

and needle assembly is best cleaned by rinsing out the last traces of reagent with a few millilitres of the solvent that has been used for the reaction. The rinsings can then be **cautiously** added to a beaker of cold water in the hood without incident. After two such rinses, the syringe and needle can be washed out with water in the normal way. Any stubborn inorganic residues formed by hydrolysis of the reagent may have to be washed out with dilute acid or alkali before final rinsing with water and thorough drying. Double-tipped needles, which will only contain traces of the reagent, can be washed in the sink immediately after use.

Air-sensitive solids
Solid reagents which are only moderately air and moisture sensitive can be handled fairly easily under an inert gas blanket provided by an inverted funnel attached to the gas line (Fig. 3.17). You must not use such a high pressure/flow rate of gas that the solid is blown all over the bench. This technique can be used to transfer solids from a reagent bottle to a sealable container for weighing, for example, or from a container to a reaction flask which can be sealed subsequently.

If your experimental procedure requires the addition of an air-sensitive solid in several portions, the best method is to transfer the reagent in a single portion, under an inert gas blanket, to a solid addition tube with a tapered glass joint. This is fitted to the reaction flask in the normal way, and portions of solid can be introduced into the flask by turning and gently tapping the tube (Fig. 3.18).

bubbler

sealed stirrer guide

inert gas

water out

clamp

condenser

solid
addition
tube

water in

clamp

Fig. 3.18 Reaction flask fitted with solid addition tube, overhead stirrer and condenser.

However, although you should be aware of the above techniques, not many solids are sufficiently air sensitive to require very special treatment. Although several solids may react violently with liquid water, lithium aluminium hydride for example, these can usually be handled in air without undue problems from atmospheric moisture.

The provision of an inert atmosphere using a balloon and a cut-down syringe barrel is particularly attractive on the microscale; a typical method for the attachment of the balloon is shown in Fig. 3.19. A short (*ca.* 2 cm) collar of thick-walled flexible tubing is pushed over the top portion of the cut-down barrel of a disposable syringe and used as a mount for a balloon which is secured in place with an elastic band. Gas is delivered to the reaction via a disposable syringe needle.

Running the reaction

Reactions involving air-sensitive reagents include the same basic stirring, heating and cooling techniques as any other reaction. The only difference is that the apparatus has to be modified so that the reaction can be carried out under an inert atmosphere. This usually means that a two- or three-necked flask is used in place of a simple single-necked round-bottomed flask, or alternatively a single-necked flask is used fitted with a Claisen, or similar, adapter. Typical apparatus set-ups for reactions requiring an inert atmosphere are discussed in more detail in the next section.

Fig. 3.19 For small-scale reactions, a balloon filled with inert gas connected to a cut-down syringe barrel via a short (*ca.* 2 cm) collar of pressure tubing and secured with an elastic band can be used to provide an inert atmosphere. Gas is introduced into the reaction vessel via a syringe needle.

Take extreme care when quenching reactions involving air or moisture sensitive reagents

At the end of the reaction, care must be taken to destroy any remaining air- or moisture-sensitive reagent that is likely to react vigorously with water, before carrying out the normal aqueous work-up (pp. 109–118). No general method can be given for this; the procedure used depends on what reagent or reagents have been involved in your reaction. Therefore an element of common sense is required at this stage, although the experimental procedures given in Part 2 of this book give precise details of what to do in specific instances.

Although the reaction might involve reagents which are air and/or moisture sensitive, the products from your reaction are very unlikely to be so air or moisture sensitive that special techniques are required **after** the reaction is over. Hence work-up and purification under air-free conditions are not normally necessary. Nevertheless, operations such as extraction, filtration, distillation and recrystallization can all be carried out under an inert atmosphere, although these techniques belong in the research laboratory rather than the teaching laboratory.

Further reading

G.B. Gill and D.A. Whiting, Guidelines for handling air sensitive compounds. *Aldrichimica Acta*, 1986, **19**, 31.

A.J. Gordon and R.J. Ford, *The Chemist's Companion. A Handbook of Practical Data, Techniques and References*, Wiley & Sons, New York, 1973.

G.W. Kramer, A.B. Levy, M.M. Midland and H.C. Brown, *Organic Syntheses via Boranes, Laboratory Operations*, Chapter 9. Wiley & Sons, New York, 1975.

C.F. Lane and G.W. Kramer, Handling air sensitive reagents. *Aldrichimica Acta*, 1977, **10**, 11.

D.D. Perrin and W.L.F. Armarego, *Purification of Laboratory Chemicals*, 4th edn, Elsevier, New York, 1996.

J.A. Riddick and W.B. Bunger, *Organic Solvents: Physical Properties and Methods of Purification*, 4th edn, Wiley & Sons, New York, 1986.

D.F. Shriver, *The Manipulation of Air Sensitive Compounds*, McGraw-Hill, New York, 1969.

In addition, many chemical companies issue technical bulletins with information about the packing and handling of their air-sensitive compounds and provision of such information is a legal requirement in many countries.

3.2 The reaction

Assembling the apparatus

Organic reactions should always be carried out in apparatus that is suitable for the task in hand. The correct choice of apparatus will allow you to combine the reactants in the right order at the right rate, stir the mixture if necessary, control the reaction temperature and, if required, exclude moisture and/or maintain an inert atmosphere. The apparatus required for an organic reaction can vary greatly in its complexity, ranging from a simple test tube or beaker in which two chemicals are mixed and heated, to a set-up involving a multi-necked flask equipped with stirrer, addition funnel, thermometer and condenser. The experimental procedures in Part 2 of this book will usually tell you what sort of apparatus to use for the reaction, with cross-reference to the basic assemblies which are detailed here.

Unless the reaction is very simple and needs just a test tube or beaker, a combination of two or more pieces of glassware will be required. It is assumed that you have access to standard-tapered joint glassware similar to the basic set described in Chapter 2. The key components are round-bottomed flasks (in various sizes), a two- or three-neck flask (if these are not available, a single-neck flask fitted with a Claisen adapter may be used), addition funnels, condensers and various adapters for fitting things like a thermometer or a gas inlet. These basic components, together with stands and clamps, can be combined in several ways to construct a range of apparatus suitable for carrying out most organic reactions. However, rather than discuss several possible permutations and combinations of glassware, we have chosen to illustrate just a few apparatus assemblies that, in our opinion, will cover most eventualities. The operations covered by these assemblies are listed below, with optional additional features given in parentheses.

- stirring a reaction mixture;
- stirring with addition (with temperature measurement);

- stirring with addition under an inert atmosphere (at low temperature);
- heating a reaction mixture (with exclusion of moisture or under an inert atmosphere);
- heating a reaction mixture with stirring;
- heating a reaction mixture with addition (with stirring);
- heating a reaction mixture with addition (liquid or solid) and stirring under an inert atmosphere;
- refluxing a reaction mixture with continuous removal of water;
- addition of gases;
- reactions in liquid ammonia.

Detailed diagrams are given for the apparatus assemblies, and in case certain pieces of glassware are not available in your laboratory, alternatives may be suggested in the text. **Whatever the apparatus, it must be adequately supported with clamps.** This is very important, since the consequences of an unsupported glass apparatus toppling over are potentially disastrous. In each of the diagrams, the recommended clamping points are clearly indicated. Ignore them at your peril!

All of the apparatus shown in pp. 94–99 (except Fig. 3.26) can be constructed from commercial microscale glassware and used in the same way.

Stirring

Most chemical reaction mixtures need stirring to mix the reagents and to aid heat transfer. In open vessels, this stirring can be done by hand using a glass rod, but it soon becomes very tedious. Likewise, efficient mixing can be achieved by swirling the reaction vessel, but again this becomes very tedious after a short while. Therefore, when constant stirring is needed for a sustained period, a stirrer motor should be used.

As described in Chapter 2, stirrer motors are of two basic types: magnetic stirrers and mechanical (or overhead) stirrers. Magnetic stirrers are easy to use, and have the advantage that they are often combined with a hotplate. A simple set-up for stirring a reaction mixture in an Erlenmeyer flask containing a magnetic stirrer bar is shown in Fig. 3.20(a). An important point to note is that, even though the flask might seem quite stable, it should be secured in a clamp. If not, the vibration of the stirrer motor may cause the flask to 'wander' towards the edge of the stirrer plate, when, at the very least, the magnetic stirrer bar will stop going round because it is so far off-centre. At worst, the unsupported flask will fall off the stirrer plate.

Magnetic stirrers are used for a range of applications, but they do have their limitations. If the liquid is very viscous, or if the reaction mixture is heterogeneous with a large amount of suspended solid, then the magnetic stirrer motor, with its relatively low torque, will not cope. In these cases a mechanical (or overhead) stirrer should be used. The higher torque motor coupled to a paddle through a stirrer shaft will usually cope with most situations where more powerful stirring is required. Mechanical stirrers should

Fig. 3.20 (a) Stirring a reaction mixture in an Erlenmeyer flask with a magnetic stirrer; (b) stirring a reaction mixture with a mechanical overhead stirrer.

also be used when very rapid stirring of a two-phase system is needed. A set-up involving a mechanical stirrer is shown in Fig. 3.20(b). If the reaction mixture is contained in a beaker, care should be taken not to use too fast a stirring rate causing the liquid to spill out of the beaker. When using overhead stirrers, it is vital to provide adequate support from clamps. The whole assembly is top heavy so a stand with a heavy base should be used. A loosely tightened clamp can also be used just above the beaker to act as a stirrer guide.

Stirring with addition

You will frequently encounter experimental procedures which require you to add one reagent to a stirred solution of another, often with some sort of temperature control. Magnetic stirrers are ideally suited for such situations, and two typical set-ups are shown in Fig. 3.21. Both incorporate a thermometer to measure the reaction temperature during the addition, but if temperature control is unimportant, the thermometer can be omitted. The first set-up (Fig. 3.21a) uses a single-neck round-bottomed flask fitted with a Claisen adapter, into which are placed a thermometer in an adapter and a pressure equalizing addition funnel. An addition funnel fitted with a pressure equalizing side arm must be used in this case since there is no other outlet to the system. If a pressure equalizing addition funnel is not available, then a normal addition funnel may be used, but the thermometer must be fitted through an adapter with a

Fig. 3.21 (a) Stirring with addition using a single-neck flask with a Claisen adapter; (b) stirring with addition using a two-neck flask.

side arm outlet. To measure the temperature of your reaction mixture the thermometer bulb should be completely immersed in the liquid. Since stirring causes a vortex, the thermometer might have to be set a little lower once the stirrer has been started. However, **do not** set the thermometer so low that the bulb is hit by the magnetic stirrer bar. Thermometer bulbs will not stand this sort of treatment, and careless assembly of the apparatus in this way will surely lead to the unwanted introduction of mercury or ethanol (depending on the thermometer) into your reaction mixture. Note the need for two clamps for adequate support; the addition funnel is off-centre so must be clamped.

The second assembly (Fig. 3.21b) uses a two-neck flask fitted with a thermometer and a pressure equalizing addition funnel. One advantage of using a two-necked flask is that only one clamp is needed, the addition funnel being directly over the clamp on the flask. If a two-neck flask is not available, then obviously a three-neck flask may be used, with the third neck stoppered. Alternatively the third neck may be left open or protected by a guard (drying) tube, thereby obviating the need for the addition funnel with the pressure equalizing arm; a simple addition funnel may be used instead. This assembly also allows the use of a cold bath (see pp. 105–108) to control the reaction temperature during the addition.

Stirring with addition under an inert atmosphere

Some organic reactions need to be run under an inert atmosphere because of the sensitivity of the starting material or reagent to moisture or air. Air- and moisture-sensitive compounds have already been discussed on pp. 79–89, along with details of how to dispense and transfer them. Reactions involving such reagents can be carried out in conventional apparatus provided it is modified to allow for the provision of an inert atmosphere. This usually means attaching the reaction vessel to a supply of inert gas (nitrogen or argon). One fairly common laboratory operation using air-sensitive reagents involves the addition of a solution of the reagent by syringe to a stirred solution of starting material, which is often maintained at low temperature under the inert atmosphere. A typical apparatus for such an operation is shown in Fig. 3.22. A three-neck flask is essential. The securely clamped flask is equipped with a septum, gas bubbler, and thermometer fitted through a thermometer adapter and side arm adapter attached to the inert gas line. Flush the flask with inert gas and introduce the solution of starting material in a **dry** solvent. Maintain the flow of inert gas and, if required, cool the reaction flask in the cooling bath (pp. 105–108). It is important to maintain a fairly rapid flow of inert gas during the cooling process, since the resulting drop in pressure in the flask will cause the mineral oil from the bubbler to be sucked back into your reaction vessel if insufficient back pressure of inert gas is provided. Once the temperature in the flask has fully equilibrated, the flow of inert gas can be reduced to a trickle as monitored by the bubbler. Start the magnetic stirrer, and then add the air-sensitive reagent by syringe through the septum.

Most microscale kits supply vial closures consisting of PTFE-lined elastomer disks which reseal following puncture by a syringe needle so reagent addition can be achieved without using pressure equalizing dropping funnels. An inert atmosphere can be provided using a balloon of nitrogen or argon connected to the apparatus via a syringe needle, a cut-down plastic syringe barrel and a short length of pressure tubing (see Fig. 3.19), or by using one of the threaded tubing adaptors available commercially.

Heating

Since the rate of a chemical reaction is increased by an increase in temperature, many organic reactions are run at elevated temperatures so that they are complete within a convenient time scale. However, the desire to complete the reaction quickly should be tempered by the need to keep side reactions, the rate of which are usually increased even more by heating, to a minimum. Some reactions generate their own heat, that is they are *exothermic*, and in these cases some degree of temperature control is necessary (pp. 105–108).

Fig. 3.22 Stirring under an inert atmosphere with addition of an air-sensitive reagent at low temperature.

However, most reactions that are run at elevated temperatures have to be carried out in apparatus that can be heated by some means, and the common sources of heat in the organic laboratory are discussed on pp. 25–33.

The most common way of conducting an organic reaction at a fixed elevated temperature is to carry it out in a boiling solvent in an apparatus equipped with a condenser, so that the solvent vapour condenses and returns to the reaction vessel. This procedure is known as *heating under reflux* or, more simply, as *refluxing*. The reaction temperature is the same as the boiling point of the solvent. It is easy to find a solvent with a suitable boiling point, but remember that the solvent should be inert and should not interfere in the reaction. Some typical arrangements for carrying out reactions in refluxing solvents are shown in Fig. 3.23. The first (Fig. 3.23a) uses a round-bottomed flask fitted with a standard water condenser, **both** of which should be clamped as shown. Always remember to add some boiling stones (anti-bumping granules) to ensure smooth boiling **before** placing the flask in the heat source. Addition of boiling stones to a liquid that is already hot and near its boiling point usually results in instant very rapid boiling. Although it may be spectacular as the solvent shoots out of the top of the condenser, as well as being

Fig. 3.23 Heating a reaction mixture under reflux: (a) with a normal water condenser; (b) under an inert atmosphere; (c) with an air condenser and drying tube.

extremely dangerous, it is annoying to have to set up your reaction again. Finally, place the flask in the heat source (heating mantle, heating bath, steam bath, etc.) and note when the solvent starts to reflux.

The second assembly (Fig. 3.23b) incorporates a minor modification so that the reflux can be carried out under an inert atmosphere. The top of the water condenser is fitted with an adapter to which the inert gas line is attached. Remove the condenser from the flask, flush it with inert gas, replace it and reduce the gas flow to a steady trickle as monitored by a bubbler. If the reaction mixture needs to be heated for only a short period (less than 30 min), then a balloon can be attached to the top of the condenser to provide a temporary inert atmosphere (see Fig. 3.11). Remember that if it is essential to exclude atmospheric moisture, then an inert gas should always be used in preference to a guard (drying) tube. The only situation where a drying tube can be used is when the reaction uses a solvent that has a boiling point greater than 140–150°C. With such high boiling solvents it is extremely unlikely that any water vapour could get into your reaction mixture. In these cases, the apparatus should also be modified to use an *air condenser* rather than a water condenser (Fig. 3.23c), although if an air condenser is not available, a normal condenser that has been drained clear of water can be used in its place.

Heating with stirring

The best way to heat a *stirred* reaction mixture is to use a magnetic stirrer hotplate and a heating bath as shown in Fig. 3.24. With modern stirrer hotplates, the temperature of the heating bath can be maintained within a very narrow range, and hence the reaction temperature can be closely controlled. Remember though that the temperature *inside* the reaction flask will be a few degrees less than that of the bath. If it is important to know the precise temperature of the reaction mixture, the apparatus will have to be modified to incorporate a thermometer in the flask. If the reaction mixture is very viscous or heterogeneous, then mechanical overhead stirring will be needed; this is discussed in the following section.

Heating with addition

Another common organic laboratory operation involves the addition of a reagent to a heated or refluxing solution of starting material. It may be that the heat of reaction causes the mixture to reflux, or that an external heat source is used, but in either case a reflux condenser is needed. Two typical assemblies are shown in Fig. 3.25 using: (a) a two-neck flask, and (b) a single-neck flask fitted with a Claisen adapter. The apparatus in Fig. 3.25(a) can be used to add a reagent to a refluxing solution in the two-neck flask. The reaction mixture is kept at reflux by heating the flask in an appropriate heat source. Figure 3.25(b) illustrates a variation which allows the reaction mixture to be stirred during the addition. Either a single-neck flask fitted with a

Fig. 3.24 (a) Heating a reaction mixture with magnetic stirring. (b) Heating a reaction with magnetic stirring on the microscale.

Claisen adapter (as shown) or a two-neck flask is used, and is fitted with the addition funnel and reflux condenser. The reaction mixture is stirred and heated to the required temperature in a heating bath on a magnetic stirrer hotplate.

If the reaction mixture requires stirring and heating during the addition of a reagent, but is very viscous or heterogeneous, then mechanical overhead stirring will be needed. The apparatus for this is shown in Fig. 3.26, and requires a three-neck flask fitted with addition funnel and reflux condenser, and, in the centre neck, a sealed stirrer guide through which the stirrer shaft passes. It is important that the stirrer adapter is sealed to prevent the escape of solvent vapour (see Fig. 2.15).

Heating and stirring with addition under an inert atmosphere

An apparatus for carrying out the addition of an air-sensitive solution to a stirred (and cooled) reaction mixture under an inert atmosphere is illustrated in Fig. 3.22. In some cases such reaction mixtures may require heating at a later stage, and therefore the apparatus needs modifying to include a reflux

Fig. 3.25 (a) Heating a reaction mixture to reflux during the addition of a reagent; (b) heating a stirred reaction mixture during the addition of a reagent.

Fig. 3.26 Heating and overhead stirring of a reaction mixture during the addition of a reagent.

condenser. One simple modification of the apparatus shown in Fig. 3.22 would involve replacing the septum and syringe with an addition funnel, and incorporating a condenser in the central neck of the flask between the flask and the bubbler. If magnetic stirring is inappropriate, then overhead stirring may be used, provided that a well-sealed stirrer is employed. A typical assembly is shown in Fig. 3.15(b). If your reaction involves the addition of an air-sensitive solid reagent, then the apparatus shown in Fig. 3.18 should be used.

Continuous removal of water

Several organic transformations involve an overall loss of water, that is, a dehydration step. Examples include the formation of an ester from an acid and an alcohol and condensation reactions of carbonyl compounds. Since many of these reactions are reversible, success is dependent on removing the water from the reaction mixture as it is formed, to displace the equilibrium. One way of doing this is to use a drying agent or dehydrating reagent in the reaction flask itself, and in certain cases this is highly successful. Another way is to take advantage of the fact that water readily forms *azeotropes* with some organic solvents, and if the reaction is conducted in such a solvent at reflux, then the vapour will contain a certain percentage of water vapour as well. For example, the azeotrope formed between water and toluene boils at 85°C (lower than both pure liquids) and the vapour contains about 80% toluene and 20% water. All that is required is an apparatus which can separate the water from the vapour and return the condensed solvent vapour to the reaction flask. A purpose-designed water separator, known as a *Dean and Stark trap* (or separator), that accomplishes this task is shown in Fig. 3.27. This par-

For a further discussion of azeotropes, see pp. 214–216

Fig. 3.27 Apparatus for continuous removal of water from a reaction mixture using a Dean and Stark water separator (trap).

ticular apparatus can only be used with solvents that are *less dense* than water, but fortunately many common organic solvents are. The complete assembly involves a round-bottomed reaction flask, which is connected to the Dean and Stark trap, on top of which is a reflux condenser. The whole apparatus should be adequately clamped, and then the flask placed on a heat source. As the reaction proceeds in the solvent, the water that is formed is carried up the trap as the azeotrope with the solvent vapour. The vapour should condense well up the condenser and to achieve this it may be necessary to prevent the heat loss from the Dean and Stark apparatus by lagging it with aluminium foil. The solvent–water azeotrope condenses and the condensed liquids fall back into the lower half of the trap. In the condensed phase, the heavier water sinks to the bottom of the trap to be retained, whilst the lighter organic solvent flows back into the reaction flask. The trap is usually graduated so that the volume of water removed from the reaction mixture can be measured. A stopcock is normally incorporated at the bottom of the trap so that if a large amount of water is formed and fills the trap, it can be run off.

Addition of gases

Very occasionally you will encounter an experiment in which one of the starting materials or reagents is a gas. The gas is added to a reaction mixture through a glass tube that dips into the solution or liquid in the reaction flask. A typical experimental set-up is shown in Fig. 3.28. The most important thing to note is that the gas supply, usually a cylinder, and the reaction vessel must be isolated from each other by two empty safety bottles. A third bottle containing a drying or purifying agent may be incorporated in between the safety bottles if necessary, although if you are using a high purity grade gas, further purification or drying is usually detrimental since it often introduces more impurities than it removes. The gas inlet tube is fitted to the flask through a thermometer adapter in a Claisen adapter, the other neck of which carries the reflux condenser. The inlet tube itself is usually a simple wide bore glass tube, although occasionally a special tube that has a small sintered glass disk at the end is used. It is particularly important to use a wide bore tube when the gas is very soluble in the reaction solvent (the solubility may cause the solvent to be sucked up the tube), or when the product of reaction of the gas with the solution is a solid (which may block the tube).

The most difficult aspect of using gaseous reagents is measuring the amount you need to use. In some cases this does not matter, for example, when a solution *saturated* with hydrogen chloride is required. In other cases, for example with a chlorination reaction, it is important to know how much chlorine is used. If the reaction is done on a large scale, then the uptake can be

Fig. 3.28 Bubbling a gas through a reaction mixture.

measured by weighing the reaction flask or small gas cylinder before and after the reaction. Otherwise it may be possible to use a flow meter to measure the gas. The most reliable method is to condense the gas in a cold trap and measure the amount of liquid; however, you need to know the density of the liquid gas at the cold bath temperature. The liquid gas is then simply allowed to evaporate into the reaction mixture. Obviously this technique can only be used with gases that are not too low boiling.

Inevitably some gas will not dissolve in, or react with, the solution in the reaction flask and will therefore escape up the condenser. It is very important that arrangements are made to deal with this; two methods are discussed below.

Toxic effluent gases must be 'scrubbed'

If the gas that you are using is particularly irritating or toxic (and most of them are), the reaction should be carried out in an efficient hood. However, it is still important that the gas should be trapped or scrubbed **before** being vented to the hood. If the gas is water soluble, one way to do this is to attach a T-piece to the top of the condenser, leave one end open and connect the other end to a tube that is attached to the water aspirator. A more reliable method, shown in Fig. 3.29, leads the gas to a beaker of water through a tube connected to an inverted funnel, which just dips below the surface of the water. An inverted funnel must be used to prevent suck-back of the water as the gas dissolves. This method also allows you to replace water with a slightly more efficient trapping/scrubbing solution. For example, acidic gases (HCl, SO_2, etc.) can be scrubbed through dilute sodium hydroxide solution, basic gases (NH_3, $MeNH_2$, etc.) through dilute sulfuric acid, and sulfurous gases (H_2S, MeSH, etc.) through an oxidizing solution such as hypochlorite (bleach).

Fig. 3.29 Absorbing effluent gas from a reaction mixture by trapping/scrubbing in aqueous solution.

Gases which are not soluble in water or which cannot be scrubbed by acids, bases or oxidants present a greater problem, and are beyond the scope of this book.

Reactions in liquid ammonia

Liquid ammonia, which boils at $-33°C$, is a good solvent for many substances, both organic and inorganic, and is therefore an excellent medium for certain reactions, particularly those involving alkali metals. Solutions of alkali metals in liquid ammonia are blue-black in colour due to the presence of solvated electrons, and hence these solutions are powerful reducing systems.

Although not difficult to carry out, reactions in liquid ammonia do require some precautions. A standard procedure which uses a special low temperature condenser is describe below. Experiments 27 and 47 illustrate the use of alkali metal–liquid ammonia reductions.

Before starting the reaction it is a good idea to mark your reaction flask with a line that indicates the required volume of liquid ammonia. Oven dry the apparatus, set up the hot glassware in an efficient hood, as shown in Fig. 3.30 and allow it to cool under a stream of dry nitrogen. For large-scale reactions it is better to use a mechanical overhead stirrer fitted through a sealed stirrer guide. If the reaction is to be carried out with the liquid ammonia refluxing, i.e. at $-33°C$, then insulate the flask with a bowl of cork chips. If the reaction is to be carried out at a lower temperature, for example at $-78°C$, then place the flask in an appropriate cooling bath. Fill the low temperature

Fig. 3.30 Reaction in liquid ammonia.

condenser with a mixture of solid CO_2 and acetone. Remove the nitrogen supply and connect the flask to an ammonia cylinder via a soda lime drying tube and two empty bottles to protect against suck-back (see Fig. 3.28). Then carefully open the cylinder valve. Liquid ammonia will start to condense from the low temperature condenser. Maintain the ammonia flow until sufficient liquid ammonia for your reaction has condensed. Do not be tempted to introduce liquid ammonia directly from the cylinder as this may introduce ferrous impurities which catalyze the conversion of the dissolved sodium into sodamide. Disconnect the ammonia supply from the flask, replace the ammonia inlet with a stopper or, if required, a nitrogen inlet, and you are ready to start the reaction. Solids, for example sodium metal, can be carefully added to the reaction flask through an open neck by quickly removing the addition funnel. Solutions of reactants are simply run in from the addition funnel, although the rate of addition should not be so fast as to cause the liquid ammonia to boil too vigorously.

Microscale low temperature condensers are now available commercially.

Temperature control

Organic reactions are usually carried out at a fixed constant temperature. It is important to be able to control the temperature of a reaction mixture for the following reasons.

- The *rate* of reaction is dependent on temperature, and a fairly narrow temperature range is required if the reaction is to proceed at a desirable rate.
- The rates of side reactions increase with increasing temperature.
- Some reactions are *exothermic*, and may run out of control.

The easiest way to conduct an organic reaction at a fixed elevated temperature is to carry it out in a boiling solvent under reflux (see pp. 96–100). However, the use of refluxing solvents is not always appropriate. For example, many reactions such as S$_N$2 displacements proceed best in dipolar aprotic solvents such as dimethyl formamide (DMF) or dimethyl sulfoxide (DMSO). These solvents decompose at reflux temperatures, and if the reaction is inconveniently slow at room temperature, then an intermediate temperature of, for example, 60 or 80°C may be needed. In this case, the reaction flask should be

Electrically heated liquid baths are best for precise temperature control

heated in an appropriate liquid heating bath. In fact, in all situations where fairly precise constant temperature control is needed, electrically heated liquid baths are undoubtedly the best. The heating bath can be any suitably sized metal container—glass dishes are best avoided—which is then heated electrically, either on a hotplate or with an immersion heater. The degree of temperature control is dependent on the heating system, but modern hotplates with in-built controls and immersion heaters attached to voltage regulators are fairly accurate (see pp. 29–30).

The choice of liquid for the heating bath depends on several factors: temperature required, toxicity, flammability, expense and ease of handling—particularly removing it from your glassware. Clearly the bath medium should be fluid, should not be too viscous at the temperature required, and should have a boiling point at least 20–30°C above that temperature. Some materials that are commonly used as heating bath fluids are listed in Table 3.1. Whatever the fluid, do not fill the bath too full. Remember the level will rise when the reaction flask is immersed in the bath.

When a reaction generates its own heat, special precautions are necessary. Indeed the control of highly exothermic reactions is quite a problem, since as the temperature rises, the rate of reaction increases and, hence, the rate of heat evolution increases. If the heat cannot be efficiently removed, the reaction temperature will increase further, and the reaction will proceed faster and faster until it blows out of the reaction vessel.

Exothermic reactions

Exothermic reactions can be controlled in two ways: by the slow addition of reagent to the reaction mixture, at such a rate that the mixture is maintained at the required temperature, or by external cooling. The first method is usually satisfactory, but there is always the danger of inadvertently adding too much reagent too quickly. With too much reagent in the reaction mixture, the exotherm may be uncontrollable. One way to avoid this is by careful monitoring of the reaction temperature. If the reaction is 'well behaved' and under control, the temperature of the mixture should rise when the reagent is added, and then start to decrease when the addition is stopped.

Controlled addition

External cooling—have the cold bath ready

However, despite taking precautions such as controlling the rate of addition, it is often necessary to use external cooling. Always get the cold bath ready **before** you start the reaction. With a suitable cold bath to hand, it is easy

Table 3.1 Heating bath fluids.

Material	Usable range (°C)	Comment
Water	0–80	Ideal within its narrow range
Ethylene glycol	0–150	Cheap. **Flammable. Low flash point**
Paraffin oil (mineral oil)	0–150	**Flammable**, produces acrid smoke above 150°C
Polyethylene glycol 400	0–250	Water soluble
Silicone oil	0–250	Much better than paraffin oil, but expensive
Glycerol	0–260	Water soluble
Wood's metal (alloy of Bi, Pb, Sn, Cd)	70–350	Solid below 70°C, but good for high temperatures. **Toxic**
Sand	50–350	Poor thermal conductivity causes problems in temperature control

to moderate a reaction by immersing the reaction vessel in the bath until the temperature of the reaction mixture is reduced.

Cold baths are also needed when a reaction has to be run below room temperature. The most suitable container for a cold bath is a straight-sided dish — a glass crystallizing dish will do, although it is breakable. If the dish is used for cold baths that are required for long periods at a temperature of less than −20°C, some sort of insulation should be used; this is conveniently done by placing the dish inside a slightly larger one and filling the gap with insulating material such as cotton wool or cork chips. For extended periods of low temperature work, a Dewar flask should be used. The cooling mixture in a cold bath is based on one of the three coolants that are routinely available in a chemistry laboratory: ice, solid CO_2 (often called dry ice, DriKold® or Cardice®) or liquid nitrogen. For temperatures down to about −20°C, an ice–salt freezing mixture may be used. This is made by mixing an inorganic salt with crushed ice in the correct ratio (Table 3.2). Although it is theoretically possible to attain temperatures as low as −40°C with such freezing mixtures, the baths are fairly inefficient and short-lived.

Use hand protection for handling low temperature baths

For more effective and lower temperature cooling, cold baths based on solid CO_2 in conjunction with an organic solvent are used. Solid CO_2 baths are made by adding small pieces of solid CO_2 to the organic solvent until a slight excess of solid CO_2 coated with frozen solvent is visible. The low temperature can only be maintained by periodic topping up with the coolant. Some commonly used cooling bath systems are given in Table 3.3, of these the acetone/CO_2 system (−78°C) is best known.

Table 3.2 Ice–salt mixtures.

Salt	Ratio (salt:ice)	Lowest temperature (approx.) (°C)
$CaCl_2 \cdot 6H_2O$	1:2.5	−10
NH_4Cl	1:4	−15
NaCl	1:3	−20
$CaCl_2 \cdot 6H_2O$	1:0.8	−40

Table 3.3 Solid CO_2 cooling baths.

Solvent	Temperature (approx.) (°C)
Ethylene glycol	−15
Acetonitrile **(toxic)**	−40
Chloroform **(toxic)**	−60
Acetone	−78

Remember that most solvents are flammable and some are toxic and baths made from them should be used in a hood.

Always use an ethanol-based low temperature thermometer when measuring low temperatures; mercury freezes at −39°C.

Further reading
For further useful information on heating and cooling baths, see: A.J. Gordon and R.J. Ford, *The Chemist's Companion. A Handbook of Practical Data, Techniques and References*, Wiley & Sons, New York, 1973.

Following the progress of a reaction

All the experimental procedures in Part 2 include an indication of how long the reaction will take to go to completion. For example, you will be told that one reaction mixture should be heated under reflux for 2 h, and another stirred at room temperature for 20 min. However, this is a slightly false situation, since in many cases you will not know *exactly* how long a reaction will take. Therefore it is much more 'scientific' to monitor the progress of the reaction yourself. In research laboratories where new reactions are being carried out, it is essential to follow their progress. In the teaching laboratory, even if not expected to monitor the reaction in detail, the good chemist always

Observe!

observes and makes notes of any changes that occur, such as colour changes, gas evolution, solid precipitation and so on. Careful observation is the keystone of experimental science.

Nowadays, chromatography is used almost universally to follow the progress of an organic reaction. Modern chromatographic analytical techniques require very little material. Therefore it is easy to withdraw small aliquots from the reaction mixture at appropriate intervals, and analyze them by one or more chromatographic techniques. In some cases it may be necessary to 'quench' the small sample of reaction mixture before carrying out the analysis. This usually means adding it to a few drops of water, which will effectively stop the reaction. This is best done in a small sample vial. Place a few drops of water in the vial, add a drop or two of the reaction mixture, followed by a few drops of an organic solvent such as diethyl ether, shake the vial and withdraw a sample from the *organic* layer — the top one in this case — for analysis. Compare the reaction mixture sample with the starting material and an authentic sample of the expected product if one is available. The chromatographic analysis is carried out using the most appropriate technique for the

Use TLC for following reactions; see also pp. 165–175

compounds involved, although thin layer chromatography (TLC) is the most widely used method. Since chromatography is also used extensively for the *purification* of organic compounds, for completeness and in order to avoid repetition, chromatographic techniques will be discussed in detail later in the section on purification (pp. 160–203).

However, chromatography is not the only way to follow the progress of an organic reaction, and many other methods can be used. For example, simple colour changes will often suffice to tell you when a reaction is complete, particularly if the starting material is coloured and the product is not. In reactions involving acids or alkalis as reagents, the consumption of the reagent can be easily followed by monitoring the pH of the reaction mixture, or by withdrawing aliquots and titrating them. Titration can also be used to follow the progress of oxidation reactions. An aliquot of reaction mixture containing the oxidizing agent is withdrawn and added to potassium iodide solution; the oxidant liberates iodine, which is titrated in the normal way using thiosulfate solution. Hence the consumption of oxidant is monitored. The list of possibilities is endless, and it is up to you, the organic chemist, to use your ingenuity to devise the most suitable method for your particular experiment.

Reaction work-up (isolation of the product)

When your organic chemical reaction is over, the product has to be isolated from the reaction mixture. The *work-up*, by which this procedure is usually known, simply refers to the *isolation* of the product from the reaction mixture, free from solvent and spent reagents, and does not imply any *purification*. Purification of the organic reaction product is carried out subsequently, and will be discussed in detail later. The choice of work-up procedure should always take into account the properties of the required product.

- *Volatility*: do not evaporate your product along with the reaction solvent.
- *Polarity*: your organic product may be water soluble; aqueous extraction may not be appropriate.
- *Chemical reactivity*: towards water, acid and base; aqueous extraction may not be appropriate.
- *Thermal stability*: distillation may be inappropriate.
- *Air sensitivity*: special handling may be required.

With the above provisos in mind, most organic reaction mixtures can be worked-up according to a single general scheme as shown in Fig. 3.31. When the product is a liquid, you may be able to isolate it by *fractional distillation* of the whole reaction mixture, although careful distillation is needed to separate the product from the reaction solvent and other volatiles. The liquid product will usually need further purification by redistillation. Just occasionally you will be lucky, and the product of your reaction will separate or crystallize from the reaction mixture as a solid. Work-up in this case simply consists of collecting the product by suction filtration. Unless the product is to be used directly in a subsequent reaction, it will usually need to be purified further, by recrystallization, for example.

However, in most cases, the work-up will involve the addition of water or ice-water to the reaction mixture. Again you may be lucky and a solid product may separate at this stage, but it is more likely that the product will have to be isolated from the aqueous mixture by *extraction* with an organic solvent such as diethyl ether or dichloromethane. The extraction is carried out in a

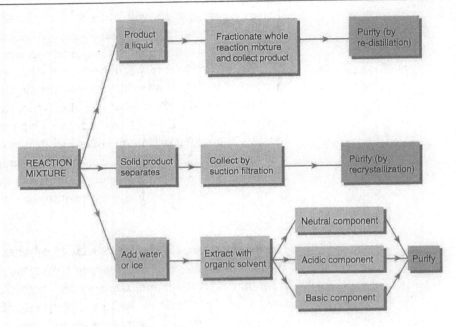

Fig. 3.31 General scheme for reaction work-up.

separatory funnel, and by carrying out multiple extractions, in combination with appropriate washes, a solution of the product in an organic solvent is isolated. The work-up can be modified at this stage to include extraction with aqueous acid or base, thereby facilitating the isolation of neutral, acidic and basic products. In either case, work-up is completed by drying the organic solution (Table 3.5, p. 127), and evaporating the solvent on the rotary evaporator (pp. 49–53) to give the crude product.

Detailed discussion of protocols for aqueous organic extractions, including the purification of neutral, acidic and basic components by extraction, is deferred until the following section (pp. 118–129). However, since you may encounter a separatory funnel for the first time during the work-up of your first organic reaction, some comments about the correct use of separatory funnels are appropriate at this point.

How to use a separatory funnel

The separatory funnel is the most commonly used piece of apparatus for carrying out routine extractions in organic chemistry. However, it is also one of the most mishandled pieces of apparatus in the organic laboratory. The correct handling of a separatory funnel requires attention to detail in all phases of the extraction and separation process. With experience, the correct manipulations should become automatic, and everyone eventually develops their own technique. Nevertheless, there are certain ground rules which should **always** be obeyed.

Fig. 3.32 A separatory funnel ready for use.

Preparing the separatory funnel

Grease lightly!

Do not grease Teflon®

Support the funnel in a ring stand

A separatory funnel is usually made of thin glass and therefore should be handled carefully. The most important part of it is the stopcock, which will be either glass or Teflon®. Glass stopcocks should be *lightly* greased before the funnel is used. Use just enough grease so that the stopcock turns easily; too much grease might clog the hole in the stopcock or contaminate the organic solution. Teflon® stopcocks are better because, owing to their low coefficient of friction, they do not need greasing. However, Teflon® is fairly soft and will deform with heat or pressure. With the stopcock in place, support the separatory funnel in a metal ring clamped to a stable stand. Ideally the ring support should be plastic coated to prevent metal–glass contact and to reduce the chance of cracking or breaking the funnel. If a coated ring is not available, the metal should be covered with some pieces of Neoprene® tubing which have been cut into short lengths and split lengthways. Get into the habit of placing an Erlenmeyer flask or beaker under the separatory funnel as soon as you have put it in its ring support. This is vital when the separatory funnel contains liquid, as it will catch any leaks from the stopcock. The complete set-up, which is ready for use, is shown in Fig. 3.32.

Check that a well-fitting stopper for the tapered glass joint at the neck of the separatory funnel is available. Opinion is divided as to whether the glass stopper should be greased or not. A *lightly* greased stopper will certainly be easier to remove, but you run the risk of introducing contamination from the grease, particularly if the organic solvent 'creeps' up the tapered joint. Wetting an *ungreased* stopper with water often prevents this solvent creep.

Transferring liquids to the separatory funnel

With the stopcock closed (**check!**), and the funnel adequately supported with an empty flask underneath it, pour the mixture to be extracted and the extraction solvent into the separatory funnel, using a long-stemmed glass funnel to minimize the chance of spillage. Remember to allow sufficient space in the funnel to mix the liquids. As a general rule, never fill the separatory funnel more than two-thirds full. If there is a large volume of liquid to extract, and a sufficiently large separatory funnel is not available, the extraction will have to be carried out in batches.

Never fill a separate funnel more than two-thirds full

Shaking out

To carry out an efficient extraction, the aqueous and organic layers have to be thoroughly mixed. This is achieved by swirling and shaking the separatory funnel. After adding the liquids to the funnel, and *before* inserting the stopper, it is a good idea initially to swirl the separatory funnel gently. Hold the funnel round the top, lift it just clear of the supporting ring and swirl it *gently*. This swirling causes some preliminary mixing of the layers, and is particularly important when aqueous carbonate or bicarbonate is being used to extract or neutralize acidic components. Carbon dioxide will be evolved, and the preliminary mixing will reduce the problems from excessive pressure building up during the extraction process. After swirling, return the separatory funnel to its support and insert the stopper.

CO_2 is evolved during extractions using aqueous carbonate and bicarbonate solutions. Guard against pressure build-up in the funnel

More vigorous swirling and shaking is required to mix the layers thoroughly, and to do this the separatory funnel has to be held in the hands clear of its support. Everyone develops their own technique for holding a separatory funnel, and one method is shown in Fig. 3.33(a). Whatever the exact grip on the funnel, the important points to note are as follows.

- Hold the funnel in *both* hands.
- Hold the body of the funnel in one hand and keep one finger over the stopper at all times.

(a) (b)

Fig. 3.33 (a) Holding a separatory funnel during shaking; (b) holding a separatory funnel during venting. **Always point the stem away from others during venting.**

- Hold the funnel around the stopcock with the other hand, so that the stopcock is kept in place and, more importantly, so that you can open and close the stopcock quickly with your fingers.
- If in doubt, practise your grip on an *empty* separatory funnel.

Never extract hot solutions

Point stem away from others

Remember—invert, vent, swirl, vent, shake, vent

To carry out the extraction, lift the separatory funnel clear of its support, adjust your grip and invert the funnel. Immediately open the stopcock to release any pressure build-up as shown in Fig. 3.33(b). Most organic solvents are fairly volatile and their vapour pressure causes build-up of pressure in the funnel. For this reason, never attempt to extract hot solutions; the greatly increased vapour pressure may cause the solvent to blow out of the funnel. Similarly, as mentioned above, pressure release is very important when doing extractions with carbonate or bicarbonate solutions, which may generate carbon dioxide. **When venting a funnel, never point the stem towards your neighbours or towards yourself.** Always aim it well away from others, preferably into a hood. After the first venting, close the stopcock, swirl the inverted funnel for a few seconds, and then vent it again. If excessive pressure build-up is evident, repeat the swirling–venting process until pressure build-up diminishes. Then, and only then, shake the funnel. Opinions vary as to the duration of shaking required to establish equilibrium between the liquids, but 20 vigorous shakes (10–20 s) are thought to be adequate. Vent the funnel at least once during the shaking process. Beware of shaking too vigorously, however, as this may encourage the formation of *emulsions* (see pp. 115–116). At the end of the shaking, vent the funnel again, make sure that the stopcock is closed and return the separatory funnel to its support stand. Immediately place an empty Erlenmeyer flask under the funnel and then allow the funnel to stand until the layers separate.

Separating the layers

Make sure which layer is which

All being well, the organic and aqueous solutions will separate into two easily visible layers in the separatory funnel. (If not, see the section on 'troubleshooting' below.) Remove the stopper, and if any organic material is stuck to the side of it, rinse this back into the funnel with a few drops of the extraction solvent from a Pasteur pipette. Do not do this if the stopper has been greased! Before running off the lower layer through the stopcock, you must be sure which layer is which. Often you may be able to tell just by the relative volumes of the two layers, or by the fact that the organic extraction solvent is much denser or less dense than water. However, the presence of dissolved inorganic and organic material can dramatically alter the densities of the aqueous and organic layers respectively, and therefore it might not be obvious which layer is which. In this case, add a few drops of water to the separatory funnel, and see which layer it goes into. With a clear interface between the layers, run off the lower layer through the stopcock. Hold the funnel as shown in Fig. 3.34 to ensure that the stopcock does not fall out, and arrange the funnel so that the tip of the stem touches the side of the Erlenmeyer flask; this reduces splashing.

Fig. 3.34 Holding a separatory funnel whilst draining the lower layer.

Do not let a vortex form

Open the stopcock *gently*; do not allow the liquid to run out too quickly as this will cause a vortex to form which will drag some of the upper layer through as well. When the lower layer is almost drained, close the stopcock, and gently swirl the separatory funnel to knock down any drops of liquid that are clinging to the glass. Open the stopcock *slowly* and carefully run off the remaining lower layer into the flask. Close the stopcock and gently tap the funnel stem to *Label all solutions immediately* dislodge the last drops into the Erlenmeyer. Label the Erlenmeyer flask *immediately*. The upper layer remaining in the separatory funnel should be poured out through the neck of the funnel into a clean Erlenmeyer, which should also be labelled immediately. The upper layer is poured from the funnel, rather than run out through the stopcock, to avoid contamination of the upper layer by the traces of material from the lower layer remaining in the stem and stopcock.

Keep everything

Always keep both solutions until you have isolated your organic product. Even experienced chemists sometimes discard the wrong layer, or discard an aqueous solution which has been incompletely extracted. It is always best to play safe, and never discard anything until you are absolutely sure that you do not need it.

Finally, wash out the separatory funnel as soon as you have finished with it. It is particularly important to remove and clean the stopcock; this will prevent it from sticking when the funnel is not in use. In fact it is better to store the funnel separately from the stopcock.

Trouble shooting

Occasionally things do not go according to plan when using separatory funnels. Some of the most commonly encountered problems are discussed below, along with some suggested remedies.

Mixture is so dark that interface is not visible

Occasionally the mixture in the separatory funnel is so dark in colour that you cannot see the interface between the two layers. If so, hold the separatory funnel up to the light, or place a small desk lamp or reading lamp directly behind it. With a brighter light source you may be able to see the interface. If that fails, start to run off the liquid *slowly* from the stopcock, and observe the flow of liquid carefully. It is usually possible to detect the changeover from water to organic solvent, or vice versa, by the change in flow properties due to differences in surface tension and viscosity.

Mixture is clear but interface is not visible

Even when the mixture is clear, the interface between the layers may not be visible. This happens when the two layers have very similar refractive indices, so that they look the same. The trick in this case is to add a pinch of powdered charcoal to the separatory funnel. This will float on top of the denser liquid, and hence the interface will be clearly marked.

Only a single layer is visible

This usually happens when the original reaction mixture, before work-up, contains large amounts of water-miscible solvents such as ethanol or tetrahydrofuran. Such solvents dissolve in water and the extraction solvent equally well, and hence a single homogeneous layer is formed in the separatory funnel. Although this can sometimes be encouraged to form two layers by adding more water and more extraction solvent, or by adding saturated sodium chloride solution, the problem is easily avoided by concentrating the original reaction mixture by evaporating the offending solvent **before** attempting aqueous work-up.

Insoluble material is visible at the interface

This is a very common problem, and in most extractions some insoluble material collects at the interface between the two layers. It is usually impossible to separate the layers without taking some of this solid into one or both of them. However, this is nothing to worry about, since the required liquid will always be processed further, and hence the insoluble impurity can be removed by filtration at a later stage.

Emulsions

Emulsions form when droplets of one solution become suspended in another, and the suspension will not separate by gravity. When this occurs in a separatory funnel, it can cause big problems. Sometimes the emulsion clears if the funnel is left undisturbed for a few minutes, and then two distinct layers will separate out. Unfortunately, most emulsions are more persistent. With such persistent emulsions, prevention is better than cure. Emulsions usually form in

Preventing emulsions

extractions involving basic solutions such as sodium hydroxide or sodium carbonate. Traces of long chain fatty acids are converted into their sodium salts, and the resulting 'soap' is a very effective emulsifying agent. Vigorous shaking also encourages the emulsification process, so in extractions involving basic components, the separatory funnel should be swirled rather than shaken, although obviously equilibrium between the liquids is reached much more slowly. In addition, if appropriate, using a weaker base such as sodium bicarbonate might help to prevent the formation of an emulsion. The tendency to form emulsions increases as electrolytes are removed from the mixture, so adding sodium chloride to the aqueous layer may prevent an emulsion. The addition of sodium chloride also has the effect of reducing the solubility of organic material in water, and of increasing the density of the aqueous layer. This latter effect may be important if the emulsion is due to the aqueous and organic solutions having very similar densities. On this basis, you can also adjust the density of the organic layer by adding pentane to reduce it, or dichloromethane to increase it. In addition, certain solvents are more likely to form emulsions than others. Benzene is particularly prone to emulsions, and is best avoided, although its toxicity generally precludes its use in any event. Chlorinated solvents (chloroform and dichloromethane) also have a tendency

Breaking emulsions

to form emulsions. If an emulsion still forms despite the precautions, it has to be broken up before an efficient extraction can be achieved. One plan of action is as follows.

- Allow the separatory funnel to stand with periodic *gentle* swirling.
- Add some saturated sodium chloride solution to the emulsion.
- Add a few drops of ethanol to the emulsion.
- Filter the whole mixture by suction; emulsions are stabilized by suspended solid, and filtration removes the solid. The same effect can be achieved by *centrifugation*.
- Transfer the mixture to an Erlenmeyer flask, and allow it to stand overnight or longer.

One of these will usually work, but you do need patience!

No product is isolated after evaporation of the organic layer

After separating the organic layer, you will usually dry the solution (pp. 127, 130–131) and then evaporate the solvent on the rotary evaporator to isolate your product. Occasionally you will be left with little or no product at this stage. This is not as disastrous as it would seem *provided that you have kept the aqueous layer* from the original work-up. What it means is that your product is sufficiently polar to have some water solubility, and therefore has been poorly extracted by the organic solvent. The first thing to do in this situation is to return the aqueous layer to the separatory funnel, and to re-extract it with a more polar organic solvent. Common extraction solvents in order of increasing polarity are: hydrocarbons (light petroleum, hexane), toluene, diethyl

For a further discussion of extraction solvents, see pp. 121–122

ether, dichloromethane, ethyl acetate. More polar solvents such as acetone or ethanol are water miscible; n-butanol, however, is largely water immiscible and can be used as a polar extraction solvent. However, it does dissolve some water, and is high boiling and hence difficult to remove from your organic product. A simple way to decrease the solubility of an organic compound in water is to add solid sodium chloride to the aqueous layer. This technique is known as *salting out* the organic compound, and is discussed further in the next section (p. 120).

Microscale solvent extraction and phase separation

Using separatory funnels on the microscale is impracticable; however, efficient extraction and phase separation can be accomplished using a Pasteur pipette and a sample tube, tapered vial, or test tube. Tapered vials are particularly suitable for this purpose because the taper allows efficient removal of the lower layer (Fig. 3.35).

Assuming a reaction has been performed in a tapered vial *in a solvent less dense than water*, open the vial and add the required quantity (typically less than 1 mL) of aqueous quench or wash solution. Use the Pasteur pipette to mix the layers, by repeatedly and rapidly filling the pipette with the entire contents (aqueous and organic) of the vial, and expelling them again. The mixture can then be allowed to settle. To remove the lower aqueous layer, insert the tip of the pipette to the bottom of the taper and slowly fill the pipette, watching

Fig. 3.35 On the microscale, the Pasteur pipette and tapered reaction vial (or tube) replace the separatory funnel. The phases are mixed intimately within the pipette; after phase separation the lower layer can be removed carefully.

the position of the meniscus carefully. The washings can be discarded and the process repeated as required.

If solvent extraction of an aqueous medium is required, transfer can be minimized using an extraction solvent that is more dense than water, such as dichloromethane. The extracts can then be combined in a second vial for washing.

Removing the upper layer efficiently is obviously more difficult because of the difference between the surface area of the meniscus and the cross-section of the pipette tip, so lower layer removal is recommended wherever possible.

3.3 Purification of organic compounds

Having worked up the reaction mixture, you will have isolated your organic product. Chemists usually refer to this as the *crude product* indicating that, in most cases, the compound will need to be purified further. To be able to purify an organic compound by separating the impurities, we have to rely on the desired compound having different properties to the impurities and we might take advantage of differences in solubility, volatility, polarity, shape and functional groups present. For example, crystallization relies on the differences in solubility between the desired compound and the impurities, whereas distillation exploits differences in volatility. Adsorption chromatography separates and purifies compounds according to their adsorption to the chromatographic material, which to a good approximation is related to the polarity of the compounds. More advanced techniques such as electrophoresis and gel filtration, which are beyond the scope of this book, separate compounds by differences in molecular charge and size, respectively. Indeed with the advent of sophisticated instruments and analytical techniques, separation science is a whole subject in itself nowadays. Our concern is merely to cover the major purification techniques that are relevant to the organic laboratory, with emphasis on the practicalities of the technique, rather than on the underlying theory. The following sections deal with the purification techniques of organic chemistry and cover extraction, crystallization, distillation and chromatography in various forms.

Extraction

Historically, extraction is one of the oldest of all chemical operations, and one which is used in everyday life. The simple act of making a cup of tea or coffee involves the extraction of various components responsible for flavour, odour and colour from tea leaves or ground coffee beans by hot water.

Extraction in the chemical sense means 'pulling out' a compound from one phase to another, usually from a liquid or a solid to another liquid. In the organic laboratory, the most common process involves the extraction of an organic compound from one liquid phase to another. The two liquid phases are usually an aqueous solution and an organic solvent, and the technique is known as *liquid–liquid extraction* or, more commonly, as *extraction*.

A simple extraction is often used in the work-up of an organic reaction mixture (see pp. 110–118), but extraction can also be used to *separate* and *purify* organic compounds. Extraction is particularly useful in the separation of acidic and basic components from an organic mixture by their reaction with dilute aqueous base or acid as appropriate. Since this relies on an acid–based chemical reaction, the technique is often called *chemically active extraction*. Whatever extraction protocol is being used, most extraction operations in the organic laboratory are carried out in *separatory funnels*, the use of which has already been discussed in the proceding section.

Aqueous–organic extraction

Before going into the experimental procedures for extracting compounds, we need to consider some of the physical chemistry theory behind the technique. When an organic compound, X, is placed in a separatory funnel with two *immiscible* liquids, such as water and dichloromethane, some of the compound will dissolve in the water and some in the dichloromethane. (We assume that X does not react with either liquid.) In more technical language, the compound is said to *partition* or distribute itself between the two liquids, and the exact amount of X in each phase clearly depends on its relative solubility in water and dichloromethane. The ratio of *concentrations* of X in each phase is known as the *partition coefficient* or *distribution coefficient* and is a constant (K) defined as

$$K = \frac{\text{Concentration in dichloromethane}}{\text{Concentration in water}}$$

which, to a rough approximation, is the same as the ratio of *solubilities* of X in dichloromethane and water measured separately.

$$K \approx \frac{\text{Solubility in dichloromethane}}{\text{Solubility in water}}$$

To illustrate this, assume that the solubility of X in dichloromethane is 35 g per 100 mL and in water is 5 g per 100 mL *at the same temperature*. Hence, the partition coefficient, K, is *approximately* given by

$$K = \frac{35\,\text{g}/100\,\text{mL}}{5\,\text{g}/100\,\text{mL}} = 7$$

Both solubilities are measured in the same units, and therefore the partition coefficient is dimensionless.

Now that we know the partition coefficient for this particular system, we can work out how much of compound X we can extract from water using dichloromethane. Suppose we have 100 mL of water containing 5 g of compound X and we are going to extract it with 100 mL of dichloromethane. How much of X will we extract? After shaking the separatory funnel until equilibrium between the two liquids is reached, assume that the amount extracted into the organic dichloromethane phase (100 mL) is x g. The amount of X remaining in the water (100 mL) is therefore $(5-x)$ g. Since

$$K = \frac{\text{Concentration in dichloromethane}}{\text{Concentration in water}}$$

we have

$$7 = \frac{x\,\text{g}/100\,\text{mL}}{(5-x)\text{g}/100\,\text{mL}}$$

and hence $x = 4.375$ g.

Therefore we can extract 4.375 g of X from 100 mL water using 100 mL of dichloromethane; the remaining 0.635 g of X will remain in the water. The process has been reasonably efficient in that we have extracted 87.5% of the compound. However, we can do better, even without using more dichloromethane. How? By dividing our 100 mL of extraction solvent dichloromethane into two 50 mL portions, and by carrying out the extraction of the water solution twice using 50 mL of fresh dichloromethane for each extraction. Calculating as before, you will find that the first extraction gives 3.889 g X, leaving 1.111 g in the water, which on the second extraction will give 0.864 g of X in the dichloromethane phase. Hence a total of 4.753 g, or 95%, of X has now been extracted.

Two or three smaller extractions are more efficient than one large one

The important conclusion from this exercise in the theory of extraction is that it is more efficient to carry out two small extractions with organic solvent than one large one. A greater number of even smaller extractions would be more efficient still, and as a general rule, provided that the partition coefficient is greater than 4 (which it is for many organic compounds in many two-phase water–solvent systems), a double or triple extraction will remove most of the organic compound from the water.

Water-soluble compounds

If the organic compound is *more* soluble in water than in the organic solvent, the partition coefficient is less than 1, and very little compound will be extracted simply by shaking up the two liquids. However, the partition coefficient of the organic compound can be changed by adding an inorganic salt, such as sodium chloride, to the aqueous solution. The theory is that the organic compound will be less soluble in sodium chloride solution than in water itself, and therefore the partition coefficient between the organic solvent and aqueous solution will now have a higher value, and the extraction into the organic solvent will be more efficient. Fortunately this theory is borne

Salting out

out in practice, and simply adding solid sodium chloride to your separatory funnel can dramatically improve the extraction of water-soluble organic compounds into an organic solvent. The technique is known as *salting out*, and was briefly referred to in the previous section.

Very occasionally you will come across an organic compound that cannot be efficiently extracted from aqueous solution. Even after salting out, the partition coefficient is still too low, and only small amounts can be extracted by each portion of organic solvent. Obviously one could carry on shaking the aqueous solution with several small portions of organic solvent, extracting, say, 2–5% of the material each time, but this is clearly going to be a long and tedious process. If you find yourself in this situation, the way out is to use a *continuous extraction* apparatus in place of your separatory funnel. A detailed discussion of continuous extraction is beyond the scope of this book, but basically the apparatus is arranged so that organic solvent continually circulates through the aqueous solution extracting a small amount of material each time, before being recycled. The extraction can run for several hours until sufficient material is obtained in the organic solvent. There are two basic designs of apparatus: one for use with solvents that are lighter than water and the other for use with solvents that are more dense than water. You are unlikely to need such an apparatus in the teaching laboratory, but if you do have serious problems in extracting your organic material from water, the apparatus may be available. Ask your instructor.

Continuous extraction

Choice of extraction solvent

In the discussion above, we looked at a typical organic extraction process which used dichloromethane as the organic solvent to extract an aqueous solution. Although water is almost always one of the liquids in the liquid–liquid extraction process, the choice of organic solvent is quite wide. Dichloromethane is, in fact, an excellent choice, because it fulfils all the main requirements for an extraction solvent: immiscibility with water, different density to water, good solubility characteristics, stability and volatility so that it can easily be removed from the organic compound by evaporation. Ideally an extraction solvent should also be non-toxic and non-flammable, but these two criteria are less easy to meet. Extraction solvents fall into two groups: those which are less dense than water and those which are more dense. Commonly used extraction solvents which fall in the first group include diethyl ether (the most common extraction solvent of all), ethyl acetate and hydrocarbons, such as light petroleum, or pentane, or toluene. Dichloromethane is the commonly used extraction solvent which is denser than water but it does have a greater tendency to form emulsions than the non-chlorinated solvents. The properties of some common extraction solvents, listed in order of increasing dielectric constant, are given in Table 3.4. Of these, diethyl ether and dichloromethane find the widest use in the organic laboratory.

Acid–base–neutral extraction

We have already mentioned the fact that *chemically active extraction* can be used in the purification of organic compounds by separating acidic, basic and

Table 3.4 Some common extraction solvents.

Solvent	Dielectric* constant	Bp (°C)	Density (gmL^{-1})†	Flammability‡	Toxicity‡	Suitability
Pentane	1.8	36.1	0.63	+++	+	Poor solvent for polar compounds; easily dried
Toluene	2.4	110.6	0.87	++	+	Prone to emulsions
Diethyl ether	4.3	34.6	0.71	+++	+	Good general extraction solvent, especially for oxygen-containing compounds; dissolves up to 1.5% water. **Prone to peroxide formation on storage**
Ethyl acetate	6.0	77.1	0.89	+++	+	Good for polar compounds; absorbs a large amount of water
Dichloromethane	8.9	39.7	1.31	Non-flammable	++	Good general extraction solvent; easily dried, but slight tendency to emulsify
1-Butanol	17.5	117.7	0.81	++	+	'Last resort' for extraction of very polar compounds; dissolves up to 20% water

* Although the dielectric constant (ε) gives some indication of the polarity of a solvent, it does not always reflect a solvent's ability to dissolve polar organic compounds.
† Water = 1.0, saturated sodium chloride solution = 1.2.
‡ + = least flammable/toxic, +++ = most flammable/toxic.

neutral components, and we now provide flow-charts and protocols for carrying out such extractions.

Separation according to acidity

The idea is that organic compounds, be they the required product or some by-product or other impurity, can be separated according to their acidity. Organic acids such as sulfonic and carboxylic acids are easily converted into their sodium salts, which are usually water soluble, by reaction with sodium bicarbonate. Weaker organic acids such as phenols require a stronger base such as sodium hydroxide. Conversely organic bases such as amines are converted into water-soluble hydrochloride salts by reaction with hydrochloric acid. The overall plan for the separation of an organic mixture into acidic, basic and neutral components is shown in outline in Fig. 3.36, and is discussed in more detail below.

To carry out the extraction procedure, you will require a selection of aqueous acidic and basic solutions. A well-equipped organic laboratory

Fig. 3.36 General outline for the separation of acidic (AH), basic (B:) and neutral (N) components of a mixture.

should have these already made up, but you may have to prepare your own solutions. What you need are:

- saturated sodium bicarbonate solution (contains about 96 g L^{-1}; $ca.$ 1 M);
- 2 M sodium hydroxide solution (contains 80 g L^{-1});
- 2 M hydrochloric acid (contains 200 mL concentrated acid L^{-1});
- saturated sodium chloride solution (contains about 360 g L^{-1}).

The extraction is carried out in a separatory funnel using the techniques already described, according to one of the following protocols. You will normally know the properties of the required organic product, i.e. whether it is acidic, basic or neutral, and therefore it is usually obvious which extraction protocol to follow. Remember, just as with a reaction work-up, never discard

Do not discard anything until you are sure you do not need it

any aqueous or organic layer from an extraction until you are sure it does not contain any of your organic product.

Isolation and purification of a neutral organic compound

The general scheme for the isolation and purification of a neutral organic compound is given in Fig. 3.37. The scheme starts with an organic solution containing the required neutral product together with some impurities. This solution may have been obtained by simply dissolving up the impure material or, more likely, will be the result of the work-up of your reaction mixture. As will become apparent, it is much better to use a solvent such as diethyl ether that is less dense than water for this extraction protocol. The scheme is self-explanatory, and involves successive extractions (washes) to remove acidic and basic impurities. After each extraction your neutral organic compound will remain in the organic layer, and therefore it is much more convenient if the aqueous solution to be run off and *eventually* discarded is the *lower* layer in your separatory funnel. Hence the preferred use of a solvent that is less dense than water for these extractions. After running off the first aqueous wash from the funnel, the next aqueous solution can be added directly to the organic layer remaining in the funnel. At the end of the extraction procedure you will be left with an organic solution containing the neutral component. The water wash removes traces of the previous acidic wash, but it is always a good idea to follow this with a final wash (extraction) with saturated sodium chloride solution, particularly if diethyl ether is the organic solvent involved, because, believe it or not, this extraction actually *dries* the organic layer! Diethyl ether, although largely immiscible with water, does dissolve 1.5% water by weight at room temperature. However, diethyl ether will not dissolve sodium chloride solution, and therefore if a diethyl ether solution containing dissolved water is washed with saturated sodium chloride solution, water is transferred from the diethyl ether to the aqueous layer. Strange, but true! The final traces of water are removed from the organic solution by drying over an appropriate drying agent (p. 126). After filtration (pp. 74–79) of the spent drying agent, the required neutral organic compound is recovered from the filtrate by evaporation of the solvent on the rotary evaporator.

Isolation and purification of an acidic organic compound

The extraction protocol for the isolation and purification of an acidic organic compound is shown in outline in Fig. 3.38. Again the overall procedure is self-explanatory, and the only thing you need to decide is which aqueous base to use in the first extraction. The choice depends on the properties of the acidic compound that you are trying to isolate and purify. Strong organic acids such as carboxylic and sulfonic acids can usually be extracted with saturated sodium bicarbonate solution, but weaker acids such as phenols can only be extracted with stronger bases such as sodium carbonate or sodium hydroxide. If you do not know the precise acidity of the compound, play safe, and use

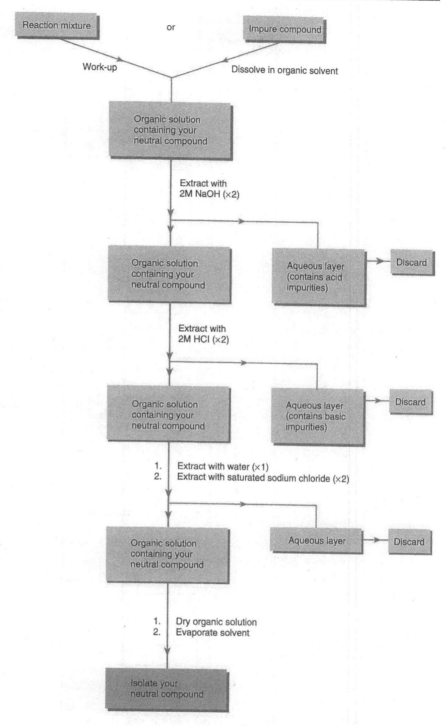

Fig. 3.37 Extraction protocol for the isolation and purification of a neutral organic compound.

Fig. 3.38 Extraction protocol for the isolation and purification of an acidic organic compound.

sodium hydroxide solution to extract it. The acidic compound is recovered from the aqueous basic layer by making the solution strongly acidic, and then extracting it with an organic solvent. The acidification is usually done by adding 2 M hydrochloric acid until the pH reaches 1–2, but if this will result in a large increase in volume, then it is better to add concentrated acid *dropwise*. Remember that the heat of the acid–base reaction will cause the aqueous solution to become quite hot. The solution should be cooled in an ice bath before extracting it. Never attempt to extract hot solutions. At the end of the extraction procedure, you will need to dry the final organic solution over an appropriate drying agent; not all drying agents are suitable for acidic compounds (see Table 3.5).

Take care when neutralizing solutions—heat evolved! Do not attempt to extract hot aqueous solutions

Isolation and purification of a basic organic compound

Basic organic compounds can be isolated and purified by using the extraction protocol shown in Fig. 3.39. The procedure is very similar to those discussed above, but obvious changes are needed as you are trying to isolate a basic compound. The basic compound is recovered from the acidic water layer by basification and extraction. Again at the very end of the process, the choice of

Table 3.5 Some common drying agents for organic solutions.*

Drying agent	Capacity†	Speed	Efficiency	Applicability
Calcium chloride	High, 90%	Slow	Poor	Use only for hydrocarbons or halides; reacts with most oxygen- and nitrogen-containing compounds; may contain CaO (basic)
Calcium sulfate (Drierite®)	Low, 7%	Very fast	Very good	Generally useful; neutral
Magnesium sulfate	High, 100%	Fast	Good	Excellent general purpose drying agent; a weak Lewis acid; should not be used for *very* acid-sensitive compounds
Molecular sieves	Moderate, 20%	Fast	Good	When freshly activated, excellent for removing most of the water, but solutions should be predried with a higher capacity agent first
Potassium carbonate	Quite high	Quite fast	Quite good	Basic; reacts with acidic compounds; good for oxygen- and nitrogen-containing compounds
Sodium sulfate	High, 75%	Slow	Poor	Mild, generally useful, but less efficient than $MgSO_4$

* These agents are for drying organic solutions, not for drying organic solvents. The drying of organic solvents is an entirely separate problem (see Appendix 2, p. 677).

† The number indicates the amount of water, as a percentage of its own weight, that a drying agent can take up.

Fig. 3.39 Extraction protocol for the isolation and purification of a basic organic compound.

drying agent for the organic solution is important. Basic compounds, particularly amines, cannot be dried over certain drying agents. The choice of drying agent for organic solutions is discussed in more detail in pp. 127, 130–131.

Extraction of solids

Solids can also be extracted with organic solvents. One very simple way of doing this is to place the solid in an Erlenmeyer flask, cover the solid with the organic solvent and allow the flask to stand with occasional swirling. The organic compound that you are interested in will be slowly leached out of the solid. The unwanted solid can then be removed from the organic solution containing your compound simply by filtration. However, this is a fairly inefficient technique, although the efficiency of the extraction can be improved by using hot solvents. A much more efficient way to extract solids is to use a *Soxhlet* apparatus (Fig. 3.40). In this, the solid to be extracted is packed into a special 'thimble' made of thick filter paper. The thimble is placed in the apparatus as shown, and the whole Soxhlet extractor is placed on top of a well-supported round-bottomed flask containing the organic solvent. A reflux condenser is placed on top of the Soxhlet extractor. The flask is heated using a water or steam bath (for flammable solvents) or some form of electrical heating, so that the solvent boils. Solvent vapour passes up the large diameter outer tube of the apparatus, and condensed solvent then drips down

Soxhlet extraction

Fig. 3.40 Soxhlet apparatus for the extraction of solids.

through the thimble containing the solid. Material is extracted out of the solid into the hot solvent. When the solution level reaches the top of the siphon tube, the solution siphons automatically through the narrow tube, and returns to the flask, where the extracted material accumulates. The process is efficient, since the same batch of solvent is repeatedly recycled through the solid. If the extraction is run for prolonged periods it is possible to extract materials that are only very slightly soluble in organic solvents. The technique is often used for the extraction of natural products from biological materials such as crushed leaves or seeds, and this particular application is illustrated in Experiment 69.

Further reading

For further detailed discussion of extraction procedures in organic chemistry, see: L.C. Craig and D. Craig, *Extraction and Distribution, Techniques of Organic Chemistry*, Vol. III (ed. by A. Weissberger), Wiley (Interscience), New York, 1950.

Solution drying

After completing the isolation or purification of an organic compound by some form of extraction, or after completing the work-up of your reaction mixture, you are left with an organic solution containing your required compound. Since the organic solution has been extracted or washed with aqueous solutions, it will undoubtedly contain some water. Although, as discussed above, the amount of water can sometimes be reduced by washing the organic solution with saturated sodium chloride solution, the last traces of water have to be removed by treatment with a drying agent. Common drying agents are anhydrous inorganic salts which readily take up water to become hydrated. At the end of the drying process, the hydrated salt is removed from the organic solution by filtration.

The complete procedure is as follows. At the end of the extraction, pour the final organic solution out of the separatory funnel into an Erlenmeyer flask as described on p. 114. Add the solid drying agent and swirl the flask. If the drying agent immediately lumps together add some more. Allow the flask to stand, with occasional swirling, for 5–20 min. The time depends on the speed with which the drying agent takes up water (Table 3.5), but you can usually tell when an excess of *anhydrous* drying agent, such as magnesium sulfate (the most commonly used agent), is present by simply swirling the flask. The *anhydrous* salt forms a cloudy suspension that settles quite slowly; the effect is often described as a 'snow storm'. If, on the other hand, only *hydrated* agent is present, the suspension settles very quickly, since the hydrated salt is usually much denser. In this case add some more drying agent. When the solution is deemed to be dry, remove the spent drying agent by filtration (pp. 74–79) and recover the organic compound from the filtrate by evaporation of the solvent on a rotary evaporator (pp. 49–53).

The most important factor in drying organic solutions is the choice of

How to tell when the solution is dry

drying agent. Ideally the solid drying agent should be totally insoluble in organic solvents, inert to a wide range of organic compounds (including solvents), and able to take up water quickly and efficiently to give a hydrated form which is an easily filterable solid. The most commonly used drying agents are listed in Table 3.5, which gives information on their *capacity* (how much water they can take up), *speed* (rate of water uptake), *efficiency* (how dry they leave the solution) and *applicability* (suitability for different classes of compound). Clearly the choice will depend on a number of factors, the most crucial of which is the nature of the organic compound that is dissolved in the solvent, and that is ultimately to be isolated. As a good general purpose drying agent, magnesium sulfate finds the widest use.

It is important to note that drying agents that are suitable for drying *organic solutions* are not usually appropriate for drying *organic solvents* for use with moisture-sensitive compounds (see pp. 79–89). The drying of organic solvents is an entirely separate problem that is referred to on pp. 81–82, and dealt with specifically in Appendix 2 (p. 677).

Solution drying on the microscale

Effective drying can be achieved in a plugged Pasteur pipette. Push a small plug of cotton or glass wool into the top of the constriction of a Pasteur pipette (see Fig. 3.9). Do not pack the plug too tightly; however, it should not simply wash through when solvent is loaded into the pipette. Solid drying agent can then be loaded into the wider section of the pipette to a depth of 1–2 cm. Using a second Pasteur pipette, wet the column evenly with clean extraction solvent, then load the solution to be dried onto the drying agent and use gentle pressure to push the solution through the bed of adsorbent. Simply fitting a teat to the top of the pipette and expelling the air will achieve sufficient pressure. Take care not to allow air back into the teat while it is still attached to the column as this will probably disrupt the filter bed, contaminating your sample. Some commercial microscale kits contain small chromatography columns which can also be used for this purpose, though a pipette is quite adequate.

Crystallization

The simplest and most effective technique for the purification of solid organic compounds is crystallization. Crystalline compounds are easy to handle, their purity is readily assessed (Chapter 4) and they are often easier to identify than liquids or oils. Crystals can be obtained in one of three ways: from the melted solid on cooling, by sublimation (pp. 159–160) or from a supersaturated solution. The last method is by far the most common in the organic laboratory.

Crystallization of organic compounds

A general flow-chart for the purification of an organic compound by *crystallization* is shown in Fig. 3.41. The process involves five stages: dissolution, filtration, crystallization, collection of the crystals, and drying the crystals. The

Fig. 3.41 Plan for purification of an organic compound by crystallization.

purity of the crystals can then be determined (Chapters 4 and 5), and if necessary further purification by *recrystallization* can be carried out. Before discussing each of the stages in the process in detail, we should briefly consider how crystallization succeeds in purifying compounds at all.

How crystallization works

The technique involves dissolving the impure solid in the minimum volume of a hot solvent and filtering to remove insoluble impurities. The resulting hot saturated solution of the compound, together with any soluble impurities, is set aside to cool slowly, whereupon crystals of pure compound will separate from solution. The solution remaining after crystallization is usually known as the *mother liquor*. Why are the crystals pure? The process of crystallization is an equilibrium: molecules in solution are in equilibrium with those in the crystal lattice. Since a crystal lattice is highly ordered, other different molecules, such as impurities, will be excluded from the lattice and will return to the solution. Therefore only molecules of the required compound are retained in the crystal lattice and the impurities will remain in solution.

Slow cooling

For a crystallization to be successful, *the solution must be allowed to cool slowly*, so that the crystals are formed slowly, and the equilibrium process which excludes the impurities is allowed to operate. If a solution is cooled rapidly, impurity molecules will be trapped or included in the rapidly growing crystal lattice. This rapid formation of solid material from solution is *precipitation*, and is not the same as crystallization.

At this stage it should be pointed out that crystallization does not always work. Substances which are grossly impure will often refuse to crystallize, and in these cases some preliminary purification by another technique, such as extraction (pp. 118–130) or chromatography (pp. 160–203), may be necessary.

Dissolution

The first problem is to dissolve the impure substance in a suitable solvent. The ideal solvent for a crystallization should not react with the compound, should be fairly volatile so that it is easy to remove from the crystals, should have a boiling point that is lower than the melting point of the compound to be crystallized, should be non-toxic and non-flammable, but most important of all, the compound should be very soluble in hot solvent and insoluble in cold solvent. In many cases, particularly when crystallizing known compounds, you will know what solvent to use because the literature or your laboratory text will tell you. In other cases, you will have to decide what solvent to use. Choosing a solvent for crystallization is not always easy, but organic chemists tend to

Like dissolves like

follow the rule that 'like dissolves like'. So, for the crystallization of non-polar substances such as hydrocarbons, use a non-polar solvent such as pentane or light petroleum. Compounds containing polar groups such as OH are best crystallized from polar OH-containing solvents such as ethanol. Indeed polar solvents are often preferred for other compounds because they tend to give better crystals. Some suggestions for crystallization solvents for the most common classes of organic compound, arranged in order of increasing polarity, are given in Table 3.6.

If the crystallization solvent is not known for certain, do not commit all your solid and attempt to dissolve it up. Rather, carry out some preliminary solubility tests. To do this, place a small quantity of the solid (*ca.* 20 mg or the

Test the solubility

Use a hood if the solvent is toxic

amount that fits on the tip of a micro-spatula) in a small test tube—an ignition tube or a 10 × 75 mm test tube is ideal—and add a few drops of solvent to the tube. If the substance dissolves easily in cold solvent, try again with a different solvent. If the substance is insoluble in cold solvent, warm the tube on a steam

Use a steam bath for heating flammable solvents

or water bath, and if the substance remains insoluble, add more solvent with continued heating. If the compound still refuses to dissolve, try again with a

Table 3.6 Suggested solvents for crystallization.

Class of compound	Suggested solvents
Hydrocarbons	Light petroleum, pentane, cyclohexane, toluene
Ethers	Diethyl ether, dichloromethane
Halides	Dichloromethane
Carbonyl compounds	Ethyl acetate, acetone
Alcohols, acids	Ethanol
Salts	Water

different solvent. Once you have found a solvent that dissolves the compound when hot, you need to check that the solid will separate again on cooling. Place the tube in a beaker of ice-water, and leave it to stand for a minute or two. If a solid forms on cooling, the solvent is probably suitable for crystallization of the bulk material. With experience, these preliminary solubility tests can be carried out quickly, and provide a satisfactory guide to the choice of crystallization solvent.

Always keep a seed crystal

Once you have found a suitable solvent, you are ready to dissolve up the solid for crystallization. Before doing so, it is a good idea to weigh the solid, if you have not already done so, so that the recovery of material from the crystallization process can be determined. If the substance is already crystalline, do not dissolve all of it. Always retain a few crystals in case they are needed for seeding purposes (see p. 136). Large crystals are often difficult to dissolve, and should be ground up before adding the crystallization solvent.

Mixed solvents for crystallization

If a suitable crystallization solvent cannot be found, then you may have to use a *mixed solvent system*. A mixed solvent system is a pair of miscible solvents, chosen so that one of them (the good solvent) dissolves the compound readily, and the other (the poor solvent) does not. For example, many moderately polar organic compounds are soluble in diethyl ether, but not in light petroleum, and therefore a mixture of the two solvents may be suitable for crystallization. There are two schools of thought on how to carry out a crystallization using mixed solvents. One method is to dissolve the solid in the minimum volume of hot good solvent, add the poor solvent dropwise until the solution starts to become slightly turbid or cloudy, and then set the solution aside to crystallize. The second method is to suspend the solid in hot poor solvent, and then add the good solvent dropwise with continued heating until the solid *just* dissolves; then set the solution aside as before. Typical mixed solvent systems that often work quite well include diethyl ether–light petroleum, dichloromethane–light petroleum, diethyl ether–acetone and ethanol–water. If possible choose a system in which the good solvent is the lower boiling solvent. One final word of warning: the use of mixed solvents often encourages *oiling out* (see p. 136), and therefore crystallization from a single solvent is preferred.

Filtration

Once your compound is in solution in a hot solvent, the solution should be filtered to remove any insoluble material. This material may be an insoluble impurity or by-product or may simply be pieces of extraneous material such as dust, glass or paper. The solution should be filtered under gravity through a fluted filter paper into an Erlenmeyer flask using the technique described on pp. 75–77.

Use hand protection for hot filtration

In some cases the solution of your organic compound will be strongly coloured by impurities. This is not a problem, provided that the coloured impurities remain in solution. However, occasionally they are adsorbed by the crystals as they form, to give an impure, coloured product. Luckily the fact that such impurity molecules are easily adsorbed can be used to remove them from solution. This process is usually known as *decolourization*, and involves treating the hot solution with activated charcoal, often known as decolourizing carbon or under the trade name Norit®. To decolourize a solution add a small quantity of activated charcoal, usually about 2% by weight of the sample, to the hot, but not boiling, solution. If the solution is at or close to its boiling point, the addition of the finely divided charcoal will cause it to boil over. Continue to heat the solution containing the charcoal for about 5–10 min with occasional swirling or stirring. By this time the impurity molecules responsible for the colour should have been adsorbed by the charcoal, and filtration of the mixture should give a decolourized solution of the organic compound. The filtration can be carried out under gravity through a fluted filter paper, although a second filtration may be necessary to remove all the fine particles of charcoal.

Decolourization

Use a steam bath for heating flammable solvents

Crystallization and what to do if no crystals are formed

Having filtered your hot solution into an Erlenmeyer flask, cover the flask with a watch glass to prevent contamination by atmospheric dust, and then set it aside so that the solution can cool slowly. The rate of cooling determines the size of the crystals, rapid cooling favouring the formation of a lot of small crystals, and slow cooling encouraging the growth of fewer, but much larger, crystals. A convenient compromise between speed of crystallization and crystal quality is to allow the hot solution to cool to room temperature by placing the flask on a surface such as glass or cork that does not conduct the heat away too quickly. The *rate* of crystallization is usually greatest at about 50°C below the melting point of the substance, and maximum formation of crystals occurs at about 100°C below the melting point. Once the crystals have formed, it is usually a good idea to cool the solution from room temperature to about 0°C by placing the Erlenmeyer in an ice bath. This will ensure that the maximum amount of crystals are obtained. It is not usually good practice to cool the solution below 0°C, unless there are special problems in getting crystals to form in the first place (see p. 136), because this results in condensation of water vapour into the solution unless special precautions are taken.

What do you do when no crystallization occurs after cooling the solution to room temperature? You should attempt to induce crystallization by one of the following methods. Add a seed crystal which was saved from the original material before dissolution. This will provide a nucleus on which other crystals can grow. If this fails, try scratching the side of the flask with a glass rod. This is thought to produce micro-fragments of glass which then serve as nuclei to induce crystallization. If this fails, try cooling the flask in an acetone–solid CO_2 bath (see p. 107), and then scratch the side of the flask as the solution warms up to room temperature. If the substance still refuses to crystallize, it probably means that you have too much solvent; the excess solvent should be boiled off (**hood — check for flames in the vicinity**), and the reduced volume of solution should be set aside again until crystallization occurs.

Seeding

Scratching

Cooling

Remove solvents in a hood and check for flames first

Oiling out

The final problem that may be encountered in crystallization is the separation of the substance as an oil rather than as crystals. This is known as *oiling out*, and usually occurs when the compound is very impure or when it has a melting point that is lower than the boiling point of the solvent. Even if the oil eventually solidifies, the compound will not be pure, and the material should be redissolved by heating the solution. You may need to add a little more solvent at this stage, or more good solvent if mixed solvents are being used. Indeed, crystallization from a slightly more dilute solution may prevent oiling out. Slower cooling also favours the formation of crystals rather than oils. If the compound completely refuses to crystallize, the chances are that it is too impure, and it should be purified by some other means such as chromatography.

Collecting the crystals

After crystallization the crystals are separated from the *mother liquor* by suction filtration, a technique which has already been discussed in detail on pp. 77–79. After filtration, the crystals should be washed with a little fresh solvent. Remember that if the crystallization has been performed using mixed solvents, the wash solvent should be the same mixture.

Remove solvents in a hood and check for flames first

Second crop will be less pure

The mother liquor from the crystallization (which is now the filtrate) may still contain a significant quantity of your organic product. In this case a second batch of crystals, known as the *second crop*, can often be obtained by concentrating the mother liquor by boiling off some of the solvent (**hood — check for flames in the vicinity**) and then allowing the solution to cool and crystallize as before. However, be warned, the second crop is usually less pure than the first simply because the impurities were concentrated in the mother liquor during the first crystallization. Do not combine the two crops of crystals until you have checked the purity of each batch.

Drying the crystals

After filtration and washing, the crystals should be dried to constant weight. Techniques for drying solids are discussed on pp. 140–143.

Special crystallization techniques

Crystallization of very small quantities

When the amount of material to be crystallized is less than about 100 mg, the normal techniques of crystallization are inappropriate because of the losses of material that would occur, particularly during filtration. To crystallize small quantities (10–100 mg) of organic compounds, place the solid in a *very small* test tube, and dissolve it up in the minimum volume of hot solvent in the usual way. It is impossible to filter very small volumes of solution using the normal technique, so another method is needed. One way is to put a small plug of cotton wool in the tip of a Pasteur pipette and then slowly draw the hot solution through the cotton wool into the pipette (Fig. 3.42a). The cotton wool will retain all but the finest of insoluble impurities. Quickly remove the wool from the end of the pipette using a pair of tweezers, and then release the hot solution from the pipette into the *pre-weighed* vessel where it will be allowed to crystallize. To avoid spills, it is safer to hold the Pasteur pipette over the crystallization vessel whilst removing the cotton wool. The mother liquor should be removed using a Pasteur pipette, taking care not to suck up any crystals (Fig. 3.42b). A small amount of wash solvent can be added, and can then be removed by pipette. The damp crystals should be dried in the same tube by placing it in a suitable drying apparatus (see Fig. 3.44).

Fig. 3.42 (a) Using a Pasteur pipette and cotton wool for filtration; (b) removing the mother liquor with a Pasteur pipette; (c) Craig tube before centrifugation; (d) Craig tube after centrifugation.

The ideal vessels for the crystallization of small quantities of material are small conical-bottomed centrifuge tubes or tubes specially designed for the purpose known as *Craig tubes*. The idea is to minimize the number of transfers and to avoid having to collect the crystals by filtration. Craig tubes (Fig. 3.42c,d) are designed so that the mother liquor from the crystallization can be removed by *centrifugation*. The hot filtrate is transferred to the Craig tube as described above, and the crystallization is allowed to proceed. When crystallization is complete, insert the well-fitting glass 'plug' of the Craig tube, place an empty inverted centrifuge tube over the Craig tube, and invert the whole, making sure that the two parts of the Craig tube do not separate. Place the tube in the centrifuge, make sure the centrifuge is balanced, and spin for 20–30 s. The centrifugation will force the mother liquor past the glass plug, but the crystals will be retained by the plug (Fig. 3.42d). The Craig tube plus crystals is then placed in a suitable drying apparatus to dry the crystals.

When the crystals are dry, the crystallization tube can be weighed, and provided that the empty weight was recorded, the weight of crystals can be determined. The crystals can be removed from the tube by inverting it over a piece of filter or weighing paper, and gently tapping it.

Craig tubes

Always balance the centrifuge rotor arm with another centrifuge tube containing enough water to make the weights equal

Fractional crystallization

Fractional crystallization is a rather special technique for separating two compounds by repeated crystallization. Although chromatography has largely supplanted fractional crystallization as a separation method, the technique still has its uses, particularly in the resolution of racemic acids or bases by separation of their crystalline diastereomeric salts formed by reaction with optically active bases or acids, respectively. A schematic plan for a fractional crystallization is shown in Fig. 3.43. The first crystallization gives crystals (C_1) and mother liquor (ML_1). These are separated in the normal way, and the crys-

Fig. 3.43 Schematic plan for fractional crystallization.

tals are recrystallized to give crystals C_2 and mother liquor ML'_2. The first mother liquor is evaporated to dryness, and the residue is redissolved and crystallized to give crystals C'_2 and mother liquor ML_2. The crystals C'_2 are combined with ML'_2, the solvent is evaporated, and the residue is crystallized further. As the scheme unfolds, pure crystals of the less soluble component are obtained and the mother liquor becomes enriched in the more soluble component. In practice it is fairly easy to obtain a pure, less soluble component after two or three crystallizations, but the more soluble component may require further purification by some other technique.

Crystals for X-ray crystallography

Good crystals are an essential requirement if the material is to be submitted for X-ray structure analysis. Therefore the growth of X-ray quality crystals is a special skill requiring considerable patience. The simplest technique is to allow the solvent to evaporate very slowly from the crystallization flask. In practice this means leaving the open flask to stand at room temperature, **in a hood if the solvent is toxic**, whilst the solvent slowly evaporates.

Allow toxic solvents to evaporate in a hood

An alternative technique for the crystallization of compounds for X-ray analysis relies on *slow diffusion* between two different solvents. In this variant on mixed solvent crystallization, it is essential that the 'good' solvent is more dense than the 'poor' solvent. Dissolve the compound in a small volume of good solvent, such as dichloromethane, in a small sample vial, the narrower the better. *Carefully* run in an equal volume of poor solvent, such as light petroleum, on top of the first solvent, stopper the vial, and set it aside. It is essential that all of this is done very carefully so that the two solvents do not mix and the interface remains clearly visible. Over the next few hours or days, diffusion between the layers will occur, and, all being well, crystals will form at the interface. This process, although rather slow, encourages the formation of good quality crystals.

A new technique for crystallizing organic compounds that give poor quality crystals or that give crystals in only small amounts in *co-crystallization* with triphenylphosphine oxide. Triphenylphosphine oxide itself gives high quality crystals, and this property is apparently carried over to the complexes it forms with a range of other organic molecules. Triphenylphosphine oxide forms complexes with most organic molecules that contain an active hydrogen (OH, NH), the complex being stabilized by hydrogen bonding to the phosphoryl P=O. The crystalline complexes are formed by dissolving equimolar amounts of your compound and triphenylphosphine oxide in toluene, and allowing the toluene to evaporate slowly. The crystals are collected in the usual way, washed quickly with a little acetone followed by light petroleum, and then dried in air. One final word of caution: having obtained beautiful crystals by this technique, do check that they are not simply triphenylphosphine oxide itself before giving them to your X-ray crystallographer!

Further reading

For further discussion of growing crystals for X-ray analysis, see: P.G. Jones, *Chem. Br.*, 1981, **17**, 222.

The co-crystallization technique was reported by: M.C. Etter and P.W. Baures, *J. Am. Chem. Soc.*, 1988, **110**, 639.

J. Hulliger, Chemistry and crystal growth, *Angew. Chem. Int. Edn.*, 1994, **33**, 143–162.

Drying solids

When an organic solid has been obtained by filtration of a reaction mixture, or when crystals have been obtained from a crystallization, the organic compound must be thoroughly dried before it can be weighed or analyzed or used in the next step of a reaction sequence. As described on p. 79, some preliminary drying can be carried out whilst the sample is still on the filter paper in the Büchner funnel. Press the filtered solid down onto the filter paper, and continue the suction for about 5 min. In this way the solid can be sucked fairly dry.

Suck the solid dry on the filter

Another simple technique for drying solids is called *air drying*. Spread the crystals or solid out on a watch glass or large piece of filter paper, and allow them to dry in the air. However, air drying is slow, especially if water or some other high boiling solvent has been used.

The *rate* of drying can be increased by increasing the rate of solvent evaporation from the solid. The simplest way to do this is to place the sample in an oven where it can be heated. Before doing this, however, you need to have a rough idea of the melting point of the compound. Organic compounds should never be heated to their melting point to dry them; for safety it is best to set the oven at about 30–50°C *below* the melting point of the compound. **Compounds that are thermally unstable should not be dried by heating**.

Never heat compounds to their melting point to dry them

Another way to increase the rate of evaporation of solvent from solids is to place the sample in an apparatus that can be evacuated by attaching it to a water aspirator or vacuum pump. Low boiling solvents are removed quickly under reduced pressure, and the drying process is reasonably efficient. The process is more efficient still if the sample is heated under reduced pressure, but you should take care that your compound will not *sublime* under these conditions. *Vacuum ovens* are useful for drying large quantities of solid materials, but for normal laboratory-scale working (200 mg to 5 g), a purpose designed *drying pistol* should be used. There are two basic types of drying pistol: the *Abderhalden* type (Fig. 3.44a) and the electrically heated type (Fig. 3.44b). Both consist of a horizontal chamber (in two parts, joined with a large diameter tapered glass joint) which can be evacuated through the stopcock. The sample to be dried is placed in a vial, which is introduced into the apparatus through the middle joint. It is a good idea to wrap a piece of copper wire around the sample vial to act as a 'handle' and to facilitate the eventual removal of the vial from the apparatus. In the Abderhalden design, the evacuated chamber is heated by hot solvent vapour from the refluxing solvent in the

Drying pistols

Fig. 3.44 (a) Abderhalden drying pistol; (b) electrically heated drying pistol.

round-bottomed flask below the apparatus. A condenser should be attached to the top of the apparatus. The degree of heating of the sample is controlled by the boiling point of the solvent used. The electrically heated design is more adaptable in that heating is provided by an outer glass furnace containing heating coils, which can be set to the desired temperature. Both designs incorporate a *desiccant* chamber in the unheated region of the tube.

Desiccants or *drying agents* are not normally needed when drying solids that are wet with organic solvents, but they are very useful when removing water from organic solids. Water removal at room temperature is carried out in a *desiccator* (Fig. 3.45), and the drying agent, such as anhydrous calcium chloride, is placed in the bottom of the desiccator. The sample to be dried is placed on a watch glass on the shelf above. When the cover is in place and the system is closed, the drying agent 'soaks up' the water from the atmosphere in the desiccator as the water evaporates from the solid. The drying process can be speeded up by evacuating the desiccator, and many desiccators are fitted with a vacuum take-off stopcock. For safety, an evacuated desiccator should be surrounded by a wire mesh cage, to prevent injury from flying glass should an implosion occur. Desiccants can also be used in drying pistols; the desiccant is placed in a tube or 'boat' in the unheated part of the apparatus as indicated in Fig. 3.44.

Put a safety cage around an evacuated desiccator

Drying agents that are commonly used in desiccators (Table 3.7) are: calcium chloride, calcium sulfate (Drierite®), potassium hydroxide, phosphorus pentoxide and concentrated sulfuric acid. Obviously great care should be taken when using some of these highly corrosive materials, and the use of concentrated sulfuric acid is best avoided. Check that the desiccant is fresh and

Fig. 3.45 Vacuum desiccator (with mesh safety cage).

Table 3.7 Common drying agents for use in desiccators.

Solvent to be removed	Desiccant
H_2O	$CaCl_2$, $CaSO_4$, silica gel, solid KOH, P_2O_5, H_2SO_4 (concentrated)
MeOH, EtOH	$CaCl_2$
Hydrocarbons, halogenated solvents	Freshly cut shavings of paraffin wax
CH_3CO_2H, aqueous HCl	Solid KOH + silica gel (kept separately)
Aqueous NH_3	H_2SO_4 (concentrated)

active. Phosphorus pentoxide is very efficient when new because it actually reacts with the water, but rapidly forms a glassy coating which markedly reduces its capacity to react with water.

The sample to be dried should be broken up on a suitably sized watch glass or petri dish to give it as large a surface area as possible, before placing it in the desiccator and evacuating the system. It is advisable to include a water trap (see Fig. 2.19, p. 38) between the water aspirator and the desiccator to prevent flooding in case of suck-back. At all times whilst under vacuum, the desiccator *must* be kept under its protective cover. At the end of the drying period, the vacuum can be released in a controlled manner by holding a filter paper to the inlet tube with the index finger and opening the stopcock. On removing the finger, air is sucked in gently through the filter paper holding it in place until the inside of the desiccator reaches atmospheric pressure, allowing the filter paper to fall off. The sample may now be removed safely. If such a precaution is not taken, the violent inrush of air will spread the sample all around the interior of the desiccator.

Release vacuum slowly

Fig. 3.46 Improvised microscale drying pistol; the vacuum connection is provided using a short length of glass tubing and a commercial threaded adapter.

A drying pistol can be improvised for drying small quantities of solid using an aspirator, a tapered or threaded reaction vial and a threaded adapter. Figure 3.46 shows a typical set-up; gentle warming of the vial in a sand or water bath can be used to increase the rate of solvent evaporation.

Distillation

The history of distillation goes back to about the second century BC when the still was invented at the school of alchemists in Alexandria for 'refining powders'. However, it was not until the twelfth century AD that the art of distillation was rediscovered as a way of producing alcoholic liquor that was much stronger than wine or beer. By the thirteenth century, distillation of alcoholic beverages (spirits) was well established. Indeed the word *alcohol* derives from the Arabic *al-koh'l*, the word for the refined powders obtained from the original stills of Alexandria.

In the organic laboratory, distillation is one of the main techniques for purifying volatile liquids. It involves vapourizing the material by heating it, and subsequently condensing the vapour back to a liquid, the *distillate*. There are various ways in which a distillation can be carried out, but in practice the choice of distillation procedure depends on the properties of the liquid that you are trying to purify and on the properties of the impurities that you are trying to separate. This section deals with the most common distillation techniques: *simple distillation, fractional distillation, distillation under reduced pressure, short path and microscale distillation and steam distillation.* In

Types of distillation

addition, *sublimation*, the purification of a solid by conversion to the vapour phase and condensation back to a solid, without going through a liquid phase, is also covered. As in other sections, the main aim is to concentrate on the practical application of the techniques, and hence a detailed discussion of the theory of distillation is inappropriate. Nevertheless, a brief consideration of the theoretical aspects of distillation is warranted.

Theoretical aspects

The *vapour pressure* of a liquid increases with temperature, and the point at which the vapour pressure equals the pressure above the liquid is defined as the *boiling point*. Pure liquids which do not decompose on heating have a sharp well-defined boiling point, although the boiling point will vary considerably with changes in pressure. A further discussion of boiling points is included on pp. 213–218, but from a practical viewpoint, if a reasonably pure liquid is distilled, the temperature of the vapour increases until it reaches the boiling point of the liquid. At this point the liquid and vapour are in thermal equilibrium with each other, and the distillation will proceed at a reasonably constant temperature. However, since we are using distillation to purify our organic compound, we are, by definition, distilling a mixture. The mixture may consist of 95% of the compound we require, together with 5% of unknown impurities, or it may be a mixture containing 50% product and 50% starting material. Whatever the situation, we need to consider the implications of the distillation of mixtures of volatile liquids.

The underlying principles of the distillation of mixtures of miscible liquids are embodied in two laws of physical chemistry: Dalton's law and Raoult's law. *Dalton's law of partial pressures* states that the total pressure of a gas, or vapour pressure of a liquid (P), is the sum of the *partial pressures* of its individual components A and B $(P_A$ and $P_B)$. So

Dalton's law

$$P = P_A + P_B$$

Raoult's law states that, at a given temperature and pressure, the partial vapour pressure of a compound in a mixture (P_A) is equal to the vapour pressure of the pure compound (P_A^{pure}) multiplied by its *mole fraction* (X_A) in the mixture:

Raoult's law

$$P_A = P_A^{pure} \times X_A$$

Hence, from both laws, the total vapour pressure of a liquid mixture is dependent on the vapour pressures of the pure components and their mole fractions in the mixture.

Dalton's law and Raoult's law are mathematical expressions of what happens during a distillation, and they describe the changes in the compositions of the boiling liquid and the vapour (and hence the distillate) with temperature as the distillation proceeds. Plots of vapour composition and liquid composition versus temperature can therefore be made. They are usually combined onto a single diagram known as a *phase diagram* or, sometimes, as a boiling point–composition diagram. An example is shown in Fig. 3.47. This figure shows the distillation of a two-component mixture of miscible liquids with: (a) markedly different boiling points (broken line), and (b) similar boiling points (full line). But what does it mean in terms of the *practical* aspects of distillation?

Assume that we start with a 1:1 mixture of the two miscible components A and B (component A having the lower boiling point) which we are to separate by simple distillation. At the start of the distillation when the liquid starts to boil, the composition of the liquid is 50 mol% of each component, and the composition of the vapour is determined by drawing a horizontal line from the liquid line to the vapour line. In the first instance, where the components have widely differing boiling points (broken line), the vapour consists of almost pure A. When most of the more volatile A has been removed from the vapour by condensation, further heating will cause a rise in temperature to the boiling point of component B. Hence the two liquids are easily separated in a *single* distillation. In practical terms this will usually be possible if the vapour pressure of the more volatile liquid is at least 10 times that of the other liquid. Translated into boiling points, this means that it is usually possible to separate, almost completely, liquids which differ in their boiling points by at least 80°C.

If the boiling points are closer (full line), the composition of the vapour as the liquid starts to boil is about 85% A and 15% B. Hence pure A cannot be obtained in a single distillation. Clearly the material containing 85% A could be subsequently redistilled to give purer A, which could be redistilled again and again until pure material was obtained. Such a series of single distillations would be extremely time consuming and tedious, so obviously an alternative

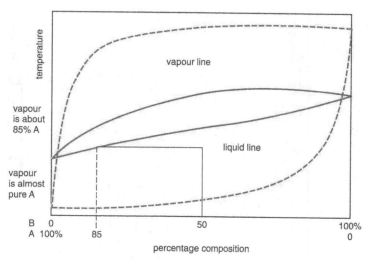

Fig. 3.47 Simple phase diagram for distillation of a two-component mixture (- - -: components with markedly different bp; —: components with similar bp).

method is needed in this situation. *Fractional distillation* is such a method, and is discussed in more detail on pp. 148–152.

Many two-component mixtures do not follow Raoult's law, and therefore do not give idealized phase diagrams. Some mixtures, particularly those in which one of the components contains a hydroxyl (OH) group, distil at a constant boiling point and with constant composition. In this case the liquids are said to form an *azeotrope* or *azeotropic mixture*, a phenomenon which is discussed in more detail on pp. 214–216. Azeotropic mixtures cannot be separated by distillation.

Azeotropes

Simple distillation

To carry out a simple distillation, set up the apparatus as shown in Fig. 3.48. The apparatus consists of a round-bottomed distillation flask (often referred to as the 'pot'), a still head, and a condenser equipped with a receiver adapter attached to the *preweighed* receiving flask. **Make sure that the apparatus is adequately supported with clamps.** The size of glassware used for the apparatus should be dictated by the *scale* of the distillation, but many laboratory operations are on the 10–100 g scale. Occasionally it will be necessary to distil smaller quantities (2–10 g), and therefore smaller glassware should be used. Glassware with size ⑤ 10 tapered joints is convenient for this purpose. For yet smaller scale distillations (50 mg to 2 g), the *short path distillation* techniques (see pp. 154–155, 158–159) should be used. Whatever the scale, always use a distillation flask that is at least 1.5 times the volume of sample.

Scale

(a) (b)

Fig. 3.48 (a) Apparatus for simple distillation. (b) Microscale distillation.

Transfer the liquid to be distilled to the distillation flask using a funnel through the neck of the still head, and add some boiling stones (anti-bumping granules) to the flask to ensure smooth boiling without 'bumping'. Fit the thermometer adapter and set the thermometer at such a height that it measures the temperature of the vapour passing over the angle of the still head, not the liquid condensing back into the flask. Heat the distillation flask in an appropriate heat source, the choice of which is influenced by both the nature and boiling point of the liquid. A water or steam bath should always be used for low boiling (less than 85°C) flammable liquids. For higher boiling liquids, an electrically heated oil bath is best. Mantles are less controllable and should only be used for the distillation of solvents. Burners are best avoided. When the liquid starts to boil, collect the condensed vapours in one or more portions, or *fractions*, in the receiving flask.

Heating

For the reasons outlined above, simple distillation can only be used to separate components that differ in boiling point by at least 80°C. More commonly, however, it is used to purify volatile components that are already fairly pure, by separating them from high boiling impurities, for example. If the liquid is relatively pure, a small amount of distillate containing the lower boiling impurities will be collected whilst the temperature at the still head is still rising; this is known as the *fore-run*. As soon as the still head temperature reaches a constant value, the main fraction can be collected, and the distillation can be continued until the bulk of the liquid has been obtained. The higher boiling impurities will remain as the residue in the distillation flask. Never attempt to distil the liquid to dryness; always leave a residue in the distillation flask. Distillation to dryness is potentially very dangerous since it involves strong heating of the material. The nature of any high boiling impurity would not be known, and hence heating it could result in a thermal decomposition reaction which may be violent.

Simple distillation will completely separate liquids that differ in boiling point by about 80°C

Never distil to dryness

If the simple distillation is being used to separate two components with widely differing boiling points, you should keep a close watch on the still head temperature. As soon as most of the more volatile compound has been collected, the temperature will start to rise, and the receiving flask should be removed, and replaced with a preweighed empty one. Collect the distillate in the second flask as long as the temperature continues to rise. This distillate will contain *both* components (*mixed fractions*), but should only account for a small fraction of the total volume. When the still head temperature becomes constant again, change the receiving flask for another preweighed empty one and collect the second component. Finally, weigh all the receiving flasks to determine the weight of each fraction. The results of a simple distillation should be recorded in a table as shown in Table 3.8.

Distilling solvents

One very common use of the simple distillation technique is in the purification of organic solvents. These are supplied in a relatively pure form which is

Table 3.8 Reporting the results of a distillation.

	bp (°C)	Weight (g)
Amount of sample to distil: 12.5 g		
Fore-run	45–88	0.5
Component A	88–90	4.8
Mixed fractions	90–180	0.9
Component B	180–183	4.2
Residue		*ca.* 2.0

adequate for most purposes, but occasionally need to be purified by distillation. For certain reactions, particularly those involving moisture-sensitive substrates, it is essential that the solvent be purified before use. In this case the purpose of distillation, as well as removing the small amounts of low and high boiling impurities, is to remove any water from the solvent. To this end a *drying agent* is often added to the distillation flask, and the solvent is said to be distilled *from* the drying agent. A list of suitable drying agents for particular solvents is given in Appendix 2 (p. 677).

If there is a regular need for distilled solvent, then it is more convenient and efficient to set up a special solvent still. An example of such a solvent still is shown in Fig. 3.49. It consists of a large distillation flask, connected to a reflux condenser via a piece of glassware which can simply be a pressure equalizing funnel modified by the inclusion of a second stopcock. Since the production of very dry solvents usually requires the exclusion of (moist) air from the apparatus, the still is fitted so that it can be operated under an inert atmosphere. With stopcock A open the solvent simply refluxes over the drying agent. When stopcock A is closed the solvent vapour passes up the narrow tube, condenses, and dry solvent collects in the central piece of the apparatus, which for convenience is often graduated. When the required volume of solvent has been collected, it can be run off, directly into the reaction flask if necessary, through stopcock B. Alternatively, smaller volumes of up to 50 mL may be drawn off by syringe through a side port closed with a septum. For safety reasons solvent stills must be closely monitored in case the water supply should fail or in case the liquid in the distillation flask should get too close to dryness.

Solvent stills must be supervised

Fractional distillation

As we have seen above, the main problem with simple distillation is that it is ineffective in the separation of compounds whose boiling points differ by less than about 80°C. One way around this problem is to carry out repeated simple redistillations until the material is adequately pure, but this is prohibitively time consuming. In practice one uses the technique of *fractional distillation*. The apparatus (Fig. 3.50) for fractional distillation only differs from that for

Fig. 3.49 Solvent still.

The fractionating column should be vertical and may need to be insulated

simple distillation in that a *fractionating column* (see below) is inserted between the distillation flask and the still head. The fractionating column should be perfectly vertical, and it may need to be insulated to prevent undue heat loss. The simplest way to do this is to wrap the column with aluminium foil, shiny side inwards. Since the intention is to collect separate fractions of distillate, a modified receiver adapter is often used at the end of the condenser. These receivers come in various shapes and styles and have rather pictorial names such as 'cows', 'pigs' or 'spiders'. One type is shown in Fig. 3.50, but they all serve the same purpose: to allow you to change over the receiving flask to collect another fraction of distillate simply by rotating the adapter without the need to remove the previous flask. The results of a fractional distillation should be reported in a table as shown for simple distillation, and should include the boiling point and weight of each fraction.

How does fractional distillation work? As the vapour from the distillation flask passes up through the fractionating column, it condenses on the column packing and revapourizes continuously. Each revapourization of the conden-

Fig. 3.50 Apparatus for fractional distillation.

sate is equivalent to a simple distillation, and therefore each of these 'separate distillations' leads to a condensate that is successively richer in the more volatile component. All being well, by the time the vapour reaches the still head, the continuous process of condensation and revapourization will have resulted in the vapour, and hence the collected distillate, being substantially enriched in the lower boiling compound. With an efficient fractionating column, the distillate may even consist of *pure* material—the ideal situation.

There are various designs of fractionating column in use in the organic laboratory; some examples are shown in Fig. 3.51. They all contain a surface on which the condensation and revapourization process can occur. This surface varies from the glass projections on the side of the Vigreux column, to the 'spiral' of the Widmer column, and columns packed with glass beads or metal turnings. The efficiency of a fractionating column depends on both its *length* and its *packing* and for columns of the same length, the efficiency is increased by increasing the *surface area* and *heat conductivity* of the packing. Hence for simple fractionating columns the efficiency increases in the order: Vigreux column, column packed with glass beads, column packed with metal turnings.

Column efficiency

In more precise terms, the efficiency of a column is expressed in *theoretical plates*, where one theoretical plate is the column that is equivalent to a single simple distillation. Therefore a column with n theoretical plates is equivalent

Theoretical plates

metal gauze to
support beads

(a)   (b)   (c)

Fig. 3.51 Some types of fractionating columns: (a) Vigreux; (b) Widmer; (c) column packed with glass beads.

to carrying out n distillations, and one can reformulate Raoult's law to account for the n-fold distillation. Without going into detail, the mathematics show that for a 1:1 mixture of compounds having a difference in vapour pressure of a factor of 3 (which represents a difference in boiling point of about 20–30°C) a fractionating column of at least three theoretical plates would be required to obtain the more volatile compound with a purity of at least 95%. In practice most laboratory fractionating columns vary from two to 15 theoretical plates. For example, a column packed with glass beads and of about 25–30 cm length will have an efficiency of about 8–10 theoretical plates, and will adequately separate compounds with boiling points as close as 20°C.

Fractional distillation can completely separate compounds that differ in bp by about 20°C

Two other factors to consider are the *throughput* and *hold-up* of the column. The throughput is the maximum volume of liquid that can be boiled up through the column per minute whilst still maintaining the all important condensation–revapourization equilibrium process within the column. For speed of operation, a high throughput is desirable. Column hold-up is the amount of liquid that is retained on the column packing when the distillation is stopped. Columns with very high surface area packings have a high hold-up and retain a substantial volume of liquid. Hence, although they are highly efficient, they are inappropriate for the fractional distillation of small quantities where loss of sample is unacceptable.

Efficiency vs hold-up

The ultimate form of fractionating column is the *spinning band column* which will separate compounds having boiling point differences of as little as

0.5°C. However, spinning band distillation requires expensive specialized apparatus that is not routinely available, and is therefore beyond the scope of this book.

Distillation under reduced pressure

Since a liquid boils when its vapour pressure equals the pressure above it, you can reduce the boiling point of a liquid by reducing the pressure under which it is distilled. This technique is known as *distillation under reduced pressure* or more simply as *vacuum distillation*. Distillation under reduced pressure is necessary when the liquid has an inconveniently high boiling point, or when the compound is likely to decompose at elevated temperatures. Unfortunately many organic compounds do undergo significant decomposition at high temperatures, and therefore it is usually recommended that the distillation be carried out under reduced pressure if the normal boiling point is greater than about 150°C.

The first thing to decide before carrying out a reduced pressure distillation is what reduction in pressure is required. As a general guide, halving the pressure will only reduce the boiling point by about 20°C. On the other hand, using a water aspirator vacuum of about 10–20 mmHg will reduce the boiling point by about 100°C, and using a vacuum pump, which will operate down to about 0.1 mmHg pressure, will reduce the boiling point by about 150°C. A slightly more accurate estimate of the boiling point of a liquid at reduced pressure can be obtained from a *nomograph* as shown in Fig. 3.52.

Two sets of apparatus for distillation under reduced pressure are shown in Fig. 3.53. Both set-ups require the use of suitable flasks that will withstand being evacuated; the flasks should be checked for star-cracks before use. A vacuum take-off receiver adapter is required for connecting the apparatus to the source of vacuum. Some pressure-measuring device should be incorporated between the apparatus and the vacuum source. The first set-up (Fig. 3.53a) uses a Claisen adapter and still head and a simple vacuum receiver adapter, whilst the second set-up (Fig. 3.53b) illustrates the use of a Claisen still head and a 'pig' type receiver adapter. The apparatus should be assembled using special vacuum grease to seal all joints—normal stopcock grease is not suitable for use under vacuum—and should then be tested for leaks by applying the vacuum *before* the sample is introduced into the distillation flask. Just as with simple distillation, you need to ensure that the liquid boils smoothly without bumping. However, boiling stones do not function under vacuum, and therefore an alternative method is needed. The only reliable way to ensure smooth boiling during a reduced pressure distillation is to use a *very fine capillary* to introduce a thin stream of air bubbles to the boiling liquid as shown in Fig. 3.53(b). It is stressed that the capillary must be very fine, so that, even under vacuum, only a thin stream of bubbles is drawn through the liquid. Obviously if the organic compound is likely to oxidize with air under these conditions, the capillary can be connected to a nitrogen supply instead. Use of

Water aspirator reduces bp by about 100°C

Vacuum pump reduces bp by about 150°C

Check for star-cracks

Preventing bumping

Use a fine capillary to stop bumping during vacuum distillation

Fig. 3.52 Nomograph for estimating the boiling point of a liquid at a particular pressure. The graph connects the boiling point at atmospheric pressure (760 mmHg) to that at reduced pressure, and a line connecting points on two of the scales intersects the third scale. For example, if the boiling point at 760 mmHg is 200°C, the intercept shows that the boiling point at 20 mmHg pressure is about 90°C.

a fine capillary works well, although it may be tricky to set up properly. A simpler technique which works in most cases is to put a small magnetic stirrer bar in the distillation flask, and stir the liquid rapidly whilst heating it under reduced pressure (Fig. 3.53a). The rapid agitation usually ensures smooth boiling. A less satisfactory method which sometimes works is to put some glass wool in the distillation pot to fill up some of the space above the liquid.

Fractions of distillate are collected in the normal way; remember to record the boiling point *and* the pressure. As with simple distillation, the distillation must not be allowed to proceed to dryness. At the end of the distillation, remove the heat source, and allow the apparatus to cool to room temperature

Allow to cool before releasing vacuum

before releasing the vacuum. If you are using a water aspirator, remember to take the usual precautions to prevent water sucking back into your apparatus.

Fractional distillation can also be carried out under reduced pressure. The apparatus shown in Fig. 3.53 should be modified to include a fractionating column.

Fig. 3.53 Apparatus for distillation under reduced pressure.

Short path distillation

One particularly useful technique for the vacuum distillation of small quantities of material in the range 50 mg to 2 g is *short path distillation*. The material to be distilled is placed in a small bulb which is connected to two other small bulbs and to a short tube which can be connected to a vacuum. The complete assembly of bulbs is shown in Fig. 3.54(a). The assembly is then placed in a special oven with just the first bulb in the heated zone as shown in Fig. 3.54(b). The bulb is heated and the assembly is rotated to prevent bumping of the liquid. Sophisticated ovens incorporate a small electric motor to rotate the bulbs. Older versions simply heat the sample, and leave the chemist to rotate the tube by hand. As the distillation proceeds, the liquid distils from one bulb to another. This is only a short distance, hence the name of the technique. This type of distillation is also referred to as *bulb to bulb distillation* or *Kugelrohr distillation* from the German *Kugel* = bulb, *Rohr* = tube. If necessary, the material can be redistilled immediately by moving the second bulb into the heated zone and allowing the liquid to distil into the third bulb. For very volatile liquids, it may be necessary to cool the receiving bulb with solid CO_2 held in a suitable container; a Neoprene® filter adapter wired onto the apparatus is ideal.

Since the distillation path is so short, no separation of volatile compounds can be achieved with this technique. Nevertheless it is an excellent technique, and finds widespread use in the purification of small quantities of liquids

Fig. 3.54 (a) Bulb-to-bulb assembly for short path distillation; (b) special oven for short path distillation.

containing involatile impurities. It is generally much more convenient than setting up a proper vacuum distillation apparatus using small glassware. Since short path distillation provides no means of measuring the precise boiling point of the liquids, the *oven* temperature is often quoted as a useful guide.

Steam distillation

Steam distillation is a useful technique for the distillation of an immiscible mixture of an organic compound and water (steam). Immiscible mixtures do not distil in the same way as miscible liquids, since each exerts its own vapour pressure *independently* of the other. Therefore the total vapour pressure is the sum of the vapour pressures of the pure individual components. (Remember that for miscible liquids it is the *partial vapour pressure* that is important.) Therefore when the sum of the individual vapour pressures equals external (atmospheric) pressure the mixture will boil at a *lower temperature* than either of the pure liquids. Hence co-distillation of an immiscible mixture of an organic compound plus water will result in the distillation of the organic compound below 100°C, even though its boiling point may be well in excess of 100°C. For example, an immiscible mixture of water and octane (boiling point = 126°C) boils at about 90°C at atmospheric pressure (760 mmHg). We can calculate the relative amounts of water and octane in the vapour phase, and hence the distillate, as follows. From tables we ascertain that the vapour pressure of water at 90°C is about 525 mmHg, and since, by definition, for immiscible liquids

$$\left(\text{Vapour pressure}\right)_{\text{total}} = \left(\text{Vapour pressure}\right)_{\text{water}} + \left(\text{Vapour pressure}\right)_{\text{octane}}$$

we have

$$760 = 525 + \left(\text{Vapour pressure}\right)_{\text{octane}}$$

Therefore, the vapour pressure of the octane is 235 mmHg. Since, for immiscible liquids, the amount (in moles) of each component in the vapour phase is directly proportional to their individual vapour pressures, we have

$$\frac{235}{525} = \frac{\text{No. of moles of octane}}{\text{No. of moles of water}}$$

and therefore the vapour, and hence the distillate, contains 235/525 = 0.448 mole octane per mole of water. Translated into weights, the distillate will contain 51 g octane per 18 g water, or about 75% octane by weight. Hence steam distillation is a very efficient way of distilling octane at a temperature that is about 35°C below its boiling point. Not surprisingly, the technique has found wide application in the distillation of substances which cannot be purified by normal distillation.

There are two ways of carrying out a steam distillation. The 'correct' method is to pass steam into the liquid in the distillation flask, which is heated as well. The water and compound co-distil, condense in the condenser, and are collected in the normal way. A normal still head and Claisen adapter can be used as shown in Fig. 3.55(a), but specially designed still heads, splash heads or swan necks as they are called, may be available in your laboratory. These have the advantage of preventing the liquid frothing and bumping over into the condenser. Provided that sufficient water and organic compound are present in the pot, the still head temperature will remain constant during a steam distillation. You will be able to tell when all the organic compound has distilled

(a)

(b)

Fig. 3.55 (a) Apparatus for steam distillation; (b) a still head for steam distillation.

by observing the distillate. When only water is distilling, the distillate in the condenser will look clear with no oily drops evident. When the distillation is completed, you have to separate the immiscible organic product from the water in the distillate. This is easily done by transferring the mixture to a separatory funnel, and separating the layers in the usual way. If the organic layer is very small in volume compared with the water layer, it is much easier to *extract* the organic compound with diethyl ether, for example. The organic layer is then separated and dried over a suitable drying agent in the normal way.

Steam can cause nasty burns

Well-equipped laboratories will have steam on tap, and therefore all you have to do is connect the steam supply to your apparatus. Keep the connecting tubes as short as possible. If there is no steam supply, a simple steam-generation apparatus can be set up as shown in Fig. 3.56(a). The steam-generating flask can be heated electrically in a mantle, or, if appropriate, using a burner. Whatever the source of steam it will contain variable amounts of condensed water, and therefore it is a good idea to incorporate a device for removing some of this water before it is transferred to the distillation flask. If this is not done, the volume of liquid in the distillation flask becomes unreasonably large. A simple way to do this is to place a separatory funnel in the steam line as shown in Fig. 3.56(b); water collects in the funnel and can be run off from time to time. Alternatively, a simple water trap can be assembled from standard glassware. One excellent design for such a trap has been described by Dr Rudolph Goetz of Michigan State University (*J. Chem. Educ.*, 1983, **60**, 424).

The 'easy' way to carry out steam distillation is simply to place a mixture of the organic compound and water in the distillation flask, and carry out a simple distillation in the usual way. The water and organic compound will co-distil in just the same way as if steam were passed into the flask. Clearly this procedure is much easier to set up, and requires a simple distillation apparatus

Fig. 3.56 (a) Apparatus for generating steam; (b) removing water from wet steam. Keep connecting tubes short.

Fig. 3.57 Alternative apparatus for steam distillation.

as shown in Fig. 3.57. Since the water in the distillation flask is not continuously being replaced by steam as it distils out, an addition funnel containing water is placed on the still head so that the water can be replenished from time to time.

Microscale distillation

All of the apparatus for simple distillation described in Figs 3.48–3.57 can be assembled on the semi-microscale using commercial glassware kits. However, separation by distillation is less convincing on the microscale (<1 mL). Even the separation of volatile materials from involatile impurities is less than straightforward because of the difficulties inherent in condensing efficiently small quantities of vapour, and minimizing the ensuing losses. Kugelrohr distillation represents the method of choice, though more economical methods have been proposed. The Hickman still is a popular alternative and the item may be found in most of the commercial microscale glassware ranges. A typical set-up features the still clamped between a reaction vial and a reflux condenser (Fig. 3.58a), but the amount of dead space is considerable and much of the distillate may be in the vapour phase at once. Vapour condenses above the still and runs down inside the wall collecting in the flange or skirt, from where it can be collected by pipette. Alternatively, direct cooling of the Hickman still can be considered. A collar can be constructed around the still using aluminium foil; this retains small chips of solid CO_2, providing a cold surface upon which vapour can condense (Fig. 3.58b). Heating can be provided using a hot sand bath, small Bunsen flame or electric hot air blower.

In the research laboratory purification would be attempted by preparative

DriKold® chips

foil collar

securing elastic

(a)   (b)

Fig. 3.58 Distillation using a Hickman still and reflux condenser (a). Alternatively, a collar made from aluminium foil may be placed around the Hickman still and secured with an elastic band (b). The collar will retain chips of solid CO_2 (DriKold®), providing a cold surface upon which vapour can condense, and a short path length so that losses of volatiles are minimized.

gas chromatography or some alternative chromatographic technique, depending on the volatility of the product.

Sublimation

Sublimation is closely related to distillation. A solid is converted into a vapour, without going through a liquid phase, which is then recondensed on a cold surface in a purified state. Not many solids sublime easily, since they usually have a very low vapour pressure. However, some solids do have an unusually high vapour pressure because of their molecular structure which results in rather weak intermolecular attractions in the solid state. The major factor that contributes to weak intermolecular forces is molecular shape, and

Spherical and cylindrical shaped molecules sublime most easily

many compounds that sublime easily have a spherical or cylindrical shape which is not ideal for strong intermolecular attraction. Hence such compounds with high vapour pressure can be purified by sublimation, provided that the impurities have a much lower vapour pressure. Just as with distillation, the rate of sublimation can be dramatically increased by heating the sample under reduced pressure, and therefore the sublimation apparatus should allow for this. The sample should never be heated to its melting point however.

A typical purpose-built apparatus for sublimation, known as a *sublimator*, is shown in Fig. 3.59(a). Essentially it is a wide glass tube with a take-off for connection to a vacuum, into which is fitted a smaller diameter tube with water inlet and outlets. The sample to be sublimed is placed in the bottom of the outer tube and heated, under vacuum if necessary. The vapour recondenses on the cold surface, often known as a *cold finger*. The apparatus is designed so that the gap between the sample and the cold finger is small. When the sublimation is complete—it is usually a fairly slow process—the cold finger can be removed carefully, and the purified solid scraped off.

If a purpose-built sublimator is not available, one can easily be improvised from standard laboratory glassware. One such design based on a Büchner filter flask is shown in Fig. 3.59(b). Variations are possible; all you need is a cold surface above the sample which is contained in a vessel that can be heated, and, if necessary, evacuated.

Chromatography

The term chromatography is derived from the fact that this technique was first used to separate pigments (Greek *chroma* = colour, *graphein* = write), but the

Fig. 3.59 Apparatus for sublimation using: (a) a purpose-built sublimator; (b) an improvised sublimator.

procedure, in its various modifications, is applicable to almost any chemical separation problem and is by no means confined to coloured compounds. The initial development of the methodology is ascribed to the Russian chemist Mikhail Tswett, who separated leaf extracts by percolation through a column packed with chalk. Since this pioneering work at the turn of the century, two Nobel Prizes have been awarded for work in the field of chromatography, such is its importance. The Swede, A. Tiselius, was awarded a Nobel Prize in 1948 in recognition of his contribution to work on electrophoresis and adsorption analysis and the Britons, A.J.P. Martin and R.L.M. Synge, were jointly awarded the Prize in 1952 for their work on partition chromatography.

Whatever the precise experimental procedure, all of the techniques depend upon the differential distribution of various components of a mixture between two phases—the *mobile phase* and the *stationary phase*. The mobile phase may be either a liquid or a gas and the stationary phase either a solid or liquid. Various combinations of these components give the main types of chromatographic techniques (Table 3.9).

There is insufficient space in this book to do justice to the detailed theory and practice of all of these techniques—and neither is that the aim. Instead, we will simply discuss some of the practical aspects of the particular variants of adsorption chromatography and vapour phase chromatography which will be used in the experimental section and which are of most general use in the organic research laboratory. There are many specialist books which concentrate on some or all of the techniques mentioned, and those who wish to read more on the subject should look at some of the references listed at the ends of the sections.

Table 3.9 Main chromatographic techniques.

Stationary phase	Mobile phase	Technique (substances separated)
Solid	Liquid	Adsorption chromatography (wide range of aliphatic and aromatic molecules)
		Reverse phase chromatography (polar organic molecules)
		Gel permeation chromatography (macromolecules)
		Ion exchange chromatography (charged molecules, amino acids)
Liquid	Liquid	Partition chromatography (thermally and acid labile organic molecules)
Liquid	Gas	Gas–liquid chromatography (volatile organic molecules)

Adsorption chromatography — a general introduction

The techniques we are going to consider in this section and which will be used in the experimental section can be categorized into *thin layer chromatography* (TLC) and *column chromatography*. The division is justified by the fact that the first technique is used almost totally for analysis, whereas the second lends itself more to preparative separations. Within the second division we will consider three techniques that are commonly useful in the laboratory — *gravity*, *'flash'* and *'dry flash'* column chromatography. To learn about other important techniques such as *preparative thin layer chromatography, dry column chromatography, ion exchange chromatography* and *gel permeation chromatography* the interested student is recommended to consult the specialist references. Let us now consider the main requirements for carrying out any type of adsorption chromatography and introduce some basic terms and principles.

The support or stationary phase

The *stationary phase* or *adsorbant* is a porous solid capable of retaining both solvents and solutes. Many different materials fill these particular requirements, but the two which enjoy most universal use are silica (SiO_2) and alumina (Al_2O_3) in highly purified and finely powdered form. Both may be supplied with a fluorescent substance (zinc sulfide) which is useful for visualizing compounds on TLC plates. This will be discussed on pp. 168–170, but, for the moment, it is sufficient to know that any grade of silica or alumina possessing the figures 254 or F_{254} will give a green fluorescence when observed under 254 nm wavelength light. Some grades of adsorbant, specifically meant for the preparation of TLC plates, where the adsorbant has to cling to a glass plate, also have the prefix G. This indicates that they contain about 15% of gypsum ($CaSO_4$, 'plaster of Paris') which acts as a binder and serves to stabilize the TLC plate. Those supports lacking this binder often have the letter H after any coding. The size and regularity of the particle diameter is very important for chromatography supports and is also indicated. The type of adsorbants most useful for standard column chromatography have particle sizes between 0.08 and 0.20 mm, whereas TLC adsorbants are much finer, and (with the exception of the technique of 'dry flash' chromatography) should not be used for column chromatography as they will pack too tightly and block solvent flow. Silica for 'flash' chromatography has a particularly regular particle size, and shows almost liquid properties at times. Thus, for example, a label bearing the description 'silica gel GF_{254}' tells us immediately that this is TLC silica possessing a fluorescer, whereas 'silica gel 60H' tells us that we are looking at an adsorbant designed for column chromatography.

Care should be exercised in handling the finer grades of silica as these are readily dispersed into the atmosphere and inhaled, and may cause respiratory problems in the long term. Such materials should always be handled in a hood and the use of a face mask is highly recommended.

The *activity* or degree to which the support holds onto adsorbed materials is dependent to some extent on the degree of moisture contained within it. The less moisture contained, the 'stickier' or more retentive the adsorbant and the higher its activity. Most silica gel is used directly from the container for column chromatography when it usually contains about 10–20% water, but TLC plates, after having been prepared from a water slurry of silica, require activation by heating to 150°C for several hours before use to drive off excess moisture. Commercially prepared TLC plates do not require this activation, however, and can be used directly. In contrast, alumina is commonly supplied as its most active form, possessing very little water. This is usually too retentive for most practical purposes and is deactivated by thoroughly mixing with a specific amount of water. The activity of such alumina is usually measured on the Brockmann scale as shown in Table 3.10, and activity grades II and III are commonly used for column chromatography.

Whilst there are many other kinds of chromatography support, these are the only two that will be used in the experimental sections.

Elution solvents

The chromatography column or plate, loaded with the material to be separated, is developed by allowing solvent to percolate through the solid adsorbant (*elution*) either by the action of gravity, pressure or capillarity. Eluting solvents of various polarities have differing abilities to displace any solute from the active sites on the support onto which the material has been adsorbed. Generally, the more polar the solvent, the more efficiently it can compete for the active sites and the more quickly the solute will move down a column or up a TLC plate. This property of solvents has been somewhat quantified by listing them in order of their ability to displace solutes from adsorbants. Such *eluotropic series* are useful as guides as to what sort of solvent or combination of solvents will be required for a particular separation. What is frequently forgotten, however, is that such a series only holds good for one particular solid support. For reference purposes two eluotropic series, for silica and alumina, are listed in Table 3.11. In the table, the absolute positions within each series do not translate across from one support to another. In

Table 3.10 Brockmann scale for chromatograph alumina activity grades.

Activity grade	I	II	III	IV	V
Water added (%)	0	3	6	10	15

Table 3.11 Eluotropic series.

	Silica	Alumina
Least polar	Cyclohexane	Pentane
	Pentane	Cyclohexane
	Toluene	Toluene
	Diethyl ether	Diethyl ether
	Ethyl acetate	Ethyl acetate
	Acetic acid	Methanol
Most polar	Methanol	Acetic acid

other words, although cyclohexane on silica is less polar than pentane on silica, this does not mean that it has exactly the same effect as pentane on alumina. In the experimental section, you will often see the term 'light petroleum' used; this refers to a petroleum fraction that consists largely of a mixture of pentanes and can be considered to have similar eluant properties to pentane itself.

Never forget to use only distilled solvents for preparative chromatography. The large quantity of solvent used compared with the amount of material to be purified means that even small amounts of impurity present in the solvent will be concentrated in the chromatographed sample which might end up being less pure than at the outset. This is particularly important for light petroleum which always contains significant amounts of high boiling residues and these will remain in your sample if you use the solvent straight from the bottle. In addition, do not forget that most chromatography solvents are volatile and flammable and many (particularly halogenated solvents) are toxic.

Avoid all flames in the vicinity of a chromatography experiment and carry out such work in a hood wherever possible.

The aim in any chromatographic technique is to use a combination of support and solvents which causes the different components of a mixture to be eluted at different rates from the support and hence effects a separation. This deceptively simple statement hides a multitude of pitfalls and difficulties. The procedures described here will permit beginners to apply the rudiments of the techniques, but there is no substitute for experience and practice in approaching new separation problems.

Further reading

For some general references to chromatographic techniques, see:

A. Braithwaite, C.B.F. Rice and F.J. Smith, *Chromatographic Methods*, 5th edn, Chapman & Hall, London, 1996; C.F. Poole and S.A. Schuette, *Contemporary Practice of Chromatography*, Elsevier, New York, 1984.

Thin layer chromatography

The TLC plate

Thin layer chromatography is largely an analytical technique used for determining the purity of materials and also for preliminary identification purposes. The results obtained using TLC can be translated to column chromatography using the same adsorbant and so TLC is also useful for determining the best solvent system for preparative separations of mixtures. As the name suggests, the adsorbant is supported as a thin coating on a flat surface which may be a glass plate or, more conveniently, a sheet of aluminium or plastic. The most useful size of plate for TLC analysis is one of about 8×2.5 cm which permits two or three samples to be spotted onto the *baseline* (a line marked about 1 cm from one end of the plate) and has sufficient length to give the best resolution in a convenient amount of time. Microscope slides are ideal for the in-house preparation of TLC plates, whereas commercial plates are usually purchased in 20×20 cm or 10×20 cm sizes and should be cut down to size for economy of time and finances. For this reason the aluminium- or plastic-backed sheets are the most convenient; cutting is best carried out with a guillotine to avoid crumbling the delicate adsorbant layer.

Micro-pipettes

In order to perform a TLC analysis it is necessary to introduce a small quantity of your material onto a TLC plate before developing it. The material is conveniently loaded as a solution using a micro-pipette. To prepare these micro-pipettes (Fig. 3.60), heat the middle of a melting point tube in a small

hold melting point tube in microburner flame

remove from flame and pull

ca. 5 cm

break here

break as indicated to get two micro-pipettes

Fig. 3.60 Making micro-pipettes for spotting TLC plates.

Always be careful with flames in the open laboratory

Care! Micro-pipettes are sharp

microburner flame until the tube softens and the flame becomes yellow (1 or 2 s). Then remove the hot tube from the flame and *quickly* pull the two halves about 5 cm apart. Allow the tube to cool and break it in half at the mid-point of the thin section to produce two micro-pipettes. These are useful items and it is best to prepare them in batches of 20 or so at a time. Practice makes perfect and in a short time you should be able to prepare uniformly sized pipettes; however even the odd shaped ones you produce initially are usually serviceable.

Spotting the plate with sample

First, make a solution of a small quantity of your sample in the least polar solvent in which it is readily soluble. Dip the narrow end of the micro-pipette into the solution of your material which will cause some to rise into the tube by capillary action. Then touch the loaded pipette *lightly* onto the silica surface at a point marked on a baseline drawn across one end of the plate about 1 cm from the end. This will cause some of the liquid in the pipette to be drawn onto the adsorbant, forming a visible ring of solvent. Blow gently on the plate to dry the spot and repeat the procedure, trying all the time to keep the baseline spot as small as possible. By this means, as much sample as is judged necessary can be spotted onto the plate. Only experience will enable you to tell when this is so—too little and you will not be able to see any spots on visualizing the plate, too much and the plate will be overloaded and all resolution will be lost. One way around this problem is to make three separate spottings on the baseline, the first with only a small amount of solution, the second with about three times as much, and the third with three times as much again. In this way you are likely to get at least one spotting with the correct amount of material (Fig. 3.61).

The most accurate results are obtained using just enough sample to visualize the spots after development. Remember that TLC is an extremely sensitive procedure and it is very easy to overload the plates.

The developing tank

There are various commercially available chromatography tanks, but for analytical TLC as commonly used in research, it is easiest and cheapest to make one using a 250 mL beaker—preferably a tall form without a spout, although this is not critically important—with a lid made from a petri dish or a watch glass (Fig. 3.62). Wide-mouthed screw cap bottles may also be used, but those with plastic lids which tend not to like the developing solvents should be ruled out! The inside of the container is lined with filter papers to aid in saturating the atmosphere with solvent vapour. However, a gap in the lining should be left in order to be able to see when the plate has been fully developed. Sufficient developing solvent is placed into this tank to wet the filter papers thoroughly and to leave about 0.5 cm of solvent in the bottom. It is important that the level of this solvent does not reach the level of the sample spotted

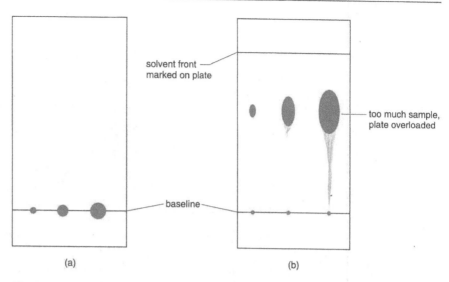

Fig. 3.61 A TLC plate spotted with three different amounts of sample: (a) before development; (b) after development.

Fig. 3.62 Simple developing tanks for TLC analysis.

onto the baseline of the plate, otherwise the material will simply be dissolved off the plate instead of being carried up it by the rising solvent.

Developing the plate

With the sample spotted onto the plate and the TLC tank charged with solvent it is time to carry out the analysis. Place the TLC plate *carefully* into the tank (making sure that it is the correct way round with the baseline at the bottom) and allow the *back* of the plate to lean against the sides of the container at a slight angle from the vertical. The baseline must be above the level of the solvent in the bottom of the container (Fig. 3.63). Allow the solvent front to rise in a horizontal straight line up the plate by virtue of capillary

Use tweezers to transfer TLC plates

solvent
ascending plate

TLC plate leaning
at a slight angle
against the sides
of the tank

sample must be spotted
onto the plate clear of
the solvent level

Fig. 3.63 Developing a TLC plate.

action until it reaches about 1 cm from the top. If the solvent front is not straight the analysis must be repeated on a new plate after checking that the filter papers lining the tank have been thoroughly wetted with solvent and are not in contact with the adsorbant at the edges of the TLC plate. Finally, *carefully* remove the plate, mark the solvent front and allow the solvent to evaporate off in the hood.

Avoid breathing solvent fumes at all times during the operation

Visualizing the developed plate

Unless the material being analyzed is coloured it will be necessary to treat the plate in some way in order to see the spots and measure the distance they have travelled. There are numerous *visualizing agents* for TLC plates, but by far the most useful means of analysis uses a combination of observation under UV light and staining with iodine vapour.

The great advantage of UV light is that it is normally non-destructive to the compounds on the plate and the analysis can be carried out without waiting for the spots to develop. However, UV light is particularly hazardous and can blind or cause unpleasant burns of the skin.

Great care must always be taken when working with UV light. Eye protection must always be worn and you must never look directly at the light source. As the wavelengths used for visualizing TLC are also damaging to the skin it is recommended that gloves should also be used.

Wear special eye protection when working with UV light

Light of 356 nm wavelength causes most aromatic molecules, or molecules possessing extended conjugation, to give out a bright purple fluorescence against a dark background. Of course, the drawback here is that not all molecules possess such chromophores and this is where the zinc sulfide fluorescer contained in some TLC adsorbants comes in very useful. When viewed under 254 nm wavelength light, the zinc sulfide in the adsorbant will fluoresce green, except where there is an eluted substance which quenches this fluorescence, giving a dark spot. Consequently, a TLC plate possessing fluorescer will show a series of dark spots on a bright-green background when viewed under

254 nm UV light. If an aromatic solvent such as toluene has been used in the elution, it is essential to dry the plate thoroughly, otherwise the residues will mask any products present. The positions of all spots which can be visualized with either wavelength of light should be noted by drawing around them lightly with a pencil.

The plate is now ready for staining with iodine. An iodine chamber can be made in the same way as the TLC tank, using a 250 mL tall-form beaker, with a petri dish as a lid, into which a few crystals of iodine are placed. Iodine vapour is toxic and the developing tank must be stored in a fume hood. Standing the plate in such a tank for about 30 min reveals the presence of any eluted compounds by the appearance of dark brown spots on a light brown background. Most compounds stain up within minutes but some may take several hours. However, it is worthwhile observing the plate at intervals, particularly the first few minutes, as some compounds (notably alcohols, acids and other halides) frequently give a negative stain initially. In these cases the white spot which first appears against the light brown background is due to the iodine actually reacting with the substance on the plate and being removed from the region. The limit of detection using iodine staining is about 50 μg of organic compound.

Iodine vapour is toxic

Some other useful staining systems are listed in Table 3.12 and others can be found by referring to the *Chemist's Companion*. Most other systems are applied to the plate in the form of a spray and staining is usually encouraged by heating. Consequently, such procedures are messy and there is a real danger of inhalation of the spray. A designated area in a hood should be set aside for such practices. Only sufficient spray should be applied to moisten the plate evenly. Alternatively, a less messy procedure is to dip the plate in the visualizing system. After dipping, the excess reagent is shaken off, and the plate allowed to dry. It must also be remembered that plastic-backed TLC plates are unsuitable for visualization procedures which involve strong heating. Likewise, aluminium-backed TLC plates should not be left for long periods in an iodine tank as the metal is attacked by the halogen, giving a dark brown deliquescent mess.

Always spray TLC plates in a hood. Many systems are corrosive

Retention factor (R_f)

A useful measurement that can be made from the developed TLC plate is the relation between the distance moved by the compound spot and the distance moved by the eluting solvent; this is the *retention factor* of the particular compound and is commonly simply referred to as its R_f (Fig. 3.64).

$$R_f = \frac{\text{Distance moved by the product spot}}{\text{Distance moved by the solvent front}}$$

Compounds which move a long way up the plate will have R_f values approaching unity, whereas those which do not move very far will have R_f values near zero. Although in theory any compound should always give the same R_f

Table 3.12 Some useful staining systems.

Staining system	Compounds visualized	Observation
Ammonia vapour	Phenols	Variously coloured spots (some coloured compounds may change colour)
5% $(NH_4)_6Mo_7O_{24}$ + 0.2% $Ce(SO_4)_2$ in 5% H_2SO_4, followed by heating to 150°C	General use	Deep-blue spots, often useful when other reagents fail
50% H_2SO_4, followed by heating to 150°C. **Corrosive**	General use	Black spots, often useful when other reagents fail
1% aqueous $FeCl_3$	Phenols and enolizable compounds	Variously coloured spots
HCl vapour	Aromatic amines	Variously coloured spots (some coloured compounds may change colour)
0.3% ninhydrin in n-BuOH with 3% AcOH, followed by heating to 125°C for 10 min	Amino acids and amines	Blue spots
0.5% 2,4-dinitrophenylhydrazine in 2 M HCl	Aldehydes and ketones	Red and yellow spots
0.5 g vanillin, 0.5 mL H_2SO_4, 9 mL EtOH	General use	Variously coloured spots
0.5% aqueous $PdCl_2$ with a few drops of concentrated HCl	Sulfur- and selenium-containing compounds	Red and yellow spots

value under given chromatographic conditions (adsorbant, eluant, temperature), it is virtually impossible to standardize the activity of the support on TLC plates. However, although rigorous application of R_f values from one analysis to another is ruled out, such values are useful to anyone following a procedure, particularly if developed in conjunction with a standard material, as they indicate the likely region to look for material on a TLC plate.

Comparisons with authentic materials and resolving close running materials
If authentic material is available, identity is best demonstrated by the technique of *double spotting*. As the unknown material is usually too precious to permit mixing some of it with another material, the preferred procedure involves spotting roughly equal amounts of the unknown and the authentic materials onto exactly the same place on the baseline (using different micropipettes of course). Usually the pure unknown and authentic materials are

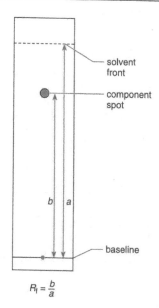

$$R_f = \frac{b}{a}$$

Fig. 3.64 Determination of the retention factor.

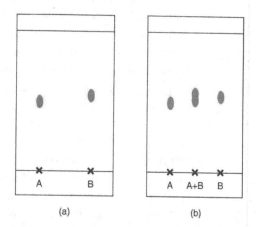

(a)   (b)

Fig. 3.65 (a) Two compounds having similar R_f values may be indistinguishable, even when run on the same TLC plate. (b) Double spotting shows the typical 'figure of eight' appearance of the two closely running but different compounds.

also run on the same plate, either side of the mixed spot. Any slight difference in R_f between the two materials will cause the mixed spot to appear as a 'figure of eight' (Fig. 3.65). If the mixed spot does not show any elongation, corroborative evidence for identity should be obtained by repeating the double spotting procedure using a different solvent system.

Such analysis can be made even more sensitive by carrying out *two-dimensional chromatography*. This involves spotting the sample at 1 cm from both edges at one corner of a square chromatography plate and carrying out

initial
point of
application

direction of
solvent flow

first development

rotation through 90° and second development

Fig. 3.66 Stages in the development of a two-dimensional chromatogram.

the first development as normal (Fig. 3.66). After the initial development, the plate is turned through 90°, with the eluted components at the bottom of the plate, and is redeveloped with a second solvent system running at right angles to the direction of the first development. This combines the advantages of analyzing the sample with two different solvent systems with the additional resolution afforded by developing the plate in two directions and provides for extremely sensitive differentiation.

An additional use of two-dimensional TLC analysis is to see whether or not the observation of several spots on TLC analysis is a result of a sample being a true mixture, or simply a consequence of decomposition on the plate, as often occurs when trying to analyze acid-sensitive compounds on silica. To check for this, spot the sample onto the corner of the plate and run it as normal in a solvent system chosen to give a good spread of the spots. Then mark the solvent front, turn the plate through 90° as before and repeat the process in the same solvent system (Fig. 3.67). If, on visualizing the plate, some of the spots (usually ill defined) do not appear on a diagonal line running from the baseline spot to the junction of the two solvent fronts, these components of the sample are not stable to the TLC conditions.

The technique of *multiple elution*, another means of separating closely running materials, is used only with preparative TLC (and then only *in extremis* when an examination of other solvent systems has not led to improved separation) as the resolving power of analytical plates is usually so high as to make recourse to this technique unnecessary. The technique simply involves developing the TLC plate using a solvent system in which the highest running component has $R_f < 0.3$ (preferably *ca.* $R_f = 0.1$), allowing the plate to dry partially and then repeating this procedure until adequate separation is achieved or the highest running spot has travelled two-thirds the distance of the plate (Fig. 3.68). Continuing any further or using a solvent system in which

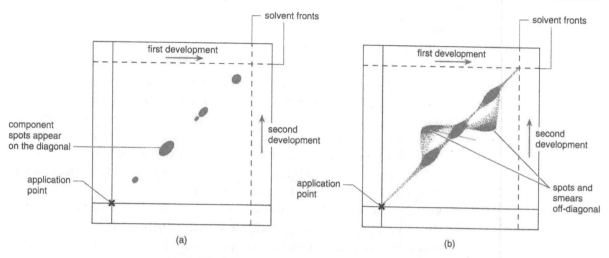

Fig. 3.67 (a) Two-dimensional thin layer chromatogram of a mixture of stable components; (b) two-dimensional chromatogram in which decomposition is occurring.

Fig. 3.68 Progress of multiple elution of a mixture of closely running components (note that, with the later elutions, the higher running spots begin to approach each other again).

the spots have R_f values higher than 0.3 actually causes the spots to run together rather than to separate. In the repeat elutions, the solvent front begins to elute the more polar material before it has reached the higher running material and this becomes the overriding effect if the developing system is too polar or the spots are too far apart.

Streaks, crescents and other strangely shaped spots

Whilst a developed TLC plate which shows a long streak instead of a clear round spot is liable to indicate that the sample is a complex mess, there are other less depressing reasons for such effects. Overloading the plate is one common reason for loss of resolution in TLC. This is usually easy to recognize if the analysis has been carried out using three spots of different amounts of material (see Fig. 3.61), as the resolution should be seen to improve with the more dilute sample. Low solubility in the eluting system is another possible cause, although if the precaution has been taken of loading the substance dissolved in the least polar solvent possible, this should not be the case.

Nonetheless, in the absence of overloading or solubility problems, some compounds still result in a smeared spot or one with the appearance of an upward pointing crescent. Such compounds are frequently those possessing strongly acidic or basic functional groups, such as amines and carboxylic acids, which cling very tenaciously to the active sites of the adsorbant (Fig. 3.69a). Much clearer TLC plates with well-defined round spots can normally be obtained with such materials if a few drops of concentrated ammonia (for amines) or formic acid (for carboxylic acids) are added to the eluting solvent.

Sometimes the spots may appear as downward pointing crescents. The most likely cause of this is careless spotting, which causes the adsorbant layer to become detached at the point of application (Fig. 3.69b). Consequently the component flows up around this blemish, carried by the rising solvent. This may also cause a visible dip in the middle of the solvent front as it rises up the plate. Flattening and doubling of spots are a consequence of using a polar solvent to apply the compound to the plate, giving a ring of sample on the baseline instead of a spot (Fig. 3.69c).

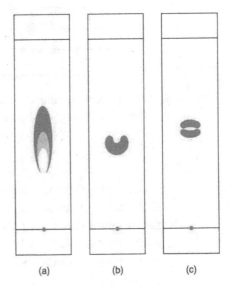

(a)   (b)   (c)

Fig. 3.69 Commonly encountered strangely shaped TLC spots from pure materials: (a) substance contains strongly acidic or basic groups; (b) adsorbant surface disturbed on application; (c) compound applied as solution in very polar solvent.

If after all this you fail to obtain a nice round spot, you have just experienced the typical TLC analysis of a failed reaction, with its one streak R_f 0–1. Tough luck!

Further reading

Among the many works giving details on the theory and practice of thin layer chromatography, see: J.C. Touchstone, *Practice of Thin Layer Chromatography*, 3rd edn, Wiley & Sons, New York, 1992; B. Fried and J. Sherma, *Handbook of Thin Layer Chromatography*, 2nd edn, Marcel Dekker, New York, 1996.

For details of adsorbants, solvent systems, visualizing agents and a lot of other very useful practical information for chromatography, see: A.J. Gordon and R.A. Ford, *The Chemist's Companion. A Handbook of Practical Data, Techniques and References*, Wiley & Sons, New York, 1972, pp. 369–407.

Gravity column chromatography

This technique, until relatively recently, was the workhorse for preparative chromatographic separation in the research laboratory. The advent of faster and (sometimes) more efficient variants has led to a decline in its use, with workers often opting for 'flash' column chromatography when a simple gravity column would be sufficient. The advantages of the gravity percolation technique are that it requires little in the way of special equipment and gives good results with a relatively low level of experimental expertise. Although slower than 'flash' or 'dry flash' column chromatography, it is possible to carry out percolation column chromatography in conjunction with other work as the amount of supervision required is much less than that for the other techniques. In addition, a percolation column requires only the most basic grades of chromatographic adsorbants, making it the most economic of the chromatographic techniques — a not inconsiderable point where large numbers of people are working, or large quantities of material need to be separated. As percolation chromatography is the progenitor to all other techniques and as it requires the lowest level of practical expertise, it is the ideal system for a newcomer to column chromatography. The aspects on pp. 160–164, dealing with stationary phases and eluting solvents, should be read before continuing with the sections on column chromatography.

The equipment

The standard apparatus for running a gravity column is shown in Fig. 3.70. The column can be simply a length of wide bore glass tubing, tapered at one end and closed with a length of flexible tubing with a screw clip. However, it is more convenient to use a column possessing a stopcock (a burette will often suffice, Fig. 3.70a). The column may possess the added sophistication of a ground glass socket for holding a solvent reservoir, or a fine porosity sintered glass disk above the stopcock to support the adsorbant (Fig. 3.70b), but these are not absolute requirements. The best stopcocks are those possessing Teflon® keys as these do not require any greasing. If the column is fitted

solvent

sand

clamps

adsorbant

clamps

sand

cotton wool

sand

glass
sinter disk

funnel containing
additional solvent

grease applied
sparingly to the edge
of the stopcock only

(a)

(b)

(c)

Fig. 3.70 Common arrangements for percolation column chromatography.

Use only the absolute minimum of grease on the stopcock and do not apply it close to the bore of the key

with an all glass stopcock, some greasing will be necessary, but it is pointless carrying out a chromatographic separation if your material ends up full of grease from the stopcock! It is preferable to use a silicone-based grease, wiping a very small amount onto the outer edges of the key (Fig. 3.70c) and then immediately wiping the key clean with a paper tissue. No excess grease should be visible. If the column does not possess a glass sinter above the stopcock, a small wad of cotton wool should be pushed firmly into the tapered end of the column (columns in frequent use normally have a resident plug of cotton wool). The cotton wool must not fit so tightly that solvent is unable to flow through the column. Before adding adsorbant, such columns require the addition of about 1 cm of fine sand, as cotton wool alone is not sufficient to retain the finer adsorbants; however, this is not necessary for columns possessing a sinter disk. The solvent reservoir is usually an addition funnel fitted into the ground glass socket or clamped above the column. The simplest collection system is a series of test tubes arranged in racks which can be pushed under the column at intervals. It is a good idea to number each tube, otherwise the result of prolonged chromatography can be a bewildering array of tubes in some obscure order which was forgotten long ago.

Choosing the solvent system

Before proceeding with the separation, you will need to have determined the best solvent system for separating the components of the mixture by TLC analysis. Realistically you will need a difference in R_f of about 0.3 between two components to stand a chance of obtaining an efficient separation using a gravity column. However, TLC adsorbant particle sizes (for silica and alumina) tend to be finer (and more retentive) than the same adsorbants when used for gravity column chromatography. Thus it is often advantageous to use a solvent combination for developing the column that is less polar than the optimum TLC solvent system. For instance, if the best TLC solvent system uses 1:1 light petroleum–diethyl ether, a suitable system for developing a column might have a 3:2 composition of light petroleum–diethyl ether.

Packing the column

The *wet packing* technique described here is so named because the adsorbant is added as a slurry in the eluting solvent. Columns may also be dry packed, but this procedure is much more likely to lead to cracking of the column due to the solvent boiling on admixture with the adsorbant.

Weigh out between 25 and 50 times the weight of adsorbant as you have crude sample for separation, using the higher weight ratio for more difficult separations or when separating less than 100 mg of sample. The size of column should be chosen such that about two-thirds of its length will be eventually packed with slurry and this may be estimated as follows:

Silica $\qquad l = \dfrac{6w}{d^2}$

Alumina $\quad l = \dfrac{2w}{d^2}$

where w = weight of adsorbant (g), l = length of column (cm) and d = internal column diameter (cm).

For example, 50 g of silica would ideally require a column of 3 cm in diameter and 35–40 cm in length. The same weight of alumina would be better used in a column of 2 cm in diameter and 25 cm in length. A 15:1–10:1 ratio of diameter to length is about the right proportion for a percolation column.

Mixing the adsorbant and solvents usually results in the liberation of a large amount of heat of hydration which is often enough to cause volatile solvents, such as diethyl ether, to boil. The mixing should therefore be carried out in a beaker of sufficient volume such that it is only one-quarter full with the dry adsorbant. In a hood add the solvent mixture with stirring until a free running slurry is obtained and then allow this to cool, stirring at intervals to remove all bubbles that may be trapped within it.

Care! Carry out slurry preparations in the hood

It is important that no air enters the packed column as this causes cracking of the slurry and results in the formation of channels through which the eluant will flow with no component separation.

Do not allow air into the column

Whilst the slurry is cooling to room temperature, fill the column to about one-third of its height with the eluting solvent mixture and run half of this through the stopcock, tapping the column gently to dislodge any trapped air bubbles (a short length of heavy duty flexible tubing is ideal for tapping the column). This operation is particularly important if you are using a column plugged with sand and cotton wool as the sand traps lots of air. Insert a filter funnel with a wide bore stem into the mouth of the column—a powder funnel is fine if it will fit. Stir up the slurry in the beaker (which by now will have settled out) to an even consistency and pour it in a steady stream into the funnel, stopping when the column is almost full. Place the beaker containing the remaining slurry underneath the column, remove the funnel, open the stopcock and allow the solvent to run into the beaker tapping the column gently as you do so. This will cause the slurry in the column to compact, dislodging any stray air bubbles. Only solvent should pass into the beaker. If any solid passes through, it will be necessary to dismantle the column, plug more firmly with cotton wool and start again. When the solvent level in the column is about 1 cm above the adsorbant layer, close the stopcock, stir up the slurry in the beaker and pour more of it into the column. Repeat the process until all of the adsorbant in the beaker has been transferred to the column. Finally, tap the column until the adsorbant surface settles no further, run out the remaining solvent to within 3 cm of the adsorbant and then carefully add a 1 cm layer of fine sand to the surface of the adsorbant to stabilize it. Your column is now ready for use.

Do not allow the column to run dry

At no time must the adsorbant in the column be permitted to run dry. If this happens, the column should be dismantled and repacked immediately.

Loading the sample

The aim of this part of the exercise is to introduce your mixture onto the top of the adsorbant column in as tight a band as possible; this requires care in minimizing the volume of solvent used to carry out the transfer. Dissolve your sample in the minimum possible volume of your elution mixture or, better still, in the least polar solvent used in the mixture if the sample is readily soluble in this. Open the column stopcock, allowing the solvent level to reach to almost the surface of the sand without touching it and then close the stopcock. Add your solution carefully to the surface of the sand using a

Add the solution slowly to the column

long pipette, taking care not to disturb the protective layer. Open the stopcock and allow the level to reach the sand layer again. Rinse out the sample container with a small amount of solvent, transfer this to the column in the same manner and repeat this procedure until all of your sample has been transferred to the top of the column. This should take about four additions. Finally, add about 3 cm of eluting solvent and allow this level to drain down to just above the layer of the sand. With the sample now introduced onto the silica, the column can be fitted with the addition funnel and filled carefully with the eluting solvent.

Eluting the column

The column is developed by allowing the eluting mixture to percolate through at a gentle rate. For most separations the maximum flow rate should not exceed 1 drop every 2 s and for difficult separations the rate should be much slower. Only experience will enable you to judge what is the correct rate for your particular problem. Fractions are collected at regular intervals; again there are no general guidelines to indicate the size of fractions, although the more difficult separations require smaller fraction sizes. Each fraction should be monitored by TLC at intervals of every five fractions or so in order to follow the progress of elution of the products. This information will help with decisions regarding flow rate and fraction size. Figure 3.71 shows the complete TLC analysis of the fractions resulting from a successful column.

Columns, once started, should ideally be finished without a break, although they may be stopped for short intervals—over lunch, for instance. Sometimes it can be possible to leave a tightly stoppered column overnight in a cool place at constant temperature. However, do not expect great things the next day as, even if the column has not cracked up, lateral diffusion of the bands will have been occurring all the time to undo your good work.

All fractions containing homogeneous material can be combined and the solvent can be removed on the rotary evaporator to furnish the purified product.

Disposal of the adsorbant

The used adsorbant must be disposed of carefully as the problems of inhalation of the powder are now worsened by the fact that it now contains adsorbed materials which have not been eluted from the column, but which may be

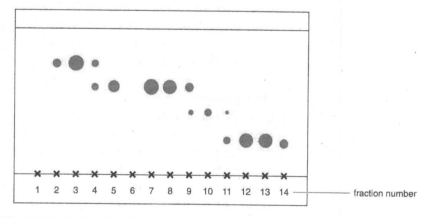

Fig. 3.71 Typical analysis by TLC of the fractions from a successful percolation column.

*Take care when disposing of
used chromatography
adsorbant*

highly toxic. The best way to empty the column is to allow the excess solvent to run out and then attach the stopcock outlet to a water aspirator in a hood to remove most of the solvent. The free running powder should be tipped carefully in a hood into a container specifically designated for chromatography residues and damped down by addition of some water.

Never dispose of chromatography residues into open bins.

'Flash' column chromatography

A more efficient preparative variant of column chromatography is that of *medium pressure chromatography*. In this technique the solvent is pushed through the column under pressure, and this faster elution rate, together with the use of a very regular fine particle adsorbant, enables an improved level of resolution to be achieved. However, the technique does require a certain amount of specialized equipment and this has tended to limit its acceptance.

In 1978 the American chemist W. Clark Still and his co-workers published a paper describing a hybrid technique between the medium pressure technique and a short column technique previously described by Rigby and Hunt in 1967. In this procedure, now simply known to chemists everywhere as 'flash' chromatography, the solvent is pushed through a relatively short column of high quality chromatography silica using gas pressure. As the pressures involved are only moderate, the technique requires very little in the way of special apparatus. Its advantages are the speed with which once tedious column chromatography can be carried out (hence the name), simplicity of operation and improved separation, particularly with larger sample sizes. Clean separation of components having R_f differences of 0.15 are possible in about 15 min and with a little more care and practice, R_f differences down to 0.1 present few problems.

Almost overnight, gravity column chromatography disappeared from research laboratories, to be replaced by 'flash' chromatography—whether the separation problem warranted it or not—and the technique is now universally used. The details below have been taken from the original paper describing the technique and, once the gravity column technique has been mastered, the transition to 'flash' chromatography should present no difficulties.

The equipment

In essence, the apparatus is the same as that used for gravity chromatography, with the additional requirement of a regulating device attached to the head of the column for controlling gas pressure, and hence elution flow rate. However, the recommended column shape is somewhat fatter than that which would be used for gravity chromatography of the same quantity of material, and has a flattened rather than a tapered bottom (Fig. 3.72). A sintered disk above the stopcock for containing the adsorbant is not recommended, as using cotton wool topped with a little sand significantly reduces the dead space at the exit

Fig. 3.72 Apparatus for 'flash' chromatography.

side of the column where remixing can occur. The top of the column may be modified to form an inbuilt solvent reservoir but this is not necessary as there is usually sufficient head space in the packed column to hold a useful quantity of solvent. The flow controller consists of a standard-taper cone fitted with a glass/Teflon® needle valve regulator which is adjustable by means of a screw thread (Fig. 3.72). All of this apparatus is commercially available but its construction poses no greater problems for a glass-blower than a standard chromatography column. As the column will be used under pressure, the glass should be thicker than normal.

Enclose flash columns in tape or webbing

The column must be wrapped in plastic webbing or adhesive tape to prevent flying glass in case of explosion when in use, and the pressure regulator must not be wired onto the column.

Before use, all equipment must be carefully checked for cracks or chips. The columns should be stored upright in racks designed for this purpose to stop the columns rolling about and banging into each other.

The adsorbant and solvent systems
The adsorbant used for separations is a high quality grade of silica with a very

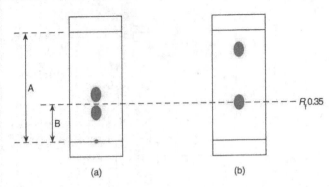

Fig. 3.73 Analytical TLC analyses of various component mixtures developed with the correct solvent combination for 'flash' chromatographic separation: (a) closely running components; (b) widely separated components.

uniform particle size of 40–63 μm. The fineness and regularity of this silica permits better packing and more efficient separations, but also leads to problems in handling the dry powder which has a tendency to disperse in the air.

Wear a face mask when handling flash silica. Handle in the hood

Flash silica must always be handled in the hood and it is recommended that a face mask is worn during transfers of this material in order to avoid accidental inhalation of any airborne powder.

The tighter packing possible with this adsorbant causes the flow rate of higher viscosity solvents to be impaired below the optimum flow rate. Wherever possible it is recommended that combinations of the following low viscosity solvents be used: light petroleum, dichloromethane, ethyl acetate or acetone. A solvent system should be chosen which gives the maximum separation of components with the desired component having an R_f value of 0.35. If the isolation of several closely running components is desired, then the solvent combination should be chosen such that the mid-point of the spots has an R_f value of 0.35. If the aim is to separate more widely separated components, the system in which the most polar material has an R_f value of 0.35 is the best choice (Fig. 3.73).

Packing the column

'Flash' chromatography columns are most simply filled using the technique of *dry packing*. The size of column and suggested fraction volumes depend on the quantity of material to be purified, and the ease of separation. Guidelines are listed in Table 3.13.

Always pack 'flash' columns in the hood

With the column in a hood, place a 0.5 cm layer of fine sand over the cotton wool plug and pour in the silica to a depth of 15 cm (for separating components with R_f differences approaching 0.1 it may be advisable to increase this depth by up to 25 cm—but no longer). Hold the column vertically and tap it

Table 3.13 Guideline size and volume parameters for 'flash' chromatography.

Sample weight (mg)		Column diameter (mm)	Suggested fraction volume (mL)
$\Delta R_f > 0.2$	$\Delta R_f < 0.2$		
100	40	10	5
400	160	20	10
900	360	30	20
1600	600	40	30
2500	1000	50	50

For details of use of gas cylinders, see pp. 64–68

Care! Pressure

Do not allow air to enter the column

carefully on a wooden surface to compact the silica which is then covered with another 0.5 cm layer of sand to protect the adsorbant surface. With the stopcock open, *and a collection vessel underneath*, introduce the chosen solvent system carefully (in the initial stages it is preferable to use a long pipette and to allow the solvent to run down the side of the column) until the head space is almost full. Attach the flow controller to a source of compressed gas (nitrogen cylinder, compressed air or a small air pump) *with the needle valve completely open* and hold it by hand on the top of the column. Force the solvent through the column using gas pressure by opening the compressed gas supply *slightly*, and then *carefully but firmly* closing the exit port on the flow controller with the forefinger. This will cause a certain amount of compaction of the silica and heat of hydration will also be produced in the initial stages. The pressure must be maintained until all of the adsorbant has been eluted with solvent, with displacement of the air, and the column has cooled down. If this procedure is not followed the column of adsorbant will crack up and will be useless. The heating effect is greatest with the larger columns containing the most silica and it is as well to practice making up a smaller size of column initially. Maintain the head pressure until the remainder of the solvent has passed through the column and the solvent surface is just above the sand layer; gently release the pressure and close the stopcock.

Loading the sample and eluting the column

Load the sample onto the column in the minimum quantity of the eluting system following the method described on p. 178 for percolation column loading. Pressure can be used to introduce the solution onto the column as described above. When all of your sample is on the silica and the head space has been topped up with solvent the column is ready to be eluted.

Before commencing the elution, make sure you have sufficient racks of test tubes readily to hand. You certainly will not have time to start arranging things during chromatography; the solvent passes through the column very quickly! Whilst the elution can be stopped during development, for instance to replenish the solvent reservoir, there is always a risk of the column cracking

Release pressure slowly

up on release of pressure and so it is as well to minimize such stoppages. Cracking frequently results from releasing excess pressure too quickly; always release the pressure slowly using the needle valve.

Never close the stopcock whilst the column is under pressure and do not close the needle valve fully

With the needle value fully open, attach the flow controller to the column with an elastic band. Open the stopcock on the column and then *carefully* close the needle valve until the solvent flows fairly rapidly through the column. This gives you both hands free for changing fractions but you must take care not to allow the pressure within the column to build up too high.

In general the solvent surface should descend at a rate of about 5 cm min^{-1} down the cylindrical body of the column for all sizes of columns. For those columns with spherical reservoirs when such a guideline is of no use, this translates into the following flow rates:

Column diameter (mm)	10	20	30	40	50
Flow rate (mL min^{-1})	4	16	35	60	100

There will be no time to follow the progress of elution during this procedure and only experience will enable you to judge when the desired component has been eluted from the column. It is always a good idea, however, to analyze all of your fractions at any stage when it proves necessary to add more solvent.

Disposal of the silica

Dispose of the silica carefully

You must exercise extreme care when emptying the used adsorbant due to its great tendency to disperse into the atmosphere when dry. The procedure described on pp. 179–180 describes a safe way to carry out this disposal, but always check for any additional rules that may be in force in the laboratory.

Further reading
B.J. Hunt and W. Rigby, *Chem. Ind. (London)*, 1967, 1868.
W.C. Still, M. Khan and A. Mitra, *J. Org. Chem.*, 1978, **43**, 2923.
D.F. Taber, *J. Org. Chem.*, 1982, **47**, 1351.

'Dry flash' column chromatography
This technique combines the speed and separation of 'flash' chromatography with use of the cheaper TLC grade silica, simple operation and absence of special apparatus requirements. In 'dry flash' column chromatography, the silica column is eluted by suction instead of using top pressure, removing the risk of bursting glassware. Additionally the column is eluted by adding predetermined volumes of solvent and is run dry before addition of the next fraction.

These features make the procedure readily adaptable to *gradient elution* and this is in fact the preferred way of developing such columns. As its name suggests, gradient elution involves developing a column with progressively more polar combinations of eluting solvent. This can confer very real time advantages for the removal of polar compounds from a column in the latter stages of a separation, without losing the separation qualities of a relatively non-polar eluting system at the beginning for the less polar components.

Do not forget that this is the *only* instance when you should allow air to get into a chromatography column during development. In fact the whole procedure appears to fly in the face of all of the principles of classic chromatography, but it can give results at least as good as the standard flash technique at much reduced cost. It is particularly useful for the separation of enormous (in chromatographic terms at least!) quantities of material—up to 50 g—although such columns should not be attempted by the inexperienced. This technique has been the subject of a certain degree of quantification by one of the authors (LMH) but has been in fairly general use in various laboratories for a long time.

The equipment

The apparatus needed is simply that for filtration under reduced pressure using a cylindrical porosity 3 sinter funnel attached to a round-bottomed flask by means of a cone and socket adapter with a side arm for attachment to a water aspirator (Fig. 3.74). The amount of sample to be purified determines the size of sinter funnel to use and the volume of fractions to collect. Suggested guidelines are shown in Table 3.14.

Choosing the solvent system

The eluting solvent system used should be that in which the desired component has an R_f value of 0.5 by TLC analysis. Although no solvent is particularly disfavoured for this technique, various combinations of hexane, diethyl ether, ethyl acetate and methanol are adequate for the majority of separations. As the system is under reduced pressure, some of the solvent collected will evaporate and may cool the receiving vessel to such an extent that

Fig. 3.74 Apparatus for 'dry flash' column chromatography.

Table 3.14 Guideline size and volume parameters for 'dry flash' chromatography.

Sinter diameter (mm)	Weight of silica (g)	Sample weight	Fraction volume (mL)
30	15	15–500 mg	10–15
40	30	500 mg–3 g	15–30
70	100	2–15 g	20–50

atmospheric moisture condenses on the apparatus. This does not affect the efficiency of the separation but, if the chromatography is prolonged, some water may find its way into the collected fractions. Use of the less volatile heptane instead of light petroleum helps somewhat in this respect.

Packing the column

Use TLC grade silica for dry flash chromatography

The silica used for this type of chromatography is TLC grade silica without the gypsum binder. This is cheaper than the silica sold for use in flash chromatography which, in any case, is too free flowing for use in these dry columns. The weight of silica recommended for each size of funnel is sufficient to leave a head space at the top of the funnel for loading solvent when the column has been packed and compacted under suction. The silica may be weighed out as indicated in the table, but it is easier just to fill the funnel to the brim with lightly packed silica. Application of suction causes the silica to compact, leaving the head space for solvent addition. During this initial compaction there is a tendency, particularly with the larger sized columns, for the silica to shrink away from the sides of the funnel or to form cracks which may remain unseen in the body of the adsorbant.

Handle silica in the hood

To ensure good packing, press down firmly on the surface with a glass stopper, particularly at the edges, using a grinding motion. Do not worry about the state of the adsorbant surface as this can be flattened off easily when finished by repeated gentle tapping around the sides of the funnel with a spatula.

When satisfied that the column has been thoroughly compacted, pre-elute the column with the least polar component of the elution system. If the packing has been carried out properly, the solvent front will be seen descending in a straight, horizontal line. Keep the silica surface covered with solvent during the pre-elution, until solvent passes into the receiving flask, and then allow the silica to be sucked dry. Remember to check the back as well as the

The column must be compacted evenly before attempting the separation

front of the column for any irregularities. If a regular solvent front is not obtained, simply suck the column dry, recompact it and repeat the pre-elution procedure. There is no excuse for attempting a separation with an improperly packed column. Note that the surface of the compacted silica is relatively stable on addition of solvent and does not require any protective layer of sand.

Loading the sample and eluting the column

Dissolve your sample in the minimum possible volume of pre-elution solvent and apply it evenly to the surface of the silica with the column under suction. Rinse the sample container and add the washings to the column until all of the sample has been transferred. If the sample does not dissolve easily in the pre-elution solvent, dissolve it in the least polar combination of the elution solvents in which it is readily soluble.

Commence gradient elution with the same solvent combination as was used to load the sample onto the column, following the guidelines in the table for the size of fraction to use (use the smaller volumes for more difficult separations). Allow the column to be sucked dry and transfer the first fraction to a test tube or any other convenient receptacle, rinsing both the flask and the stem of the funnel. Whilst the column is being sucked dry, prepare the next fraction, increasing the quantity of the more polar component by about 5%. Repeat the elution procedure. Continue the gradient elution in this manner until eluting with the pure, more polar component alone, and then continue with this as necessary. It is often advantageous to interrupt the gradient elution temporarily when the desired component is eluting from the column and continue with the same solvent mixture for a few fractions.

The progress of the separation should be followed by TLC analysis of the fractions. However, as a rough guide, the desired product is usually eluted from the column when the gradient elution reaches that solvent mixture in which the material would have an R_f value of 0.5 on TLC. When quantities of material of more than about 100 mg are purified, elution of product from the column is often indicated by frothing on the underside of the sinter. If the product is a solid, it may crystallize out in the stem of the funnel or the receiving flask, particularly with separations of larger quantities of material. Be sure to rinse thoroughly both the flask and the funnel stem between fractions, and check that the solid does not obstruct elution from the column.

The typically low degree of lateral diffusion of the product bands with this technique usually means that pure compounds elute in relatively few fractions, reducing the number of cross-contaminated fractions. The material recovery from the column should be excellent if the crude sample does not contain polymeric material.

Disposal of the silica

After the elution is complete, suck the silica dry and then transfer it to the silica residues bin. Generally a sharp tap with the funnel held upside down will cause the whole of the adsorbant to fall out as a single plug of material. As always, care should be taken not to produce large quantities of silica dust in the atmosphere of the laboratory.

Take care with the disposal of used silica

Further reading

L.M. Harwood, *Aldrichimica Acta*, 1985, **18**, 25.

For a technique using TLC grade silica and a combination of suction and head pressure to elute the column, see: Z. Zsótér, T. Eszenyi and T. Tímár, *J. Org. Chem.*, 1994, **59**, 672

High performance liquid chromatography

It would need a series of books to attempt to do justice to the whole range of chromatographic separation techniques. In this chapter, we have simply attempted to deal with the practical aspects of those techniques which are commonly encountered in the laboratory, or which are used in the experiments described in Part 2 of this book. Nonetheless, it would not be proper to leave this section on adsorption chromatography without at least a cursory mention of the ultimate application of this branch of chromatography—high performance (or pressure) liquid chromatography.

As one interpretation of the acronym HPLC suggests, this highly efficient technique once again uses solvent under pressure to elute the column. Although generally used as an analytical system, larger capacity columns having almost as good resolving power can be used in preparative systems. These systems are commercially available and the fine details vary from model to model but the general features are shown diagrammatically in Fig. 3.75. The general arrangement and operation bears more than a passing resemblance to gas chromatography (pp. 191–203), but HPLC is the more powerful analytical technique as it permits analysis of non-volatile and thermally labile compounds. However, development of the technique had to await the technology for preparing the specialized stationary phases so crucial for success.

Fig. 3.75 Schematic of a typical HPLC set-up with low pressure solvent mixing.

The equipment

The column is a stainless steel tube packed with a special stationary phase consisting of extremely fine, regularly sized, spherical particles with a very high ratio of surface area to mass, usually in the range $200–300 \, m^2 \, g^{-1}$. Owing to the small size of the particles, typically $5–10 \, \mu m$ in diameter, any solvent contained in the matrix of each particle is close to the external solvent and equilibration can take place readily. It is this which makes HPLC much more efficient than column chromatography using supports, in which the much larger particles have deep interstices predominantly filled with stagnant, non-equilibrating solvent. The technique may use a standard adsorption column or a *reversed phase* column. In reverse phase chromatography a highly polar solvent system is used for elution. Under such conditions polar compounds prefer to stay in the mobile phase and are eluted before non-polar materials which have a greater affinity for the stationary phase—the reverse of usual adsorption systems. Another very exciting development uses stationary phases in which the surface has been covalently linked to a chiral material. Such *chiral bonded phase supports* permit the analytical separation of enantiomers, and the potential for such chiral columns seems boundless.

These customized stationary phases are expensive, but the columns are designed to be reusable, and so the set-up always possesses a pre-column filter to remove particulate or polymeric matter before it contaminates the main column. Typically, analytical columns are 10–25 cm long with an internal diameter of 4–6 mm and may be surrounded by a thermostatted bath for extremely accurate work. Owing to the small size of the column the 'dead space' in the connections between the outlet and the detector must be kept to an absolute minimum in order to avoid remixing of components after elution from the column.

As a consequence of the highly packed nature of the stationary phase in these columns, pressures of anything up to 7000 psi are necessary to force the eluting solvent along the column. The pump must be capable of maintaining a constant flow of solvent with no pressure surges and it must also be constructed of material which can withstand a wide range of organic solvents. The pump is also designed to permit the precise choice of a particular rate from a wide range of flow rates.

The solvents used for HPLC must be highly pure, contain no solid matter and will require degassing immediately before use by sonification or by displacement of dissolved gases with helium. Any formation of air bubbles within the system totally upsets the pressure maintenance. Elution may be with a single solvent or a mixture of solvents when the process is described as *isochratic*, or the composition of the eluting system can be varied with time to permit *gradient elution*. The mixing of solvents for gradient elution may be carried out either at the low pressure side of the system, before the pump, or in the high pressure part. Both arrangements have their advantages and disadvantages and both require microprocessor control.

Samples for analysis are introduced onto the column by injection through a multiport valve which permits precise, repeatable sample loading with minimal disturbance of solvent flow. Basically, a solution of the sample is injected into an isolated, fixed volume loop of tubing which, on turning the valve, becomes part of the solvent delivery system. Sample in excess of that required to fill the loop is led to waste (Fig. 3.76). So-called *external loop* injection ports permit variation of the volume of sample introduced into the column.

The normal means of detecting the eluted components is by using a UV detector placed close to the outlet from the column. This permits continuous, instantaneous monitoring of the effluent from the column with the results being transmitted to a chart recorder; but this, of course, rules out the use of any solvent which has even a weak absorption in the UV region to be analyzed and imposes stringent purity requirements on all solvents. The most convenient type of detector is one which can be varied to monitor any specific wavelength desired. Common practice involves the simultaneous analysis of two different wavelengths as the impurities may possess different chromophores to the component of interest and may pass undetected if just one wavelength is observed. An alternative, but less frequently encountered means of monitoring column output, is to measure the refractive index of the eluant and to compare this with the pure solvent system. Perhaps the ultimate in separation–analysis techniques involves the coupling of the HPLC output to a mass spectrometer (pp. 373–378). This technique of *LC/MS* combines the ability to separate very complex mixtures with the extreme analytical sensitivity of mass spectrometry. The major problem with the technique has been the development of an interface between the liquid eluant from the column and the very low pressure within the mass spectrometer which will permit the selective introduction of the separated components and removal of the undesirable carrier solvents. It is perhaps worth reflecting on the extreme cost and sophistication of this arrangement, compared with the basic percolation column set-up, to appreciate the enormous advances which have been made in separation and analytical technology.

Fig. 3.76 Schematic diagram of the operation of an internal loop injection port for HPLC: (a) injection of sample; (b) introduction onto column.

Practical points for HPLC use

Every individual item of equipment used in HPLC is both delicate and expensive, and extreme care must be taken by anyone using such a set-up—that is if they want the chance to use it on future occasions! The most important 'do nots' are the following.

• Never start work on an HPLC set-up without first obtaining permission from the person responsible for its upkeep and giving instructions on its correct use.

• Do not be tempted to rush the degassing of the solvents; a few minutes skipped here will invariably cause several hours of extra work once air bubbles have got into the system. Check the solvent reservoir periodically and do not allow it to run dry.

• Never forget to use a pre-column filter and always check the age of the filter presently in use. If in doubt, clean the filter and put in fresh adsorbant. If at all possible, carry out a preliminary clean-up on your sample before the analysis—a simple filtration through a Pasteur pipette filled with a little TLC silica will be sufficient.

• Do not force the pump to work at very high rates of eluant flow. This will cause the stationary phase to compact and the resultant increase in back pressure can result in leaking joints or damage to the pump. When increasing flow rates, do so slowly, or the instantaneous back pressure developed might also damage the pump.

• If in doubt about anything, ask the person in charge for direction. Do not attempt to find out by trial and error as mistakes in HPLC are always costly in time, money and popularity.

Further reading

A. Braithwaite, C.B.F. Rice and F.J. Smith, *Chromatographic Methods*, 5th edn, Chapman & Hall, London, 1996.

P.R. Brown and A. Weston, *HPLC and CE: Principles and Practice*, Academic Press, London, 1997.

C.K. Lim (ed.) *HPLC of Small Molecules—a Practical Approach*, IRL Press, Oxford, 1986.

C.F. Simpson (ed.) *Practical High Performance Liquid Chromatography*, Heyden & Son, London, 1976.

Gas chromatography (gas–liquid chromatography)

Usually referred to as GC or GLC, gas chromatography is widely used in the resolution of mixtures of volatile compounds (or volatile derivatives if the parent compounds are insufficiently volatile) which may differ in boiling point by only a fraction of a degree. It is predominantly used as an analytical technique but, in its preparative form, provides an excellent alternative to fractional distillation for up to tens of grams of material.

It is probably easiest to think of GC as a hybrid between chromatography and distillation. The sample to be analyzed is volatilized and swept by a stream of *carrier gas* through a heated column containing an absorbant support impregnated with an involatile liquid which acts as the *stationary phase* (Fig. 3.77). *Packed column GC* is carried out using columns made of stainless steel or glass tubing, usually between 2 and 6 m in length with inside diameters of about 3–5 mm. In order to fit inside the heating oven, the columns are coiled. As with all other types of chromatography using packed columns, the packing resists any flow through it and so limits the length of column (and hence degree of separation) that can be used. *Capillary column GC*, in which the stationary phase is bonded to the walls of a long capillary tube, permits far greater selectivity. The reduced resistance to flow along such columns enables lengths of up to 50 m to be used with phenomenal increases in resolving power.

As in chromatography, the components of the mixture partition between the stationary phase and the carrier gas due to a combination of volatility and the degree with which they interact with the stationary phase. The separated components are then eluted from the column and pass over a detector. The lapsed time between injection onto the column and the exit of a particular component is referred to as the *retention time* and, just like the R_f of a compound in TLC, is diagnostically useful for a given column and set of conditions. To continue the analogy between adsorption chromatography and GC, increasing the rate of flow of carrier gas is equivalent to increasing the rate of elution of a chromatography column. Raising the oven temperature surrounding the column increases the rate of elution in GC in the same way as using a more polar solvent in column chromatography. The direct equivalent of gradient elution is called *temperature programming* in which the oven temperature may be increased during the analysis to accelerate the rate of elution of the less mobile components of a mixture. Increasing the amount of stationary phase loaded onto the solid support has the same effect on retention

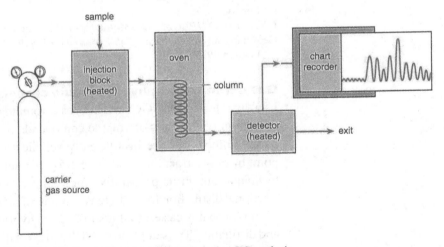

Fig. 3.77 Schematic diagram of the set-up for GC analysis.

of components as using a more active grade of adsorbant in column chromatography.

The carrier gas

The carrier gas is required to be inert to the column material and components of the sample. Depending on the detector, nitrogen, hydrogen, helium or argon may be used. In the case of flame ionization detectors, where the sample issuing from the column is burnt, the carrier gas is a mixture of hydrogen and air or nitrogen. Alternatively, on some machines fitted with flame ionization detectors, the hydrogen and air are introduced at the exit of the column just before the detector. Helium, with its low viscosity, is generally the carrier gas of choice for capillary columns. Flow rates must be controlled rigorously if retention time measurements are to have any meaning.

Packed columns and supports

The column consists of a length of glass or stainless steel tubing, coiled into several turns for convenience. The internal diameter varies from 3 to 5 mm and the length is usually between 2 and 6 m. Generally, separation efficiency increases with length and decreases with diameter, but at the same time, the greater resistance to flow in the longer columns demands a wider bore tube. The tube is filled with a porous support whose role is to absorb the stationary phase and present as large a surface area as possible. As might be expected, better efficiency of separation is obtained with supports consisting of small regularly sized particles. However, working against this is the greater pressure drop which occurs down the column when these more closely packed materials are used. The usual types of support are made from firebrick-derived materials (Chromosorb P) which are most suitable for use with non-polar hydrocarbon materials, or diatomaceous earth (Chromosorb W) which are better for use with molecules containing active hydrogens such as acids, amines and alcohols. These supports are first impregnated with the stationary phase and are then packed evenly into the column.

Stationary phase in packed column GC

As with solid–liquid chromatography, the stationary phase plays a very important role and hundreds of stationary phases have been developed in response to specific separation problems. The prime requirements are that a stationary phase should be thermally stable, unreactive and involatile over the working range of the column. All stationary phases can be classified as either *polar* or *non-polar*. Non-polar phases separate components largely on the basis of their differing boiling points, whereas polar phases may also impose dipole–dipole interactions in varying degrees on the compounds passing over them. In deciding which type of phase to use for a particular separation problem, it is helpful to remember that non-polar compounds are most suited to non-polar situations and vice versa. Another important consideration is the maximum temperature at which the stationary phase can be used before it starts to become volatile. Operating at higher temperatures will cause the stationary phase to begin to detach from the support, resulting in *stripping* and degradation of the column and swamping of the detector system. A brief list of commonly used stationary phases is given in Table 3.15 but for more comprehensive listings the reader is referred to the appropriate sections in *The Chemist's Companion* or the wide range of commercial literature available.

Capillary columns

The development of capillary columns has largely eliminated the limitations of packed column GC associated with pressure drop along the column. As

Table 3.15 Commonly used stationary phases for GC.

Stationary phase (type)	Property	Maximum operating temperature (°C)	Applications
Squalane (hydrocarbon)	Non-polar	150	General, halocarbons, hydrocarbons
Apiezon (hydrocarbon)	Non-polar	280(L), 200(M), 200(N)	General, hydrocarbons
SE-30 (methylsilicone)	Non-polar	350	Non-polar, high molecular weight compounds, silylated derivatives
OV-1, OV-101 (dimethylsilicone)	Non-polar	300–350	Non-polar, high molecular weight compounds
Carbowax® 20 M (polyglycol)	Polar	225	Low molecular weight, polar compounds
PEGA (polyethyleneglycol adipate)	Polar	180	Low molecular weight, polar compounds
DEGS (diethyleneglycol succinate)	Polar	190	Low molecular weight, polar compounds
OV-17 (50:50 dimethylsilicone: diphenylsilicone)	Intermediate	350	Low molecular weight, polar compounds, high molecular weight hydrocarbons
DC-550 (silicone oil)	Intermediate	275	Low molecular weight, polar compounds, high molecular weight hydrocarbons

their name suggests, these columns—first proposed by M.J.E. Golay—consist of a fine bore tube, usually made of silica with an internal diameter of less than 0.5 mm, the walls of which are coated with the stationary phase. As the unfilled centre permits relatively free passage of gas, there is a markedly reduced pressure drop down such columns, and lengths of 25–50 m are usual. The resolution efficiency of these columns (often referred to as the number of *theoretical plates* by analogy with distillation) is greatly superior to that of packed columns. Capillary columns possessing 500 000 theoretical plates are not uncommon as opposed to the absolute maximum of about 20 000 for packed columns. Other salient features of capillary columns compared with the equivalent packed columns may be listed as follows.

- Smaller sample sizes are necessary.
- Limits of detection are the same as packed columns, although less material is used due to the sharpness of the peaks.
- Elution times for equivalent resolutions are up to 10 times shorter.
- Column temperatures are usually about 20°C lower than those required for the corresponding packed columns.
- Almost any sample mixture can be separated using one of four stationary phases: OV-101, SE-30 (non-polar samples), OV-17 (medium polarity samples) and Carbowax® 20 M (polar samples).

The stationary phase may be deposited either as a thin film directly onto the internal wall of the tube, or adsorbed onto a support which is applied to the tube. In the case of *bonded phase capillary columns* the stationary phase is further stabilized by being covalently linked to the support. The mechanical properties of the silica when drawn out into a capillary, particularly when coated with a protective resin, result in a flexible, resilient column which can be crumpled in the hand without breaking or deforming (practise this trick at your peril, however, these columns are expensive!).

The oven

Very stringent demands are placed on the functioning of the oven as the temperature of the column has a direct effect on the retention times of the components. The oven must be capable of maintaining an accurate temperature in a range from slightly above ambient temperature to about 300°C. In addition, the temperature throughout the whole volume of the oven must be constant so that the total column length is at the same temperature. For this reason an internal fan is fitted to circulate air. The heater must also be able to produce accurate, reproducible heating rates of anything up to 40°C min^{-1} and, at the same time, the walls of the oven must have minimal heat capacity in order to keep temperature overshoot to an absolute minimum. This feature is particularly important in stepped temperature programmes, when an initial phase of temperature increase is followed by a period of steady temperature, before proceeding with a second temperature increase.

Detector and response factors

Various types of detector are used, but the most commonly encountered is the *flame ionization detector*. As the name suggests, the gas issuing from the column is burnt and the ions in the flame are detected and translated into an electric current. When a compound is eluted from the column, this causes an increase in the production of ions, with a corresponding increase in the current sent to the chart recorder. It is tempting to measure the areas under the peaks which make up the GC trace and conclude that these reflect the relative quantities of material present in the original mixture. Unfortunately, different compounds give rise to different amounts of ions when they burn, so this assumption cannot be made. Compounds containing sulfur, for instance, are notoriously poorly detected by flame ionization detectors. To quantify GC traces it is necessary to standardize the peak area due to a known quantity of each component against an internal standard in order to obtain the *response factor* in each case. This is a time-consuming exercise which may not always be possible to carry out if authentic materials are not available. However, to a first order of approximation, it may be assumed that isomers or compounds of the same structural type will have closely similar response factors and relative peak areas can be compared. That this is not really a valid assumption can be seen from the following flame ionization detector response factors for some straight-chain primary alcohols relative to ethanol:

Comparing peak areas in GC traces is not a reliable method of determining relative quantities of components

Alcohol	Ethanol	Propanol	Butanol	Pentanol
Response factor	1.00	1.41	1.63	1.97

If an automatic integrator is not available, treatment of the peaks as if they are triangles is usually permissible if the baseline is flat. An alternative method is to photocopy the trace (with enlargement if possible) and cut out and weigh the various peaks on an analytical balance.

Sample preparation

The sample should be made up as a solution in dichloromethane, toluene, or acetone to a concentration of $1–2\,mg\,mL^{-1}$. The solution must be free of any particulate matter which could block the syringe. Obviously the sample should be volatile enough to permit analysis by GC, but if not, it may be possible to convert it to a suitably volatile derivative.

Derivatization of involatile or polar compounds

As well as increasing the volatility of components to be analyzed, derivatization might also help if excessive 'tailing' of the peaks is observed—often the case with compounds capable of hydrogen bonding. By far the commonest derivatization technique is to silylate any free acid, alcohol or amine groups. Many reagents have been developed for this but the most reactive are doubly silylated derivatives of amides. Both BSTFA (*N,O*-bis(trimethylsilyl)trifluoroacetamide) and BSA (*N,O*-bis(trimethylsilyl)acetamide) trimethylsilylate alcohols, acids or amines rapidly and quantitatively.

OSi(CH₃)₃

CF₃ — NSi(CH₃)₃

BSTFA

OSi(CH₃)₃

CH₃ — NSi(CH₃)₃

BSA

To carry out such a derivatization before analysis, dissolve a small quantity of the sample (1–2 mg) in 4 drops of dry pyridine contained in a 2 mL screw cap vial and add excess of the silylating reagent (*ca.* 20 μL). After 15 min at room temperature, the mixture can be diluted to 1 mL with the requisite solvent and the solution injected directly onto the column.

Alkylation and acylation are other commonly used derivatization techniques, but usually they have no advantage over silylation.

Introducing the sample onto the column

Samples are introduced onto the column via the injection port (Fig. 3.78) which consists of an adapter over the inlet end of the column carrying a septum which is pierced using a microlitre syringe containing a solution of the sample.

Treat GC syringes with great care

Syringes for GC analysis are high precision instruments designed to deliver (as opposed to just containing) exact amounts of liquid in microlitre quantities. With this aim, the dead space in the bore of the needle is minimized by a fine wire which runs from the tip of the plunger to the tip of the needle when the plunger is fully depressed. This fine wire is very easily damaged if the plunger is withdrawn too far from the barrel and will require expensive repair work.

Never dismantle the microlitre syringe and take care not to bend or kink the needle

Some syringes may be fitted with a device which only permits the plunger to be pulled back a certain distance (Fig. 3.79a). If not, it is recommended that

Fig. 3.78 Cross-section through a GC injection port.

(a)   (b)

Fig. 3.79 (a) A typical syringe for GC analysis with a fitting for limiting plunger withdrawal; (b) technique for holding the syringe with one hand during rinsing and filling.

you hold the syringe in one hand only when rinsing and filling it. To do this, grasp the barrel of the syringe between the thumb and third and fourth fingers and hold the plunger with the index and forefingers (Fig. 3.79b). In this way, it is possible to take up the sample, but it is not possible to pull the plunger out too far. After a little practice, this technique soon becomes second nature.

Keep the syringe thoroughly clean at all times

As the syringe cannot be dismantled in the normal course of events, it must be thoroughly cleaned whenever it is used, *both before and after use*. Rinse the syringe out initially at least 10 times in pure sample solvent, by filling to its maximum volume and then expressing the contents of the barrel as a tiny drop of liquid. Similarly rinse out the syringe with your dissolved sample, but on the final filling, push the plunger down to the volume required for analysis (between 0.5 and 5 μL, and usually 1 μL). Now, *holding the syringe with both hands* (Fig. 3.80) push the needle slowly through the septum of the inlet port *without injecting the sample*, until the syringe barrel almost touches the metal surround of the port. *Perform this operation slowly, otherwise you will bend the needle and ruin the syringe.* The wire running the length of the needle ensures that no liquid resides in that region of the syringe, subsequently boiling off onto the column before the main body of the sample can be injected.

Take care not to burn your hands on the metal of the injection port which will be at a temperature close to that of the oven

In one smooth movement, quickly push the plunger fully into the barrel, make a mark on the chart recorder to show the actual point of introduction of the sample, and then withdraw the syringe. *Immediately rinse out the syringe 10 times with pure solvent.*

use both hands

pierce septum
without injecting

inject with a smooth,
rapid movement

Fig. 3.80 Injecting the sample onto the column.

Your sample is now on the column and you are waiting impatiently to see the result of the analysis on the chart recorder. If things are working well, you might hope to see a trace looking something like Fig. 3.81—the peaks will be even sharper if you are using a capillary column. Knowing the rate at which the chart recorder paper is moving permits the retention time for each peak to be read off directly from the horizontal axis.

Common problems
Unfortunately, there are many reasons why you might not see anything like the trace in Fig. 3.81 and a few common problems are mentioned here.

No peaks visible or only very small peaks. If no peaks appear at all, check the recorder is connected up correctly and switched on. If all appears correct, either you have not injected enough sample or, more likely, the sensitivity of the detector is not high enough. This is controlled using the *attenuator*, which perversely enough, gives higher detection sensitivities when at lower settings. The most sensitive setting is 1 and the infinity position cuts out any response altogether. Normally you should operate between positions 4 and 64 on the attenuator.

Some or all peaks off scale. Do not worry about the first peak being off scale—this is the solvent peak—but all the other peaks should be on scale if you wish to measure peak areas. Either you are injecting too much sample, or you have the attenuator set at too sensitive a position. It is usually simple to differentiate between these possibilities as concentrated samples tend to give read-outs

Fig. 3.81 Idealized GC trace of a sample mixture.

with a very smooth baseline, whereas high sensitivity attenuator settings result in a noisy baseline.

Irregularly shaped peaks. The ideal shape of the peaks should be gaussian or nearly so; the pen should rise and descend smoothly and symmetrically when drawing out the peak. If the peak shows noticeable tailing (Fig. 3.82a), this is often evidence that you have a mismatch between the sample being analyzed and the column stationary phase and support. This might be remedied by silylating the sample to remove any hydrogen-bonding groups, or it may be easier to opt for a less polar column. If the leading edge of the peak rises sluggishly and erratically, followed by a rapid drop at the trailing edge, giving a broad peak with a 'shark's fin' effect (Fig. 3.82b), this is a sure sign of column overload and much less sample should be injected. Owing to lateral diffusion which occurs in any chromatographic process, it is natural that some peak broadening, with consequent loss of peak height, will occur with later eluting components. When long retention times lead to the peaks becoming indistinguishable from the baseline then use of temperature programming is called for (Fig. 3.83).

Baseline drift. A baseline which drifts upward, particularly during the latter stages of a temperature programme, indicates that the stationary phase is beginning to 'strip' from the column. Lower oven temperatures are necessary to avoid ruining the column.

Appearance of spurious peaks. Remember that impurities do not count as spurious peaks! However, if the trace shows broad peaks which crop up at unpredictable intervals, this is a sign that the previous users have contami-

Fig. 3.82 Typical irregularities in peak shapes: (a) tailing peaks; (b) shark's fin peaks.

Fig. 3.83 Typical packed column GC traces: (a) isothermal conditions; (b) same sample analyzed with temperature programming—passage of the later components is speeded up by increasing the oven temperature.

nated the column with polymeric material, or that the person immediately prior to you has not allowed all the components to elute off the column before shutting it down. As some molecules take an exceedingly long time to be eluted from the column, the person who has just used the column may not be to blame. Report the state of the column to the person responsible for the apparatus—do not attempt to remonstrate with anyone yourself! After a day's use, it is usual to 'bake out' the column. This involves heating the oven overnight to near the maximum working temperature of the column with the carrier gas flowing through it.

The appearance of erratic, sharp spikes on the trace is usually caused by electrical interference from some other piece of apparatus; these spikes do not usually interfere with your result. Do not attempt to find the source of interference by switching off any electrical instruments in the vicinity!

Variable retention times. If repeated injections do not give very close retention times for the eluted peaks, something is likely to be wrong with the supply of carrier gas. If the retention times increase, it is probable that the gas supply is running out and needs renewing. If the times vary erratically, check the state of the septum in the injection port, which is liable to be leaking.

Variable peak areas. If repeated injections show wild variations in the heights of the peaks on the trace, do not blame the apparatus as this is almost certainly due to poor injection technique. Either you are not taking up the same amount of sample each time, or you are not injecting all of it onto the column. It is useless having the apparatus in perfect condition if your technique does not give repeatable results. This only comes with practice and care.

Co-injection as an indication of identity

In order to compare an unknown compound with a sample of authentic material to see if they have identical retention times, it is necessary to carry out simultaneous analysis of the unknown and the authentic material. Preparing a mixed solution of the two materials requires some care to ensure that neither component predominates by too much. If one component of the mixture is present in a large excess over the other, its peak will totally dominate the trace and will swamp any shoulder due to a closely running component. This will give the impression that the two compounds are identical. Often the components are too precious to sacrifice to a potentially mixed solution. In this case each should be dissolved separately to give solutions of roughly equal concentrations. An equal volume of each should be removed using the microlitre syringe for simultaneous injection onto the column.

Remember that, whilst the appearance of a double peak on co-injection tells you that the two components are definitely different, the observation of a single peak only *indicates* identity. Other supportive evidence must be found as the unavoidable peak broadening which occurs with packed columns means that two different compounds might have overlapping peaks.

Further reading
A. Braithwaite, C.B.F. Rice and F.J. Smith, *Chromatographic Methods*, 5th edn, Chapman & Hall, London, 1996, Chapter 5.

For the proposal of the potential of capillary columns, see: M.J.E. Golay, *Gas Chromatography* (ed. R.P.W. Scott), Butterworths, London, 1958, p. 36.

For texts dealing with capillary GC, see: W. Jennings, *Gas Chromatography with Glass Capillary Columns*, 2nd edn, Academic Press, London, 1980; D.W. Grant, *Capillary Gas Chromatography*, Wiley & Sons, New York, 1996.

For texts dealing with gas chromatography, see: A.J. Gordon and R.A. Ford, *The Chemist's Companion. A Handbook of Practical Data, Techniques and References*, Wiley & Sons,

New York, 1973; G. Schonburg, *Gas Chromatography*, VCH, 1990; P. Baugh, *Gas Chromatography*, IRL Press, Oxford, 1993; I.A. Fowlis, *Gas Chromatography*, 2nd edn, Wiley & Sons, New York, 1995; W. Jennings, E. Mittlefehldt and P. Stemple, *Analytical Gas Chromatography*, 2nd edn, Academic Press, London, 1997.

For further details of preparing derivatives for GC analysis, see: K. Blau and J.M. Halket (eds) *Handbook of Derivatives for Chromatography*, 2nd edn, Wiley & Sons, New York, 1993; D.R. Knapp, *Handbook of Analytical Derivatization Reactions*, Wiley & Sons, New York, 1979.

Chapter 4

Qualitative Analysis of Organic Compounds

4.1

Purity

Why bother to analyze compounds?

All scientists observe systems, make observations and draw conclusions from their results. It is this protocol which, if rigorously adhered to in the laboratory, is most likely to turn a chance observation into an important discovery. However, before any meaningful results can be obtained, the scientist must know for certain exactly what is under scrutiny, otherwise any results obtained are simply a worthless jumble of irreproducible facts. Organic chemists are no exception to this general situation and, as the systems usually under study in the laboratory are chemical substances, the worker must ensure at the outset the nature of the material under investigation, and whether it is indeed a single substance or a mixture of components.

All this may seem obvious, but the regularity with which students commence analyzing an unknown before actually ensuring the purity of their sample makes this reminder very necessary. Nobody would dream of undertaking an analysis of the active constituents contained in the extract of some obscure species of tropical plant without first making a thorough examination of the complexity of the extract. Likewise, the fact that a sample has been taken from a bottle on a shelf is no assurance of purity or even that the substance is what the label says it is! Quite apart from the contrived machinations of academics devising unknown mixtures for analysis in the teaching laboratory, labelling mistakes occur only too frequently; particularly in samples which have been relabelled or repackaged after purchase. Additionally, it must be remembered that most organic chemicals degrade on storage and, whilst the age of the sample might be known, its stability under the specific conditions of storage is impossible to estimate. Consequently, even commercial samples, apparently pristine in their original wrapping, should always be checked for purity before use. Too frequently this apparently self-evident precaution is overlooked by even the most experienced research chemists—often to their downfall. The least important consequences of such poor technique are erroneous results, lowered yields or wasted laboratory time; the potential for disaster is only too obvious.

It might be argued that, with the introduction of sensitive, non-destructive spectroscopic techniques (Chapter 5), there is little need for new generations of chemists to learn the art of qualitative analysis. However, apart from the practical requirements in the research laboratory which may or may not be equipped with the latest elaborate piece of spectroscopic hardware, there are other reasons for learning these techniques which apply specifically to anyone wishing to become a worthwhile chemist. The identification of an unknown compound encapsulates the events which occur during any scientific investigation, no matter how short or how grand. The cyclic sequence of test–observe–propose/extrapolate–verify/disprove teaches us good scientific practice, and if a certain amount of inspired guesswork occurs, that only mirrors the serendipity which takes place in research a good deal more frequently than most would care to admit!

The techniques required to test for functional groups and to prepare derivatives provide the student with excellent training in the various manipulative techniques of small-scale experimental work that will be required later on in the teaching and research laboratory. In addition to this, as the characterization of functional groups depends on their specific features of structure and reactivity, qualitative analysis allows us to see at first hand the chemical consequences of the presence of a particular moiety in a molecule and contributes to the general understanding that separates the good practical chemist from the nondescript. It is for these profound pedagogical reasons that the descriptions of analytical techniques precede the preparative experiments in this book.

This chapter is broken down into sections covering criteria of purity and qualitative analysis. Although frequently spectroscopic analysis alone can provide the full structure of an unknown substance, the prudent chemist will nonetheless carry out some confirmatory chemical tests to check the presence of the proposed functionalities.

Laboratory safety

It is most important when analyzing an unknown compound never to forget that its properties as well as its chemical identity are unknown. 'Safety first' is always the motto in the laboratory and never more so than when handling unidentified materials which may be toxic, corrosive, flammable or explosive.

Care is paramount when carrying out analyses on unknown materials which must always be treated as potentially hazardous to health.

Remember that the absence of known toxic effects for a chemical can never constitute an absolute assurance of its safety (the perennial problem of the pharmaceutical industry where legislation appears to demand this) and some compounds possess hazardous properties, such as carcinogenicity, which may not manifest themselves in any obvious way until many years later when it is too late.

Criteria of purity

The ancient alchemists believed that all matter was made up of various combinations of four components—earth, air, fire and water. As far as the organic chemist is concerned, the vast majority of the compounds handled regularly in the laboratory are either solid or liquid, and the physical properties relating to these two states (melting point, boiling point, refractive index) are frequently used as indications of the purity of a compound. Another physical property which holds if the molecule is optically active is the degree by which a solution of the substance will rotate plane polarized light under standard conditions ($[\alpha]_D$). We will consider the practical aspects of determining these parameters in the first part of this chapter.

Analytical techniques which have already been dealt with in Chapter 3, which depend on a combination of physical properties of the compound (polarity, volatility, solubility, shape, functional groups present), are the chromatographic techniques, particularly thin layer chromatography (TLC, see pp. 165–175) and gas chromatography (GC, see pp. 191–203). These techniques, relying as they do on the interplay of a whole range of properties, are highly selective and permit distinction between very similar substances. In addition, they use very little material and (particularly in the case of TLC) are very quick and easy to use, giving reliable results within minutes.

There is also an analysis which is still regarded as the touchstone for purity of organic substances—quantitative elemental microanalysis. This technique is a measure of the bulk contents of a sample but suffers from the disadvantages of requiring expensive specialized apparatus and highly skilled operators, which certainly puts it outside the realm of the teaching laboratory. However, it is probably the fact that it is outside the scope of the ability of most chemists to microanalyze their own samples that is its strong point. In a world where the pressure for success grows daily, microanalysis is a technique in which the second person carrying out the analysis acts effectively as an independent witness, verifying the validity of the results claimed by the first.

Melting point

The melting point of a solid substance can give an indication of its degree of purity and can also assist greatly in its identification. Whilst not always strictly true, it is considered that a sharp melting point range (<2°C) between the first appearance of drops of liquid within the sample to the disappearance of the last trace of solid constitutes good evidence for believing a substance to be pure. Rarely, however, a mixture might give a sharp melting point if the components are present in the exact proportions to form a *eutectic mixture* (see below).

Conversely a broad melting point, whilst strong evidence for lack of purity, can result if a pure substance decomposes on heating, thus introducing impurities. Darkening of the sample or evolution of a gas is an indication that this is occurring. Dissolution of the compound in residual or occluded recrystallization solvent will also give what appears to be a broad melting point and is a commonly encountered situation in the teaching laboratory!

Melting point range

To explain why impure compounds have a broad melting point range let us consider a hypothetical phase diagram of a mixture containing two components having different melting points (A = 90°C, B = 110°C) (Fig. 4.1).

In the phase diagram, the mixture corresponding to 70% A and 30% B has the lowest melting point (74°C — the *eutectic temperature*). A mixture of A and B having exactly this composition would appear to have a sharp melting point at this reduced temperature. However, suppose that A is an impurity in B and is present to the extent of 5%. Melting will first occur at 74°C and the liquid formed will have the eutectic composition containing 70% A — in other words much higher than in the original mixture containing only 5% A. The mixture will continue to melt at 74°C until all of the impurity A is in the liquid phase. The total amount of material which will have melted at this point is

$$A + B = 5\% + \left(30/70 \times 5\right)\%$$
$$= 7.1\%$$

This initial melting would probably not be visible to the naked eye, and at this stage the remaining solid, representing 92.9% of the original mixture, consists totally of B. As the temperature rises the remaining solid begins to melt, adding to the amount of B in the liquid until the first drop is observed — let us say that this occurs when 30% of the mixture has melted. At this point the melt will contain five parts of A and 25 parts of B (approximately 17% A, 83% B). From the phase diagram it can be seen that the melting point of a mixture containing 83% B would be roughly 104°C and this would be recorded as the start

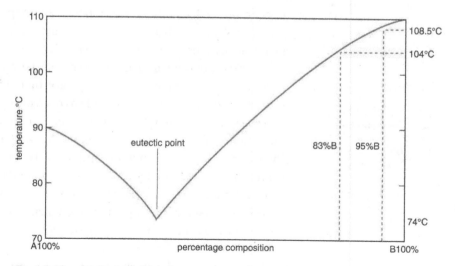

Fig. 4.1 Simple phase diagram for a two-component mixture.

of melting. As the temperature rises, B will continue to melt according to the phase diagram until the last crystal of B melts to give a liquid containing 95% B and 5% A (the original composition). This will occur at approximately 108.5°C. The melting point range would thus be recorded as 104.0–108.5°C; broader and depressed compared with that of pure B.

Mixed melting point as a means of preliminary identification

The melting point of a pure substance can be used to provide an indication of its possible structure by comparing the melting point obtained with those contained in data tables. Usually, some knowledge of the chemical reactivity of the unknown is also to hand and it is frequently possible to narrow the field to one or two prime candidates having similar melting points. The assignment may be verified or disproved by making an intimate mixture of the unknown with a pure sample of the proposed material in approximately equal proportions and recording the melting point of this mixture. If the substances are identical then the melting point will be unchanged. However, if they are different the melting point of the mixture will be depressed compared with that of the unknown as the introduction of the impurity lowers and broadens the melting point range. This technique is particularly handy when several possible candidate compounds have quoted melting points within one or two degrees of the observed value (for example benzoic acid, 121°C, and succinic anhydride, 120°C).

Experimental procedures for recording melting points

Capillary tube method

At its simplest, this consists of placing a small amount of the substance, contained in a capillary tube, into a heating bath with a means of measuring the temperature of the bath. Various refinements are possible and numerous commercial systems are available which may use an electrically heated oil bath or metal block as the heat transmission medium (Fig. 4.2).

However, before the melting point can be measured, it is necessary to introduce your sample into the capillary tube. Commercial melting point tubes are available in which one end has been presealed, but it is more usual to utilize a simple open-ended capillary and seal it oneself—*before* introducing the sample, of course! The tube should be sealed by just touching the hot (blue) flame of a microburner with the tube pointing slightly upwards to prevent the flow and condensation into the body of the tube of any water vapour driven off by the heating (Fig. 4.3). Care should be taken not to permit a globule of glass to develop on the sealed end as this may prevent the introduction of the tube through any preset hole in a commercial apparatus and may also slow down heat transfer to the solid.

Make sure that the sample is dry and has been ground to a fine powder. Press the open end of the cooled melting point tube into a small pile of the

Familiarize yourself with the apparatus in your laboratory

Care! Hot surfaces

Care! Always check for solvents or flammable materials

Fig. 4.2 Examples of apparatus used for capillary tube melting point determination.

tube tilted to prevent
water condensation inside

stages for
correct sealing

WRONG!
Tube has been
over-heated

Fig. 4.3 Sealing a melting point capillary tube.

sample on a clean glass surface, such as a watch glass, causing a plug of the material to become wedged into the mouth of the tube. To move this to the sealed end, stand a length of glass tubing about 50 cm long on the bench and drop the tube, sealed end first, down it. The force of impact on the bench will not be sufficient to break the melting point tube, but it will cause the solid to be transferred to the sealed end. Repeat this procedure until about 3 mm of the tube has been packed with sample.

An alternative procedure for moving your sample to the sealed end of the capillary involves rubbing the tube with a rough surface, such as the milled edge of a coin or the serrated edge of a glass file, when the vibrations shake the sample to the bottom.

On attempting to record a melting point, it may be observed that the solid sublimes before melting (indicated by a ring of solid appearing at the point where the tube leaves the heating medium). In this instance, it may be possible to obtain a melting point by using a closed capillary prepared by sealing the open end after introduction of the sample. Needless to say, as this will involve the development of pressure within the tube, such a procedure must never be carried out in anything larger than the standard capillary tube where the relative thickness of the glass compared with the internal volume permits safe operation.

As it is assumed that the temperature of the medium equates with that of the sample under investigation, it follows that the sample must be held close to the point of measurement and adequate heat distribution must be assured within the transmission medium. All commercial apparatus is designed to meet these criteria, but none of the features will be of any use if the temperature is increased too rapidly, as the sample must be allowed to come to equilibrium with its surroundings. It is usually acceptable (indeed necessary with thermally unstable compounds) to approach rapidly to within 20°C of the expected melting point and to then slow down the rate of heating such that the temperature is increased at no more than 2°C each minute—the slower the better. Some pieces of apparatus have built-in booster heaters for this purpose. It is best to be aware that the temperature of the heating bath will normally continue to rise at a relatively rapid rate for some time after the heating has been reduced owing to residual heat within the heating element. Therefore it may be necessary to slow down the heating some way below the expected melting point. The best practice (particularly if, as is usually the case, the melting point is unknown) is to carry out an initial rapid but approximate determination, followed by an accurate determination in which the melting point is approached slowly from about 20°C below the value expected.

Always increase the temperature slowly near the expected melting point

It is necessary to observe the sample carefully before the melting point and note faithfully any changes in appearance (for example darkening) and the temperature at which they occur. This is normally made easier by the positioning of a magnifying lens in the apparatus. Above all, it is necessary not to fall prey to any preconceived ideas, but to record all of your observations objectively. This maxim always applies in the laboratory, but it appears that waiting for a substance to melt brings out the worst in some people—do not be impatient!

The first sign that your sample is about to melt is usually a contraction in volume of the sample, which may result in it pulling away from the walls of the tube, although no liquid will be visible at this stage. This phenomenon is referred to as *sintering* and the temperature at which this occurs should be noted. The first droplet of liquid should then be visible within a few degrees of the sintering point and this is considered to be the commencement of melting. The completion of melting is taken to be the point at which the last crystal disappears. These two readings constitute the melting point range (Fig. 4.4).

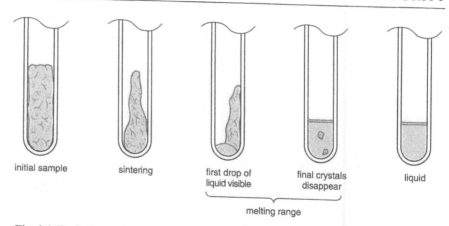

Fig. 4.4 Typical sample changes in the region of its melting point.

As soon as your sample has melted and the three readings and other observations have been noted, the apparatus should be allowed to cool and the sample should be disposed of carefully, as directed by the laboratory for disposal of sharp materials. In otherwise clean and tidy laboratories, there is frequently a mess of discarded capillary tubes around the communal melting point apparatus. This is not only slovenly, but potentially hazardous should a worker be cut accidently.

Always clean up your mess after you

Heated block method

This general heading covers two very different pieces of commercial apparatus which may be encountered. One permits rapid approximate determination of melting points (for example, to obtain an initial approximate melting point, or to enable instructors to check on students' claims!), and the other permits very accurate readings on small amounts of sample.

In the first case, the apparatus consists essentially of a metallic strip which is heated by an electric current in such a way that a temperature gradient is set up. Along the strip is a pointer which can be moved along a calibrated temperature scale (Fig. 4.5a). A small amount of compound is sprinkled onto that area of the plate corresponding to a temperature close to, but lower than, the suspected melting point of the sample. This is then spread along the plate using the pointer until a transition from solid to liquid is observed, enabling a melting point to be read off from the scale. Of course, such an apparatus can only give very approximate values, as the solid–liquid transition is often difficult to detect with precision and, more importantly, the actual temperature at any point on the metal strip depends on the temperature of the room and the absence of draughts. It is also generally forgotten that the apparatus requires time to come to equilibration (about 30 min). Nonetheless, many instructors have found that merely switching on such an apparatus will convince an adamant student that the recorded melting point might require checking!

Fig. 4.5 (a) Kofler hotbench. (b) Koflerblock and viewing microscope.

Care! Hot surfaces

At all times treat such apparatus with care, as the exposed metal surface is very hot. Cleaning such apparatus between samples is problematical, and is best carried out carefully using a paper tissue held with tongs, with a much more thorough cleaning at the end of the laboratory session after the apparatus has been unplugged and allowed to cool down.

The more precise systems, of which the Kofler block apparatus (Fig. 4.5b) is an example, utilizes a very small amount of sample sandwiched between two microscope cover slips in intimate contact with a heated metal block. The sample is observed through a magnifying lens or microscope which permits very detailed observation of the beginning and end of the melting. Sintering will not be obvious in such a sample and the onset of melting can be rapid and unexpected. Draughts must be avoided and, in the case of the Kofler apparatus, a glass plate may be supplied to cover the heating block. Kofler blocks are provided with a microscope for viewing the sample. The microscope must always be focused by first lowering the tip down to the glass cover and then moving upwards. Ignoring this precaution will result in repeated, costly breakages of the glass cover. Great care must be exercised in the handling of the microscope cover slips as a deposition of grease from the hands will constitute a considerable impurity with regard to the amount of sample used. It is important to use as little sample as possible (preferably one crystal) and to press the two cover slips tightly together. If this is not done some of the

Do not contaminate the cover slips used for holding the sample

sample will be in contact with the glass and some will not, with the consequence that a broad melting point range may be observed. Extra care must be taken with the thermometers used in such pieces of apparatus as they are extremely expensive.

Calibration of the melting point apparatus — the 'corrected melting point'

It stands to reason that, for a quoted melting point to have any scientific value, it must be a reproducible value regardless of the apparatus with which it has been measured. Unfortunately we do not live in such an ideal world and different pieces of apparatus, particularly thermometers, may lead to measurements which vary to some extent. Frequently organic chemists are willing to accept small discrepancies of, say 1°C, from a quoted literature value if the melting range is sharp, and the word 'uncorrected' may often be seen applied to melting point data in research literature. To correct any particular apparatus involves the determination of the melting points of a number of standard samples on the apparatus and the preparation of a calibration graph across its working temperature range. Corrected melting points can then be obtained from the graph, which is special to the apparatus, its environment and its component parts — a broken thermometer, for instance, will necessitate a new calibration graph. As poor technique (for instance heating the sample too quickly) can have a much larger effect on the measurement of a melting point than any inbuilt errors of the apparatus, it is not likely that you will be expected to correct your values in the teaching laboratory. In any case, the probable identity of an unknown is always best checked by a mixed melting point rather than by simply comparing with literature values. Nonetheless, you should be aware of the practice of correcting melting points.

Boiling point

Pure liquids which distil without decomposition will possess a sharp, constant boiling point, and will leave no residue on distillation to dryness. However, this property is very susceptible to fluctuations in atmospheric pressure and consequently an experimental determination of a boiling point may differ by several degrees from that reported in the literature. Indeed, as already discussed, the lowering of the boiling point of a substance with pressure is frequently used to advantage in the laboratory in reduced pressure distillation of thermolabile or high boiling compounds and in the removal of solvents using a rotary evaporator.

The effects of impurities on the boiling point of a liquid depend on the nature of the impurity and may commonly lead to a sharp boiling point. Therefore, it is dangerous to interpret a sharp, steady boiling point as evidence of purity in a liquid sample. As an obvious example, an involatile impurity leaves the boiling point of the distilling liquid unaffected (although the pot temperature will be higher than that of the boiling point of the pure liquid and the contaminant will remain as a residue after distillation). Unfortunately, the relationship between the temperatures of the liquid in the pot and the distilling vapour is not a reliable indication of the presence of impurities owing to the ease with which superheating can occur during a distillation.

The effects of volatile impurities on the boiling point of a mixture can vary depending on the nature and proportion of the volatile components present, but are generally manifested in one of three ways.

- The boiling point rises steadily over a certain boiling range.
- The boiling point appears to rise in a series of definite steps with detectable steady temperatures at intervals.
- The whole mixture boils at one steady temperature.

The second effect is really just an extreme case of the first and both can be illustrated by considering the phase diagram for the distillation of an ideal two-component solution as depicted in Fig. 3.47 and discussed on pp. 144–146.

It is rarely the case experimentally that a single distillation is sufficient to separate two components to an acceptable degree of purity; however, the use of a *fractionating column* can permit efficient separation of materials having boiling points as close as 20°C (pp. 148–152). The more efficient *spinning band* columns will permit separations of components having boiling point differences of as little as 0.5°C, but these are costly, highly specialized pieces of apparatus. The techniques for carrying out simple and fractional distillation are discussed in Chapter 3.

Azeotropes or constant boiling point mixtures

In some instances the components of a mixture form a constant boiling mixture which has a fixed composition and sharp boiling point (referred to as an *azeotrope*) and, in such a case, simple distillation is not sufficient to obtain the two liquid components of the mixture in pure form. Two types of azeotrope exist, namely the *minimum boiling azeotrope* and the *maximum boiling azeotrope*. These phenomena are common in both inorganic and organic systems, but it is usually the case that one of the components possesses a hydroxyl group. Examples of such azeotropes include the following:

- *Minimum boiling azeotropes*:
  95.6% ethanol/4.4% water (78.2°C/760 mmHg),
  60.5% benzene/39.5% methanol (58.3°C/760 mmHg).
- *Maximum boiling azeotropes*:
  79.8% water/20.2% hydrogen chloride (108.6°C/760 mmHg),
  77.5% formic acid/22.5% water (107.1°C/760 mmHg).

The forms of the phase diagrams corresponding to systems which yield minimum and maximum boiling azeotropic mixtures are shown diagrammatically in Fig. 4.6.

As can be seen from the diagram of the minimum boiling point azeotropic system, all other component mixtures boil at a higher temperature than the azeotropic composition, and so the azeotrope will always be the first to distil and will continue to do so until one of the components is exhausted.

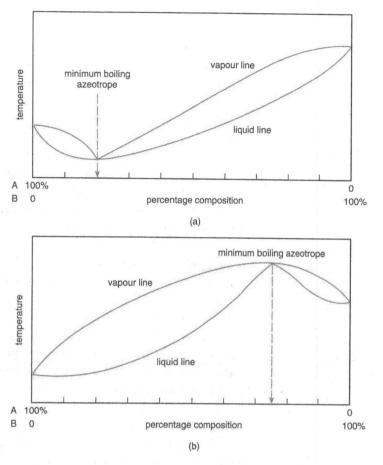

Fig. 4.6 Phase diagrams for a binary mixture forming (a) a minimum boiling point azeotrope; (b) a maximum boiling point azeotrope.

In the case of the maximum boiling point azeotropic system, attempted distillation will result in the initial removal of that component which is present in excess of the azeotropic composition. When the residue in the pot eventually reaches the azeotropic composition this mixture distils.

Azeotropes are frequently, but not always, a nuisance to the chemist — some can be quite useful. Water and benzene or toluene form minimum boiling azeotropes which can be used for removing water from systems (91.1% benzene/8.9% water has bp 69.4°C/760 mmHg; 79.8% toluene/20.2% water has bp 85.0°C/760 mmHg). The Dean and Stark apparatus (Fig. 3.27) has been designed to utilize these properties and provides an ingenious method of continuously removing water that is produced in equilibrating reactions, such as ketalization and enamine formation, in order to drive them to completion. The apparatus takes account of the facts that the azeotropes contain more water than will actually dissolve in the organic solvent at room temperature, and that water is denser than either benzene or toluene. The azeotrope compositions show that toluene is the more efficient for removing water and this, coupled with the high toxicity of benzene, makes toluene the solvent of choice for procedures involving azeotropic removal of water (albeit that its higher boiling point can sometimes be troublesome with sensitive materials).

More complex azeotropic mixtures exist and have also found use. For instance, anhydrous or 'absolute' ethanol used to be obtained by adding benzene to ethanol and removing the initial minimum boiling *ternary azeotrope* (three-component constant boiling mixture) consisting of 7.4% water, 18.5% ethanol and 74.1% benzene. Such alcohol contains traces of residual benzene which render it totally unsuitable for human consumption and also preclude its use as a solvent for UV spectroscopy.

Boiling point determination

If sufficient quantities of material are available, the boiling point can be determined by simple distillation, recording the still head temperature. Although this will frequently be the case, such a procedure is not applicable for boiling point determinations of limited quantities of compound and for such instances the following approach is recommended. *Do not forget, however, that any boiling point is meaningless if quoted without the pressure under which the determination has been carried out.*

See pp. 146–159 for distillation techniques

Microscale determination of boiling point

The boiling point of smaller quantities of liquid may be determined using the following technique. Seal a 5 cm length of 4 mm inside diameter thin-walled glass tubing at one end to make a small test tube and attach it to a thermometer with tape or an elastic band such that the sealed end of the tube is level with the bulb of the thermometer. Similarly seal the end of a melting point tube, cut the tube about 2 cm from the sealed end and place this, *open end first*, inside the first tube. Immerse the thermometer and attached tubes in an oil bath provided with means for heating and stirring, making sure that the elastic band does not touch the oil. Finally, using a pipette, introduce the liquid whose boiling point is to be determined to a depth of about 1 cm (Fig. 4.7).

Heat the oil bath with stirring and observe the tip of the inner tube carefully. Initially, a slow, erratic stream of air bubbles will be seen to leave the tube as the air inside warms up and expands, but this will eventually be replaced by a steady rapid stream of bubbles as the liquid reaches its boiling point. At this point, stop the heating but leave the sample in the oil bath, the temperature of which will continue to rise for a short while, depending on the rate of heating and the actual temperature of the bath. As the temperature begins to fall, examine the tube closely and record the temperature at which the stream of bubbles stops and liquid just begins to rise up within the inner capillary tube — this is the boiling point of the liquid. After allowing the bath to cool to about 20°C below the recorded boiling point, a second 2 cm sealed melting point

Fig. 4.7 Microscale determination of boiling point.

tube can be introduced into the liquid, and the procedure repeated using the new tube to obtain a confirmatory value. *Remember to record the prevailing atmospheric pressure when determining the boiling point.*

It is worthwhile considering how this experiment works. Initially, the heating bath causes the vapour pressure above the surface of the liquid to increase, resulting in the slow, erratic evolution of air and the gradual replacement of the air within the capillary with solvent vapour. Eventually the heating bath exceeds the boiling point of the liquid, which boils, causing the constant rapid stream of bubbles to be observed. When the bath is allowed to cool down to the boiling point of the liquid, the vapour pressure within the capillary becomes equal to ambient pressure and the liquid commences rising up the tube. Therefore the whole experiment is a very clever application of the fact that liquids boil when their vapour pressure equals that of the prevailing pressure above the liquid surface.

Quoting bath temperatures in short path distillations

The microscale boiling point described above is very neat, but the chances are that you will never actually use it, except perhaps as a laboratory exercise when being introduced to experimental techniques! The truth is that chemists are no different from the rest of the world in having an aversion to doing any more than the absolute minimum, and this certainly applies to determining the boiling points of small quantities of samples. What you will see frequently reported in the literature are bath temperature boiling points for materials which have been purified by short path distillation (see pp. 154–155). This is, of course, a measurement of the pot temperature and the boiling point of the compound cannot be derived from it. Nonetheless, this value is of use to others who may be following the procedure and so is a valid piece of information. However, it must always be borne in mind that the actual boiling point of the compound is somewhat lower than the reported bath temperature, particularly if the experiment is being carried out on a scale which permits a more standard distillation procedure where the still head temperature can be observed. In several experiments described in this book you will find the bath temperature has been quoted if a short path distillation is to be used to purify the product.

Refractive index

Another characteristic physical property of a liquid which can be used as a diagnostic feature is its refractive index. Quoting refractive indices is rapidly falling into disuse as a means of contributory evidence for purity or identity in the face of more sophisticated methods of spectroscopic analysis. It is not the aim of this book to enter into the debate as to whether the loss of such a practice is to be lamented or not! However, we must all be aware of falling into the trap of relying on increasingly sophisticated instrumentation and losing contact with the basic physical properties of compounds, as it is such awareness and 'feel' that make a good experimentalist. Certainly, refractive index determination should be part of every practical training programme — even if the technique may never be used very frequently in later life.

Refractive indices are conveniently determined using an *Abbé refractometer*, and are always quoted as n_D^t, where the subscript relates to the wavelength of the light used for the analysis (standardized to the D line of sodium at 589.3 nm) and the superscript refers to the temperature at which the determination was made (often standardized to 20°C although it is frequently sufficient to measure at room temperature as long as the temperature is stated). The great advantage of the Abbé refractometer is that it can operate using ordinary white light. The instrument gives a reading corrected to 589.3 nm and can compensate for dispersion effects resulting from the fact that the incident light is not monochromatic. It is not necessary to go into the details behind the operation of the refractometer, but as it relies critically on the quality and alignment of the prism faces on which the liquid sample is placed, *great care must always be taken not to mark or scratch the prisms and to clean the faces with soft paper tissue or cotton wool before and immediately after use.* This is another one of those cases where instant, official unpopularity will result from a moment's carelessness in the laboratory.

Take care of the prism surfaces

Using the Abbé refractometer

To determine the refractive index of your sample it is first necessary to deposit a thin film of the liquid between the prism surfaces in intimate contact with them. Expose the two prism surfaces by opening the clip and allowing the bottom prism in its mounting to swing down (Fig. 4.8a). Clean both surfaces

Fig. 4.8 The Abbé refractometer. (Redrawn by kind permission of Cambridge Instruments, Cambridge, UK.)

Always clean the apparatus thoroughly before and after use.

Take care with flammable solvents

thoroughly using tissue or cotton wool soaked in acetone (**flammable solvent**), held in a pair of solvent-resistant plastic tweezers. This avoids recontaminating the surfaces with grease from the hands. *Never use metal tweezers* which will scratch the surfaces if protruding through the soaked pad. Dry the surfaces thoroughly with a second pad, looking for the disappearance of interference patterns due to the presence of very thin layers of residual solvent. Dip a fire-glazed glass rod (or better a Teflon® rod) into your sample and touch the small amount of liquid adhering to the tip onto the ground glass surface of the bottom prism (*never the top prism*). It may be necessary to repeat this once or twice in order to transfer enough sample such that the prism surfaces will be completely covered when the apparatus is closed. When sufficient sample has been transferred, clamp the prisms together again. *Do not* give in to the temptation to smear out the sample over the prism surface with the glass rod as this will inevitably lead to scratching; the liquid will be spread out by the action of bringing the prisms together. As the prisms come very closely together, only a small amount of sample is necessary. One final word of warning: the tempting looking tubes which project from the prism housings are for thermostatically regulating the temperature of the sample if so desired and should *not* be used to introduce your sample!

Next it is necessary to focus on the set of cross-wires which are visible on looking down the eyepiece (or perhaps not, depending on the eyesight of the previous user). Do this by moving the eyepiece up and down carefully with a rotating motion, and when satisfied, turn the mirror under the microscope stage to get the best illumination from a suitably placed light source. Rotate the prism housing by means of the large knurled head screw at the side of the apparatus until the field appears partly light and partly dark in which the boundary may possess a more or less coloured fringe (Fig. 4.9a). Adjust the milled ring at the base of the microscope in order to get a sharp boundary, lacking any colour, between light and dark (Fig. 4.9b), and finally set the boundary exactly on the intersection of the cross-wires. It is the sharpness of this boundary which is affected by the optical quality of the prism surfaces; scratched or worn prisms make for a diffuse boundary. If insufficient sample has been placed on the prism it may be impossible to see any light–dark boundary, or the boundary may be visible in only part of the field of view (Fig. 4.9c). This situation can be simply rectified by putting some more sample onto the bottom prism as described above. The refractive index of the liquid can now be read off the scale using the magnifying eyepiece and the temperature at which the measurement was made must also be noted. The scale is normally divided to the third decimal place and the fourth decimal place can be obtained by estimation. Finally, open the prism box, clean the sufaces thoroughly with solvent, dry them carefully and close the box again, ready for the next person to use the refractometer.

Specific rotation

Substances having molecular dissymmetry are termed *chiral* and, if *resolved* into *enantiomers*, they possess the property of rotating the plane of plane polarized light as it passes through them. Such molecules are said to be *optically active*. The commonest cause of optical activity is the presence of an asymmetric carbon atom within the molecule but other structural features such as helicity (helicenes, *E*-cycloalkenes), orthogonality (biphenyls, allenes, spiranes) and extended tetrahedra (adamantanes possessing four different

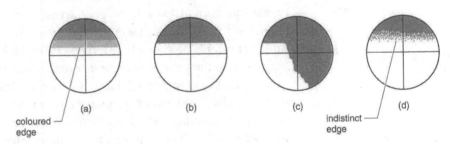

coloured edge   (a)   (b)   (c)   (d)   indistinct edge

Fig. 4.9 Appearance of the field of view using an Abbé refractometer: (a) before compensation for dispersion effects; (b) after compensation for dispersion effects; (c) insufficient sample on prism surfaces; (d) using an instrument with poor quality optical surfaces.

bridgehead substituents) also result in molecular dissymmetry leading to the potential for optical activity. As optical activity is an integral part of living systems and much of organic chemistry is involved with the isolation, study and synthesis of natural products, the organic chemist will usually need to measure an optical rotation at some stage.

The instrument used to measure optical rotation is called a *polarimeter*, and the principle of its operation is easy to understand. Plane polarized light is obtained by passing light from a sodium lamp (commonly measurements are made using the 589.3 nm D line of sodium) through a *polarizer*. This light is then passed through the sample, either as the neat liquid or in solution, which causes the polarization plane to be rotated to some extent depending on the optical activity of the sample. Nowadays, polarimeters are automatic and give this α value as a digital read-out and this permits the *specific rotation* of the sample to be calculated using the following formula

$$[\alpha]_D^t = \frac{100\alpha}{l\,c}$$

where $[\alpha]_D^t$ is the specific rotation at $t°C$, α is the number of degrees through which the incident beam has been rotated, l is the length of the sample tube in *decimetres* (1 dm = 10 cm, usually tubes are 1 dm long to make the calculation very easy) and c is the concentration of the sample in g per 100 mL.

The specific rotation of a neat liquid is given by the following expression

$$[\alpha]_D^t = \frac{\alpha}{l\,d}$$

where d is the density of the sample. By convention the specific rotation is quoted as a dimensionless figure. The units are $°cm^2 g^{-1}$; *not* degrees as is often seen in the literature!

When quoting the specific rotation of a sample, it is necessary to give the concentration of the solution and the solvent used as well as the temperature at which the measurement was made, as all of these factors affect the value obtained. For example, the specific rotation of an enantiomer of menthol might be quoted as: $[\alpha]_D^{20} = +49.2$ ($c = 5$, EtOH). The + sign before the value indicates that the plane of the incident light has been rotated in a *clockwise* manner and such substances are said to be *dextrorotatory* and given the prefix *d-*. The above sample is therefore *d*-menthol; its enantiomer is termed *laevorotatory*, indicated by the prefix *l-*. All of this can get rather confusing, not only because of the rather strange units used in the expressions for deriving $[\alpha]_D$, but also because the prefixes L- and D- are used to describe the absolute configuration of the highest numbered asymmetric carbon atom in sugars and the absolute configuration at the α-position of amino acids. Remember that *l-* and *d-* refer to a physical property—the ability of a compound to rotate plane polarized light—and L- and D- refer to molecular structure.

Automatic polarimeters are costly and delicate and you must seek instruction on the use of the particular instrument in your laboratory before attempting to use it alone. It is first necessary to zero the instrument with the solvent-filled cell in place and then a series of readings is taken with the same cell containing the sample. The sets of readings are averaged to give the value for the rotation. Remember that it is imperative to use the same cell for all measurements and that the cell should always be inserted the same way round into the polarimeter. There is frequently a good deal of oscillation of the last figure on the digital read-out, particularly with dilute samples or with those which are turbid. The average of the extremes of these oscillations should be taken.

It is the degree of care in preparing the sample that determines whether a reliable result will be obtained or not. It goes without saying that the sample must be made up accurately (usually a concentration of 2–5 g per 100 mL is about the right region to aim for) in a graduated flask. A 10 mL flask is normally convenient, as this results in an acceptable compromise between obtaining sufficient accuracy in the measurements and not requiring too much sample (which should be recovered afterwards in any event). The solution, when made up, must be totally free of suspended particles otherwise the dispersion of the polarimeter beam will make it difficult to obtain an accurate reading.

Cloudy solutions are no good for optical rotation measurements

A common type of sample cell used is an accurate tube of 1 dm (10 cm) in length closed at each end with optically flat glass plates and fitted with a central opening for filling (Fig. 4.10a). Such cells usually have a nominal capacity of 5 mL, but it will be necessary to make up more solution than this of course. Variations on this pattern include cells which are multiples of the standard 1 dm length, narrow bore micro-cells requiring only about 1 mL of solution (useful when limited quantities of material are available) which may be jacketed to permit measurements at a standard temperature (Fig. 4.10b).

Filling the cell demands a fair measure of care. It is imperative to avoid any air bubbles in the tube and, whilst this is not difficult with the centre-filled tubes, the narrow bore tubes, with openings at either end, sometimes encourage stubborn bubbles to cling to the inner walls. In such instances gently rocking the tube usually does the trick, and it is as well to do this under all cir-

All air bubbles must be removed from the sample

(a)   (b)

Fig. 4.10 (a) Standard polarimeter sample cell; (b) jacketed cell.

cumstances in order to remove any rogue bubbles. At all times avoid touching the end plates of the tube—the grease on your hands is optically active and will also result in dispersion of the beam.

When the measurement has been made, the sample should be recovered and the cell should be washed thoroughly in solvent and dried with a stream of nitrogen from a cylinder. Do not use compressed air lines to dry the cells as these are full of oil and grit and the tube will end up dirtier than at the outset.

Never dry apparatus using compressed air

One final word of warning is required regarding the values of specific rotation. Publications concerned with methods of enantioselective synthesis of optically active molecules often quote a specific rotation for a compound which is higher than that previously reported in the literature, implying this to be evidence of the higher optical purity of their product. Whilst this may well be true, traces of impurities having high specific rotations of the same sign as the major product will have dramatic effects on the $[\alpha]_D$ value of the bulk sample. Analysis by specific rotation alone is insufficient; there must always be additional confirmatory evidence of the homogeneity of the sample before such values can be meaningful.

Just because your $[\alpha]_D$ is higher does not necessarily mean your product is purer

Further reading

For discussions of the structural basis of optical activity in organic molecules, see: E.L. Eliel, S.H. Wilen and L.N. Mander *Stereochemistry of Carbon Compounds*, Wiley & Sons, New York, 1994, Chapters 3–8, 11, 13, 14.

J. March *Advanced Organic Chemistry*, 4th edn, Wiley & Sons, London, 1994, Chapter 4.

Chromatography: the problems of purity and identity versus homogeneity and a few hints

The practical aspects of carrying out chromatographic purification and analysis have been dealt with already in pp. 160–203. In this section we will address a little bit of philosophy and look at a few additional practical tricks.

The vexed problems of absolute proof of purity and identity using chromatography

How can a chemist *prove* that their compound is pure or that their compound is *identical* with an authentic sample? The straight answer is that demonstration of purity or identity to any degree of certainty is not possible using a single chromatographic analytical technique because such an analysis can only be considered to give meaningful information if more than one component is detected. If more than one spot is visible on the TLC plate or more than one peak is recorded on the GC trace then we do indeed have irrefutable evidence of contamination. However, a single spot on a TLC plate or a single peak on a GC trace, whilst an *indication* of purity (or identity in the case of a mixed analysis), can never in itself constitute *proof* of purity, as the *absence* of additional spots is a *negative result*. It can always be argued that the impurities have all eluted coincidentally to the same degree in the analysis system and that the observation of only one component is simply a consequence of the failure of the system to resolve the various constituents. Here we will consider briefly the sort of things the chemist can try in chromatographic analysis to increase the odds of being correct in assuming purity or identity.

Variation of TLC solvent systems or GC temperature programmes

If TLC analysis of a compound still indicates homogeneity when carried out using a second solvent system, or if GC analysis still shows only one peak on changing the temperature programme, this is stronger support for the conclusion that the compound is indeed pure. The counter-argument now depends on the constituents coincidentally having the same mobilities under two different analysis systems—a much less likely proposition.

A simple procedure which often works with TLC analysis is to carry out one analysis using an appropriate mixture of non-halogenated solvents to give an R_f value of approximately 0.5 (hexane, ether, ethyl acetate, methanol, for instance) and a second analysis with one of the components replaced by a halogenated solvent (for example, dichloromethane or chloroform for diethyl ether). It seems that, if two compounds have coincidentally identical R_f values in one such system, they may often be separated in the other. Of course, this will not work in every case, but it is quite a good first try and it is often useful to bear this in mind. To demonstrate identity when an authentic sample is available, it is necessary to carry out TLC analysis on mixtures of the authentic and unknown solutions, as even running two samples side by side on the same plate does not permit a sufficient degree of distinction (see Fig. 3.65). If the unknown is too precious to permit mixing some of it with another material, the two solutions can be spotted onto exactly the same point on the TLC plate (using different micro-pipettes of course) (see Fig. 3.65). Such analysis can be made even more sensitive by carrying it out as two-dimensional chromatography (see Fig. 3.66).

In GC analysis, the equivalent variation to changing eluting solvents can be considered to be changing the temperature programme. Again, substituting for a particular temperature programme, with a steady oven temperature set at the mid-point of the programme (or vice versa), sometimes has the desired effect. For purposes of attempting to demonstrate identity, it is necessary to carry out co-injection of the unknown and the authentic material. As before, if you do not want to mix the unknown with the authentic, a permissible technique involves taking up some of the unknown solution in the syringe, followed by a **very small** bubble of air (air destroys stationary phases) and then some of the authentic solution. In between taking up the two samples the needle should be wiped on a tissue; this and the small bubble of air minimize any cross-contamination.

Variation of stationary phases

Thin layer chromatography is frequently carried out on silica which is a relatively acidic support. Use of alumina-coated plates, in which the support is alkaline, often produces surprising variations in mobility (see solvent eluotropic series for both silica and alumina, (Table 3.11, p. 164). There are other frequently used TLC supports, but silica and alumina are probably the most useful for the organic chemist concerned with non-zwitterionic aliphatic and aromatic molecules.

The same principle applies to GC and, although it is rather a nuisance to have to change columns on a single machine, it is usually the case that several machines will be available, having complementary columns. If cast away on a desert island and able to take only two packed columns for GC analysis, the chemist would probably choose a column containing a relatively polar stationary phase such as polyethylene glycol adipate (PEGA) or Carbowax®, and a non-polar stationary phase such as SE-30 or OV-101. As a very simplistic approximation, non-polar stationary phases tend to separate molecules on the basis of their relative volatility, whereas the more polar stationary phases superimpose dipole–dipole interactions onto the volatility effect.

Capillary columns (pp. 194–195) are now frequently used as they possess a much larger number of theoretical plates than the equivalent packed columns and will sometimes resolve single broad peaks into a distressing number of components!

Use of different visualizing agents in TLC

Different visualizing systems often show very different colour reactions with different functional groups and so even compounds which co-elute may be distinguished from one another. The actual systems which are often used are discussed more fully in Table 3.12 (p. 170).

Conclusion

In the preceding sections of this chapter, we have looked at various criteria of purity which depend on the physical properties of the materials under study. In isolation, any one of these techniques will not permit the chemist to say with certainty anything about the purity or identity of any compound being studied; however, combinations of techniques do lend support to any provisional conclusions. The advantages of such techniques are that they are relatively rapid in execution and the apparatus required is usually readily to hand in the laboratory. Their main disadvantage is that, for *identification* purposes, it is necessary to have available an authentic sample, or data on the authentic material, before any conclusions can be made. Therefore the greatest use for these techniques is in permitting estimations of likely purity—or more correctly, any lack of it. In the next chapter we will consider the various techniques of spectroscopic analysis and how these can be used, usually in combination, to determine the structures of materials without any prior knowledge, except perhaps their provenance and probable degree of purity. Spectroscopic analysis requires much more expensive apparatus but, without doubt, the accuracy, sensitivity and non-destructive nature of these techniques have been the main reasons for the massive strides which have been made in research in organic chemistry over the last four or five decades.

4.2 Determining structure using chemical methods

The above discussion of the merits of spectroscopic analysis might have convinced you that there is never any need to carry out chemical analysis; do not allow yourself to be lulled into this false conclusion! Whilst it is true that modern structure determination relies very heavily on spectroscopic studies, increasingly with the more direct expedient of X-ray crystallographic analysis for the more complex materials, this does not remove the need for confirmatory chemical evidence. In addition, the derivatization procedures, designed specifically for forming highly crystalline compounds, are ideal for use in conjunction with X-ray work if the unknown itself is not crystalline.

It cannot be stressed strongly enough that the processes and logic involved in the chemical determination of the structure of an unknown provide the perfect chemical training. In essence, chemical analysis involves the use of degradative techniques to produce simpler and more readily analyzed compounds from an unknown. Its success therefore hinges on the ability to work with small quantities of material, and the accurate observation and interpretation of the results obtained. The development of these practical and theoretical skills provides the cornerstone for any chemical training.

The investigation of an unknown can be divided into four main stages.
- Preliminary observation of general physical characteristics of the material.
- Estimation of purity—with purification if necessary—and determination of the physical constants (melting or boiling point and refractive index).
- Identification of the elements and key functional groups present within the structure.
- Tentative proposal of candidate structures on the basis of the results from the first three stages and confirmation of identity by degradation or derivatization to furnish recognizable structures.

The classic means of carrying out these steps involves relatively small-scale work, with milligrams of material being used for each test. This approach will be described in the first part of this section. However, many of the degradative and derivatization reactions can be carried out on the microscale using analysis by TLC. The process of carrying out *in situ* chemical reactions on TLC plates (reaction thin layer chromatography, RTLC), which requires extremely small quantities of material, will be described in the latter part of this section. Needless to say, TLC can also be used for purity analysis of the original unknown and is also suited for the purification of small quantities of material.

Qualitative analysis

The procedures described in the following pages should be applied to any unknown and, on the basis of the results obtained, other confirmatory tests should be carried out. No rigid guidelines can be laid down here and the success of the analysis relies totally on the initiative and ability of the investigator—you. Negative results are as important in directing you to the correct conclusion as positive results.

NOTE: never forget that any unknown material has potentially dangerous properties and should be treated with all the precautions required for toxic and flammable materials.

Preliminary observation of general physical characteristics

Whilst the more specific physical properties of melting point or boiling point and refractive index will be crucial for the final identification of your material, the simple observation as to whether the material is solid or liquid is an important first guide for likely candidate structures.

Treat all unknown compounds with caution

Many procedures suggest that the odour (even the taste in some older texts!) of the compound should be noted. **This practice is strongly discouraged due to the likely toxicity of the unknown.** Many materials have disagreeable odours at the very least and many are intensely lachrymatory or worse. Any advantage from the minimal information obtained in this manner is heavily offset by the risks involved. Whilst any odour noticeable during handling should not be ignored, smelling the sample must be avoided.

Never sniff chemicals

Care! Check for flammable solvents

Heat a very small amount of the material on the tip of a spatula in a microburner flame. A luminous, sooty flame indicates that the compound possesses a high degree of unsaturation and may be aromatic, whereas a less coloured or blue flame indicates an aliphatic compound. Halogenated or highly oxygenated compounds often burn with difficulty or not at all. A residue remaining after burning is indicative of a metal salt and additional evidence for this can be obtained by testing the pH of the moistened residue — metal salt residues are often alkaline.

Solubility in distilled water is an indication that the compound either has a low molecular weight (particularly if a liquid) or possesses hydrophilic groups such as $-CO_2H$, NH_2 or $-OH$. Most monofunctional compounds with up to five carbon atoms show noticeable water solubility. A few crystals or a drop of liquid should be added to 0.5 mL of distilled water in a small test tube. Dissolution to give an acidic solution (pH 2–4) is evidence that the unknown is a carboxylic or a sulfonic acid. Compounds such as phenols are too weakly acidic to be detected in this manner. An alkaline solution (pH 10–12) indicates an aliphatic amine but, once again, heterocyclic bases such as pyridine and most aromatic amines are difficult to spot by this method.

Take care with corrosive reagents

If the compound is insoluble in distilled water, it should be similarly tested for solubility in aqueous acids and bases. Solubility in saturated sodium bicarbonate solution indicates the presence of a carboxylic or sulfonic acid, whereas insolubility in this weakly basic reagent but solubility in 2 M sodium hydroxide is evidence for a phenol or enolic material such as a 1,3-diketone. An intensification or appearance of colour on dissolution in the base often indicates that the material is aromatic. Solubility in 2 M hydrochloric acid is evidence for an amino compound or a heteroaromatic base. Any change in colour — often becoming weaker — can point to the presence of an aromatic amine. Any unknown insoluble in all of the reagents so far should also be checked for solubility in concentrated sulfuric acid (**take care!**). Most oxygenated and unsaturated aliphatic materials are soluble, whereas alkanes and unactivated aromatic compounds are insoluble. This can be a particularly useful piece of information. The general solubility behaviour of common classes of organic compounds is shown schematically in Fig. 4.11.

Take care with flammable solvents

The solubility of the material in some common organic solvents should also be examined to obtain an impression of its likely polarity. Light petroleum, dichloromethane, ethyl acetate and ethanol provide a representative range of solvents. Each test is easily carried out using 5–10 mg of the unknown in 0.5 mL of solvent and solubility in both cold and hot solvent should be examined. This information will be very helpful in deciding on the choice of solvent for recrystallization for solid unknowns (see pp. 131–140).

Purification and determination of physical constants

There is no point in analyzing impure material and so the very next thing you must do is to purify your material to homogeneity. Most organic compounds degrade to some extent on storage and so it is always good practice to carry out preliminary purification before proceeding with the analysis. (In the research situation, extensive purification will normally have been necessary to obtain the compound in the first place.) Any brown colouration in your sample is usually an indication that some degradation has occurred and this should disappear on purification. However, colours which persist after purification indicate the presence of chromophoric groups in the molecule, most commonly associated with aromatic structures.

For a full discussion of purification by crystallization and distillation, see the appropriate sections in Chapter 3

If the material is a solid it should be recrystallized to constant melting point and the melting point of the purified material should be noted. Impure low melting solids may appear as a mixture of crystals and liquid and should be purified by low temperature recrystallization. Liquids should be distilled using the standard distillation procedure if sufficient material is available, or a

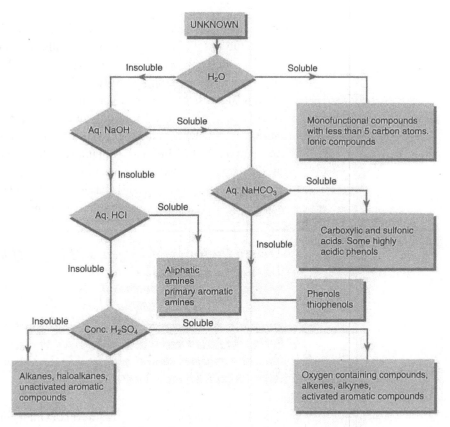

Fig. 4.11 Solubility behaviour of common classes of organic compounds.

short path or microscale distillation apparatus if not. If the material decomposes on attempted distillation at atmospheric pressure (indicated by extensive darkening or evolution of fumes) it will require reduced pressure distillation. If only a small amount of material is available, an accurate boiling point can be determined using the small-scale procedure previously described (pp. 216–217). In addition, the refractive indices of pure liquids should be measured routinely.

At the completion of these two phases of observations, you should have some impression of the overall properties of your unknown—its degree of unsaturation, whether it is acidic, neutral or basic, and an idea of its polarity. In addition, you will have the specific information relating to its physical constants for confirmatory evidence in the final analysis. The next stage is to determine the elemental constitution and the types of functional group present in the molecule.

Qualitative determination of elemental composition

In addition to the usual elements of carbon, hydrogen and oxygen, commonly encountered elements in organic molecules are nitrogen, sulfur, phosphorus and halogens. These may be detected using the *Lassaigne fusion* technique where the unknown is heated with metallic sodium, or by *Middleton's fusion* using sodium carbonate and zinc in place of sodium. Middleton's method is the less hazardous, being more suitable for use in crowded teaching laboratories, and it is also considered to be superior to Lassaigne fusion for the analysis of volatile compounds. The disadvantage of Middleton's method is that very pure zinc powder is required if spurious positive results for sulfur and halogens are not to be obtained. A blank test should always be carried out on the stock material when it is first prepared.

In both methods analysis is based on the conversion of the heteroatoms to inorganic salts such as cyanide, sulfide or halide.

Determination of nitrogen, sulfur, phosphorus and halogens by Lassaigne sodium fusion

NOTE: *owing to its potentially hazardous nature, the fusion operation should be carried out behind a safety screen in a hood designated for this procedure. No other work should be allowed to take place in the same hood during the fusion and it is recommended that gloves be worn for this operation. The analyses should also be carried out in a hood although, at this stage, individuals may share the same hood.*

The analysis may involve the evolution of small amounts of hydrogen cyanide and hydrogen sulfide. It should be borne in mind that the toxicity of hydrogen sulfide is about the same order of magnitude as that of hydrogen cyanide. Fortunately, its repulsive smell serves as adequate warning of its presence. For both reasons, detecting hydrogen sulfide by its odour—although at times unavoidable—is not recommended.

Equipment	safety screen, microburner, test tube holder, 6 × soda glass test tubes 5 cm × 1 cm, evaporating basin, crucible tongs, 10 cm × 10 cm wire gauze, tripod; apparatus for filtration

Materials		
unknown sample		
sodium metal	4 mm cube	**flammable, corrosive**
iron (II) sulfate		
aqueous sulfuric acid (5%)		**corrosive**
aqueous disodium pentacyanonitrosyl ferrate (0.1%) (sodium nitroprusside, sodium nitroferricyanide)*		**toxic**
aqueous nitric acid (5%)		**corrosive**
aqueous silver nitrate solution (5%)*		**corrosive**

Continued

Box cont.

chlorine water* (an equivalent reagent may be prepared from 10% aqueous NaOCl, acidified with one-fifth of its volume of 10% aqueous HCl)	**corrosive**
ammonia solution (conc. *ca.* 30%)	**corrosive, toxic, lachrymator**
ammonium molybdate reagent* (prepared by dissolving 4.5 g $(NH_4)_2MoO_4$ in 4 mL concentrated ammonia solution, adding 12 g NH_4NO_3 and diluting the mixture to 100 mL)	**toxic, irritant**
zirconium–alizarin red S paper* (for the preparation of this paper see the section in part 4 on fluorine detection)	

The reagents marked (*) are most conveniently prepared as stock solutions on the day of the experiment

Procedure

1. Sodium fusion

HOOD
SAFETY SCREEN

Place about 20 mg of your sample in the bottom of a small soda glass test tube, using a pipette for liquid samples to ensure that no sample is smeared on the upper part of the tube. Add 10 mL of distilled water to an evaporating basin, and place this in the hood behind the safety screen. Using a test tube holder which supports the tube firmly (crucible tongs allow the tube to rock and are not suitable), introduce a piece of sodium about the size of a small pea —

[1]*Care!*

roughly a 4 mm cube — into the mouth of the test tube,[1] without allowing it to come into contact with the substance at the bottom. With the safety screen in place and the front of the fume hood pulled well down, heat the sodium gently over a small microburner flame until it melts and runs down into the sample. There may be a very vigorous reaction when the molten sodium touches the sample, particularly if halogens are present. Heat the tube gently for 1 min, and then heat more strongly until the bottom 2 cm of the tube glows red hot. Holding the gauze with tongs in your free hand, drop the red-hot tube into the water in the evaporating basin and immediately place the gauze on top.[1] (The tube will shatter on contact with the water, releasing any unreacted sodium, and the gauze stops the loss of any material.) Allow any excess sodium to react and when the reaction has subsided, place the evaporating basin on the gauze

[2]*See Fig. 3.6*

on a tripod and boil the solution for 2 min. Filter the solution whilst hot,[2] to remove the broken glass and charred material, and pour an equal quantity of the colourless, alkaline filtrate into five test tubes.

2. Sulfur

Add 2 mL of the disodium pentacyanonitrosyl ferrate stock solution to one of the test tubes. A purple colouration which fades slowly on standing indicates sulfur is present. If a stock solution is not available, dissolve a small crystal of the reagent in 2 mL of distilled water and add this to your sample.

3. Nitrogen

Add *ca.* 200 mg of iron (II) sulfate to the second test tube, heat the solution to boiling and add sufficient dilute sulfuric acid to dissolve any precipitate and make the solution acid. The formation of a deep blue precipitate or colouration (Prussian blue) indicates the presence of nitrogen. If the colour of the mixture makes it impossible to tell if any blue colouration has been formed, filter the mixture, washing the filter paper with distilled water, and examine the residue for the blue colouration.

4. Halogens

To the third test tube, add sufficient nitric acid to render the solution acidic and boil the mixture until its volume has been halved. (The heating has the effect of removing any HCN or H_2S if cyanides or sulfides are present which would interfere with this test. It may be omitted if nitrogen and sulfur have been shown to be absent.) Add 1 mL of the silver nitrate solution to this mixture. The observation of a white or yellowish precipitate indicates the presence of halogen. To identify the halogen present, add chlorine water dropwise to the fourth tube with gentle shaking. The appearance of a brown colouration indicates bromine or iodine. In the latter case, addition of excess chlorine water will cause the brown colouration to disappear as the iodine is further oxidized to iodate. Confirmation may be obtained by adding concentrated ammonia solution to the third tube containing the precipitate. Total dissolution is indicative of iodine; by the process of elimination, a sample which gives a white precipitate with silver nitrate, but no colouration on treatment with chlorine water, must contain chlorine. In addition the white precipitate will be unaffected by the ammonia solution.

Fluorine is not frequently encountered in undergraduate qualitative analyses due to the toxicity of many compounds which contain it. Fluorine will not be detected by the standard tests for halogens and, if it is desired to test for its presence, the following additional procedure should be carried out.

Acidify *ca.* 2 mL of the filtrate with glacial acetic acid, reduce the volume of the solution to one-half by boiling, and spot the resultant mixture onto zirconium–alizarin red S paper. The appearance of a yellow spot on the red paper is a positive result indicating the presence of fluorine, although the presence of phosphate or sulfate ions in the filtrate can interfere with this result.

The zirconium–alizarin red S paper can be prepared by dipping filter paper sequentially into 5% aqueous zirconium nitrate, 5% aqueous hydrochloric acid and 2% aqueous alizarin red S solution (sodium alizarin sulfonate), followed by drying in air.

5. Phosphorus

Acidify the sample in the fifth test tube with dilute nitric acid and boil the mixture for 2 min. Add an equal volume of the ammonium molybdate solution, warm the mixture to *ca.* 40–50°C and allow to stand. The formation of a yellow precipitate indicates the presence of phosphorus.

Determination of nitrogen, sulfur and halogens by sodium carbonate–zinc fusion (Middleton's method)

In this method nitrogen and halogens are converted to sodium cyanide and sodium halides, respectively, and these are detected in the same manner as in the Lassaigne fusion. Any sulfur present is converted to zinc sulfide which is decomposed with dilute acid and the H_2S liberated is detected with lead acetate paper. Although less hazardous than the Lassaigne fusion, the analysis must be carried out in the hood.

Equipment   (as for the Lassaigne fusion)

Materials
unknown sample
zinc powder–sodium carbonate mixture
aqueous lead (II) acetate (5%)   **cancer suspect agent, toxic**
reagents for nitrogen and halogen analysis as used in the Lassaigne fusion
It is recommended that the zinc powder–sodium carbonate mixture be prepared as a stock reagent by grinding intimately together 25 g of anhydrous sodium carbonate and 50 g of high purity grade zinc powder. This quantity is sufficient for about a dozen experiments and a blank test should be carried out on the reagent to confirm the absence of halogens and sulfur

---

Procedure

1. Fusion

HOOD

In a test tube mix your unknown (*ca.* 100 mg) with sufficient of the zinc–sodium carbonate reagent to fill the tube to a depth of 1 cm. Without further mixing, top up with a further 2 cm of the reagent. Place about 10 mL of water in the evaporating dish to receive the hot tube after fusion and place this behind the safety screen. With the tube held horizontally, gently heat the reagent nearest the open end of the tube and slowly increase the rate of heating until this region becomes red hot. Gradually permit the heating to extend the length of the tube until the whole mass is at red heat. **Too rapid heating at this stage may cause vigorous evolution of gases and the ejection of red-hot solid from the tube. Stop heating temporarily if this appears likely.** Finally, heat the tube in the vertical position for 2 min and then drop it into *Care!* the water contained in the evaporating dish.[1] Boil the contents of the dish for 2 min and then filter the hot mixture.[2] Retain the residue (which will be required for the sulfur test) and split the filtrate equally into three test tubes.

2. Nitrogen

Test the filtrate in one of the tubes in the same manner as described in the Lassaigne fusion.

3. Halogens

Test the other two tubes for halogens in the same manner as described in the Lassaigne fusion.

4. Sulfur

Wash out the evaporating dish and return the residue in the filter paper to it. Add about 10 mL of 5% hydrochloric acid to the residue and cover the evaporating dish with a filter paper moistened with the lead acetate solution. The formation of a brown stain on the paper indicates the presence of sulfur in the original sample. ∎

Other investigations

With the information from these three stages of analysis to hand, you are now in a position to make preliminary proposals as to the nature of your unknown. When looking for candidate structures on the basis of the melting point or boiling point you have recorded for your unknown, it is necessary to include for consideration compounds which have values within 5°C of that which you have obtained.

Frequently, at this stage you will be required to report your preliminary findings and proposals to an instructor in order to avoid wasting time following erroneous conclusions. You may also at this stage be able to obtain or study spectroscopic data (IR, NMR, MS) associated with your unknown in order to corroborate your findings and direct your thinking (Chapter 5). Even the most basic spectroscopic examination will be of great help at this stage; for instance, examination of the IR spectrum of a suspected alcohol or ketone will immediately support or disprove your initial proposal.

For the sake of this exercise, however, it will be assumed that you do not have access to any spectroscopic data and are relying solely on chemical evidence. Whatever your situation, it is now necessary to pinpoint the actual compound from your list of candidate structures. This will involve the preparation of at least two derivatives and, obviously, the type of functional group present (alcohol, ketone, amine, etc.) will dictate the type of derivative to prepare. However, you should bear in mind that the particular derivatives chosen ought to have melting points that enable clear differentiation between other possible structures within that series.

Functional group identification

Your unknown will probably possess functionality which will place it in one or more of the classes of compounds listed in Table 4.1. Except in the teaching laboratory, it is rare for an unknown to possess just one functional group and you must always be aware of the possibility that more than one functional group may be present. Although the classification in Table 4.1 only holds for monofunctional compounds, the sequence of analysis described here can be applied to any unknown.

From the experimental results so far, you will have a general idea about the types of functional groups present in your unknown. Firstly, it is necessary to confirm the presence of these functional groups; then crystalline derivatives can be prepared to identify the actual substance by comparison of melting points with literature values. The ideal derivative should be simply and quickly prepared by a high yielding, unambiguous route and should also be easily purified and identified. As these manipulations are normally carried out on relatively small amounts of material, this requires a solid derivative with a sharp and definite melting point, preferably between 50 and 250°C. In this work, you would be well advised not to jump to premature conclusions about the likely identity of your compound. Always prepare one derivative and check that its properties agree with those expected before leaping into the preparation of the second confirmatory derivative. Much student time is wasted in qualitative analysis by attempting to prepare two unsuitable derivatives at the same time.

The tests performed so far will have enabled you to pinpoint fairly accurately any class of compound showing acidic or basic properties, and the choice of which confirmatory tests to carry out and which derivatives to prepare should be easy. This situation also holds for neutral compounds containing a halogen or nitrogen. However, neutral compounds lacking nitrogen, sulfur, phosphorus or a halogen require further investigation. The order of the confirmatory tests for these functional groups is very important and should not be varied. It follows a logical sequence of events, with each test building on the results of the previous ones. The testing order follows the reactivity of the functional groups, with the most reactive groups being checked for first. Consequently, *positive results with the later tests in the sequence will be meaningful only if the earlier tests have proved negative*, as the more reactive functionalities will interfere to give spurious positive results.

Neutral compounds in which nitrogen, halogens, sulfur and phosphorus are absent

Aldehydes and ketones

Both classes of compounds will give crystalline derivatives called *hydrazones* when reacted with 2,4-dinitrophenylhydrazine. If the crystalline product is yellow, this indicates a saturated carbonyl compound; an orange precipitate

Table 4.1 Common classes of monofunctional organic compounds.

Neutral compounds	Acidic compounds	Basic compounds
C, H, O compounds	*C, H, O compounds*	*C, H, N compounds*
Aldehydes	Carboxylic acids	Amines
Ketones	Anhydrides	Nitrogen heterocycles
Esters	Phenols (weakly acidic)	
Alcohols		*C, H, N, halogen*
Ethers	*C, H, O, halogen compounds*	*compounds*
	Acyl halides	Quaternary ammonium
C, H compounds		salts
Alkenes	*C, H, S compounds*	
Alkynes	Aryl thiols (weakly acidic)*	
Arenes		
Alkanes	*C, H, S, O compounds*	
	Sulfonic acids	
C, H, halogen compounds		
Halides		
C, H, N, O compounds		
Nitro compounds		
Amides		
C, H, N compounds		
Nitriles		
C, H, S compounds		
Thioethers*		
Thiols*		
C, H, O, S compounds		
Sulfoxides		
Sulfones		
C, H, P compounds		
Phosphines*		
C, H, O, P compounds		
Phosphonates		
Phosphites*		

*These compounds are generally unsuitable for use in the teaching laboratory for reasons of odour or toxicity.

indicates an α,β-unsaturated system and a red precipitate indicates an aromatic ketone or aldehyde.

yellow, orange or red precipitate

If this test is positive, differentiation between ketones and aldehydes is possible due to the fact that aldehydes are oxidized to carboxylic acids under mild conditions, whereas ketones are not. Systems used for this differentiation include chromic acid oxidation and *Tollen's*, *Fehling's* and *Benedict's* reagents; only the Tollen's procedure will be described here.

$$RCHO \xrightarrow{2Ag(NH_3)_2OH} RCO_2NH_4 + 3NH_3 + H_2O + Ag\downarrow$$

black precipitate
or
silver mirror

If you suspect that your unknown is a methyl ketone, confirmatory evidence for this can be obtained by carrying out the *iodoform reaction*. A note of caution is necessary here, however. Alcohols which can be oxidized to methyl ketones will also give a positive result in the iodoform reaction, and so the iodoform reaction must only be applied after confirmation of the presence of a carbonyl group.

pale yellow precipitate

2,4-Dinitrophenylhydrazone formation (Brady's test)
To the unknown (2–3 drops of liquid or *ca.* 50 mg of solid) dissolved in a few drops of methanol, add 1 mL of Brady's reagent* and shake. If no precipitate is formed, boil the mixture for 1 min and cool in ice. The appearance of a yellow, orange or red precipitate of the 2,4-dinitrophenylhydrazone indicates the presence of a carbonyl compound.

Differentiation between aldehydes and ketones (Tollen's test)
To the unknown (2–3 drops of liquid or *ca.* 50 mg of solid) add 0.5 mL of freshly prepared Tollen's reagent.† The formation of a black precipitate or a

*Brady's reagent. This is best prepared as a stock solution by dissolving 2,4-dinitrophenyl-hydrazine (1.0 g) in concentrated sulfuric acid (5 mL), adding this solution slowly with stirring to a mixture of water (7.0 mL) and absolute ethanol (25 mL), and filtering to remove any suspended solid.

†Tollen's reagent. This reagent must be prepared immediately before use from the following stock solutions: (Continued on p. 238.)

silver mirror on the walls of the test tube, either immediately or on warming in a beaker of hot water, constitutes a positive test for an aldehyde. The silver mirror will only form if the test tube has been thoroughly cleaned.

Test for methyl ketones or compounds capable of being converted to them (iodoform reaction)

Dissolve the unknown (2–3 drops of liquid, *ca.* 50 mg of solid) in aqueous dioxan (1:1) and add 2 mL of 3 M aqueous sodium hydroxide, followed by 3 mL of iodine solution.* A positive result is indicated by the disappearance of the brown colouration and the formation of a pale yellow precipitate (mp 119°C) which has a characteristic pervasive antiseptic odour which should be detectable without the need to smell the reaction directly.

Do not smell the reaction mixture directly

If an aldehyde or ketone is found to be present, suitable derivatives to prepare are *2,4-dinitrophenylhydrazones*, *oximes* (p. 254). Other derivatives which may be prepared include *phenylhydrazones*, *4-nitrophenylhydrazones*, *semicarbozones* and *dimedone derivatives* (aldehydes only).

Esters

Esters react with hydroxylamine to produce hydroxamic acids which give a purple or deep red colouration with iron (III) chloride. Carboxylic acids and anhydrides, acyl halides and phenolic or enolic compounds may interfere with this test. These can all be ruled out, however, by their solubility in aqueous sodium hydroxide. The derivatization procedure for esters relies upon saponification to the constituent acid and alcohol, followed by separation and preparation of suitable derivatives of both of these (pp. 268–269 and 255–257).

hydroxamic acid   red/purple complex

Test for esters

To the unknown (2–3 drops of liquid or *ca.* 50 mg of solid) add a saturated ethanolic solution of hydroxylamine hydrochloride (10 drops) and 20%

Cont.
silver nitrate (2.5 g) in distilled water (42 mL) — solution A,
potassium hydroxide (3.0 g) in distilled water (42 mL) — solution B,
concentrated ammonia solution (30%).
Add the concentrated ammonia solution to solution A (3 mL) until the initial brown precipitate has almost totally redissolved to give a greyish slightly cloudy solution. Add solution B (3 mL) to this and then add more concentrated ammonia solution until the mixture is almost clear again.

NOTE: excess reagent must not be stored as it decomposes on standing to yield a potentially explosive solid.

*Iodine solution. A stock solution may be prepared by dissolving iodine (25 g) in a solution of potassium iodide (50 g) in distilled water (200 mL).

ethanolic potassium hydroxide (10 drops). Heat the mixture to boiling, acidify with 5% hydrochloric acid and to this add a 5% solution of iron (III) chloride dropwise. A deep red or purple colouration due to the formation of an iron (III) salt of the hydroxamic acid is a positive result.

Alcohols and ethers

A neutral compound containing only carbon, hydrogen and oxygen which is neither a carbonyl compound nor an ester is liable to be an alcohol or an ether. These two classes of compounds may be distinguished from each other by the use of acetyl chloride, which reacts vigorously with alcohols to form an ester and evolve hydrogen chloride, which may be detected with indicator paper. Ethers are unreactive, but adventitious water will interfere, giving a seemingly positive result. If in doubt, dry your compound and always use a dry test tube. Phenols, carboxylic acids and amines will also react with acetyl chloride but should have been ruled out due to their non-neutrality.

$$ROH \xrightarrow{CH_3COCl} RO-\overset{O}{\overset{\|}{C}}-CH_3 + HCl\uparrow$$

If an alcohol containing the $-CH(OH)CH_3$ group is suspected, the iodoform reaction may be applied. Primary, secondary and tertiary alcohols may be distinguished using Lucas' reagent which converts tertiary alcohols rapidly to the insoluble chloride, secondary alcohols more slowly and primary alcohols not at all.

$$ROH \xrightarrow{ZnCl_2, \text{ conc. HCl}} RCl\downarrow$$

Suitable crystalline derivatives of alcohols are *urethanes* (pp. 255–256) and *3,5-dinitrobenzoates* (pp. 256–257).

Reaction with acetyl chloride

HOOD

In a dry test tube place the unknown (*ca.* 0.5 mL of liquid or 500 mg of solid — most alcohols encountered will be liquid) and add acetyl chloride (0.3 mL) dropwise by pipette. A reaction, indicated by the mixture becoming warm and the evolution of hydrogen chloride, is a positive indication for an alcohol.

Differentiation between primary, secondary and tertiary alcohols (Lucas' test)

HOOD

To the unknown (0.5 mL) in a test tube, add 3 mL of Lucas' reagent,* close the tube with a cork, shake for 15 s and allow to stand. Observe the mixture after 5 min when the following results may be seen.

---

*Lucas' reagent. A stock solution may be prepared by adding anhydrous zinc chloride (68 g) in portions to concentrated hydrochloric acid (45 mL) with cooling. This must be carried out in the hood.

- Solution totally clear (some darkening may occur) — *primary alcohol.*
- Solution becomes gradually cloudy (*ca.* 5–10 min) — *secondary alcohol.*
- Solution goes cloudy immediately — *tertiary alcohol.*

This test has its drawbacks, however. Allyl alcohols give results similar to secondary alcohols and the biphasic mixtures resulting from water-insoluble primary and secondary alcohols may be mistaken for a positive result for a tertiary alcohol. Preparation of derivatives is the only sure way to identify the alcohol.

Test for ethers

Ethers are difficult compounds to identify simply. However, if you think that your neutral unknown contains oxygen (e.g. by solubility in conc. H_2SO_4) and the functional group tests thus far have proved negative, it is likely to be an ether. Owing to their inertness, ethers are difficult compounds to derivatize. Symmetrical ethers can be cleaved with 3,5-dinitrobenzoyl chloride in the presence of zinc chloride and the crystalline 3,5-dinitrobenzoates can be characterized (p. 258). Unsymmetrical ethers are problematical, however, and identification in the absence of spectroscopic data relies mainly on their physical properties.

Alkenes and alkynes

Tests for unsaturated hydrocarbons are based on their ready ability to undergo electrophilic addition reactions. A simple test involves shaking with a solution of bromine water and observing whether or not the solution is decolourized. However, this test is not unequivocal as some alkenes react only very slowly with this reagent.

A better test is to look for decolourization of a solution of potassium permanganate (*Baeyer test*), but this test must only be carried out after determining the absence of other easily oxidized groups such as aldehydes.

Test for unsaturation using aqueous potassium permanganate (Baeyer test)
Dissolve the unknown (2–3 drops of liquid or *ca.* 50 mg of solid) in ethanol (2 mL) and add 1 drop of a 0.1 M solution of potassium permanganate. If the purple colouration is discharged with the formation of a brown/black precipitate of manganese dioxide, continue adding the solution dropwise, counting

the drops, until the purple colouration persists. Repeat this procedure with a blank solution of ethanol; a significant difference in the number of drops needed for persistence of the purple colour indicates the presence of an unsaturated hydrocarbon.

Both alkenes and alkynes may be derivatized by the formation of their crystalline addition products with 2,4-dinitrobenzenesulfenyl chloride (pp. 258–260).

Alkanes and arenes

Both alkanes and simple arenes are insoluble in concentrated sulfuric acid, whereas alkenes and alkynes undergo sulfonation to give soluble products. Although some polyalkylated aromatic compounds are also sufficiently reactive to be sulfonated and therefore dissolve, these should give a negative reaction with the test for unsaturation using bromine water. Distinction between alkanes and arenes is possible by reacting with chloroform in the presence of anhydrous aluminium chloride. Alkanes are unreactive and give little or no colour change, whereas arenes undergo a series of Friedel–Crafts alkylations resulting in colour changes which are frequently quite characteristic.

$$\text{ArH} \xrightarrow{\text{CHCl}_3, \text{ AlCl}_3} \text{Ar}_3\text{CH}$$

Owing to the chemical inertness of aliphatic hydrocarbons there are no satisfactory derivatization procedures and so identification relies heavily on the observation of physical properties. Aromatic hydrocarbons may be nitrated or any alkyl side chains may be oxidized with alkaline potassium permanganate to give aromatic acids. In a two-step procedure, aromatic compounds may be converted to the corresponding *sulfonamide* via chlorosulfonylation (pp. 260–261) and treatment of the resultant arylsulfonyl chloride with ammonia. Another convenient means of derivatizing aromatic compounds involves the formation of the 1:1 π-complex with 1,3,5-trinitrobenzene (p. 261).

Distinction between alkanes and arenes

Dissolve the unknown (3 drops of liquid or *ca.* 100 mg of solid) in dry chloroform (1 mL) in a clean dry test tube and wet the sides of the tube by shaking vigorously. Add a spatula tip of powdered anhydrous aluminium chloride to the tube so that it clings to the wet sides. The observation of a bright colouration, ranging from red to blue, where the three components have come into contact is a positive test for an aromatic compound. These colours are often characteristic of particular classes of arene and examples are given in Table 4.2.

Neutral compounds containing a halogen

The fusion test will have shown which halogen is present in your unknown, but

Table 4.2 Colour reactions of aromatic compounds with $AlCl_3$–$CHCl_3$.

Compound class	Colour
Benzene and alkylated derivatives	Orange to red
Naphthalene	Blue
Anthracene	Green
Phenanthrene	Purple
Biphenyl	Purple

it is also possible to obtain evidence about the degree of substitution of the carbon to which the halogen is attached by reacting it with ethanolic silver nitrate. As reaction proceeds via an S_N1 mechanism to give the alkyl nitrate and silver halide, tertiary halides are much more reactive than secondary halides, and these in turn are more reactive than primary halides. Benzylic and allylic halides, which ionize readily to generate resonance stabilized cations react with silver nitrate at a similar rate to tertiary halides, but halogens at sp^2 hybridized centres, such as vinyl or aryl halides, are unreactive. The rate of reaction is judged by observing the rate of formation of a precipitate of silver halide.

$$RX \xrightarrow{AgNO_3, EtOH} R-ONO_2 + AgX \downarrow$$

$X = Cl, Br, I$ white (X=Cl), cream (X=Br) or yellow (X=I) precipitate

If an aromatic halide is suspected, the $AlCl_3$–$CHCl_3$ test for an aromatic ring may be applied to the unknown; an orange or red colouration being a positive result for the aromatic ring. Primary and secondary aliphatic bromides and iodides may be characterized as S-alkylated thiouronium salts (p. 263). Chlorides react poorly but the yield can be improved by adding some potassium iodide to the reaction mixture. Tertiary halides give anomalous results, however, but you may rely on physical data to characterize these. Aromatic halides are best converted to their 2,4-dinitro derivatives which are high melting point solids (p. 264).

Ethanolic silver nitrate test for distinguishing tertiary, secondary, primary and aryl halides

Add 1 drop of the halide to a 0.1 M solution of silver nitrate in ethanol (2 mL) and leave the mixture at room temperature for 5 min. If no white or cream precipitate is observed, warm the mixture in a water bath and observe any change. Tertiary halides normally react in the cold, whereas secondary and primary halides require heating, with primary halides giving a much more slowly formed precipitate. Aromatic halides give no precipitate. Iodides are the most reactive, and bromides are more reactive than chlorides. This test may give spurious positive results if a carboxylic acid group is present, owing to the formation of an insoluble silver salt, and so should only be applied to neutral compounds. (There is a method for ruling out this possibility but a slight error in the procedure might lead to an explosive reaction. It is better just to use this test for compounds that are known to be neutral.)

Neutral compounds containing nitrogen

Three common classes of compounds fall into this category: nitriles, amides and nitro compounds. If you believe your unknown to be one of these, it is simplest to test first for the presence of a nitro group.

Nitro compounds

Both aliphatic and aromatic nitro compounds are oxidizing agents and their presence can be detected using freshly prepared iron(II) hydroxide which is oxidized to the brown iron(III) hydroxide.

$$RNO_2 \xrightarrow[\substack{\text{greenish-blue} \\ \text{solid}}]{Fe(OH)_2} RNH_2 + Fe(OH)_3 \downarrow$$

brown precipitate

Hydroxylamines, alkyl nitrates, alkyl nitrites and nitroso compounds also give this reaction, but are less likely to be encountered in the teaching laboratory (nitroso compounds must never be used in the laboratory as they are potent carcinogens).

Characterization of nitro compounds is a relatively lengthy procedure involving reduction to the corresponding amines (pp. 264–265) and derivatization of the amine. Aromatic compounds possessing alkyl substituents may be oxidized to the corresponding aromatic carboxylic acids if preferred.

Iron(II) hydroxide test

Add the unknown (2 drops of liquid or *ca.* 50 mg of solid) to a freshly prepared solution of 5% aqueous iron(II) ammonium sulfate (2 mL) in a test tube. Add 1 M sulfuric acid (3 drops) followed by a 2 M ethanolic solution of potassium hydroxide (1 mL), stopper the tube and shake it. If the initially formed blue precipitate turns brown within 1 min this is a positive result for the presence of a nitro group. Any slight darkening or greenish colour forming during this time does not constitute a positive test.

Nitriles and amides

Both primary amides and nitriles may be hydrolyzed to carboxylic acid salts and ammonia with aqueous sodium hydroxide. The two can usually be distinguished by the rate of hydrolysis, as nitriles are more slowly hydrolyzed than primary amides in base (amides are intermediates in the hydrolysis of nitriles). Nitriles are relatively easily hydrolyzed by warming in concentrated sulfuric acid.

$$RCONH_2 \xrightarrow{\text{aq. NaOH}} RCO_2^- + NH_3 \uparrow$$

$$RCN \xrightarrow{\text{aq. } H_2SO_4} RCO_2H + NH_4^+$$

Another aid to differentiation is that nitriles are usually liquids, whereas amides are almost invariably solids. Access to IR data would also permit ready differentiation between the two types of functionality. Characterization of primary amides and nitriles consists of hydrolysis to their corresponding acids whereas secondary and tertiary amides also necessitate identification of the amine component (pp. 271–274).

Alkaline hydrolysis

Add the unknown (4–5 drops of liquid or *ca.* 100 mg of solid) to 2 M aqueous sodium hydroxide (2 mL) and boil the mixture. Test for the evolution of ammonia with damp litmus or universal indicator paper. The rapid evolution of ammonia is indicative of a primary amide, slower evolution indicates a nitrile.

Neutral compounds possessing sulfur

No sane analysis course in a teaching laboratory will include thiols or thioethers due to their repulsive odours. Should one ever come your way, you will not need, or want, to prepare any derivatives. This is one instance when you will have no choice but to smell the compound! Sulfoxides and sulfones, however, are odourless and may well appear in a laboratory course. Generally sulfoxides are crystalline solids, whereas sulfones are liquids. Having decided that your unknown is a neutral compound that contains sulfur, it should be possible to identify it on the basis of its physical properties. Sulfoxides may be distinguished from sulfones by oxidation with potassium permanganate, but only if other easily oxidized groups are absent.

Acidic compounds in which halogens and sulfur are absent

The solubility tests using aqueous sodium bicarbonate and aqueous sodium hydroxide will have given a good indication whether or not your unknown is a phenol or a carboxylic acid. One source of confusion might come from the low rate of hydrolysis of some anhydrides. If in doubt, shake the tube containing the unknown and sodium bicarbonate, leave it for a few minutes and look for the steady evolution of small bubbles of carbon dioxide. Simple phenols ($pK_a = 9$–11) are weaker acids than carbonic acid ($pK_a = 6.35$) and so do not displace carbon dioxide from its salts. The few exceptions are phenols possessing electron-withdrawing groups in the 2- and 4-positions such as 2,4,6-trinitrophenol (picric acid, $pK_a = 0.38$). These tend to be brightly coloured solids, however, and should be readily recognizable.

Carboxylic acids and anhydrides

The liberation of carbon dioxide from aqueous sodium bicarbonate, coupled with the absence of halogens or sulfur, is sufficient evidence to justify proposing that your unknown is a carboxylic acid or anhydride. The two may be differentiated from each other using thionyl chloride which does not react with anhydrides, but converts carboxylic acids to acyl chlorides with the liberation of sulfur dioxide and hydrogen chloride. A positive result for a carboxylic acid is a steady, continuous evolution of gas; but remember that any moisture will react with the thionyl chloride giving a spurious result.

$$RCO_2H \xrightarrow{SOCl_2} RCOCl + HCl\uparrow + SO_2\uparrow$$

Differentiation between a carboxylic acid and an anhydride

Place the unknown (3 drops of liquid or *ca.* 50 mg of solid) in a dry test tube. Add 3 drops of thionyl chloride using a pipette, allowing the reagent to run down the side of the test tube. Observe the mixture; a steady fizzing and evolution of gas at the point where the unknown and the thionyl chloride meet indicates a carboxylic acid is present. Any slow evolution of gas may be due to moisture present in the sample but should cease fairly rapidly.

Carboxylic acids may be derivatized by conversion into the corresponding *phenacyl esters* ($RCO_2CH_2(CO)Ar$) which are easy to prepare and highly crystalline (pp. 268–269). The 4-bromophenacyl and 4-phenylphenacyl esters are commonly prepared. Another popular derivatization procedure is the preparation of the *S-benzylisothiouronium* salt. However, this suffers from the drawback that the *S*-benzylisothiouronium chloride used to prepare the derivative decomposes to the extremely malodorous benzyl thiol if the reaction conditions are allowed to become too alkaline.

Anhydrides may be characterized by hydrolysis to the corresponding acid (pp. 269–270) (unsymmetrical anhydrides pose too many problems for simple qualitative analysis) or may be converted to *N*-phenyl amides, often referred to as *anilides*. The carboxylic acid products from hydrolysis may of course be derivatized further.

Phenols

Insolubility in aqueous sodium hydrogen carbonate but solubility in aqueous sodium hydroxide indicates a phenol. Simple phenols give moderately strong blue or purple colour reactions with iron(III) chloride whereas polyhydroxylated aromatic molecules give more varied colours, or are oxidized if the hydroxyl groups have a 1,4-relationship to each other. The colour reaction is much less strong than the intense purple colouration given by esters or 1,3-dicarbonyl compound derivatives with this reagent and can be used to distinguish between phenol and 1,3-dicarbonyl compounds which may show similar acidity.

HOOD

Many phenols yield crystalline *benzoates* when reacted with benzoyl chloride in aqueous sodium hydroxide (*Schotten–Baumann reaction*, see pp. 272–273) and *3,5-dinitrobenzoates* are also commonly prepared; in this instance the reaction proceeds best in pyridine solution. An indirect derivatization procedure makes use of the high reactivity of phenols towards electrophilic aromatic substitution to prepare crystalline polybrominated derivatives using an excess of an aqueous solution of bromine (pp. 262–263). This procedure is only suited to simple phenols, however, as polyhydroxylated aromatics undergo ready oxidation and any deactivating groups on the aromatic ring inhibit reaction. Other derivatives which are often prepared are *aryloxyacetic acids* (p. 257).

Acidic compounds possessing halogen

The only monofunctional compounds which fall into this category are the acyl halides, their acidic properties being a consequence of ready hydrolysis to carboxylic acids and hydrogen chloride. They are simply distinguished from carboxylic acids possessing a halogen substituent by their vigorous reaction with water to evolve a hydrogen halide. Derivatization procedures are the same as for anhydrides.

Acidic compounds possessing sulfur

The common strongly acidic monofunctional compounds which fall into this category are the sulfonic acids and these are derivatized in very much the same manner as carboxylic acids, giving *S*-benzylisothiouronium salts (p. 268). Alternatively they may be converted via the sulfonyl chloride (pp. 274–275) to sulfonamides (pp. 273–274). Another derivative commonly prepared is the *p-toluidine salt*, obtained by reaction of the sodium salt of the sulfonic acid with 4-methylaniline (*p*-toluidine) (p. 275).

Aryl thiols are weakly acidic ($pK_a = 6$–8) and dissolve in aqueous sodium hydroxide. The presence of such a compound will manifest itself without the need for any rigorous chemical analysis, however. As previously stated, the use of any thiol as an unknown in a class experiment is really not a practical proposition due to the repulsive odours of these compounds.

Basic compounds

The basic organic compounds are all amines of one sort or another. If the unknown contains a halogen and dissolves in water to give an alkaline solution, it is a quaternary ammonium halide. These compounds are crystalline and, whilst it may be sufficient to compare the melting point of the unknown with literature values, quaternary ammonium salts are frequently hygroscopic and in such cases are not amenable to simple analysis. Aliphatic amines dissolve in water to give a strongly alkaline solution. Primary, secondary and tertiary amines may be distinguished by *Hinsberg's method* in which the amine is reacted with an arylsulfonyl chloride (pp. 273–274). Primary and secondary amines both react to give sulfonamides; those derived from primary amines possess a relatively acidic proton on the nitrogen and dissolve in aqueous alkali, whereas those derived from secondary amines are insoluble in base. Tertiary amines react to yield water-soluble salts of the arylsulfonic acid.

$$RNH_2 \xrightarrow{ArSO_2Cl} RNHSO_2Ar \xrightarrow{aq.\ NaOH} \underset{soluble}{RNSO_2ArNa^+}$$

$$R_2NH \xrightarrow{ArSO_2Cl} R_2NSO_2Ar \xrightarrow{aq.\ NaOH} no\ reaction$$

$$R_3N \xrightarrow{ArSO_2Cl} R_3\overset{+}{N}SO_2Ar\ Cl^-$$

A quicker means of distinction, involving reaction of the amine with nitrous acid, is *not* recommended as secondary amines react with this reagent to give a class of compounds called nitrosamines of which many members are potent carcinogens.

$$RNH_2 \xrightarrow[HCl]{aq.\ NaNO_2} \left[R-\overset{+}{N}\equiv N \right] \xrightarrow{H_2O} ROH + N_2\uparrow$$
$$\underset{\substack{unstable \\ diazonium\ salt}}{}$$

$$R_2NH \xrightarrow[HCl]{aq.\ NaNO_2} R_2N-N=O \underset{(carcinogen)}{\overset{nitrosamine}{}}$$

$$R_3N \xrightarrow[HCl]{aq.\ NaNO_2} \overset{+}{R_3NH}\ Cl^-$$

Benzoylation under *Schotten–Baumann* conditions (pp. 272–273) and acetylation with acetic anhydride (pp. 271–272) are suitable derivatization procedures for aliphatic and aromatic primary and secondary amines. Other derivatives which might be prepared include formamides, phenylthioureas and picrates. The crystalline 1:1 molecular complexes with picric acid are also suitable derivatives for tertiary amines (p. 274).

Reaction thin layer chromatography for ultra small-scale characterization of functional groups

Before continuing with this section or attempting any characterizations using RTLC, you should read pp. 165–175 which describe the various techniques and procedures of analysis using thin layer chromatography.

The technique of RTLC, which permits the simple and rapid characterization of several important functional groups and requires only minute quantities of material, can be traced back to the work of J.M. Miller and J.G. Kirchner in 1953. In essence, the unknown is spotted onto the baseline of a TLC plate and then over-spotted with the characterization reagent. After allowing some time for the reaction to proceed, the TLC plate is developed alongside samples of the unknown and reagent as standards, and is visualized as usual.

The technique can be considered to be a natural extension of the procedure for following the progress of a reaction by TLC. The difference in this case is that the reaction is allowed to take place on the TLC plate itself instead of in a flask. A new spot appearing in the mixed sample which does not have a counterpart in either of the two standard samples indicates reaction of the unknown with the reagent and gives a good indication of the presence of the functional group — 'good indication' — but not proof.

There are perfectly good reasons why a reaction may occur on the TLC plate which does not involve the particular derivatization reaction which is being examined; hydrolysis or dehydration brought about by acid in a reagent for instance. With a little thought, however, such side reactions may be minimized and the technique can provide good experimental evidence for functionality using quantities of material which would be difficult or impossible to analyze using classic or even spectroscopic analysis. Table 4.3 shows a list of

Table 4.3 Derivatization and functionalization procedures amenable for use in RTLC.

Reaction	Reagent system
Acetylation of alcohols	Acetic anhydride Acetyl chloride
Benzoylation of alcohols	Benzoyl chloride
Dehydration	Sulfuric acid (concentrated)
Derivatization of alcohols	3,5-Dinitrobenzoyl chloride Phenyl isocyanate
Derivatization of carbonyl compounds	2,4-Dinitrophenylhydrazine
Halogenation of alkenes or phenols	Bromine
Catalytic hydrogenation	H_2/catalyst
Methylation of acids	Methanol/sulfuric acid (concentrated) Diazomethane
Nitration	Nitric acid (concentrated)
Oxidation	Chromium(VI) oxide/glacial acetic acid 30% Hydrogen peroxide Ozone Peracid
Reduction	Lithium aluminium hydride Sodium borohydride Tin(II) chloride

reactions which may be carried out using the technique. Modifications of the basic procedure such as *elatography* involve applying the reagent to the plate as a band through which the unknown passes on development. Alternatively the reagent can be included in the stationary phase or the eluting solvent. These more complex procedures have been reviewed by Beroza (1977) and those interested are directed to this article. The simple double spotting technique will be sufficient for our needs (Fig. 4.12).

Procedure

The analysis is carried out in exactly the same way as a normal TLC analysis with the one difference that a certain period of time is allowed to elapse between double spotting the reagent with the unknown and developing the TLC plate. To encourage reaction even more, the TLC plate may be warmed *gently*, but this should be avoided wherever possible, as organic compounds are highly prone to aerial oxidation when highly dispersed on the adsorbant. Incomplete reaction before development is indicated by the presence of a new spot accompanied by a spot corresponding to residual starting material. On leaving the plate for a longer period before developing or increasing the amount of reagent applied, the new spot should appear to increase at the expense of that corresponding to unreacted starting material.

As well as allowing time for the reaction to proceed, the spots must also be as dry as possible before development, otherwise the residual solvents in

A = PhCH$_2$OH
B = A + C
C = CH$_3$COCl in diethyl ether

A = PhCHO
B = A + C
C = NaBH$_4$ in methanol

(a)

(b)

Fig. 4.12 Examples of RTLC analysis: (a) esterification of benzyl alcohol with acetyl chloride; (b) reduction of benzaldehyde with methanolic sodium borohydride (adsorbant, silica G$_{254}$; eluting system, diethyl ether–light petroleum 1:1; visualization, 254 mm UV light).

which the reagent was applied will interfere with the analysis. When the reagent is dissolved in a high boiling point solvent, or the unknown is a sensitive material, it is frequently advantageous to apply the reagent first, dry the plate and apply the unknown afterwards. This order of application is also worth trying when the reagent is dissolved in a polar solvent. This will avoid enlarging the unknown spot on application of the reagent, and will remove problems due to subsequent distortion of the spots on the developed chromatogram (see Fig. 3.69, p. 174). Some reagents, for example Brady's reagent, tail badly if too much is spotted onto the plate and it is advisable to find the optimum quantity of reagent to use before carrying out the analysis. In the cases where gaseous reagents are used (catalytic hydrogenation, oxidation), the unknown is spotted onto the plate and the gas is played onto the spot in a slow stream using a Pasteur pipette before development of the plate.

The solvent system should be such that the unknown has an R_f value of *ca.* 0.5, but any solvent that undergoes reaction with the derivatizing reagent is precluded. For instance, acetone cannot be used for the development of reductions using hydride reagents and likewise methanol for chromium(VI) oxide oxidations.

The use of two-dimensional TLC provides additional sophistication in searching for a compound possessing a specific functional group within a mixture of compounds (see Fig. 3.66, p. 172). The mixture is first spotted in the corner of a square TLC plate and the first development is carried out as usual. The plate is then dried and a line of reagent is applied carefully to the whole of the new baseline for the second development. After drying and reaction, the plate is developed a second time at 90° to the first. The developed plate should be compared with a two-dimensional analysis of the same mixture carried out without the intermediate *in situ* reaction.

The next paragraphs contain some practical advice for carrying out the TLC reactions listed in Table 4.3, but it is impossible to generalize the procedures. Each individual case will require optimization of eluting solvent composition and stationary phase as well as optimization of the quantities of reagent to use, and the length of time between application and development.

Acetylation and benzoylation of alcohols

All these RTLC analyses should be carried out in a hood

The acylating agents are added as 10% solutions in dry ethyl ether to the unknown, previously spotted onto the TLC plate, and the solvent is allowed to evaporate. Reactions with acetyl chloride may be developed as soon as the spot appears to be dry. Reactions with acetic anhydride and benzoyl chloride are better left for 5 min before drying the spot with a current of air and developing the plate. The ester products will be less polar than the starting alcohols in the vast majority of cases. Use of alumina TLC plates may be advantageous with acid-sensitive alcohols.

Dehydration

Apply a small quantity of neat concentrated sulfuric acid to the unknown spot. The TLC plate may be developed after 30 s. As the products may be much less polar than the starting alcohols, it is usually more practical to check for disappearance of starting material than for the appearance of new spots. Any residual starting material may have a slightly different R_f value to that of the standard due to interference by the concentrated acid on the baseline.

Derivatization of alcohols

Apply the 3,5-dinitrobenzoyl chloride or the isocyanate as 10% solutions in dry diethyl ether. Allow the solvent to evaporate and allow at least 5 min for reaction before development.

Derivatization of carbonyl compounds

Brady's reagent is spotted onto the plate first, and the spot is allowed to become almost dry, using a stream of air to encourage drying. The unknown is spotted onto the reagent and the plates are developed after 5 min. An advantage of using Brady's reagent is that the 2,4-dinitrophenyl-hydrazones are visible to the naked eye. The disadvantage of these derivatives is their relative insolubility in common solvents with the effect that it is very easy to overload TLC plates.

Bromination of unsaturated hydrocarbons

Care!

A 5% solution of bromine in acetic acid is applied to the unknown spot on the TLC plate and the acetic acid and excess bromine are removed with a current of air. Development proceeds as soon as the spot appears dry.

Catalytic hydrogenation

Care! No naked flames

A solution of the unknown in diethyl ether, in which the catalyst has been suspended, is spotted onto the plate and the solvent is allowed to evaporate. In the hood, a slow stream of hydrogen is played onto the spot for 15 min with the tip of the Pasteur pipette held 2 mm from the surface of the plate. The plate may be developed immediately after this period. Reductions of double bonds may give products with very similar R_f values to the starting material, but these frequently visualize differently with some spray reagents; it is necessary to experiment.

Methylation of carboxylic acids

A small quantity of concentrated sulfuric acid is spotted onto the plate, followed by a 5% solution of the carboxylic acid in methanol. After 5 min the plate is developed. The esters are less polar than the starting acids. The use of diazomethane for RTLC has been described but is not recommended. Although it methylates carboxylic acids instantly, its toxicity, volatility and explosive nature do not make it an easy reagent to manipulate in this manner. Above all, a micro-pipette must *never* be dipped into a solution of diazomethane as rough surfaces can catalyze an explosive decomposition.

Nitration

Phenols may be nitrated by co-spotting with concentrated nitric and then drying the plate in a current of warm air. Development of the plate proceeds as soon as the spot appears dry.

Oxidation

Care! Oxidants

Chromium(VI) oxide or peracetic acid are applied to the unknown as solutions in acetic acid, and hydrogen peroxide is applied as the 30% aqueous solution. The plates are dried in a current of warm air after 5 min and developed.

Reduction

Care! Solutions of metal hydrides are highly flammable and react vigorously with water

A freshly prepared saturated ethereal solution of lithium aluminium hydride or freshly prepared 5% methanolic sodium borohydride are spotted onto the unknown. The spots are allowed to dry and the plate is developed after 5 min. Owing to their different reducing abilities, a combination of these two systems allows the differentiation of ketones and aldehydes from esters and carboxylic acids, the latter two being unaffected by sodium borohydride; whereas all are reduced by lithium aluminium hydride.

Tin(II) chloride, applied as a solution in glacial acetic acid, may be used for the reduction of aromatic nitro compounds to anilines. The solvent is removed with gentle warming and the plate is developed after 5 min.

Further reading

The following works provide further introductions to the techniques of RTLC and contain many useful references:

M. Beroza, *Chimia (Supplement) — Column Chromatography* (ed. E.Sz. Kovatz), *Chimia*, 1977, p. 92.

K. Blau, and G.S. King, *Handbook of Derivatives for Chromatography*, Heyden, London, 1977, p. 323.

A.M. Osmam, M. El-Gorby Younes, and F.M. Ata, *J. Chem U.A.R.*, 1970, **13**, 273.

J.C. Touchstone, *Practice of Thin Layer Chromatography*, Wiley (Interscience), New York, 1983, p. 214.

Preparation of derivatives

The confirmation of which functional groups are present in your unknown, together with the knowledge of its physical properties, should enable you to narrow the range of possible candidate structures. Indeed, it is possible that the data available to you will only fit for one particular substance. However, as generic compounds having melting points or boiling points within 5°C of that obtained from your unknown must be included for consideration, it is likely that you will still have two or more structures as possible candidates. It is now time to prepare two derivatives of your unknown and compare the melting points of these with literature values. Tables of melting points of derivatives have not been included in this book as it would be impossible to provide anything like a comprehensive list for each functional group that might be encountered. Besides which, an important part of the exercise of identifying your unknown is using the chemical literature. There are many sources of such information, some more complete than others, but no single work is exhaustive. Some, such as the *CRC Handbook, Vogel's Textbook* and the *Dictionary of Organic Compounds*, are particularly useful for this kind of information and it is highly likely that the details you require will be contained somewhere within one of these works; the full details of these are given at the end of this section.

The choice of which derivative to prepare will be largely governed by the functional groups within the molecule; an extreme category being the alkanes which cannot be derivatized. Nonetheless, it is usual that you will be presented with a choice of possibilities and it is up to you to decide. Whilst convenience of preparation should be borne in mind, a paramount consideration is that the derivative should not have a melting point much lower than 50°C, as crystallization of the crude material might be difficult, causing purification problems. Even more important is the need for a derivative having a melting point sufficiently different from that of the same derivative of other candidate structures. For example, an unknown alcohol with a boiling point of 99°C might be 1-propanol (bp 97°C) or 2-butanol (bp 99°C). The respective 3,5-dinitrobenzoate esters of these alcohols have melting points of 74°C and 75°C and therefore will not permit differentiation between the two candidate structures. However, their 1-naphthylurethane derivatives have melting points of 80°C and 97°C respectively, which will permit this distinction, and so these should be prepared.

The following list of derivatization procedures is not comprehensive but has attempted to include those which are most convenient and useful. The procedures are listed by functional group, more or less in the same order as the characterizations have been described. All require filtration with suction (pp. 77–79) and small-scale recrystallization (pp. 137–138) at some stage, and some involve distillation (pp. 146–159) or periods of reflux (pp. 96–100). The level of difficulty of the procedures calls for some prior experience with basic manipulative techniques and your attention is drawn to the hazards associated with some of the reagents used. Where appropriate, suggested quantities of reagents are given in the materials section, and the smaller volumes of liquid reagents quoted may be estimated accurately enough using a simple 1 mL graduated Pasteur pipette. The derivatizations may be carried out on slightly larger or smaller scales by modifying the quantities pro rata, but if you want to change the scale by a factor of 10 or more, consult an instructor before proceeding.

Aldehydes and ketones

Preparation of dinitrophenylhydrazones

Equipment	Apparatus for filtration and recrystallization	
Materials		
unknown sample	*ca.* 0.20 g	
2,4-dinitrophenylhydrazine	0.25 g	**toxic**
sulfuric acid (98%)	0.50 mL	**corrosive, oxidizer**
ethanol		**flammable, toxic**

Procedure

Add ethanol (5 mL) to the 2,4-dinitrophenylhydrazine in a 25 mL Erlenmeyer flask and add the concentrated sulfuric acid cautiously to the suspension with constant swirling during the addition.[1] Dissolve the unknown carbonyl compound in a small volume of ethanol and to this add the clear supernatant[2] of the 2,4-dinitrophenylhydrazine reagent. Warm the mixture if no solid separates immediately, and then allow to stand for 10 min. If a precipitate still does not form, add water dropwise until precipitation occurs. Filter off the solid with suction and wash it with 1:1 aqueous methanol (5 mL). Recrystallize the solid from ethanol or ethyl acetate to constant melting point.

[1]*Care! Exothermic*

[2]*Do not transfer undissolved solid*

Preparation of oximes

Equipment	apparatus for filtration and recrystallization	
Materials		
unknown sample	*ca.* 0.5 g	
hydroxylamine hydrochloride	1.0 g	**corrosive**
sodium acetate trihydrate	2.0 g	
ethanol		**flammable, toxic**

Procedure

Dissolve the hydroxylamine hydrochloride and sodium acetate in 5 mL of distilled water in a 25 mL Erlenmeyer flask, and to this solution add the unknown carbonyl compound. If the unknown is not soluble in the aqueous system, add ethanol dropwise until solution occurs. Swirl the mixture with warming for 10 min on a water bath and then cool in ice. Filter off the precipitated solid with suction and recrystallize to constant melting point from ethanol, ethyl acetate or aqueous ethanol.

∎

Alcohols and phenols

Many of the derivatives for characterizing alcohols (3,5-dinitrobenzoates, urethanes) may be used equally successfully for phenols. Phenols may also be characterized directly as benzoate esters, by adapting the Schotten–Baumann procedure described for derivatizing amines (pp. 272–273), and as aryloxy-acetic acid derivatives; they can also be characterized indirectly by bromination of the aromatic ring (pp. 262–263).

Preparation of urethanes

$$ROH \ + \ ArN{=}C{=}O \longrightarrow$$

$$\left(Ar = \quad Ph{-} , \quad \right)$$

Both naphthyl and phenyl urethanes are useful derivatives of alcohols, but phenyl isocyanate used for the preparation of the latter derivatives is highly lachrymatory and is also readily decomposed by any moisture to form diphenylurea (mp 238°C) which can interfere with the derivatization. 1-Naphthyl isocyanate is more stable to hydrolysis (dinaphthylurea, mp 297°C) and is less lachrymatory, and consequently is the reagent of choice for urethane preparation. A further advantage is that the 1-naphthylurethane derivatives have higher melting points than the phenyl analogues. The procedure below is readily adapted for the preparation of phenylurethanes and may also be used for preparing urethane derivatives of phenols.

Equipment	apparatus for filtration and recrystallization		
Materials			
unknown alcohol	*ca.* 1.0 g		
1-naphthyl isocyanate	0.5 mL		**lachrymator,**
light petroleum (bp 40–60°C)			**flammable**

HOOD

Procedure

Measure the alcohol into a dry test tube and add the 1-naphthyl isocyanate to it in one portion. *Loosely* plug the mouth of the tube with cotton wool, shake to mix the contents and allow to stand for 5 min with occasional shaking. If no solid separates during this period, warm briefly on a water bath and cool the mixture in ice, scratching the sides of the tube with a glass rod to encourage crystal formation. Filter off the solid with suction and recrystallize it to constant melting point from light petroleum, after first removing any 1-naphthylurea which is insoluble in the light petroleum. If crystallization of the reaction mixture cannot be induced by the heating–scratching procedure, digest the whole mixture with light petroleum, filtering off any insoluble material, and remove the solvent on the rotary evaporator to furnish crude urethane suitable for further recrystallization.

Preparation of 3,5-dinitrobenzoates

$$ROH \; + \quad \text{(3,5-dinitrobenzoyl chloride, —COCl)} \quad \longrightarrow \quad \text{(3,5-dinitrobenzoate, —CO}_2\text{R)} \; + \; HCl$$

3,5-Dinitrobenzoate esters are suitable derivatives for both alcohols and phenols for which the following general procedure is applicable. However, this is not necessary for volatile alcohols which can be derivatized simply by heating with twice the weight of 3,5-dinitrobenzoyl chloride for 10 min and cooling the mixture.

Equipment	apparatus for filtration, recrystallization and extraction	
Materials		
unknown alcohol or phenol	*ca.* 0.5 mL (0.5 g if solid)	
3,5-dinitrobenzoyl chloride	1.0 g	**lachrymator, corrosive**
pyridine	2.0 mL	**flammable, irritant**
diethyl ether		**flammable, irritant**
light petroleum (bp 40–60°C)		**flammable**
ethanol (alternative recrystallizing solvent to light petroleum)		**flammable, toxic**
aqueous hydrochloric acid (5%)		**corrosive**
aqueous sodium hydroxide (5%)		**corrosive**

Procedure

HOOD

Place the unknown, the 3,5-dinitrobenzoyl chloride and the pyridine in a test tube. Stopper the tube loosely with cotton wool and heat the mixture on a water bath for 15 min (30 min if the unknown is believed to be a tertiary alcohol). Allow the mixture to cool, add diethyl ether (20 mL) to the mixture and extract with dilute hydrochloric acid (3 × 25 mL) to remove pyridine. Wash the organic phase with dilute sodium hydroxide solution (25 mL) to remove any 3,5-dinitrobenzoic acid (and unreacted phenol if the unknown is phenolic) and dry over MgSO₄. Filter the solution and remove the solvent on the rotary evaporator. Recrystallize the residue from light petroleum or aqueous ethanol.

Phenol characterization by aryloxyacetic acid preparation

$$ArONa + ClCH_2CO_2Na \longrightarrow [ArOCH_2CO_2Na] \xrightarrow{H^+} ArOCH_2CO_2H$$

Equipment	apparatus for filtration, recrystallization and extraction	
Materials		
unknown phenol	ca. 0.20 g	
chloroacetic acid	0.25 g	corrosive, toxic
sodium hydroxide	0.25 g	corrosive
diethyl ether		flammable, irritant
ethanol		flammable, toxic
aqueous hydrochloric acid (5%)		corrosive
aqueous sodium carbonate (5%)		corrosive

Procedure

HOOD

Measure the phenol and sodium hydroxide into a test tube and then add water (1 mL) and the chloroacetic acid. Heat the mixture on a steam bath and add sufficient water to render the mixture homogeneous. Continue to heat the mixture for 1 h, allow to cool and then acidify by dropwise addition of dilute hydrochloric acid. Filter off with suction any solid which precipitates and recrystallize it to constant melting point from aqueous ethanol. If no solid forms on acidification, extract the acidic solution with diethyl ether (2 × 10 mL). Wash the combined organic phases with water (2 × 10 mL) to remove excess chloroacetic acid and then with 5% aqueous sodium carbonate[1] (3 × 10 mL) to extract the aryloxyacetic acid derivative as its sodium salt.

[1] Care CO₂ evolved

Cautiously acidify this aqueous extract,[1] filter off the precipitate with suction and recrystallize from aqueous ethanol. ∎

Ethers

Owing to their lack of reactivity, ethers are difficult compounds to derivatize, particularly unsymmetrical aliphatic ethers, where it is necessary to rely on the physical constants of the unknown for characterization. However, if the ether is believed to be symmetrical it is possible to carry out a one-pot cleavage of the ether linkage and obtain the 3,5-dinitrobenzoate ester derivative of the cleavage products. If the ether is aromatic, there is scope for characterization by electrophilic substitution of the aromatic ring. Bromination is a convenient procedure and that described for derivatization of phenols may be followed (pp. 262–263).

Cleavage of an ether and derivatization of the resulting alcohol

$$R-O-R \xrightarrow[ZnCl_2]{} RCl + \text{(3,5-dinitrobenzoate)}-CO_2R$$

Equipment	apparatus for reflux (with protection from atmospheric moisture), filtration and recrystallization

Materials		
unknown symmetrical ether	*ca.* 2.0 mL	
3,5-dinitrobenzoyl ether	1.0 g	**lachrymator, corrosive**
anhydrous zinc chloride	0.3 g	**irritant, toxic**
ethanol		**flammable, toxic**
aqueous sodium carbonate (10%)		**corrosive**

Procedure

HOOD

Weigh out the zinc chloride rapidly, grind it to a fine powder and add this to a dry 25 mL round-bottomed flask. Add the 3,5-dinitrobenzoyl chloride followed by the ether and arrange the apparatus for reflux with protection from atmospheric moisture. Heat the mixture on a boiling water bath for 1 h and allow to cool. Dismantle the apparatus, carefully add 5 mL of aqueous sodium carbonate[1] to the residue and heat the mixture on the boiling water bath, with stirring, for 1 min. When evolution of gas subsides, add a further 5 mL and repeat the process until a total of 20 mL of sodium carbonate solution has been added. Allow the mixture to cool and filter off the solid residue with suction. Recrystallize the product to constant melting point from aqueous ethanol. ∎

[1]Care! Exothermic

Alkenes and alkynes

Alkenes and alkynes may be characterized conveniently by preparing the crystalline adducts with 2,4-dinitrobenzenesulfenyl chloride. Moreover, as addition to the unsaturated linkage is stereospecifically *anti*, it is possible to differentiate between *E*- and *Z*-alkenes which give isomeric adducts possessing different melting points. However, owing to the lack of other suitable general derivatization procedures for alkenes and alkynes, it will be necessary also to rely on the physical constants of the unknown.

Derivatization of alkenes

Equipment	apparatus for filtration and recrystallization	
Materials		
unknown alkene	*ca.* 0.3 g	
2,4-dinitrobenzenesulfenyl chloride	0.2 g	**lachrymator, corrosive**
glacial acetic acid	3.0 mL	**corrosive**
ethanol		**flammable, toxic**

Procedure

HOOD

Dissolve the 2,4-dinitrobenzenesulfenyl chloride and the unknown alkene in 3 mL of glacial acetic acid in a test tube and heat for 15 min on a steam bath. Allow the mixture to cool, pour onto crushed ice and stir until the precipitated product becomes solid. Filter off the crude derivative with suction and recrystallize it to constant melting point from ethanol.

Derivatization of alkynes

Equipment	apparatus for filtration and recrystallization	
Materials		
unknown alkyne	*ca.* 3.0 mL	
2,4-dinitrobenzenesulfenyl chloride	1.5 g	**lachrymator, corrosive**
1,2-dichloroethane	15 mL	**cancer suspect agent, flammable**
ethanol		**flammable, toxic**

HOOD

Procedure

Dissolve the 2,4-dinitrobenzenesulfenyl chloride in the 1,2-dichloroethane in a 25 mL Erlenmeyer flask, loosely stopper and cool in ice for 15 min. Add the alkyne and allow the mixture to stand at 0°C for 2 h (refrigerator) or until a crystalline product is formed. Filter off the product with suction and recrystallize it from ethanol to constant melting point. If the crude material is dark in colour, it may be helpful to decolourize with charcoal before proceeding with the recrystallization. ∎

Aromatic hydrocarbons

Aromatic compounds may be converted to the corresponding sulfonamides in a two-step process by first reacting with chlorosulfonic acid followed by addition of ammonia. If the unknown is believed to possess an electron-rich aromatic ring, it is usually possible to obtain a crystalline complex with 1,3,5-trinitrobenzene, although other planar electron-poor aromatic compounds which may be used include picric acid (2,4,6-trinitrophenol) and styphnic acid (2,4,6-trinitroresorcinol). If alkyl groups are present, another option may be to degrade these oxidatively to the corresponding carboxylic acid. Other procedures involving bromination or nitration are less generally applicable for preparing crystalline derivatives. However, bromination can be used with phenols which are not readily oxidized and nitration may prove useful for indirect derivatization of aromatic halides (p. 264).

Preparation of sulfonamides

$$ArH \xrightarrow{ClSO_3H} ArSO_2Cl \xrightarrow{NH_3} ArSO_2NH_2$$

Equipment	apparatus for filtration, recrystallization and extraction	
Materials		
unknown aromatic sample	*ca.* 1.0 g	
chlorosulfonic acid	3.0 mL	**corrosive, toxic**
chloroform		**cancer suspect agent, toxic**
ethanol		**flammable, toxic**
aqueous ammonia (conc., 30%)	10 mL	**lachrymator, corrosive, toxic**

Procedure

HOOD
[1]*Care! Corrosive*

Dissolve the unknown in the chloroform and add the chlorosulfonic acid dropwise[1] with cooling in an ice bath. After the evolution of hydrogen chloride fumes has slowed down, allow the mixture to stand at room temperature for 30 min with periodic gentle shaking, and then pour onto crushed ice. Separate the lower chloroform layer, adding a little more chloroform if necessary, and dry the solution over $MgSO_4$. Filter off the drying agent and remove the solvent on the rotary evaporator in a 50 mL round-bottomed flask. Add the ammonia[2] to the residue and heat the mixture on a steam bath for 10 min. Add 25 mL of water to the mixture and break up any lumps of solid with a glass rod. Filter off the crude sulfonamide with suction and recrystallize to constant melting point from aqueous ethanol.

[2]*Care! Lachrymator*

Preparation of 1,3,5-trinitrobenzene adducts

Equipment	apparatus for filtration and recrystallization	
Materials		
unknown aromatic sample	*ca.* 0.2 g	
1,3,5-trinitrobenzene	0.2 g	**flammable**
Note: *1,3,5-trinitrobenzene is potentially explosive. Do not heat or grind the solid and do not handle in quantities greater than recommended*		
ethanol		**flammable, toxic**

Procedure

[1]*Do not expose to heat!*

Dissolve the unknown in 1 mL of ethanol and add this to a solution of the 1,3,5-trinitrobenzene[1] dissolved in cold ethanol (2 mL). Cool the mixture in ice, filter off the precipitate solid with suction and recrystallize it to constant melting point from ethanol.

Oxidation of side chains of aromatic substrates

Any alkyl group possessing at least one benzylic hydrogen can be degraded to the carboxylic acid group by oxidation on refluxing with alkaline potassium permanganate. However, many aromatic compounds such as phenols and anilines will not withstand such vigorous reaction conditions. Compounds possessing more than two alkyl side chains usually require inconveniently long periods of time for complete oxidation.

Equipment	apparatus for filtration, recrystallization and reflux	
Materials		
unknown aromatic sample	*ca.* 0.5 g	
potassium permanganate	2.0 g	**irritant, oxidizer**
sodium carbonate	0.5 g	**corrosive**
ethanol		**flammable, toxic**
aqueous sulfuric acid (5%)		**corrosive**
saturated aqueous sodium bisulfite		**irritant**

Procedure

[1]See Fig. 3.23a

Check for flammable materials in the area

Measure the unknown, potassium permanganate and sodium carbonate into a 100 mL round-bottomed flask and add 50 mL of water. Set the apparatus for reflux[1] and reflux vigorously over a microburner until the purple colour of the oxidizing agent has been replaced by a black precipitate of manganese dioxide (or 2 h whichever is the shorter period). Cool the mixture, acidify with 5% aqueous sulfuric acid and add saturated sodium bisulfite solution with shaking until the manganese dioxide has been removed. Filter the mixture with suction and recrystallize the residue to constant melting point from water or aqueous ethanol.

Bromination of phenols

This procedure is really only suitable for phenolic compounds possessing one hydroxyl group as bromine–acetic acid will oxidize the more sensitive polyhydroxylated substrates. The number and position of the bromine atoms introduced depend on the substrate; phenol itself readily yields the 2,4,6-tribromo derivative.

Equipment	apparatus for filtration and recrystallization

Materials

unknown phenol	*ca.* 0.5 g	
aqueous solution of bromine*		**corrosive**
ethanol		**flammable, toxic**
saturated aqueous sodium bisulfite		**irritant**

NOTE: *extreme caution must be exercised when using bromine as its volatility, density and highly irritant properties make it extremely difficult to handle. Always wear gloves and manipulate bromine in the hood*

*The aqueous bromine reagent is conveniently prepared as a stock solution by dissolving potassium bromide (10 g) in water (50 mL) followed by the addition of bromine (2 mL).

Procedure

HOOD

[1]*Care! Corrosive*

Dissolve the phenol in ethanol (5 mL) and add the aqueous bromine reagent dropwise,[1] shaking the reaction mixture until a permanent yellow colouration just appears. Add water (20 mL) to this mixture and filter off the precipitate with suction. If the precipitate is yellow in colour due to residual bromine, wash it on the filter with saturated aqueous sodium bisulfite (5 mL) followed by water (3 × 15 mL). Recrystallize the crude material to constant melting point from ethanol or aqueous ethanol. ∎

Halides

Halides are relatively inert compounds from the point of view of efficient derivatization, but primary and secondary halides form crystalline *S*-alkylisothiouronium salts; the normally slow reaction of chlorides is increased by adding an inorganic iodide to the reaction mixture. Tertiary halides do not give such derivatives and their characterization presents difficulties, particularly in view of their tendency towards elimination. Halides may be converted into a wide range of easily characterized compounds by first converting them into the corresponding Grignard reagent, but this procedure is sometimes difficult on a small scale. Aromatic halides may be derivatized indirectly by electrophilic substitution of the aromatic nucleus or by oxidation of any alkyl side chains (pp. 261–262).

Preparation of S-alkylisothiouronium picrates

Equipment	apparatus for filtration, recrystallization and reflux	
Materials		
unknown halide sample	*ca.* 0.2 g	
thiourea	0.2 g	**cancer suspect agent, toxic**
picric acid (2,4,6-trinitrophenol)	0.2 g	**flammable, toxic**
ethanol		**flammable, toxic**
potassium iodide (for use with alkyl chlorides)	0.2 g	

Procedure

HOOD

[1]*See Fig. 3.23a*

Place the thiourea, unknown and ethanol (10 mL) in a 25 mL round-bottomed flask and set the apparatus for reflux[1] and heat the mixture. If the unknown is a chloride, add the potassium iodide at the beginning of the reflux period, together with sufficient water to produce a homogeneous solution when the mixture is refluxing. After 30 min (primary bromides and iodides) or 2 h (chlorides or secondary bromides and iodides) at reflux, cool the mixture temporarily; add the picric acid and return to reflux until a clear solution is formed. At this point cool the mixture to obtain the crystalline picrate salt, adding several drops of water if crystallization does not occur spontaneously. Filter off the crude derivative with suction and recrystallize it to constant melting point from ethanol.

Nitration of aromatic halides

This procedure may also be used to derivatize alkylated aromatic compounds but the conditions are much too extreme for use with activated aromatic compounds.

Equipment	apparatus for filtration and recrystallization		
Materials			
unknown aromatic halide	*ca.* 0.5 g		
sulfuric acid (conc.)	3 mL	**corrosive, oxidizer**	
fuming nitric acid (*ca.* 90%)	3 mL	**corrosive, oxidizer**	
NOTE: *extreme care must be exercised when handling fuming nitric acid. Always wear gloves and handle in the hood*			
ethanol		**flammable, toxic**	

Procedure

HOOD

[1]*Care! Highly corrosive*

Add the unknown to the sulfuric acid in a test tube and *cautiously* add the fuming nitric acid dropwise.[1] Heat the mixture on a water bath for 15 min and then pour onto ice-water. Filter off the precipitated material with suction and recrystallize it to constant melting point from aqueous ethanol. ∎

Nitro compounds

The usual derivatization procedure involves reducing the nitro compound to an amine and then characterizing the primary amine as an amide or *p*-toluidine salt. Most unknowns possessing a nitro group which are likely to appear in the teaching laboratory are aromatic nitro compounds, and so indirect methods of derivatization such as nitration (above) or oxidation of alkyl side chains (pp. 261–262) may be used.

Polynitrated aromatic compounds may be dangerously explosive. Consult an instructor before attempting such a derivatization.

Owing to the deactivating effect of the electron-withdrawing nitro group on the aromatic ring, relatively forcing conditions are needed to effect electrophilic substitution reactions.

Reduction to primary amines

$$RNO_2 \xrightarrow{\text{Sn / HCl}} RNH_2$$

The standard means of reducing nitro groups uses tin–hydrochloric acid from which the reduced product is extracted after basification.

Equipment	apparatus for filtration, distillation and reflux	

Materials

unknown nitro compound	*ca.* 1.0 g	
mossy tin	3.0 g	
ethanol		flammable, toxic
diethyl ether		flammable, irritant
hydrochloric acid (10%)	30 mL	corrosive
aqueous sodium hydroxide (20%)		corrosive

Procedure

HOOD

[1]*See Fig. 3.23a*

[2]*Care! Heat evolved*

Weigh the unknown and the mossy tin into a 50 mL round-bottomed flask and arrange for reflux.[1] Add 10 mL of the hydrochloric acid down the condenser, shake thoroughly and heat this mixture on the steam bath. If the unknown is insoluble in the aqueous system, add ethanol (4 mL) to aid solution. Add the remainder of the hydrochloric acid in 10 mL portions at 10 min intervals, shaking the flask after each addition. After the final portion of acid has been added, and the mixture heated for 10 min, allow the flask to cool and decant the supernatant into 40% sodium hydroxide (10 mL) with cooling in ice.[2] If the mixture still contains solid tin salts, stir the mixture vigorously and add further 40% sodium hydroxide until any residual tin salts dissolve. Extract the alkaline mixture with diethyl ether (3 × 10 mL), combine the organic extracts and dry over $MgSO_4$. Filter and remove the solvent on the rotary evaporator to furnish the crude amine. Further derivatization should follow the procedures described on pp. 271–274. ∎

Esters, amides and nitriles

Esters are considered in this section because, in common with amides and nitriles, they are characterized by hydrolysis. In the case of primary amides and nitriles, it is only necessary to characterize the acid, but with esters it is also necessary to characterize the alcohol produced on saponification. Similarly, with secondary and tertiary amides, the amine moiety must be identified. Derivatization of alcohols has already been discussed (pp. 255–257) and derivatization of acids is considered on pp. 268–269. Moreover, many acids are crystalline and can be considered as derivatives in their own right. Primary amides and esters are most efficiently hydrolyzed with aqueous base, but nitriles and substituted amides are hydrolyzed more effectively under acidic conditions.

Hydrolysis of esters

$$R^1CO_2R^2 \xrightarrow{\text{KOH}} R^2OH + R^1CO_2K \xrightarrow{\text{H}^+} R^1CO_2H$$

Equipment	apparatus for filtration, distillation and reflux	
Materials		
unknown ester	*ca.* 1 mL (1.0 g if solid)	
diethylene glycol (2-hydroxyethyl ether)	3 mL	**irritant**
potassium hydroxide	1.0 g	**corrosive**
sulfuric acid (20%)		**corrosive**

Procedure

[1]See Fig. 3.23(a)

[2]See Fig. 3.48

Measure the potassium hydroxide and the diethylene glycol into a 25 mL round-bottomed flask and heat the mixture gently with a small flame until the mixture becomes homogeneous. Add the ester and a boiling stone, arrange the apparatus for reflux[1] and heat until only one liquid layer is visible (*ca.* 5 min), ignoring any solid which may remain. Allow the flask to cool and arrange for distillation.[2] Distil the alcohol from the mixture, with fairly strong heating if necessary, but do not allow the diethylene glycol to distil (bp 245°C). Note the still head temperature at which the alcohol distils to help you to make a preliminary identification and to decide which derivatives to prepare. Allow the residue containing the potassium salt of the acid to cool, add water (10 mL) and acidify with 20% sulfuric acid. If a solid precipitates, filter it off with suction, washing the residue with cold water (3 × 5 mL) and characterize the acid as appropriate. If a precipitate does not form, the aqueous phase should be made neutral to phenolphthalein and the solution of the potassium salt should be used to prepare a derivative (see pp. 268–269).

Hydrolysis of primary amides with aqueous base

$$RCONH_2 \xrightarrow{\text{aq. NaOH}} RCO_2Na + NH_3 \xrightarrow[H^+]{} RCO_2H$$

Primary amides hydrolyze efficiently under alkaline conditions, but the hydrolysis of secondary or tertiary amides is better attempted under the acidic conditions described for hydrolysis of nitriles.

Equipment	apparatus for filtration	
Materials		
unknown primary amide	*ca.* 0.5 g	
aqueous sodium hydroxide (10%)	10 mL	**corrosive**
aqueous sulfuric acid (20%)		**corrosive**

Procedure

HOOD

Measure the unknown and the aqueous sodium hydroxide into a 50 mL Erlenmeyer flask and heat the mixture on a steam bath for 30 min during which time ammonia is evolved. Acidify the residual solution, filtering off with suction any precipitated acid for derivatization. If no precipitate is formed on acidification, neutralize the mixture towards phenolphthalein and use this solution to prepare a derivative of the acid (pp. 268–269).

Acidic hydrolysis of nitriles and secondary or tertiary amides

$$RCN \xrightarrow{H_3O^+} RCO_2H + \overset{+}{N}H_4$$

$$R^1\overset{\overset{\displaystyle O}{\|}}{C}NR^2R^3 \xrightarrow{H_3O^+} R^1CO_2H + R^2R^3\overset{+}{N}H_2$$

Equipment	apparatus for filtration, extraction and reflux	
Materials		
unknown nitrile or amide	*ca.* 0.5 g	
sulfuric acid (conc.)	5.0 mL	**corrosive, oxidizer**
diethyl ether		**flammable, irritant**
aqueous sodium hydroxide (20%)		**corrosive**

Procedure

[1] *See Fig. 3.23(a)*

[2] *Care! Exothermic*

Place the unknown and the concentrated sulfuric acid in a 50 mL round-bottomed flask, attach a reflux condenser and heat to *ca.* 50°C for 30 min.[1] Allow the mixture to cool and **cautiously** add water[2] (15 mL) down the condenser. Reflux the resulting mixture for 1 h and cool in ice. Filter off with suction any acid which precipitates and characterize it. If no solid precipitates, extract the mixture with diethyl ether (3 × 10 mL), combine the organic extracts and dry them over MgSO$_4$. Filter the mixture, remove the solvent on the rotary evaporator and use the residue of crude acid directly for derivatization. If the unknown is a secondary or tertiary amide, the amine component contained in the acidic aqueous phase as a salt may be isolated. Basify the layer with aqueous sodium hydroxide and extract it with diethyl ether (3 × 10 mL). This solution can be used to prepare derivatives of the amine directly. Removal of the solvent should not be attempted as the lower homologues of primary and secondary amines are highly volatile. Some amines are extracted from water only with great difficulty and the yield of amine may be very low in such instances.

◼

Carboxylic acids

Preparation of **S-Benzylisothiouronium salts**

S-Benzylisothiouronium chloride reacts with the sodium salt of the acid to produce the salt. It is important not to allow the reaction medium to become too alkaline as this causes the liberation of benzyl thiol which possesses a particularly penetrating and repulsive odour. This procedure may also be used for characterizing sulfonic acids.

Equipment	apparatus for filtration and recrystallization	
Materials		
unknown carboxylic acid	*ca.* 0.2 g	
S-benzylisothiouronium chloride	0.8 g	toxic
ethanol		flammable, toxic
aqueous sodium hydroxide solution (5%)		corrosive
aqueous hydrochloric acid (1%)		corrosive

Procedure

HOOD

Stench!

Dissolve or suspend the unknown acid in water (0.5 mL) in a test tube and add the sodium hydroxide solution until the mixture is just alkaline when tested with phenolphthalein. Neutralize the excess alkali by adding dilute hydrochloric acid—**do not proceed if the solution is alkaline**.[1] Add to this a solution of the S-benzylisothiouronium chloride in water (2 mL) and cool the mixture in ice until the derivative precipitates. Filter off the solid with suction and recrystallize it to constant melting point from aqueous ethanol.

Preparation of 4-bromophenacyl esters

The sodium salt of the acid can also be used in the preparation of the 4-phenylphenacyl esters.

Equipment	apparatus for filtration, recrystallization and reflux	
Materials		
unknown carboxylic acid	*ca.* 0.2 g	
4′-bromophenacyl bromide	0.2 g	**lachrymator, corrosive**
(2,4′-dibromoacetophenone)		
aqueous sodium hydroxide (5%)		**corrosive**
aqueous hydrochloric acid (1%)		**corrosive**
ethanol		**flammable, toxic**

Procedure

HOOD

Prepare a solution of the sodium salt of the acid in a 25 mL round-bottomed flask as described on p. 268. Dissolve the 4′-bromophenacyl bromide in ethanol (5 mL), add this to the flask and reflux the mixture for 1 h.[1] Add more ethanol during the reflux period if necessary to maintain a homogeneous mixture. (If the unknown is a dicarboxylic acid it is advisable to double the reflux period.) At the end of this period, cool the solution and filter off the pre-cipitated product with suction. Recrystallize the solid to constant melting point from aqueous ethanol. ∎

[1]*See Fig. 3.23(a)*

Acid anhydrides and acid halides

Both acid anhydrides and halides are hydrolyzed to the corresponding carboxylic acids which may be characterized as such, or derivatized using the procedures outlined previously. Anhydrides and halides also react very readily with aromatic amines such as aniline or 4-methylaniline (*p*-toluidine) to furnish crystalline *anilides* (*N*-phenylamides) and *toluidides* respectively. (This derivatization is also suitable for carboxylic acids, after first being con-verted to acid chlorides by heating with excess thionyl chloride for 30 min, fol-lowed by removal of excess thionyl chloride.) Only symmetrical acid anhydrides are readily amenable to analysis by such procedures. Acid halides react very readily with concentrated aqueous ammonia to furnish primary amides although this procedure is less useful for anhydrides.

Hydrolysis of anhydrides and halides to carboxylic acids

Equipment	apparatus for filtration and recrystallization	
Materials		
unknown acid anhydride or halide	*ca.* 0.20 mL (0.2 g)	
aqueous sodium hydroxide (10%)		**corrosive**
aqueous hydrochloric acid (10%)		**corrosive**

Procedure

Add the unknown anhydride or halide dropwise to the aqueous sodium hydroxide (3 mL) in a test tube with swirling.[1] After the initial vigorous reaction has subsided, heat the mixture on the water bath for 15 min or until the contents of the tube become homogeneous. Allow to cool, acidify the reaction mixture with hydrochloric acid and filter off the precipitate with suction. Alternatively, if no precipitate forms, the acid may be derivatized via its sodium salt (pp. 268–269) by adding aqueous sodium hydroxide until the solution is just alkaline to phenolphthalein.

Preparation of anilides and toluidides

$$R^1COX \quad \xrightarrow{\quad H_2N-\!\!\!\langle\rangle\!\!-R^2 \quad} \quad R^1\!\!\underset{O}{\overset{}{C}}\!\!-NH-\!\!\!\langle\rangle\!\!-R^2$$

$$X = Cl, OCR^1 \; ; R^2 = H, Me$$

Equipment	apparatus for filtration and recrystallization

Materials		
unknown acid anhydride or halide	*ca.* 0.2 mL	
aniline (or 4-methylaniline)	0.2 mL (0.20 g)	**cancer suspect agent, irritant, toxic**
ethanol		**flammable, toxic**
aqueous hydrochloric acid (5%)		**corrosive**

Procedure

HOOD

Add the aniline (or 4-methylaniline) to the unknown acid anhydride or halide in a test tube with shaking and then heat the contents on a steam bath for 5 min. Add dilute hydrochloric acid (2 mL) to dissolve excess aromatic amine, breaking up any lumps of solid with a glass rod to ensure the thorough removal of amine. Filter the crude material with suction, washing it with water (2 × 10 mL) and recrystallize it to constant melting point from ethanol or aqueous ethanol.

Conversion of acid halides (and carboxylic acids) to primary amides

Equipment	apparatus for filtration and recrystallization

Materials		
unknown acid halide	*ca.* 0.2 mL	
ammonia solution (conc., 30%)		**lachrymator, corrosive, toxic**
ethanol		**flammable, toxic**

Procedure

HOOD

[1]Care! Vigorous reaction

Add the unknown acid halide dropwise to the concentrated ammonia solution (2 mL) in a test tube.[1] Allow the reaction mixture to cool and filter off the precipitate of amide with suction, washing the residue with water (2 × 5 mL). Recrystallize the crude material to constant melting point from ethanol or aqueous ethanol.

HOOD

[2]Care! Lachrymator

Adaptation for derivatization of carboxylic acids. Prepare the crude acid chloride by heating a mixture of the carboxylic acid (0.2 g or 0.2 mL) and thionyl chloride (2 mL)[2] for 30 min in a thick-walled test tube. Remove the excess of thionyl chloride by attaching the test tube to a water aspirator and heating the mixture gently with continuous shaking. Use the residue for conversion to the amide as described above. This procedure is not applicable for carboxylic acids which form volatile halides. ∎

Amines

Primary and secondary amines are readily acylated to form the corresponding amides with both acetic anhydride or benzoyl chloride under aqueous conditions. The reaction with benzoyl chloride in the presence of aqueous sodium hydroxide is often referred to as the *Schotten–Baumann reaction* and it is equally applicable to the preparation of benzoate esters of phenols. Primary and secondary amines react in a similar manner with arylsulfonyl chlorides to furnish sulfonamides and this reaction forms the basis of the *Hinsberg method* of distinction of primary, secondary and tertiary amines. Tertiary amines do not undergo these reactions and probably the best method for derivatizing these compounds is to form a crystalline salt with picric acid (2,4,6-trinitrophenol). Tertiary amines may also be derivatized as their quaternary ammonium salts, but these derivatives are frequently hygroscopic and difficult to handle. In addition, their preparation involves the use of the volatile and highly toxic iodomethane and this procedure is not recommended for the teaching laboratory.

Acetylation of primary and secondary amines

$$R^1R^2NH \xrightarrow[\text{aq.NaOAc}]{(CH_3CO)_2O} R^1R^2N\overset{\displaystyle O}{\underset{}{\|}}CH_3$$

R^2 = alkyl, aryl, H

The following method involves acetylation under aqueous conditions and usually gives excellent results, even with some 2,6-disubstituted anilines which are frequently sluggish towards acylation due to steric hindrance.

Equipment	apparatus for filtration and recrystallization

Materials

unknown primary or secondary amine	*ca.* 0.2 mL (0.2 g)	
acetic anhydride	2 mL	**lachrymator, corrosive**
hydrated sodium acetate	2.0 g	
aqueous hydrochloric acid (10%)		**corrosive**
ethanol		**flammable, toxic**

Procedure

HOOD

Dissolve the amine in hydrochloric acid (3 mL) in a 25 mL Erlenmeyer flask, add the sodium acetate and make the solution volume up to about 10 mL with water. Add a few pieces of crushed ice followed by the acetic anhydride and swirl the mixture. Stopper and shake the flask until the ice has melted and then leave the mixture for a further 15 min, re-stoppering and shaking at 5 min intervals. Collect the solid amide by filtration with suction, wash it with water (5 mL), and recrystallize it to constant melting point from aqueous ethanol.

Benzoylation of primary and secondary amines (Schotten–Baumann reaction)

$$R^1R^2NH \xrightarrow{\text{PhCOCl, aq.NaOH}} R^1R^2N\overset{\displaystyle O}{\underset{}{\|}}Ph$$

$$R^2 = \text{alkyl, aryl, H}$$

This procedure is equally applicable to the benzoylation of phenols. Failure of the reaction is generally the consequence of overgenerous use of the benzoyl chloride. Benzoyl chloride is particularly lachrymatory and, for both reasons, excesses of the reagent are to be avoided. Always handle it in the hood and destroy any residual material with concentrated ammonia solution.

Equipment	apparatus for filtration and recrystallization

Materials

unknown primary or secondary amine	*ca.* 0.2 mL (0.2 g)	
benzoyl chloride	0.4 mL	**lachrymator, corrosive**
aqueous sodium hydroxide (10%)		**corrosive**
ethanol		**flammable, toxic**
ammonia solution (conc., 30%)		**lachrymator, corrosive, toxic**

Procedure

HOOD

Add the amine to the aqueous sodium hydroxide (3 mL) in a 10 mL round-bottomed flask capable of being tightly closed with a ground glass stopper. Add a portion of the benzoyl chloride[1] (*ca.* 0.1 mL) by pipette, stopper the flask securely, and shake vigorously for 2 min.[2] Repeat this procedure until all of the benzoyl chloride has been added and then leave the mixture to stand for 10 min. Destroy any residues of the reagent in the pipette by washing with concentrated ammonia.[1] Check the reaction mixture is still alkaline, adding more aqueous sodium hydroxide if not, and filter off the precipitated solid with suction. Wash the residue with water (10 mL) and recrystallize it to constant melting point from aqueous ethanol.

Preparation of sulfonamides from primary and secondary amines (Hinsberg's distinction)

$$R^1R^2NH \xrightarrow{\text{ArSO}_2\text{Cl, base}} R^1R^2NSO_2Ar$$

$$Ar = Ph\text{-}\xi \quad , \quad CH_3\text{-}\langle\text{---}\rangle\text{-}\xi$$

Most primary and secondary amines may be sulfonylated using an aqueous system corresponding to the Schotten–Baumann type conditions for benzoylation. To do this, substitute the same quantity of benzenesulfonyl chloride or *p*-toluenesulfonyl chloride for the benzoyl chloride and follow the instructions given in the previous procedure. However, some aromatic amines substituted with electron-withdrawing groups (for example, 2-nitroaniline) are such weak nucleophiles that the majority of the sulfonyl chloride will be hydrolyzed under aqueous conditions instead of forming the sulfonamide. For these reluctant amines the following procedure should give excellent results. Whilst it may be used for the sulfonylation of all primary and secondary amines, the simpler aqueous procedure is to be preferred for any but the least reactive substrates.

Equipment	apparatus for filtration, recrystallization and reflux

Materials		
unknown primary or secondary amine	*ca.* 0.5 mL (0.5 g)	
benzenesulfonyl chloride (*alternatively p-toluenesulfonyl chloride (1.0 g) may be used observing the same precautions with regard to its toxicity*)	0.7 mL	**corrosive, toxic**
pyridine	4 mL	**flammable, irritant**
ethanol		**flammable, toxic**
aqueous hydrochloric acid (5%)		**corrosive**

Procedure

Measure the amine, sulfonyl chloride and pyridine into a 10 mL round-

[1]See Fig. 3.23(a)

bottomed flask, attach a reflux condenser[1] and heat the mixture on a steam bath for 30 min. Pour the hot reaction mixture into dilute hydrochloric acid (25 mL) and stir with a glass rod until the product crystallizes. Filter off the solid with suction, wash the residue with water (10 mL) and recrystallize it to constant melting point from ethanol or aqueous ethanol.

Preparation of amine–picrate complexes

Crystalline 1:1 complexes of amines with picric acid may be prepared for any class of amine, but these derivatives are most important for tertiary amines.

Equipment	apparatus for filtration and recrystallization	
Materials		
unknown amine	*ca.* 0.3 mL (0.3 g)	
saturated ethanolic solution of picric acid	5 mL	**flammable, toxic**
(2,4,6-trinitrophenol)		
ethanol		**flammable, toxic**

Procedure

Dissolve the amine in sufficient ethanol in a test tube to give a totally homogeneous solution (*ca.* 5 mL) and to this add the solution of picric acid. Heat the mixture on a hot water bath for 5 min and then allow it to cool. Filter off the precipitate with suction and recrystallize the product to constant melting point from ethanol. ∎

Sulfonic acids

Sulfonic acids are frequently derivatized as sulfonamides by conversion to sulfonyl chlorides using phosphorus pentachloride followed by reaction with concentrated ammonia or an amine (pp. 273–274). The *S*-benzylisothiouronium salts may be prepared using the procedure described for carboxylic acids (p. 268), and the crystalline salts formed with *p*-toluidine are also useful derivatives.

Conversion of sulfonic acids to sulfonyl chlorides for further derivatization

Equipment	apparatus for reflux	
Materials		
unknown sulfonic acid	*ca.* 1.0 g	
phosphorus pentachloride	2.5 g	**corrosive**
NOTE: *phosphorus pentachloride is readily hydrolyzed by atmospheric*		
moisture, liberating hydrogen chloride. Always use this reagent in the hood		
toluene	20 mL	**flammable, toxic**

Procedure

HOOD

Mix the sulfonic acid and phosphorus pentachloride in a dry 25 mL round-bottomed flask, attach a reflux condenser, plug the mouth of the condenser loosely with cotton wool and heat the mixture on an oil bath to 150°C for 30 min.[1] Remove the flask from the heating bath and allow to cool for 2 min. Add toluene (20 mL) down the condenser and heat the mixture to reflux for 5 min. Allow the mixture to cool to room temperature and carefully decant the supernatant liquid into a clean 25 mL round-bottomed flask and remove the toluene on the rotary evaporator. The residue of crude sulfonyl chloride may be used directly for further derivatization.

[1]*See Fig. 3.23(a)*

Preparation of p-*toluidine salts*

Equipment	apparatus for filtration and recrystallization	
Materials		
unknown sulfonic acid	*ca.* 0.5 g	
4-methylaniline (*p*-toluidine)	0.3 g	**cancer suspect agent, irritant, toxic**
hydrochloric acid (conc., 36%)		**corrosive**

Procedure

Dissolve the sulfonic acid in the minimum volume of hot water and add to it a solution of *p*-toluidine in concentrated hydrochloric acid (*ca.* 1.0 mL). Heat the mixture on a steam bath and add more water if necessary to obtain a homogeneous solution. Allow the mixture to cool and filter off the precipitate with suction. Recrystallize the solid to constant melting point from water acidified with one or two drops of concentrated hydrochloric acid.

Further reading

The following references should provide the necessary data required for identification of unknowns. In addition, Furniss *et al.* (1989) provides additional derivatization procedures:

Aldrich Catalog Handbook of Fine Chemicals, Aldrich-Sigma Co. Ltd, Milwaukee, USA.

J. Buckingham and F. MacDonald (eds) *Dictionary of Organic Compounds*, Vols 1–9, 6th edn, Chapman & Hall, London, 1996.

T.J. Bruno, *CRC Handbook of Basic Tables for Chemical Analysis*, CRC Press, Boca Raton, 1989.

CRC Handbook of Chemistry and Physics, CRC Press, Boca Raton. (This extremely useful reference work is published annually but the tables of physical constants or organic compounds do not change appreciably from year to year.)

B.S. Furniss, A.J. Hannaford, V. Rogers, P.W.G. Smith and A.R. Tatchell, *Vogel's Textbook of Practical Organic Chemistry*, 5th edn, Longman, London, 1989.

Chapter 5

Spectroscopic Analysis of Organic Compounds

Absorption spectroscopy

Spectroscopic methods, introduced during the middle of the twentieth century, now play a fundamental role in the solution of many problems in organic chemistry. Of the four spectroscopic techniques most widely used by practising organic chemists—ultraviolet (UV) spectroscopy, infrared (IR) spectroscopy, nuclear magnetic resonance (NMR) and mass spectrometry (MS)—UV spectroscopy is historically the most important, having been introduced in the 1930s. The 1940s saw the advent of IR spectroscopy, and this was followed by MS and NMR in the 1950s and early 1960s. The use of these techniques, which enable recovery of the compound, has revolutionized structural organic chemistry, and their impact cannot be overstated. Although the techniques are usually used in combination, many would argue that NMR, looking as it does at carbon and hydrogen (the elements most relevant to organic chemists), has had the single greatest effect on organic chemistry.

In the following sections we will look at the four spectroscopic techniques in turn, dealing with them not in the order of historical development (i.e. UV spectroscopy first), but in the order that reflects common practice in the organic laboratory for the collection of spectroscopic data: IR spectroscopy, NMR, UV spectroscopy and MS. Many teaching laboratories now possess IR, NMR and UV spectrometers for students to use themselves; MS, however, requires expensive special instrumentation.

Of the four spectroscopic techniques, three of them (IR, NMR and UV) come under the general heading of *absorption spectroscopy*, the absorption of electromagnetic radiation by the sample under study over a range of wavelengths, while MS is fundamentally different to these in that it does not involve the absorption of radiation. Although the theory of spectroscopy will be dealt with in detail in other parts of your course, and in your lecture texts, a brief discussion of the theory behind the techniques is needed here.

Electromagnetic radiation can be specified by wavelength (λ), frequency (v) or energy (E). Wavelength and frequency are related by the well-known equation:

$$\lambda v = c$$

where c is the speed of light. Hence wavelength and frequency are inversely proportional; long wavelengths corresponding to low frequencies and vice versa. Organic molecules absorb electromagnetic radiation over a wide range of wavelengths, and this absorption occurs in discrete 'packets' of energy known as *quanta*. When a molecule absorbs radiation energy it enters an energetically *excited state*, and the difference in energy (ΔE) between the ground state and the excited state is given by

$$\Delta E = h\nu$$

where ν is the frequency of the absorbed radiation and h is Planck's constant (6.626×10^{-34} Js). Promotion of a molecule to an excited state can only occur when a quantum of the correct amount of energy is supplied, that is when the electromagnetic radiation has precisely the right energy (frequency). From the above equation, high frequency radiation (short wavelength) has higher energy than low frequency radiation. The energy absorbed by an organic molecule is displayed in either mechanical or electronic motion, the nature of which depends on the energy of the radiation. The *electromagnetic spectrum* (the wavelengths, energies and associated effects) is shown in Fig. 5.1.

When a molecule absorbs low energy radiation in the radiowave region, nuclear spin transitions occur, and this is the basis of NMR spectroscopy. More energetic radiation in the microwave region causes rotation about bonds, although microwave spectroscopy is not widely used by organic chemists. IR radiation causes vibration of the molecular framework, whilst visible radiation

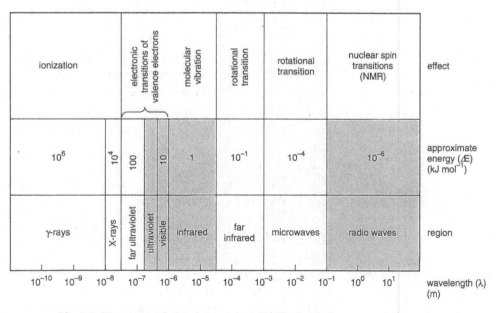

Fig. 5.1 The electromagnetic spectrum: the shaded areas represent the regions of most interest to organic chemists.

and UV radiation cause electronic transitions—the promotion of an electron from a bonding or lone pair orbital to an antibonding orbital. Radiation in the X-ray and γ-ray regions of the spectrum causes electronic transitions of core electrons and ionization. Indeed, such high energy radiation is often known as ionizing radiation, and exposure to it is highly dangerous.

In essence, absorption spectroscopy involves the irradiation of a sample, and the observation of how the absorption varies with the wavelength of the radiation. The instrument used for this is called a *spectrometer*, and is designed to look at one particular region of the electromagnetic spectrum. The output from a spectrometer is usually recorded onto calibrated paper in the form of a plot of wavelength (or frequency) against absorption of energy. This plot, simply referred to as the *spectrum*, consists of a series of peaks or bands which correspond to absorption of radiation at that particular wavelength, and which can be interpreted in terms of the molecular structure of the sample under investigation. It should also be remembered that the magnitude of the absorption is directly proportional to the amount of sample.

Infrared spectroscopy

The IR region of the electromagnetic spectrum corresponds to wavelengths in the range 2×10^{-4} to 1×10^{-6} m. Although this is outside the range visible to the human eye, IR radiation can be detected by its warming effect on the skin. The energies associated with IR radiation, in the range 4–40 kJ, cause vibrations, either of the whole molecule, or of individual bonds or functional groups within the molecule. There are several *modes of molecular vibration*, and these are often described in such terms as stretching, bending, scissoring, rocking and wagging. However, for the purposes of this brief discussion we will only consider the simple stretching of a bond X–Y. To a good approximation, such a two-atom system can be considered as two balls connected by a spring; therefore *Hooke's law* will be obeyed. Thus the frequency of vibration (stretching) of the bond X–Y is directly proportional to the strength of the bond, and inversely proportional to the masses of both X and Y. Consequently different bonds belonging to different groups within the molecule will vibrate at different frequencies and many organic functional groups can be readily identified by their IR absorption properties. The stronger the bond, the higher the vibration frequency. Hence double bonds vibrate at higher frequencies than single bonds between like pairs of atoms, and strong bonds such as O–H, N–H and C–H vibrate at higher frequencies than weaker bonds such as C–C and C–O. Also the heavier the atoms, the lower the vibration frequency of the bond between them. Hence in deuterated compounds, the C–D bonds involving the heavier isotope vibrate at lower frequency than the C–H bonds. Similarly in moving down the periodic table, S–H bonds vibrate at lower frequency than O–H bonds.

Hooke's law

The stronger the bond, the higher the vibration frequency

The heavier the atoms, the lower the vibration frequency

The position of an IR absorption peak can be specified in terms of wavelength, usually expressed in *microns* ($1\,\mu m = 10^{-6}\,m$), or in terms of frequency. The latter is preferred since we usually talk about vibration frequencies of bonds, and nowadays IR absorptions are always measured in frequency units by *wavenumber* ($\bar{v}$), expressed in *reciprocal centimetres* (cm^{-1}). However, you may still see IR spectra described in microns, particularly in the older literature, and you have to be prepared to convert these into the more familiar reciprocal centimetre units. The conversion is given by:

$$\text{Wavenumber}\left(\text{cm}^{-1}\right) = \frac{1}{\text{Wavelength}\left(\text{cm}\right)} = \frac{10\,000}{\text{Wavelength}\left(\mu m\right)}$$

Remember the higher the wavenumber, the higher the frequency, and the lower the wavelength.

The majority of functional groups relevant to organic chemistry absorb radiation within a fairly narrow range of the IR region, 600–4000 cm^{-1}, and therefore most simple spectrometers operate only within this range.

The spectrometer

Most IR spectrometers operate on the double beam principle, and a typical example of such a spectrometer is shown schematically in Fig. 5.2. The source of radiation is an electrically heated glowing wire which emits throughout the whole frequency range of the instrument. Mirror optics are used to split the beam into two beams of equal intensity. One beam passes through a cell containing the sample to be examined, whilst the other passes through a reference cell containing the solvent (this may be missing altogether). After passing through the cells, a rotating segmented mirror alternately allows light from each of the two beams to enter the *monochromator*. The monochromator is a device, based on a prism or grating, which scans through the range of the instrument, usually from high to low frequency, but only allows one frequency of radiation through the slit and into the *detector* at any one time. The scan-

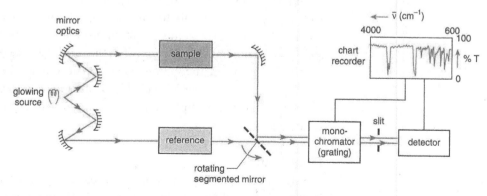

Fig. 5.2 Schematic representation of a double-beam IR spectrometer.

ning mechanism is coupled to the chart recorder and moves the pen along the frequency scale (x axis) of the paper, with high frequency ($4000\,cm^{-1}$) at the left of the paper. It should be noted that the frequency scale on the paper may not be linear throughout the whole 4000–$600\,cm^{-1}$ range. Many spectrometers divide the range into two separate linear scales; one between 4000 and $2000\,cm^{-1}$, and another, more expanded scale, between 2000 and $600\,cm^{-1}$. The signal from the detector, which is proportional to the difference in light intensity between the sample and reference beams, is fed to the chart recorder and moves the pen along the y axis of the paper. This vertical scale on the IR spectrum is usually calibrated in *percentage transmittance* (%T), with 100% transmittance (no absorption) at the top of the paper. At the frequency at which the sample absorbs the IR radiation, the detector response is recorded as a reduction in %T, a dip, on the chart.

In recent years a new type of IR spectroscopy, known as Fourier transform infrared (FTIR) spectroscopy, has been developed. Although the final spectrum looks almost identical to one that is obtained on a double beam instrument, the spectrometer operates on an entirely different principle. Light, often from a laser source, covering the whole range of IR frequencies, is passed through the sample. A second beam, which has travelled along a longer path length, is combined with the first beam to produce a complex interference pattern which looks nothing like a spectrum. Technology then takes over, and the on-board microcomputer performs a Fourier transformation on a series of these interference patterns to convert them into a conventional plot of absorption against frequency. FTIR has many advantages over the traditional method: sensitivity (very small samples can be examined), resolution (not dependent on optical properties of gratings, slits and prisms), time (the whole spectral range is measured in a few seconds), and the flexibility that comes with the on-board computer (allows subtraction of one spectrum from another, digital plots of data and so on).

FTIR

For a further application of Fourier transforms, see section on NMR, pp. 306–356

Preparing the sample

Infrared spectra can be recorded on liquids, solids and even gases, although we will only be concerned with the first two. Spectra of liquids can be recorded on the *neat liquid*, or as *solutions* in an appropriate solvent, whereas spectra of solids can be obtained in *solution*, or in the *solid state* as a *mull* or *KBr disk*. To record the spectrum, the sample must be placed in the beam of the IR spectrometer in a suitable sample cell. Unfortunately glass is opaque to IR radiation, and therefore sample cells are usually made out of sodium chloride, which is IR transparent.

NaCl is transparent to IR

Neat liquids

The IR spectrum of a pure liquid is most easily determined as a *thin film* between two *sodium chloride plates*. The sodium chloride plates commonly used for this purpose are circular, about 20–25 mm in diameter and 5 mm thick, with a polished flat surface. The plates are cut from a large crystal of sodium chloride, and hence are expensive. Unfortunately they are also rather fragile, and sensitive to moisture. Exposure to moisture from wet samples, damp hands or even atmospheric moisture causes the polished surfaces of the plates to become fogged. Such fogged plates produce poor IR spectra, and should be repolished. Never attempt to polish plates yourself without first seeking expert advice. To prevent damage to plates, they should be stored, wrapped in tissue or cotton wool, in a desiccator, or in a screw-capped jar that contains some drying agent. Handle the plates only by their edges, and ensure that all your samples are free from water.

To record the IR spectrum of a neat liquid, place 1 or 2 drops of the liquid in the centre of a sodium chloride plate using a Pasteur pipette as shown in Fig. 5.3a. Place the second plate on top (Fig. 5.3b), and *gently* squeeze the plates together so that the liquid spreads out into a thin film. Holding the plates by their edges, mount them in a sample holder (Fig. 5.3c). Most sample holders have a top cover plate which can be *gently* screwed down to hold the plates in place. Place the sample holder in the sample beam (usually the front beam) of the IR spectrometer, and record the spectrum (see below). When recording the spectrum of a thin film, it is not necessary to put anything in the reference beam of the spectrometer. After running the spectrum, clean the plates with an anhydrous solvent, such as dichloromethane, dry them on a soft tissue, and return them to their storage jar or desiccator. If you need to recover the sample, you must wash the liquid off the plates with dichloromethane into a suitable receptacle, and then evaporate off the

(a)   (b)   (c)

Fig. 5.3 Obtaining the IR spectrum on a neat liquid: (a) 1 or 2 drops of the liquid are placed in the centre of a sodium chloride plate; (b) a second plate is placed on top, and the plates are *gently* squeezed together; (c) the two plates are mounted in the sample holder (top cover plate omitted for clarity).

solvent. However, in these circumstances it is much better to run the IR spectrum using the solution method.

Solutions

IR spectra of both liquids and solids can be obtained in solution. The compound is dissolved in an appropriate solvent (see below), and the solution is placed in a special IR *solution cell* (Fig. 5.4a). The solution cell consists of two rectangular sodium chloride plates sealed together to give a gap of uniform and accurately known dimensions, usually in the range 0.05–0.2 mm. The sodium chloride plates are held together by two metal cover plates which incorporate two syringe ports for filling and flushing the cells. Solution cells usually come in pairs, the second cell precisely matching the first. Like the plates used for thin films, sodium chloride solution cells are fragile and moisture sensitive, and because of the precision machining required in their manufacture, they are also very expensive. Handle them with care.

Solution cells must match

The choice of solvent for solution IR spectra is quite restrictive. No solvent is ideal because all organic solvents absorb at some point in the IR spectral range. Traditionally three solvents have been recommended for IR spectroscopy: carbon tetrachloride, carbon disulfide and chloroform. All three are **toxic**, and although carbon tetrachloride occasionally could give better resolved spectra than chloroform, it is no longer commercially available due to environmental legislation and, in addition, it is rather a poor solvent for many organic compounds. Carbon disulfide is far too hazardous for general use because of its extremely low flash point; indeed, it is our opinion that

Solvents for IR

Fig. 5.4 Obtaining the IR spectrum of a solution: (a) the sodium chloride solution cell; (b) filling the cell through the lower syringe port; (c) flushing the cell after use through the top syringe port.

carbon disulfide should never be used in the teaching laboratory. That only leaves chloroform, which although a **cancer suspect agent**, can be used in the organic laboratory, **provided due regard is paid to its potential toxicity**. Commercial chloroform contains ethanol as a stabilizer, and therefore must be purified before use as a solvent for IR spectroscopy. The purification is easily and quickly accomplished by passing the solvent down a short column of alumina as described in Appendix 2. The IR spectrum of pure chloroform is shown in Fig. 5.5, and consists of two strong absorptions centred at 1216 and 759 cm^{-1}. In practice, this means that when running solution spectra in chloroform, no useful information about the absorptions of the sample can be obtained in the ranges 1200–1250 and 650–800 cm^{-1}. However, this is not a serious limitation. If chloroform is considered too toxic, use dichloromethane.

Remember, chloroform is toxic

To run a solution IR spectrum, make up a 5–10% solution of the compound in pure chloroform. The internal volume of the solution cells is quite small, so 0.2–0.5 mL of solution is plenty. If the sample is a liquid, a solution of about 10% concentration can easily be approximated by adding 1 drop of liquid to 9 drops of chloroform. If the sample is a solid, it is best to weigh it out, bearing in mind the difficulty in estimating weights by eye; dissolve 10–20 mg of solid in 0.1–0.2 mL of chloroform. To transfer the solution to the IR cell, draw it up into a 0.5 or 1.0 mL syringe, remove the needle, and holding the cell by its top edges slightly inclined from the vertical, fill the cell through the

Fig. 5.5 IR spectrum of chloroform.

lower syringe port (Fig. 5.4b). As the liquid enters, air is displaced through the top port. It is important that the cell is filled beyond the top of the window, and that no air bubbles are present. Having filled the cell, gently but firmly stopper the two syringe ports with the small Teflon® stoppers. Clean out the syringe with fresh chloroform, and fill the reference cell with pure chloroform. Place the sample cell in the sample beam of the IR spectrometer, the reference cell in the reference beam, and record the spectrum. If the cells are perfectly matched, the absorptions due to solvent in the sample and reference cells will cancel each other out, and these peaks will not appear on the final spectrum. However, despite this cancelling, do not forget that you cannot obtain information about the absorption of the sample in the region where chloroform is opaque to IR radiation (see above). After running the spectrum, clean the cells out immediately by flushing with fresh chloroform as shown in Fig. 5.4c. The original solution and washings can be collected as shown, and, if necessary, the sample can be recovered by evaporation of the solvent. Dry the cells by drawing air through with either an empty syringe or by attaching the outlet to a water aspirator. Never dry solution cells by attaching them to the compressed air line; the air stream from compressors is inevitably contaminated with dirt and grease. Finally, return the clean, dry cells to a desiccator.

Mulls

Spectra obtained from samples in the solid state look different from spectra obtained on the same compound in solution

Infrared spectra of solid samples can also be recorded in the solid phase. However, it should be borne in mind that, in the solid state, intermolecular forces are particularly strong, and will affect the vibrational properties of the molecule; the IR spectrum obtained on a compound in the solid state may look quite different from that obtained in solution (see Fig. 5.14). This is particularly true for compounds containing polar functional groups that can participate in hydrogen bonding. Because of these additional complications associated with the solid state, many organic chemists prefer, as a matter of course, to run IR spectra in dilute solution.

Before you can record the IR spectrum of a solid sample, the solid must be made transparent to IR radiation. One way to do this is to prepare a *mull* by grinding the solid with an inert carrier agent. The usual carrier agent is a liquid hydrocarbon oil (paraffin oil, mineral oil); the commercial material most commonly used is known as Nujol®. Nujol® shows the characteristic absorptions associated with the C–C and C–H vibrations of hydrocarbons, and its IR spectrum is shown in Fig. 5.6. The spectrum consists of four major peaks centred at 2922, 2854, 1461 and 1377 cm^{-1}. Obviously when recording the IR spectrum of a Nujol® mull, the C–H and C–C vibrations of the sample will be obscured by those of the mulling agent. If it is important to examine the C–H vibration region (*ca.* 3000 cm^{-1}) of your sample, then hexachlorobutadiene can be used as an alternative mulling agent since, as can be seen from its IR spectrum in Fig. 5.7, it is transparent in this region.

To prepare a Nujol® (or hexachlorobutadiene) mull, place about 5 mg of

Fig. 5.6 IR spectrum of Nujol®.

Solid must be finely ground

the solid in a small agate mortar, and grind it to fine powder using the agate pestle. It is very important that the solid be finely ground since large particles cause reflection and scattering of the radiation. Ideally the particle size should be less than the shortest wavelength of the radiation, in other words less than 2.5 μm (4000 cm^{-1}). Because of this requirement for finely ground samples, it is better to grind the sample *before* adding the mulling agent. Having ground the sample, add 1 small drop of Nujol®, and continue to grind the sample until the mull takes on a thick pasty consistency. If the mull is too thick, add another drop of Nujol®. Chemists very quickly develop their own technique for transferring the mull to the sodium chloride plates, but one of the best methods is to use a thin flexible piece of metal such as a razor blade (**mind your fingers!**). Spatulas are generally too thick and inflexible. Scrape the mull out of the mortar, and place it as a blob in the centre of the circular sodium chloride plate (*cf.* Fig. 5.3a) or, better, as a thin line along the plate diameter. Never attempt to spread the mull over the whole surface of the plate. Place the second plate on top, and gently but firmly squeeze the plates together to distribute the sample evenly into a thin layer between the plates, taking care not to scratch the plates with any solid that may remain in the mull. Place the plates in the sample holder in the sample beam, and with nothing in the reference beam, record the spectrum. After running the spectrum, clean the plates

Do not add too much Nujol®— add it 1 drop at a time

Fig. 5.7 IR spectrum of hexachlorobutadiene.

with a tissue soaked in dichloromethane, and return them to their desiccator or jar. It is not easy to recover the sample from Nujol® mulls.

KBr disks

The second way to record IR spectra of samples in the solid state is in the form of a KBr disk or wafer. Potassium bromide is completely transparent throughout the IR range, and therefore has advantages if the absorptions of the mulling agent interfere. However, special equipment in the form of a hydraulic press is needed, and this may not be available in your laboratory. To prepare a KBr disk, grind about 2 mg of sample in a small agate mortar. Add 300–400 mg of pure spectroscopic grade KBr, and mix, but *do not grind*, with the sample. Place the mixture in the die of the press, and subject it to high pressure (*ca.* 1000 bar) for a few minutes. This causes the KBr to become fluid, resulting in the formation of a very fragile translucent disk, which can be removed from the die with tweezers and placed in the sample beam of the IR spectrometer; the spectrum can then be recorded.

KBr disks are fragile: handle them carefully

The design of hydraulic press varies, but a typical example is shown in Fig. 5.8a. It consists of a hydraulic ram (which can be pumped up by hand to the required pressure) on which is placed a die of appropriate diameter, usually in the range 7–13 mm. Since KBr is hygroscopic, the die often incorporates an

Fig. 5.8 (a) A typical hydraulic press and die for preparing KBr disks; (b) a small low cost press for preparing KBr disks.

outlet for connection to a vacuum so that the sample can be pressed in the absence of atmospheric moisture. If your laboratory does not possess a purpose-designed hydraulic press, various low cost small presses are available. One design is shown in Fig. 5.8b. The press consists of a thick metal casing with a threaded central hole, at the centre of which is a small (1 mm) diameter hole leading to a vacuum take-off. Two machined bolts with flattened polished faces complete the press. One bolt is screwed into place, the sample is placed in the press on the end of the bolt, and the second bolt is screwed down on top of it. Grip the whole assembly in a vice, and tighten the bolts with a spanner or wrench to press the disk. After a few minutes, loosen and remove the bolts. The press is designed so that is can be placed directly into the sample beam of the instrument, so that there is no need to attempt to remove the fragile disk from the press. If carefully prepared, KBr disks give excellent results. However, there are two notes of warning. Since KBr is hygroscopic, the spectra often show an O–H absorption, and before assigning this to your sample, remember that it may be due to the absorbed water in the disk. Secondly, KBr disks may give different spectra from those of the same solid obtained as a mull (see Fig. 5.14), and direct comparison of solid state spectra is not possible unless they were prepared in the same way.

KBr is hygroscopic!

Running the spectrum

One of the great advantages of IR spectroscopy is that highly satisfactory spectra can be recorded on relatively low cost instruments, thereby bringing the technique within the range of most organic laboratories. IR spectrometers usually require very little adjustment, and have relatively few controls.

Although one instrument will differ slightly from another, the general protocol for running an IR spectrum is as follows. Before starting the scan, check that the chart paper is positioned correctly with respect to the horizontal position of the pen. If not, the position of the paper must be adjusted. The only other controls that you need to worry about are the *100% control*, the scan speed/stop/start control and, occasionally, the *gain control*. Having placed your sample (and reference if necessary) in the spectrometer, adjust the vertical position of the pen to about 95%T using the 100% control. Select a scan speed; often the choice is just fast or slow, and press the scan start button. At the end of the run the scan will stop automatically. At this stage it is as well to check the calibration. Remove the sample (and reference) and replace it with a standard reference sample of polystyrene film. Back up the chart paper and superimpose a section of the reference spectrum on that of your sample. Polystyrene has a very sharp, but strong, absorption at $1602\,cm^{-1}$, and it is normal to record only this section of the reference spectrum. If the calibration is out, then the appropriate correction factor must be applied to all peak positions. Occasionally you should check the *gain* of the spectrometer, and this is done with no sample in the beam. Set the pen position to 90%T using the 100% control, and place your hand in the sample beam so that the pen dips to about 70%T. Quickly remove your hand, and the pen should immediately and quickly return to the 90%T mark after overshooting it by 1 or 2%. If the pen returns sluggishly or badly overshoots, the gain should be adjusted using the gain control. Some instruments have a *gain check* button, and pressing this replaces putting your hand in the beam.

Polystyrene as reference

It is rare that serious problems are encountered in using IR spectrometers, and poor spectra are usually the fault of poor samples rather than the instrument. The two most common minor problems are spectra in which the peaks are too strong, i.e. a lot of the peaks are in the 0–10%T range, and the reverse problem of spectra with very weak 70–90%T peaks. The first problem is due to too much sample, and is easily corrected if a neat liquid is being used, by squeezing the plates together to make a thinner film. If a solution is being used, dilute the sample with more solvent. If a Nujol® mull is being used, squeeze the plates together to make a thinner film, or, if that fails, remake the mull using less sample or more Nujol®. Similarly if a KBr disk is being used, remake the disk using more KBr. To deal with the problem of weak spectra, the reverse procedures apply—add more sample. The only possible problem in this respect is with neat liquids; if the liquid is volatile, it may evaporate from between the plates in the warmth of the sample beam. In such cases, the spectrum must be recorded in solution.

Interpreting the spectrum
The interpretation of IR spectra can be carried out at different levels according to why you ran the spectrum in the first place. If you know what the compound is, the interpretation may consist of confirming the presence of the

characteristic peaks associated with the vibrational absorptions of certain functional groups, and confirming the absence of others. Alternatively, since every organic compound has a unique IR spectrum, the interpretation may simply involve comparing your spectrum, peak for peak, with a published spectrum of the same compound, thereby confirming its identity. However, if you do not know what the compound is, the spectrum must be analyzed much more thoroughly in order to extract the maximum amount of information from it. Although it is rarely possible to assign the complete structure of an unknown compound from its IR spectrum alone, you will be able to identify certain bond types and functional groups which, in combination with other data, will lead to the correct structure.

Initial deductions

Whatever level of interpretation is required, the analysis of IR spectra follows a few simple guidelines. These guidelines become second nature, and you will soon learn what to look for first when confronted with an IR spectrum. When analyzing an IR spectrum, always proceed as follows:

Where to look first

1 Start at the high frequency (4000 cm^{-1}) end, as many of the common functional groups of organic chemistry absorb in the high frequency half of the IR spectroscopic range.

2 Look at the largest peaks first; these are usually the most structurally significant.

3 Do not try to identify every peak; smaller peaks are often overtones (harmonics) or even 'noise'.

4 Note the absences of peaks; the absence of a strong peak in a key area of the spectrum is as equally diagnostic as the presence of peaks.

Having some idea of what peaks to look at first, you need to assign them to specific bond types or functional groups within the molecule. Fortunately these assignments are greatly facilitated by the fact that a vast body of IR spectroscopic data has been accumulated over the last 40 years. These data have been combined into *correlation tables* which link peak position with various types of functional groups; correlation tables for the major functional groups of organic chemistry are included in Appendix 3. In order to analyze *Division of the spectroscopic range* your IR spectrum using the correlation tables, it is convenient to divide the IR spectroscopic range (4000–600 cm^{-1}) into smaller sections, and the key dividing point is 1500 cm^{-1}. The region to the right (lower frequencies) of this line is usually complex, consisting of many peaks, and is therefore difficult to interpret. Although some functional groups do show characteristic absorptions in this range (Table 5.1), many of the absorptions correspond to vibrations of the molecule as a whole, and since these are unique to the particular compound, this part of the spectrum is known as the *fingerprint region*. The region to the left (higher frequencies) of 1500 cm^{-1} is much more useful, since it is here that most of the common functional groups of organic chemistry absorb. For convenience, this 4000–1500 cm^{-1} region of the spectrum is further subdivided

Table 5.1 IR correlation table.

Frequency (cm⁻¹)	Functional group	Comment
4000–2500 region		
3600	O–H	Free, non-H-bonded; sharp
3500–3000	O–H	H-bonded; broad peak
	N–H	Amine or amide; often broad
3300	≡C–H	Sharp
3100–2700	C–H	Variable intensity
3500–2500	COO–H	Carboxylic acids; broad
2500	S–H	Weak
2500–1900 region		
2350	CO_2	Carbon dioxide from path-length imbalance and not your sample!
2200	C≡C, C≡N	Often weak
2200–1900	X=Y=Z	Allene, isocyanate, azide, diazo groups, etc; strong
1900–1500 region		
1850–1650	C=O	Strong
1650–1500	C=C, C=N	Variable intensity
1600	C=C (aromatic)	Often weak
1550	–NO₂	Strong
1500–600 region		
(fingerprint region)		
1350	–NO₂	Strong
	–SO₂–	Strong
1300–1250	⟩P=O	Strong
1300–1000	C–O	Alcohol, ether, ester; strong
1150	–SO₂–	Strong
850–700	Aromatic C–H	*o-, m-, p-*disubstituted benzenes
800–700	C–Cl	Usually strong

into three smaller portions (4000–2500, 2500–1900 and 1900–1500 cm⁻¹), the division being based on the type of functional group which absorbs there. The various regions of the IR spectroscopic range, together with the bond and functional group types associated with them, are shown schematically in Fig. 5.9.

The information contained in this simple correlation chart is also given, in slightly more detail, in tabular form in the IR correlation table (Table 5.1). These types of correlation charts and tables form the basis of the analysis and interpretation of IR spectra, and from them you should learn to locate the important regions in the spectrum. Do not try to remember the exact vibration frequency of every functional group and bond type, but rather get to recognize the O–H/N–H, C–H and C=O regions. Use Fig. 5.9 and Table 5.1 to

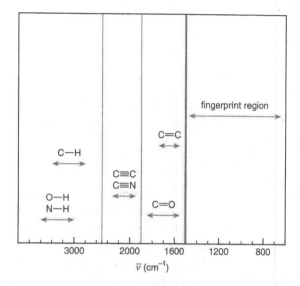

Fig. 5.9 Simple IR correlation chart showing the major regions of the spectroscopic range.

help you make your initial deductions about the presence, or absence, of certain types of groups within your molecule. Having done this, carry out a more thorough analysis of your spectrum using the more detailed correlation tables in Appendix 3. Expanded versions of these tables are widely available in standard spectroscopy texts, and most of your lecture texts will contain some IR correlation tables.

More detailed analysis

The 4000–2500 region

This is the region where bonds to hydrogen usually absorb, and hence C–H, O–H and N–H bonds all show stretching absorptions in this range. Because of the effect of atomic mass on vibration frequency, the higher frequency absorptions are the O–H and N–H absorptions. Therefore as you 'read' the spectrum from left to right, the first peaks that you might encounter around $3500\,cm^{-1}$ are likely to be due to O–H or N–H stretching. Peaks in this region of the spectrum are highly diagnostic; if no peaks are present then the compound does not contain such functional groups. One note of warning: beware of small peaks in the 3600–$3200\,cm^{-1}$ range since these could possibly be overtones of strong carbonyl peaks in the 1800–$1600\,cm^{-1}$ range.

O–H (Appendix 3, Table A3)

The O–H group of alcohols and phenols absorbs in the range 3500–$3000\,cm^{-1}$. It is rare to observe the absorption of the 'free' O–H group—if present it is a sharp band at about $3600\,cm^{-1}$—since both alcohols and phenols are usually

Hydrogen bonds

H-bonded dimer of
a carboxylic acid

*Intermolecular vs
intramolecular hydrogen
bonding: distinguish by dilution*

involved in hydrogen bonding. The resulting polymeric hydrogen-bonded aggregates manifest themselves as broad peaks in the IR spectrum. The appearance of these broad peaks varies according to the type of hydrogen bonding involved. Carboxylic acids, for example, form strongly hydrogen-bonded dimers, which result in the O–H stretching absorption being extremely broad, reaching down to about 2500 cm^{-1}. The position of O–H absorptions can also depend on whether the hydrogen bond is intermolecular or intramolecular. However, you can distinguish between these possibilities by running the IR spectra in chloroform solution at different sample concentrations. In relatively concentrated solution both intermolecular and intramolecular hydrogen bonds are possible. Intramolecular hydrogen bonds are unaffected by dilution, and therefore the position of absorption remains the same. Intermolecular hydrogen bonds, on the other hand, are broken on dilution, and therefore the broad band they produce will disappear on dilution of the sample to be replaced by the sharper, higher frequency, free O–H band. In the solid state, the O–H absorption band is always broad. The positions of various types of O–H groups are given in Table A3 in Appendix 3, and some examples of IR spectra of compounds containing O–H bonds are shown in Figs 5.10–5.12.

Figure 5.10 shows the IR spectrum of a simple alcohol, 2-methylcyclohexanol (*cis/trans* mixture) run in the liquid phase. The most striking feature of the

Fig. 5.10 IR spectrum of 2-methylcyclohexanol.

2-methylcyclohexanol

2-chlorophenol

2-hydroxybenzaldehyde
(salicylaldehyde)

(intramolecular H-bond)

cyclohexanecarboxylic
acid

spectrum is the strong broad absorption centred at 3353 cm⁻¹, typical of the O–H stretching frequency of hydrogen-bonded alcohols. The presence of such a band in the IR spectrum of an unknown compound would be strongly indicative of an alcohol group, but since alcohols necessarily contain a C–O bond, you should immediately check for the presence of this to confirm your initial deduction. Compounds with C–O bonds (alcohols, ethers, esters) show a strong absorption due to C–O stretching in the range 1300–1000 cm⁻¹, although the unambiguous assignment of the C–O absorption is complicated by the fact that other functional groups also absorb in this region (see Table 5.1). However, the *absence* of a strong peak in this region does suggest that there is no C–O bond in your molecule, and hence your initial deduction about the alcoholic O–H group is probably wrong; the assumed O–H may in fact be N–H (see p. 295). In the example shown in Fig. 5.10 there are three strong bands around 1050 cm⁻¹, probably due to C–O stretching.

Continuing with the analysis, moving to the right of the O–H peak, there are only two more significant peaks above the fingerprint region at 2927 and 2857 cm⁻¹. These are aliphatic C–H stretching absorptions (see below and Table A5 in Appendix 3). Detailed analysis of the fingerprint region is not usually possible, although in this case the C–H bending deformation absorption at 1451 cm⁻¹ is clearly seen.

Figure 5.11a shows the IR spectrum of a phenol, 2-chlorophenol, in the liquid phase. Starting our analysis from the 4000 cm⁻¹ end, the first peak we come to is a broad peak centred at 3522 cm⁻¹. Again this would strongly suggest a hydrogen-bonded O–H group. The only other significant peak above the fingerprint region is at 1586 cm⁻¹; this is associated with the aromatic ring C=C absorptions (see also Table A8 in Appendix 3). The lack of strong C–H absorptions at about 3000 cm⁻¹, seen in the previous example, should also be noted. Aromatic C–H stretching absorptions are much weaker than aliphatic stretching absorptions.

Figure 5.11b shows the liquid phase IR spectrum of another phenol, salicylaldehyde (2-hydroxybenzaldehyde), and nicely illustrates the effect of hydrogen bonding on the position and appearance of the O–H absorptions. As indicated by the structure, the phenolic O–H of salicylaldehyde is strongly intramolecularly hydrogen bonded to the aldehyde carbonyl. The effect of this is seen in the spectrum; the O–H peak is broader and at a lower frequency than the other phenol (Fig. 5.11a). The effect of intramolecular hydrogen bonding is also seen on the position of the C=O stretching absorption which, at 1667 cm⁻¹, is lower than expected for an aromatic aldehyde (see below). Since the O–H group is intramolecularly hydrogen bonded, dilution of the sample would have no effect on the appearance of the spectrum.

Figure 5.12 shows the IR spectrum of cyclohexanecarboxylic acid. The spectrum is dominated by the intense broad absorption from 3500 to 2500 cm⁻¹ corresponding to the O–H stretch of the carboxyl group. This broad band is highly characteristic of carboxylic acids, but the assignment can be confirmed

Fig. 5.11 (a) IR spectrum of 2-chlorophenol; (b) IR spectrum of salicylaldehyde.

Fig. 5.12 IR spectrum of cyclohexanecarboxylic acid.

by the presence of a strong peak in the $1700\,cm^{-1}$ region corresponding to the C=O stretching absorption—$1703\,cm^{-1}$ in the present example. It should be noted that although the COOH peak is broad and intense, the strong C–H stretching absorptions are still clearly seen at 2932 and $2857\,cm^{-1}$.

N–H (Appendix 3, Table A4)

O–H or N–H?

As can be seen from Fig. 5.9 and Table 5.1, the stretching frequency of N–H bonds occurs in the same region of the spectrum as that of O–H bonds. This can lead to confusion and possible misinterpretation. However, there are a number of ways in which a distinction may be made. We have already seen that the O–H stretch of alcohols and acids is *always* accompanied by a C–O and C=O stretch, respectively, thereby confirming O–H assignments in the $3500\,cm^{-1}$ region. In addition, the N–H absorption is usually less intense than the O–H, and since N–H bonds do not participate in hydrogen bonding as readily as O–H, the peaks are usually sharper. The positions of various types of N–H absorptions are detailed in Table A4 of Appendix 3, and some examples of IR spectra of compounds containing N–H bonds are shown below.

Figure 5.13 shows the IR spectrum of a primary amine, cyclohexylamine. The spectrum was recorded on the neat liquid. The first absorption consists of

Fig. 5.13 IR spectrum of cyclohexylamine.

cyclohexylamine

two sharp peaks at 3354 and 3279 cm⁻¹ superimposed on a broader band. These correspond to N–H stretching absorptions, the underlying broadness being due to hydrogen bonding. Primary amines always give two bands, whereas secondary amines with only one N–H bond give a single peak; tertiary amines, lacking N–H bonds, of course, are transparent in this region. Amines also show N–H bending absorptions of medium intensity in the 1650–1550 cm⁻¹ region, and you should always look for this peak to confirm your initial assignment of the N–H stretching peak. In the present example, the peak is seen at 1600 cm⁻¹. The only other peaks outside the fingerprint region in the spectrum of cyclohexylamine are the by now familiar strong C–H stretching absorptions at 2927 and 2853 cm⁻¹. The C–H bending deformation at 1450 cm⁻¹ is seen within the fingerprint region.

N-phenylethanamide (acetanilide)

Primary and secondary amides also contain N–H bonds, and the IR spectrum of a typical secondary amide, N-phenylethanamide (acetanilide) is shown in Fig. 5.14. The example also illustrates the effect of running IR spectra with the sample in different phases; some differences between the spectra recorded in chloroform solution (Fig. 5.14a), in the solid state as a Nujol® mull (Fig. 5.14b) and as a KBr disk (Fig. 5.14c) should be immediately apparent. As usual we start our analysis from the high frequency end, and focus on the peaks in the 3300 cm⁻¹ region. The solution spectrum shows two peaks at 3436

Fig. 5.14 IR spectrum of *N*-phenylethanamide (acetanilide): (a) in chloroform solution; (b) as a Nujol® mull; (c) as a KBr disk.

NHCCH₃

(KBr)

Fig. 5.14 *Continued.*

and 3318 cm⁻¹ due to N–H stretching. In the solid state spectra, the N–H absorption is lowered to 3295 cm⁻¹. The tentative assignment of a peak to an amide N–H *must* be confirmed by locating the corresponding C=O stretching absorption. The relevant peaks occur in the carbonyl region of the spectrum; amides show two peaks in this range, referred to as amide I (higher frequency) and amide II. Again the positions of the peaks are dependent on the method of sample preparation, and they appear at lower frequency in the solid state. In the present example, the solution spectrum shows the amide I peak at 1685 cm⁻¹. Amide II which is usually less intense is probably the peak at 1525 cm⁻¹. In the solid state spectra, the amide I peak occurs at 1666 cm⁻¹. Other differences between the spectra that should be noted are as follows: the presence of chloroform peaks due to imperfectly matched cells in Fig. 5.14a; the presence of Nujol® peaks in Fig. 5.14b—the peaks at 1461 and 1377 cm⁻¹ are hidden; the absence of Nujol® C–H peaks in the KBr spectrum; the general broadening of the N–H region up to 3500 cm⁻¹ in the KBr spectrum probably due to the presence of water in the sample as KBr is hygroscopic.

C–H (Appendix 3, Table A5)

The vast majority of organic molecules contain C–H bonds, and therefore their IR spectra contain peaks due to C–H vibration absorptions. The C–H

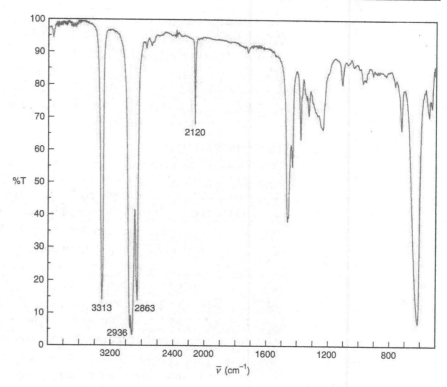

$HC \equiv C(CH_2)_4CH_3$

Fig. 5.15 IR spectrum of 1-heptyne.

Strength, and hence absorption frequency, of C–H bond depends on hybridization of C

$C_5H_{11}C \equiv CH$

1-heptyne

stretching absorption occurs at the high frequency end of the spectrum in the range 3300–2700 cm^{-1}, the exact position depending, amongst other things, on the strength of the C–H bond in question. Since the strength of a C–H bond depends on the hybridization of the carbon atom involved, we can use IR spectroscopy to identify different types of C–H bond. The strongest C–H bonds are those involving sp hybridized carbons, the stronger bond resulting from orbitals with a high degree of s-character. Hence the highest frequency C–H stretching absorptions are exhibited by terminal alkynes. The absorption is always sharp, usually quite intense, and occurs around 3300 cm^{-1}. Figure 5.15 shows the IR spectrum of 1-heptyne, and the acetylenic C–H is clearly seen at 3313 cm^{-1}. The presence of a terminal acetylene can be confirmed by locating the C≡C stretching absorption. This occurs in the range 2150–2100 cm^{-1} (2120 in the present example), although it is often rather weak in intensity, and may be missed. The other characteristic peaks in Fig. 5.15 are the aliphatic C–H stretching absorptions at 2936 and 2863 cm^{-1}.

C–H bonds involving sp^2 hybridized carbon atoms absorb at just above 3000 cm^{-1}, whilst as we have seen several times already (Figs 5.10, 5.12, 5.13, for example), bonds to sp^3 carbons absorb just below 3000 cm^{-1} in the range 2950–2850 cm^{-1}. In terms of peak intensity, C–H absorptions involving sp^3 carbons are usually very strong, whilst those involving sp^2 carbons are much weaker. Aromatic C–H bonds give particularly weak IR bands (Fig. 5.11a), and are often not clearly visible. The aldehyde–CHO group deserves special mention; aldehydes usually show two weak bands in the range 2900–2700 cm⁻¹ due to C–H stretching, and these are visible in the spectrum of salicylaldehyde (Fig. 5.11b) at 2847 and 2752 cm⁻¹. Although these aldehyde C–H bands are not completely diagnostic, the presence of an aldehyde is easily confirmed by locating the strong C=O band.

The 2500–1900 region

This region of the spectrum is comparatively easy to interpret since, of the functional groups that you are likely to encounter, only alkynes and nitriles absorb in this region. The other functional groups which absorb here are much less common, and are of the cumulene type, X=Y=Z, such as isocyanates (RN=C=O), azides (RN=$\overset{+}{N}$=$\bar{N}$), diazo compounds (R₂C=$\overset{+}{N}$=$\bar{N}$), ketenes (R₂C=C=O), carbodiimides (RN=C=NR) and allenes (R₂C=C=CR₂). One very simple cumulene is carbon dioxide (O=C=O) which absorbs at about 2350 cm⁻¹. IR spectra quite often contain a small peak or pair of peaks around 2350 cm⁻¹; these may be puzzling at first sight until you remember that any slight inequalities in path length in the spectrometer will result in imperfect subtraction of sample and reference beams, and hence a peak due to atmospheric carbon dioxide will appear in the spectrum (see Fig. 5.18a).

C≡C (Appendix 3, Table A6)

As we have already seen in Fig. 5.15, terminal alkynes absorb in the range 2150–2100 cm⁻¹. In non-terminal alkynes this absorption moves to a slightly higher frequency (2250–2150 cm⁻¹), although as with terminal alkynes, the band is often weak. The intensity of the C≡C stretching absorption in both types of alkyne is increased if the triple bond is conjugated to an alkene or carbonyl. In symmetrical, or nearly symmetrical, alkynes, which have a zero or very small dipole moment, the C≡C stretching absorption is usually absent.

C≡N (Appendix 3, Table A6)

$$\underset{\text{ethyl cyanoacetate}}{CH_3CH_2O\overset{\overset{\displaystyle O}{\displaystyle \|}}{C}CH_2CN}$$

Nitriles exhibit similar triple bond stretching absorptions to alkynes, although the C≡N bond absorbs at a slightly higher frequency in the range 2270–2200 cm⁻¹. Again the absorption band is often very weak. Figure 5.16 shows the IR spectrum of ethyl cyanoacetate recorded as a thin film. Starting from the left we can interpret the spectrum as follows: the weak bands at around 3500 cm⁻¹ are overtones of the strong carbonyl peak at around 1750 cm⁻¹; the two bands at 2987 and 2937 cm⁻¹ are the familiar strong sp³ C–H stretching absorptions; the nitrile peak is at 2266 cm⁻¹; the ester carbonyl has a very strong absorption at 1747 cm⁻¹; and the associated C–O stretch is probably the strong peak at 1201 cm⁻¹.

The 1900–1500 region

This is the region where double bonds absorb IR radiation, and detailed cor-

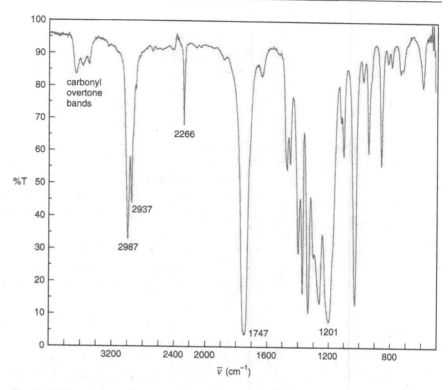

CH₃CH₂OCCH₂C≡N
‖
O

Fig. 5.16 IR spectrum of ethyl cyanoacetate.

relation tables for C=O and other double bonds are given in Tables A7 and A8 in Appendix 3. The carbonyl group has a large dipole moment, and has an intense C=O stretching absorption. Therefore the presence of a strong peak in your spectrum at around 1700 cm⁻¹ is highly indicative of a carbonyl group. Indeed the absorption is so strong that the overtones can usually be seen at around 3500 cm⁻¹. Since the exact type of carbonyl group can often be inferred from the precise position of its IR absorption, careful analysis of this region of the spectrum is usually very helpful in assigning structures to unknown compounds. Carbon–carbon and carbon–nitrogen double bonds usually absorb at lower frequency than carbonyl groups.

C=O (Appendix 3, Table A7)

All carbonyl-containing compounds show a strong band corresponding to the C=O stretching absorption in the range 1800–1600 cm⁻¹. The exact position of the peak varies according to the specific functional group and its environment. For detailed correlation values see Table A7 in Appendix 3, but rather than trying to remember all these values, you may find it more useful to remember some general guidelines as to the position of the carbonyl group in various compounds. These can be summarized as follows.

cyclobutanone
1780 cm^{-1}

cyclopentanone
1746 cm^{-1}

cyclohexanone
1713 cm^{-1}

1 In compounds of the type RCO.X, the more electronegative the group X, the higher the frequency of the carbonyl absorption. Thus acid anhydrides (X=OCOR), acid chlorides (X=Cl) and esters (X=OR) all absorb at higher frequency than ketones (X=carbon).

2 When the carbonyl group is in a ring, the smaller the ring, and hence the greater the compression of the carbonyl bond angle, the higher the frequency; six-membered rings and larger give carbonyl absorptions similar to acyclic analogues.

3 If the carbonyl group is conjugated to a C=C bond, the carbonyl frequency is lowered by 40–15 cm^{-1} (except for amides).

4 Hydrogen bonding to the carbonyl oxygen lowers the frequency by about 50 cm^{-1}.

Some examples of IR spectra of compounds containing carbonyl groups are shown in Figs. 5.11b, 5.12, 5.14 and 5.16–5.18. The examples are chosen to illustrate the major types of carbonyl functional group, and to exemplify the above guidelines.

Figure 5.11b shows the IR spectrum of an aromatic aldehyde, salicylaldehyde. The carbonyl absorption is at 1667 cm^{-1}; this is lower than normal for an aromatic aldehyde (1715–1695 cm^{-1}) because of the hydrogen bonding to the adjacent hydroxyl. As has already been discussed, aldehydes also show C–H absorptions in the range 2900–2700 cm^{-1}.

Figure 5.12 shows the IR spectrum of a carboxylic acid, and Fig. 5.14 shows an amide. These spectra have already been discussed, and you will find that the positions of the carbonyl peaks conform to those expected from the correlation table in Appendix 3.

The spectrum of an ester is shown in Fig. 5.16; the carbonyl peak is at 1747 cm^{-1}. Esters can usually be distinguished from ketones by the presence of the associated C–O stretch, which ketones do not possess.

Figure 5.17 shows the IR spectra of two simple cyclic ketones, cyclopentanone and cyclohexanone, and illustrates the effect of ring size on the position of the carbonyl absorption. Ring strain shifts the C=O absorption to a higher frequency, and hence in cyclopentanone the peak is at 1746 cm^{-1} (Fig. 5.17a). Cyclohexanone, a relatively unstrained ketone, shows a C=O peak at 1713 cm^{-1} (Fig. 5.17b), a value typical of an acyclic ketone. In cyclobutanone, however, the effect of increased strain is to shift the C=O absorption to about 1780 cm^{-1}. Apart from the differences in carbonyl absorption, the spectra of both ketones show weak absorptions at around 3500 cm^{-1} due to overtones of the carbonyl peak, and similar C–H absorptions in the 2970–2860 cm^{-1} range, although there are obvious differences in the fingerprint region.

Figure 5.18a shows the IR spectrum of butanal (butyraldehyde), the analysis of which is fairly straightforward, as follows: typical strong sp^3 C–H stretching absorptions at 2962 and 2876 cm^{-1}, a small shoulder on the side of the 2876 peak which may be the aldehyde C–H stretch, and the strong carbonyl peak at 1714 cm^{-1}. Since the second aldehyde peak is obscured by the adjacent strong

CH$_3$CH$_2$CH$_2$CHO

butanal
1714 cm^{-1}

Fig. 5.17 (a) IR spectrum of cyclopentanone; (b) IR spectrum of cyclohexanone.

CH₃CH₂CH₂CHO

Fig. 5.18 (a) IR spectrum of butanal (butyraldehyde); (b) IR spectrum of butenal (crotonaldehyde).

C–H peak, this spectrum also illustrates the dangers of relying on small peaks for structural assignments. The pair of small peaks at about 2350 cm^{-1} is due to carbon dioxide!

Figure 5.18b shows the spectrum of butenal (crotonaldehyde), and nicely illustrates the effect of conjugation on the position of the C=O absorption, which is to lower the frequency by about 25 cm^{-1} to 1690 cm^{-1}. It should also be noted that the C–H region lacks the strong C–H stretches associated with sp^3 C–H bonds, the sp^2 C–H absorptions being much weaker. Hence the two aldehyde bands are more easily seen. The strong band at 1642 cm^{-1} is due to the C=C stretching absorption.

CH$_3$CH=CHCHO

but-2-enal

1690 cm^{-1}

C=C (Appendix 3, Table A8)

Although C–C single bond absorption is not particularly useful for structure determination, the absorptions of C=C double bonds are quite useful. Most compounds containing C=C bonds show stretching absorptions in the 1680–1500 cm^{-1} region of the spectrum. Remember that the C=C bond is weaker than the C≡C bond, and therefore absorbs at a lower frequency. Simple alkenes show a weakish absorption in the range 1680–1640 cm^{-1}. Conjugation with another double bond increases the intensity of, and lowers the frequency of, the absorption. Therefore the C=C bond in α, β-unsaturated carbonyl compounds is usually easy to pick out (1642 cm^{-1} in Fig. 5.18b), although it is weaker than the associated carbonyl peak. Conjugation of the C=C bond with a lone pair of electrons, as in enamines and enol ethers, also increases the intensity of the C=C absorption, but *increases* the frequency. Aromatic C=C bonds are a special case, and most aromatic compounds show two or three bands in the region 1600–1500 cm^{-1}. The reason that aromatic C=C bonds absorb at lower frequency than aliphatic C=C bonds is that the reduced π-overlap associated with aromatic delocalization means that the aromatic C=C bond is not a true double bond, and is therefore weaker than an alkene C=C bond. The presence of two or three bands in this region of the spectrum is often diagnostic of an aromatic compound (*cf.* Fig. 5.11), the presence of which can usually be confirmed by additional strong bands in the 850–730 cm^{-1} region of the spectrum. These bands result from out-of-plane aromatic C–H vibrations, the position of the bands being dependent on the number of adjacent aromatic protons. Hence, in principle, differently substituted aromatic compounds can be identified by the positions of these IR absorptions. For example, *ortho*-substituted benzenes with four adjacent hydrogens show a strong band in the range 770–735 cm^{-1}, and although this absorption can be seen in the spectra of the *ortho*-substituted phenols shown in Fig. 5.11, the general complexity of the fingerprint region often makes such unambiguous interpretations impossible.

Conjugation increases intensity of C=C absorption

The fingerprint region

By its very nature, the fingerprint region of an IR spectrum is complex, and detailed analysis is not usually possible. However, as we have seen, some useful information can be extracted from this region of the spectrum; for example, the distinction between ester and ketone carbonyls can be made by looking for the ester C–O absorption in the fingerprint region. Other functional groups of organic chemistry such as nitro- and sulfonyl also show characteristic absorptions in the fingerprint region, and the more important of these are summarized in Table A9 in Appendix 3.

Further reading

A selection of reference books that contain sections on IR spectroscopy is given below:

L.J. Bellamy, *The Infrared Spectra of Complex Molecules*, 2nd edn, Chapman & Hall, London, 1981.

L.D. Field S. Sternhell and J. Kalman, *Organic Structures from Spectra*, 2nd edn, Wiley & Sons, New York, 1995.

L.M. Harwood and T.D.W. Claridge, *Introduction to Organic Spectroscopy*, Oxford University Press, Oxford, Chapter 3, 1996.

C.J. Pouchert (ed.) *The Aldrich Library of Infrared Spectra*, 3rd edn, Aldrich Chemical Co. Inc., Milwaukee, USA, 1981.

C.J. Pouchert (ed.) *The Aldrich Library of FT-IR Spectra*, Aldrich Chemical Co. Inc., Milwaukee, USA, 1985.

R.M. Silverstein, G.C. Bassler and T.C. Morrill, *Spectrometric Identification of Organic Compounds*, 5th edn, Wiley & Sons, New York, 1991.

D.H. Williams and I. Fleming, *Spectroscopic Methods in Organic Chemistry*, 5th edn, McGraw-Hill, Maidenhead, 1995.

For a discussion of FT-IR spectroscopy, see: P.R. Griffiths and J.A. de Haseth, *Fourier Transform Infrared Spectrometry*, Wiley & Sons, New York, 1986. S.F. Johnston, *Fourier Transform Infrared: a Constantly Evolving Technology*, Ellis Horwood, Chichester, 1991.

5.3 Nuclear magnetic resonance spectroscopy

It is no exaggeration to say that the development of NMR spectroscopy has been the single largest factor contributing to the rapid progress in organic chemistry during the second half of the twentieth century. Prior to about 1955, all organic structures had to be determined by combinations of chemical tests and degradations—such as those described in Chapter 4—supplemented where possible by the small amount of information available from optical absorption measurements. As a consequence, structure determination was the major activity (at least when measured by the time spent in its performance) of organic chemists. During the pre-NMR period of chemistry it would not have been at all unusual for a complete research project for a graduate student to be the elucidation of the structure of a single natural product of only moderate complexity. The great difficulties associated with the determination of structures by chemical means naturally diverted effort away from other, perhaps more central problems of organic chemistry, such as the synthesis of complex molecules and the investigation of the intermediates and mechanisms of organic reactions.

Circumstances are quite different now, as NMR (in conjunction with the other physical methods described in this chapter) permits the straightforward determination of the structure of most small-to-medium organic molecules (say with molecular weights below 1000) in a very short time. This is especially true in synthetic work, where the range of structures to be considered is naturally restricted by the known compositions of the reactants. As a result, it becomes possible to try out new reactions on a small scale, and to discover much about what has happened during the reaction (or even what is happening as it takes place) without the lengthy purification and degradations required in earlier times. The pace of chemical experimentation and discovery can therefore be much faster.

NMR instrumentation is quite expensive, but nevertheless it is fairly common for teaching laboratories to possess at least a rudimentary spectrometer. Even if your laboratory lacks this facility, you should be provided with NMR spectra of the materials you handle. It is most important to get into the habit of examining these and trying to understand the information they contain, and especially to relate the changes in the spectra to the reactions you are doing. In this way it is easy to develop an appreciation of NMR spectroscopy suitable for everyday application to organic chemistry. Do not fall into the trap of viewing NMR as a rather disconnected, perhaps disconcertingly physical subject, remote from the thinking of organic chemists. In reality we shall see that there is a strong connection between the kinds of information contained in NMR spectra and the way in which organic structures are represented—which is of course what makes the technique so useful. The physical theory of NMR is an intriguing subject that forms a major research area in its own right, but if you find yourself attracted by this aspect there are many specialized texts available and some of these are listed at the end of this section. To understand NMR at a level useful for organic chemistry the following very simple physical model will suffice.

Nuclear resonance comes about because the nuclei of at least one of the isotopes of most elements possess *magnetic moments* (in other words, they behave like small bar magnets). The magnetic moment arises because the nucleus may have 'spin', and is also charged, so that if you like you can think of it as a tiny loop of electric current (Fig. 5.19). When placed in a constant magnetic field, the energy of the nuclear magnetic moment obviously depends on the orientation of the nucleus with respect to that field (just as bar magnets attract or repel according to their relative orientation), and on the microscopic nuclear scale only certain energies are permitted (that is, the energy is quantized). Application of electromagnetic radiation at a suitable frequency can stimulate transitions between the nuclear energy levels, which as usual provides the basis for any form of spectroscopy.

NMR thus differs from other kinds of absorption spectroscopy only with

Nuclear 'spin'

307

Fig. 5.19 Three ways of picturing a nucleus: as a spinning, charged ball (top), a loop of current (middle) and a bar magnet (bottom).

respect to the requirement for the sample to be subjected to an external magnetic field. So by analogy with IR, for instance, we can devise an experimental set-up to measure the resonances (Fig. 5.20).

The aim here is to find the combinations of external field and applied frequency that cause absorption of the electromagnetic energy by the sample; we may conveniently achieve this by holding one parameter static (say, the field) and varying the other (i.e. the frequency). This is the most obvious way to perform NMR, and is most likely to be the way a basic instrument, as may be found in a teaching laboratory, will work. Later we will see that there is an alternative approach that offers distinct advantages. However, in the main you will probably find it useful to keep in mind the analogy with the more 'obvious' IR or UV measurements, and imagine NMR spectra to be obtained by varying the frequency of applied electromagnetic radiation while the sample sits in a constant magnetic field. This measurement mode is known as the *continuous wave* (CW) method, with *frequency sweep*.

The fundamental properties of a nucleus of significance for NMR are clearly its spin, characterized by quantum number I that can take integral or half-integral values (for example, $0, 1/2, 1, 3/2 \ldots$), and the relationship between its angular momentum and its magnetic moment, a parameter known as the *gyromagnetic ratio*, often represented by γ. From our point of view, we are obviously concerned that I should not be zero, because then there is no spin and hence no magnetic moment; however, it also turns out that nuclei with $I > 1/2$ have rather inconvenient NMR properties, so that we will, in practice, only be investigating nuclei for which $I = 1/2$. The normal isotope of hydrogen (^{1}H) is, fortunately, such a nucleus, but we are not so lucky with the element of

Fig. 5.20 Schematic diagram of a simple NMR spectrometer.

greatest importance to organic chemistry (carbon!) as its most abundant isotope (^{12}C) has $I = 0$, as do all nuclei with even atomic number and mass. However, natural carbon contains around 1.1% ^{13}C, which does have $I = \frac{1}{2}$, so that NMR of carbon is possible, although with more difficulty and with significantly different information content in the resulting spectra (of which more later). The number of quantized energy states allowed for a nucleus with spin I is $2I + 1$, so that spin $\frac{1}{2}$ nuclei can only be in either of two states. In the 'bar magnet' picture (Fig. 5.21) you can think of these two states as corresponding with parallel and antiparallel arrangements of the magnet relative to the static field; the lower energy (parallel) state is often labelled α, whereas that of higher energy (antiparallel) state is represented as β. The NMR resonance corresponds with a flip of the magnet from parallel to antiparallel, or in other words with transitions from α to β. We will find shortly that this rather simplistic picture helps us to understand some very important interactions that make NMR distinctively different from other kinds of spectroscopy.

The frequency at which nuclei 'resonate' depends on the applied magnetic field

For practical applied field strengths (typically in the range 1.4–14 tesla), nuclear resonances are found to occur in the radiofrequency region (for instance, protons resonate around 60 MHz at a field strength of 1.4 tesla), and the resonant frequency is directly proportional to the field (so in a 14 tesla magnet the proton frequency increases to 600 MHz). Different nuclei have

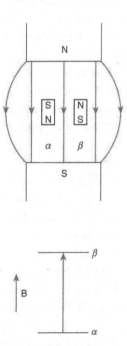

Fig. 5.21 Using the 'bar magnet' picture, we can see that the two orientations of the nuclei relative to the static field will have different energies (top). Transitions between the resulting energy levels are responsible for the NMR absorption (bottom).

different gyromagnetic ratios and hence different NMR frequencies (for example, ^{13}C resonates at about one-quarter of the frequency of ^1H for the same applied field). These gross changes from one nucleus to another are of practical significance in that they affect the ease with which NMR measurements can be made, but otherwise they are not relevant from the point of view of structure determination. It is the much more subtle changes in frequency depending on various aspects of the environment of the nuclei that are chemically interesting.

Preparing the sample

Before proceeding to investigate the use of NMR spectra, it is appropriate to discover how they are obtained in practice. This section covers sample preparation techniques that you will need to use yourself in your day-to-day application of NMR to routine problems.

NMR specialists are often regarded as mildly eccentric by the organic chemists who consult them, because despite having ordinary, harmless views on most topics, they seem to suffer from a highly specific form of paranoia when it comes to the preparation of NMR samples. The object is to put the sample, in solution, in a tube and you might suppose that there is not much room for error on the chemist's part. However if you reflect for a moment on the nature of the NMR experiment it should become clear that the spectroscopist's paranoia is not entirely misplaced. Throughout the discussion of coupling on pp. 326–328, frequent reference will be made to interactions that cause line splittings of 1 or 2 Hz. Now, this measurement might be made on a spectrometer with an operating frequency of 500 MHz, and so detection of a 1 Hz frequency difference is a measurement accurate to 2 parts in 10^9 (equivalent to measuring the distance between the earth and the moon to within a few centimetres). Considerable effort is required to construct and maintain instrumentation capable of measurements of this kind, so it is a shame if easily avoided problems related to sample quality are allowed to degrade performance.

High resolution NMR spectra are always obtained on samples in solution. In preparing a sample for NMR spectroscopy it is necessary to select a solvent, arrange that the solute concentration is appropriate to the measurement to be attempted, and eliminate, so far as possible, any contaminants that might affect the homogeneity of the field in the region of the sample. The third point is particularly important, and means taking care to remove solid particles that might be suspended in the solution, because these distort the static magnetic field and hence degrade the resolution of the spectrometer.

Many solvents are suitable for use in NMR spectroscopy, but it is necessary to replace any hydrogen they contain with deuterium. This is in order that the solvent proton signal does not obscure the much weaker signals from the solute, and also because, on advanced spectrometers, the NMR resonance of the deuterated solvent (^2H has $I = 1$) is used as a reference to stabilize the

15–25 cm

5 mm

3–5 cm

Fig. 5.22 NMR sample tube—typical dimensions.

instrument. All the usual organic solvents are available in deuterated form, although in some cases at considerable cost (Table 5.2). For routine applications of proton NMR, chloroform-*d* (CDCl$_3$) is the most versatile and economic solvent.

Samples for proton NMR are usually prepared in glass tubes of 15–25 cm length and 5 mm outside diameter, which are specially made for NMR spectroscopy (Fig. 5.22). The volume of solvent to be placed in the tube varies depending on the model of spectrometer in use, but is typically 0.4–0.7 mL. Do not make the mistake of *filling* the tube! Only a small portion of the total length (about 3–5 cm) should contain solution. On a 60 MHz CW instrument it will probably be necessary to use at least 25 mg of substance in order to obtain adequate spectra, which is far more material than is needed for other spectroscopic techniques. On a modern, high-field instrument this quantity may be reduced to less than 1 mg, but even so NMR is a method of rather low sensitivity.

In order to avoid problems with floating particles in the sample, it is good practice to prepare the solution in a small vial, and then filter it directly into the NMR tube. This can conveniently be done using a Pasteur pipette with a small plug of cotton wool pushed into the narrow section (Fig. 5.23). Take care that the sample is compatible with these materials; if it is not, glass wool can be used instead, but this does not make such an effective filter.

For dilute samples, signals due to both residual proteated solvent and dissolved water can obscure significant regions of the spectrum (see the spectra of solvents in Table A16 in Appendix 3). The latter is often the more objectionable of the two, and so it is sometimes helpful to combine the filtration of the sample with drying using sodium sulfate or alumina above the plug in the pipette. Once again you should consider whether the sample will be adversely

Table 5.2 Properties of some deuterated NMR solvents.

Solvent	Relative cost*	mp (°C)	bp (°C)	δ¹H
Acetone-*d*⁶	10	−93	55	2.05
Acetonitrile-*d*³	15	−48	81	1.95
Benzene-*d*⁶	10	7	79	7.16
Chloroform-*d*	1	−64	61	7.27
Dichloromethane-*d*²	20	−97	40	5.32
Dimethyl sulfoxide-*d*⁶	10	18	190	2.50
Methanol-*d*⁴	15	−98	65	3.31
Pyridine-*d*⁵	40	−42	114	8.71, 7.55, 7.19
Tetrahydrofuran-*d*⁸	100	−106	65	3.58, 1.73
Toluene-*d*⁸	20	−93	110	7.1–6.9, 2.09

*The relative cost column gives approximate costs per unit weight, relative to that for chloroform-*d*.

Fig. 5.23 A convenient arrangement for filtering NMR samples.

affected by any drying agent chosen. Molecular sieves are not very suitable for drying NMR samples, as they sometimes contain fine dust that is difficult to remove by filtration.

Once the sample is in the tube, the tube is sealed with a plastic cap and mounted in a turbine assembly before being placed in the spectrometer (Fig. 5.24). This is in order to allow the tube to be spun at fairly high speed (20–30 Hz) about its vertical axis, which helps to average out inhomogeneities in the magnetic field. Care should be taken to ensure that the outside of the tube and turbine assembly are clean before introducing them into the spectrometer, because contamination in the active region of the instrument is very detrimental and hard to remove. The spinning of the sample, although essential if high resolution spectra are to be obtained, sometimes introduces artefacts into the spectrum in the form of satellite lines separated from the real lines by one or two multiples of the spinning speed (Fig. 5.25). These satellites, known as *spinning sidebands*, should never be more than a few per cent of the height of the main peaks; if they are bigger, the spectrometer is in need of adjustment. Spinning sidebands can sometimes be confused with other small, genuine peaks. If this is a problem the sidebands can readily be identified by re-running the spectrum with altered spinning speed, in which case the sidebands move while the real peaks do not.

Samples for ^{13}C NMR were traditionally prepared in 10 or 15 mm outside

Fig. 5.24 NMR tube mounted in the turbine assembly.

Fig. 5.25 Spinning sidebands at two different spinning speeds. With faster spinning (top) the sidebands are weaker and further from the main line.

Fig. 5.26 Typical arrangement for ¹³C NMR, using a large diameter tube, 1–3 mL of sample and a vortex suppressor.

diameter tubes, which require a solvent volume of 1–3 mL in order to allow the use of large amounts of substance (around 150–200 mg) to compensate for the much lower signal strength obtained with this nucleus (see pp. 341–345). However, it is now common to find 'dual purpose' spectrometers that permit the measurement of ¹H and ¹³C spectra on the same sample and, for these instruments, 5 mm tubes are used in both cases. When the larger tubes are necessary, it is virtually essential to employ a plastic or glass plug known as a *vortex suppressor*, in order to prevent the spinning of the sample creating a whirlpool in the solution. The vortex suppressor is introduced after the solution, and is pushed down until it just contacts the liquid surface (Fig. 5.26). Plastic types, made from PTFE (Teflon®), are a close fit in the tube and usually have a small hole through the centre to let trapped air escape; the glass ones are looser fitting and float on the surface of the solution. Both kinds incorporate a hook or threaded hole so that they can be fished out after the experiment is finished.

Obtaining the spectrum

There are two kinds of NMR spectrometer in widespread use at present. In the teaching laboratory you are most likely to find CW instruments, which use permanent magnets and obtain the spectrum by sweeping either the field or the frequency as described on pp. 307–308. Operation of this kind of instrument is not substantially different from the use of an IR absorption spectrometer. The sample is introduced as described above, and the instrument sweeps through the spectroscopic region plotting out the signals as it goes. There will be controls to allow the selection of the sweep range, alteration of the sensitivity and adjustment of the magnetic field homogeneity, amongst others, but these are instrument-specific and cannot be described here.

In the research laboratory, CW spectrometers have been virtually supplanted by machines that work on an entirely different principle in order to offset a major problem with NMR that has already been mentioned: low sensitivity. The sensitivity of NMR is so low that it is unsatisfactory even when every aspect of the spectrometer has been carefully optimized. It is therefore useful to employ *signal averaging* to improve further the signal-to-noise ratio. It can be shown, by analyzing the statistical properties of the electrical noise in the NMR spectra, that by repeating the analysis and summing the results, the sensitivity increases as the square root of the number of repetitions (in other words, doing the experiment four times gives twice as good a result).

Now, this can certainly be attempted on a CW spectrometer, but unfortunately it proves to be inefficient because of the time taken to sweep through the spectrum. An alternative, and much better, approach is to measure *all* the NMR resonances simultaneously. This can be achieved by applying a short, intense pulse of radio energy to the sample, which is absorbed by all of the nuclei present. After the pulse, the sample *emits* signals for a time, while the various transitions return to their equilibrium state. The

Fig. 5.27 Typical line shape obtained on a CW spectrometer. The 'wiggles' following the line are absent from spectra obtained in FT mode.

resulting signal, called a *free induction decay* (FID), consists of a superimposition of all the resonances from the sample, which have to be unscrambled in order to obtain the familiar presentation in the form of a spectrum. The unscrambling is done by an arithmetical process known as *Fourier transformation*, and so this experiment mode is referred to as *FT NMR*. The point of the exercise is to increase the speed of the measurement in order to make signal averaging efficient.

The above description will scarcely give you more than a flavour of what is involved in FT NMR, but regrettably there is insufficient space to provide more details. FT spectrometers are characterized by much higher sensitivity than equivalent CW instruments. In addition, the FT technique tends to be used on more advanced systems with high magnetic field strengths, so the effective difference is even more noticeable. Very high magnetic fields, from about 4.5 tesla upwards, are obtained using *superconducting magnets*, in which a current flows in a coil of wire immersed in a bath of liquid helium. After being established, such magnets require no power, and have very good properties with respect to stability and homogeneity of the field. Apart from differing in terms of signal-to-noise ratio and peak separation, the spectra obtained on low field CW and high field FT instruments are basically similar, the only major distinction being the appearance in CW spectra of 'ringing' patterns after the lines (Fig. 5.27). For clarity, some of the spectra in this chapter have been obtained on high field FT instruments, but the worked examples in Figs 5.54 and 5.55 were run at 60 MHz in CW mode.

Interpreting the spectrum

Main features

Homing in on the resonances of a single nuclear species such as ^1H, we generally find that not all nuclei in a molecule resonate at exactly the same frequency. By scanning through the expected range within which the resonances fall (which is known from past experience), we obtain a spectrum containing peaks corresponding to the different absorption frequencies. The origin of these differences will be surveyed in the following sections, but we can quickly gain some perspective on the usefulness of NMR spectroscopy by considering three facts (until further notice, the discussion will now be concerned solely with ^1H NMR).

1 *Peak positions depend on chemical environment*. For instance, in benzyl acetate the methyl group contributes a signal in a different position to the benzylic CH_2 (Fig. 5.28). This variation in frequency is known as the *chemical shift*, in recognition of its link with chemical structure.

2 *Peak intensities depend on the number of contributing nuclei* (subject to certain experimental conditions, which will normally be met in ^1H NMR). This means that the methyl resonance of benzyl acetate will be 1.5 times stronger

Fig. 5.28 Proton spectrum of benzyl acetate.

Fig. 5.29 Part of the proton spectrum of Z-3-chloropropenoic acid, showing the splitting of each alkene signal into a doublet.

than that due to the CH_2. However, you have to be careful about what is meant by 'peak intensity'; a point which is discussed later.

3 *Peaks have a fine structure related to the presence of neighbouring nuclei.* In Z-3-chloropropenoic acid (β-chloroacrylic acid) each of the two alkene protons exhibits a signal consisting of two lines of slightly different frequency (Fig. 5.29). This phenomenon, known as *coupling*, reflects the fact that each proton is in some sense 'aware' of the fact that its neighbour can be in one of two states (i.e. α or β).

These three things are all we need to understand. We will examine the significance and application of these aspects of NMR in detail, but it is quite exciting to notice immediately how the information in NMR spectra is peculiarly well suited to structure determination. The fact that chemical shifts reflect the chemical environments of nuclei is obviously useful. However, it is not so different from the observation that, for instance, certain IR bands

NMR permits elucidation of molecular 'connectivity'

reflect the presence of functional groups. What *is* different, and is unique to NMR, is the coupling interaction that reveals relationships between pairs of nuclei. We will see that coupling depends essentially on the existence of paths of *bonds* through which the interaction is relayed, and of course mapping out paths of bonds is just what structural elucidation is about. It is this feature above all that makes NMR useful in chemistry.

Measuring chemical shifts

The two spectra we have seen so far contained no indication of the separation between the various peaks, but obviously this will normally be required. Your first thought might be that the natural thing to do is to measure the exact frequency of each resonance, in a similar fashion to the presentation of IR spectra; however, although this is possible there are two reasons why it is not satisfactory. Firstly, the absolute frequency of the resonances depends on the static field, and this varies (widely) between spectrometers, comparison of spectra obtained on different instruments would be difficult and, since the use of NMR rests in part on the comparison of known spectra with that of the unknown, this is quite unacceptable. Secondly, it turns out that the variations in frequency due to chemical shifts are very small (typically less than 1000 Hz for protons at 60 MHz), so that making absolute frequency measurements to a suitable degree of accuracy and reproducibility is technically difficult. The solution to these problems is to measure shifts *relative* to a reference NMR signal, and to express them as *fractional* changes. So, if the reference signal has frequency F_{ref} and an NMR resonance is found at F, its chemical shift δ is *defined* as

Frequencies are always measured relative to a reference signal

$$\delta = \left(F - F_{ref} \right) / F_{ref}$$

Notice that this definition implies that signals at higher frequency than the reference have positive chemical shifts. This choice of 'direction' for the scale, which has now been agreed as an IUPAC convention, has not always been consistently adopted in the past, so that some care is needed when working with data from old literature (in practice this problem is mainly encountered for nuclei other than ^1H and ^{13}C). Another scale which may be encountered in older literature, but which is now not used, is represented as τ and is defined as $\tau = 10 - \delta$ (the historical origin of this confusion lies in the possibility of measuring NMR spectra by varying either the frequency or the field; τ is the 'field sweep' version). All chemical shifts in this book are expressed on the δ scale.

The δ scale clearly depends on the choice of a reference signal, and for both ^1H and ^{13}C NMR the universally agreed standard is the methyl resonance of tetramethylsilane (TMS). On rudimentary spectrometers this substance, which is conveniently inert and volatile (for subsequent ease of removal), is generally added to the sample so that the correct referencing of the spectrum can be checked directly. Whenever proton chemical shifts are quoted you can assume, in the absence of any statement to the contrary, that they are relative to TMS. Clearly, from the definition of δ the shift of TMS itself is 0. Some further rather subtle points regarding chemical shift referencing are discussed on pp. 350–351.

The range of proton shifts is of the order of hundreds of hertz at 60 MHz, as indicated above, so that the most convenient units for δ are 'parts per million' (ppm). Protons in the majority of organic structures have chemical shifts that fall within the range 0–10 ppm, although a significant minority are found outside this region in both the positive and negative directions. By convention, NMR spectra are presented so that the δ scale increases *from right to left*. We now have enough information to put a scale on the benzyl acetate spectrum (Fig. 5.30).

There is a final point of notation regarding chemical shifts which is rather confusing, as it again has its origin in the historical distinction between field and frequency sweep spectra. Regrettably, it is still in widespread use and you must be aware of it. Resonances with high (positive) chemical shifts (on the δ scale, which is a frequency scale) are often referred to as being at 'low field'. So, the left-hand end of Fig. 5.30 would commonly be described as 'the low field end', whereas the methyl resonance of benzyl acetate is found 'to high field' of that due to the CH_2. Because it is confusing, this terminology will not be used again in this book, but you will certainly encounter it in conversation and in the literature. Beware of the chaos that may result from careless use of such terms!

Fig. 5.30 The conventional presentation of a proton spectrum covering the range 0–10 ppm with δ increasing from right to left.

The meaning of chemical shifts

Chemical shifts arise because of the local magnetic properties of molecules. That is, the static field at the site of each nucleus is not quite the same as the external field applied to the sample. The essential character of this effect is that the nuclei are, to a greater or lesser extent, *shielded* from the external field by the magnetic behaviour of their surrounding electrons. They therefore resonate at lower frequency than would an equivalent 'naked' nucleus. Variations in structure, and particularly those that influence the electron density in different parts of the molecule, alter the extent of this shielding and hence give rise to chemical shifts. There is a well-developed theory to explain these variations in shielding, but from the perspective of organic chemistry all that is needed is empirical information concerning the influence of different structural features on chemical shifts. This has been built up from the measurement of the spectra of many compounds of known structure, and is recorded in the form of tables of shift data (for instance, those in Appendix 3).

Nuclei experience 'local' magnetic fields which differ slightly from the applied magnetic field

Data tables are the primary source of shift information, but it is neither pleasant nor desirable to spend much time poring over such collections of numbers. For the routine interpretation of proton NMR spectra it is fortunately much more important to have an appreciation of general trends than to be able to remember the exact shifts of specific compounds. It is also essential not to make the mistake of attaching too much significance to the exact values of chemical shifts. Beginners often use tables, such as Tables A10 and A11 in Appendix 3, to estimate shifts to several decimal places, and then base structural conclusions on the equality or otherwise of these predictions with the signals found in the unknown. This approach, although unfortunately common, is fundamentally wrong; the correlations do not always correspond that well. Estimated shifts should be used as a *guide*, to help you to find your way around a spectrum; other, more substantial evidence, principally derived from patterns of coupling, must be used to support suggested structures. You can best build up familiarity with the typical chemical shift ranges for different structural fragments simply by regular use of NMR spectra in conjunction with your practical work, but as a starting point the following guidelines may be helpful.

Rough chemical shifts values can be estimated by combining a knowledge of the basic areas of the spectrum in which different groups resonate, with a feel for the variations induced by substituents. We will see that the effectiveness of substituent groups in influencing chemical shifts correlates quite well with familiar chemical concepts such as electronegativity and the strength of inductive and mesomeric effects, so that the necessary categorization of groups should already be familiar to you. The essential theme that runs through all of what follows is that reduction in the electron density around a nucleus moves its chemical shift to higher frequency (i.e. more positive δ or the left of the spectrum), by virtue of increasing its exposure to the applied field (*deshielding*). (**Warning**: this is a naïve view,

Lowering the electron density around a nucleus (deshielding) causes resonance at higher frequencies

and there are many special cases and exceptions, but it works well enough to be of some value.) We will use terms such as 'shifted to high frequency', 'deshielded' or 'increased chemical shift' to indicate the displacement of peaks towards the left-hand end of the spectrum. The following discussion is not intended to be a comprehensive survey of the variation of shifts with structure, which you can readily find in texts, but rather is an overview to get you started.

Basic shift ranges

To begin with it is helpful to identify three regions within the typical 0–10 ppm range of proton chemical shifts that are particularly characteristic of different groups in the absence of modification by substituents. The majority of protons in organic structures fall into one of these three types:

0–2 ppm	Alkane protons (the aliphatic region)
5–6 ppm	Alkene protons (the olefinic region)
7–8 ppm	Arene protons (the aromatic region)

Some special cases, such as protons bound to heteroatoms, are discussed later. These basic values are then modified according to the various trends mentioned below. In following this approach it is important to keep in mind that the aim is to establish *very roughly* the region in the spectrum in which a particular type of proton might reasonably be found to resonate. Arguments based on these trends, or on the more detailed additivity rules summarized in Table A11 in Appendix 3, work best in non-rigid systems for which the influence of various substituents is averaged over a wide range of conformations. In rigid molecules, *anisotropic* (uneven) magnetic effects around certain kinds of bond or functional group can cause wide deviations from the expected shift ranges, and some examples of these will be discussed later. You should not be surprised to find protons in rigid systems resonating up to about 1 ppm away from their estimated positions, but deviations much greater than this should be treated as a cause for suspicion that the assignment or structure is wrong.

Substituent effects

The basic resonance frequencies are modified by many factors, of which the most important are the following.

1 *In aliphatic compounds, increased branching leads to increased shift* (i.e. δ *increases in the series* $CH_3 < CH_2 < CH$). For example, in 2-methylbutane, the methyl groups resonate near $\delta\,0.9$, the methylene at $\delta\,1.2$ and the methine at δ 1.45 (Fig. 5.31).

2 *Substitution by electronegative elements causes increased shift, and the degree of the shift correlates roughly with electronegativity.* So, for instance, while an aliphatic methyl group would resonate around $\delta\,0.8$, the methyl resonance of methylamine is found at $\delta\,2.3$ and that of methanol is at $\delta\,3.3$. This effect, which as you can see is quite strong for protons adjacent to the heteroatom, is also propagated with rapidly reducing intensity to more distant protons—for example, examine the shifts indicated for 1-nitropentane (Fig. 5.32).

Fig. 5.31 Proton spectrum of 2-methylbutane at 500 MHz.

Fig. 5.32 Chemical shifts of methylene protons in 1-nitropentane at increasing distances from the electron-withdrawing substituent.

3 *Substitution by electropositive elements causes decreased shift.* This is much less commonly observed in practice, as many compounds in which carbon is bound to a more electropositive element are reactive organometallic species. It is, however, the reason that the TMS resonance occurs at lower frequency than those of most other normal organic compounds.

4 *Substitution by unsaturated groups causes increased shift.* Vinyl substitution generally produces an increase in shift of about 1 ppm (e.g. allylic methyl groups typically resonate around $\delta 1.6$) while aryl groups and carbonyls have a stronger effect (e.g. the methyl groups of toluene and acetone are both found close to $\delta 2.2$).

5 *In unsaturated compounds, mesomeric effects can also influence shifts.* The direction of the shift depends on whether the substituent has a $+M$ or $-M$ effect, and the locations at which it is most effective can be predicted by drawing resonance structures, or by 'arrow pushing'. For instance, the introduction of a methoxyl substituent on a benzene ring causes a *decrease* in the

MeO

H δ5.3

OMe

Fig. 5.33 The strongly deshielded methine proton of benzaldehyde dimethylacetal.

Anisotropic effects

shift of the 2 and 4 protons by about 0.5 ppm, but has much less effect on the protons in the 3 position.

All these effects are roughly additive, so that a CH group bearing three strongly deshielding substituents such as 2 × MeO and Ph might be found straying into the 'alkene' part of the spectrum. For example, the methine proton of benzaldehyde dimethylacetal resonates at δ5.3 (Fig. 5.33).

Certain bonds or groups are found to have characteristic effects on the shifts of nearby protons that are spatially *anisotropic*; in other words, you get different effects in different places. Because they are dependent on the relative spatial arrangement of groups, the analysis of these shifts can be particularly useful. A simple way to picture the variation in shift around such groups is to divide their surroundings into two regions, separated by a boundary in the shape of two cones with their points meeting (Fig. 5.34). Protons located on one side of this boundary will experience increased chemical shift (indicated by a + sign in the figure), while protons on the other side experience the opposite effect. *The orientation of the cones relative to the group, and the location of the + and −regions, depends on the group.* Figure 5.34 illustrates the pattern of shielding and deshielding regions for several common groups (deshielding = increased shift = +).

A common and strong effect of this kind is associated with the carbonyl group (Fig. 5.34d). As a result of lying in the strongest part of the deshielding region surrounding the C=O bond, aldehyde protons are found to resonate in

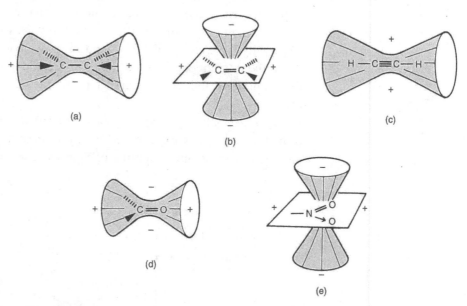

Fig. 5.34 Anisotropic magnetic fields surrounding carbon–carbon single, double and triple bonds (a)–(c) and carbonyl and nitro groups (d, e). + = regions of increased shift; − = regions of decreased shift. (Adapted from H. Günther, *NMR Spectroscopy*, 2nd edn, Wiley & Sons New York, 1995, with kind permission.)

(a)

(b)

Fig. 5.35 (a) Cyclophanes, and (b) $4n + 2$ electron annulenes show abnormal chemical shift positions for 'inside' and 'outside' protons.

'Ring currents' in aromatic systems

Protons on heteroatoms

the range 9–11 ppm (of course, it would be expected that the inductive effect of the carbonyl group would cause a shift in this direction, but not to such a great extent). Similarly, in α,β-unsaturated carbonyl compounds, β-substituents *cis* to the carbonyl are shifted to higher frequency than the equivalent *trans* substituents.

Another very important anisotropic effect of this kind is associated with aromatic rings (Fig. 5.35). Here substituents around the outside edge of the ring (in particular, those directly attached to it) are in the deshielding region. This is the reason that shifts of aromatic protons are typically higher than those of alkenes. The existence of the opposite shielding region can be demonstrated with rather contrived compounds, such as cyclophanes (Fig. 5.35a), in which the protons in the middle of the methylene chain are found to resonate at abnormally low frequency. It is also evident in the astonishing difference in shift between the 'inside' ($\delta - 2.99$) and 'outside' ($\delta 9.28$) protons of large aromatic systems such as [18]-annulene (Fig. 5.35b). This effect, which is found to be characteristic of cyclic conjugated π systems containing $4n + 2$ electrons, can be explained in a simple way by imagining that the external field induces a flow of the π electrons around the ring. This *ring current* then generates a local magnetic field which is in the same direction as the static field outside the ring, and in the opposite direction within it (Fig. 5.36).

Protons attached directly to atoms such as nitrogen or oxygen do have characteristic shifts, but the situation here is complicated by the fact that such protons may be involved in interactions such as hydrogen bonding and chemical exchange. As a result, the shifts become strongly dependent on the precise conditions of the measurement. The values recorded in Table A13 (Appendix 3) are typical of those found under average observation conditions (i.e. without taking special precautions to exclude water, acids or bases from the sample). The following factors often alter the shift and appearance of such peaks.

1 *Hydrogen bonding causes very strong shifts to high frequency.* The degree of hydrogen bonding experienced by a proton may vary either because of intramolecular factors, or because of changes of solvent, pH or temperature.

Fig. 5.36 Magnetic fields surrounding a benzene ring. B_0 represents the applied field, B_1 represents the induced field.

Fig. 5.37 The strongly hydrogen-bonded phenolic proton of 2-hydroxybenzaldehyde resonates at an anomalously high frequency. Also see p. 293.

Rates of chemical exchange are sometimes accelerated by traces of acid

For example, phenolic protons typically resonate around δ 5–6, but in 2-hydroxybenzaldehyde (salicylaldehyde) the strong hydrogen bond from the hydroxyl to the adjacent carbonyl group shifts the resonance to δ 11.1 (Fig. 5.37). Carboxylic acids commonly exist as hydrogen-bonded dimers in solutions of moderate concentration, and in this form they have resonances in the region δ 12–14; however, if the dimer can be broken up by dilution or change of solvent polarity, shifts to low frequency of many parts per million can be obtained.

2 *Chemical exchange can cause averaging of resonance positions.* The effects arising from chemical exchange are discussed in more detail later (pp. 345–347) but for the moment we need only consider the observation that, if a proton finds itself alternating between two different chemical environments at a sufficient rate, then its chemical shift becomes the average of the shifts appropriate to those environments. The two cases of interest here are exchange amongst acidic protons within a molecule (e.g. several OH or NH groups), and exchange between such protons and those of water, which is always present in NMR samples to a greater or lesser extent. The rate of this kind of exchange is strongly affected by acid or base catalysis, so that surprising variations may be found between samples containing different batches of the same compound. A highly purified substance may exhibit separate resonances for each of several hydroxyl protons, but on another occasion the presence of a trace of acid may accelerate exchange so that the peaks merge into one. Fast exchange with dissolved water, which resonates around δ 1.6 in chloroform solution, may 'pull' the shifts of acidic protons to lower frequency.

3 *Exchange may broaden peaks.* When exchange is not quite fast enough to achieve complete averaging, the resonances involved may be broadened (see pp. 345–347 for more details). As a general rule, OH and amino-NH resonances in average organic samples do show unusually broad lines as a result of this effect, but clearly changes in solvent, temperature or purity will influence their appearance strongly. The exchange properties of OH and NH protons can be used in a diagnostic test for their presence; this is discussed on pp. 347–348.

4 *Protons attached to nitrogen are broadened for a special reason.* While the common broadness of amino-NH protons can reasonably be attributed to the effect of chemical exchange, it is often found that *amide* protons are also broad; however, it can readily be demonstrated that amide protons are not in fast exchange in the absence of base catalysis. The reason for their broadness is that ^{14}N is an NMR-active isotope with spin 1, and a combination of coupling and the special properties of nuclei with $I > \frac{1}{2}$ leads to the broadening. It is not particularly necessary to appreciate the technicalities behind this effect, but it is important to realize that the broadness of amide protons is not normally due to exchange. An analogous broadening of ^{13}C resonances of carbon attached to nitrogen in certain functional groups can also sometimes be seen.

Some special cases

A few important groupings give rise to shifts that do not fit very well into the pattern described above. Cyclopropanes, which are often regarded in chemical terms as falling somewhere between alkanes and alkenes, do not show such behaviour with respect to their NMR signals. Cyclopropyl methylene resonances are found around δ 0.2 in the absence of deshielding substituents on the ring, and since compounds containing silicon are the only other common species that resonate in this region the observation of such a signal is quite diagnostic. This effect has also been attributed to the existence of a ring current, as in aromatic compounds, but with the difference that since

Protons attached to small rings resonate at lower frequency than expected

the cyclopropyl protons are out of the plane of the ring they fall in the shielding region. Similar shifts to low frequency are seen in other three-membered ring compounds; contrast, for instance, the methylene resonance of oxirane (ethylene oxide, δ 2.54) with that of ethanol (δ 3.59). In four-membered rings the effect, although present, is much smaller.

Alkyne protons also resonate at lower frequency than might at first be expected, with monoalkyl-substituted compounds appearing around δ 1.7–1.9 (see Fig. 5.34c). As *substituents*, however, triple bonds cause the expected shifts to high frequency, leading to the rather surprising observation that in propyne the methyl group and the alkyne proton have the same shift (δ 1.8).

Peaks that should not be there

Aside from the various peaks due to your sample, you are very likely to encounter resonances in NMR spectra due to assorted impurities. Three very common types will be mentioned here; they can all be avoided by good experimental technique!

Take care to remove solvents from your sample

Nice crystalline solids are often assumed to be pure, but they can still contain large residues of the last solvent in which they were dissolved. Peaks of the common solvents, such as diethyl ether, ethyl acetate and acetone, are readily identified in proton NMR spectra, and as long as they are not too intense they are tolerable. However, since solvents are generally of low molecular weight, it does not require a very high percentage of solvent in mass terms to generate very strong NMR signals, and these may obscure regions of the spectrum. Impurities at this level are also unacceptable in samples intended for elemental analysis. In crystalline samples the solvent is often trapped within the crystal, and so it cannot be removed unless the sample is ground to a fine powder. Subsequent pumping under high vacuum for several hours will remove solvents with boiling points below 100°C at atmospheric pressure. Removal of solvent from viscous, liquid samples is much more difficult. The best method, if the material is sufficiently volatile, is short path distillation (pp. 154–155). Failing that, prolonged pumping under high vacuum will be needed. For the removal of spurious peaks from the proton spectrum another alternative is to evaporate solutions repeatedly in a proton-free solvent, such as carbon tetrachloride. Unfortunately, although this is very effective as a way of cleaning up the proton spectrum, it does not help to improve the accuracy of elemental analysis or the yield of your reaction!

A second very common impurity is also solvent-related. Some commercial solvents, particularly the various hydrocarbon fractions, contain a proportion of very involatile material. If small amounts of sample are exposed to relatively large volumes of such solvent, as may easily happen when carrying out chromatography for instance, then the involatile residue may accumulate to an unacceptable extent. These impurities, which are wax-like polymers, give rise to a broad peak in the proton spectrum around $\delta 1.2$ and a weaker triplet at about $\delta 0.8$. This problem can be avoided by using the solvent purification procedures described in Appendix 2.

Impure solvents leave contaminants which give broad absorptions around $\delta 1.2$ and $\delta 0.8$

Finally, most samples are exposed at some stage to apparatus with ground-glass joints. If these are treated with a silicone-based vacuum grease, this inevitably finds its way into the sample and gives rise to peaks at $\delta 0.1$–0.2. To avoid this contamination, which is difficult to remove subsequently, it is best to avoid greasing joints wherever possible. Grease is not necessary on any non-moving joint in a system which will work at atmospheric pressure or will only be used under rough vacuum (e.g. for drying samples). Moving ground glass joints (stopcocks) have to be greased, but these are being superseded by more modern alternatives which use a Teflon® key.

Silicone grease causes signals at $\delta 0.1$–0.2

Measuring peak intensities

The relative intensities of the peaks in a proton NMR spectrum reflect the number of nuclei contributing to them. This information can be used as an assignment aid, for which it is only necessary to determine the relative intensities to the nearest integer multiple, so that sets of equivalent protons can be identified. It can also be used in a more quantitative way to measure the concentrations of different species present in a solution, in which case considerable care may be necessary in order to obtain sufficiently accurate results. It is not appropriate to discuss the latter application here, except to issue a warning. The familiar use of peak intensities to count groups of equivalent protons often leads chemists to have an over optimistic view of the potential of NMR to yield quantitative results with respect to peak intensities. Many conditions, which in routinely obtained spectra are most unlikely to be met, determine whether measurements accurate to better than a few per cent can be made. It *is* possible to use NMR for accurate quantitative analysis, but special care must be taken in choosing experimental conditions.

It is difficult to measure peak intensities accurately. NMR integrations are usually for guidance only

For the former application, however, it can be assumed that routine ^{1}H spectra will provide adequate information. Since NMR signals may be split into several lines by coupling, and since the widths of the lines may vary for a number of reasons, it is necessary to measure areas rather than just peak heights in order to make this comparison. This can be done either by numerical analysis of the spectrum (typical on an advanced spectrometer), or by electronic summation of the signal as it is obtained (typical on a rudimentary spectrometer). Either way the result is presented in the form of an integral, which is usually plotted directly over the spectrum (Fig. 5.38). The size of the

57.9   23.1   35.4

δ ppm

Fig. 5.38 Spectrum of benzyl acetate including the integral. The ratio of the peaks should be $5:2:3$, and in fact is found to be $5.01:2.00:3.06$ in this case.

integral can be measured with a ruler, counted by means of a graticule on the chart paper, or, on a modern computer-controlled spectrometer, displayed in numerical form, as in this example. The measurement will be fairly crude, with perhaps an error of up to ±10%, but should be adequate for counting groups of protons.

The origin of coupling

Imagine measuring the NMR transitions of a proton which has a neighbour. The neighbour can be in one of two states, and, viewing these states as two orientations of a magnet, there are in effect two different types of molecule whose spectra are being measured. In some molecules the neighbour proton is aligned parallel to the external field, while in others it is antiparallel. In order to understand the effect this has on the spectrum of the first proton, we need to consider two questions: how many of the neighbours are in each state, and what influence does the neighbour's state have on the magnetic field experienced by the original proton?

The first question can be answered by comparing the energies of NMR transitions, which are very low, with the general thermal energy in the sample. A Boltzmann distribution is established between the upper and lower levels of the transitions, or in other words between the two orientations of the magnets. With a very small energy difference, the difference in populations of the two states is also small, so that to all intents and purposes we can assume that half the molecules have the neighbour proton in the α-state, while for the

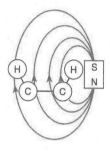

Fig. 5.39 The direct, or dipolar, interaction between two protons reverses as the nuclei change from the α- to the β-state.

Neighbouring nuclei 'couple' with each other

other half the neighbour proton is in the β-state. This is not quite true of course—otherwise it would not be possible to measure the NMR absorption at all—but the excess in the lower energy state is only of the order of 1 part in 10^5 for protons in presently available magnetic fields.

The answer to the second question proves to be slightly more subtle. The most obvious influence of one proton on the other is its direct magnetic interaction: the neighbour proton has a magnetic field, in which the first proton sits, and the direction of this field reverses between the α- and β-states (Fig. 5.39). However, since NMR spectra are measured in solution, we have to allow for the fact that the complete molecule can move freely relative to the static field. This means that the direct interaction, which is known as the *dipolar coupling*, is averaged over all possible relative orientations of the two protons, and because of the symmetry of the field surrounding each nucleus its average value is zero. In order for there to be any remaining interaction between the protons, it is therefore necessary to find a mechanism which is not affected by the molecular motion, and this is obtained by remembering that the nuclei are surrounded by electrons. The state of the neighbour proton can influence the electrons around it, which in turn can influence the field at the proton to be measured, as long as a suitable network of bonds is available to relay the information (we will see what qualifies as a 'suitable network' later). This pathway *through the bonds* leads to an effect which is not cancelled out by motion relative to the static field, and it is the origin of the coupling we observe in solution-state NMR which is known as *scalar coupling*.

Therefore half of the molecules have the neighbour proton in the α-state, and if we measure the spectrum of these molecules we obtain a resonance line for the observed proton. The other half have the neighbour proton in the β-state, and this change influences the static field at the observed proton if there is a suitable path of bonds linking the two. These molecules therefore contribute a resonance line at a different frequency, with the net result that the signal for the observed proton appears as a *doublet*, consisting of two lines of equal intensity. The argument works equally well in reverse, of course, so the signal for the neighbour proton is also split into a doublet. This is the typical pattern of *first-order* coupling, which is an approximation to reality: the resonances of a pair of coupled protons each split into two lines of equal intensity. Although it is not obvious from the preceding discussion, the nature of the coupling interaction is such that the degree of splitting of the signals of each of the coupling partners is equal. Thus the separation between the lines in either doublet can be measured to give us a parameter known as the *coupling constant J* (Fig. 5.40). This is the physical principle; the chemical application arises because of the dependence of coupling on the presence of bonds.

Fig. 5.40 First-order coupling. Each partner in a coupling has its signal split into two lines separated by J Hz.

Measuring coupling constants

Just as for chemical shifts, quantitative measurements of coupling constants are required so that they may be correlated with structural features. There is, however, a vital distinction. Coupling is an interaction within the molecule under consideration, and as such it is *independent of the applied field*. It is therefore essential to measure coupling constants in terms of the actual frequency differences between lines, which are typically in the range 0–20 Hz for proton–proton couplings. Line separations that arise from coupling must *never* be converted to parts per million, because the result would then vary from one spectrometer to another.

Coupling constants between nuclei do not depend on the applied magnetic field

Coupling constants can be measured directly from the spectrum as line separations, *provided that the first-order approximation applies*. This requires that all the chemical shift differences between the coupled protons (measured in hertz) are much larger than all the relevant coupling constants. Guidelines for determining whether first-order analysis is applicable will be presented later. For the moment, it should be noted that increasing the static field increases frequency differences without changing coupling constants, so that first-order analysis is more likely to be possible on spectrometers with stronger magnets. This is one of several motivations for using such instruments.

Coupling constants vary in sign as well as in magnitude, which seems a little mysterious, but in fact has a simple physical interpretation. In the discussion so far we have argued that the state of a neighbour proton (α or β) influences the field at the observed proton, and hence causes its resonance to be split into two lines. While the magnitude of J reflects the strength of this effect, the sign of J reflects its direction. Therefore, suppose that for some particular structure it is found that resonances from molecules in which the neighbour protons are α are at higher frequency than those in which the neighbour protons are β. Then in another structure which gives rise to a coupling of opposite sign, the reverse will be true and the β-neighbours will cause resonance at higher frequency. Either circumstance may arise in practice because of the indirect way in which the interaction is relayed through the molecule. Determination of the sign of J generally requires either detailed analysis of complex coupling patterns, or special experimental techniques; therefore it is not normal to obtain this information in routine applications of NMR. However, it is necessary to appreciate that coupling constants have a sign, because substituent effects that increase the coupling constant (in the sense of making it more positive) may make its absolute value (which is what we observe) bigger or smaller according to whether the basic starting value is positive or negative.

Coupling constants have sign as well as size

Typical coupling patterns

So far we have only considered the interaction between a pair of protons. In realistic chemical structures much more complex patterns of coupling arise, and within the first-order approximation the resulting multiplet patterns can be derived in a straightforward way. Each additional coupling causes further splitting of the lines, so that coupling to one, two or three distinct neighbours

'First-order' splitting patterns

Fig. 5.41 First-order splitting patterns arising from coupling to one, two or three nuclei with distinct coupling constants J_1–J_3.

gives patterns of two, four or eight lines, respectively (Fig. 5.41), and so on for further couplings. The coupling constants can still be obtained directly from the line separations, as indicated in the figure.

The chemical shift of a proton involved in coupling is taken to be the location at which its resonance would be found in the absence of the coupling, or in other words the centre of the multiplet in these first-order cases.

Another common circumstance is equal coupling to two or more protons. This may arise due to accidental equality of certain coupling constants, or out of necessity if several protons are indistinguishable, for example the three protons of a methyl group. The same procedure can be applied to derive the multiplet pattern, but with the difference that some lines are now coincident (Fig. 5.42). There are therefore fewer lines in the multiplet than would be obtained from coupling to an equal number of non-equivalent protons, and the intensities of the lines reflect the number of degenerate transitions that contribute to them. The single coupling constant characteristic of the system is reproduced in each of the line separations.

The result of calculating the multiplet patterns can be summarized in a simple rule: coupling to n equivalent protons leads to a multiplet with $n+1$ lines whose relative intensities are given by the $(n+1)$th row of Pascal's triangle:

Coupling to n equivalent leads to multiplet with n +1 lines

$$
\begin{array}{c}
1 \\
1\ 1 \\
1\ 2\ 1 \\
1\ 3\ 3\ 1 \\
1\ 4\ 6\ 4\ 1 \\
1\ 5\ 10\ 10\ 5\ 1 \\
1\ 6\ 15\ 20\ 15\ 6\ 1
\end{array}
$$

Fig. 5.42 The patterns arising from coupling to two or three equivalent nuclei.

Fig. 5.43 'Double triplet' patterns with the single coupling (a) greater than and (b) less than the sum of the couplings to the two equivalent nuclei.

Cases up to $n = 6$ are easily imagined (e.g. the methine of an isopropyl group). The $n = 2$ and $n = 3$ patterns (1:2:1 triplet and 1:3:3:1 quartet) are extremely common and easily recognized, which makes the identification of ethyl groups, for instance, very straightforward.

The final extension of these ideas to a mixture of coupling of an equivalent group or groups and other non-equivalent couplings follows in a straightforward way. For instance, a proton flanked on one side by a methylene and on the other by a methine may appear as a 'double triplet', in which the disposition of the various components will depend on the relative values of the coupling constants (Fig. 5.43).

With experience it becomes quite easy to pick out characteristic patterns of this kind even in complex spectra. Of course, the patterns presented here are idealized, and on a real spectrometer it will not necessarily be possible to resolve all the different lines expected within a multiplet.

Only nuclei which are close neighbours show measurable couplings

Coupling and chemical structure

Various correlations of the magnitude of *J* with structural features have been obtained, but the most important fact about coupling can be summarized very simply: *it is only large over paths of two or three bonds.* 'Large' in this context means greater than about 2 Hz. The existence of such a coupling between two protons is a good indication that they are in either a *geminal* or *vicinal* relationship to one another (Fig. 5.44). However, in some circumstances such protons can show small or undetectable coupling, so that the reverse conclusion that pairs of protons which appear not to be coupled are more than three bonds apart cannot be so readily drawn. For structure determination *vicinal* couplings are particularly important, because they define a link between protons attached to two adjacent carbon atoms. Mapping out the relationship between carbon atoms obviously plays a large part in defining the structure of organic molecules.

The average value of three-bond proton–proton coupling (^3J) in a freely rotating system (e.g. an ethyl group) is about +7 Hz. This can be modified by substituents attached to the H–C–C–H fragment, the general trend being that electronegative substituents cause a reduction in ^3J. However, this is quite a small effect in saturated systems, the change generally being less than 1 Hz. Much more interesting variations are found in rigid molecules, in which the coupling constant depends on the dihedral and valence angles (ϕ and θ, Fig. 5.45) and the C–C bond length. The dependence on the dihedral angle can be summarized in the *Karplus–Conroy* curve (Fig. 5.46), in which the key features are that the coupling is a maximum for *syn*- and *anti*-periplanar arrangements of the protons (with the latter invariably leading to larger coupling), but falls to a small value for a dihedral angle of about 90°. The H–C–C valence

Vicinal coupling

Fig. 5.44 The observation of a 'large' coupling between protons usually indicates that they are in one of these two relationships.

Fig. 5.45 Definition of the dihedral angle ϕ and valence angle θ.

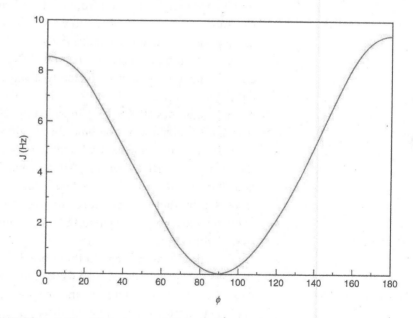

Fig. 5.46 The relationship between vicinal coupling constants and the dihedral angle ϕ. The values of J at $\phi = 0°$ and $\phi = 180°$ may be altered by substituent effects, but the shape of the curve remains the same.

angle dependence is such that larger angles lead to smaller coupling; for instance in acyclic alkenes the coupling between *cis* protons is about 10–12 Hz, whereas for cyclopropenes the widening of the H–C=C angle required by the three-membered ring reduces the coupling to about 1 Hz. An increase in the C–C bond length also leads to a decrease in ^3J.

The form of the Karplus–Conroy curve leads to some very useful applications of ^3J measurements to stereochemical problems. *Cis-* and *trans*-alkenes clearly have H–C=C–H dihedral angles of 0° and 180° respectively, so that it is predicted that the coupling should be larger in *trans* compounds. This is found to be the case in practice, with *cis* couplings typically in the range 9–12 Hz and *trans* couplings in the range 14–16 Hz. Similarly, in rigid cyclohexanes in the chair form, protons in an *axial–axial* relationship invariably show larger coupling than either *axial–equatorial* or *equatorial–equatorial* pairs. Typical values for these and other couplings are given in Table A14 (Appendix 3).

Geminal coupling

Geminal (^2J) coupling constants are found to have a wide range of values between –20 and +40 Hz. However, the most common cases observed in everyday structures are saturated methylene groups, which in the absence of the substituent effects described below, show couplings of around –12 Hz, and terminal alkenes, which show small couplings of around ±2 Hz. The main factors that contribute to the very wide variation in *geminal* coupling are hybridization, substitution by electronegative groups and substitution by π-bonds.

Change in hybridization from sp3 to sp2, and the addition of electronegative substituents at the carbon to which the protons are attached, both cause an increase in ^2J, that is, a change *in the positive direction*. Therefore, the *magnitude* of ^2J initially decreases from its basic value of around 12 Hz as these effects come into play, but sufficiently strong influences may eventually cause an increase in magnitude as the value passes beyond zero. For instance, in methylene imines ($RN=CH_2$), in which the effects of hybridization and electronegative substitution combine, the ^2J value is +16.5 Hz.

Substitution by adjacent π-bonds and by electronegative substituents β to the carbon to which the protons are attached both cause a decrease in ^2J, that is, a change *in the negative direction*. Therefore the *magnitude* of ^2J is usually increased by these effects in sp3 hybridized systems, for which the starting value is almost always negative, but may be increased or decreased in the case of sp2 hybridization.

Long-range coupling

Couplings over more than three bonds are usually less than 2 Hz, but, as we have seen, geminal and vicinal couplings can also fall in this region in some cases. Thus it is important to be able to spot cases in which long-range coupling is likely to occur, and fortunately these can be classified into a few structural types. In saturated systems, significant couplings over four and five bonds are most common when the path of bonds involved is held in a rigid zig-zag arrangement (Fig. 5.47). Four-bond coupling of this kind is often referred to as

Fig. 5.47 The 'W' arrangement of bonds most favourable for four-bond coupling.

Fig. 5.48 Four-bond coupling may also be large in strained rings.

Connecting up couplings

Coupled nuclei must show a common coupling constant

W coupling, for obvious reasons. If the path of bonds is also in a strained ring system, ^4J values can become quite large, for example around 7 Hz for the indicated protons in bicyclo[2.1.1]hexane (Fig. 5.48).

In unsaturated compounds, four-bond allylic coupling (over the path H–C=C–C–H) of around 1–2 Hz is common. Even when this does not appear as a line splitting, it is often responsible for an increase in line width for groups adjacent to alkenes or aromatic rings. coupling over more than four bonds is often found in conjugated alkenes, because such substances naturally tend to adopt the favourable 'W' arrangement.

The interpretation of the values of coupling constants in the light of the effects described above is really a rather specialized aspect of this part of NMR. For the purposes of structure determination it is sufficient to check that the coupling under investigation is the right size to be a short-range (^2J or ^3J) effect. The problem then is to work out which signal elsewhere in the spectrum is due to the proton responsible for the coupling, so that its couplings can be examined in turn in order to continue the chain of assignments. In a simple molecule this may be a trivial question; for instance, in ethyl acetate the methyl and methylene of the ethyl group are the only participants in coupling, and this is immediately obvious from the spectrum. In general, however, connecting up the couplings is the major difficulty to be overcome in interpreting NMR spectra.

One obvious way to tackle this problem is to use the fact that the splittings at each end of a coupling have to be equal. Therefore if it is required to find which proton is responsible for a 6 Hz splitting in a multiplet, then the rest of the spectrum can be searched for a matching splitting. There are two limitations to this approach: it cannot be guaranteed that the other part of the coupling will give rise to a readily identifiable multiplet in a complex spectrum, and since coupling constants only have a fairly narrow range of values, the likelihood of confusion with other couplings is high. Because of these difficulties, considerable attention has been paid to the discovery of experimental methods for identifying coupling partners unambiguously. The traditional solution to this problem, known as *homonuclear decoupling* will be described here, while a more recent and extremely powerful alternative method based on *two-dimensional NMR* is introduced briefly on pp. 354–355.

The essence of the homonuclear decoupling experiment is that the coupling of one proton is 'deactivated' by continuous irradiation at its resonance frequency during the measurement of the NMR spectrum. You can think of this irradiation as bringing about constant, rapid transitions between the α- and β-states of the proton to be decoupled, so that the distinction between the two is effectively lost. All the splittings due to this proton elsewhere in the spectrum then disappear, so that comparison of the spectra obtained with and without decoupling allows the coupling partners to be identified immediately (Fig. 5.49). The limitations of this technique are that a new experiment is needed for each signal in the spectrum, and practical difficulties may be

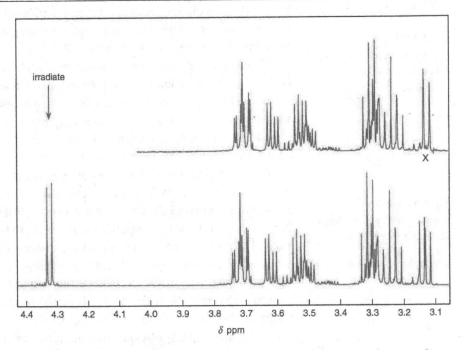

Fig. 5.49 Use of homonuclear decoupling to identify coupling partners in a complex spectrum. The lower trace is the normal spectrum, while in the top trace the doublet at δ 4.32 has been irradiated during the acquisition, causing one splitting to disappear from a double doublet at δ 3.13 (marked X in the top trace).

encountered in achieving selective irradiation of a signal resonance or in identifying the resulting changes in a complex spectrum. These problems are absent from the two-dimensional experiment described later.

Failure of the first-order model

The very simple model we have used to explain coupling patterns so far works well as long as all the shift differences involved in the spin system are much larger than all the coupling constants. When this ceases to be true, care is needed to avoid drawing incorrect conclusions from the appearance of multiplets. The essential character of the first-order approximation is that it attributes each line in the spectrum to a transition of a single nucleus. When the magnitude of the coupling interaction becomes comparable with chemical shift differences this is no longer true, and the lines in the spectrum arise because of transitions involving mixtures of the wave functions of all the nuclei involved in the spin system. It is not appropriate to discuss the theoretical basis of this process here, but it is essential to appreciate the important consequences of it, which are as follows.

1 *Peak intensities no longer follow the first-order rules of Pascal's triangle.*
2 *Line separations are not necessarily equal to coupling constants.*
3 *Chemical shifts are not necessarily at the centre of multiplets.*

Chemical shifts and coupling constants can still be extracted from spectra which deviate from first-order coupling, but a more detailed analysis is necessary. This can be done by hand for small spin systems, and for more complex cases computer programs are available that make the process essentially routine. However, for most straightforward chemical applications there is no particular need to extract these parameters; the essential thing is to avoid measuring line separations and calling them coupling constants when they are not. Therefore you need to be able to recognize the symptoms of deviation from first-order coupling, and these can be illustrated with a few common cases.

For first-order splitting
$\Delta\delta \geqslant 10\Delta J$

The first-order model begins to fail when the smallest shift differences in a spin system are about 10 times the largest coupling constants. For instance, on a 60 MHz spectrometer, shift differences of less than about 1.5 ppm are likely to give rise to breakdown of the first-order approximation, while at 500 MHz peaks as little as 0.2 ppm apart may still show first-order coupling. As shifts fall below this point, the position, intensity and number of lines in the spectrum may change. For instance, for two coupled protons the first-order model predicts two doublets, with equal intensity for all four lines. As the shift difference between the protons falls, a quantum-mechanical calculation predicts that the inner pair of lines should grow in intensity at the expense of the outer pair, until, as the shifts coincide, the outer lines disappear completely, leaving a single resonance for the two protons (Fig. 5.50). This behaviour is confirmed in

Two-spin systems

Fig. 5.50 The progressive change from an AX pattern (a), through various AB quartets, to a single line for two equivalent protons (f). The spectra were simulated with $J_{AX} = 10\,Hz$ and $\delta_A - \delta_B$ varied in the sequence: (a) effectively infinite (forced X approximation), (b) 50 Hz, (c) 34 Hz, (d) 14 Hz, (e) 5 Hz, (f) 0 Hz.

practice. In this simple case the line separation (between each of the outer pairs of lines) remains equal to J, but the chemical shifts move from the centre of each of the doublets to their 'centres of gravity' with respect to the unequal peak heights. The 'slope' of the multiplets towards each other, known as the *roof effect*, is quite characteristic of breakdown of the first-order model, and in addition aids in locating the coupling partner by examination of the direction of slope.

It might be supposed that limitless possibilities exist for coupling patterns once the first-order restriction has been removed. In fact, a surprising number of real cases can be related to only a few typical patterns. To aid in categorizing these patterns, a notation has been developed that expresses the character of the spin system independently of the specific values of shifts and coupling constants. In this notation, the first-order two-spin case is described as an AX system. The choice of letters at opposite ends of the alphabet indicates first-order coupling. As the first-order approximation fails, letters next to each other are selected, so the characteristic four-line pattern with the inner lines stronger than the outer lines is referred to as an AB quartet. Once the shifts coincide, the system degenerates to A_2. The disappearance of the outer lines as the system changes from AB to A_2 illustrates a general principle that equivalent nuclei cannot show any splitting due to their mutual coupling (but see the discussion of chemical and magnetic equivalence later, to find out what 'equivalent' really means).

Three-spin systems

The three-spin case in which all shift differences are small relative to the coupling constants (an ABC system) leads to rather complicated splitting patterns. However, it is very common to encounter situations in which two nuclei are close in shift, while one is substantially different: the ABX system. Figure 5.51 illustrates the variation in both the 'AB part' and the 'X part' of such a spectrum as a function of the shift difference between A and B.

An interesting feature of these spectra is the rather harmless appearance of the X signal, which in most cases looks like a simple double doublet. **Beware!** The line separations in this multiplet are not necessarily equal to coupling constants, as is clear in this case since the spectra have all been simulated with $J_{BX} = 0$. Only the top spectrum shows the patterns that would be predicted, apart from the roof effect in the AB part, by the first-order model.

Some of the AB patterns look as if each of the two protons is split by proton X (for example, spectra (b) and (c) in Fig. 5.51), but this is completely untrue. In addition, for some values of the AB shift difference, the AB part of the spectrum has rather few strong lines. In a real spectrum, in which the weak outer lines might easily be lost in noise or under other signals, such patterns can be quite confusing. This effect is referred to as *deceptive simplicity*. Clearly you must watch out for this, because it is very easy to draw false conclusions.

Beware of deceptively simple multiplets

A particularly subtle cause of failure of the first-order rules arises when protons have the same shift but still cannot be regarded as equivalent from an NMR point of view. To appreciate this, consider the difference between the

'AB' part   'X' part

Fig. 5.51 Simulated ABX spectra with the following parameters: $J_{AB} = 16\,Hz$, $J_{AX} = 7$ Hz, $J_{BX} = 0\,Hz$. $\delta_A - \delta_B$ was varied in the sequence: (a) 40 Hz, (b) 20 Hz, (c) 15 Hz, (d) 10 Hz, (e) 5 Hz.

Chemical and magnetic equivalence

protons in a methyl group and the 2 and 6 protons of a 1,4-disubstituted benzene ring (Fig. 5.52). In both cases the chemical shifts of the groups of protons have to be the same by symmetry, so they can be described as *chemically equivalent*. However, to be *truly* equivalent, from the perspective of NMR, *all* their magnetic interactions (both shifts and couplings) have to be the same. Now, for the methyl group this will certainly be so, since any coupling experienced by one of the three protons will also be experienced by the others. The methyl protons are thus *magnetically equivalent*, and an adjacent proton widely differing in shift will be split into a quartet in accord with the first-order rules.

For the pair of protons on the aromatic ring the situation is quite different. Consider the interaction of the 2 and 6 protons with proton 3. For the 2 proton this is a three-bond relationship, so the coupling constant will be fairly large;

Fig. 5.52 Protons of a methyl group are both chemically and magnetically equivalent, but the protons of 1,4-disubstituted benzene rings are magnetically inequivalent, even though the chemical shifts of the pairs of protons (H_2, H_6) and (H_3, H_5) must be the same.

however, for proton 6 it is a five-bond coupling. Thus their interactions *are not identical*. The situation is not ameliorated by the fact that the 6–5 coupling must equal the 2–3 coupling; magnetic equivalence requires that *all* interactions to each other magnetic nucleus *treated individually* must be equal. In the letter notation, magnetically inequivalent protons are distinguished by use of a prime ('); therefore, assuming a large shift difference between the 2,6 and 3,5 positions, this case would be described as an AA'XX' system. The calculated spectrum (Fig. 5.53) is radically different from that of either an A_2X_2 system (two triplets) or a pair of superimposed AX systems (two doublets), either of which might have been suggested to model this case had the magnetic inequivalence not been recognized.

The moral of this section is that care is needed to avoid false interpretation of NMR spectra. This is especially true for spectra obtained at low field, which are exactly the type that you are likely to need to interpret in your first encounters with NMR. Things become much easier with higher fields, although, of course, the complexity of the problems being tackled usually increases proportionately.

Working with ¹H NMR

Even if you have read the previous pages assiduously, you are probably still at a loss as to how to proceed when actually faced with a spectrum for the first time. The purpose of this section is to demonstrate the analysis of proton spectra using a couple of examples. In one case we will assume that the structure is already known, so that the object of the exercise is just to assign the peaks. This is a very common requirement, for instance, when checking the spectrum of a starting material. For the second example we will try to work out the structure from the spectrum.

Figure 5.54 is the 250 MHz FT spectrum of 4-(1-methylpropyl)phenol. The

Fig. 5.53 Simulated AA'XX' spectrum with $J_{AX} = J_{A'X'} = 7\,Hz$, $J_{AA'} = J_{XX'} = 2.5\,Hz$, $J_{AX'} = J_{A'X} = 1\,Hz$ (typical for a 1,4-disubstituted aromatic ring).

Fig. 5.54 The first example spectrum: 4-(1-methylpropyl)phenol.

first thing to do in assigning this spectrum is to split it into sections corresponding to groups of protons, either mentally or by drawing lines on the chart. The obvious groups in this case are centred on δ 6.90, 5.90, 2.55, 1.50, 1.15 and 0.80. From the integration (which is not reproduced in the figure), the number of protons contributing to each group can then be determined, as follows:

δ6.90: 4H, δ5.90: 1H, δ2.55: 1H, δ1.50: 2H, δ1.15: 3H, δ0.80: 3H

In this simple compound the assignments can be made rapidly on the basis of shifts, and then confirmed by examination of the coupling patterns. The peaks at δ 6.90 must be due to the four aromatic protons, whereas the single, broad resonance at δ 5.90 is in the typical region for phenolic hydroxyl protons. Of the remaining aliphatic resonances, the two 3H groups should presumably correspond to the methyls. Indeed they are at a low chemical shift, whereas the methine adjacent to the aromatic ring is shifted to high frequency and the methylene falls somewhere in between. It is also reasonable that the methyl nearer the aromatic ring (which must be the δ1.15 doublet) is found to have a larger shift than that in the ethyl group.

Finally, we should examine the coupling patterns. The aromatic protons form an AA′BB′ system, which typically leads to a spectrum with four strong lines and a number of weaker ones. One of the methyl resonances is a triplet and the other a doublet, in accord with the structure. The methine is split into

339

six lines as it is adjacent to methyl and methylene groups. The methylene resonance partly overlaps with the δ 1.15 methyl, but it is still possible to discern four of the five lines that it would be expected to show on a first-order analysis. However, there are also signs of other partially resolved splittings (e.g. the lump on the side of the second line from the left), so it is best to attribute this peak as a *multiplet*, a term which implies no commitment as to the exact pattern of coupling. If you wanted a formal record of this assignment, you might then present it like this: δ (250 MHz, CDCl$_3$) 6.90 (4H, AA'BB', Ar), 5.90 (1H, s, br, ArO<u>H</u>), 2.55 (1H, sext., J 7 Hz, CH$_3$C<u>H</u>CH$_2$), 1.50 (2H, m, CHC<u>H</u>$_2$CH$_3$), 1.15 (3H, d, J 7 Hz, C<u>H</u>$_3$CHCH$_2$), 0.80 (3H, t, J 7 Hz, CHCH$_2$C<u>H</u>$_3$). The abbreviations in the parentheses are: d, doublet; t, triplet; sext. sextet; m, multiplet; s, br, broad singlet (see pp. 403–404 for more details on the recording of NMR data in notebook form).

For the spectrum of an unknown, such as Fig. 5.55, we initially proceed in the same way and split the signals into groups. In this case there are clearly discernible multiplets centred on δ 4.20, 3.75, 3.50, 2.60 and 1.20 (once again the integration is not reproduced in the figure, but these were found to have relative intensities 1 : 1 : 1 : 1 : 3). Next, we need to decide what structural fragments might give rise to each group. The signal at δ 1.20 is most likely due to a methyl group (or groups—remember we only have the relative numbers of protons at present), while the remaining signals are probably various methylenes or methines. In addition, all the other signals have quite large shifts to high frequency, implying that these groups are adjacent to electron-withdrawing sub-

Fig. 5.55 Spectrum of an unknown compound (250 MHz).

stituents. The three groups at $\delta 4.20$, $\delta 3.75$ and $\delta 3.50$ are, in fact, at such high frequency that the protons that give rise to them must almost certainly be directly adjacent to an electronegative atom such as oxygen or chlorine.

This is about as far as we can go without risking over-interpretation of the data; the next thing to do is to take account of any other available information. The formula of this compound, obtained from its mass spectrum, is $C_7H_{14}O_3$, and IR spectroscopy shows the presence of an ester carbonyl. The formula implies one double-bond equivalent, taken up by the carbonyl, so there will be no further unsaturation or rings. The formula also tells us that the actual number of protons contributing to each peak is double the relative number obtained from integration. We now have to take the plunge and come up with a possible structure. With the additional knowledge that the multiplet at $\delta 1.20$ is due to two methyl groups we can go a little further with the identification of structural fragments. Examining the $\delta 1.20$ resonance closely, it can be seen to consist of two overlapping triplets. Thus, we must have two ethyl fragments in the structure and we need to look for the corresponding methylene signals which are visible as quartets at $\delta 4.20$ and $\delta 3.50$. Given that both the ethyl CH_2 groups are at high frequency, we can assume two CH_3CH_2O- subunits in the molecule, one of which is presumably part of the ester (because there are only three oxygens in the formula altogether), giving CH_3CH_2O- and $-COOCH_2CH_3$ fragments so far. This leaves only $-CH_2CH_2-$ to accommodate, and clearly the only way these fragments can be put together is as ethyl 3-ethoxypropanoate.

With this structure in mind, we can make some further sense of the spectrum. The triplet at $\delta 2.60$ must be due to the CH_2 adjacent to the carbonyl, because of its shift. The other CH_2 triplet at $\delta 3.75$ corresponds to a CH_2 adjacent to an oxygen. This relationship also explains why the two CH_2 groups couple with each other but with no other groups. Therefore everything is quite consistent with the proposed structure. This is a very simple example, but it illustrates the three main stages of structure elucidation.

1 *Make initial inferences from the spectra (NMR, IR, UV, MS).*
2 *Assemble the fragments into candidate structures.*
3 *Check the candidates against a more detailed analysis of the spectra.*

In realistic cases the second stage is the most difficult, and it is here that the connectivity information available from the detection of coupling in NMR spectra is extremely useful. In our simple example there was only one way the fragments could fit together, but in general this will not be so, and it will be necessary to use coupling patterns to help to decide on the right combinations of fragments.

ethyl 3-ethoxypropanoate

13C NMR

Since only 1.1% of natural carbon consists of ^{13}C, the character of ^{13}C NMR spectroscopy is considerably different from that ^1H NMR. The first striking difference is that sensitivity is much lower: use of FT NMR and signal averag-

Obtaining ¹³C NMR spectra requires more sample than for ¹H NMR spectra

In 'natural abundance' spectra C–C coupling is not visible

ing is essential for the detection of ¹³C, and even then, sample quantities need to be about 10 times greater than for proton observation. The low proportion of the NMR-active isotope also means that homonuclear coupling is not observed; it certainly exists, but the probability of finding two adjacent ¹³C nuclei is negligible. Therefore the information content of basic ¹³C spectra is limited to carbon chemical shifts and the coupling with ¹H—*heteronuclear coupling*. This section surveys briefly how these can be exploited.

Coupling to protons has a major and in some ways undesirable effect on ¹³C spectra. The ¹J values for directly attached protons are large (135–210 Hz), whereas ²J and ³J values are generally in the 0–15 Hz range. Carbon atoms in average organic structures are often within two or three bonds of a considerable number of protons, so that the heteronuclear coupling leads to extensive splitting of the carbon lines. This, in turn, complicates the spectrum, especially since the large ¹J couplings tend to cause multiplets to overlap, and it also degrades sensitivity. It is therefore usual to remove completely coupling with the protons by use of *broad-band proton decoupling*. This is essentially similar to the homonuclear decoupling described on pp. 333–334, but with suitable adjustments to the irradiation method to make the effect non-selective. The peaks in carbon spectra obtained under conditions of broad-band proton decoupling consist of sharp, single lines (Fig. 5.56), from which the chemical shifts can easily be determined.

Carbon chemical shifts follow very similar trends to those of protons, but the range of δ values involved is larger (about 0–200 ppm). A very useful rule

Fig. 5.56 ¹³C spectrum (with broadband proton decoupling) of myrtenol. The small signal at δ 77 is due to the solvent, CDCl₃; it is split into three lines because of the coupling to deuterium ($I = 1$).

of thumb to aid interpreting ^{13}C shifts is that they are about 20 times greater than the shifts of protons in analogous environments. So, for example, the alkene region of ^1H spectra is around $\delta\,5$, whereas in ^{13}C spectra it is in the region of $\delta\,100$. Since the relative chemical shift range is 20 times larger than that of ^1H, while the actual carbon frequency is only four times smaller in the same static field, the absolute shift range (in hertz) is also large. This, together with the freedom from coupling, means that even complex molecules yield well-resolved ^{13}C spectra, in which each distinct carbon site contributes a single peak to the spectrum. It is therefore often possible to use the ^{13}C spectrum to count the number of carbons in a molecule. Unfortunately, for technical reasons related to the use of signal averaging and broad-band proton decoupling, the peak intensities in ^{13}C spectra, obtained under normal conditions, do not reflect the number of contributing nuclei, so that identification of groups of equivalent nuclei is not so straightforward as in ^1H NMR.

Signal intensities in ^{13}C spectra do not reflect number of carbons

A very useful classification of the resonances in a ^{13}C spectrum according to the number of protons attached to each carbon can be obtained in any of several ways. A crude method identified *quaternary* carbons on the grounds that their resonances are usually weaker than those of proton-bearing nuclei; for example, the peaks at $\delta\,148$ and $\delta\,37$ in Fig. 5.56. This is clearly a rather vague criterion, but nevertheless it can be helpful in the everyday interpretation of ^{13}C spectra. More well-defined information can be obtained either by the *off-resonance decoupling* experiment, or by *spectrum editing*.

Quaternary carbons give low intensity signals

Off-resonance decoupling was the original technique used to determine the number of protons attached to each carbon, and involves *partial* decoupling of protons, such that the two- and three-bond couplings are more or less removed, whereas the one-bond couplings are scaled down to a manageable value. Peaks then appear as singlets, doublets, triplets or quartets according to whether they are due to quaternary, methine, methylene or methyl carbons respectively (Fig. 5.57).

Off-resonance ^{13}C spectra show couplings to attached protons

The sensitivity of this experiment is rather low, because of the splitting and broadening of the lines, and in complex spectra identification of the multiplicities may not be straightforward. It is also vital to realize that the line separations in an off-resonance proton-decoupled ^{13}C spectrum *do not equal* $^1J_{HC}$; the splittings are scaled down by some unknown factor.

In the more recently developed and vastly superior spectrum editing technique, actual subspectra containing only resonances due to methine, methylene or methyl carbons are obtained (Fig. 5.58). Quaternary carbons can be identified in the original spectrum by elimination, on assignment of all the other resonances, or by some separate technique. The mechanism of this experiment is too subtle to describe here, but the major advantage is that the spectra are obtained with broad-band decoupling, so that sensitivity and resolution are not compromised.

Because of the lack of homonuclear coupling information, ^{13}C NMR does not play such a prominent role as ^1H NMR in routine chemical applications.

Fig. 5.57 Low frequency part of the ¹³C spectrum of myrtenol, with broadband (bottom) and off-resonance (top) proton decoupling. The assignment of the peaks as singlets, doublets, etc. is mostly obvious, but even in this simple compound the off-resonance experiment is not totally clear. The result for the two peaks near $\delta 31$ is confused by the fact that their multiplets overlap in the off-resonance experiment, and one of the two does not appear as a clean triplet owing to a large shift difference between its attached protons.

Fig. 5.58 Spectrum editing applied to the spectrum of myrtenol. (a) Normal ¹³C spectrum acquired with broad-band proton decoupling; (b) CH carbons; (c) CH_2 carbons; (d) CH_3 carbons. Quaternary carbons (including that of the solvent $CDCl_3$, as its protons have been replaced by deuterium) do not appear in the edited spectra.

The determination of the numbers of different types of carbons is probably the most useful aspect of the technique in this area. However, in more advanced structure determination, and particularly in conjunction with two-dimensional techniques, the ability of ^{13}C NMR to resolve distinct peaks for each carbon in the majority of complex molecules becomes extremely important.

Further features of NMR

Why are the peaks in the spectrum of this amide broad?

Because the frequency differences involved in NMR are so small, some quite surprising things can happen to the spectra when nuclei do not wait around long enough for us to measure their resonances. This effect has already been mentioned briefly on p. 323 (in the discussion of protons on heteroatoms), but because it is both puzzling and useful it warrants a little further discussion. The essential principle is that to discriminate between resonances separated by F Hz, it is necessary to be able to make the measurement for at least $1/F$ s. Now, in IR spectroscopy, for instance, where the frequency differences involved are of the order of 10^{12}–10^{14} Hz (tens to thousands of cm^{-1}), this does not impose much of a condition on the length of the measurement. Things are quite different for NMR, in which it might be necessary for a nucleus to maintain exactly the same resonance frequency for a second or more in order for us to be able to make an adequate measurement.

Therefore processes with a time scale in the millisecond to second range can significantly affect NMR spectra. Most overall molecular motions (translations, rotations, etc.) occur much faster than this in solution, so that we see averaged spectra with respect to them. However, some internal motions, such as certain conformational changes and a wide variety of chemical reactions, do occur on this *NMR time scale*.

Exchanging systems — 'dynamic' NMR

It is helpful to distinguish three rate regimes in terms of their effects on the NMR spectrum. If a process interchanging a nucleus between two environments in which it has NMR frequencies differing by F Hz occurs with a rate constant k much greater than F s^{-1}, then a completely averaged spectrum is obtained and the effect of the process is concealed. Conversely, if the rate constant is much less than F, there are effectively two distinct species in the solution, each with its own characteristic signal. Once again, the existence of the exchange process is not immediately apparent from the spectrum. In between, when k and F are comparable, a kind of partial averaging arises, leading to broadening of the lines. If the rate is varied, for instance by varying the temperature, it is possible to observe the transition between the three types of spectrum (Fig. 5.59).

Analysis of the line shapes in the *intermediate exchange* regime is a very powerful method for obtaining rate constants of processes that are too fast to investigate by more conventional means, but this is too specialized an applica-

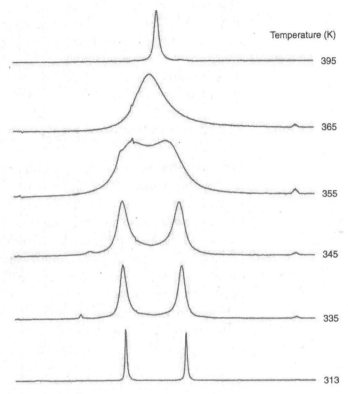

Temperature (K)

395

365

355

345

335

313

Fig. 5.59 Proton spectra of the *N*-methyl groups of *N*, *N*-dimethylacetamide. As the temperature is increased, the rate of rotation about the C–N bond becomes comparable with the frequency difference between the peaks, they gradually broaden and coalesce, and eventually an averaged spectrum is obtained.

tion to discuss here. However, you will need to be able to spot the effects of exchange and to understand how they vary according to the spectrometer field strength, sample temperature and observed nucleus. All these follow naturally from the relationship between the frequency difference between the exchanging sites, the rate of exchange and the appearance of the spectrum. So, for instance, a spectrum that appears broad on a low field spectrometer may become sharp (with double the number of peaks) at high field, because the peak separations have been increased, while the rate of the exchange process remains constant. You might like to compare this change with photography of a humming bird: with a slow film, and hence long exposure time, the wings appear blurred, but on changing to a fast film and shortening the exposure they can be photographed in the extreme positions of the wing beat.

Similarly, a compound may quite easily have a broad proton spectrum but show perfectly sharp peaks for ^{13}C, or vice versa, because the peak separations are different for the two nuclei. Some peaks in the spectrum can be doubled, some broadened and some unaffected, according to the different influences that the exchange process has on their chemical shifts. When you are not concerned with rate measurements, these broadening effects can be quite annoying, since they make the spectrum hard to interpret. They are common for acidic protons, as mentioned on p. 323. Problems may also sometimes arise as a result of conformational changes: rotations about single bonds are usually fast on the NMR time scale, but a common exception to this, which explains the title to this section, is found for amides. Here the partial double-bond character of the amide bond raises the barrier to rotation and makes the process sufficiently slow so that it often causes peak doubling or broadening in NMR spectra. If a properly resolved spectrum is required in such a case, then it is necessary to change to either slow or fast exchange (preferably the latter, because then there will only be one set of peaks in the spectrum). This can be achieved by altering the temperature, or by changing to a spectrometer of different field strength (lowering the field strength is equivalent in its effect to raising the temperature).

Exchange can also have an indirect broadening effect on nuclei via coupling. For instance, when acidic protons are broadened by exchange amongst themselves or with water in the sample, this process clearly will not affect the chemical shift of any other protons in the molecule and so will not change their line shapes directly. However, protons coupled to the exchanging proton may be influenced in a way that can be understood as follows. Imagine a proton adjacent to an OH group; its signal is split by the *vicinal* coupling into the usual kind of doublet, one line arising from molecules in which the hydroxyl proton is α and the other from molecules in which the hydroxyl proton is β. When the hydroxyl is exchanged, the replacement proton has an equal chance of being α or β, so that molecules which had been contributing to one of the doublet components may find themselves contributing to the other after the exchange. There is, in effect, an internal exchange going on between the two lines of the doublet, and if the rate constant is much greater than their separation the coupling will be lost. The rapid averaging of the α- and β- states is akin to the effect of the homonuclear decoupling experiment described on pp. 333–334, and the result is the same: the doublet collapses to a singlet. At intermediate exchange rates the lines of the doublet are broadened, and in practice it is quite common to see this effect for nuclei coupled to acidic protons.

Other useful techniques

Useful extra information can often be obtained from NMR spectra by performing simple tests or chemical reactions directly on the sample. For instance, the fact that acidic protons (e.g. those in hydroxyl or amino groups) exchange rapidly with water can be used to aid in their assignment. After obtaining a proton spectrum, a small amount of D_2O (1–2 drops) is mixed with the sample. For solvents which are not completely miscible with water the sample should be shaken vigorously and then allowed to stand for a few moments to separate. The spectrum is then re-run, and since the acidic protons will have been replaced by deuterium, their peaks should have disappeared

D_2O exchange

(Fig. 5.60). Amines, alcohols and carboxylic acids usually exchange instantly when treated in this way, while amides exchange slowly or not at all. Amide signals can be located in a further experiment, by adding a trace of base to the sample (e.g. a drop of sodium deuteroxide solution, prepared by dissolving sodium in D_2O — *care!*). A side effect of the D_2O exchange experiment is the removal of the line broadening effect due to coupling with acidic protons (described at the end of the previous section), and it may sometimes be desirable to perform the exchange solely for this reason.

Another straightforward technique also uses the presence of hydroxyl and amino groups to aid in making assignments. After obtaining the original spectrum, the sample is treated with an excess of trifluoroacetic anhydride (**care!** — in practice a few drops should be sufficient). This reagent is highly reactive, and will usually acylate primary and secondary amines and alcohols almost instantly. In addition, it does not contribute extra resonances to the spectrum, but because of the powerful electron-withdrawing character of the

Acylation

Fig. 5.60 D_2O exchange experiment on 2-phenylethanol. The lower trace is the normal spectrum; D_2O was added to the sample before obtaining the upper spectrum. The peak at $\delta 1.7$ has almost disappeared, and is therefore assigned to the hydroxyl resonance. The new peak at $\delta 4.7$ is due to residual HDO in the D_2O (note that this signal is due to *droplets* of water, and is in a different place to the typical signal obtained for water dissolved in $CDCl_3$ which occurs at $\delta 1.57$).

trifluoroacetyl group it has a strong effect on the resonances of the original compound. Resonances α- to the site (or sites) of acylation will be shifted to high δ by about 0.7–0.9 ppm, while β- and γ-protons will also show significant changes. These shifts can help in assignment of the spectrum, or they may simply be used to improve the peak separation for a compound whose basic spectrum is poorly resolved.

Manipulating chemical shifts

It often happens that peaks in a proton spectrum overlap, even at high field. When faced with this problem all is not lost, because there are a number of techniques available for altering shifts. The most straightforward and highly recommended approach is to try another solvent. Any change of solvent is likely to alter shifts significantly, but particularly strong effects are found with the aromatic solvents benzene, toluene and pyridine. This is a consequence of the magnetic anisotropy typical of aromatic systems; different parts of the solute will naturally have different interactions with solvent molecules, and hence may find themselves in shielding or deshielding regions. For samples which have previously been run in $CDCl_3$, benzene is often a suitable alternative solvent, and its use can have spectacular results (Fig. 5.61). Toluene, although slightly less attractive from an NMR point of view because of its greater spread of residual solvent peaks, may sometimes be preferred on the grounds of reduced carcinogenicity. Pyridine is suitable for many more polar solutes, but it is toxic and unpleasant to handle.

Changing the NMR solvent

Fig. 5.61 Part of the proton spectrum of a fairly complex molecule run in (a) $CDCl_3$, and (b) benzene-d^6. The broad singlet at $\delta 1.57$ in (a) is due to water in the $CDCl_3$. The triplet at $\delta 1.26$ in (a) is shifted off-scale in (b).

A more sophisticated approach to chemical shift control employs *shift reagents*. These are paramagnetic complexes of certain lanthanides, such as europium and ytterbium, with ligands designed to make them soluble in organic solvents. When added to NMR samples, they coordinate weakly to polar functional groups, such as esters and ketones, and create a strong local magnetic field that can produce large shift changes. There are very many shift reagents available, and you should refer to specialized literature for further information; however a useful practical hint regarding their use is to proceed with care. It is necessary to achieve a fine balance between the desired shift change and the undesirable side effect that follows from their paramagnetism: line broadening. Small incremental additions, starting with much less than one molar equivalent of the reagent, give the best results. Re-examine the spectrum after each addition, and stop as soon as the desired simplification has been achieved, or the line broadening effect becomes too strong. Problems are likely to occur with compounds containing strongly coordinating groups such as carboxylic acids, because then the shift reagent becomes too strongly bound.

Apart from their basic use in attempting to simplify unresolved spectra, shift reagents have another very important application to the study of enantiomeric purity. Shift reagents with chiral ligands are available in optically active form, and if these bind a substrate possessing an asymmetric centre, two diastereomeric complexes can be formed from its enantiomers. In principle these will exhibit different shifts and, as long as the actual difference is sufficient, the ratio of the enantiomers can be measured in a straightforward way. If this technique is to be used to estimate optical purity, it is essential to start with a racemic mixture and to establish the combination of reagent and concentration that gives the best separation of peaks. The purified enantiomers can then be assayed under the same conditions. It is hopeless to start with a substance expected to be 99% optically pure, add some chiral shift reagent and then take the absence of any new peaks as proof of purity!

The basic principle behind chemical shift measurement was introduced on pp. 316–318: comparison of the observed signals with that of a reference substance. Unfortunately, things are not quite as simple as they may at first appear, and it is important that you should not have any misconceptions about the 'accuracy' of chemical shift determinations. It is not, in fact, necessary to measure shifts very accurately at all, *except* when it is required to demonstrate the identity of two substances (e.g. a natural product and its synthetic counterpart). The guidelines for estimating shifts are accurate to a few tenths of a part per million at best and so in routine structure determination the problems described in this section are inconsequential. For proof of identity, and when using literature data for exact comparison purposes (and, for that matter, when reporting your own data that others may use), more care is necessary.

The primary reference substance for proton and carbon NMR is tetramethylsilane (TMS). On low field CW spectrometers, for which the sample concentration is quite high, it is common to add this material to the sample. Referencing may then take the form of aligning the TMS peak with a chart mark, and at this level of accuracy the effects described here will rarely prove troublesome. On more advanced machines the spectrum will be stored in a computer, and referencing is then the numerical process of assigning the correct shift value to the reference line. With lower sample concentrations such as are typical on FT instruments it is convenient, and quite acceptable, to take the known shift of the residual solvent signal as the reference (but see the warning about D_2O below). Either way, this process is known as *internal referencing*, as the reference substance is in the sample. The alternative mode, known as *external referencing*, involves measuring the spectrum of the reference separately, and then comparing it somehow with that of the unknown. On a modern instrument, which has field stabilization using the deuterium resonance of the solvent, external referencing can comprise measurement of the absolute frequencies of the NMR lines and then calculation of their shifts on the basis of some previous calibration experiment.

Internal and external referencing

All these approaches are more than adequate for routine shift measurement. A computer-controlled FT spectrometer may encourage you to record and interpret shifts to higher levels of accuracy, by displaying them to hundredths of a part per million or better, but consider whether this is meaningful. All of the measurements presume that the shift of the reference substance is absolutely fixed, but clearly this is not true. For a start, there is no reason why TMS should have the same resonance frequency when dissolved in chloroform as it does in benzene. Furthermore, the shift of the reference may be altered by the presence of the sample, and vice versa. External referencing presumably avoids this problem, but still we need to define some kind of standard conditions for the reference sample. What if the sample shifts themselves are concentration dependent, as they may well be? Should we define a standard sample concentration, too? Clearly there is more to the accurate measurement of shifts than meets the eye.

So what *can* be done with chemical shifts? Those of a physical turn of mind like to convert everything to standard conditions, by introducing corrections for solvent susceptibility, extrapolating sample and reference concentrations to infinite dilution, etc. For normal organic applications, however, it is sufficient to be aware of the problem and to work round it in various ways. Obviously, comparisons can best be made when conditions are similar. Therefore it is important to try to identify the measurement conditions used to obtain data you find in the literature, and to quote the conditions when you report data. 'Conditions' should include field strength and solvent, and ideally also concentration, temperature, the reference peak used and the shift that was assigned to it (because for peaks other than that of TMS there is no absolute agreement on what shift to use). Regrettably it is not common to find the last three items reported in literature data. When you cannot discover all the details of the experiment, consider the likely accuracy of any comparisons you make, on the basis of whatever information is available. In practice, the various problems described above are not too significant for reasonably dilute samples in organic solvents, but they are much more pronounced in D_2O solution. Here the solvent shift can be strongly influenced by solute concentration, pH and temperature, so internal referencing using the residual solvent peak is unreliable. Changes in the solvent shift also affect the field stabilization of an FT spectrometer, so that external referencing may be equally invalid. Water-soluble reference compounds, such as the sodium salt of 3-(trimethylsilyl)propionic acid (TSP), are available and should be used when reproducible measurements are required. Another handy, water-soluble substance that gives a single, sharp peak and is more easily removed than TSP is 1,4-dioxan.

For proof of identity by NMR it is vital that the measurements are made under identical conditions. This is best achieved by measuring the substances to be compared in the same sample. In other words, obtain a spectrum of the authentic material, and then add an equal quantity of the comparison substance to the sample and repeat the measurement. This maximizes the chance of discovering differences between the two, for if they are identical there should be no extra peaks in the spectrum. If the sample concentration is kept constant during the addition, then the two spectra should be exactly the same.

Advanced techniques

We have already seen an NMR experiment that goes beyond the simple measurement of a spectrum: homonuclear decoupling. This is one example of a vast array of more complicated experimental techniques available in NMR spectroscopy. With the advent of FT NMR spectroscopy, some particularly exciting progress in the design of new experiments has occurred, and totally changed the way in which organic chemists use NMR. There is no space here to give you any of the theoretical background to the more advanced NMR experiments, but it seems appropriate to describe the information available from two of the most useful. One is by no means new, but technological progress has steadily made its use more practical (the nuclear Overhauser effect), while the other is the most important example of the new class of *two-dimensional* NMR experiments (COSY).

Nuclear Overhauser effect

The great thing about the nuclear Overhauser effect (NOE) is that it gives information complementary to that obtained from couplings. Couplings tell us about the bonding relationships in a structure, but the NOE is a direct, through-space effect, and helps in the determination of molecular geometry. In an NOE experiment, the *intensities* of resonances are measured after one peak in the spectrum has been irradiated for a time. Changes in intensity occur because the whole system tries to stay at thermal equilibrium: irradiating a peak reduces the population differences across its transitions to zero, so that in order to maintain the same net population difference for the system the differences for other transitions increase, and hence the corresponding peaks become stronger. The mechanism by which this happens turns out to be strongly distance dependent, so that it is generally found that only the resonances of protons fairly close to that which was irradiated change in intensity.

To clarify the intensity changes that occur during an NOE experiment, which can never be more than 50% and are more typically 1–10%, it is usual to employ *difference spectroscopy*. In this technique two spectra are recorded under identical conditions, except that in one spectrum a peak is irradiated for a time before acquiring the spectrum, while in the other it is not. Subtracting the latter 'blank' experiment from the one with irradiation generates the difference spectrum, in which only peaks that changed intensity should appear (Fig. 5.62). In this example, the stereochemistry of *E*- and *Z*-methylbutenedioic acids was determined by the observation of a much larger NOE from the methyl group to the alkene proton in the *Z*-compound. The main difficulty in using NOE measurements in practice is that, although the effect always varies with distance, it is also influenced by many extraneous factors. Thus, when examining a single effect in one compound, it is difficult to gauge whether it shoxuld be considered as 'large' or 'small'. The best circumstance is to be able to compare effects in geometrical isomers, as in the above example. It is then reasonable to take the isomer with the larger NOE as being the one in which the protons involved are closer together.

Fig. 5.62 Normal spectra of *E*- and *Z*-methylbutenedioic acid and the corresponding NOE difference spectra obtained after irradiating the methyl group in each compound. The NOE spectra are plotted to the same absolute scale so that the size of the enhancements can be compared directly.

353

Two-dimensional NMR experiments are exclusive to FT spectrometers, and produce a kind of map rather than a simple spectrum (Fig. 5.63). The two axes of the rectangular spectrum both represent frequency, while the contours represent amplitude; so where there are contours, there are peaks. In a COSY experiment both axes correspond to proton chemical shifts (although this need not be the case in general). The idea of the two-dimensional experiment is to clarify the relationships between nuclei that are engaged in some kind of interaction, by mapping out the connections between them directly. There are two kinds of peak in Fig. 5.63: those which have the same shift in each frequency dimension and hence lie along the diagonal of the spectrum, and those with different shifts in each dimension. The latter kind, known as *cross-peaks*, are the most informative, as we shall see momentarily.

Fig. 5.63 Part of the COSY spectrum of the same compound as used for the example of homonuclear decoupling in Fig. 5.49. The connection between the doublet at δ4.33 and its partner is identified by way of the cross-peak, as indicated by the broken line drawn on the spectrum.

The diagonal peaks in a COSY spectrum correspond to the normal one-dimensional proton spectrum of the sample, and serve as a reference point for making assignments (examine the one-dimensional spectrum plotted at the top of Fig. 5.63, and see how each multiplet has a corresponding 'blob' on the diagonal of the two-dimensional plot). The cross-peaks link signals that are coupled in square patterns. Therefore, if you know the assignment of one reso-nance, you can trace a path through the spin system to which it belongs by alternating between diagonal and cross-peaks, as indicated in the figure. This method has several advantages over a series of homonuclear decoupling experiments, which could be considered as an alternative way of getting the same information. Decoupling requires both that the target peak can be irra-diated selectively, and that the ensuing effect occurs in a tractable region of the spectrum. In a COSY experiment, even if the signals of both coupling part-ners are hidden in complex spectral regions, the cross-peak between them is still likely to be identifiable. Cross-peaks are generally well resolved even in spectra of large molecules, because two different shifts contribute to their location; there is much more 'space' in a COSY spectrum over which to spread the peaks. An additional advantage is that the COSY experiment requires the same time to perform regardless of the number of correlations it contains; whereas the more decouplings you need to carry out, the more time you must spend on the experiment. This is analogous to the advantage of FT over CW NMR discussed on pp. 313–314.

COSY, and a similar experiment that correlates ^{13}C shifts with those of their attached protons, have passed into standard use in research laboratories already. They make the mapping out of the vital coupling relationships in organic compounds very straightforward, and render structure elucidation of complex products even more feasible than before.

Further reading

Introductory theory

L.M. Harwood and T.D.W, Claridge, *Introduction to Organic Spectroscopy*, Oxford University Press, Oxford, 1996, Chapters 4 and 5.

Proton NMR

H. Günther, *NMR Spectroscopy*, 2nd edn, Wiley & Sons, New York, 1995.

L.M. Jackman and S. Sternhall, *Applications of Nuclear Magnetic Resonance Spectroscopy in Organic Chemistry*, 2nd edn, Pergamon, Oxford, 1969.

D.H. Williams and I. Fleming, *Spectroscopic Methods in Organic Chemistry*, 5th edn, McGraw-Hill, Maidenhead, 1995.

Carbon NMR

R.J. Abraham and P. Loftus, *Proton and Carbon-13 NMR Spectroscopy—an Integrated Approach*, 2nd edn, Heyden, London, 1988.

C.J. Pouchert and J. Behnke (eds), *The Aldrich Library of ¹³C and ¹H FT-NMR Spectra*. Aldrich Chemical Co., Milwaukee, 1992.

Data tables
E. Pretsch, J. Seibl, W. Simon and T. Clerc, *Tables of Spectral Data for Structure Determination of Organic Compounds*, 2nd edn, Springer-Verlag, Berlin, 1989.

Practical techniques
S.A. Richards, *Laboratory Guide to Proton NMR Spectroscopy*, Blackwell Scientific Publications, Oxford, 1988.

Shift reagents
R.E. Sievers (ed.) *NMR Shift Reagents*, Academic Press, New York, 1973.

Exchanging systems
J. Sandstrom, *Dynamic NMR Spectroscopy*, Academic Press, New York, 1982.

Advanced techniques
D. Canet, *Nuclear Magnetic Resonance, Concepts and Methods* (English Translation). Wiley & Sons, New York, 1996.

A.E. Derome, *Modern NMR Techniques for Chemistry Research*, Elsevier, Oxford, 1987.

H. Friebolin, *One and Two-Dimensional NMR Spectroscopy*, 2nd edn, VCH, Weinheim, 1993.

J.K.M. Sanders and B.K. Hunter, *Modern NMR Spectroscopy*, 2nd edn, Oxford University Press, Oxford, 1987.

5.4

Ultraviolet spectroscopy

UV and visible regions

Ultraviolet spectroscopy was the first method of spectroscopic analysis to make an impact on organic chemistry. The UV region of the electromagnetic spectrum comprises radiation with wavelengths from just below 10^{-7} and up to about 3.5×10^{-7} m. As can be seen from Fig. 5.1, this region borders the visible region of the spectrum, which stretches on up to about 8×10^{-7} m. Hence UV light has a shorter wavelength, higher frequency, and therefore higher energy than visible light. UV spectroscopy is usually extended into the visible region to study the absorptions which give rise to coloured organic compounds. This is not a problem from the practical point of view since both UV and visible regions can be measured on a single instrument (see later). When extended into the visible region, the technique is more correctly called ultraviolet–visible (UV–VIS) spectroscopy, although the simpler term UV spectroscopy is widely used to cover both regions. For the purposes of the present discussion we will refer simply to UV spectroscopy, and following common practice we will use *nanometres* as the units of wavelength (1 nm = 10^{-9} m).

Although the UV region of the electromagnetic spectrum stretches down to below 100 nm, we will only be concerned with wavelengths in the range 200–700 nm, the longer wavelengths (350 nm upwards) corresponding to visible light. The higher frequency, higher energy radiation below 200 nm is absorbed by oxygen molecules in the atmosphere, and therefore the study of this region of the spectrum requires special instrumentation which can operate with the sample in a vacuum. This region of the spectrum, normally called the *far UV* or, because of the experimental requirements, *vacuum UV*, is rarely used by organic chemists.

As we have already seen (pp. 276–277), the energy (E) of electromagnetic radiation is related to its frequency (v) by the equation:

$$E = hv$$

where h is Planck's constant. Since frequency is related to wavelength by the speed of light, we can derive a simple relationship between energy and wavelength by inserting a value for Planck's constant. Thus:

$$E\left(\text{kJ mol}^{-1}\right) = \frac{118\,825}{\lambda\left(\text{nm}\right)}$$

Hence the energies associated with the wavelengths of interest (200–700 nm) fall in the range 170–600 kJ mol^{-1}, and these cause electronic transitions within organic molecules. The detailed theory of electronic transitions incorporates rules, known as *selection rules*, to indicate which transitions are allowed and which are forbidden on the basis of molecular symmetry. This theory is quite complicated and is way beyond the scope of this book; you should consult your appropriate lecture text.

Electronic transitions

The electronic transitions that concern organic chemists are those involving the excitation (promotion) of an electron from a bonding or lone-pair orbital to a non-bonding or antibonding orbital. The energy, and hence the wavelength of radiation required, to cause the promotion of an electron, depend on the energy difference between the two relevant orbitals, which in turn depends on the type of electrons involved. Organic chemists are mainly interested in three types of electron: those in (single) σ-bonds, those in (double) π-bonds and lone-pair electrons. Hence, for example, a π-electron can be promoted from a bonding orbital (π) to an antibonding orbital (π^*), and in notation form this is described as a $\pi \rightarrow \pi^*$ *transition*. There are several other types of transition which are possible, and the more important ones are shown in Table 5.3, together with the wavelength of radiation required to cause the transition.

The first thing that should be apparent from Table 5.3 is that only one of the transitions (the last one) actually falls in our 200–700 nm range, and as it happens, this n $\rightarrow \pi^*$ transition of the carbonyl group is 'forbidden' and therefore gives rise to a very weak absorption. (This 'forbidden' transition can only be seen because the molecular symmetry that forbids it is broken by molecu-

Table 5.3 Common electronic transitions relevant to UV spectroscopy.

Electron type	Example	Transition notation	Approx. wavelength (nm)
σ	C–C	$\sigma \rightarrow \sigma^*$	150
π	C=C isolated	$\pi \rightarrow \pi^*$	180
Lone pair	O	$n \rightarrow \sigma^*$	185
	N	$n \rightarrow \sigma^*$	195
	C=O	$n \rightarrow \sigma^*$	190
	C=O	$n \rightarrow \pi^*$	300

Conjugation

lar vibrations.) Thus electrons in isolated systems usually require radiation well outside the UV range to excite them, and it is in the study of *conjugated* systems, such as dienes, α,β-unsaturated carbonyl compounds and aromatics, that UV spectroscopy comes into its own. The presence of an *isolated* C = C or C = O bond in a compound is much better established by NMR or IR than by UV.

Why then do organic molecules containing conjugated functional groups absorb at longer wavelengths in the observable UV range? As a simple example let us compare ethene and butadiene. In general, π-electrons are much more easily excited than σ-electrons (Table 5.3), so as far as UV spectroscopy is concerned we need only consider the π-system, and its associated molecular orbitals. The molecular orbitals of ethene comprise the HOMO, which contains the two π-electrons, and the LUMO, which is unoccupied. Therefore the simplest possible transition of a π-electron is from the HOMO to the LUMO, and this represents the $\pi \rightarrow \pi^*$ transition for ethene. The energy difference between these orbitals is about 690 kJ mol^{-1}, and therefore from the equation

$$E = \frac{118\,825}{\lambda}$$

we can calculate that, in order to effect this transition, we would need radiation with a wavelength of 172 nm, below the normal UV range. The energy levels for ethene are shown schematically in Fig. 5.64a; the σ and σ^* orbitals are below and above the π and π^* orbitals respectively, and are not shown. The much larger energy gap between the σ and σ^* orbitals means that the $\sigma \rightarrow \sigma^*$ transition would require even shorter wavelength radiation.

Butadiene, on the other hand, has four molecular orbitals associated with the π-system (Fig. 5.64b). Since the HOMO is higher in energy than that of ethene, and the LUMO is lower in energy, the energy gap between the two orbitals is only about 544 kJ mol^{-1}. Hence, less energy is needed to effect the

Fig. 5.64 (a) Energy levels of ethene π-orbitals; (b) energy levels of butadiene π-orbitals.

$\pi \rightarrow \pi^*$ transition in butadiene than in ethene, and the transition will occur on absorption of radiation of wavelength 218 nm, inside the normal UV range. With increasing conjugation, the HOMO LUMO energy difference progressively decreases, and therefore the wavelength of light needed to cause the $\pi \rightarrow \pi^*$ transition increases.

Chromophores

In such molecules it is the π-system that is responsible for the absorption of UV radiation, and the functional group or collection of functional groups responsible for the absorption is referred to as a *chromophore* (Greek: *chroma* = colour). Complex molecules can, of course, contain more than one chromophore. Hence, the effect of conjugation on the chromophore, often described as extending the chromophore by conjugation, is to shift the position of maximum absorption to a longer wavelength. Such shifts to longer wavelengths are often called *red shifts or bathochromic shifts*; shifts to shorter wavelengths are called *blue shifts* or *hypsochromic shifts*. However, do not let the jargon confuse you: the important point to remember is that *extending a chromophore by conjugation causes an increase in the wavelength of absorption*. This is a general rule with no exceptions; *the more double bonds there are in conjugation, the longer the wavelength of absorption*.

Red/blue shifts
Bathochromic/hypsochromic shifts

Conjugation causes an increase in the wavelength of absorption

As an extreme example of the effects of conjugation, consider lycopene, a natural product that can be isolated from tomatoes, which contains 11 conjugated C = C bonds. The absorption maximum occurs at 470 nm, well into the visible region; the compound strongly absorbs blue light and therefore appears red. Indeed such compounds are responsible for the bright orange and red colours of carrots, tomatoes, and so on. This association of molecular structure with colour is, of course, central to the chemistry of dyestuffs and photographic materials, and is vital for vision where the photoreceptors in the eye contain a pigment called *rhodopsin* which absorbs in the visible region at 498 nm.

lycopene

rhodopsin

$CH=N-$opsin

So far we have restricted our discussion to the *position* of the absorption, that is, at what wavelength the chromophore absorbs. The other variable is the efficiency with which a compound absorbs light, in other words the *intensity* of absorption. Amongst other factors, this is related to the probability of the particular electronic transition occurring; this takes us back to the complex selection rules referred to earlier. The only point to note is that certain forbidden transitions, notably the n $\rightarrow$ π^* transition of the C = O group, do have weak, but observable absorptions. However, from the *practical* point of view, there are two empirical laws which have been derived concerning absorption intensity. Individually these are known as Lambert's law and Beer's law. However, it is common practice for them to be combined into the *Beer–Lambert law* which states that the absorbance (A) of a sample at a particular wavelength is proportional to the concentration (c) of the sample (in moles per litre) and the path length (l) of the light through the sample (in centimetres). Absorbance (A), or optical density (OD) as it is sometimes called, is further defined as the logarithm of the ratio of the intensity of the incident light (I_0) to the intensity of transmitted light (I). Hence:

Absorption intensity

Beer–Lambert law

$$A = \log_{10}\left(\frac{I_0}{I}\right) = \varepsilon c l$$

The constant ε is called the *molar extinction coefficient*, and is a measure of how strongly the compound absorbs at that wavelength. In general, we find that *the longer the chromophore, the more intense the absorption* and hence the higher the value of ε. From the above equation we can see that ε has the rather meaningless units of $1000\,cm^2\,mol^{-1}$, but, by convention, these are never expressed. Provided that the concentration of the sample is known, ε is readily calculated; conversely, if the ε value for a compound is known at a given wavelength, measuring the absorbance at this wavelength permits the determination of the concentration of the sample. This is what makes UV spectroscopy such an important quantitative tool in analytical chemistry.

The instrument

Like IR spectrometers, most UV spectrometers operate on the double-beam principle, with one beam passing through the sample and the other passing through a reference cell. A typical example of such an instrument is shown schematically in Fig. 5.65. Most spectrometers use two lamps, one emitting in the UV range 200 nm to *ca.* 330 nm, and one for the visible part of the spectroscopic range *ca.* 330 nm to 700 nm. The light from the source passes through the *monochromator*. This consists essentially of a prism or a grating for breaking down the beam into its component wavelengths and allowing one wavelength at a time to pass through. The light emerging from the monochromator is then further divided into two beams of equal intensity, with one beam passing through a solution of the compound to be examined in the sample cell, and the other beam passing through the reference cell which contains pure solvent. After passing through the cells, the light arrives at the detector, which measures the ratio of the intensity of the reference beam (the incident intensity, I_0) to the intensity of the sample beam (the transmitted intensity, I). Hence the detector measures the quantity I_0/I. However, on most machines the output from the detector is automatically converted and plotted on the chart recorder y axis as $\log_{10}(I_0/I)$—the absorbance (A). Therefore, as the instrument scans the wavelength range, a plot—the UV spectrum—of absorbance (A) against wavelength (λ, in nanometres) is obtained. The appearance of UV spectra contrasts sharply with that of IR and NMR spectra, in that they usually consist of rather broad peaks, and often only one peak.

The absorbance scale on most spectrometers will run from 0 to 1 or from 0 to 2. In regions of the spectrum where the sample does not absorb light, $I = I_0$, $(I_0/I) = 1$, and hence $A = 0$. At the other extreme, if the sample absorbs very strongly, I is small and hence the ratio I_0/I is large. The value of the ratio that

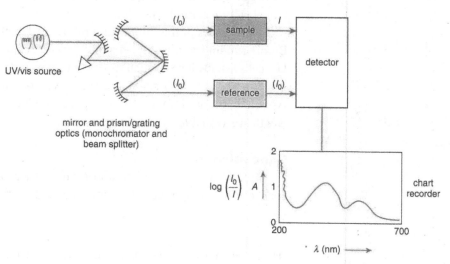

Fig. 5.65 Schematic representation of a double-beam ultraviolet spectrometer.

the instrument can tolerate is 10 ($\log_{10} 10 = 1$) or 100 ($\log_{10} 100 = 2$) depending on whether the maximum on the absorbance scale is 1 or 2. If the absorbance is too great, the chart recorder pen will move off-scale, and the only way round this is to dilute the sample.

Preparing the sample

Although spectrometers can measure the UV spectra on solid samples by reflecting light off the solid surface (reflectance spectroscopy), organic chemists routinely record UV spectra on solutions of the compound contained in a special cell. Therefore in preparing samples for UV spectroscopy, the three factors we have to consider are the *type of cell*, the *concentration* of the solution and which *solvent* to use.

Cells

You must use quartz cells for measurements in the UV range

Cells for UV spectroscopy are made out of quartz, glass or plastic. Whereas quartz is transparent throughout the 200–700 nm range, both glass and plastic, which 'cut-off' somewhere between 350 and 300 nm, are opaque to the shorter wavelengths, and can only be used in the visible range of the spectrum. Therefore, to study the UV part of the spectroscopic range, quartz cells have to be used. This is unfortunate since quartz cells are both fragile and much more expensive than glass or plastic cells, and they *must* be handled carefully. Plastic cells, although cheap, can only be used with certain solvents, usually water or alcohols. Whatever the material, standard UV cells are about 1 cm square and about 3 cm high (Fig. 5.66). The faces that are placed in the beam are polished, and the cell is constructed so as to give a path length of exactly 1 cm. The other two faces are often 'frosted' or of ground glass to distinguish

Handle cells by non-polished edges

them from the polished faces. Always handle cells by these faces to avoid putting fingerprints on the clear polished faces. Cells come in pairs, the individual cells accurately matching one another, so that there are no problems with differences in the sample and reference beams due to unmatched cells. Before running your UV spectrum, always check that you have matched cells. UV cells usually have a small stopper of some sort, often made out of Teflon®, which seals well with slight pressure—do not ram the stopper in too far. Although standard UV cells have a path length of 1 cm, cells of different path length are available.

Teflon® stopper

polished face

light

ground glass face

1 cm path length

Fig. 5.66 Standard 1 cm UV cell.

Concentration

As we have already seen, the absorbance of a sample is proportional to its concentration and to the path length, and is given by

$$A = \varepsilon c l$$

If you are using a standard UV cell, $l = 1$, and hence

$$A = \varepsilon c$$

K

Since the maximum value of A that the spectrometer can usually cope with is 2, you need to choose a concentration that will keep within these limits. Unfortunately this requires some knowledge of the value of the extinction coefficient, ε, at the wavelength of maximum absorption—i.e. how strongly will the compound absorb? This is not as difficult to estimate as you might think, and you will soon develop a feel for how certain types of organic compounds absorb UV light. You will presumably already have some idea about what sort of compound you are dealing with, either by knowing its origin or by examining its IR and NMR spectra. For the purposes of the present discussion, suffice it to say that it is not at all uncommon for an organic compound to have an ε value of 10 000 or more. Putting the values $l = 1$ and $\varepsilon = 10\,000$ into the Beer–Lambert law, we can see that to give an absorbance (A) of 1, we require a solution of concentration of 10^{-4} M (0.0001 M). This simple example illustrates one of the great strengths of UV spectroscopy; the fact that you can use *very dilute solutions* requiring very small quantities of compound. In the example above, if we assume a molecular weight of 200, we need only 0.2 mg of compound to make up 10 mL of solution of the required concentration. This obviously places considerable demands on the actual experimental technique in making up such solutions, and this is discussed in more detail later in this section.

One problem in obtaining UV spectra is that your compound may have two or more chromophores with widely differing extinction coefficients, a situation which is in fact quite common. For example, the compound may have a chromophore with an extinction coefficient of 10 000 absorbing at 250 nm, and it may also have a much weaker intensity, 'forbidden' absorption with $\varepsilon = 100$, due to another chromophore at, say, 350 nm. If we were to run the spectrum using a solution of 0.0001 M concentration, we would see a large peak ($A = 1$) for the shorter wavelength absorption, but the second chromophore would have an absorbance of 0.01 and a very small peak that could easily be missed.

Use solutions of two different concentrations

The only way round this problem is to run the UV spectrum on samples of two different concentrations; a difference factor of 100 is usually appropriate. Make up the more concentrated solution first, and run the spectrum. Even though some peaks may go off-scale you will see the small ones. Then dilute the sample and re-run the spectrum; this technique was used to obtain the UV spectrum of isophorone shown in Fig. 5.67.

Solvent

The prime requirement for a solvent for UV spectroscopy is that it should be transparent to radiation over the complete UV range. Fortunately most common organic solvents meet this requirement, the only differences between them being the point at which they 'cut-off' at the short wavelength end of the range. Since spectrometers operate on the double beam principle, any absorptions due to solvent are cancelled out at the detector. Although the solvents do not contain any chromophores, they do of course constitute effec-

Fig. 5.67 UV spectrum of isophorone: (a) at a concentration of 6.2 mg per 10 mL; (b) diluted by a factor of 100.

Table 5.4 Cut-off points for solvents for UV spectroscopy.

Solvent	Approx. cut-off point (nm)
Water	190
Hexane	200
Ethanol	205
Dichloromethane	220
Chloroform	240

tively 100% of the sample; there comes a point at which the 1 cm path length of the solvent absorbs so strongly that no light of that particular wavelength, or shorter, will be transmitted through the sample. The cut-off points for various solvents are given in Table 5.4, and it is this which leads to the feature known as *end absorption* in UV spectra.

The most commonly used solvent for UV spectroscopy is ethanol, usually the commercially available 95% grade. Ethanol is cheap, a good solvent for a wide range of organic compounds, and is transparent down to about 205 nm. Although it is **toxic** and **flammable**, it can be handled safely, provided that due regard is paid to the potential hazards. Whatever solvent is used it must be free from impurities that might absorb in the UV region. UV spectroscopy is very sensitive and so even a tiny amount of impurity can cause problems if it has a large ε value. This is particularly true of hydrocarbon solvents which may contain aromatic impurities. To reassure chemists, many solvents are sold as 'spectroscopic grade' or 'spectrophotometric grade', the absorption proper-

Beware of UV absorbing contaminants in your solvents. In particular, never use 'absolute' ethanol ties of which are clearly defined and guaranteed. You must never use 'absolute' or commercially dried ethanol, as this may have been dried azeotropically with benzene, traces of which remain in the ethanol and interfere with the spectrum.

The solvent also affects the wavelength of maximum absorption and the appearance of UV spectra. This is because many electronic transitions lead to an excited state which is more polar than the ground state, and therefore polar solvents, such as ethanol, will stabilize the excited state by dipole interactions to a greater extent than the ground state. Non-polar solvents, such as hexane, have little or no dipole interactions. Hence the energy difference between the two electronic states will be slightly smaller in ethanol than in hexane, and therefore the absorption maximum will be at a longer wavelength in ethanol than in hexane. This shift to longer wavelength (*bathochromic shift*) in moving from a non-polar solvent to a polar solvent can be as much as 20 nm. Solvent effects on the absorption maxima of α,β-unsaturated ketones are given in detail in Table A19 in Appendix 3. Molecules containing isolated carbonyl groups often show the reverse solvent effect; the absorption moves to a shorter wavelength on increasing the polarity of the solvent. This is because polar hydroxylic solvents, such as ethanol, form stronger hydrogen bonds to the ground state, and therefore stabilize the ground state to a greater extent than the excited state. In addition to the effects on the wavelength of absorption, non-polar solvents often lead to UV spectra which show more fine structure than those run in ethanol.

Making up the sample

The fact that UV spectra can be run on very dilute solutions is one of the great assets of the technique: however, it is also one of the potential pitfalls from the practical point of view. How do you make up such dilute solutions with accurately known concentration? The answer is by dilution.

Treat analytical balances with care

See section on weighing on pp. 70–72

To make up solutions for UV spectroscopy, you need an accurate analytical balance reading to 0.01 mg, some volumetric flasks (preferably 10 mL) and a 1 mL pipette. Remember that the volume of standard UV cells is only about 3 mL, so there is no need to make up several hundred millilitres of solution. Weigh out *accurately* about 1 mg of your compound on the analytical balance into an appropriate container. It does not matter whether you end up with 1.27 or 0.93 mg, as long as you know exactly what the weight is. Transfer the material to a 10 mL volumetric flask, taking care to rinse it all in with portions of the solvent if necessary, and then make up the volume to 10 mL with solvent. (Alternatively, if your laboratory does not have a balance that can weigh to 0.01 mg, you should weigh out accurately about 10 mg of compound, and dissolve it in 100 mL of solvent in a 100 mL volumetric flask.) Label the flask immediately, so that you know its concentration. This solution is likely to be too concentrated, so it is as well to make up at least one, and preferably two, more solutions before going to the instrument. This is easily done by

Never suck up liquids into pipettes by mouth

dilution. Pipette out exactly 1 mL from the first solution (use a pipette filler), and transfer it to a second 10 mL volumetric flask. Make up the volume to 10 mL, and label the flask. Using a clean pipette, withdraw 1 mL of the second solution and transfer it to a third 10 mL volumetric flask. Make up the volume to 10 mL, and label the flask. You now have three solutions with accurately known concentrations of approximately 1, 0.1 and 0.01 mg per 10 mL. As with all quantitative analytical work, you must take great care that no impurities are introduced, either during the weighing, or the making up of the solutions.

Avoid contamination

Running the spectrum

Ultraviolet spectrometers are quite simple to operate, and have relatively few controls. The controls usually allow you to adjust the wavelength range of the scan, the absorbance range ($A = 1$ or 2), the scan speed and the expansion along the x axis (how many centimetres of chart paper correspond to 10 nm). There will also be a baseline adjusting control, which may have been preset. If this adjustment is correct, the spectrometer will produce a nice straight line at the $A = 0$ mark when pure solvent is placed in both sample and reference cells. With the machine turned on, both the UV and visible lamps should be lit; if not, check that they are not linked to separate switches.

Using a clean Pasteur pipette fill the sample cell with the most concentrated of your solutions and, holding the cell by the edges, place it in the sample beam of the spectrometer. Fill the reference cell with pure solvent, using a clean Pasteur pipette, ensuring that you use the same batch of solvent used to make up the solution in the first place. Likewise, place the reference cell in the reference beam, holding the cell by the edges.

Most spectrometers scan from long to short wavelength. If the compound is colourless, there is no point scanning the whole of the visible range, and you should start the scan at 450 nm; however, for coloured compounds you must scan the whole range. Select the wavelength from which you want to scan, and press the start button. As the spectrometer scans to shorter wavelength there may be a slight hiccup as the lamps switch over; this switch-over point can be seen at 325 nm in the spectra shown in Figs 5.67 and 5.69.

The chances are that your first solution will be too concentrated and therefore some of the peaks will go off-scale. In this case, remove the sample cell, discard the solution, wash the cell with a little solvent, then with 1 or 2 mL of the more dilute solution; and finally refill it with the more dilute solution. There is no need to change the reference cell. In most cases one of your three solutions will give a suitable spectrum, but in exceptional cases, particularly if the compound is very strongly coloured, you may have to make extra dilutions. Do not worry if the peaks start to go off-scale below about 220 nm; this usually happens. Most organic molecules, the solvent included, start to absorb strongly below this wavelength, and this is generally referred to as *end absorption*. After running the spectrum you should calibrate the instrument by

End absorption

running a reference sample which has a sharp absorption at an accurately known wavelength. The common reference material used is *holmium glass*, which has a sharp peak at 360.8 nm.

Interpreting the spectrum

Ultraviolet spectra look relatively simple and straightforward compared with IR and NMR spectra. They consist of broad peaks, and indeed many may only be a single peak. The initial data that should be extracted from your spectrum are as follows.

1 The wavelength or wavelengths at which the absorption reaches a maximum, referred to as λ_{max}.

2 The absorbance, A, at each of the maxima.

Knowing the concentration of the solution, the molecular weight of the compound and the path length of the cell, you should then calculate the value of the extinction coefficient, ε, at each maximum. The whole process is best illustrated with an actual example. Figure 5.67 shows the UV spectrum of isophorone recorded in ethanol solution at two different concentrations in a cell of path length 1 cm. Spectrum (a) was obtained on a solution containing 6.2 mg per 10 mL; this solution was then diluted 100-fold to obtain spectrum (b). Note that the absorption at 300 nm is only visible in the spectrum of the more concentrated sample; this absorption, which is due to a 'forbidden' transition, would have been missed if the spectrum had only been recorded on the dilute solution. The 'allowed' $\pi \rightarrow \pi^*$ transition gives rise to a much stronger absorption at 234 nm. The spectrum is simple, and we can immediately read off the values of λ_{max} and the absorbance A. The molecular weight of isophorone is 138.2, and using the Beer–Lambert law

$$A = \varepsilon c l$$

we can see that for the absorption at 234 nm, $A = 0.52$, and hence

$$\varepsilon = \frac{A}{cl} = \frac{0.52 \times 138.2}{0.0062 \times 1} = 11\,590 \ \left(\text{to four significant figures}\right)$$

Similarly for the absorption at 300 nm, we can calculate ε as 71.

UV spectroscopic data are usually quoted in the form: λ_{max} (solvent) (ε) nm. Alternatively, the extinction coefficient is often quoted as its logarithm (to base 10). Hence we should quote the UV data for the $\pi \rightarrow \pi^*$ transition of isophorone as λ_{max} (EtOH) 234 (ε 11 590) nm or λ_{max} (EtOH) 234 (log ε 4.06).

So far the analysis of the spectrum has simply been a matter of reading off the λ_{max} and calculating ε values for all the peaks. We now need to interpret these in terms of the structural features and functional groups of the compound under study. Nowadays despite its historical importance as the first spectroscopic method of organic chemistry, UV spectroscopy is rarely used as the prime spectroscopic tool for structure determination. Therefore by the time that you run your UV spectrum you will know exactly what your compound is, or at least have some idea about its structure. Nonetheless UV spectroscopy remains a useful confirmatory technique, and occasionally still provides the key evidence—for instance in distinguishing between α,β-unsaturated ketones and other types of unsaturated ketones.

The types of compound giving rise to characteristic UV spectra that can be interpreted in terms of distinct chromophores arising from functional groups within the molecule are those with conjugated systems: dienes, α,β-unsaturated carbonyl compounds and aromatics. Unfortunately, you cannot correlate a peak at, say, 265 nm in the UV spectrum with one particular functional group in the same way as you can correlate an IR peak at, say, 1700 cm^{-1} with a carbonyl group. However, when faced with a UV spectrum, there are some general guidelines that will help you to make some initial deductions. These are listed below.

1 Starting at the short wavelength end, ignore the end absorption. Peaks with λ_{max} of less than about 220 nm cannot usually be interpreted unambiguously.

2 If the spectrum is very simple with essentially one main peak absorbing below 300 nm with an ε value in the range 10 000–20 000, the compound probably contains a very simple conjugated system such as a diene or an enone, the $\pi \rightarrow \pi^*$ transition of which is responsible for the absorption. Less intense bands in this region (ε, 2000–10 000) may suggest an aromatic system. Obviously these possibilities would be readily distinguished by IR or NMR spectroscopy.

3 If the spectrum is more complex and extends into the visible region, the molecule contains an extended chromophore such as a polyene, an aromatic ring with conjugating substituents, or a polycyclic aromatic system.

At this stage you can abandon the analysis/interpretation of your UV spectrum, and simply say that it is consistent with certain structural features in your compound, and confirms previous assignments made from IR or NMR spectroscopy. However, it is possible to take the analysis a stage further, because there are some very useful correlations between structure and UV absorption maxima. These empirical rules, first formulated by R.B. Woodward in 1941 and subsequently modified by L.F. Fieser, are known as the *Woodward rules* or the *Woodward–Fieser rules*, and enable us to predict the λ_{max} values for conjugated dienes and α,β-unsaturated carbonyl compounds. The rules were further developed by A.I. Scott in one of the classic works on UV spectroscopy, *Interpretation of the Ultraviolet Spectra of Natural Products*, published in 1964.

In effect the rules assign a λ_{max} value to the $\pi \rightarrow \pi^*$ transition of the parent chromophore, and tabulate increments for the effect of added substituents. Substituents which are not chromophores in their own right, but which alter the λ_{max} value of a chromophore, are known as *auxochromes*. The simplest types of auxochromes are alkyl groups, which cause a small (5–10 nm) bathochromic shift (to longer wavelength) when attached to a chromophore.

Woodward rules

Auxochromes

Similarly other groups act as auxochromes: OR, OCOR, SR, NR$_2$ and halogen all cause bathochromic shifts. The addition of extra unsaturation in the form of another double or triple bond obviously causes a much larger shift to longer wavelength. The rules for diene absorptions are given in Table A17 in Appendix 3, and list the values for the parent chromophore according to whether the diene is acyclic or cyclic, together with the increments due to various auxochromes. The analogous rules for α,β-unsaturated ketones are given in Table A18; however, there is an additional complication here, since with carbonyl groups, the position of maximum absorption is subject to changes in solvent polarity as discussed earlier. The effects of solvent on the absorption maxima of α,β-unsaturated ketones are shown in Table A 19 in the form of the correction factors needed to 'convert' the λ_{max} to that expected in ethanol. There is no solvent effect with dienes.

The application of Woodward's rules is best illustrated with a few examples, although you must remember that the rules only predict the lowest $\pi \rightarrow \pi^*$ transition.

Example 1. Cholesta-3,5-diene

Parent (heteroannular) diene	214
Substituents:	
2–3 bond (ring residue)	5
6–7 bond (ring residue)	5
5–10 bond (ring residue)	5
Exocyclic double bond	5
Calculated λ_{max}	234 nm

The observed value is 235 nm.

Example 2. Cholesta-5,7-diene-1,3-diol

Parent (homoannular) diene	253
Substituents:	
4–5 bond (ring residue)	5
8–9 bond (ring residue)	5
5–10 bond (ring residue)	5
8–14 bond (ring residue)	5
Calculated λ_{max}	273 nm

The observed value is 272 nm.

Example 3. Dihydrojasmone

Parent α,β-unsaturated five-ring ketone	202
α-Substituents: alkyl group	10
β-Substituents:	
alkyl group	12
ring residue	12
Calculated λ_{max} (EtOH)	236 nm

The observed value is 237 nm.

Example 4. Rotundifolene

Parent α,β-unsaturated acyclic ketone	215
α-Substituents: ring residue	10
β-Substituents: two alkyl groups	24
Exocyclic double bond	5
Calculated λ_{max} (EtOH)	254 nm

The observed value is 260 nm.

The other types of compound that give useful UV spectra are aromatic molecules, but unfortunately simple quantitative rules for the prediction of their spectra do not exist. However, there are a number of general guidelines that will assist you in the interpretation of the UV spectra of aromatic compounds.

Aromatic compounds

1 In monosubstituted benzenes, conjugating substituents, such as CH = CH or COR, which extend the chromophore increase both the wavelength and intensity of the absorption. This is, of course, the general rule that applies to all compounds.

2 Alkyl substituents have a small bathochromic effect.

3 Substituents with lone pairs of electrons also cause bathochromic shifts. The effect is a result of the interaction of the aromatic π-system with the substituent lone pair, and the magnitude of the bathochromic shift is related to the substituent's ability as a donor. Thus the effect of substituents decreases in the order: $NH_2 > OH > Cl$.

4 In polysubstituted benzenes, the combined effects of substituents may be considerably greater than that expected on the basis of the individual effect of each substituent. As an example of this consider 4-methoxybenzaldehyde (Fig. 5.68). Since the two substituents are 'complementary' with the methoxy-

Fig. 5.68 'Complementary' substitution in 4-methoxybenzaldehyde.

releasing and the aldehyde-withdrawing electrons, and they are *para* related, we can write a resonance form in which the conjugation is considerably extended. This extends the chromophore, and the observed λ_{max} is greater than would be expected from the *individual* effects of the groups. When the groups are *meta* or *ortho* related, the effect on the chromophore is much less dramatic, and the observed λ_{max} values are much closer to those expected from the individual effects of the substituents. Similarly if the two substituents are non-complementary, in other words both are electron-releasing or electron-withdrawing, the chromophore is not affected to the same extent.

5 Bicyclic and polycyclic aromatic systems absorb at much longer wavelengths than monocyclic compounds.

There are two types of aromatic compound that can usually be readily identified from their UV spectra: phenols and anilines. We have already referred to the effect of interaction of the aromatic π-system with substituent lone pairs of electrons, and in comparing the long wavelength λ_{max} values for benzene, phenol and aniline, we find that they occur at 254, 270 and 280 nm, respectively. The interaction of the phenolic oxygen with the π-system increases considerably in the phenolate anion, since there are now two non-bonding pairs of electrons, and there is a large *bathochromic* shift in the absorption maximum. Hence the UV spectrum of a phenol should change dramatically if a base is added to the sample to deprotonate the phenolic OH. This effect is illustrated in Fig. 5.69, which shows the UV spectrum of 4-

Phenols and bathochromic shifts

Fig. 5.69 UV spectra of 4-nitrophenol: (a) in ethanol; (b) in ethanol with added sodium hydroxide solution.

nitrophenol run in ethanol, and the changes that occur on adding sodium hydroxide to the solution. On addition of base the λ_{max} value increases from 310 to 400 nm. Note that the *intensity* of absorption also increases. In this particular case the change in absorption properties on addition of base is so dramatic as to be visible to the human eye; the original dilute ethanol solution of 4-nitrophenol is *very* faintly yellow, but the colour deepens considerably when a drop of sodium hydroxide solution is added.

The reverse arguments apply with anilines. Because of the greater donor ability of nitrogen over oxygen, the nitrogen lone pair has a greater interaction with the π-system. However, we can remove this interaction by protonating the nitrogen. The resulting anilinium cation no longer has non-bonding electrons to interact with the aromatic system, and therefore shows a *hyp-*

Anilines and hypsochromic shifts

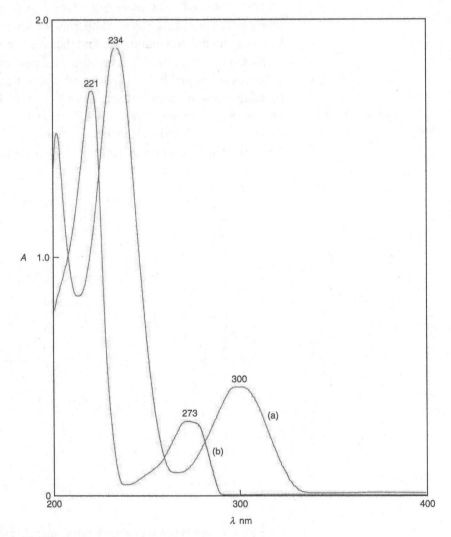

Fig. 5.70 UV spectra of 4-methoxyaniline: (a) in ethanol; (b) in ethanol with added hydrochloric acid.

sochromic shift (to shorter wavelength) in the UV spectrum. Hence the UV spectrum of an aniline should change if an acid is added to the solution to protonate the NH_2 group. This effect is illustrated in Fig. 5.70, which shows the UV spectrum of 4-methoxyaniline in ethanol and the changes which occur on addition of hydrochloric acid. The long wavelength absorption at 300 nm moves to 273 nm with a decrease in intensity on addition of the acid. Such simple experimental tricks are very useful in the identification of these functional groups.

Further reading

Organic Electronic Spectral Data, Vols 1–31, Wiley & Sons, New York, 1960–1989.

Sadtler Handbook of Ultraviolet Spectra, Sadtler, Pennsylvania, 1979.

L.M. Harwood and T.D.W. Claridge, *Introduction to Organic Spectroscopy*, Oxford University Press, Oxford, 1996, Chapter 7.

A.I. Scott, *Interpretation of the Ultraviolet Spectra of Natural Products*, Pergamon, Oxford, 1964.

R.M. Silverstein, G.C. Bassler and T.C. Morrill, *Spectrometric Identification of Organic Compounds*, 6th edn, Wiley & Sons, New York, 1998.

S. Sternhell and J. Kalman, *Organic Structures from Spectra*, 2nd edn, Wiley & Sons, New York, 1995.

D.H. Williams and I. Fleming, *Spectroscopic Methods in Organic Chemistry*, 5th edn, McGraw-Hill, Maidenhead, 1995.

5.5 Mass spectrometry

Mass spectrometry is concerned with the determination of the molecular mass of the sample in question—a particularly useful piece of information for the organic chemist which the other spectroscopic techniques cannot provide. The basic principle by which the individual molecules are 'weighed' is very simple and was first demonstrated by Wien in 1898. The sample is first converted into positive ions by being bombarded with high energy electrons which remove an electron from the molecule on impact. The positive ions are then accelerated by an electrical potential and pass through a magnetic field which causes them to be deflected from their initial straight line of flight. The degree of deviation depends on the magnetic field strength, the charge on the ion and its momentum. It is not difficult to appreciate intuitively that lighter ions will be deflected more than heavier ions for a given magnetic field strength and ionic charge, and very simple application of classic mechanics permits the following relationship to be derived.

$$\frac{m}{z} = \frac{H^2 R^2}{2V}$$

where m = mass of the ion, z = charge on the ion, H = applied magnetic field strength, R = radius of arc of deflection, and V = applied accelerating voltage.

Of course, the whole procedure only works in the absence of energy exchanges resulting from intermolecular collisions; therefore the analysis has to be carried out under extremely high dilution conditions, necessitating a very high vacuum. As it examines individual species and not the bulk sample, mass spectrometry readily distinguishes between isotopes of the same element and this is also useful for the organic chemist.

In addition to giving the molecular weight of the substance under examination (the *molecular ion*), mass spectrometry enables a detailed analysis of molecular structure to be made. Under the fairly brutal conditions of electron impact ionization, the molecules tend to undergo cleavage either at weak bonds or to give particularly stable fragments in very predictable ways. Consequently, it is usually possible to infer molecular structure by analysis of the breakdown pattern in the mass spectrum of an unknown. Some molecules are so sensitive that none survive the conditions of electron impact ionization intact and therefore a molecular ion is not obtained in the mass spectrum. Naturally this can be very misleading and also deprives the chemist of the one piece of information that cannot be obtained by the other spectroscopic techniques—the molecular weight of the substance. Fortunately there are 'softer' ionization techniques available which allow the molecular ion to be observed by using lower energy electron beams or a pre-ionized gas.

Machines of higher resolving power, referred to as *double-focusing* instruments, permit the accurate measurement of molecular masses to within a few parts per million. With this precision it is possible to obtain the actual atomic constitution of the molecule by differentiation between different species which have the same integral molecular mass. Such measurements permit a very good guess at the molecular formula of even rather complex substances, and this technique provides an alternative to microanalysis for determining elemental composition—of particular importance when only small amounts (less than $500\,\mu g$) of material are available.

Mass spectrometry requires only a very small amount of sample; less than a microgram is needed for the analysis itself. The actual amount of sample required is therefore really only a function of the limitations of manipulation rather than the analysis. This makes mass spectrometry effectively a non-destructive technique.

Computers are central to mass spectrometry. An important feature of commercial machines is the computing hardware available to manage the wealth of data that can be extracted from the mass spectrum of a compound, but a discussion of such aspects is beyond the scope of this book.

The instrument

Organic chemists can thank the petroleum industry for providing the impetus to move mass spectrometry from the realm of the physicists into the organic chemistry laboratory for use as an analytical tool. Mass spectroscopic analysis proved ideal for providing rapid solutions to the problems of differentiating between members of homologous series of alkanes and alkenes. From this sprang the large range of commercial machines which are able to cope with an enormous spread of chemical structures and molecular weights.

All instruments, whatever additional sophistication they might possess, require a very high vacuum (around 10^{-6} mmHg) to operate, at the same time permitting the introduction of sample. It is this requirement, placing very stringent demands on the design, engineering and operation of a mass spectrometer, which makes these instruments extremely sensitive to misuse. For this reason, organic chemists are usually kept well clear of the machine, and its operation is left to those who have been fully trained. Mass spectrometry is very rarely available 'hands-on', although with the advent of more robust pumping systems this situation is beginning to change, at least in some research laboratories.

The resolution in the type of instrument used to obtain a standard mass spectrum of organic molecules by electron impact ionization can be achieved by the *single focusing* arrangement depicted in Fig. 5.71.

A small quantity of the sample to be analyzed is introduced through the inlet port as a vapour where it meets a beam of high energy electrons (*ca.* 70 eV). Whilst electrons of about 10 eV possess sufficient energy to cause ionization of the molecule, the higher energy electrons used can rupture bonds within the molecule, causing its fragmentation and giving a much more informative spectrum than one which just contains the molecular ion. The positive ions produced in the ionization chamber are then accelerated by a high voltage (4–8 kV) and focused into a tight beam. The collimated beam then passes through a strong magnetic field disposed at right angles to its path which causes the ions to be deflected in an arc. Lighter ions are deflected to a greater extent than heavier ions with the same charge, and the separated ion beams are collected and the intensity of each beam is measured (Fig. 5.72).

To record the entire range of molecular masses, either the accelerating potential or (more commonly) the magnetic field strength is varied, in order to focus each ion beam in turn onto the detector where the positive ions combine with electrons. This sets up a current proportional to the intensity of

Fig. 5.71 Schematic diagram depicting the layout of a single focusing mass spectrometer.

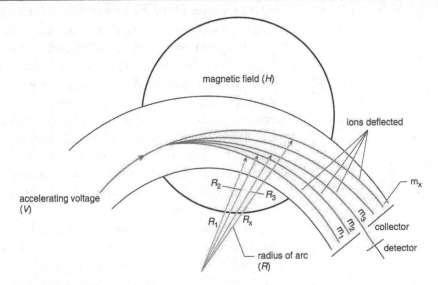

Fig. 5.72 Positively charged ions are deflected to varying degrees by an applied magnetic field according to their mass.

Fig. 5.73 Schematic diagram showing the principal features of a double-focusing mass spectrometer.

the ion beam and measurement of this gives the *relative abundance* of the ions produced by that particular fragmentation process. The relative abundance of each ion formed is, of course, dependent on the ease of the fragmentation process which gives rise to it, and is an important diagnostic feature of the mass spectrum of a molecule.

The construction of the *double-focusing* instrument is similar to the single-focusing system except than an additional electrostatic analyzer is placed after the magnetic analyzer (Fig. 5.73). After the ions have been sorted according to their mass by the magnetic analyzer, the electrostatic analyzer separates ions of the same mass but possessing different energy. This enhances resolution by refocusing the small energy spread that is found within each collection of ions of the same integral mass. To increase resolution further, the slits on the collector are narrower than in the single focusing instrument, enabling much greater discrimination in the analysis of the ion beams. Unfortunately, this higher selectivity is won at the cost of sensitivity because the narrower slit means that fewer ions can be sampled at any one time. The sensitivity problem is overcome by using electron multipliers in conjunction with the collector, making it possible to detect ion currents as low as 10^{-18} A.

Other means of mass analysis are also available in addition to deflection of ions by a magnetic field as just described. Other systems include *time of flight spectrometers* and *ion-cyclotron spectrometers*; however, by far the commonest alternative to magnetic sector spectrometers are those using a *quadrupole mass filter*. The advantage of this system is that it is robust and compact, making it suitable for 'hands-on' bench-top machines. In addition, its fast molecular weight scanning capability renders it ideal for use in GC–MS systems and such quadrupole instruments are rapidly gaining acceptance. However, there is insufficient space to cover these systems here and those interested in the principles governing the operation of such instruments are directed to the references at the end of this section.

A development which is proving to be a very powerful technique is *on-line GC–MS*. As its name suggests, this involves connecting the outlet from a gas chromatograph directly to the inlet of a mass spectrometer, permitting the analysis of very complex mixtures. However, the need for selective removal of the carrier gas from the effluent before introduction of the sample into the high vacuum of the mass spectrometer results in many additional technical difficulties. Several designs of GC–MS interface exist, but one commonly encountered arrangement uses a jet molecular separator in which the column effluent gas exits through a fine jet and impinges onto a sharp-edged collector nozzle (Fig. 5.74). The lighter components of the mixture diffuse more quickly to the periphery and are removed. The sharp-edged collector nozzle, a small

Fig. 5.74 Jet molecular separator interface, GC–MS.

distance from the jet, only permits passage of the innermost part of the jet (containing the heavier molecules) into the mass spectrometer.

In *directly coupled GC–MS* systems the use of highly efficient vacuum pumps, combined with the reduced rate of gas throughput in capillary GC, now mean that it is possible for the chromatography effluent gases to enter the mass spectrometer without the necessity for an interface.

Combined high performance liquid chromatography (HPLC)–MS instruments are also available which take the output from a liquid chromatography column directly into a mass spectrometer. The problems associated with GC–MS pale into insignificance against those encountered in the selective removal of the eluant solvents from purified components after HPLC. However, the prize of being able to analyze mixtures which are not volatile enough to be separated by vapour phase chromatography makes the additional instrumental complication all worthwhile.

It has not been possible in these paragraphs to do more than mention a few of the extensions of mass spectrometry which now make up the sophisticated analytical arsenal available to organic chemists. The limitation on the technique is the stability of molecules to conditions in which they are volatile enough to pass through the mass spectrometer. As the kinds of molecules of interest to chemists grow in complexity and sensitivity, so new techniques are developed to analyze them by mass spectrometry. Whilst many of these techniques involve extremely complex instrumentation, what is considered as 'state-of-the-art' today has a habit of becoming routine very rapidly in mass spectrometry. There is insufficient space to give procedures such as *field desorption spectrometry*, *field ionization spectrometry*, *fast atom bombardment*, *electroscopy*, *thermospray* and MALDI, even the cursory treatment which has been afforded to the basic mass spectrometric techniques in this book. The references given at the end of this section contain useful additional information.

Preparing the sample

Avoiding contamination

As far as most organic chemists are concerned, preparation of the sample simply involves placing a suitable quantity in a labelled tube and submitting it for analysis. However, the very high sensitivity of mass spectrometry underlines the need to avoid contamination of the sample at all costs. Many a pure sample has given an unacceptable or misleading mass spectrum because of thoughtlessness in preparing the sample for analysis. The problem stems from the almost ubiquitous use of additives to maintain pliability in plastics — particularly those used to make push-caps for specimen tubes. The plasticizers leach perniciously into the sample if allowed to come into contact with it, and give a whole series of spurious peaks in the mass spectrum. *Be warned! Never use push-cap tubes to submit samples for mass spectrometry.* The types of

Beware of plasticizers!

Table 5.5 Common impurity peaks encountered in mass spectra.

Contaminant	Peaks observed (m/z)
(a) Plasticizers	
n-Butyl phthalate	149, 205, 223, 278
n-Octyl phthalate	149, 167, 279
Tri-n-butyl acetyl citrate	129, 185, 259, 429
Tributyl phosphate	99, 155, 211
(b) Antioxidants	
2,6-Di-t-butyl-p-cresol	205, 220
(c) Stopcock grease	
Silicone grease	133, 207, 281, 355, 429
(d) Air	18 (H_2O), 28 (N_2), 32 (O_2), 40 (Ar), 44 (CO_2)

plasticizers used (Table 5.5) have molecular weights in the region 200–300, precisely the sort of region of interest to organic chemists. The best tubes to use for mass spectrometry samples are those having screw-caps with an aluminum-covered inner liner to the cap. However, plastic push-caps are not the only source of plasticizers and you should not allow your sample to come into contact with anything made of flexible polymer such as pipette bulbs or even plastic-backed TLC plates. Impurities which are frequently encountered in mass spectra of apparently rigorously purified samples are silicone grease and polymeric hydrocarbons. The usual sources of these materials are over-liberally greased stopcocks on chromatography columns or separatory funnels; however, care should also be taken when sealing flasks with commercially available paraffin film, traces of which can find their way into the sample. Hydrocarbons often give a whole series of peaks separated by 14 mass units whose intensities gradually decrease with increasing molecular weight. As these tend not to give a definite molecular ion the presence of these peaks is usually unsatisfactory rather than misleading; however, samples giving a weak molecular ion can be swamped by the background contamination. Silicone grease is a different affair, giving very distinct peaks in the mass spectrum. Finally, many plastics contain added antioxidants, usually hindered phenols, to slow down atmospheric degradation and increase their useful life. Although only present in trace amounts, these are readily leached by organic materials with which they come into contact. You should learn to recognize and distrust any peaks corresponding to those in Table 5.5.

Sample submission

Although the technique requires only a vanishingly small amount of sample for analysis, have pity on the operator and supply at least enough sample to see — this makes life much easier when trying to extract the sample from the tube! In addition, the more sample you supply the less will be the effect of any chance contamination on the resultant spectrum. At the same time, there is no need to supply grams of material; usually a few milligrams of a crystalline solid or a little more of a viscous oil will suffice. Whenever possible, liquid samples should be supplied in containers with a conical or hemispherical bottom in which the sample accumulates for easy removal. Never forget to label your tube clearly with your name, where you can be contacted, the possible structure of your sample and any dangerous properties it may possess. Normally it will be necessary to fill in a form with all of these details and also to fill in a booking sheet. Courtesy and common sense should always be paramount with sample submission to any analytical service; once goodwill between yourself and the operator has been lost it is nearly impossible to regain it!

Submit samples in a manner which makes it easy for the operator to handle them

Never submit noxious or toxic materials for analysis without first discussing your intentions with the operator.

Always check before submitting noxious materials for analysis

Derivatizing samples for GC–MS

The common derivatization procedures for GC–MS involve the conversion of polar groups such as alcohols, amines and carboxylic acids into the silylated, acetylated or methylated derivatives, and some procedures are described on pp. 196–197. Derivatization is used in mass spectrometry, not only for rendering the material more volatile, but also to give a more abundant molecular ion peak or clearer fragmentation pattern.

Running the spectrum

Introducing the sample

The choice of method for introducing the sample into the mass spectrometer is usually dictated by the physical properties of the substance under investigation. All systems are designed to permit the material to be introduced in a controlled and measured way without destroying the vacuum within the instrument or requiring extended periods of additional evacuation. Moderately volatile samples can be introduced by a *heated inlet* in which the material diffuses into a reservoir maintained at *ca.* 10^{-2} mmHg and a temperature of up to 350°C. The reservoir is attached to the ultra-low pressure part of the mass spectrometer by a porous disk which allows the sample in the reservoir to bleed into the ionization chamber (Fig. 5.75). The drawback of this arrangement is that thermally unstable compounds may undergo decomposition on the container walls before being introduced into the ion chamber.

Heated inlet

A septum inlet may be used for liquids, but materials of low thermal stability are usually introduced into the mass spectrometer using a *direct insertion probe*. The sample is loaded onto the ceramic tip of the probe contained in a glass capillary, and this is then passed through a vacuum lock into the ioniza-

Direct insertion

Fig. 5.75 Sample introduction by a heated inlet system.

Fig. 5.76 Direct insertion probe for thermally unstable materials.

tion chamber where the sample is exposed to the electron beam (Fig. 5.76). The tip of the probe can also be heated by means of a platinum element to extend the temperature range of samples which can be analyzed.

Recording and calibrating spectra

The mass spectrum is scanned over the full range from low to high mass in the magnetic sector instrument (high to low mass with quadrupole instruments). Recording is usually stopped before the lowest ion $m/z = 12$, corresponding to C^+, is reached.

Peak counting on photographic charts

Older spectrometers produce the spectra as photographic charts which require each peak to be counted by eye. A recognizable starting point is therefore necessary. You should look for nitrogen and oxygen molecular ions at $m/z = 28$ and 32 as a pair of peaks with relative intensities of roughly $4:1$ (see Table 5.5). Another useful calibration point is the closely spaced double peak that occurs at $m/z = 40$ due to the presence of argon and the $C_3H_4^+$ fragment ion from the introduced sample. Although the peaks on photographic charts are widely separated at low molecular mass, they close up at high mass and it becomes difficult to count them at molecular masses higher than about 300. When counting, you should not be misled by the appearance of any small peaks which appear at the mid-point between expected peaks, as these are

Fig. 5.77 The mass spectrum of benzoic acid presented as a photographic chart. Note the metastable peaks at $m/z = 56.47$ ($105 \rightarrow 77$) and 90.37 ($122 \rightarrow 105$) and the doubly charged ion peak at $m/z = 52.5$. The peaks close up with increasing mass and the major peaks on the top trace are off-scale and have been truncated.

due to doubly charged odd molecular weight ions ($m/2z$) which have been detected. To ease peak counting, especially in 'empty' areas in the sample spectrum, a spectrum of perfluorokerosene is often included against the unknown spectrum, or a scale of mass units may be marked on the bottom of the chart.

Perfluorokerosene contains a regular series of peaks separated by 12 or 14 mass units in a molecular weight range of 19–800 mass units. Photographic charts normally present the spectrum as a series of superimposed traces of increasing sensitivity. By this means it is usually possible to count the peaks using the most sensitive trace at the same time as identifying the major fragmentation ions (Fig. 5.77). However, it is not very easy to measure the relative abundances of the fragment peaks.

The photographic charts fade if left exposed to bright light, so always roll them up when not needed and store them in a dark place.

Bar graphs

A more convenient representation of the mass spectrum is given by a bar graph, plotting relative abundance of the ions against their mass. (This is the form in which mass spectra will be depicted in this book). The spectrum is normalized to give the most abundant ion (the *base peak*) an intensity of 100% (Fig. 5.78). One drawback to this method of presentation is that the wide variation in peak intensities in a mass spectrum can cause important peaks such as the molecular ion to be too small to be observed. This can be overcome by magnifying the high molecular weight end of the spectrum to render small but important peaks visible. Another disadvantage of this presentation is that it gives no information on any metastable peaks (pp. 388–389), as it only shows peaks occurring at integral values.

A third form of output presents the data in tabular form but, although this contains all of the necessary data, the fact that the information is not in a pictorial format makes it difficult to assimilate at a glance.

Fig. 5.78 Mass spectrum of benzoic acid represented as a bar graph.

Fig. 5.79 Isotope abundances for carbon, silicon, sulfur, chlorine and bromine.

Interpretation of spectra

Isotopes

Before we can start to discuss the extraction of data from the mass spectrum of an unknown, it is necessary to consider the consequences of the isotopic constitution of the constituent elements of the sample. Of the elements likely to be encountered in your sample, only fluorine, iodine and phosphorus are monoisotopic. However, with the exception of the elements shown in Fig. 5.79, most others can be considered to be effectively monoisotopic due to the low abundance of their minor constituent isotopes.

Let us discuss the effect of a polyisotopic element on the appearance of the mass spectrum by considering a monobrominated compound. Bromine consists of two isotopes (^{79}Br, ^{81}Br) in roughly equal amounts, and therefore the molecular ion, or any species containing bromine, will appear in the mass spectrum as a pair of equal intensity peaks separated by two mass units (Fig. 5.80a). It is not difficult to see that a species containing two atoms of bromine will appear as three peaks (each separated by two mass units) of approximate intensity 1:2:1 (Fig. 5.80b). Likewise tribrominated species will give four peaks of intensity 1:4:4:1 (Fig. 5.80c). Parts d–f show the equivalent isotope patterns for species containing one, two and three chlorine atoms (76% ^{35}Cl, 24% ^{37}Cl).

The relative intensity of peaks resulting from the presence of atoms of an element with two isotopes in a molecule can be calculated using a binomial expansion

$$\left(a+b\right)^n$$

where a = the abundance of the light isotope, b = the abundance of the heavy isotope, and n = the number of atoms of the element.

These isotope patterns are quite useful when examining mass spectra of molecules containing chlorine or bromine. However, the 1.1% ^{13}C isotope naturally present in organic molecules can be a trap for the unwary chemist when it comes to deciding which is the molecular ion of the compound under investigation. If a molecule contains 10 carbon atoms, there is a 1.1% chance that any of them will be a ^{13}C isotope and there is a $10 \times 1.1\%$ chance that the molecule will contain one ^{13}C atom somewhere. Consequently, if we forget the possibility of other polyisotopic elements being present, the molecular ion (M$^{+\cdot}$) will be accompanied by another peak at (M + 1) of about one-tenth its intensity (see Figs 5.77 and 5.78). *Do not mistake the ^{13}C peak at M + 1 for the molecular ion.* With larger molecules this ^{13}C peak becomes more and more important and peaks due to molecules containing two or more ^{13}C isotopes start to become visible at M + 2, M + 3 and so on, complicating the situation still further. However, for the usual size of C,H,N,O-containing organic molecule encountered, the molecular ion will be the largest of the peaks at the high molecular weight limit.

Look out for the ^{13}C peak at M + 1

The molecular ion

The first, and arguably the most important, piece of information that can be obtained from the mass spectrum is the molecular ion (M$^{+\cdot}$) which corresponds to the molecular weight of the unknown. In deciding which peak actu-

Fig. 5.80 Isotope patterns of species: (a) Br; (b) Br$_2$; (c) Br$_3$; (d) Cl; (e) Cl$_2$; (f) Cl$_3$.

ally corresponds to the molecular ion, it is important to remember the possibility of polyisotopic atoms and not to be tricked by the ^{13}C peak.

The nitrogen rule

Most organic molecules have molecular weights that are even, with the common exceptions to this rule being those compounds which contain odd numbers of nitrogen atoms—a consequence of nitrogen having an even atomic weight and an odd valency. However, whilst the observation of an odd molecular ion in a mass spectrum run under electron impact conditions indicates the presence of nitrogen in the molecule, this need not be the situation. It may be that this highest molecular weight peak is actually a fragment ion, with the true molecular ion being too unstable to be observed. You should particularly suspect this if the 'molecular ion' loses any fragment between 3 and 14 mass units. These would correspond to highly unfavourable events, such as multiple losses of hydrogen atoms or the formation of high energy species. For this latter reason, loss of methylene (CH_2) is almost never observed, and so that appearance of a fragment ion at 14 mass units below the highest peak is clear evidence that the true molecular ion is not being observed. This can be checked by repeating the electron impact spectrum under 'softer' ionizing conditions (using lower energy electrons of, say, 20 eV) to see if the molecular ion becomes visible.

If the molecular ion is still not observed, the spectrum can be obtained using even milder *chemical ionization* conditions. This technique is carried out by introducing the sample at low pressure (10^{-4} mmHg) into the ionization chamber in the presence of excess ammonia or methane at a pressure of 1 mmHg. Electron impact causes preferential ionization of the gas which can then undergo intermolecular proton transfer under the relatively high concentrations in the ionization chamber to furnish NH_4^+ or CH_5^+. These species can protonate the sample under conditions which are sufficiently mild so that fragmentation of the resultant MH^+ *quasi-molecular ion* does not occur. With ammonia the highest peak is often at M + 18 due to the formation of the MNH_4^+ species. However, electrophilic additions are much less common with methane and any such peaks are usually small compared with MH^+.

Some substances, particularly amines and polyols, show a tendency to carry out a similar sort of intermolecular protonation process under standard electron impact conditions. This results in a diminished molecular ion with a larger than predicted M + 1 peak, and is most noticeable when the substance itself has a molecular ion which is unstable with regard to fragmentation (Fig. 5.81).

As a general rule of thumb, aromatic compounds give strong molecular ions (exceptions are bromides, iodides, benzylic halides and aryl ketones, although these usually give easily detected molecular ions). Molecular ions which are very weak or totally absent can be expected in spectra obtained from tertiary alcohols and halides, and branched or long chain alkanes.

Fig. 5.81 Mass spectrum of cyclohexylamine showing an M + 1 peak due to intermolecular self-protonation.

Common fragmentation pathways

When a molecule is ionized by electron impact with 70 eV electrons, more energy can be imparted than is needed to remove an electron. In the absence of intermolecular interactions, this excess electronic energy of the excited state is transferred to ground-state vibrational energy, and can result in fragmentation of the molecule. The energy transferred in any impact can vary up to the maximum energy of the ionizing electrons. This leads to a range of different decomposition pathways, giving fragment ions which provide a characteristic fingerprint of the compound.

Fragmentation peaks are important for structural elucidation

Under any given conditions, the degree to which a particular fragmentation occurs, and hence the relative abundance of the peaks corresponding to the fragments, depends to a large extent on the facility of the cleavage process. Generally, one-bond cleavages occur more readily than those which involve simultaneous breaking of more than one bond, as the latter process imposes strict conformational constraints on the molecule. One-bond cleavages from C,H,O compounds will result in odd mass fragment ions, whereas two-bond cleavages, with the loss of a neutral molecule, will give even-mass fragments. A list of some of the more frequently encountered fragmentations is given in Appendix 3, but this is by no means exhaustive and other more complete tables may be found in the works listed on pp. 395–396. However, some particular fragmentations are so important that they deserve special mention here.

Tropylium ion = 91

Any aromatic molecule containing a benzyl group will show a very important fragment (usually the base peak) at $m/z = 91$. This corresponds to formation of the highly stabilized tropylium species, either directly or by rearrangement of the benzyl cation. Usually the tropylium peak is accompanied by a peak at $m/z = 65$ due to a second fragmentation resulting in loss of ethyne.

Compounds possessing acyl groups will give important fragment peaks at m/z corresponding to formation of the acylium cation. For instance, acetates and methyl ketones give a strong peak at $m/z = 43$ and benzoates or phenyl ketones give an equivalent peak at $m/z = 105$. Usually these species are accompanied by peaks corresponding to loss of carbon monoxide.

Acetyl ion = 43
Benzoyl ion = 105

Among the two-bond fragmentation processes, one of the most documented is the *McLafferty rearrangement* which occurs with ketones and esters in which a hydrogen substituent is present γ to the carbonyl group. The molecular ion can be considered to undergo a reverse-ene reaction, with the charge usually residing on the portion retaining the carbonyl atoms.

X=H, alkyl, aryl, OR

The *retro-Diels–Alder* reaction is an important fragmentation which occurs with cyclohexenes, commonly leaving the charge on the diene component.

In general, if an elimination can occur to furnish a small stable neutral molecule then this will happen, particularly in molecules where one-bond cleavages are not favoured. In particular, alcohols lose water giving a peak at $M - 18$ and acetates lose acetic acid to give a peak at $M - 60$.

In fragmentation reactions it is possible to predict which fragment will be lost as the neutral moiety and which will retain the charge and be detected in the mass spectrometer. The *Stephenson–Audier rule* states that in a fragmentation reaction, the positive charge will reside on the moiety which has the lowest ionization potential. The easiest way of applying this rule is to remember the approximation that the greater possibility a fragment has for resonance stabilization, the lower its ionization potential (Fig. 5.82).

Metastable peaks

These are a special kind of fragment peak which are seen in spectra recorded on photographic chart paper. They are much less common than normal fragmentation peaks, are characteristically broad and occur at non-integral positions in the spectrum. Metastable peaks can be clearly seen at $m/z = 56.47$ and 90.37 in the spectrum of benzoic acid in Fig. 5.77.

Metastable peaks are the result of fragmentations which occur outside the ionization chamber but before the magnetic analyzer of the spectrometer. The qualitative result of such a fragmentation can be appreciated without the need for rigorous mathematical treatment. When fragmentation occurs in the field-free zone, the parent ion has already experienced a period of time within the accelerating voltage. On fragmentation, the daughter ion keeps the velocity but has a lower mass than the parent ion. This means that the daughter ion has

Fig. 5.82 Illustrations of the Stephenson–Audier rule.

a momentum which results in a measured mass lower than its actual mass. The actual relationship which can be derived is as follows:

$$m^* = \frac{\left(m_2\right)^2}{m_1}$$

where m_1 = the parent ion mass, m_2 = the daughter ion mass, and m^* = the metastable peak position.

The reason for the low abundance of metastable peaks can also be understood qualitatively. The rate constant for the fragmentation to furnish a metastable peak must be such as to allow the reaction to occur in the field-free region before the magnetic analyzer. If it occurs at a faster rate, the daughter ion is formed in the ionization chamber and gives a normal peak; if it occurs within the analyzer the ion peak is not transmitted to the detector. It turns out that very few ions have the type of lifetime (*ca.* 10^4–10^6) which fits the above constraints, and so only relatively few metastable peaks are recorded.

The mathematical relationship relates the position of the metastable peak to the masses of the parent and daughter ions. Unfortunately we only have one equation and two unknowns and so this has to be solved in a trial-and-error manner by inserting possible values for m_1 and m_2. However, to make life a little easier nomographs such as that shown in Fig. 5.83 have been developed, enabling values of m_1 and m_2 to be read off by placing a ruler at the value for m^*. Fortunately, the particular fragment ions m_1 and m_2 are usually abundant in the mass spectrum and this helps in choosing the likely parent and daughter ions. In addition, differences between m_1 and m_2 of less than 15 mass units can be ruled out.

High resolution mass measurement

Chemists usually quote atomic weights to no greater accuracy than one decimal place. However, using the non-integral atomic weight values based on ^{12}C = 12.000000, it is clearly possible to differentiate between atomic combinations having the same integral mass if the molecular mass can be measured with sufficient accuracy. If we consider species having an integral mass of 28, the accurate molecular mass values are as follows: CO = 27.99492; C_2H_4 = 28.03123; N_2 = 28.00616; and CH_2N = 28.01870. Consequently, it is possible to distinguish any of these from the others with a high resolution mass spectrometer. Conversely, if the mass of an unknown substance can be measured accurately (to around 1 ppm) it is possible to propose atomic combinations giving molecular mass values which agree with the measured result. This job is readily carried out using a computer, and it is frequently the case that a unique combination of elements fits the result, or all but one combination can be discarded on chemical grounds. This permits elemental

Fig. 5.83 Nomograph for relating metastable peaks to parent and daughter ions (after J.H. Benyon).

analysis by mass spectroscopy with all the attendant advantages of economy of sample.

Procedure for interpreting the spectrum of an unknown

It is impossible to give a foolproof procedure for interpreting any mass spectrum that you will encounter, and there is no substitute for experience. The flow diagram in Fig. 5.84 might help to put you on the right track, particularly with the types of compound you are liable to encounter in the early stages of your training, such as those listed below.

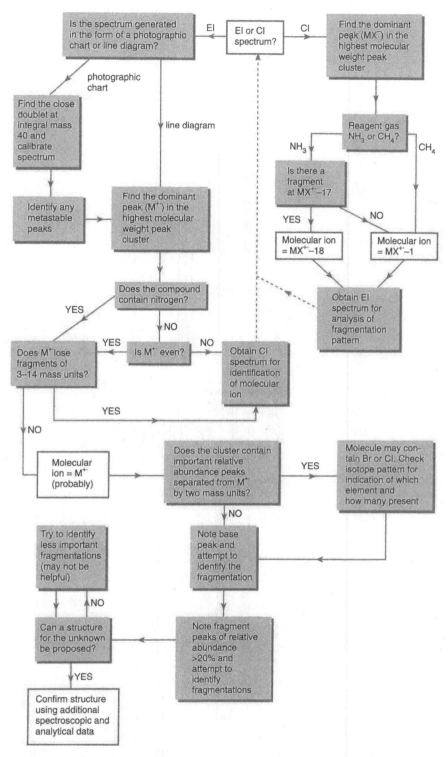

Fig. 5.84 Flow diagram of the suggested protocol for the interpretation of mass spectra. CI, chemical ionization; El, electron impact.

Examples

2,4-Pentanedione

Points to note

Highest peak $(M^{+\bullet}) = m/z$ 114.

Base peak $= m/z$ 43 $(CH_3C\equiv O^+)$.

Important fragment ions at m/z 71 $(M^{+\bullet} - 43)$, 41 $(C_3H_5^+)$, 39 $(C_3H_3^+)$.

2-Octanone

Points to note

Highest peak (M$^{+\bullet}$) = m/z 128.

Base peak = m/z 43 (CH$_3$C≡O$^+$).

Important fragment ions at m/z 113 (M$^{+\bullet}$ − 15), 85 (M$^{+\bullet}$ − 43), 58 [H$_2$C=C(OH)CH$_3$]$^{+\bullet}$ (McLafferty rearrangement).

Propanamide

Points to note

Highest peak (MH$^+$) = m/z 74 due to intermolecular self-protonation. (M$^{+\bullet}$) = m/z 73 (odd molecular weight — nitrogen present).

Base peak = m/z 44 (O=C=NH$_2^+$).

Important fragment ions at m/z 57 (M$^{+\bullet}$ − NH$_2^\bullet$) (McLafferty rearrangement), 29 (C$_2$H$_5^+$), 27 (C$_2$H$_3^+$).

Benzyl acetate

Points to note

Highest peak ($M^{+\bullet}$) = m/z 134.

Base peaks = m/z 91 (tropylium ion), 43 ($CH_3C\equiv O^+$).

Important fragment ions at m/z 92 (loss of $CH_2=C=O$ from molecular ion), 65 (loss of $CH\equiv CH$ from tropylium ion).

1,4-Dibromobenzene

Points to note

Highest peak cluster = m/z 234/236/238.

Important fragment ions at m/z 155/157 ($C_6H_4Br^+$), 75 ($C_6H_3^+$). The appearance of the molecular ion region indicates the presence of two atoms of bromine in the molecule. The pair of roughly equal intensity fragments at m/z 155/157 indicates the presence of one atom of bromine.

1,3-Dichloro-5-nitrobenzene

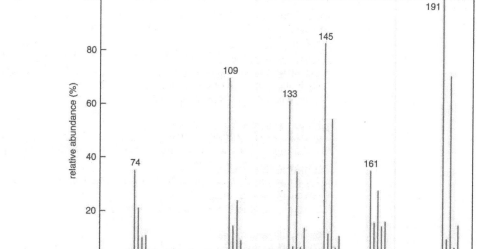

Points to note

Highest peak cluster = m/z 191/193/195 (odd molecular weight—nitrogen present).

Base peak = m/z 191 ($M^{+\bullet}$).

Important fragment ions at m/z 161/163/165 ($M^{+\bullet}$ − $^{\bullet}NO$), 145/147/149 ($M^{+\bullet}$ − $^{\bullet}NO_2$), 133/135/137, 109/111 ($M^{+\bullet}$ − $^{\bullet}NO_2$, HCl), 74 ($C_6H_2^{\bullet}N$). The appearance of the molecular ion and fragment peak clusters at $m/z > 133$ indicates the presence of two atoms of chlorine. The fragment peak cluster at m/z 109/111 indicates one chlorine atom to be present.

Further reading

A.J. Gordon and R.A. Ford, *The Chemist's Companion. A Handbook of Practical Data, Techniques and References*, Wiley & Sons, New York, 1973.

L.M. Harwood and T.D.W. Claridge, *Introduction to Organic Spectroscopy*, Oxford University Press, Oxford, 1996, Chapter 6.

I. Howe, D.H. Williams and R.D. Bowen, *Mass Spectrometry*, 2nd edn, McGraw-Hill, Maidenhead, 1981.

E. Pretsch, J. Seibl, W. Simon and T. Clerc, *Tables of Spectral Data for Structure Determination of Organic Compounds*, 2nd edn, Springer-Verlag, Berlin, 1989.

D.H. Williams and I. Fleming, *Spectroscopic Methods in Organic Chemistry*, 5th edn, McGraw-Hill, Maidenhead, 1995.

Further experimental aspects
J.R. Chapman, *Practical Organic Mass Spectroscopy*, Wiley & Sons, New York, 1985.

Mass spectrometry
The following specialist books discuss some of the principles and techniques for the more sophisticated developments in mass spectrometry:

H.D. Beckey, *Principles of Field Ionisation and Field Desorption Spectroscopy*, Pergamon, Oxford, 1977.

J.R. Chapman, *Practical Organic Mass Spectrometry*, 2nd edn, Wiley & Sons, New York, 1995.

R.B. Cole, *Electrospray Ionization Mass Spectrometry*, Wiley & Sons, New York, 1997.

A.G. Harrison, *Chemical Ionization Mass Spectrometry*, CRC Press, Boca Raton, 1983.

E. De Hoffmann, J. Charette and V. Strooband, *Mass Spectrometry: Principles and Application*, Wiley & Sons, New York, 1996.

GC–MS interfacing methods
F.W. Karasek and R.E. Clement, *Basic Gas Chromatography–Mass Spectrometry*, Elsevier, Amsterdam, 1991.

F.G. Kitson, B.S. Larsen and C.N. McEwan, *Gas Chromatography–Mass Spectrometry*, Academic Press, London, 1996.

R.D. Smith and H.R. Udseth, *Chem. Br.*, 1988, **24**, 350.

Computer programs
For a computer program predicting the relative intensities of peaks for any given number of isotopes, see: B. Dombek, J. Lowther and E. Carberry, *J. Chem. Educ.*, 1971, **48**, 729.

For a description of a computer program for the analysis of metastable ions, see: L.E. Brady, *J. Chem. Educ.*, 1971, **48**, 469.

Chapter 6

Keeping Records: the Laboratory Notebook and Chemical Literature

Despite what some theoreticians would have us believe, chemistry is founded on experimental work. An investigative sequence begins with a hypothesis which is tested by experiment and, on the basis of the observed results, is ratified, modified or discarded. At every stage of this process, the accurate and unbiased recording of results is crucial to success. However, whilst it is true that such rational analysis can lead the scientist towards his or her goal, this happy sequence of events occurs much less frequently than many would care to admit. Serendipity frequently plays a central role in scientific discovery, and is often put down by others to simple good fortune. This overlooks the fact that many important chance discoveries can be ascribed largely to a combination of perseverance and meticulous technique. From penicillin to polythene, accurate observations of seemingly unimportant experimental results have led to discoveries of immeasurable importance.

Discovery is only part of the story, however. Having made the all-important experimental observations, transmitting this information clearly to other workers in the field is of equal importance. The record of your observations must be made in such a manner that others as well as yourself can repeat the work at a later stage. Omission of a small detail, such as the degree of purity of a particular reagent, can often render a procedure irreproducible, invalidating your claims and leaving you exposed to criticism. The scientific community is rightly suspicious of results which can only be obtained in the hands of one particular worker!

Therefore, as an experimentalist, your laboratory notebook is your most valuable asset. In it you must record everything that you do and see in the laboratory which pertains to your work, no matter how trivial or superfluous it might seem at that moment. Time and again, results which might not have appeared to be directly relevant to the investigation *at the time* have proved to have deep significance when re-examined at a later stage.

It is sometimes difficult to consider experiments which do not give the expected or desired result to be as vital as those which do proceed in the predicted manner. Remember that there is a reason for everything, and if a reaction does not follow the expected course, then it is necessary to reconsider the premise that led to the experiment in the first place. Do not be tempted to attempt to bend the facts to fit in with some preconceived notion of what ought to happen. In this respect, it is crucial that you observe and record results impartially and without bias. Always record what you actually observe, and not what you have been told will happen, or what you expect or want to see. Above all, record your results in a way which will be clear, not only to yourself, but to others as well.

Remember—honesty, accuracy and clarity, in that order, are the three prerequisites when undertaking and reporting experimental work.

The laboratory notebook

Style and layout

The following passages contain suggestions as to how you should record your work in the laboratory. Whilst these follow generally accepted guidelines, they may not tally completely with instructions given to you by your institution. If differences exist, always follow the rules of the establishment in which you are working. Remember, in the teaching laboratory, it is the instructor's assessment of your reports that will determine your class position at the end of the course and, in research, your notebook is a lasting record of your efforts—successful or otherwise.

Use a sturdy notebook

As your notebook has to contain a permanent record of your work, it must be made to last. The book should be bound with a strong spine that will not break under repeated opening and closing. The pages should be numbered and sewn into the spine so that they do not drop out with continued use. A good durable cover is a necessity to protect the contents from wear and tear and from any water splashes when on the laboratory bench. It is a good idea to cover the book with clear adhesive film to provide additional waterproofing.

Do not use loose sheets of papers—even for rough notes

Never record your observations on sheets of loose paper for copying into your notebook at a later stage as these are too easily lost during the course of a working day. Likewise, clip binders or spiral bound notebooks are not suitable for recording your work as the sheets may be torn out easily, either by careless handling or intentionally. Always write in ink, not in pencil which fades with time and can be erased. However, you must remember not to use water-soluble ink, otherwise your precious notes will be rapidly obliterated if you spill water onto the open book. Cross out any mistakes boldly, but in a manner which does not totally obscure what was written in the first place. Whilst desirable, the requirement for an absolutely neat notebook is secondary to the necessity for accurate reporting. *Never* tear pages out of your book; like a ship's log, whatever goes into your book must stay in. The only exceptions to this rule are notebooks fitted with duplicate pages for use with carbon paper. With this arrangement the copy may be removed for storage in a safe place. In some universities, and in all commercial enterprises, the laboratory notebook remains the property of the institution and is a legal document which can be

Do not erase mistakes totally—or tear out pages

Your notebook is a legal document

used for evidence after an accident or to indicate prior knowledge in patent disputes — always bear this in mind.

The outside cover of the book should have your name on it, together with the general subject matter it contains and a means by which it can be returned to you if lost (for instance, the address of the department). It is convenient if your name and the contents are also written on the spine, to help in finding the book when it is stacked in a pile or on a shelf.

Write all observations directly into your notebook

Leave the first few pages of the book clear for an index of contents and then use the remaining pages consecutively. Always write your observations directly into the notebook *as they are made* and do not rely on your memory at a later stage as it is highly likely that you will forget some of the details in the intervening period. The best arrangement is to write your rough notes, weighings and any observations on the left-hand pages of the book and to write the actual report on the right-hand pages (Fig. 6.1).

The top of every page should have your name and the date entered on it, and the first page of each experiment should begin with a brief title describing its aim. Underneath the title, there should be a scheme depicting structural formulae with the molecular weight of each compound clearly noted. It helps if this scheme is emphasized by drawing a box around it. Underneath this, the quantities of compounds and reagents to be used (by weight as well as by the number of moles) together with their purity and source should be noted, together with a listing of the apparatus to be used. In this section you should include any literature references relevant to the procedure. All of these details should be put into the book *before* starting the experiment as, in this manner, you will be made to think in advance about the experiment.

Keep reports concise

Whilst your laboratory notebook should contain all information pertinent to the experiment being undertaken, keep the writing concise and avoid unnecessary verbosity. If following a set of specific instructions, it is usually unnecessary to write out the whole procedure again, a simple reference will suffice, but any variations (things rarely go exactly as laid out in the manuals) must be faithfully described. This is of particular importance if, at some later stage, you need to explain why you did not obtain the predicted result!

During the course of the experiment, keep a record of your actions, together with any observations, as rough notes on the left-hand pages. These can be transcribed into a more legible form on the right-hand pages, either when time permits during the course of the experiment, or at the end of the day. Never leave the updating of your book for another day as, by then, the details will no longer be clear in your mind. Any thin layer chromatography (TLC) analyses should be drawn faithfully into the book with shading to show the appearance of the spots, together with a note of how they have been visualized.

When recording and reporting your observations during the qualitative analysis of an unknown, it is best to employ a tabular layout as shown in

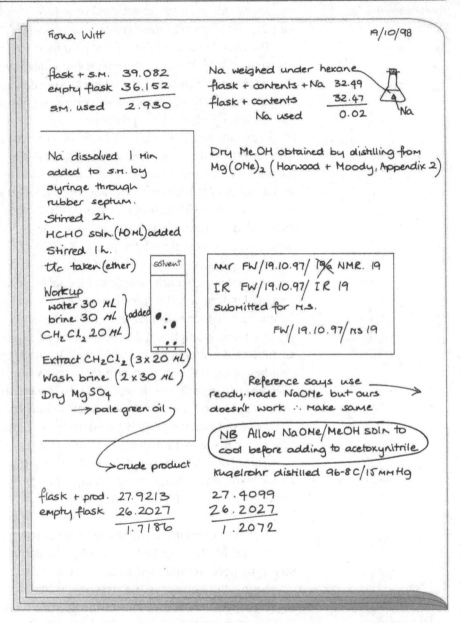

Fig. 6.1 Enter all preliminary observations on the left-hand pages of your notebook, and write the final report on the right-hand pages.

Fig. 6.2. In this manner, you will learn to fall into a set order for carrying out the tests, and this will result in more efficient use of laboratory time and make it less likely that you will forget to carry out a crucial test.

Spectra should be filed in separate folders, and reference numbers for any spectra taken during the course of the experiment should be recorded in the notebook. Do not stick the spectra in your book as this will cause the spine to tear, in time; file them separately. A coding system which is concise — but at the

File spectra separately

Fiona Witt
Experiment ⑲   19/10/98

7-Oxabicyclo [2.2.1] hept-5-en-2-one by basic hydrolysis of
2-acetoxy [2.2.1] hept-5-ene-2-carbonitrile
(Black, KA ; Vogel, P ; Helv Chim Acta 1984, 67, 1612-1615)

Diels-Alder adduct   MW   179.2 (from expt.18), 2.93g (16.3 mmol)
Sodium metal   23 (Aldrich), 0.02g (0.9 mmol)
Methanol (anhydrous)- redistilled from Mg(OMe)₂   25 mL
Formaldehyde solution 37% (Aldrich), 10 mL

Apparatus · 50 mL rb flask, mag. stirrer, N₂ line, syringes

Methanolic sodium methoxide, prepared by dissolving sodium
(0.02g, 0.9 mmol) in dry methanol (5 mL), was added to a
stirred soln. of the acetoxynitrile (2.93g, 16.3 mmol) in dry
MeOH (20 mL), under N₂, at 20°C. The solution was
stirred for 2h at room temp. Formaldehyde solution
(10 mL of 37% solution) was added and the mixture
was stirred for 1h further.

TLC (ether, molybdate spray):   ← very strong
                                                            spot

The solution was diluted with ice-water (30 mL), satd. NaCl (30 mL)
and CH₂Cl₂ (20 mL). Organic + aqueous phases were separated,
the aqueous phase was extracted with CH₂Cl₂ (3 × 20 mL). The
combined CH₂Cl₂ phases were washed with satd. NaCl (2 × 30 mL)
and dried over MgSO₄. Solvent was evaporated → pale green
oil (1.72g, 96%)

   → nmr FW/19.10.98/NMR 19 shows reqd. product
                              sufficiently pure to continue
                              to next step.

IR FW/19.10.98/IR 19
Mass spec. obtained FW/19.10.98/MS.19

Purified by Kugelrohr bulb-to-bulb distillation (bp 96-98°C/15 mmHg,
obtained as colourless oil 1.21g, 67%   Lit 90°/15 mmHg)

Fig. 6.1 Continued.

same time enables you to locate readily any spectroscopic data associated
with an experiment—uses your initials, the date, the technique used and a
number for the component being analyzed (for example FW/19.10.97/
NMR19). This reference should enable you to find the pages in your notebook
on which the experiment has been recorded as well as the position of the spectrum in its folder. All samples prepared or studied should be listed, together
with their reference number, in the index at the front of the notebook against

Fig. 6.2 Use a tabular format for recording results of qualitative analysis investigations.

Use a cross-referencing system to collate spectra and experiments

the page number on which the experiment is described. This cross-referencing system enables you to find a particular spectrum or experimental procedure rapidly and will become increasingly important as you progress through your teaching course and into research. Starting such a system at the very beginning will save much frustration in the long term, and will avoid the embarrassment of rummaging through a mountain of paper, looking for a particularly elusive spectrum, whilst the instructor or your research supervisor breathes down your neck impatiently!

Reporting spectroscopic and microanalytical data

The practical aspects of recording spectroscopic data on your samples are dealt with in Chapter 5. Such results are usually reported by listing the important features of each spectrum in a shorthand notation. Uniformity in presentation of these results is necessary to enable ready interpretation and to avoid ambiguity. The following formats are recommended but, once again, you must always follow the style laid down by your institute where differences of opinion occur. Please note that the preferred term is '*spectroscopic*' and not '*spectral*' which may imply that your results are ghostly! For once, do not follow the rather dubious example of the many experienced organic chemists all around the world who ought to know better.

Infrared spectra

The position of maximum absorption (v_{max}) is quoted for sharp peaks such as those due to carbonyl absorptions. Broad peaks, for instance hydroxyl absorptions, should be quoted as a range. Peak absorption positions in IR spectra are recorded as their *wavenumber* (cm⁻¹) which, as the units indicate, is the reciprocal of the wavelength. The strength of the absorption can be indicated using the letters w (weak), m (medium) and s (strong) after the position of each peak quoted. 'Weak' usually refers to peaks having less than 10% absorbance, and 'strong' refers to those having greater than about 80% absorbance—the exact judgement is rather subjective. Remember that it is not usual practice to quote every peak in the IR spectrum, particularly in the fingerprint region. The method of preparing the sample for analysis must also be given before quoting the absorption positions. The terms 'neat' or 'thin film' are used for pure liquid samples placed between sodium chloride plates. Solids may have been obtained as a 'mull' in a specified mulling agent (Nujol® or hexachlorobutadiene), or as a KBr disk. Solution spectra can be indicated by stating the solvent used (usually $CHCl_3$). For example, an IR spectrum of 7-oxabicyclo[2.2.1]hept-5-en-2-one quoted in this manner would be written as follows:

IR, v_{max} (thin film), 3700–3250 (m), 3020 (m), 1750 (s), 1635 (w) cm⁻¹

Nuclear magnetic resonance spectra

It is always necessary to quote the operating frequency of the instrument used (in MHz) and the solvent in which the sample was dissolved. Chemical shift values are reported using the δ-scale against tetramethylsilane (TMS) = 0.0 ppm. The relative number of protons contributing to the absorption is given to the nearest integer, together with any multiplicity of the absorption and related coupling constants.

For multiplets which show interpretable first-order splittings, the chemical shift at which the absorption would have occurred in the absence of splittings is quoted. For uninterpretable multiplets an absorption range is sufficient. The type of splitting is denoted as d (doublet), t (triplet), q (quartet), quint (quintet), sext (sextet) and m (multiplet), with additional qualifications such as dd (double doublet) and br (or broad). Peaks removable on treatment with D_2O need to be specified. The coupling constant J is quoted in hertz, and for multiplets from which several different values can be obtained these are listed progressively as J, J', J'' and so on. Thus the NMR spectrum of 7-oxabicyclo[2.2.1]hept-5-en-2-one would be reported as follows:

NMR δ_H (200 MHz, $CDCl_3$), 1.90 (1 H, d, J 16.0 Hz), 2.28 (1 H, dd, J 15 Hz, J' 5 Hz), 4.50 (1 H, s, br), 5.38 (1 H, d, br, J 5 Hz), 6.40 (1 H, dd J 5.5 Hz, J' 1.5 Hz), 6.68 (1 H, dt, J 5.5 Hz, J' 1.0 Hz)

An equivalent format applies to the recording of ^{13}C spectra which may be obtained as both 'proton coupled' or 'broadband decoupled' spectra, with the exception that coupling constants are not quoted in proton coupled ^{13}C spectra.

Mass spectra

The particular technique used to obtain the mass spectrum (electron impact (EI) or chemical ionization (CI)) must always be quoted, together with the ionizing reagent used if the spectrum was obtained under chemical ionization conditions. The peak positions are quoted as m/z and, wherever possible, their relative abundances should be given compared with the most abundant peak (the *base peak*). The molecular ion is denoted $M^{+\bullet}$, or if chemical ionization has been used, MH^+, MNH_4^+ or MCH_5^+, depending on the reagent system used to carry out the ionization. There is usually little point in listing peaks below about 15% relative abundance (other than the molecular ion which may be of low abundance), nor any with m/z less than 40.

Accurate mass measurements should be reported, together with the expected value for the molecule being examined and an estimation of the margin of error in the measurement in parts per million. Once again let us consider 7-oxabicyclo[2.2.1]hept-2-en-5-one:

m/z (EI) 110 ($M^{+\bullet}$, 4%), 68 (100%)
Accurate mass: found 110.0367, $C_6H_6O_2$ requires 110.0368 (2 ppm error)

Ultraviolet spectra

The two important pieces of information obtained from the UV spectrum of a compound are the wavelength at maximum absorption (λ_{max} (nm)) and the *extinction coefficient* which possesses the units of 1000 cm^2 mol^{-1} (not surprisingly these are never expressed by convention). A peak may appear as an ill-defined maximum superimposed on a stronger absorption and the λ_{max} position is often qualified with 'sh' denoting that it is a shoulder. Obviously it is necessary to note the solvent in which the sample has been dissolved. An example of the format for quoting a UV spectrum is given in Chapter 5.

Microanalytical data

You are unlikely to be required to produce microanalytical data as proof of purity until you begin to carry out research, when it is still considered (quite rightly) to be one of the important pieces of information for total characterization of a new substance. Carbon, hydrogen and nitrogen are determined by combustion analysis, with the combustion products being estimated by gas chromatography. This technique permits estimation of these elements with an

Acceptable C, H, N analysis must have results within 0.3% of expected values

accuracy in the region of ±0.3% and an acceptable analysis therefore requires the recorded results to be within 0.3% of those expected. Estimation of oxygen requires special facilities (C, H, N combustion analysis is carried out in an atmosphere of oxygen) and is usually not undertaken. Other elements such as halogens, sulfur and phosphorus are determined titrimetrically, and the lower accuracy in their estimation means that a greater error of up to 0.5% is usually acceptable.

The style of reporting microanalytical data which is commonly adopted quotes both the required values (or calculated values if the compound has been previously reported) and the results found by the analysis to within ±0.1%. There is no point in quoting calculated values to any greater degree of precision than this as the analysis techniques do not warrant it; however, you must always calculate the values using accurate atomic weight values (±0.001) before rounding off the final result and quoting it as follows:

C_7H_8O. Calculated (or required) C, 77.7; H, 7.5%. Found C, 77.8; H, 7.3%

Calculating yields

The theoretical yield of a reaction is decided by the limiting reagent present. When this material is used up, the reaction necessarily stops no matter how much of the other constituents remain. Therefore a little thought is necessary here to determine which reagents are being used in excess in the reaction and which is the limiting reagent before calculating the theoretical yield. The actual yield obtained after isolation and purification of the product is calculated as a percentage of the maximum theoretical yield:

The yield is based on the limiting reagent

$$\text{Percentage yield} = \frac{\text{Yield of pure product}}{\text{Theoretical yield}} \times 100$$

Quoting a percentage yield permits an estimate to be made of the efficiency of the reaction which is independent of the scale on which the reaction was carried out. Yields of 50–80% are in the range of moderate to good depending on the optimism of the reporter, and yields greater than 80% are usually considered to be excellent. Yields of 100% are impossible to obtain in practice as some losses are inevitable during work-up. Thus yields which approach this figure (>99%) should be quoted as 'quantitative'. Sometimes the quoted yield is accompanied by the phrase '*accounting for recovered starting material*'. As it implies, the yield here has been calculated on the basis of material converted, rather than the amount initially placed in the reaction vessel. Although this somewhat cosmetic treatment is justified on the grounds that the recovered material can be used again, this practice has the effect of giving an impression that the reaction is more efficient than is actually the case. You must be on your guard for such statements when planning multi-step syntheses to avoid running out of material before reaching your target.

Quote percentage yields to the nearest whole number

When presenting the yield always round off the figure to the nearest whole number, as the way in which reagents are measured does not warrant greater precision—despite the fact that your calculator can give you an answer to several decimal places!

Data sheets

It is a good idea to record the full spectroscopic data for every compound you prepare on a data sheet (Fig. 6.3). Just as with writing up a notebook, record data continuously during your work. This will remove the rather arduous task of transcribing all of your data on completion of the project. This practice is worth cultivating in the teaching laboratory and it is usually obligatory for the research student.

Get into the habit of filling in data sheets regularly

The action of filling in a data sheet will make you aware of any pieces of information, such as a melting point, that still need to be obtained whilst you have material available. All too often, research workers reach the stage of writing up their thesis before realizing that some compounds are incompletely characterized: this usually necessitates the preparation of a new batch of material.

Filling in a data sheet will also make you examine your spectra carefully, and will help you to bring to light any discrepancies or interesting features which might otherwise pass unnoticed as the spectra linger in some file at the back of a drawer. In any event, the practice in interpreting your data will help you to develop your technique and, on the principle of 'never keeping all your eggs in one basket', this set of data sheets which can be kept apart from your original spectra provides a useful safeguard against loss or destruction, for instance in a laboratory fire.

References

You must always record in your notebook all references that are needed to perform the experiment. Of particular importance are the literature sources of the physical properties of known compounds. The observed values must never be simply stated without including the literature data for comparison together with the source reference.

Every detail of the reference must be quoted

When citing a reference it is important to quote it fully and not to be tempted to leave out some of the authors' names, replacing them with *et al*. If there is an error somewhere in the reference, it will be possible to track down the correct reference using the combination of authors. If just one author is cited, this job can become quite a long one, whereas there are likely to be many less references with the specific combination of authors in your reference. Styles of quoting literature mainly fall into two main categories, depending on which side of the Atlantic you are working. In the United States, the standard format follows that laid down by the American Chemical Society and is as follows:

Name of compound   Compound ref. no. FW/19.10.98/19

7-oxabicyclo[2.2.1] hept-5-en-2-one

Structure   Compound description   colourless oil

M.p./b.p. 96-98°C / 15 mmHg (lit 90°C, 15mmHg)

Molecular formula/weight $C_6H_6O_2$, MW 110

High resolution

Mass spectrum

Analysis:
  Found: C, 65.40% H 5.40%
  Requires: C, 65.45% H, 5.49%

$[\alpha]_D^{20}$ racemic

H n.m.r. 200   MHz $CDCl_3$

δ_H 6.68, 1H, dt , J 1,5.5Hz , H6
  6.40, 1H dd , J 1.5, 5.5Hz , H5
  5.38, 1H, bd, J 5Hz, H4
  4.50, 1H, bs, H1
  2.28 , 1H, dd , J 5, 15 Hz , H3 exo
  1.90, 1H, d , J 16Hz , H3 endo

Infra-red spectrum (thin film)

ν_{Max} 3700-3250 (m), 3020 (m), 1750 (s) C=O, 1635 (m) C=C

Mass spectrum EI / CI / IBEI / DCI / FI / FD / FAB

110 (M+, 4%), 68 ($\overline{CH=CHCH_2OOH_2}$, 100%)

Other data:

Fig. 6.3 A typical data sheet.

Katsuki, K; Sharpless, K.B; *J. Am. Chem. Soc.*, **1980**, *102*, 5974–5976.

When writing by hand, italics and bold print can be indicated by underlining with straight and wavy lines respectively.

The other common format is that adopted by the Royal Society of Chemistry in Britain. Typically, the American and British formats differ from each other in several ways!

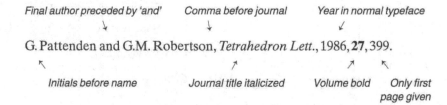

G. Pattenden and G.M. Robertson, *Tetrahedron Lett.*, 1986, **27**, 399.

Each particular journal will demand that references conform to their 'house style' and your institution may also require you to use a particular format. If not, it is perhaps best to conform to that most popular in your particular country. A list of generally approved abbreviations for journal titles is given in Table 6.1, p. 413; however, when writing a paper for publication, always verify the abbreviations required by the journal to which you intend to send the paper. Software is now available to help you to switch reference formatting from one style to another.

6.2 The research report

At the completion of a research project it is necessary to produce a report which encapsulates precisely the aims and achievements of the work, including all experimental details. Such a report may be for the eyes of your instructor or research adviser, or it may be for publication in a journal to be read throughout the world. Whatever its target audience, the production of a clear report in the required standard format will be very much simpler if you have conscientiously noted all of your results in your notebook, and kept your data sheets up to date. There are no hard and fast rules for the format required in a report, but some general points are outlined here to cover a few of the common requirements.

The report must have a title which concisely summarizes the aims of the work and will alert readers to its contents, for instance 'Studies on the intermolecular Diels–Alder reactions of furans'. As articles are often abstracted for content by searching for '*keywords*' in the title, the correct choice of title can make the difference between your article being noticed by chemists or passing into obscurity. Most journals require a brief abstract of the work to be inserted before the main body of the text. Whilst brief, this must contain all of the salient features of the work, otherwise someone scanning the abstract may fail to realize the true contents of the paper.

The report itself should begin with a concise but complete review of all relevant work that has been carried out previously, referencing and giving due credit to work carried out by other workers. Sufficient background material should be given for someone who is not a specialist in the field to be able to grasp the problem. Frequently the area will have been the subject of reviews by others and it is often sufficient to give references to these reviews followed by the phrase 'and references cited therein'. Each citation in the body of the text is marked by a numerical superscript and the references themselves are grouped together at the end of the report or at the foot of the page containing the reference work.

The main body of the report contains the 'results and discussion' section, where the work is presented and conclusions are drawn, with supporting evidence. It is the presentation of this section which distinguishes between good and bad reports. Take care to use the correct terminology, without falling into the trap of using too much jargon—the aim is to inform, not mystify. The presentation should be scholarly and any arguments must be presented logically. Only reasonable conclusions should be drawn, with experimental support being given at all times. Explanations for reactions which did not go as planned are just as important as those for 'successful' reactions. What exactly constitutes a 'scholarly' presentation is difficult to define, and it is best to ask a more experienced chemist to comment on your efforts whilst in draft form, before preparing the final copy.

The last part of this section should contain a summary which encapsulates the final conclusions of the work and discusses implications and future aims. In a report submitted to a journal, it is usual at this point to acknowledge any financial assistance, gifts of chemicals and technical assistance given by individuals.

The experimental section should begin with a listing of all the instrumentation used in the recording of the spectroscopic data, the sources of the compounds used and details about any purification and analytical processes used. If a standard work-up procedure is used throughout the experiments, this can be described here and then be referred to in individual experiments as 'usual work-up' to save repetition.

The experiments should be listed in the order in which the compounds appear in the results and discussion section, even though this may not always be the order in which they were actually prepared during the project. If a series of related compounds have been prepared using the same procedure, it

Titles and abstracts are important for conveying the content of the report

Always review earlier work, giving due credit to other workers

Present results and conclusions logically with clear reasoning

Experimental section

is acceptable to write out one general procedure and then list the individual spectroscopic and analytical data for each compound afterwards.

Styles vary between departments and from journal to journal, but the usually accepted practice is to present the experimental section in the third person, passive past tense. In other words, 'The experiment was carried out' and not 'I carried out the experiment'. This does vary, however, and some journals prefer the experimental section to be written in the present tense. In any case, it is important to read the instructions to authors which are published in the journals before submitting papers to them. Non-adherence to the required style could result in rejection of the paper.

Whether writing a report for an adviser or for publication in a journal, the details given in the experimental section must be sufficient for another chemist to be able to repeat your work. The names of all compounds should be written out in full and the quantity of each as weight or volume, as well as number of moles, should be given in parentheses after the name. Any danger-

Clear hazard warnings

ous properties must be highlighted by adding ***Caution!*** followed by an indication of the danger (***Toxic***, ***Explosive***). SI units should be used (although organic chemists are rather bad at this and you are still likely to see kilocalories being used instead of kilojoules) and any abbreviations must follow the SI recommendations. The yield of product quoted must be the actual yield obtained in the experiment and must give an indication of purity of the isolated material (crude, recrystallized). Chromatography supports and elution systems are required and the full physical data of the compound prepared must be presented following the formats outlined on pp. 402–405. An example of the style of reporting an experimental procedure is as follows.

Preparation of 7-oxabicyclo[2.2.1]hept-5-en-4-one (2)[12]

Methanolic sodium methoxide, prepared by dissolving sodium (0.20 g, 0.9 mmol) in freshly dried methanol (5 mL), was added via syringe to a stirred solution of the nitrile (1) (2.93 g, 16.3 mmol) in dry methanol (20 mL) at 20°C. After stirring for 2 h, formaldehyde solution (10 mL, 30%) was added and the mixture was stirred for 1 h. The mixture was cooled to 0°C using an ice-water bath, and was quenched with ice-water (30 mL). Usual work-up gave, after drying ($MgSO_4$) and removal of solvents at reduced pressure, crude (2) as a pale green oil (1.72 g, 96%). Pure material was obtained by short path distillation (1.21 g, 67%); bp 96–98°C/15 mmHg, (lit.[12] 90°C/15 mmHg).

IR v_{max} (thin film) 3700–3250 (m), 3020 (m), 1750 (s), 1635 (w) cm^{-1}.

NMR (200 MHz, $CDCl_3$), 1.90 (1 H, d, J 16.0 Hz), 2.28 (1 H, dd, J 15 Hz, J' 5 Hz), 4.50 (1 H, s, br), 5.38 (1 H, d, br, J 5 Hz), 6.40 (1 H, dd, J 5.5 Hz, J' 1.5 Hz), 6.68 (1 H, dt, J 5.5 Hz, J' 1.0 Hz).

m/z (EI) 110 (M$^+$, 4%), 68 (100%).

Accurate mass: found 110.0367, $C_6H_6O_2$ requires 110.0368 (2 ppm error).

References

No research report is complete without a full listing of all pertinent literature. This should be referenced in the body of the text using numerical superscripts and then listed in numerical order at the end of the report. You must include references to all material necessary for readers to familiarize themselves with the background to your work, as well as specific details relating to your project. You should only refer to the actual articles you have used in carrying out the work and preparing the report. For instance, do not quote a reference from *Croat. Chem. Acta* if you actually gleaned your information from a summary of the article in *Chemical Abstracts*—quote both references. Likewise, if a review article was your source of information, reference the review, followed by the phrase 'and references cited therein', to alert the reader to the fact that it may be necessary to read further.

Remember whatever the details of style and format, your report must be accurate, clear and concise at all stages.

Further reading
The following books and articles contain useful hints on keeping a laboratory notebook and writing up reports:

R. Barrass, *Scientists Must Write*, Chapman & Hall, London, 1978.

B.E. Cain, *The Basics of Technical Communicating*, American Chemical Society, Washington, 1998.

J.S. Dodd (ed.) *The ACS Style Guide, a manual for Authors and Editors*, American Chemical Society, Washington, 1986.

H. Ebel, C. Bliefert and W. Russey, *The Art of Scientific Writing*, VCH, Deerfield Beach, 1987.

A. Eisenberg, Keeping a laboratory notebook, *J. Chem. Educ.*, 1982, **52**, 1045.

P.A. Ongley, Improve your English, *Chem. Br.*, 1984, **20**, 323.

J.M. Pratt, Writing a thesis, *Chem. Br.*, 1984, **20**, 1114.

R. Schoenfeld, *The Chemist's English*, VCH, Weinheim, 1986.

McGraw-Hill Dictionary of Scientific and Technical Terms, 5th edn, McGraw-Hill, New York, 1993.

The Oxford Dictionary for Scientific Writers and Editors, Oxford University Press, Oxford, 1991.

6.3   Chemical literature

The chemical literature is huge, and getting bigger. Over 500 000 papers are added to the literature of chemistry every year, to say nothing of books and patents. Much of this literature is now held on computer databases adding to the vast store of published knowledge to draw on. There will be many occasions on which you have to consult this store of knowledge, but before marching into your departmental or campus library and consulting books, journals and computer databases at random, you should attempt to plan your search of the literature in advance. This planning will save you considerable time, but to do this you need to know: (i) what type of literature is available, and (ii) what is the most appropriate for your particular problem. This short section is designed to help you to find your way through the literature of organic chemistry, by a brief discussion of points (i) and (ii) above. Some common text books (e.g. March, *Advanced Organic Chemistry*) also contain a brief overview of, and guide to, the literature of organic chemistry.

With the recent rapid developments in information technology and the advent of the Internet, an increasing amount of information that is useful to organic chemists is available on the World Wide Web in electronic form. There are a number of Internet sites that are relevant to organic chemists; these contain listings of databases and other sources of information. Most national chemical societies (e.g. the American Chemical Society and the Royal Society of Chemistry) maintain their own Internet site, as do a number of major chemistry publishers. Since all of these sites are under constant development, a discussion of this rapidly moving area is beyond the scope of this book. If you are interested in accessing such information, please consult your university Internet expert. Alternatively, just start surfing.

Primary literature

This is the place where chemists publish their original research results in the form of communications and papers. *Communications* are intended for important new advances in the subject, and are published fairly quickly, but usually without experimental detail. *Papers*, on the other hand, are intended to be detailed accounts of the research, containing a full discussion of the background to the work, the results and their significance, and *importantly* the experimental details.

Most nations that are engaged in serious chemical research have learned societies which publish chemical journals; in addition, there are a number of respected commercial publishers who also produce chemistry journals. Table 6.1 lists the major journals which are relevant to organic chemistry, although the list is by no means comprehensive. The table also shows the approved style of journal abbreviations defined in *Chemical Abstracts Service Source Index (CASSI)* and based on internationally recognized systems. Always use the approved journal abbreviation.

Use approved journal abbreviations

The primary literature is indispensable for finding precise details of how certain reactions have been carried out, and the properties of the products. However, you cannot go to the relevant reference immediately; you need another source to find the reference. This other source is either the *review literature* or one of the *major reference works*.

Review literature

There are several journals and series which contain review articles on organic chemistry. These cover such topics as classes of compounds, synthetic methods, individual reactions and so on. They are a valuable source of information and, of course, of references to the primary literature. Table 6.2 lists the major sources of reviews in organic chemistry, although again the list is not comprehensive.

Table 6.1 The primary literature of organic chemistry.

Journal title	Abbreviation
Acta Chemica Scandinavica	*Acta Chem. Scand.*
Angewandte Chemie, International Edition	*Angew. Chem. Int. Edn Engl.*
Australian Journal of Chemistry	*Aust. J. Chem.*
Bulletin of the Chemical Society of Japan	*Bull. Chem. Soc. Jpn.*
Bulletin de la Société Chimique de France	*Bull. Soc. Chim. Fr.*
Canadian Journal of Chemistry	*Can. J. Chem.*
Chemische Berichte	*Chem. Ber.*
Chemistry Letters	*Chem. Lett.*
Gazzetta Chimica Italiana	*Gazz. Chim. Ital.*
Helvetica Chimica Acta	*Helv. Chim. Acta*
Heterocycles	*Heterocycles*
Journal of the American Chemical Society	*J. Am. Chem. Soc.*
Journal of the Chemical Society, Chemical Communications	*Chem. Commun.*
Journal of the Chemical Society, Perkin Transactions 1	*J. Chem. Soc. Perkin Trans. 1*
Journal of Heterocyclic Chemistry	*J. Heterocycl. Chem.*
Journal of Medicinal Chemistry	*J. Med. Chem.*
Journal of Organic Chemistry	*J. Org. Chem.*
Journal of Organometallic Chemistry	*J. Organomet. Chem.*
Liebigs Annalen der Chemie	*Ann. Chem.*
Monatshefte für Chemie	*Monatsh. Chem.*
Recueil des Travaux Chimique des Pays-Bas	*Recl. Trav. Chim. Pays-Bas*
Synlett	*Synlett*
Synthesis	*Synthesis*
Synthetic Communications	*Synth. Commun.*
Tetrahedron	*Tetrahedron*
Tetrahedron: Asymmetry	*Tetrahedron: Asymmetry*
Tetrahedron Letters	*Tetrahedron Lett.*

Major reference works

There are a number of major reference works for organic chemistry, each running to many volumes. These are the main source of references to the primary literature, and anyone who works in chemistry eventually has to get to know their way around these works, particularly *Chemical Abstracts*. The major reference works are summarized below.

The Dictionary of Organic Compounds (DOC)

This is a useful source of data on relatively common compounds. The most recent edition (the 6th) was published in 1996, and regular supplements are issued. DOC contains information on over 170 000 organic compounds,

Table 6.2 The review literature of organic chemistry.

Review title	Abbreviation
Accounts of Chemical Research	*Acc. Chem. Res.*
Advances in Heterocyclic Chemistry	*Adv. Heterocycl. Chem.*
Advances in Organometallic Chemistry	*Adv. Organomet. Chem.*
Advances in Physical Organic Chemistry	*Adv. Phys. Org. Chem.*
Annual Reports (on the Progress of Chemistry), Section B, Organic Chemistry	*Annu. Rep. Prog. Chem. Sect. B*
Chemical Reviews	*Chem. Rev.*
Chemical Society Reviews	*Chem., Soc. Rev.*
Methods of Organic Synthesis	*Meth. Org. Syn.*
Organic Reactions	*Org. React.*
Organic Reaction Mechanisms	*Org. React. Mech.*
Specialist Periodical Reports (SPR)	*Specialist Periodical Reports (SPR)*
Synthesis	*Synthesis*
Synthetic Methods of Organic Chemistry (Theilheimer)	*Synthetic Methods of Organic Chemistry (Theilheimer)*
Tetrahedron Reports	*Tetrahedron Reports*
Topics in Stereochemistry	*Top. Stereochem.*

together with a name and formula index. The information includes name, formula and structure of compound, mp or bp, rotation (if relevant), mp of simple derivatives, and references to its preparation and properties. DOC is available in electronic form on a CD-ROM.

Handbuch der Organischen Chemie (Beilstein)

This major reference work deals with individual compounds, and is indispensable for the early literature of organic chemistry. It is published in German although new editions are produced in English, in several parts:

Hauptwerk (main edition) abbreviated to	H	up to 1910
1ᵉ Erganzungswerk (1st supplement)	EI	1910–1919
2ᵉ Erganzungswerk (2nd supplement)	EII	1920–1929
3ᵉ Erganzungswerk (3rd supplement)	EIII	1930–1949
4ᵉ Erganzungswerk (4th supplement)	EIV	1950–1959
5ᵉ Erganzungswerk (5th supplement)	EV	1960–1979

Each part of the work is divided into 27 volumes ('Band') by subject areas; thus volumes 1–4 cover acyclic compounds; volumes 5–16 cover carbocyclic compounds and volumes 17–27 cover heterocyclic compounds. For some volumes, the 3rd and 4th supplements are combined. The compounds are further divided into about 5000 classifications ('Systemnummer'), so that a given compound (and very closely related ones) always appears in the same volume under the same Systemnummer. Having located the correct entry, you will find methods of preparation, physical properties and chemical reactions of the compound, together with references to the primary literature. Unfortunately many chemists are put off using Beilstein because they think it is too complicated. To remedy this the publishers have produced a small guide, *How to use Beilstein*, in English and a 2000 word German dictionary; both of these are freely available. An example of using Beilstein is given later in this section. Like *Chemical Abstracts* (see below), Beilstein is now available on-line.

Chemical Abstracts (CA)

This is the comprehensive abstracting service run by the American Chemical Society, and reckons to abstract all papers, books, patents and conference proceedings covering the whole of chemistry. *Chemical Abstracts* started in 1907, and a new issue of about 10000 abstracts appears every week. Each abstract contains key information from the primary literature source: authors, reference, brief resumé of the work (in English), and language of the original. A volume consists of 26 weekly issues, and each completed volume has associated *Author, Subject, Chemical Substance* and *Formula Indexes*. Every 5 years, a *Collective Index* covering the preceding 10 volumes, is published, and it is these *collective indexes* that are the most use in searching the literature. In the period 1947 onwards, collective indexes have appeared as follows:

5th Collective Index	1947–1956	Volumes 41–50
6th Collective Index	1957–1961	Volumes 51–55
7th Collective Index	1962–1966	Volumes 56–65
8th Collective Index	1967–1971	Volumes 66–75
9th Collective Index	1972–1976	Volumes 76–85
10th Collective Index	1977–1981	Volumes 86–95
11th Collective Index	1982–1986	Volumes 96–105
12th Collective Index	1987–1991	Volumes 106–115
13th Collective Index	1992–1996	Volumes 116–125

Chemical Abstracts is the largest single source of information relating to chemistry, and is therefore invaluable in locating the original literature on a particular problem. In recent years it has become possible to search this vast database by computer using the CAS ONLINE service, although the database is only complete from 1967 onwards. Therefore do not get used to relying on computer literature searches totally, since for earlier work you must still use the hard copy abstracts or Beilstein.

Science Citation Index (SCI)

This index, published regularly, enables you to find work in a closely related area given a reference to the original (or early) work in the field. The citation index then leads to all subsequent papers which cite the original reference. Again, this is available on-line.

In addition to the above, regularly updated, reference works, there are a number of other major reference works relevant to organic chemistry. These are encyclopedia-type works, and include the following.

Rodd's *Chemistry of Carbon Compounds* (2nd edn); over 30 volumes published from the mid-1960s to date; covers organic compounds by compound class.

Elsevier's *Encyclopedia of Organic Chemistry*; a multi-volume work, particularly useful for the literature on carbocyclic compounds with two or more rings.

Houben-Weyl's *Methoden der Organischen Chemie* (in German); published in several volumes, and deals with compound classes, with emphasis on experimental aspects.

Fieser's *Reagents for Organic Synthesis*; 17 volumes to date, lists organic reagents alphabetically, together with examples of their use, and references to the primary literature.

Comprehensive Organic Chemistry, Comprehensive Organometallic Chemistry, Comprehensive Heterocyclic Chemistry (I and II), Comprehensive Organic Synthesis, Comprehensive Organic Functional Group Transformations, and *Encyclopedia of Reagents for Organic Synthesis* are all multi-volume works containing review chapters written by experts in the field.

Compilations of spectroscopic data, such as *The Aldrich Library of IR Spectra, The Aldrich Library of NMR Spectra*, the *DMS Atlas of IR Spectra, Organic Electronic Spectral Data* and the *Eight Peak Index of Mass Spectra* are particularly useful in finding reference spectra of fairly common compounds.

How to use the literature

To find a specific compound
The best method is to use the formula indexes of DOC, Beilstein and CA.

1 Work out the molecular formula of the compound; most indexes use the system: C, H (both in ascending order), then other elements alphabetically.

2 Consult the formula index of DOC (and latest supplements); compounds of that molecular formula will be listed. Make sure you consider all the possible names for your compound, since the indexers may not have used the same name. If the compound is present, look up the appropriate page in the appropriate volume, and retrieve the information.

For example, find the mp of 1-naphthol, and any crystalline derivatives:

Formula = $C_{10}H_8O$

Formula Index → 1-naphthol N-00193

N-00193 (in volume 4) → **Answer**
1-naphthol mp 94°C
benzoate mp 56°C
3,5-dinitrobenzoate mp 217.4°C

If the compound is not in the DOC, go to Beilstein for pre-1950 literature and to CA for post-1950 work.

3 Start with the formula index ('Generalformelregister') of the second supplement (EII) of Beilstein; this is cumulative for the main edition, and the 1st and 2nd supplements. Compounds of that molecular formula will be listed with their German name; make sure you recognize the German name for your compound! Turn up the appropriate pages, and obtain the information. To look up the compound in the 3rd and 4th supplements, go to the same volume (Band) number, find the part that pertains to the correct Systemnummer, and look up the formula index.

For example, find a method of preparation of O-benzylhydroxylamine, $C_6H_5CH_2ONH_2$:

Formula = C_7H_9NO

EII Formelregister	$\rightarrow$	**6**, 440; I 222 (refers to volume 6 of main work and 1st supplement)
6, 440	$\rightarrow$	Systemnumber 528
	$\rightarrow$	**Answer** Plenty of information and references
I 222	$\rightarrow$	More information

To find more recent references, go to the formula indexes of volume 6 of the 3rd and 4th supplements that pertain to Systemnummer 528:

EIII Band 6 (Systemnummer 525–533)	$\rightarrow$	1552 (p. 1552 in that volume) more information
EIV Band 6 (Systemnummer 524–528)	$\rightarrow$	2562 (p. 2562 in that volume) more information

4 Go to the *Formula Index* of CA and use the collective indexes; but whether to start with the most recent and work backwards, or to start with the earliest and work forwards is a matter of choice—sometimes you intuitively feel that the most likely source of references will be in the most recent volumes. Having checked the collective indexes, do not forget to check the most recent individual volume indexes. When using the CA *Formula Index* it is essential that you consult the relevant *Index Guide*. CA has had the unfortunate habit of changing the way in which it names compounds, so you must look up the *Index Guide* to find the correct CA name for that particular period.

Having found your compound in the *Formula Index*, this will lead you to the appropriate volume of abstracts and to the abstract itself. At this point you may be able to decide whether it is worth looking up the original reference, or whether to go on to the next abstract. To be certain of obtaining all the information, you may have to look up several original references.

For example, find the preparation and properties of 7b-methyl-7bH-cyclopent[cd]indene, a recent addition to the interesting family of novel 10π-aromatic compounds:

Formula = $C_{12}H_{10}$
Compound is fairly recent, so work backwards through CA.
11th Collective Index	→	9 references
10th Collective Index	→	1 reference
Volume 106 Index	→	0 references
Volume 107 Index	→	0 references
Look up Abstracts	→	**Answer**
		10 references to the primary literature

To find information on a type of compound or reaction

For this type of literature search it is best to use the review literature, or to consult one of the encyclopedia-type works.

For more recent references on such a topic, try sources such as the latest volumes of *Annual Reports*, the Royal Society of Chemistry *Specialist Periodical Reports on General and Synthetic Methods* or Fieser's *Reagents for Organic Synthesis*.

Conclusion

The purpose of this section has been to alert you to the types of literature, and to provide some guidelines as to how to search for information in the chemical literature. Further guidelines are given in the references below. No foolproof method of finding chemical information exists, and those of you who remain in chemistry will eventually develop your own system of literature searching. You may even end up having an information scientist to do the job for you, although this removes the element of serendipity, in which the adjacent paper turns out to be more interesting to you than the one the search led to!

Further reading
J. March, *Advanced Organic Chemistry*, 4th edn, Wiley & Sons, New York, 1992.
R.E. Maizell, *How to Find Chemical Information*, 3nd edn, Wiley & Sons, New York, 1998.
Y. Wolman, *Chemical Information: a Practical Guide to Utilization*, Wiley & Sons, New York, 1983.

However, the Diels–Alder reaction is not the only pericyclic reaction to have found use in organic chemistry and this section includes experiments which illustrate other important pericyclic reactions such as [2+2]-cycloadditions, [3,3]-sigmatropic rearrangements, and 1,3-dipolar cyclo-additions.

Experiment 60　　　*Diels–Alder preparation of cis-cyclohex-4-ene-1,2-dicarboxylic acid*

The simplest diene substrate for the Diels–Alder reaction, 1,3-butadiene, is a gas at room temperature and pressure (bp −4.5°C) and consequently its handling requires specialized procedures. However, it can be generated readily *in situ* by means of cheletropic extrusion of sulfur dioxide from 2,5-dihydrothiophene-1,1-dioxide (frequently referred to as butadiene sulfone or sulfolene) which is a stable solid at room temperature. It is prepared by the addition of sulfur dioxide to butadiene under the effect of heat and pressure; the addition and elimination reactions are simply the reverse of one another.

Heating 2,5-dihydrothiophene-1,1-dioxide to *ca.* 140°C results in the dissociation reaction and presents us with an experimentally convenient laboratory source of butadiene which can be trapped, as it is generated, by reactive dienophiles, such as butenedioic anhydride (maleic anhydride). The Diels–Alder adduct formed in this instance can be hydrolyzed readily to the dicarboxylic acid by heating with water.

Level	1	
Time	3 h	
Equipment	apparatus for suction filtration, recrystallization	

Materials

2,5-dihydrothiophene-1,1-dioxide (butadiene sulfone, sulfolene) (FW 118.2)	2.4 g (20 mmol)	**irritant**
butenedioic anhydride (maleic anhydride) (FW 98.1)	2.0 g (20 mmol)	**corrosive**
bis(2-methoxyethyl)ether (diglyme)	2 mL	

Procedure

HOOD

1. Preparation of cis-cyclohex-4-ene-1,2-dicarboxylic anhydride

Into a large test tube weigh the 2,5-dihydrothiophene-1,1-dioxide and butenedioic anhydride and add the bis(2-methoxyethyl)ether. Stir the mixture with a 360°C thermometer and clamp the tube vertically with the thermometer remaining in the mixture. Warm the mixture *gently* with a small flame,[1] stirring constantly with the thermometer and observe the temperature. At about 140°C the mixture begins to evolve bubbles of sulfur dioxide; at this point, stop heating and allow the exothermic reaction to continue. When the reaction begins to moderate, as evidenced by a drop in temperature, maintain the temperature at 150–160°C with intermittent heating until the evolution of bubbles finally subsides (*ca.* 5 min). Cool the reaction by placing the end of the test tube in a water bath and stir the contents with the thermometer to induce partial crystallization. Add cold water (*ca.* 25 mL), stir the mixture and filter it with suction,[2] washing the crystals with two further 25 mL portions of water. Leave the crystals on the funnel and continue suction for several minutes to remove as much excess moisture as possible. Weigh the slightly moist product, remove 1.0 g for the hydrolysis experiment, and dry the remainder of the product in a vacuum desiccator over P_2O_5.[3] Record the weight of the dried product and calculate the percentage yield, knowing the initial weight of total moist product and accounting for the fact that 1.0 g of damp product has been removed. Record the mp of your product.

[1] *Check for flammable solvents before lighting burner; alternatively use a heat gun*

[2] *See Fig. 3.7*

[3] *Commence the next experiment*

2. Hydrolysis of initial anhydride adduct to cis-cyclohex-4-ene-1,2-dicarboxylic acid

Place the 1.0 g portion of moist adduct in a large test tube, add a boiling stone and water (10 mL), and boil the mixture over a small flame until the crystals of the adduct have totally dissolved. Remove the boiling chip with a spatula and cool the test tube in an ice bath (5 min). Filter off the crystals with suction, wash them with a small volume (*ca.* 5 mL) of chilled water, and dry with suction until excess moisture has been removed. Finally, dry the crystals in a vacuum desiccator over P_2O_5. Record the mp and calculate the yield of product based upon the actual amount of starting material contained in the moist material used for the hydrolysis (calculate this from your weights of material before and after drying in the first experiment). ∎

MICROSCALE

Level	1
Time	3 h
Equipment	apparatus for suction filtration

Materials		
2,5-dihydrothiophene-1,1-dioxide (butadiene sulfone, sulfolene) (FW 118.2)	120 mg (1 mmol)	irritant
butenedioic anhydride (maleic anhydride) (FW 98.1)	100 mg (1 mmol)	corrosive
bis(2-methoxyethyl)ether (diglyme)	0.2 mL	

Procedure

Weigh the 2,5-dihydrothiophene-1,1-dioxide and maleic anhydride into a test tube and add the diglyme. Stir the mixture with a 360°C thermometer and clamp the tube vertically with the thermometer remaining in the mixture. Warm the mixture gently with a small flame[1] or hot air blower, stirring constantly with the thermometer and observe the temperature. At about 140°C the mixture begins to evolve bubbles of sulfur dioxide; at this point, stop heating and allow the exothermic reaction to continue. When the reaction begins to moderate, as evinced by a drop in temperature, maintain the temperature at 150–160°C with intermittent heating until the evolution of bubbles ceases finally (*ca.* 5 min). Cool the reaction by placing the end of the test tube in a water bath and stir the contents with the thermometer to allow partial crystallization. Add cold water (*ca.* 1.5 mL), stir the mixture and filter at the pump using a micro-Hirsch funnel,[2] washing the crystals with portions of water (2 × 1 mL). Suck the crystals as dry as possible and dry in a vacuum dessicator over phosphorus pentoxide.[3] Weigh the dried product and record the mp and yield of the dry product.

[1] *Check for flammable solvents before lighting burner*

[2] *See Fig. 3.7*

[3] *See Fig. 3.45*

Problems

1 What conformation must be adopted by the diene for cycloaddition of a dienophilic component to occur? Explain why this accounts for the unreactivity of 2Z,4Z-hexadiene in the Diels–Alder reaction.

2 In the Diels–Alder reaction of cyclopentadiene with butenedioic anhydride, what are the two possible stereochemistries of the adduct? Which of the two products would you predict to be the most stable? Explain why it is the *least* stable adduct which is formed preferentially in this reaction.

3 What diene and dienophile would be required as starting materials for the eventual synthesis of the following compounds via Diels–Alder cycloaddition?

4 What are the ultimate organic products when the following dienes are heated strongly with diethyl butynedioate (diethyl acetylenedicarboxylate)?

Experiment 61

Preparation of 2,3-dimethyl-1,3-butadiene and its Diels–Alder reaction with butenedioic anhydride (maleic anhydride)

In this experiment the diene required for the Diels–Alder reaction is prepared by acid-catalyzed elimination of two molecules of water from 2,3-dimethylbutan-2,3-diol (pinacol). A by-product of this reaction is 3,3-dimethylbutane-2-one (pinacolone) formed by an acid-catalyzed 1,2-alkyl migration of the diol, but this does not interfere with the Diels–Alder reaction. (This competing reaction, known as the *pinacol–pinacolone rearrangement* is the archetype of a whole class of such migrations called *Wagner–Merwein shifts*.) The rearrangement pathway predominates over the desired elimination reaction but redistillation of the crude product provides enough material in sufficient purity to carry out the Diels–Alder reaction, albeit in poor yield.

Experiment 16   *Preparation of 4-bromomethylbenzoic acid by radical substitution and conversion to 4-methoxymethylbenzoic acid by nucleophilic substitution*

A convenient procedure for generating bromine radicals utilizes *N*-bromo-succinimide as the bromine source and benzoyl peroxide as the initiator. Heating benzoyl peroxide causes homolytic cleavage of the labile peroxide linkage, giving radicals which react with the *N*-bromosuccinimide, breaking the relatively weak N—Br bond to generate bromine radicals. The HBr generated by benzylic hydrogen atom abstraction from the 4-methylbenzoic acid reacts with more *N*-bromosuccinimide to form molecular bromine which in turn combines with the benzyl radical to furnish the product and another bromide radical. Thus, the bromine atoms function as the chain carrier in this reaction.

Unlike most benzyl halides, the 4-bromomethylbenzoic acid prepared in this experiment is not lachrymatory, making it suitable for use in a laboratory procedure. Nonetheless, the product is a potential skin irritant and due caution should be exercised in its handling.

Benzyl halides undergo ready substitution and this can be demonstrated in an optional experiment by converting the brominated product to 4-methoxymethylbenzoic acid using methanolic potassium hydroxide.

Level	3
Time	2×3h
Equipment	stirrer/hotplate; apparatus for reflux (×2)
Instruments	IR, NMR

Materials

1. Preparation of 4-bromomethylbenzoic acid

4-methylbenzoic acid (*p*-toluic acid) (FW 136.2)	2.72 g (20 mmol)	**toxic**
N-bromosuccinimide (FW 178.0)	3.60 g (20 mmol)	**irritant**
benzoyl peroxide (FW 242.2)	0.20 g	**explosive**

NOTE: *benzoyl peroxide is an oxidizing agent and liable to explode if heated or ground as the dry solid. Handle with extreme caution*

Continued

Box cont.

chlorobenzene		flammable
light petroleum (bp 40–60°C)		flammable
2. *Preparation of 4-methoxymethylbenzoic acid*		
methanol	25 mL	flammable, toxic
potassium hydroxide pellets	1.1 g (20 mmol)	corrosive

Procedure

1. *Preparation of 4-bromomethylbenzoic acid*

Place the 4-methylbenzoic acid and N-bromosuccinimide in a 100 mL round-bottomed flask. Add the benzoyl peroxide,[1] taking care that none sticks to the ground glass joint of the flask. Finally, add 25 mL chlorobenzene by pipette and wash down any solids which may be adhering to the sides of the flask, paying particular attention to the ground glass joint. Arrange the apparatus for reflux[2] and heat gently over a small flame for 1 h with occasional (*ca.* every 5 min) vigorous swirling[3] in order to ensure good mixing. After this period, cool the flask and contents in an ice bath (*ca.* 10 min) and filter off the precipitated products with suction.[4] Wash the residue on the funnel with light petroleum (3 × 10 mL), and transfer the solid to a beaker. Add water (50 mL), stir the slurry thoroughly to dissolve the succinimide present, and filter the mixture under suction, washing the solid residue successively with water (2 × 10 mL) and light petroleum (2 × 10 mL). Leave the product on the funnel with suction to dry as thoroughly as possible and record the yield and mp of the crude material. Obtain the IR ($CHCl_3$) and NMR ($CDCl_3$) spectra of your product. The crude material is of sufficient purity to use in the following experiment but, if time permits, may be recrystallized from ethyl acetate.

[1]*Care! Potentially explosive*

[2]*See Fig. 3.23(a)*

[3]*Care! Chlorobenzene boils at 132°C*

[4]*See Fig. 3.7*

2. *Preparation of 4-methoxymethylbenzoic acid (optional)*

Place the potassium hydroxide pellets and the methanol in a 100 mL round-bottomed flask and add 1.1 g of the 4-bromomethylbenzoic acid prepared in the previous experiment. Set the apparatus for reflux with a calcium chloride guard tube and heat gently for 45 min.[5] Remove the methanol at reduced pressure on the rotary evaporator with gentle warming[6] and dissolve the alkaline residue in water (30 mL). Acidify the mixture with dilute hydrochloric acid and filter the precipitated product. Wash the solid with light petroleum (2 × 15 mL) and dry with suction on the funnel. Record the yield and mp of your crude product and then recrystallize it from water. As before, filter the precipitated product with suction, wash the crystalline solid with light petroleum (2 × 15 mL) and dry on the funnel with suction. Obtain the IR ($CHCl_3$) and NMR ($CDCl_3$) spectra of the purified product and compare its mp with that of the crude material.

[5]*See Fig. 3.23(c)*

[6]*Bumping may occur if heating is too strong*

See Exp. 51

MICROSCALE

Level	3
Time	2×3 h
Equipment	stirrer/hotplate; apparatus for reflux, Craig tube recrystallization

Materials

1. Preparation of 4-bromomethylbenzoic acid

4-methylbenzoic acid (*p*-toluic acid) (FW 136.2)	136 mg (1.0 mmol)	**toxic**
N-bromosuccinimide (FW 178.0)	180 mg (1 mmol)	**irritant**
benzoyl peroxide (FW 242.2)	10 mg	**explosive**

NOTE: *benzoyl peroxide is an oxidizing agent and liable to explode if heated or ground as the dry solid. Handle with extreme caution, even when using the small quantities required in this experiment*

chlorobenzene	**flammable**
light petroleum (bp 40–60°C)	**flammable**

2. Preparation of 4-methoxymethylbenzoic acid

methanol	25 mL	**flammable, toxic**
potassium hydroxide pellets	1.1 g (20 mmol)	**corrosive**

Procedure

1. Preparation of 4-bromomethylbenzoic acid

Place the toluic acid and the *N*-bromosuccinimide in a 3 mL conical reaction vial containing a spin vane. Add the dibenzoyl peroxide,[1] carefully avoiding any contact with ground glass surfaces. Add the chlorobenzene from a Pasteur pipette, using the solvent to rinse any traces of the peroxide into the base of the vial. Heat the mixture at reflux[2] for 1 h with vigorous stirring. Cool the flask in an ice bath and remove the liquid carefully using a drawn out Pasteur pipette. Wash the solid by slurrying with light petroleum ether (3×0.5 mL) then transfer the solid to a Craig tube. Add water (1 mL) and stir the slurry thoroughly to dissolve the succinimide. Filter by centrifugation,[3] washing the solid with water (2×0.5 mL), then light petroleum ether (2×0.5 mL), and centrifuging after each washing. Dry the solid rapidly *in vacuo*[4] and reserve a TLC sample for later use.

2. Preparation of 4-methoxymethylbenzoic acid

Prepare a solution of potassium hydroxide in methanol and transfer 1.25 mL of the solution to a 3 mL reaction vial. Add bromomethylbenzoic acid (55 mg) prepared in the previous experiment. Set the apparatus for reflux with a calcium chloride guard tube[5] and heat gently for 45 min with stirring. Remove the methanol with a gentle vacuum[6] and dissolve the residue in water (1.0–1.5 mL). Transfer the solution to a Craig tube and acidify by adding concentrated

[1] *Care! Potentially explosive*

[2] *See Fig. 3.24*

[3] *See pp. 137–138*

[4] *See Fig. 3.46*

[5] *See Fig. 3.24*

[6] *Bumping may occur if heating is too strong*

hydrochloric acid carefully one drop at a time testing the pH between drops. Filter the precipitated solid by centrifugation. Wash the solid with light petroleum ether (2×0.75 mL), centrifuging after each washing. Transfer the solid to a vial and dry *in vacuo*. Record the melting point and TLC against the starting material and the intermediate bromomethyl compound.

Problems

1 Assign the important absorptions in the IR spectra and interpret the NMR spectra of your products.

2 Write out the full mechanism for the radical chain reaction which is occurring in the conversion of 4-methylbenzoic acid to 4-bromomethylbenzoic acid.

3 Kerosene consists mainly of C_{11} and C_{12} hydrocarbons and finds use as a fuel for jet engines although it is not suitable for automobiles. However, catalytic cracking will convert it to shorter chain hydrocarbons. The process involves the formation of radical intermediates and results in two smaller molecules, one of which is an alkene. Write out a mechanism for the overall process below:

$$C_{11}H_{24} \xrightarrow{\text{heat, catalyst}} C_9H_{20} + C_2H_4$$

4 Suggest reaction pathways for the following transformations:

Further reading

For the procedure on which this experiment is based, see: E.S. Olson, *J. Chem. Educ.*, 1980, **57**, 157.

D.L. Tuleen and B.A. Hess, *J. Chem. Educ.*, 1971, **48**, 476.

residue repeatedly with hot petroleum (25 mL portions) until no further material is extracted. (This can be verified by looking for the absence of oily streaks on the ground glass after decanting the petroleum.) Save a second sample and concentrate the remainder of the solution to 25 mL on the rotary evaporator. Add a crystal of iodine, reflux the solution[5] for 30 min to effect isomerization and allow to cool. Decolourize the mixture with 25% sodium metabisulfite solution (10 mL), remove the lower aqueous phase, and add methanol (25 mL) to the organic phase remaining in the separatory funnel. If two phases do not form, add water dropwise until this occurs. Separate the upper layer of petroleum, dry over $MgSO_4$, filter and remove the solvent on the rotary evaporator in a preweighed flask. Record the yield and mp of the crystalline product and recrystallize from ethanol. Carry out TLC analysis[6] of the two aliquots obtained during the course of the experiment and the final sample. Use a TLC plate pre-coated with silica, elute with light petroleum and observe the developed plate under UV light[7] and, after standing over iodine, noting the R_f value. Obtain the NMR ($CDCl_3$) and UV (EtOH) spectra.

[5]See Fig. 3.23(a)

[6]See Chapter 3

[7]Care! Eye protection

Problems

1 Discuss the mode of action of phase transfer catalysts, particularly with regard to this experiment.
2 From the TLC and spectroscopic evidence, comment upon the purity or otherwise of your material. what purpose is served by trituration of the initial reaction material with petroleum? Which is the major isomer of 1,2-diphenylethene formed in the reaction.
3 *E*-1,2-diphenylethene demonstrates very weak oestrogenic activity. The related *E*-1,2-di(4-hydroxyphenyl)ethene is much more active in this respect and is also called stilboestrol. The *Z*-isomers of these compounds are inactive. Suggest a reason for this activity.

Further reading

The authors thank Dr D.C.C. Smith, University of Manchester, for supplying details upon which this experiment is based.

For a review of the Wittig reaction, see the references given on p. 561.

For reviews and monographs of phase transfer catalysis, see: E.V. Dehmlow and S.S. Dehmlow, *Phase Transfer Catalysis*, 2nd edn, Verlag Chemie, Deerfield Beach, Florida, 1983; J.M. McIntosh, *J. Chem. Educ.*, 1978, **55**, 235; E.V. Dehmlow, *Angew. Chem. Int. Ed. Engl.*, 1977, **16**, 493.

Experiment 51   *Preparation of 4-vinylbenzoic acid by a Wittig reaction in aqueous medium*

In this second example of an aqueous Wittig reaction, the ylid is generated in the presence of a large excess of a reactive aldehyde. The ylid is stabilized by virtue of the electron-withdrawing carboxylic acid group on the aromatic ring and is resistant to hydrolysis. The phosphonium salt is prepared from 4-bromomethylbenzoic acid which, being non-volatile, is relatively safe to handle, although it still has irritant properties. This starting material may be prepared according to the procedure described in Experiment 16; it is also available commercially.

Level	1
Time	3 h
Equipment	magnetic stirrer; apparatus for suction filtration, reflux, TLC

Materials

1. Preparation of phosphonium salt

4-bromomethylbenzoic acid (FW 215.1)	4.30 g (20 mmol)	lachrymator, irritant
triphenylphosphine (FW 262.3)	5.20 g (20 mmol)	irritant
acetone		flammable
diethyl ether		flammable, irritant

2. Preparation of 4-vinylbenzoic acid

formaldehyde (37% aqueous solution) (FW 30.0)	32 mL	cancer suspect agent, toxic
This represents a large excess of formaldehyde		
4-carboxybenzyltriphenyl- phosphonium bromide	3.76 g (8 mmol)	irritant
sodium hydroxide pellets	2.5 g	corrosive, hygroscopic
ethanol		flammable, toxic
hydrochloric acid (conc.)		corrosive

Procedure

1. Preparation of 4-carboxybenzyltriphenylphosphonium bromide

HOOD
[1]*Wear gloves*
[2]*See Fig. 3.23(a)*

[3]*See Fig. 3.7*
[4]*This can be done during Part 2*

Dissolve the bromomethylbenzoic acid[1] and the triphenylphosphine in 60 mL acetone in a 100 mL round-bottomed flask and reflux the mixture[2] for 45 min. After this time, cool the reaction mixture and filter off the precipitated phosphonium salt with suction.[3] Wash the solid with diethyl ether (2 × 20 mL) on the sinter and dry it with suction. Record the yield and mp[4] of the product, which is sufficiently pure to use directly in the next stage.

HOOD

2. Preparation of 4-vinylbenzoic acid

Place the 4-carboxybenzyltriphenylphosphonium bromide (3.76 g, 8 mmol), aqueous formaldehyde and 15 mL water in a 250 mL Erlenmeyer flask equipped with a magnetic stirrer bar. Clamp the flask, stir vigorously and add a solution of the sodium hydroxide in 15 mL water over *ca.* 10 min. Stir the mixture for an additional 45 min and filter off the precipitate with suction,[3] washing it with water. Acidify the combined filtrate and washings with concentrated hydrochloric acid and filter off the resultant precipitate of crude product with suction.[3] Recrystallize the product from aqueous ethanol and record the yield and mp of the material obtained. Record an IR (Nujol®) spectrum of the purified material, and run a TLC of the product (silica gel, dichloromethane–ethyl acetate (1:1)) and compare its R_f with that of the starting material. ∎

MICROSCALE

Level	1
Time	3 h
Equipment	magnetic stirrer; apparatus for suction filtration (micro-Hirsch and side arm tube), Craig tube recrystallization

Materials

1. Preparation of phosphonium salt

4-bromomethylbenzoic acid (FW 215.1)	108 mg (0.5 mmol)	lachrymator, irritant
triphenylphosphine (FW 262.3)	130 mg (0.5 mmol)	irritant
acetone		flammable
diethyl ether		flammable, irritant

2. Preparation of 4-vinylbenzoic acid

formaldehyde (37% aqueous solution) (FW 30.0)	0.8 mL	cancer suspect agent, toxic

This represents a large excess of formaldehyde

4-carboxybenzyltriphenylphosphonium bromide	94 mg (0.25 mmol)	irritant
sodium hydroxide (16.7% w/v)	0.375 mL	corrosive, hygroscopic
ethanol		flammable, toxic
hydrochloric acid (conc.)		corrosive
Celite® or Hyflo®	ca. 100 mg	irritant dust

Procedure

HOOD

[1]Wear gloves

[2]See Fig. 3.24

[3]See Fig. 3.7

[4]This can be done during Part 2

HOOD

[5]See Fig. 3.9

1. Preparation of 4-carboxybenzyltriphenylphosphonium bromide

Dissolve the 4-bromomethylbenzoic acid[1] and the triphenylphosphine in the acetone in a 3 mL reaction vial and reflux the mixture[2] for 45 min. After this time, cool the reaction mixture and collect the precipitated phosphonium salt at the pump using a micro-Hirsch funnel.[3] Wash the solid at the pump with diethyl ether (2 × 0.5 mL) and suck dry. Record the yield and mp.[4]

2. Preparation of 4-vinylbenzoic acid

Place the phosphonium salt (94 mg, 0.25 mmol), the aqueous formaldehyde and water (0.375 mL) in a small test tube containing a small stirrer bead, and add the sodium hydroxide solution. Stir the solution for an additional 45 min, then remove the precipitate by filtration through a short plug of Celite®,[5]

⁶See pp. 137–138

washing the filter bed with water (2 × 0.2 mL). Collect the filtrate and the washings in a 2 mL Craig tube. Acidify the tube contents with concentrated hydrochloric acid and collect the precipitated product by centrifugation.⁶ Recrystallize the crude product from aqueous ethanol in a Craig tube and record the yield and mp.

Problems

1 Assign the main absorptions in the IR spectrum of 4-vinylbenzoic acid.
2 Explain why it is possible to generate the ylid with aqueous sodium hydroxide in this example.
3 If an aldehyde other than formaldehyde were to be used, what would be the geometry of the double bond in the major product and why?

Experiment 52

A Wittig reaction involving preparation and isolation of a stabilized ylid: conversion of 1-bromobutyrolactone to α-methylenebutyrolactone

In the following experiment it is possible to isolate the intermediate ylid after its generation with aqueous sodium carbonate. The mildness of the reaction conditions and the relative stability of the phosphorane are a reflection of the presence of an electron-withdrawing group (the lactone moiety) on the carbon α- to the phosphorus, which permits additional resonance delocalization of the carbanion.

Wittig reactions of stabilized ylids with aldehydes (other than formaldehyde of course) favour the thermodynamically more stable E-product. This is considered to be a consequence of reversibility of the initial nucleophilic addition step, with one betaine selectively collapsing to products and the other betaine reverting to starting materials.

Procedure

Dissolve the sodium hydroxide in water (0.12 mL) in a 1 mL reaction vial containing a spin vane. Allow the solution to cool and then add *ca.* 0.02 mL of the benzaldehyde followed by *ca.* 20 mg of hydroxylamine hydrochloride. Stopper the flask and stir vigorously, briefly stopping the stirring at 5 min intervals to add further portions of benzaldehyde and hydroxylamine until both reagents have been added completely. The reaction mixture will become warm, giving a homogeneous solution with no almond odour, indicating total consumption of the benzaldehyde. Neutralize the mixture by the addition of ethanoic acid[1] and allow the mixture to cool before extracting with diethyl ether (2 × 1.2 mL). Separate the organic extracts, dry by passing through a column of $MgSO_4$,[2] into a preweighed reaction vial and remove the solvent *in vacuo*. Record the yield of product.

[1] *If a precipitate of sodium acetate forms, add more water*

[2] *See Fig. 3.9*

Problems

1 Write a mechanism for the formation of oximes from aldehydes and hydroxylamine.

2 Reaction of unsymmetrical ketones with hydroxylamine gives a mixture of oxime isomers:

Describe how you might distinguish the two possible products.

3 Compare and contrast the IR spectra of benzaldehyde and benzaldoxine.

Further reading

For other reactions of hydroxylamine, see: EROS, 2760.

Experiment 6   *Preparation of 4-bromoaniline (p-bromoaniline)*

The aromatic ring of aniline is very electron rich due to the ability of the lone pair on the nitrogen to be delocalized into the π-system, and consequently aniline undergoes very ready electrophilic substitution reactions. Even with aqueous bromine in the cold, polysubstitution occurs to give 2,4,6-tribromoaniline and other more reactive reagents such as nitric acid react so vigorously that they lead to decomposition of the aniline.

However, 'tying up' the nitrogen lone pair, by derivatizing the aniline as an amide, lowers the reactivity of the system to the point where controlled mono-substitution reactions can be carried out. In amides, an important contribution towards resonance stabilization comes from delocalization of the nitrogen lone pair onto the amide oxygen, making the lone pair less available to the aromatic ring.

An additional advantage of the derivatization procedure results from the increased steric bulk of the amide group, favouring substitution at the 4-position over the 2-positions which it shields. Consequently, the advantages of increased control over the degree and position of substitution far outweigh the disadvantages of the extra steps involved in the preparation and hydrolysis of the amide—an example of a protection–deprotection sequence.

In this experiment, the aniline is first converted to N-phenylethanamide (acetanilide) which is then brominated in the 4-position. After bromination, the amide group is hydrolyzed back to the amine to furnish the desired 4-bromoaniline. Notice that, even with the amide group present, the aromatic ring is sufficiently electron rich to undergo aromatic substitution with bromine, without the need for a Lewis acid catalyst to be added to the reaction mixture.

Level	1
Time	$2 \times 3\,h$
Equipment	apparatus for stirring, suction filtration, reflux

Materials

1. Preparation of N-phenylethanamide (acetanilide)

aniline (FW 93.1)	10 mL, 10 g (0.11 mmol)	**cancer suspect agent, toxic**
ethanoic anhydride (FW 102.1)	12 mL, 12 g (0.12 mol)	**corrosive, irritant**
glacial ethanoic acid (FW 60.1)	25 mL	**corrosive, irritant**

2. Preparation of N-(4-bromophenyl)ethanamide (p-bromoacetanilide)

| N-phenylethanamide (FW 135.2) | 5 g (37 mmol) | |

Continued

Box cont.

bromine (FW 159.8)	2.1 mL, 6 g (38 mmol)	corrosive, toxic

NOTE: *bromine is highly toxic and corrosive. Its volatility combined with its density make it very difficult to handle. Always wear gloves and measure out in the hood*

glacial ethanoic acid	2 × 25 mL	corrosive, toxic
sodium metabisulfite	1–2 g	irritant

3. Preparation of 4-bromoaniline

N-(4-bromophenyl)ethanamide (FW 214.1)	5 g (23 mmol)	
hydrochloric acid (5 M)	50 mL	corrosive
sodium hydroxide solution (25%)		corrosive
pH indicator paper		

Procedure

HOOD

[1]Care! Exothermic

1. Preparation of N-phenylethanamide (acetanilide)

Place the ethanoic acid in a flask and add the aniline followed by the ethanoic anhydride.[1] Mix well and allow the solution to stand at room temperature for 5 min. Dilute with 100–200 mL of water until crystallization of the product occurs. When this is complete filter off the colourless lustrous crystals of N-phenylethanamide, dry in air and record the yield. Although the material is pure enough for further use, a portion should be recrystallized from aqueous ethanol and the mp of the purified material determined.

HOOD

[2]Care! Wear gloves

2. Preparation of N-(4-bromophenyl)ethanamide (p-bromoacetanilide)

Dissolve the N-phenylethanamide and bromine in separate 25 mL portions of ethanoic acid, then add the bromine solution[2] over 5 min to the acetanilide solution while stirring. The bromine colour disappears and the product may begin to crystallize out. Allow the mixture to stand at room temperature for 15 min and then pour into 300 mL of cold water.[3] Stir well, adding 1–2 g of sodium metabisulfite to remove any remaining bromine. Filter off the product by suction[4] and record the yield of crude dry material. The product is sufficiently pure for use in the final stage, but a portion should be recrystallized from aqueous ethanol and the mp determined.[5] (If a brown colouration persists at this point add a little activated charcoal during the recrystallization then filter whilst hot.)[6]

[3]Product certainly crystallizes out now

[4]See Fig. 3.7

[5]May be left at this stage

[6]See Fig. 3.6

3. Preparation of 4-bromoaniline

Place the N-(4-bromophenyl)ethanamide in a 100 mL round-bottomed flask and add the hydrochloric acid. Fit a reflux condenser[7] and allow the mixture to boil until all the solid dissolves and then heat for a further 10 min. Cool the solution in ice and cautiously make alkaline by the addition of sodium hydroxide (use pH paper).[8] The product separates as an oil which solidifies on

[7]See Fig. 3.23(a)

[8]Care! Exothermic

cooling and scratching. When all has crystallized, filter by suction,[4] wash with a little water and recrystallize from a mixture of water and ethanol. Charcoal may again be used at this point to remove coloured impurities if present. The amine is susceptible to oxidation by air, particularly when wet or in solution, but the dry solid will keep indefinitely. Record the mp and yield of your purified material. ∎

MICROSCALE

Level	1
Time	$2 \times 3\,h$
Equipment	apparatus for stirring, Craig tube recrystallization, reflux

Materials

1.   Preparation of N-phenylethanamide (acetanilide)

aniline (FW 93.1)	0.20 mL,	**cancer suspect agent, toxic**
	200 mg (2.2 mmol)	
ethanoic anhydride (FW 102.1)	0.24 mL,	**corrosive, irritant**
	240 mg (2.4 mmol)	
glacial ethanoic acid (FW 60.1)	0.50 mL	**corrosive, irritant**

2.   Preparation of N-(4-bromophenyl)ethanamide (p-bromoacetanilide)

N-phenylethanamide (FW 135.2)	100 mg (0.74 mmol)	
bromine (FW 159.8)	0.42 mL,	**corrosive, toxic**
	1.20 g (7.6 mmol)	

NOTE: *bromine is highly toxic and corrosive. Its volatility combined with its high density make it very difficult to handle, particularly when small quantities are involved. Always wear gloves and measure out in the hood. Alternatively, make up a larger quantity than you require for a single experiment of a standard solution in glacial acetic acid by weighing accurately and using a volumetric flask*

glacial ethanoic acid (60.1)	5.5 mL	**corrosive, irritant**
sodium metabisulfite	50–100 mg	**irritant**

3.   Preparation of 4-bromoaniline

N-(4-bromophenyl)ethanamide (FW 214.1)	100 mg (0.47 mmol)	
hydrochloric acid (5 M)	1 mL	**corrosive**
sodium hydroxide solution (25%)		**corrosive**
pH indicator paper		

HOOD

Procedure

1.   Preparation of N-phenylethanamide (acetanilide)

Place the ethanoic acid in a 2 mL Craig tube and add the aniline followed by the ethanoic anhydride.[1] Mix well using a Pasteur pipette and allow to stand at room temperature. Dilute with water (0.5 mL) and leave to stand to allow

[1]*Care! Exothermic*

complete crystallization of the product. Collect the colourless crystals by centrifugation[2] and air dry. Record the yield, and recrystallize a small sample (*ca.* 30 mg) from aqueous ethanol.

2. Preparation of N-(4-bromophenyl)ethanamide (p-bromoacetanilide)

Dissolve the acetanilide in ethanoic acid (0.5 mL) in a Craig tube containing a tiny stirrer bead, then add bromine solution[3] (0.5 mL) slowly over 5 min to the stirred solution. Allow the decolourized solution to stand at room temperature for 15 min, remove the stirrer bead with tweezers, then add cold water (1 mL) by pipette and mix thoroughly.[4] Add small portions (*ca.* 40 mg) of sodium metabisulfite to remove any remaining bromine. Filter by centrifugation[2] and air dry the product.[5]

[3]Care! Wear gloves

[4]Product certainly crystallizes out now

[5]May be left at this stage

3. Preparation of 4-bromoaniline

Place the bromoacetanilide in a 3 mL reaction vial and add the hydrochloric acid. Fit a reflux condenser[6] and heat the mixture until all the solid dissolves, then heat for a further 10 min. Transfer the hot solution to a Craig tube and allow to cool, finishing the cooling in a beaker of ice. Cautiously make the solution alkaline by the addition of sodium hydroxide solution.[7] The product separates as an oil which solidifies on cooling and scratching. When all the material has crystallized, filter by centrifugation,[2] wash the solid with a little (0.25 mL) water, recentrifuge and recrystallize the solid from aqueous ethanol. Collect the recrystallized material by centrifugation, dry the solid *in vacuo* and record the mp.

[6]See Fig. 3.24

[7]Care! Exothermic

Problems

1 Write mechanistic equations for each step in the preparation of *p*-bromoaniline from aniline. Why does bromination of acetanilide stop at the monobromo stage?

2 Predict products of bromination of the following:

Indicate which might be expected to react with bromine in ethanoic acid ('molecular bromination') and which would need a Lewis acid catalyst.

7.2 Reactions of alkenes

The chemistry of alkenes is dominated by the properties of the C=C bond. Hence alkenes undergo a range of addition reactions which are initiated by electrophilic attack on the electron-rich double bond. For example, the addi-

Appendix 1 Hazardous Properties of Chemicals

The hazardous properties of some 100 commonly encountered laboratory solvents, reagents and chemicals are described in tabular form. The table contains information under the following headings.

Name: the common name for the chemical.

Warnings: the standard hazard warnings: flammable, corrosive, etc.

Handling: precautions required in handling the chemicals (see pp. 5–11): **S** refers to standard precautions, i.e. avoid breathing the vapour, avoid contact with skin and eyes, avoid breathing the dust; **C** refers to suspected carcinogen.

Effects: effects immediately apparent: **E**, eyes; **S**, skin; **RS**, respiratory system; **N**, nausea; **D**, dizziness or drowsiness.

First aid: immediate treatment required in the event of an accident involving the chemical (see pp. 12–13): **S** refers to standard treatment, i.e. flush affected eyes or skin with copious amounts of cold water, remove any contaminated clothing, and summon medical assistance for eye injuries.

Water: reaction of compound with water: **R**, reacts; **VR**, violent reaction; **M**, miscible or soluble; **I**, immiscible or insoluble.

Special: any special hazards or precautions not noted elsewhere.

Name	Warnings	Handling	Effects	First aid	Water	Special
Acetic acid	Flammable Highly corrosive	S	E, S, RS	S	M	
Acetic anhydride	Flammable Corrosive Lachrymator	S	E, S, RS	S	R	
Acetone	Highly flammable Irritant	S	E, D	S	M	
Acetyl chloride	Highly flammable Corrosive	S	E, S, RS	S	VR	
Allyl bromide (or chloride)	Highly flammable Extremely toxic Irritant, lachrymator	S	E, S, RS, D	S	I	
Alumina	Irritant	S	RS	S	I	
Aluminium chloride	Corrosive	S, keep dry	E, S	S	VR	Moisture sensitive
Ammonia gas	Flammable Toxic Corrosive	S	E, RS	S	M	Liquefied gas
Ammonium hydroxide	Corrosive Toxic	S	E, S, RS	S	M	
Aniline (and aromatic amines)	Extremely toxic Cancer suspect agent	S, C	S, D	S	I	
Benzaldehyde	Irritant Toxic	S	E	S	I	Easily oxidized
Benzene	Highly flammable Extremely toxic Cancer suspect agent	S, C	E, S, D	S	I	
Benzoyl chloride (and aroyl chlorides)	Corrosive Lachrymator	S	E, S, RS	S	R	
Benzyl bromide (and chloride)	Corrosive Lachrymator	S	E, RS	S	I	
Biphenyl	Irritant	S	RS, E	S	I	
Bromine	Extremely toxic Highly corrosive Oxidizer	S	E, S, RS	S	Slightly soluble	Reacts with many organic materials
Bromobenzene	Flammable Irritant	S	D	S	I	

Continued

Appendix 1 cont.

Name	Warnings	Handling	Effects	First aid	Water	Special
Bromoethane	Flammable Irritant Cancer suspect agent	SC	E, RS, D	S	I	
N-Bromosuccinimide	Cancer suspect agent, corrosive Irritant	S, keep dry	E, S, RS	S	I	Moisture sensitive
t-Butanol	Highly flammable Irritant	S	E, RS	S	M	
Butyl-lithium (in hexane)	Flammable Pyrophoric	S, keep dry	E, S	S	VR	Work under inert atmosphere
Carbon tetrachloride	Extremely toxic Cancer suspect agent	S, C	E, RS, S D, N	S	I	
Chlorobenzene	Flammable Irritant	S	D, S	S	I	
Chloroform	Extremely toxic Cancer suspect agent	S, C	E, D, N	S	I	
3-Chloroperbenzoic acid	Oxidizer Irritant	S	RS, S	S	I	Explosion risk
Chromium (VI) oxide	Oxidizer Corrosive Cancer suspect agent	S, C	RS, S	S	M	
Copper salts	Toxic Irritant	S	E, RS	S	M	
Cyanides	Extremely toxic	Not for general use	Fatal	Antidote needed	M	
Cyclohexane	Highly flammable Irritant	S	E, S, RS	S	I	
Cyclohexanone	Flammable Harmful	S	E, S, RS	S	I	
Cyclopentadiene (dicyclopentadiene)	Highly flammable Harmful, stench	S	RS	S	I	Exothermic dimerization
Dichloromethane	Toxic Irritant	S	E, RS	S	I	
Dicyclohexylcarbodiimide	Toxic Irritant	S, keep dry	E, S	S	R	Causes skin reactions

Continued on p. 672

Cont.

Name	Warnings	Handling	Effects	First aid	Water	Special
Diethyl ether	Highly flammable Irritant	S	D, RS	S	I	Forms explosive peroxides
Diethyl malonate	Harmful	S	E, RS	S	I	
Diisopropylamine	Highly flammable Corrosive	S	E, RS, S	S	M	
Dimethylformamide	Harmful Irritant	S	E, S, RS	S	M	
Dimethylsulfoxide	Harmful Irritant	S	E, S	S	M	Hygroscopic; absorbed through skin
2,4-Dinitrophenylhydrazine	Harmful Flammable	S	S	S	I	Explosion risk
Dioxan	Highly flammable Cancer suspect agent	S, C	E, D	S	M	Forms explosive peroxides
Ethane-1,2-diol	Harmful	S	RS	S	M	Hygroscopic
Ethanol	Highly flammable Toxic	S	Well known	S	M	
Ethyl ethanoate	Highly flammable Irritant	S	E, RS	S	I	
Ethyl 3-oxobutanoate	Irritant	S	E, RS	S	I	
Ethyl chloroethanoate acetate	Toxic Lachrymator	S	E, RS, S	S	I	
Ethyl chloroformate	Highly flammable Toxic Irritant	S	E, RS	S	I	
Ferric chloride	Irritant Corrosive	S	E, S	S	M	
Formaldehyde (aqueous solution)	Toxic Cancer suspect agent	S, C	D, RS	S	M	
Hexane (and light petroleum)	Highly flammable Irritant Toxic	S	RS	S	I	
Hydrazine hydrate	Flammable Corrosive Cancer suspect agent	S, C	E, S	S	M	

Continued

Appendix 1 cont.

Name	Warnings	Handling	Effects	First aid	Water	Special
Hydrochloric acid	Corrosive Toxic	S	E, RS, S	S	M	
Hydrogen	Highly flammable	Special	Asphyxiant	S	I	Forms explosive mixtures with air; compressed gas
Hydrogen peroxide	Oxidizer Corrosive	S	E, S	S	M	Reacts with many organic materials
Hydroxylamine hydrochloride	Corrosive Irritant	S	E, S	S	M	Explodes when heated
Iodine	Corrosive	S	E, RS, S	S	I	Reacts with many organic materials
Iodomethane	Extremely toxic Cancer suspect agent	S, C	D, E, S	S	I	Very volatile
Lead salts	Toxic	S	N	S	M/I	
Lithium	Reacts violently with water	S, keep dry	S	S	VR	
Lithium aluminium hydride	Reacts violently with water Flammable	S, keep dry	S	S	VR	
Magnesium	Highly flammable	S	S	S	R (slow)	Explosion risk
Magnesium sulfate	Irritant	S	RS	S	M	Hygroscopic
Maleic anhydride	Harmful Irritant	S	E, RS, S	S	R	Moisture sensitive
Manganese dioxide	Oxidizer Irritant	S	RS	S	I	
Mercury	Extremely toxic	S	N	S	I	High vapour pressure
Mercury salts	Extremely toxic	S	E, N	S	M/I	
Methanol	Highly flammable Extremely toxic	S	D, E, RS	S	M	
Methylamine (solutions)	Flammable Corrosive	S	E, RS, S	S	M	

Continued on p. 674

Cont.

Name	Warnings	Handling	Effects	First aid	Water	Special
Nitric acid	Highly corrosive Oxidizer	S	E, S, RS	S	M	
Perchloric acid (and perchlorates)	Corrosive Oxidizer Explosive	S	E, S, RS	S	M	Explosion risk
Peroxides and peracids	Oxidizer	S	RS, S	S	M/I	Explosion risk
Petroleum ether (light petroleum)	Highly flammable	S	E, RS	S	I	
Phenol (and substituted phenols)	Extremely toxic Highly corrosive	S	E, S, RS	S	M	Absorbed through the skin
Phosphoryl chloride (phosphorus oxychloride)	Corrosive Irritant	S	E, S, RS	S	R	Moisture sensitive
Phthalic anhydride	Irritant	S	E, RS	S	R	Moisture sensitive
Picric acid (and other polynitro aromatics)	Toxic Explosive	S	S	S	M	Explosion risk
Piperidine	Highly flammable Toxic Corrosive	S	E, RS, S	S	M	
Potassium	Reacts violently with water	S, keep dry	S	S	VR	
Potassium hydroxide	Highly corrosive Toxic	S	E, S	S	M	
Potassium permanganate	Oxidizer Corrosive	S	S	S	M	Explosion risk
Pyridine	Highly flammable Harmful	S	E, D, N, RS	S	M	Stench
Pyrrolidine	Highly flammable Corrosive Irritant	S	RS, S	S	M	
Semicarbazide hydrochloride	Cancer suspect agent	S, C	S	S	M	
Silica gel	Irritant	S	RS	S	I	
Silver nitrate	Corrosive Toxic Oxidizer	S	E, S	S	M	

Continued

Appendix 1 cont.

Name	Warnings	Handling	Effects	First aid	Water	Special
Sodium	Reacts explosively with water	S	S	S	VR	
Sodium borohydride	Flammable Harmful	S	RS	S	R	Evolves H_2 with acids
Sodium carbonate	Corrosive	S	S	S	M	
Sodium hydride	Reacts violently with water	S	S	S	VR	
Sodium hydroxide	Corrosive Toxic	S	E, S	S	M	
Sodium hypochlorite (bleach)	Oxidizer Corrosive	S	E, S	S	M	Can liberate Cl_2
Sodium iodide	Irritant	S	S	S	M	Liberates I_2 with oxidizers
Sodium nitrite	Toxic Oxidizer	S	E, S	S	M	Liberates nitrous fumes with acids
Sodium sulfate	Irritant	S	S	S	M	Hygroscopic
Styrene	Flammable Toxic	S	E, RS	S	I	
Sulfuric acid	Highly corrosive Oxidizer	S	E, S	S	M	
Tetrahydrofuran	Highly flammable Irritant	S	D, E, RS	S	M	Forms explosive peroxides
Thionyl chloride	Corrosive Irritant Lachrymator	S	E, RS, S	S	VR	
Toluene	Highly flammable Irritant	S	D, E, RS, S	S	I	
Toluene-4-sulfonic acid	Corrosive Toxic	S	E, S	S	M	
Toluene-4-sulfonyl chloride	Corrosive	S	E, S	S	R	Moisture sensitive
Triethylamine	Highly flammable Corrosive	S	E, RS, S	S	M	

Continued on p. 676

Cont.

Name	Warnings	Handling	Effects	First aid	Water	Special
Trimethylchlorosilane	Highly flammable Corrosive Irritant	S	E, S, RS	S	VR	
Triphenylphosphine	Irritant	S	RS	S	I	
Xylene	Flammable Toxic	S	E, RS	S	I	
Zinc (dust)	Flammable	S	RS	S	I	Liberates H_2 with acids

Appendix 2 **Organic Solvents**

Table A1 Properties of common laboratory solvents.

Solvent*	Bp (760 mmHg) (°C)	Mp (°C)	Flashpoint (°C)	Density, d^{20} (g mL^{-1})	Refractive index, n_D	Dielectric constant, ε	Toxicity, TLV† (ppm)	Hazards
Acetone	56.2	−95.3	−30	0.790	1.3588	20.7	1000	Flammable
Acetonitrile (methyl cyanide)	81.6	−45.2	5	0.786	1.3442	37.5	40	Flammable Lachrymator
Benzene‡	80.1	5.5	−11	0.874	1.5011	2.3	8	Carcinogen Flammable
1-Butanol (n-butyl alcohol)	117.3	−89.5	35	0.810	1.3993	17.5	100	Flammable Irritant
2-Butanol (s-butyl alcohol)	99.5	−114.7	26	0.808	1.3978	16.6	100	Flammable Irritant
Carbon tetrachloride	76.5	−22.9	None	1.594	1.4601	2.2	10	Carcinogen Highly toxic
Chloroform	61.7	−63.5	None	1.483	1.4460	4.8	10	Carcinogen Photosensitive
Cyclohexane	80.7	6.6	−18	0.779	1.4266	2.0	300	Flammable Irritant
1,2-Dichloroethane (ethylene dichloride)	83.5	−35.4	15	1.235	1.4448	10.4	20	Carcinogen Flammable
Dichloromethane (methylene chloride)	39.8	−95.1	None	1.327	1.4242	8.9	200	Toxic Irritant
Diethyl ether	34.5	−116.2	−40	0.714	1.3526	4.3	400	Flammable Irritant Forms peroxides
Dimethoxyethane (glyme, ethylene glycol dimethyl ether)	83.0	−58.0	0	0.863	1.3796	7.2		Flammable Forms peroxides
N,N-Dimethyl-formamide	157.0	−60.5	57	0.949	1.4305	36.7	20	Irritant

Continued on p. 678

Table A1 *Cont.*

Solvent*	Bp (760 mmHg) (°C)	Mp (°C)	Flashpoint (°C)	Density, d^{20} (g mL^{-1})	Refractive index, n_D	Dielectric constant, ε	Toxicity, TLV† (ppm)	Hazards
Dimethylsulfoxide	189.0	18.5	95	1.101	1.4770	46.7		Irritant Readily adsorbed
1,4-Dioxan	101.3	11.8	12	1.034	1.4224	2.2	50	Carcinogen Flammable
Ethanoic acid	117.9	16.6		1.049	1.3716	6.2	10	Corrosive
Ethanol (ethyl alcohol)	78.5	−117.3	8	0.789	1.3611	24.6	1000	Flammable Toxic
Ethyl ethanoate	77.1	−83.6	−3	0.900	1.3723	6.0	400	Flammable Irritant
n-Hexane	69.0	−95.0	−23	0.660	1.3751	1.9	50	Flammable Irritant Toxic
Methanol (methyl alcohol)	65.0	−93.9	11	0.791	1.3288	32.7	200	Flammable Toxic
2-Methyl-2-propanol (*t*-butyl alcohol)	82.2	25.5	4	0.789	1.3878	12.7	100	Flammable
n-Pentane	36.1	−129.7	−49	0.626	1.3575	1.8	600	Flammable
1-Propanol (*n*-propyl alcohol)	97.4	−126.5	15	0.804	1.3850	20.3	200	Flammable Irritant
2-Propanol (isopropyl alcohol)	82.4	−89.5	22	0.786	1.3776	19.9	400	Flammable Irritant
Pyridine	115.5	−41.6	20	0.982	1.5095	12.4	5	Flammable Irritant
Tetrahydrofuran	67.0	−108.6	−17	0.889	1.4050	7.6	200	Flammable Irritant Forms peroxides
Toluene	110.6	−95.0	4	0.867	1.4961	2.4	200	Flammable Irritant
Xylene (isomers)	138–144	<−45	~25	~0.87	~1.50	2.4	200	Flammable Irritant

* Purification procedures are described (see Table A2).

† Threshold limit value: time-weighted average concentration for a normal 8 h working day to which nearly all workers may be repeatedly exposed without adverse effects. Absence of a quoted value must not be interpreted as absence of toxicity.

‡ Benzene has been proved to be a causative agent for leukaemia and its use should be avoided whenever possible. In particular, the use of benzene as a solvent is proscribed and toluene should be substituted, with due modification, in any procedure calling for benzene solvent.

For further information, see: I.M. Smallwood, *Handbook of Organic Solvent Properties*, Arnold, London, 1996; A. Collings and S.G. Luxon (eds), *Safe Use of Solvents*, Academic Press, New York, 1982.

Table A2 Purification procedures for commonly used laboratory solvents.

Solvent	Purification procedure	Hazards, boiling range, comments
(a) Aliphatic hydrocarbons		
Cyclohexane Hexane Light petroleum Pentane	If contaminated with olefins (particularly light petroleum) shake with concentrated sulfuric acid (1/10 volume of solvent), separate and wash with water. Dry (MgSO$_4$) and distil, discarding the initial fore-run which contains water	Flammable Hexane is toxic Cyclohexane: 79–82°C Hexane: 67–71°C Light petroleum: collect fraction distilling below 60°C Pentane: 35–37°C Light petroleum must always be distilled before use Distilled hydrocarbons may be stored in dark bottles more or less indefinitely without special precautions
(b) Aromatic hydrocarbons		
Benzene Toluene Xylene	Distil, rejecting milky fore-run (*ca.* 5%).	Benzene is carcinogenic Flammable Benzene: 79–81°C Toluene: 109–111°C Xylene: *ortho-* 143–146°C 　　　*meta-* 138–140°C 　　　*para-* 137–139°C Store as aliphatic hydrocarbons Use toluene in place of benzene wherever possible
(c) Chlorinated hydrocarbons		
Chloroform 1,2-Dichloroethane Dichloromethane	Distil, discarding wet fore-run (*ca.* 5%). Chloroform required for IR analyses should be passed through Activity I alumina immediately before use (25 g alumina : 500 mL chloroform).	Chloroform and 1,2-dichloroethane are possible carcinogens Never treat halogenated solvents with sodium as an explosion will result Chloroform is decomposed by light forming phosgene and rendering the solvent acidic Store as aliphatic hydrocarbons Chloroform should only be kept for limited periods in dark glass containers
(d) Ethers		
Diethyl ether	Test for peroxides by shaking for 1 min with acidified	Flammable

Continued on p. 680

Cont.

Solvent	Purification procedure	Hazards, boiling range, comments
Dimethoxyethane 1,4-Dioxan Tetrahydrofuran	10% aqueous potassium iodide. If positive (yellow colour) shake with 1/5 volume 5% aqueous sodium bisulfite until test for peroxides is negative. Small volumes may then be purified by passage through Activity I alumina. Dry by standing over potassium hydroxide pellets overnight and then over sodium wire. Very dry ethers are obtained by refluxing the sodium-dried material (1 L) over sodium (3 g) and benzophenone (1 g) until the mixture develops the deep purple colour of the sodium benzophenone ketyl. Distil and use immediately. Never distil to dryness. Never distil without verifying absence of peroxides	**Readily form explosive peroxides on storage** Diethyl ether: 33–35°C 1,2-Dimethoxymethane: 82–85°C Tetrahydrofuran: 64–66°C Diethyl ether may be kept over sodium wire. Ultra-dry solvents should be used immediately Always check for peroxides before distillation—distrust old or partially filled bottles in particular Such distillations need care and attention, and should only be carried out by experienced personnel
(e) Alcohols Ethanol Methanol	Add magnesium (5 g) to 50 mL alcohol in a 2 L round-bottomed flask. Add 0.5 g of iodine and heat to reflux until the iodine colour has disappeared. Be ready to remove the flask from the source of heat if the reaction becomes too vigorous. Make up the mixture to 1 L with alcohol and reflux for 0.5 h with protection from the atmosphere. Distil and use the dry alcohol immediately	**Flammable** Ethanol: 77–79°C Methanol: 63–66°C Use ultra-dry alcohols immediately
1-Butanol 2-Butanol	Distil, discarding initial fore-run (*ca.*10%) which contains water. Very dry material may be obtained by refluxing over and distilling from calcium hydride	1-Butanol: 115–119°C 2-Butanol: 98–101°C Use ultra-dry alcohols immediately
2-Methyl-2-propanol (*t*-butyl alcohol)	As for butanols, except that care must be taken to avoid blocking the condenser	2-Methyl-2-propanol: 81–83°C If the alcohol solidifies in cold weather, it should be melted by standing in warm (*ca.* 40°C) water. Do not heat the container more strongly
1-Propanol 2-Propanol	Distil, discarding initial fore-run (*ca.*10%) which contains water. Very dry material may be obtained by using the magnesium alkoxide method described for methanol and ethanol	1-Propanol: 96–98°C 2-Propanol: 81–84°C Use ultra-dry alcohols immediately

Continued

Table A2 *Cont.*

Solvent	Purification procedure	Hazards, boiling range, comments
(f) Miscellaneous		
Acetone	Dry over anhydrous calcium sulfate. Distil	Flammable Acetone: 55–57°C
Acetic acid	Add 5% acetic anhydride and 2% chromium (VI) oxide. Reflux and fractionate	Corrosive Ethanoic acid: 117–119°C Store in a screw-capped bottle
Acetonitrile	Dry over anhydrous potassium carbonate. Small quantities may be purified by passage through Activity I alumina. Larger quantities can be distilled from phosphorus pentoxide	Flammable Lachrymator Acetonitrile: 80–83°C Small volumes may be stored for short periods over 3Å molecular sieves. Seal the stopper with paraffin film
Dimethylformamide Dimethylsulfoxide	Stir over calcium hydride and distil *in vacuo*. Do not distil at atmospheric pressure as these solvents decompose	Irritant Toxic by skin absorption Hygroscopic Dimethylformamide: 41–43°C/ 10 mmHg, 53–56°C/20 mmHg Dimethylsulfoxide: 83–86°C/ 12 mmHg, 49–51°C/20 mmHg Dried solvent should be used immediately
Ethyl ethanoate	Stir over anhydrous potassium carbonate. Filter and distil	Flammable Ethyl acetate: 76–78°C Store over 5 Å sieves in screw-capped bottles
Pyridine Diisopropylamine	Dry for 24 h over potassium hydroxide pellets. Decant and distil from barium oxide or calcium hydride	Flammable Hygroscopic Pyridine: 114–117°C Diisopropylamine: 82–85°C Store over 5 Å sieves in screw-capped bottles

Note: This table contains guidelines for purification procedures. Further details may be found in the references below. The purification of certain solvents such as benzene, carbon disulfide and hexamethylphosphoramide should only be attempted by experienced workers, and only then after taking into account the very special hazardous properties associated with these solvents (procedures for purifying the latter two solvents are not given in this appendix).

With the exception of light petroleum, it is usually unnecessary to carry out extensive purification of solvents intended for extraction purposes. However, solvents intended for use in chromatography or recrystallization procedures require distillation before use. Owing to the presence of an appreciable proportion of high boiling residues in light petroleum, this solvent must always be distilled. Solvents for use with moisture-sensitive reagents require rigorous drying and distillation just prior to use.

All purifications involving reflux over a reagent followed by distillation, are most conveniently carried out using a solvent still expressly designed for such procedures (see Fig. 3.49).

References

For full details of purification procedures of these and other laboratory solvents, see: A.J. Gordon and R.A. Ford, *The Chemists' Companion*, Wiley (Interscience), New York, 1972, pp. 430–436;

D.D. Perrin and W.L.F. Armarego, *Purification of Laboratory Chemicals*, 3rd edn, Pergamon, New York, 1988.

Appendix 3 **Spectroscopic Correlation Tables**

IR correlation tables

Table A3   O–H bonds

Table A4   N–H bonds

Table A5   C–H bonds

Table A6   X≡Y bonds

Table A7   C=O bonds

Table A8   C=C bonds

Table A9   Other functional groups

NMR correlation tables

Table A10   Approximate proton chemical shifts of methyl groups CH_3–X

Table A11   Incremental rules for estimating the proton shifts of methylene and methine groups

Table A12   Incremental rules for estimating the chemical shifts of alkene protons

Table A13   Chemical shifts of some acidic protons

Table A14   Some proton–proton coupling constants

Table A15 ^{13}C chemical shift ranges

Table A16   Residual proton signals of common deuterated NMR solvents

UV correlation tables

Table A17   Woodward rules for UV absorption maxima of dienes

Table A18   Woodward rules for UV absorption maxima of α,β-unsaturated ketones in ethanol

Table A19   Solvent correction for UV absorption maxima of α,β-unsaturated ketones

MS correlation tables

Table A20   One-bond cleavage processes associated with common functional groups

Table A21   Common fragmentations

Table A22   Common fragment ions

IR correlation tables

Table A3 O–H bonds.

Group	Frequency (cm⁻¹)	Appearance	Comment
Free O–H	3600	Sharp	Usually only seen in dilute solution
Alcohol or phenol O–H (intermolecularly H-bonded)	3500–3100	Broad, strong	Sharpens on dilution of solution; look for alcohol C–O band (1300–1000)
Alcohol or phenol O–H (intramolecularly H-bonded)	3400–2500	Broad	Unaffected by dilution of solution
Carboxylic acid COO–H	3500–2500	Very broad	Always accompanied by strong C=O band (1730–1680)

Table A4 N–H bonds.

Group	Frequency (cm⁻¹)	Appearance	Comment
Amine N–H	3500–3000	Usually sharper and weaker than O–H	Two bands for primary amines; secondary amines much weaker; look for N–H bending band (1650–1550)
Amide CONH₂	3500–3300	Two bands (sharp)	In solid state occur at lower frequency; always accompanied by strong C=O bands (1700–1510)
Amide CONH (and lactams)	3450–3300	Two bands	As above; only one band for lactams
Amine salts NH₃⁺	3200–3000	Broad	Also show strong N–H bending (1600)

Table A5 C–H bonds.

Group	Frequency (cm⁻¹)	Appearance	Comment
–C≡C–H	3300	Sharp, quite intense	C–H stretch; look for triple bond absorption (2150–2100)
C=C–H	3100–3000	Weak	C–H stretch; easily obscured by stronger bands; look for C=C bands (1680–1500)
	1000–850	Strong	C–H out-of-plane deformation
Aromatic C–H	3050–3000	Weak	Often obscured; look for aromatic C=C peaks (1600–1500)
	850–730	Strong	C–H out-of-plane deformations; can often distinguish between o-, m- and p-substituted benzenes
sp³C–H	2980–2840	Strong	Two bands; C–H stretch
	1480–1420	Strong	C–H deformations
Aldehyde C–H	2900–2700	Often weak	Two bands; always accompanied by strong C=O peak (1740–1680)

Table A6 X≡Y bonds.

Group	Frequency (cm⁻¹)	Appearance	Comment
Non-terminal alkynes	2250–2150	Often weak	Intensity increased by conjugation; absent if alkyne is symmetrical or nearly symmetrical
Terminal alkynes	2150–2100	Often weak	Intensity increased by conjugation; look for the sharp C–H stretch (3300)
Nitriles	2270–2200	Often weak	

Table A7 C=O bonds.

Group	Frequency (cm⁻¹)	Appearance	Comment
Acid anhydrides	1850–1800 and 1790–1740	Strong	Two bands separated by about 60 cm⁻¹; lowered by 20 cm⁻¹ on conjugation
Acid chlorides	1815–1790	Strong	Lowered by 40–25 cm⁻¹ on conjugation
Esters	1750–1730	Strong	Lowered by about 20 cm⁻¹ on conjugation; look for strong C–O band (1300–1000)
Lactones: six-ring	1750–1730	Strong	And larger rings
Lactones: five-ring	1780–1760	Strong	Four-ring at 1830–1810
Aldehydes	1740–1695	Strong	Lowered by conjugation and H-bonding; look for C–H stretch (2900–2700)
Ketones: saturated	1730–1700	Strong	All classes lowered by H-bonding
Ketones: unsaturated	1700–1670	Strong	
Ketones: six-ring	1730–1700	Strong	And larger rings
Ketones: five-ring	1750–1740	Strong	Four-ring at 1790–1770
Carboxylic acids	1730–1700	Strong	Lowered by 20 cm⁻¹ on conjugation; always accompanied by broad O–H stretch (3500–2500)
Amides: primary	1690 and 1600	Strong; two bands	Values given are for solution; lowered in solid state; amide II less intense; look for N–H stretch (3500–3000); amide carbonyls are not lowered by conjugation
Amides: secondary	1700–1670 and 1550–1500	Strong; two bands	Lowered in solid state; amide II less intense; look for N–H stretch
Amides: tertiary	1670–1630	Strong	No N–H stretch!
Lactams: six-ring	1670	Strong	And larger rings
Lactams: five-ring	1700	Strong	Four-ring at 1760–1740

Table A8 C=C bonds.

Group	Frequency (cm⁻¹)	Appearance	Comment
Alkene C=C	1680–1640	Often weak	Absent in symmetrical alkenes
Diene C=C	1650–1600	Strong; two bands	Intensity increased by conjugation
Alkene C=C conjugated to aromatic ring	1640–1620	Medium intensity	
Alkene C=C conjugated to C=O	1650–1590	Strong	Intensity increased by conjugation; always accompanied by stronger C=O peak
Alkene C=C conjugated to lone pair of electrons (enamines, enol ethers)	1700–1650	Strong	Intensity increased by conjugation
Aromatic C=C	1600–1500	Two or three bands of medium intensity	Look for stronger C–H deformations (850–730)

Table A9 Other functional groups.

Group	Frequency (cm⁻¹)	Appearance	Comment
S–H	2500	Weak	
C=N	1700–1620	Often strong	Difficult to distinguish from C=C and (sometimes) C=O
–NO₂	1550 and 1350	Strong	
–SO₂–	1350 and 1150	Strong	
C–O	1300–1000	Strong	Esters (look for associated C=O), ethers, alcohols (look for associated O–H)
≡P=O	1300–1250	Strong	
–SiMe₃	1270	Strong	
C=S	1250–1050	Strong	
C–Cl	800–700	Strong	

NMR correlation tables

Table A10 Approximate proton chemical shifts of methyl groups CH_3-X.

X	δ	X	δ
Alkyl	0.90	OH	3.40
C=C	1.70	OR	3.25
C≡C	1.80	OAr	3.75
Ar	2.35	OAc	3.70
F	4.30	OCOAr	3.90
Cl	3.05	COR	2.10
Br	2.70	COAr	2.60
I	2.15	CHO	2.20
SH	2.00	CO_2H	2.10
SR	2.10	CO_2R	2.00
NH_2	2.50	CN	2.00
NHAc	2.70	$CONH_2$	2.00
NO_2	4.30		

Table A11 Incremental rules for estimating the proton shifts of methylene and methine groups (after E. Pretsch, T. Clerc, J. Seibl and W. Simon, *Tables of Spectral Data for the Structure Determination of Organic Compounds,* 2nd edn. Springer–Verlag, Berlin, 1989).

$$\delta CH_2R_1R_2 = 1.25 + \Delta_1 + \Delta_2;$$
$$\delta CHR_1R_2R_3 = 1.50 + \Delta_1 + \Delta_2 + \Delta_3$$

R	Δ	R	Δ
Alkyl	0.0	NR_2	1.0
C=C	0.8	NO_2	3.0
C≡C	0.9	SR	1.0
Ar	1.3	COR	1.2
OH	1.7	CO_2H	0.8
OR	1.5	CO_2R	0.7
OAr	2.3	Cl	2.0
OAc	2.7	Br	1.9
OCOAr	2.9	I	1.4
CN	1.2		

Note: these estimates are much more reliable for methylene groups than for methines.

Table A12 Incremental rules for estimating the chemical shifts of alkene protons (from U.E. Matter, C. Pascual, E. Pretsch, A. Pross, W. Simon and S. Sternhell, *Tetrahedron*, 1969, **25**, 691).

$$\delta C=CH = 5.25 + \Delta_{gem} = \Delta_{cis} = \Delta_{trans}$$

R	Δ_{gem}	Δ_{cis}	Δ_{trans}
Alkyl	0.45	−0.22	−0.28
Alkyl (ring)	0.69	−0.25	0.28
CH_2OR	0.64	−0.01	−0.02
CH_2Hal	0.70	0.11	−0.04
CH_2CN, CH_2COR	0.69	−0.08	−0.06
CH_2Ar	1.05	−0.29	−0.32
CH_2NR_2	0.58	−0.10	−0.08
C=C (isol.)	1.00	−0.09	−0.23
C=C (conj.)	1.24	0.02	−0.05
C≡C	0.47	0.38	0.12
Ar	1.38	0.36	−0.07
CN	0.27	0.75	0.55
COR (isol.)	1.10	1.12	0.87
COR (conj.)	1.06	0.91	0.74
CO_2H (isol.)	0.97	1.41	0.71
CO_2H (conj.)	0.80	0.98	0.32
CO_2R (isol.)	0.80	1.18	0.55
CO_2R (conj.)	0.78	1.01	0.46
CHO	1.02	0.95	1.17
$CONR_2$	1.37	0.98	0.46
OR	1.22	−1.07	−1.21
OAr, OC=C	1.21	−0.60	−1.00
OCOR	2.11	−0.35	−0.64
Cl	1.08	0.18	0.13
Br	1.07	0.45	0.55
I	1.14	0.81	0.88
NR_2	0.80	−1.26	−1.21
NRCOR	2.08	−0.57	−0.72
SR	1.11	−0.29	−0.13
SO_2	1.55	1.16	0.93

Note: the values designated 'conj.' are used when either the alkene or the substituent is involved in further conjugation. The values 'Alkyl (ring)' are used when the alkene and the alkyl group are both part of the same five- or six-membered ring.

Table A13 Chemical shifts of some acidic protons (very variable according to conditions).

	δ		δ
RCO$_2$H	8–14	RCONHR	5–12
ROH	0.5–4.5	ArOH	5–7
RNHR	1–5	ArNHR	3–6
RSH	1–2	ArSH	3–4
Oxime	9–12		

Table A14 Some proton–proton coupling constants.

	$|J|$ (typical range) (Hz)
H–C–H (*geminal*)	10–15
H–C–C–H (*vicinal*, free rotation)	≈7
C=Ch–CH	5–7
C=CH–Ch=C	10–13
HC=CH (*cis*)	9–12
HC=CH (*trans*)	14–16
C=CHH (*geminal*)	1–2
Cyclohexane, three-bond, *ax–ax*	10–13
Cyclohexane, *ax–eq* and *eq–eq*	2–5
Phenyl, 1,2	7–8
Phenyl, 1,3	1–2
Phenyl, 1,4	0–1
CH=C–CH (allylic)	1–2
CH≡C–CH	2–3
CH–C≡C–CH	0–1

Table A15 ^{13}C chemical shift ranges.

	δ		δ
Alkanes	0–50	Ketone C=O	190–220
Alkenes	100–140	Aldehyde C=O	185–205
Alkynes	75–105	Acid C=O	165–185
Arenes	115–145	Ester C=O	155–180
CH$_3$–C=C	5–30	Amide C=O	155–180
CH$_3$–O	50–60	C≡N	110–125
CH$_3$–(Cl,Br)	10–25	CH$_3$–I	–21
CH$_3$–N	15–45	CH$_3$–F	75
RCH$_2$–C=C	25–55	R$_2$CH–C=C	35–65
RCH$_2$–O	35–75	R$_2$CH–O	65–90
RCH$_2$–N	40–60	R$_2$CH–N	50–70
RCH$_2$–S	25–45	R$_2$CH–S	55–65
R$_3$C–C=C	30–50	R$_3$C–O	75–85
R$_3$C–N	65–75	R$_3$C–S	55–75

Table A16 Residual proton signals of common deuterated NMR solvents.

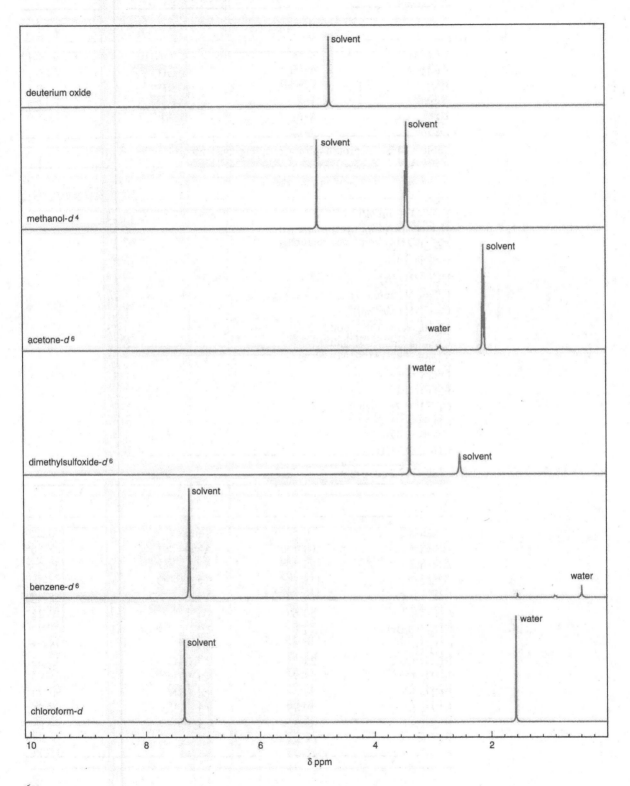

UV correlation tables

Table A17 Woodward rules for the UV absorption maxima of dienes.

Acyclic diene e.g.	Heteroannular diene e.g.	Homoannular diene e.g.

Value for parent acyclic diene		214 nm
Value for parent heteroannular diene		214
Value for parent homoannular diene		253

Increments to be added

If an additional double bond extends conjugation	30
If one of the diene double bonds is exocyclic	5

Increments to be added for substituents (auxochromes)

Alkyl group	5
Ring residue	5
Halogen (Cl, Br)	5
Alkoxy group (OR)	6
Acyloxy group (OCOR)	0
Alkylthio group (SR)	30
Dialkylamino group (NR_2)	60

Table A18 Woodward rules for the UV absorption maxima of α,β-unsaturated ketones in ethanol.*

Acyclic	Six-ring	Five-ring

	Five-ring
Value for parent acyclic α,β-unsaturated ketone	215 nm
Value for parent six-ring α,β-unsaturated ketone	215
Value for parent five-ring α,β-unsaturated ketone	202

Increments to be added

If an additional double bond extends conjugation	30
If one of the double bond is exocyclic	5

Increments to be added for α-substituents (auxochromes)

Alkyl group	10
Ring residue	10
Hydroxyl group (OH)	35
Alkoxy group (OR)	35
Acyloxy group (OCOR)	6
Chloro group (Cl)	15
Bromo group (Br)	25

Increments to be added for β-substituents (auxochromes)

Alkyl group	12
Ring residue	12
Hydroxyl group (OH)	30
Alkoxy group (OR)	30
Acyloxy group (OCOR)	6
Chloro group (Cl)	12
Bromo group (Br)	30
Alkylthio group (SR)	85
Dialkylamino group (NR_2)	95

* For values in other solvents a solvent correction must be applied (see Table A19).

Table A19 Solvent correction for UV absorption maxima of α,β-unsaturated ketones.

The rules for the absorption maxima of α,β-unsaturated ketones apply to spectra that are run in ethanol. To calculate the expected λ_{max} in other solvents, proceed as follows:

1 using Table A18, calculate the expected λ_{max} in ethanol;
2 subtract the solvent correction factor given below

Solvent	Correction (nm)
Water	−8
Methanol	0
Hexane	11
Chloroform	1

MS correlation tables

Table A20 One-bond cleavage processes associated with common functional groups.

Functional group	Fragmentation

Alcohol

$$\left[\begin{array}{c} R \\ HC-OH \\ R \end{array}\right]^{+\cdot} \xrightarrow{-R\bullet} R-\overset{+}{\underset{H}{C}}=OH$$

Amine

$$\left[\begin{array}{c} R^1 \\ N-CH_2R^2 \\ R^{1'} \end{array}\right]^{+\cdot} \xrightarrow{-R^2\bullet} \begin{array}{c} R^1 \\ \overset{+}{N}=CH_2 \\ R^{1'} \end{array} \xrightarrow{\quad} R^1-\overset{+}{\underset{H}{N}}=CH_2$$

Ester

$$\left[\begin{array}{c} R^1 \\ C=O \\ R^2O \end{array}\right]^{+\cdot} \begin{array}{l} \xrightarrow{-OR^2\bullet} R^1-\overset{+}{C}\equiv O \qquad \text{major} \\ \xrightarrow{-R^1\bullet} \overset{+}{O}\equiv C-OR^2 \qquad \text{minor} \end{array}$$

Ether

$$\left[\begin{array}{c} R^1 \\ HC-OR^2 \\ R^1 \end{array}\right]^{+\cdot} \xrightarrow{-R^1\bullet} R^1-\overset{+}{\underset{H}{C}}=OR^2 \xrightarrow{\quad} R^1-\overset{+}{\underset{H}{C}}=\overset{\cdot\cdot}{O}H$$

Halide

$$\left[\begin{array}{c} R-X \end{array}\right]^{+\cdot} \xrightarrow{-X\bullet} R^+ \qquad (R = \text{aryl or tertiary alkyl})$$

$$\left[\begin{array}{cc} R^1 & R^3 \\ HC-CX & \\ R^2 & R^4 \end{array}\right]^{+\cdot} \xrightarrow{-HX} \left[\begin{array}{cc} R^1 & R^3 \\ & \\ R^2 & R^4 \end{array}\right]^{+\cdot}$$

Ketal

$$\left[\begin{array}{c} R \\ R \end{array}\bigcirc\bigcirc\right]^{+\cdot} \xrightarrow{-R\bullet} R-C\bigcirc^{+}$$

Table A21 Common fragmentations.

m/z	Possible fragment lost and conclusion
M – 1, M – 2	H, H$_2$
M – 14	M is not the molecular ion. Loss of CH$_2$ disfavoured
M – 15	CH$_3$
M – 17	OH, NH$_3$
M – 18	H$_2$O loss from alcohol, aldehyde, ketone
M – 26	CN, C$_2$H$_2$
M – 28	CO, C$_2$H$_4$, N$_2$
M – 29	C$_2$H$_5$, CHO
M – 30	NO, C$_2$H$_6$
M – 31	CH$_3$O
M – 35	Cl
M – 42	CH$_2$CO loss from methyl ketone or aromatic acetate C$_3$H$_6$
M – 43	CH$_3$CO loss from methyl ketone C$_3$H$_7$
M – 44	CO$_2$
M – 45	C$_2$H$_5$O, CO$_2$H
M – 46	NO$_2$
M – 55	C$_4$H$_7$ from butyl ester
M – 60	CH$_3$CO$_2$H loss from acetate, HCO$_2$CH$_3$ from tertiary esters, CH$_2$NO$_2$
M – 77	C$_6$H$_5$
M – 79	Br
M – 81	
M – 91	PhCH$_2$ (tropylium), C$_6$H$_5$N
M – 93	CH$_2$Br
M – 105	PhCO
M – 127	I

Table A22 Common fragment ions.

m/z	Possible fragment and conclusion
15	CH_3^+
18	$H_2O^{+\cdot}$
26	$C_2H_2^{+\cdot}$
28	$CO^{+\cdot}, C_2H_4^{+\cdot}, N_2^{+\cdot}, CH_2N^{+\cdot}$
29	$CHO^+, C_2H_5^+$
30	$CH_2=NH_2^+$ (primary amine)
31	$CH_2=OH^+$ (primary alcohol)
36/38	$HCl^{+\cdot}$
40	$Ar^{+\cdot}, C_3H_4^+$ (useful reference peak)
43	$CH_3CO^+, C_3H_7^+$
44	$O=C=NH_2^+$ (primary amide), $CO_2^{+\cdot}$
	$CH_2=CHOH^{+\cdot}$ (aldehyde)
45	$CH_2=OCH_3^+, CH_3CH=OH^+$ (ether or alcohol)
49/51	CH_2Cl^+
58	$CH_2=C(OH)CH_3^{+\cdot}$ (methyl ketone)
59	$CO_2CH_3^+$ (methyl ester), $CH_2=C(OH)NH_2^+$ (primary amide), $CH_2=OC_2H_5^+$
65	C_5H_5 (fragmentation from tropylium ion—$PhCH_2X$)
73	$(CH_3)_3Si^+$
77	$C_6H_5^+$
79/81	Br^+
80/81	HBr^+
81	
85	(tetrahydropyranyl ether)
91	Tropylium ion ($PhCH_2X$)
93/95	CH_2Br^+
127	I^+
128	$HI^{+\cdot}$
149	(from plasticizer contaminating sample)

The Periodic Table A23

key to chart

- new notation
- previous IUPAC form
- CAS version

atomic number	50 +2 +4
symbol	Sn
1995 atomic weight	118.710 −18−18−4
	oxidation states
	electron configuration

Group 1 IA	2 IIA		3 IIIA IIIB	4 IVA IVB	5 VA VB	6 VIA VIB	7 VIIA VIIB	8 VIIIA VIII	9 VIIIA VIII	10	11 IB IB	12 IIB IIB	13 IIIB IIIA	14 IVB IVA	15 VB VA	16 VIB VIA	17 VIIB VIIA	18 VIIIA	Shell
1 +1 −1 **H** 1.00794 1																		2 0 **He** 4.002602 2	K
3 + **Li** 6.941 2−1	4 +2 **Be** 9.012182 2−2												5 +3 **B** 10.811 2−3	6 **C** 12.0107 2−4	7 **N** 14.00674 2−5	8 −2 **O** 15.9994 2−6	9 **F** 18.9934032 2−7	10 0 **Ne** 20.1791 2−8	K−L
11 +1 **Na** 22.91970 2−2−1	12 +2 **Mg** 24.3050 2−8−2												13 +3 **Al** 26.981538 2−8−3	14 **Si** 28.0855 2−8−4	15 **P** 30.971761 2−8−5	16 **S** 32.066 2−8−6	17 **Cl** 35.4527 2−8−7	18 0 **Ar** 39.918 2−8−8	K−L−M
19 +1 **K** 39.0983 −8−8−1	20 +2 **Ca** 40.078 −8−8−2		21 +3 **Sc** 44.955910 −8−9−2	22 +2 +3 +4 **Ti** 47.867 −8−10−2	23 +2 +3 +4 +5 **V** 50.9415 −8−11−2	24 +2 +3 +6 **Cr** 51.9961 −8−13−1	25 +2 +3 +4 +6 +7 **Mn** 54.938049 −8−13−2	26 +2 +3 **Fe** 55.845 −8−13−2	27 +2 +3 **Co** 58.933200 −8−15−2	28 +2 +3 **Ni** 58.6934 −8−16−2	29 +1 +2 **Cu** 63.546 −8−18−1	30 +2 **Zn** 65.39 −8−18−2	31 +3 **Ga** 69.723 −8−18−3	32 +2 +4 **Ge** 72.61 −8−18−4	33 +3 +5 −3 **As** 74.92160 −8−18−5	34 +4 +6 −2 **Se** 78.96 −8−18−6	35 +1 +5 −1 **Br** 79.904 −8−18−7	36 0 **Kr** 83.80 −8−18−8	−L−M−N
37 +1 **Rb** 85.4678 −18−8−1	38 +2 **Sr** 87.62 −18−8−2		39 +3 **Y** 88.90585 −18−9−2	40 +4 **Zr** 91.224 −18−20−2	41 +3 +5 **Nb** 92.90638 −18−12−1	42 +6 **Mo** 95.94 −18−13−1	43 +7 **Tc** (98) −18−13−2	44 +3 **Ru** 101.07 −18−15−1	45 +3 **Rh** 102.90550 −18−16−1	46 +2 +4 **Pd** 106.42 −18−18−0	47 +1 **Ag** 107.8682 −18−18−1	48 +2 **Cd** 112.411 −18−18−2	49 +3 **In** 114.818 −18−18−3	50 +2 +4 **Sn** 118.710 −18−18−4	51 +3 +5 −3 **Sb** 121.760 −18−18−5	52 +4 +6 −2 **Te** 127.60 −18−18−6	53 +1 +5 +7 −1 **I** 126.90447 −18−18−7	54 0 **Xe** 131.29 −18−18−8	−M−N−O
55 +1 **Cs** 132.90545 −18−8−1	56 +2 **Ba** 137.327 −18−8−2	57* +3 **La** 138.9055 18−9−2	72 +4 **Hf** 178.49 −32−10−2	73 +5 **Ta** 180.5479 −32−11−2	74 +6 **W** 183.84 −32−12−2	75 +4 +6 +7 **Re** 186.307 −32−13−2	76 +3 +4 **Os** 190.23 −32−14−2	77 +3 +4 **Ir** 191.217 −32−15−2	78 +2 +4 **Pt** 195.078 −32−17−1	79 +1 +3 **Au** 196.96655 −32−18−1	80 +1 +2 **Hg** 200.59 −32−18−2	81 +1 +3 **Tl** 204.3833 −32−18−3	82 +2 +4 **Pb** 207.2 −32−18−4	83 +3 +5 **Bi** 208.98038 −32−18−5	84 +2 +4 **Po** (209) −32−18−6	85 **At** (210) −32−18−7	86 0 **Rn** (222) −32−18−8	−N−O−P
87 +1 **Fr** (223) −18−8−1	88 +2 **Ra** (226) −18−8−2	89** +3 **Ac** (227) −18−9−2	104 +4 **Unq** (261) −32−10−2	105 **Unp** (262) −32−11−2	106 **Unh** (263) −32−12−2	107 **Uns** (262) −32−19−2	108 **Uno** (265) −32−14−2	109 **Une** (266) −32−15−2	110 **Uun** (269) −32−16−2									−O−P−Q

Lanthanides*

58 +3 +4 **Ce** 140.116 −19−8−2	59 +3 **Pr** 140.90765 −21−8−2	60 +3 **Nd** 144.24 −22−8−2	61 +3 **Pm** (237) −23−8−2	62 +2 +3 **Sm** 150.36 −24−8−2	63 +2 +3 **Eu** 151.964 −25−8−2	64 +3 **Gd** 157.25 −25−9−2	65 +3 **Tb** 158.92534 −27−8−2	66 +3 **Dy** 162.50 −28−8−2	67 +3 **Ho** 164.93032 −29−8−2	68 +3 **Er** 167.26 −30−8−2	69 +3 **Tm** 168.93421 −31−8−2	70 +2 +3 **Yb** 173.04 −32−8−2	71 +3 **Lu** 174.967 −32−9−2

Shell: −N−O−P

Actinides**

90 +4 **Th** 232.0381 −18−10−2	91 +5 +4 **Pa** 231.03588 −20−9−2	92 +3 +4 +5 +6 **U** 218.0289 −21−9−2	93 +3 +4 +5 +6 **Np** (237) −22−9−2	94 +3 +4 +5 +6 **Pu** (241) −24−8−2	95 +3 +4 +5 +6 **Am** (243) −25−8−2	96 +3 **Cm** (247) −25−9−2	97 +3 +4 **Bk** (247) −26−9−2	98 +3 +4 **Cf** (251) −28−8−2	99 +3 **Es** (252) −29−8−2	100 +3 **Fm** (257) −30−8−2	101 +2 +3 **Md** (258) −31−8−2	102 +2 +3 **No** (259) −32−8−2	103 +3 **Lr** (262) −32−9−2

Shell: −O−P−Q

The new IUPAC format numbers the groups from 1 to 18. The previous IUPAC numbering system and the system used by Chemical Abstracts Service (CAS) are also shown. For radioactive elements that do not occur in nature, the mass number of the most stable isotope is given in parentheses.

References 1. G. I. Leigh, Editor, *Nomenclature of Inorganic Chemistry*, Blackwell Science Publications, Oxford, 1990.
2. *Chemical and Engineering News*, 63(5), 27, 1985.
3. Atomic Weights of the Elements, 1995. *Pure & Appl. Chem.*, 68, 2339, 1996.

Index of Chemicals

Acesulpham® 633–4
acetaldehyde (ethanal) 533–4
acetanilide (*N*-phenylethanamide)
    296–8, 440–3
acetic acid (ethanoic acid) 57, 59, 142,
    164, 251, 252, 262, 430–3, 452–3,
    625–6, 670, 677, 681
    glacial 232, 248, 252, 259, 438–9,
        440–3, 492–3, 517, 543–4, 545–6,
        600–2, 605–7, 625–6, 644–6, 664–5
acetic anhydride (ethanoic anhydride)
    247, 248, 250, 271–2, 440–3, 547–8,
    550–2, 586–8, 647–8, 670, 681
acetone 7, 16, 22, 24, 43–5, 59, 105, 107,
    116, 134, 136, 139, 182, 196, 219,
    250, 311, 465–6, 478–9, 497, 524–5,
    532, 537–9, 540–1, 543–4, 557,
    564–6, 578–80, 605–7, 623, 653–4,
    670, 677, 681, 690
acetonitrile (methyl cyanide) 107, 311,
    631–3, 658–9, 677, 681
acetophenone 654–7, 662–5
acetophenone azine 662–5
cis-2-acetoxycyclohexanol 452–3
acetyl chloride 239, 248, 249, 250, 586–8,
    670
2-acetylcyclohexanone 547–8
allyl bromide (3-bromoprop-1-ene)
    423, 553–4, 605–7, 670
allyl chloride 670
2-allylphenol 605–9
allyl phenyl ether (2-propenyloxy-
    benzene) 605–9
alumina 162–3, 177, 491, 640–1, 670, 679,
    680, 681
aluminium chloride 9, 241, 481, 583–5,
    586–90, 670
3-aminoacetophenone 480–1
2-aminobenzoic acid (anthranilic acid)
    516–18, 597–600
1-aminobenzotriazole 597
ammonia
    gas 9, 66, 103, 170, 241, 243, 260, 266–
        7, 385, 391, 642, 670
    liquid 104–5, 428, 497–8, 553–4
    solution 142, 231–2, 260–1, 270,
        634–5
        concentrated 238, 269, 270–1,
            272–3, 520
ammonium acetate 644–6

ammonium chloride 107, 553–4, 558–9,
    577–80
ammonium hydroxide 9, 645–6, 670
ammonium molybdate 170, 231, 233
ammonium nitrate 231
amyl alcohol (3-methylbutan-1-ol)
    430–3
aniline 9, 269, 270, 371, 440–3, 670
anthracene 242
anthranilic acid (2-aminobenzoic acid)
    516–18, 597–600
argon 64, 82, 95
aryloxyacetic acid 257–8
arylsulfonyl chloride 246–7
Aspartame® 633–4
aspirin 612–13

barium oxide 681
benzaldehyde 249, 427–9, 535–6, 537–9,
    562–3, 638–9, 642, 644–6, 662–5,
    670
benzaldehyde azine 662–5
benzaldehyde dimethylacetal 321
benzaldoxime 427–9, 609–11
benzene 7, 9, 10, 116, 214–6, 242, 311,
    349, 371, 423, 670, 677–8, 679,
    681–2, 690
benzenediazonium-2-carboxylate
    597–600
benzenesulfonyl chloride 273–4
benzhydrol (diphenylmethanol) 473–5
benzil 642, 644–6
benzoic acid 382–3, 562, 651–2
benzoin 477–9
benzophenone 473–5, 557–9, 680
1,4-benzoquinone 601–2
benzoyl chloride 246, 248, 250, 272–3,
    585, 625–6, 670
2-benzoyloxyacetophenone 624–6
benzoyl peroxide 463–4, 468–71
benzopyrene 10
benzyl acetate 314–5, 317, 326, 394
benzyl alcohol 249
benzyl bromide 670
benzyl chloride 569–71, 577–80, 670
O-benzylhydroxylamine 417
S-benzylisothiouronium chloride 245,
    268
2-benzylpyridine 643–4
benzyl thiol 245, 268

benzyltrimethylammonium chloride
    604
benzyltriphenylphosphonium chloride
    562–3
benzyne (1,2-didehydrobenzene)
    597–600
bicyclo[3.2.0]hept-2-en-6-one 600–2
bicyclo[2.1.1]hexane 333
biphenyl 242, 670
γ-bisabolene 616
(*N,O*-bis(trimethylsilyl)acetamide)
    196–7
(*N,O*-bis(trimethylsilyl)
    trifluoroacetamide) 196–7
bleach (sodium hypochlorite) 8, 104,
    231, 609–10, 645, 675
borane 462
borane dimethylsulfide 461–2
boron trifluoride 583
boron trifluoride etherate 586–9
bromine 9, 248, 383–4, 391
    solid 517, 670
    solution 246, 251, 262–3, 439–43
    water 240, 492–3, 614–15
p-bromoacetanilide (*N*-(4-
    bromophenyl)ethanamide)
    440–3
4-bromoacetophenone 518–21
4-bromoaniline (*p*-bromoaniline)
    439–43
bromobenzene 523–5, 585, 670
4-bromobenzophenone 584–5
1-bromobutane 465–6
2-bromobutane 526–7
1-bromobutyrolactone 566–8
trans-2-bromocyclohexanol 447–50
bromoethane 671
bromohydrin 447–50
4-bromomethylbenzoic acid 468–71,
    564–6
2-bromopentane 444, 628–9
4-bromophenacyl bromide (2,4-
    dibromoacetophenone) 268–9
4-bromophenacyl ester 268–9
N-(4-bromophenyl)ethanamide (*p*-
    bromoacetanilide) 440–3
3-bromoprop-1-ene (allyl bromide)
    423, 553–4, 605–7, 670
N-bromosuccinimide 447–50, 468–71,
    574–80, 671

bromotrichloromethane 462–4
butadiene 358–9, 591–2
butadiene sulfone (sulfolene) (2,5-
    dihydrothiophene-1,1-dioxide)
    591–2
butanal (butyraldehyde) 302, 304
1-butanol (*n*-butyl alcohol) 117, 122,
    170, 677, 680
2-butanol (*s*-butyl alcohol) 253, 433–4,
    671, 677, 680
butenal (crotonaldehyde) 304–5
butenedioic anhydride (maleic
    anhydride) 592–4, 594–7, 673
but-2-enoic acid (crotonic acid)
    433–4
n-butyl alcohol (1-butanol) 117, 122,
    170, 677, 680
s-butyl alcohol (2-butanol) 253, 433–4,
    671, 677, 680
t-butyl alcohol (2-methyl-2-propanol)
    678, 680
s-butyl but-2-enoate (*s*-butyl crotonate)
    433–4, 525–7
t-butyl chloride (2-chloro-2-methyl
    propane) 530–2
s-butyl crotonate (*s*-butyl but-2-enoate)
    433–4, 525–7
4-*t*-butylcyclohexanone 475–7
t-butylhydroperoxide 458–60
n-butyl-lithium 84, 529–33, 555–7,
    558–9, 561, 577–80, 671
butylmagnesium bromide 525
s-butyl 3-methylheptanoate 525–7
n-butyl phthalate 379
n-butyraldehyde (butanal) 302, 304
butyric acid 10
butyrolactone 485–8

caffein 619–20
calcium chloride 82, 107, 127, 141–2,
    469, 470, 524, 526, 528, 541, 547–8,
    589, 625
calcium hydride 680
calcium oxide 127
calcium sulfate 127, 141–2, 162, 681
camphor 616
ε-caprolactone 514–15
carbon 229, 383–4
    activated 511–12
carbon dioxide
    gas 83, 245, 290, 300, 516–18, 536, 597,
        641
    solid 43–5, 59, 105, 107, 136, 154, 158,
        487, 497, 532, 557
carbon disulfide 8, 27, 282, 681–2
carbon monoxide 387–9, 641
carbon tetrachloride 10, 282, 487, 550–2,
    671, 677, 679
4-carboxybenzyltriphenylphosphonium
    bromide 564–5
carvone 494–6
cerium sulfate 170
chlorine 66, 103, 383–4, 391, 675
    water 231–2
chloroacetic acid 257–8

β-chloroacrylic acid (*Z*-3-
    chloropropenoic acid) 315
chlorobenzene 469–70, 671
chloroform 3, 9, 10, 107, 116, 241, 260–1,
    282–4, 297, 311, 348–9, 423,
    499–500, 511–12, 547–8, 586–8,
    603–5, 620–1, 658–9, 671, 677, 679,
    690
2-chloro-2-methyl propane) (*t*-butyl
    chloride) 530–2
3-chloroperbenzoic acid 671
2-chlorophenol 293–4
3-chlorophenol 650
4-chlorophenol 650
chloroplatinic acid (hydrogen
    hexachloroplatinate) 492–3
Z-3-chloropropenoic acid (β-
    chloroacrylic acid) 315
chlorosulfonic acid 260, 260–1, 634–5
chlorotrimethylsilane 549–552, 555
cholesta-3,5-diene 369
cholesta-5,7-diene-1,3-diol 369
cholesterol (3β-hydroxy-5α,6α-
    epoxycholestane) 455–8, 491–3
chromic acid 22, 237, 501–7
chromium (VI) oxide 8, 248, 250, 252,
    507–10, 634–5, 671, 681
trans-chrysanthemic acid 616
cinnamaldehyde (*E*-3-phenylpropenal)
    570–1
cinnamic acid (*E*-3-phenylpropenoic
    acid) 535–7
cinnamyl alcohol (*E*-3-phenyl-2-
    propenol) 510–13
cinnamyl aldehyde (*E*-3-phenyl-2-
    propenal) 510–13
copper (II) acetate monohydrate
    638–9
copper (II) chloride 636–7
copper phthalocyanine 636–7
copper (II) sulfate 55
3-cresol 650
4-cresol 650
crotonaldehyde (butenal) 304–5
crotonic acid (but-2-enoic acid) 433–4
cyanin 624
cyclamate 633–4
cycloheptanone 631–3
cycloheptatriene 646–9
cyclohexane 59, 134, 164, 463, 671, 677,
    679
cyclohexanecarboxylic acid 293, 295,
    434–5
cis-cyclohexane-1,2-diol 451–3
trans-cyclohexane-1,2-diol 447–50,
    451
cyclohexanone 302–3, 546–8, 572–4,
    659–62, 671
cyclohexene 444, 447–50, 452–3
cyclohexene oxide 448–50
cis-cyclohex-4-ene-1,2-dicarboxylic acid
    591–4
cyclohexylamine 295–6, 386
cyclopentadiene 600–2, 671
cyclopentanone 302–3

daphnetoxin 617
1-deuterio-1-phenylethanol 654–7
deuterium oxide 347–52, 690
1,5-diazabicyclo[4.3.0]non-5-ene 636–7
diazomethane 248, 252
2,4-dibromoacetophenone (4-
    bromophenacyl bromide) 268–9
1,4-dibromobenzene 394–5
trans-1,2-dibromocyclohexane 444
2,6-di-*t*-butyl-*p*-cresol 379
1,2-dichlorethane 679
dichloroacetyl chloride 600–2
7,7-dichlorobicyclo[3.2.0]hept-2-en-6-
    one 600–2
dichlorocarbene 603–5
(2,2-dichlorocyclopropyl)benzene
    603–4
1,2-dichloroethane (ethylene
    dichloride) 259–60, 677
dichloroketene 600–2
dichloromethane (methylene chloride)
    58, 109, 116, 119–122, 134, 182,
    196, 228, 311, 454–5, 456–8,
    459–60, 473–5, 478–9, 507–10,
    514–15, 562, 578–80, 586–8,
    609–10, 614–15, 618, 631–3, 641,
    647–8, 653–4, 658–9, 671, 677,
    679
1,3-dichloro-5-nitrobenzene 395
dicyclohexylcarbodiimide 501, 671
dicyclopentadiene 601–2, 671
1,2-didehydrobenzene (benzyne)
    597–600
4,6-diethoxycarbonyl-3-
    methylcyclohex-2-enone 545–6
diethyl benzylphosphonate 569–71
diethylene glycol (2-hydroxyethyl
    ether) 266, 489
diethyleneglycol succinate 194
diethyl ether 7–8, 121–2, 124, 134, 164,
    177, 256–8, 265, 267, 430–3, 433–4,
    438–9, 448–50, 452–3, 461–2,
    465–6, 475–7, 480–1, 482–5, 487,
    490, 495–6, 502–7, 538–9, 540–1,
    545–6, 547–8, 558–9, 564–6, 572–
    4, 577–80, 585, 589–90, 598–600,
    601–2, 604, 605–7, 620–1, 628–9,
    634–5, 643–4, 664–5, 671, 677,
    680
    anhydrous 484–5, 497–8, 508–10,
        524–5, 526–7, 528–9, 530–2, 553–
        4, 567–8, 628–9, 631–3, 647–8,
        655–7
diethyl malonate (diethyl
    propanedioate) 540–2, 672
diethyl propanedioate (diethyl
    malonate) 540–2, 672
diethyl tartrate 458–60
diglyme (2-methoxyethyl ether) 461–2,
    592–4, 636–7
7,8-dihydrocarvone 494–6
dihydrojasmone 370
1,4-dihydronaphthalene-1,4-endoxide
    597–600
dihydroquinine phthalazine 454–5

2,5-dihydrothiophene-1,1-dioxide (butadiene sulfone, sulfolene) 591–2
diisobutylaluminium hydride (hydridobis(2-methylpropyl)-aluminium) 33, 473, 485–8
diisopropylamine 555–7, 672, 681
1,3-diketone 228
dimedone (5,5-dimethylcyclohexane-1,3-dione) 540–2
2,5-dimethoxybenzyl alcohol 530–2
dimethoxyethane (glyme, ethylene glycol dimethyl ether) 677, 680
1,2-dimethoxyethane 567–8, 597–600
N,N-dimethylacetamide 346
dimethylamine 542–4
3-(N,N-dimethylaminomethyl)indole (gramine) 542–4
1,2-dimethylbenzene (o-xylene) 496–8
2,3-dimethyl-1,3-butadiene 594–7
2,3-dimethylbutan-2,3-diol (pinacol) 594–7
2,3-dimethylbutane-2-one (pinacolone) 594–7
1,2-dimethyl-1,4-cyclohexadiene 497–8
5,5-dimethylcyclohexane-1,3-dione (dimedone) 540–2
4,5-dimethyl-cis-cyclohex-4-ene-1,2-dicarboxylic anhydride 596
3-(1,1-dimethyl)ethyl-2,2,4,4-tetramethylpentan-3-ol (tri-t-butylcarbinol) 529–33
dimethylformamide 105, 542–4, 549–552, 567–8, 638–9, 672, 681
N,N-dimethylformamide 677
(E)-3,7-dimethyl-2,6-octadien-1-ol (geraniol) 458–60, 616
dimethylsilicone 194
dimethyl sulfate 9, 10
dimethyl sulfide 10, 59, 572, 631–3
dimethyl sulfoxide 59, 105, 311, 489, 501, 572–4, 672, 678, 681, 690
dimethylsulfoxonium methylide 572–4
dinaphthylurea 255
2,4-dinitrobenzenesulfenyl chloride 258–9
2,4-dinitrobenzenesulfonyl chloride 241
3,5-dinitrobenzoate 256–7
3,5-dinitrobenzoyl chloride 240, 248, 251, 256–7
3,5-dinitrobenzoyl ether 258–9
2,4-dinitrophenylhydrazine 170, 235, 248, 254, 437, 672
2,4-dinitrophenylhydrazone 237–8, 254
2-[(2,4-dinitrophenyl)methyl]pyridine 642–4
dioxan 238, 653–4, 672
1,4-dioxan 352, 678, 680
2,2-diphenylacetic acid 482–5
9,10-diphenylanthracene 641
E,E-1,4-diphenyl-1,3-butadiene 569–71
4,4-diphenylbut-3-en-2-one 523–5
E-diphenylethene (stilbene) 561–3

trans-1,2-diphenylethene (trans-stilbene) 453–5
Z-1,2-diphenylethene 562
1,2-diphenylethene-1,2-diol 454–5
3,5-diphenylisoxazoline 609–11
diphenylmethanol (benzhydrol) 473–5
2,6-diphenyl-4-(2,4,6-triphenylpyridinio) phenolate 653–4
diphenylurea 255
dipotassium osmate 454–5
disodium pentacyanonitrosyl ferrate 230–2

(2S,3S)-epoxygeraniol 460
ethanal (acetaldehyde) 533–4
ethane-1,2-diol (ethylene glycol) 106, 107, 436–7, 672
ethanoic acid (acetic acid) 57, 59, 142, 164, 251, 252, 262, 430–3, 452–3, 625–6, 670, 677, 681
    glacial 232, 248, 252, 259, 438–9, 440–3, 492–3, 517, 543–4, 545–6, 600–2, 605–7, 625–6, 644–6, 664–5
ethanol (ethyl alcohol) 7, 108, 115, 116, 117, 134, 142, 170, 214–6, 228, 240–1, 242, 254–65, 268–74, 283, 324, 364–5, 372, 441, 443, 472, 473–81, 493, 494–6, 511–12, 519–20, 526–7, 529, 530–2, 538–9, 562, 564–6, 571, 583, 598–600, 601–2, 610, 620, 623, 643–4, 645–6, 653–4, 664–5, 672, 678, 680, 692–3
    absolute 497–8, 540–1, 647–8
ethene 358–9
ethyl acetate 7, 116, 121–2, 134, 164, 182, 185, 228, 254, 333, 448–50, 473–5, 499–500, 538–9, 562, 567–8, 601–2, 672, 678, 681
ethyl acetoacetate (ethyl 3-oxobutanoate) 436–7, 498–500, 545–6, 558–9, 672
ethyl alcohol (ethanol) 7, 108, 115, 116, 117, 134, 142, 170, 214–6, 228, 240–1, 242, 254–65, 268–74, 283, 324, 364–5, 372, 441, 443, 472, 473–81, 493, 494–6, 511–12, 519–20, 526–7, 529, 530–2, 538–9, 562, 564–6, 571, 583, 598–600, 601–2, 610, 620, 623, 643–4, 645–6, 653–4, 664–5, 672, 678, 680, 692–3
    absolute 497–8, 540–1, 647–8
ethyl bromoacetate 10
ethyl chloroacetate 672
ethyl chloroformate 528–9, 672
ethyl cyanoacetate 300–1
ethyl 1,3-dithiane-2-carboxylate 574–80, 577–80
ethylene 389
ethylene dichloride (1,2-dichloroethane) 259–60, 677
ethylene glycol (ethane-1,2-diol) 106, 107, 436–7, 672
ethylene glycol dimethyl ether (dimethoxyethane) 677, 680

ethylene oxide (oxirane) 324
ethyl ether 250
(S)-ethyl 3-hydroxybutanoate 498–500
ethyl 5-hydroxy-3-oxo-5,5-diphenylpentanoate 558–9
ethyl 3-oxobutanoate (ethyl acetoacetate) 436–7, 498–500, 558–9
ethyl 3-oxobutanoate ethylene ketal 523–5
ethyl phenyl ketone (propiophenone) 489–90, 555–7
ethyl phenylpropynoate (ethyl phenylpropiolate) 528–9
ethyl phenylpyruvate 574–80
eugenol 613–15

ferric chloride 170, 672
ferrocene 586–9
flavone 589, 624–7
flavonol 624
fluoroboric acid 646–9
fluorine 383
formaldehyde 10, 410, 542–4, 545–6, 564–6, 672
formic acid 214
2-furanaldehyde (furfural) 513–15, 659–62
furan 597–600
2-furanmethanol (furfuryl alcohol) 513–15
furfural (2-furanaldehyde) 513–15, 659–62
furfuryl alcohol (2-furanmethanol) 513–15

geraniol ((E)-3,7-dimethyl-2,6-octadien-1-ol) 458–60, 616
glycerol 106
glyme (dimethoxyethane) 677, 680
gramine (3-(N,N-dimethylaminomethyl)indole) 542–4
guajol 616

haem 637–8
haemoglobin 637–8
1-heptanol 507–10
1-heptyne 299–300
hexachlorobutadiene 284–6
hexamethylacetone (2,2,4,4-tetramethylpentan-3-one) 530–3
hexamethylphosphoramide 681–2
hexane-1,2-diol 514–15
hexane 7, 9, 10, 84, 116, 185–6, 452–3, 557, 577–80, 586–8, 594–6, 601–2, 631–3, 658–9, 671, 672, 678, 679
hexan-2-ol 444–6
1-hexene 444–6
hydrazine 10
    hydrate 489–900, 663–5, 672
hydridobis(2-methylpropyl)-aluminium (diisobutylaluminium hydride) 33, 473, 485–8
hydrobromic acid 8, 594–6, 605–7

hydrobromous acid 447
hydrochloric acid 8, 122–5, 128, 142, 170, 214, 228–9, 231, 232, 234, 239, 247, 256–8, 264–5, 268–70, 271–2, 273–4, 372–3, 441, 469, 475–7, 478, 489, 490, 507–10, 528–9, 535–6, 547–8, 553–4, 604, 605–7, 625–6, 628–9, 631–3, 650, 655–7, 672
   concentrated 170, 239, 275, 470–1, 473–5, 479–81, 514–15, 517, 520, 524–5, 526–7, 536, 540–1, 547–8, 564–6, 589–90, 598–600, 614–15, 664–5
hydrogen 8, 64, 229, 248, 251, 491–6, 558–9, 570–1, 572–4, 673, 675, 676
hydrogen bromide 444
hydrogen chloride 9, 11, 64, 102, 103, 170, 239, 245, 246, 274–5, 489, 600–2, 641
hydrogen cyanide 230, 232
hydrogen hexachloroplatinate (chloroplatinic acid) 492–3
hydrogen peroxide 8, 59, 248, 252, 456, 641, 673
hydrogen sulfide 9, 103–4, 230, 232, 233
hydroquinone 642
2-hydroxyacetophenone 589–90, 624–6
4-hydroxyacetophenone 589–90, 650
2-hydroxybenzaldehyde (salicylaldehyde) 293–4, 302, 323
4-hydroxybutanal 485–8
ortho-hydroxydibenzoylmethane 624–6
3β-hydroxy-5α,6α-epoxycholestane (cholesterol) 455–8, 491–3
2-hydroxyethyl ether (diethylene glycol) 266, 489
hydroxylamine 238
hydroxylamine hydrochloride 238, 254–5, 438–9, 519–20, 673
2-hydroxypyridine 658–9
2-hydroxytetrahydrofuran 485–8

indigo 622–4
indole 10, 542–4
indole-3-carboxaldehyde 542, 544
indoxyl 622
iodine 57, 168–9, 238, 383, 452–3, 463, 465–6, 524–5, 562, 563, 631, 673, 675
1-iodobutane 465–6
iodomethane 9, 10, 423, 630–3, 673
iron (II) ammonium sulfate 243
iron (II) hydroxide 243
iron (III) chloride 238–9, 245, 478–9
iron (II) sulfate 230–2, 430–3
*iso*amyl acetate (3-methyl-1-butyl ethanoate) 430–3, 627
*iso*amyl acetate 430–3, 627
*iso*amyl nitrite 597–600
*iso*menthone 505
*iso*phorone 363–4, 673

cis-jasmone 600

lanosterol 616
lead (II) acetate 233–4
light petroleum (petroleum ether) 7, 116, 121, 134, 139, 177, 182, 228, 249, 255–6, 256–7, 469–71, 473–9, 482–5, 524–5, 535–6, 538–9, 540–1, 558–9, 562, 567–8, 572–4, 578–80, 585, 590, 598–600, 601–2, 605–7, 614–15, 625–6, 645–6, 672, 674, 679, 682
limonene 616–18
lithium 530–2, 553–4, 673
lithium aluminium hydride (lithium tetrahydroaluminate) 8, 89, 248, 252, 434, 472, 481–5, 485, 655–7, 673
lithium diisopropylamide 555–7
lithium hydride 481
lithium tetrahydroaluminate (lithium aluminium hydride) 8, 89, 248, 252, 434, 472, 481–5, 485, 655–7, 673
lithium tri-*t*-butoxyaluminium hydride 472
lophine (2,4,5-triphenylimidazole) 642, 644–6
lycopene 359–60, 613–15

magnesium 8, 523–5, 526–7, 628–9, 630–3, 673, 680
magnesium alkoxide 680
magnesium monoperoxyphthalate 456–8
magnesium oxide 620–1
magnesium sulfate 127, 130–1, 257, 260–1, 265, 267, 410, 434, 439, 446, 452–3, 455, 457–8, 460, 462, 465–6, 476, 477, 479, 481, 483, 487, 498, 500, 502, 506, 524–5, 529, 531, 532, 538, 546, 551, 557, 559, 562, 563, 571, 574, 578, 579, 585, 590, 595, 598, 600, 602, 604, 607, 610, 614–15, 618, 629, 631, 644, 656, 664, 673, 679
maleic anhydride (butenedioic anhydride) 592–4, 594–7, 673
malonic acid (propanedioic acid) 535–6
manganese dioxide 240, 262, 510–13, 673
menthol 505–7
menthone 505–7
mercury 673
mesityl oxide (4-methylpent-3-en-2-one) 540–2
methane 385, 391
methanesulfonamide 454–5
methanethiol 104
methanol (methyl alcohol) 7, 9, 142, 164, 185, 214, 237, 248, 250, 251, 252, 254, 311, 319, 410, 452–3, 463–4, 469–70, 472, 487, 514–15, 543–4, 562, 567–8, 586–8, 614–15, 620–1, 625–6, 638–9, 653–4, 662, 673, 678, 680, 690

4-methoxyaniline 372–3
4-methoxybenzaldehyde 370–1
2-methoxyethyl ether (diglyme) 461–2, 592–4, 636–7
4-methoxymethylbenzoic acid 468–71
4-methoxyphenol 650
methyl alcohol (methanol) 7, 9, 142, 164, 185, 214, 237, 248, 250, 251, 252, 254, 311, 319, 410, 452–3, 463–4, 469–70, 472, 487, 514–15, 543–4, 562, 567–8, 586–8, 614–15, 620–1, 625–6, 638–9, 653–4, 662, 673, 678, 680, 690
methylamine 103, 319, 434–5, 673
4-methylaniline (*p*-toluidine) 246, 269, 270, 274–5
methyl benzoate 581–3
4-methylbenzoic acid (*p*-toluic acid) 468–71
2-methylbutane 319–40
3-methylbutan-1-ol (amyl alcohol) 430–3
methylbutenedioic acid 353
3-methyl-1-butyl ethanoate (isoamyl acetate) 430–3, 627
methyl chloracetate 631–3
methyl cyanide (acetonitrile) 107, 311, 631–3, 658–9, 677, 681
1-methylcycloheptanol 630–3
1-methylcycloheptene 631–3
N-methylcyclohexanecarboxamide 434–5, 484–5
2-methylcyclohexanol 501–5, 2923
2-methylcyclohexanone 501–5, 549–552, 555–7
3-methylcyclohex-2-enone 545–6, 553–4
N-methylcyclohexylmethylamine 434, 484–5
7b-methyl-7b*H*-cyclopent[*cd*]indene 417–8
α-methylenebutyrolactone 566–8
methylene chloride (dichloromethane) 58, 109, 116, 119–122, 134, 182, 196, 228, 311, 454–5, 456–8, 459–60, 473–5, 478–9, 507–10, 514–15, 562, 578–80, 586–8, 609–10, 614–15, 618, 631–3, 641, 647–8, 653–4, 658–9, 671, 677, 679
methylenecyclohexane oxide (1-oxaspiro[2.5]octane) 571–4
3-methylheptanoic acid 526–7
3-methylheptan-3-ol 627–9
4-methylheptan-3-one 627–9
methyl-lithium 549
N-methylmorpholine-*N*-oxide 450
methyl 3-nitrobenzoate 582–3
methyl 9-oxodec-2-enoate 630–3
4-methylpent-3-en-2-one (mesityl oxide) 540–2
2-methyl-2-propanol (*t*-butyl alcohol) 678, 680
4-(1-methylpropyl)phenol 338–9
methylsilicone 194

methyl (triphenylphorphoranylidene) acetate 630–3
myrtenol 342–4

naphthalene 242
2-naphthylamine 10
1-naphthyl isocyanate 255–6
nickel 491
ninhydrin 170
nitric acid 8, 22, 230–3, 439, 674
  concentrated 248, 252, 581–3
  fuming 264, 643–4
3-nitroacetophenone 479–81
2-nitroaniline 273
2-nitrobenzaldehyde 622–3
nitrobenzene 9
nitrogen 229–234, 389, 391
  gas 62, 64, 82–3, 95, 105, 461–2, 463, 495, 573–4, 578, 586–8, 597, 602
  liquid 41, 43–5, 107
1-nitropentane 319–21
3-nitrophenol 650
4-nitrophenol 371–2
1-(3-nitrophenyl)ethanol 480–1
2-[(4-nitrophenyl)methyl]pyridine 642–4
6-nitrosaccharin 633–5
4-nitrotoluene 634–5
4-nitrotoluene-2-sulfonyl chloride 634–5
nitrous acid 247

octan-1-ol 461–2
2-octanone 392–3
1-octene 461–2
n-octyl phthalate 379
orthophosphoric acid 583
osmium tetroxide 450–1, 453–5
7-oxabicyclo[4.1.0]heptane 447
7-oxabicyclo[2.2.1]hept-5-en-4-one 410
oxalyl chloride 9, 501, 640–1
1-oxaspiro[2.5]octane (methylenecyclohexane oxide) 571–4
oxime 254–5, 689
oxirane (ethylene oxide) 324
7-oxo-octanal 631–3
7-oxo-octanoic acid 547–8
oxygen 229
  gas 64, 82–3, 561
  liquid 41, 43–5
ozone 8, 57, 248

palladium 491
palladium chloride 170
paraformaldehyde 545–6, 567–8
pentane 121–2, 134, 164, 550–2, 556–7, 678, 679
2,4-pentanedione 392
1-pentene 444
peracetic acid 252, 456
perchloric acid 550–2, 674
perfluorokerosene 382
perylene 641

petroleum ether (light petroleum) 7, 116, 121, 134, 139, 177, 182, 228, 249, 255–6, 256–7, 469–71, 473–9, 482–5, 524–5, 535–6, 538–9, 540–1, 558–9, 562, 567–8, 572–4, 578–80, 585, 590, 598–600, 601–2, 605–7, 614–15, 625–6, 645–6, 672, 674, 679, 682
phenanthrene 242
phenol 9, 371, 605–7, 650–2, 674
phenyl acetate 589–90
phenylacetic acid 10
phenylacetylene 528–9
N-phenylethanamide (acetanilide) 296–8, 440–3
1-phenylethanol 654–7
2-phenylethanol 348
phenylhydrazine 9, 10
phenyl isocyanate 248, 255
phenylmagnesium bromide 523–5
E-3-phenylpropenal (cinnamaldehyde) 570–1
E-3-phenyl-2-propenal (cinnamyl aldehyde) 510–13
E-3-phenylpropenoic acid (cinnamic acid) 535–7
E-3-phenyl-2-propenol (cinnamyl alcohol) 510–13
phosphoric acid 8
phosphorus 229–33, 383
phosphorus oxychloride (phosphoryl chloride) 542–4, 674
phosphorus pentachloride 274–5
phosphorus pentoxide 141–2, 508, 592–3, 681
phosphoryl chloride (phosphorus oxychloride) 542–4, 674
phthalic anhydride 674
phthalimide 516–18
phthalonitrile 636–7
picric acid (2,4,6-trinitrophenol) 8, 244, 247, 260, 263, 274, 674
pinacol (2,3-dimethylbutan-2,3-diol) 594–7
pinacolone (2,3-dimethylbutane-2-one) 594–7
α-pinene 616
β-pinene 462–4
piperidine 535–6, 545–6, 674
platinum 491
platinum (IV) chloride 57
platinum (IV) oxide monohydrate 491–3
polyethylene glycol 27–8, 106
polyethyleneglycol adipate 194
polyphosphoric acid 519–20
potassium 8, 674
potassium bisulfate 631–3
potassium bromide 262, 286–7, 297
potassium t-butoxide 489, 603
potassium carbonate 127, 436–7, 452–3, 478–9, 484–5, 535–6, 562, 605, 681
potassium cyanide 9
potassium ferricyanide 454–5, 645–6
potassium hydroxide

solid 141–2, 265–6, 469–70, 489–90, 526–7, 540–1, 624–6, 645–6, 674, 680, 681
solution 9, 238, 239, 243, 454–5, 468, 547–8, 605–7
potassium iodide 57, 238, 242, 263, 680
potassium permanganate 8, 240–1, 244, 261–2, 450–1, 511, 655–7, 674
progesterone 617
propanal (propionaldehyde) 628–9
propanamide 393
propanedioic acid (malonic acid) 535–6
propanoic acid 638–9
propanoic anhydride 646–9
1-propanol (n-propyl alcohol) 253, 678, 680
2-propanol 570, 653–4, 680
2-(prop-2-enyl)-3-methylcyclohexanone 553–4
2-propenyloxy-benzene (allyl phenyl ether) 605–9
propionaldehyde (propanal) 628–9
propiophenone (ethyl phenyl ketone) 489–90, 555–7
n-propyl alcohol (1-propanol) 253, 678, 680
n-propylbenzene 489–90
propyne 324
pyridine 10, 197, 228, 246, 256–7, 273–4, 311, 349, 507–10, 535–6, 624–6, 647–8, 674, 678, 681
pyridinium chlorochromate 507–10
pyridinium dichromate 507
2-pyridone 658–9
pyrrole 638–9
pyrrolidine 9, 547–8, 551–2, 674
pyrrolidine enamine 550–2
1-pyrrolidinocyclohexene 547–8

rhodium 491
rhodium (III) chloride trihydrate 494–6
rhodopsin 360
rotundifolene 370
ruthenium 491

saccharin 633–4
salicylaldehyde (2-hydroxy-benzaldehyde) 293–4, 302, 323
semicarbazide 248
semicarbazide hydrochloride 10, 251, 661–2, 674
silica
  gel 163, 508–10, 524–5, 567–8, 586–8, 614–15, 674
  powder 162, 177–9, 181–2, 184, 186–7, 249, 495–6, 631
silicon 383
silicone oil 106, 194
silver acetate 452–3
silver (I) carbonate 513–5
silver nitrate 230–2, 238, 242–3, 513–14, 674
sodium 8, 105, 230–3, 410, 497–8, 528–9, 530–2, 540–1, 675, 680

sodium acetate 251, 254–5, 271–2, 519–20
sodium alizarin sulfonate 232
sodium bicarbonate 6, 122–4, 228–9, 244–5, 452–3, 456–8, 506–7, 524–5, 526–7, 528–9, 551–2, 556–7, 578–80, 614, 631–3, 661–2
sodium bisulfate 6
sodium bisulfite 261–3, 465–6, 680
sodium borohydride 57, 59, 248, 249, 252, 472, 472–9, 485, 675
sodium bromide 465
sodium carbonate 6, 9, 116, 124, 233, 257–8, 258–9, 261–2, 430–3, 433–4, 502–5, 513, 514–15, 566–8, 601–2, 675
sodium chloride
  saturated solution 115, 123–8, 130, 434, 456–8, 460, 526–7, 553–4, 572–4, 614–15
  solid 107, 116, 117, 120, 499–500
sodium cyanide 9, 233
sodium cyanoborohydride 472
sodium deuteroxide 348
sodium dichromate dihydrate 501–7, 628–9
sodium dithionite (sodium hydrosulfite) 622–3
sodium ethoxide 489
sodium hydride 557–9, 570–1, 573–4, 675
sodium hydrogen carbonate 245
sodium hydrosulfite (sodium dithionite) 622–3
sodium hydroxide
  solid 257–8, 438–9, 448–50, 517, 538–9, 564–6, 675
  solution 9, 103, 116, 122–7, 228–9, 238, 243–5, 244–7, 256–7, 265–70, 272–3, 372, 436–7, 445–6, 448–50, 456–8, 459–60, 480–1, 538–9, 543–4, 545–6, 561–3, 562, 585, 589–90, 598–600, 603–4, 605–7, 614–15, 620, 623, 628–9, 643–4, 650, 655–7
sodium hypochlorite (bleach) 8, 104, 231, 609–10, 645, 675
sodium iodide 465–6, 675
sodium metabisulfite 441, 562
sodium methoxide 410
sodium nitrate 492–3
sodium nitrite 247, 675

sodium nitroferricyanide 230
sodium nitroprusside 230
sodium sulfate 127, 675
sodium sulfite 454–5, 456–8
sodium tetraborate decahydrate 650
squalane 194
stannic chloride 583
stilbene (E-diphenylethene) 561–3
trans-stilbene (trans-1,2-diphenylethene) 453–5
styphnic acid (2,4,6-trinitroresorcinol) 260
styrene (vinylbenzene) 603–5, 609–10, 675
sucrose 499–500, 633–4
sulfonamide 260–1
sulfur 229–234, 383
sulfur dioxide 103, 245, 591–4
sulfuric acid 8, 22, 103, 170, 230–2, 243–4, 261–2, 266–7, 444–6, 448–50, 454–5, 620, 675
  concentrated 141–2, 228–9, 240, 241, 248, 251, 254, 264, 267, 433–4, 501–7, 545–6, 581–3, 625–6, 628–9, 634–5, 643–4

tetrahydrofuran 7, 115, 311, 448–50, 492–3, 653–4, 675, 678, 680
  anhydrous 556–7, 558–9, 577–80
2,2,4,4-tetramethylpentan-3-one (hexamethylacetone) 530–3
tetramethylsilane 351
tetraphenylporphin 637–9
5,10,15,20-tetraphenylporphinato-copper (II) 639
theobromine 619–21
thionyl chloride 9, 10, 245, 269, 271, 434–5, 675
thiourea 10, 263
tin 264–5, 479–81
tin (II) chloride 248, 252
titanium tetraisopropoxide 458–60
toluene 7, 116, 121–2, 134, 139, 164, 169, 196, 214–6, 274–5, 311, 349, 433–4, 435–7, 480–1, 489, 511–12, 514–15, 547–8, 614–15, 631–3, 642, 645–6, 653–4, 675, 678, 679
  anhydrous 487, 495, 551–2
toluene-4-sulfonic acid 436–7, 547–8, 551–2, 675
toluene-4-sulfonyl chloride 675
p-toluene-4-sulfonyl chloride 273–4

p-toluic acid (4-methylbenzoic acid) 468–71
p-toluidine (4-methylaniline) 246, 269, 270, 274–5
2,4,6-tribromoaniline 439
tri-n-butyl acetyl citrate phthalate 379
tri-t-butylcarbinol (3-(1,1-dimethyl)ethyl-2,2,4,4-tetramethylpentan-3-ol) 529–33
tributyl phosphate 379
7-trichloromethyl-8-bromo-Δ¹-p-menthane 462–4
triethylamine 9, 549–552, 601–2, 609–10, 675
triethylene glycol 489–90
triethyl phosphite 569–71
trifluoroacetic anhydride 348–9
trimethylamine-N-oxide 461–2
trimethylchlorosilane 675
(trimethylsilyl)propionic acid 352
trimethylsulfoxonium iodide 572–4
1,3,5-trinitrobenzene 241, 260–1
2,4,6-trinitrophenol (picric acid) 8, 244, 247, 260, 263, 274, 674
2,4,6-trinitroresorcinol (styphnic acid) 260
2,4,5-triphenylimidazole (lophine) 642, 644–6
triphenylmethanol 646–9
triphenylmethyl fluoroborate 646–9
triphenylphosphine 59, 494–6, 560, 564–6, 567–8, 631–3, 676
triphenylphosphine oxide 139, 631
tropylium fluoroborate 646–9
turpentine 463

valeric acid 627
vanillin 170, 499
vinblastine 612–13
vinylbenzene (styrene) 603–5, 609–10, 675
4-vinylbenzoic acid 563–6
vinyl chloride 10

xylene 676, 678, 679
o-xylene (1,2-dimethylbenzene) 496–8

zinc 59, 230, 233, 489, 600–2, 676
zinc chloride 239, 240, 258–9
zinc sulfide 162, 168, 233
zirconium nitrate 232

General Index

Please note: page references to figures appear in *italic* type and those for tables appear in **bold** type.

Abbé refractometer 218–20
Abderhalden drying pistol 140–1
absorption spectroscopy 276–372
    see also infrared spectroscopy;
        nuclear magnetic resonance
        spectroscopy; ultraviolet
        spectroscopy
accident procedures 12–14
acetophenone azine, equilibrium
        constants 664
acetylation
    alcohols **248**, 250
    amines 271–2
    cyclohexanone 546–8
    ferrocene 586–9
    Friedel–Crafts reaction 586–9
acetylide anions 528–9
acid anhydrides
    derivatization procedures 269–71
    hydrolysis 269–70
    infrared spectroscopy 302, **685**
    qualitative analysis 245
acid chlorides, infrared spectroscopy
        302, **685**
acid dissociation constants, phenols
        649–52
acid halides
    conversion to primary amides 270–1
    derivatization procedures 269–71
    hydrolysis 269–70
acidic compounds, separation 119,
        121–7
acylation
    Friedel–Crafts reaction 583–5
acyl halides, qualitative analysis 238,
        245, 246
Adam's catalyst 491–3
addition reactions
    alkenes 443–64
    cycloadditions 600–2, 609–11
    enolate anions 533–5
    free radical 462–4
    Michael addition 540–2
adsorption, of solvents **678, 681**
adsorption chromatography 118, **161**,
        162–88

elution solvents 163–4
stationary phases 162–3
see also column chromatography; thin
        layer chromatography
air condensers 98
air drying 140
air-sensitive reagents 70, 79–91
    dispensing and transfer 83–9
    handling 486
    liquids 83–8
    reactions 89–91, 95, *96*
    solids 88–9
alcohols
    crystallization solvents **134**
    derivatization procedures 253, 255–7
    infrared spectroscopy **290**, 291–5,
        684, 686
    mass spectrometry 380, **694–6**
    oxidation 501–15
        biological 501
    proton magnetic resonance
        spectroscopy 348
    qualitative analysis 237, 239–40
    reaction thin layer chromatography
        acetylation **248**, 250
        benzoylation **248**, 250
aldehydes
    derivatization procedures 254–5
    infrared spectroscopy 293–4, 300,
        302, 304–5, **684–5**
    mass spectrometry fragmentation
        695–6
    nuclear magnetic resonance
        spectroscopy **689**
    qualitative analysis 235, 236–9, 240
    reaction thin layer chromatography
        252
    reduction to methylene 488–90
    thin layer chromatography *171*
aldol condensation 533–5, 557–9
aliphatic compounds, proton magnetic
        resonance spectroscopy 319–20
alkaline hydrolysis 244
alkanes
    mass spectrometry 374
    nuclear magnetic resonance
        spectroscopy 319, **689**
    qualitative analysis 228–9, 241–2
alkenes
    addition reactions 443–64

derivatization procedures 258–9
functional group interconversions
        443–64
hydration 444–6, 461–2
hydroboration oxidation 461–2
hydrogenation
    catalytic 54
    reaction thin layer chromatography
        248
infrared spectroscopy 305, **684, 686**
isomer differentiation 258–9
mass spectrometry 374
nuclear magnetic resonance
        spectroscopy 319, 321, 332,
        689
qualitative analysis *229*, 240–1
S-alkylated thiouronium salts
    S-benzylisothiouronium salts 268
    picrates 263, 274
    qualitative analysis 242
alkylation
    Friedel–Crafts reaction 241, 584
    reductive 553–4
alkyl nitrates, qualitative analysis 243
alkyl nitrites, qualitative analysis 243
alkynes
    catalytic hydrogenation 54
    derivatization procedures 258–60
    infrared spectroscopy 300, **684–5**
    nuclear magnetic resonance
        spectroscopy 324, **689**
    qualitative analysis *229*, 240–1
allenes
    infrared spectroscopy **290**, 300
    specific rotation 220
allyl alcohols, qualitative analysis 240
2-allylphenol, preparation and reactions
        605–9
amides
    derivatization procedures 265–7
    hydrolysis 266–7
    infrared spectroscopy **290**, 295–8,
        302, **684–5**
    mass spectrometry fragmentation
        696
    nuclear magnetic resonance
        spectroscopy 323, 348, **689**
    qualitative analysis 243–4
amines
    acetylation 271–2

amines, *continued*
  amine–picrate complex preparation
    274
  benzoylation 246, 247, 255, 272–3
  derivatization procedures 271–2
  infrared spectroscopy **290**, 295–8, **684**
  mass spectrometry 380, 385, **694, 696**
  proton magnetic resonance
    spectroscopy 323, 348
  qualitative analysis 228–9, 239, 243,
    246–7
  reduction of nitro compounds 264–5
  separation 122
  sulfonamide preparation 246, 273–4
  thin layer chromatography *171*
2-aminobenzoic acid, preparation
  516–8
ammonia, liquid 104–5, 428, 497–8,
  553–4
anilides
  preparation 270
  qualitative analysis 245
anilines
  derivatization procedures 439–43
  reaction thin layer chromatography
    252
  ultraviolet spectroscopy 371–3
antioxidants, mass spectrometry
  impurities 379
apparatus
  assembly 91–105
  see also glassware
arenes
  nuclear magnetic resonance
    spectroscopy 319, **689**
  qualitative analysis 241–2
Argyropelecus (fish), bioluminescence
  639
aromatic compounds
  halide nitration 264
  hydrocarbons
    derivatization procedures 260–2
    oxidation of side chains 261–2
  infrared spectroscopy 305, **684, 686**
  mass spectrometry 385–6
  proton nuclear magnetic resonance
    spectroscopy 322–3, 337–8
  ultraviolet spectroscopy 358, 368,
    370–1
aromatic electrophilic substitution
  580–90
artificial sweeteners 633–5
aryl compounds, proton magnetic
  resonance spectroscopy 320
aryloxyacetic acids
  preparation 257
  qualitative analysis 246
arylsulfonyl chlorides, qualitative
  analysis 241, 246–7
aryl thiols, qualitative analysis 246
Atta texana (Texas leaf cutting ant) 628
Attenburrow reagent 510–11
azeotropes 100–1, 146, 214–16
azides, infrared spectroscopy **290**, 300
azines, equilibrium constants 662–5

Baeyer test 240–1
Baker–Venkataraman rearrangement
  624
balances 70–1
basic compounds, separation 127–9
Beckmann rearrangement 518–21
Beer–Lambert law 360, 367, 656
*Beilstein (Handbuch der Organischen
  Chemie)* 414–15
Benedict's reagent 237
benzaldehyde, condensation with
  acetone 537–9
benzaldehyde azine, equilibrium
  constants 662–5
E-benzaldoxime, preparation 437–9
benzenes
  infrared spectroscopy **290**, 305
  proton nuclear magnetic resonance
    spectroscopy 322–3, 337–8
  ultraviolet spectroscopy 370–1
benzoates, qualitative analysis 245
benzoin, stereospecific reduction 477–9
benzophenone, reduction 473–5
benzoylation
  alcohols **248**, 250
  amines 246, 247, 255, 272–3
  phenols 272–3
benzyne, Diels–Alder reaction with
  furan 597–600
biphenyls, specific rotation 220
Birch reduction 497–8
boiling point 213–8, 228–9, 234
  bath temperatures in short path
    distillation 217–18
  constant boiling point mixtures 214–
    16
  determination 216–18
    microscale 216–18
  distillation 144–6
  impurity effects 213–14
  nomographs 152–3
  organic solvents **122, 677–81**
bonds
  carbon–carbon bond-forming
    reactions 522–611
  1-deuterio-1-phenylethanol 654–57
  infrared spectroscopy 278–9, 290–306
bottle carriers 70
Brady's test 237, 250, 251
Brockmann scale 163
bromides, qualitative analysis 242
bromination
  ethers 258
  phenols 260, 262–3
  unsaturated hydrocarbons 251
bromine, handling 262
4-bromoaniline, preparation 439–43
4-bromobenzophenone, preparation
  584–5
4-bromomethylbenzoic acid,
  preparation 467–71
S-bromophenacyl esters, preparation
  268–9
Brown procedure 57
Büchner funnels 77–9

Bunsen burners 6, 26, 81
burettes 55–6
burners 6, 25–7, 70
burning
  accident procedures 12
  burns 9, 13
s-butyl but-2-enoate, preparation 433–4
4-*t*-butylcyclohexanone, reduction 475–
  6
t-butyl-lithium, generation and
  estimation 529–33
s-butyl 3-methylheptanoate,
  preparation 5257
butyrolactone, reduction 485–8

caffein, isolation from tea 619–21
cancer suspect agents 9–10, 423, **670–6**
  solvents 283, 349, **677–81**
cannula technique 87
carbanions
  heteroatom-stabilized 560–80
  see also enolate ions
carbenes, generation 603–5
carbocations, preparation and
  properties 646–8
carbodiimides, infrared spectroscopy
  300
carbonyl compounds
  addition of enolate anions 533–5
  condensation 560–1
  crystallization solvents **134**
  1,3-dicarbonyl derivatives 245
  infrared spectroscopy 305
  mass spectrometry 387
  proton magnetic resonance
    spectroscopy 320, 321, 323
  qualitative analysis 235, 236–9
  reaction thin layer chromatography
    248, 251
  simple transformations 429–43
  tautomeric systems 658–9
  ultraviolet spectroscopy 358, 368–9
carbon–carbon bond-forming reactions
  522–611
  aromatic electrophilic substitution
    580–90
  enolate anions 533–59
  Grignard reagents 522–33
  heteroatom-stabilized carbanions
    560–80
  organolithium reagents 522–33
  pericyclic reactions 590–611
carboxylic acids
  conversion to primary amides 270–1
  derivatization procedures 268–9,
    269–71
  infrared spectroscopy **290**, 292–5,
    302, **684–5**
  mass spectrometry 380
  methylation **248**, 251–2
  proton magnetic resonance
    spectroscopy 323, 348
  qualitative analysis 228–9, 238, 239,
    242–5, 246
  separation 122, 124

carcinogenic reagents 9–10, 423, **670–6**
  solvents 283, 349, **677–81**
Carpino reagent 511
carvone, selective homogeneous
      reduction 494–6
catalytic hydrogenation 54–7, 428,
      490–6
  Adams' catalyst 491–3
  burettes 55–6
  carvone 494–6
  cholesterol 491–3
  low pressure apparatus *54*
  microscale 57
  reaction thin layer chromatography
      248, 250, 251
  safety procedures 55–7
  Wilkinson's catalyst 494–6
Celite® 513–5
centrifugation, crystallization 138
Chemical Abstracts 415
chemically active extraction 119, 121–9
chemiluminescence 639–41
chemoselectivity, 3-nitroacetophenone
      reduction 479–81
chlorides, qualitative analysis 242
chlorine-liberating reagents **675**
chloroform
  infrared spectroscopy 283–4
  purification 283
chlorosulfonylation, qualitative analysis
      241
cholesterol
  hydrogenation 491–3
  peracid epoxidation 455–8
chromatography
  adsorption 118, 162–88
  high performance liquid
      chromatography 188–91, 378
  purity determination 223–5
  reaction monitoring 108
  techniques **161**
  see also column chromatography; dry
      flash chromatography; flash
      chromatography; gas
      chromatography; high
      performance liquid
      chromatography; thin layer
      chromatography
citrus fruit, limonene isolation 616–9
Claisen adapters 152, *154*
Claisen rearrangement 605–9
Claisen–Schmidt reaction 537–9
clamps and holders 23–5, 92
  rotary evaporators 50
Clemmensen reduction 489
clothing
  burning 12
  laboratory safety 5
  see also protective clothing
cloves, eugenol isolation 613–4
¹³C nuclear magnetic resonance
      spectroscopy 312–13, 341–5,
      689
cocoa, theobromine isolation 619–21
co-crystallization 139

coding systems, pressurized gas
      cylinders 66
cold baths 106–7
colour
  changes during reactions 108–9
  decolourization 135
  phthalocyanines 636
  ultraviolet spectroscopy 359–60,
      372–3
  see also photochromism;
      piezochromism;
      thermochromism
column chromatography 175–88, 428
  column packing 177–8, 182–3
  flash 180–4
    dry flash 184–8, 615
  gradient elution 184–5, 187
  gravity 175–80
  methyl 9-oxodec-2-enoate 630–3
compressed gases 5, 64–8
condensation
  aldol condensation 533–5, 557–9
  base-catalyzed 545–6
  carbonyl compounds 560–1
  Claisen Schmidt reaction 537–9
conjugated systems, ultraviolet
      spectroscopy 358–60, 370–2,
      691–2
Cope rearrangement 605
copper phthalocyanine, preparation
      636–7
cork rings 23
correlation tables
  infrared spectroscopy **290–1**, 683,
      684–6
  mass spectrometry 683, **694–6**
  nuclear magnetic resonance
      spectroscopy 683, **687–90**
  ultraviolet spectroscopy 683, **691–3**
corrosive reagents 5–6, 8–9, **670–6**
  handling 70
  liquefied gases 66
  solvents **677–8, 681**
Craig tube 138
crystallization 76, 118, 131–40
  centrifugation 138
  co-crystallization 139
  cooling 135–6
  crystal drying 136
  fractional 138–9
  mother liquor 132, 136
  oiling out 134, 136
  recrystallization 132
  scratching 136
  seeding 136
  small scale 137–8
  solvents 133–4
  for X-ray crystallography 139–40
cumulenes, infrared spectroscopy
      300
cycloadditions 600–2, 609–11
E-cycloalkenes, specific rotation 220
cyclohexane-1,2-diol
  cis preparation 451–3
  trans preparation 447–50

cyclohexanes, nuclear magnetic
      resonance spectroscopy 332, **689**
cyclohexanone
  acetylation 546–8
  competitive semicarbazone
      formation 659–62
cis-cyclohex-4-ene-1,2-dicarboxylic
      acid, Diels Alder preparation
      591–4
cyclohexenes, mass spectrometry 387
cyclophanes, proton magnetic
      resonance spectroscopy 322
cyclopropanes, proton magnetic
      resonance spectroscopy 324
cyclopropenes, proton magnetic
      resonance spectroscopy 332
Cypridina (crustacean),
      bioluminescence 639

Dalton's Law 144–5
databases, chemical literature 411–12
data sheets, record keeping 406, *407*
Dean and Stark apparatus *101*, 215–16,
      433, 436
decolourization 135
degassing
  photolysis samples 62, 63
  solvents 189, 191
dehydration
  continuous removal of water 100–4,
      428
  drying agents 100, **127**
  reaction thin layer chromatography
      248, 251
density, organic solvents **122, 677–81**
derivatization
  functional group characterization
      252–75
    reaction thin layer chromatography
      248–52
  gas chromatography 196–7, 200
  mass spectrometry 380
desiccators 141–2
  see also drying
deuterated solvents **311**, 347–8, 352, **690**
1-deuterio-1-phenylethanol, kinetic
      isotope effect 654–57
dianions, aldol condensation 557–9
diaphragm regulator, pressurized gas
      cylinders 67–8
diazo compounds, infrared spectroscopy
      290, 300
1,3-dicarbonyl compound derivatives,
      qualitative analysis 245
7,7-dichlorobicyclo[3.2.0]hept-2-en-6-
      one, preparation 600–2
dichlorocarbene, generation 603–5
(2,2-dichlorocyclopropyl)benzene,
      preparation 603–5
dielectric constant, organic solvents
      122, 677–81
Diels–Alder reactions 590–600, 609–11
  retro 387
dienes
  infrared spectroscopy **686**

dienes, continued
 mass spectrometry 387
 ultraviolet spectroscopy 358, 368–9,
  691.
dihydroxylation 453–5
dimedone derivatives, qualitative
  analysis 238
1,2-dimethylbenzene, Birch reduction
  497–8
2,3-dimethyl-1,3-butadiene, preparation
  594–7
5,5-dimethylcyclohexane-1,3-dione,
  synthesis 540–2
(*E*)-3,7-dimethyl-2,6-octadien-1-ol,
  Sharpless epoxidation 458–60
Dimroth's dye 653
3,5-dinitrobenzoates
 preparation 256–8
2,4-dinitrophenylhydrazones,
  preparation 254
 reaction thin layer chromatography
  251
2-[(2,4-dinitrophenyl)methyl]pyridine,
  synthesis 642–4
cis-1,2-diols, stereospecific synthesis
  450–1
diphenylacetic acid, reduction 481–3
E,E-1,4-diphenyl-1,3-butadiene,
  preparation 568–71
E-diphenylethene, preparation 561–3
trans-1,2-diphenylethene, asymmetric
  dihydroxylation 453–5
3,5-diphenylisoxazoline, preparation
  609–11
diphenylmethanol, preparation 473–5
direct photolysis 60
dissolution 133–4
 see also solubility
dissolving metal reduction 496–500
distillation 143–59
 capillaries 152–3
 trans-cyclohexane-1,2-diol
  preparation 447–50
 2,3-dimethyl-1,3-butadiene
  preparation 594–6
 from drying agents 148
 1-heptanol oxidation 507–10
 hexan-2-ol preparation 444–6
 history 143
 insect pheromone synthesis 627–33
 1-iodobutane preparation 465–6
 3-methyl-1-butyl ethanoate
  preparation 430–3
 2-methylcyclohexanol oxidation
  501–5
 3-methylcyclohex-2-enone
  preparation 545–5
 microscale 158–9
 pear-shaped flasks 27
 record keeping **148**
 under reduced pressure 152–4, 153,
  428
  2-allylphenol preparation 605–9
  s-butyl 3-methylheptanoate
   preparation 525–7

s-butyl but-2-enoate preparation
  433–4
(2,2-dichlorocyclopropyl)benzene
  preparation 603–5
E,E-1,4-diphenyl-1,3-butadiene
  preparation 569–71
enol derivatives 549–52
ethylene ketals 436–7
ethyl phenylpropynoate
  preparation 528–9
menthol oxidation 505–7
simple 428
solvents 81–2, 147–8, 682
steam 155–8, 428, 589–90, 613–5,
  616–9
theory 144–6
see also fractional distillation; short
  path distillation
double-ended needle technique 87
drug development 612
dry flash column chromatography
  184–8, 615
drying 140–3
 air drying 140
 crystallization 136
 desiccators 141–2
 drying agents 100, **127**, 141–2, 148,
  311–12
 glassware 20–3, 81, 87–8
 pistols 140–1, 143
 solution drying 130–1
 solvents 81–2
dyes
 preparation 622–4
 solvatochromic 652–4

elatography 249
electrical heating
 baths 27–30
 mantles 6, 29, *30*
electromagnetic radiation 276–8, 357
 electromagnetic spectrum *277*, 356–7
 electronic transitions 357–9
electron impact ionization *see* mass
  spectrometry
electrophilic reactions
 addition 240
 aromatic substitution 542, 580–90
 reagents 647
electrophoresis 118
elemental composition
 qualitative analysis 229–34
 quantitative elemental microanalysis
  206
eluotropic series 163–4
emulsions, product isolation 113, 115–6
enamines 546–52
enantiomers 220–3
enolate anions
 additions to carbonyl compounds
  533–5
 carbon–carbon bond-forming
  reactions 533–59
 lithium diisopropylamide as base
  555–7

enolic compounds
 derivative preparation 549–52
 nuclear magnetic resonance
  spectroscopy 549–52, 555–7
 qualitative analysis 228, 238
enones, reductive alkylation 553–4
environment
 hazardous waste disposal 10–11,
  179–80, 184, 187
epoxidation
 peracid 455–8
 Sharpless 453–5, 458–60
equilibrium constant
 azines 662–5
 nuclear magnetic resonance
  spectroscopy 662–5
esterification 430–4
 reaction thin layer chromatography
  249
esters
 derivatization procedures 265–6
 infrared spectroscopy **290**, 302, **685–6**
 mass spectrometry 387, **694–6**
 nuclear magnetic resonance
  spectroscopy **689**
 preparation 430–4
 qualitative analysis 238–9, 245
 reaction thin layer chromatography
  252
 saponification 265–6
ethanol-based thermometers 108
ethers
 crystallization solvents **134**
 derivatization procedures 257–8
 infrared spectroscopy **290, 686**
 mass spectrometry fragmentation
  694, 696
 qualitative analysis 237, 239–40
ethyl 3-oxobutanoate, reduction 498–
  500
ethyl phenylpropynoate, preparation
  528–9
ethyl phenylpyruvate, synthesis 574–9
eugenol, isolation 613–6
eutectic mixtures 206–7
evaporation, rotary evaporators 49–54
exothermic reactions
 chemiluminescence 639
 dimerization **671**
 temperature control 96, 105, 106
experiments
 illustrating particular techniques
  428
 listed 424–6
 scale 70
 sequence 427
explosion risks 24
 chemiluminescence 639
 ozonolysis 58–9
 polynitrated aromatic compounds
  264
 pressurized gas cylinders 64
 reagents 5–6, 252, 261, **671–5**,
  697–80
extraction *see* solvent extraction

eyes
  chemical hazards 13
  protection 4–5, 61–3

Fehling's reagent 237
ferrocene, Friedel–Crafts acetylation
  586–9
Fetizon's reagent 513–5
filtration 74–9
  column *80*
  crystallization 135
  gel 118
Finkelstein reaction 465–6
fire extinguishers 12
fire hazards 5–6
  accident procedures 12
first aid, hazardous chemicals **669–76**
Fischer–Johns apparatus 212
flame ionization detectors 195–6
flammable reagents 5–6, 7–8, **670–6**
  handling 70
  pyrophoric 80, **671**
  solvents 5–6, 7–8, 25–6, **122**, 364,
    677–81
  unknown compounds 205, 227
flash column chromatography 180–4
flashpoint, organic solvents **677–81**
flavone, synthesis 624–7
fluorescence 640–1
formamides, qualitative analysis 247
formula indexes 416–17
Fourier transform spectroscopy
  infrared 280
  nuclear magnetic resonance 341–2,
    352–5
fractional distillation 109, 148–52, 428
  s-butyl but-2-enoate preparation
    433–4
  fractionating columns 149–51, 214
    spinning band columns 151–2
free radical reactions
  addition 462–4
  substitution 467–71
Friedel–Crafts reaction
  acetylation 586–9
  acylation 583–5
  alkylation 241, 584
Fries rearrangement, phenyl acetate
  589–90
fume hoods 6, 9–10, 70
  extraction systems 24–5
  weighing operations 71
fuming nitric acid, handling 264
functional groups
  common classes **236**
  derivative preparation 252–75
  infrared spectroscopy 279, 289–306,
    684–6
  interconversion 270–1, 429–521
    alkene reactions 443–64
    oxidation 500–15
    rearrangement 515–21
    reduction 472–500
    simple transformations 429–43
    substitution 464–71

qualitative analysis 205, 235–47
reaction thin layer chromatography
  247–52
2-furanaldehyde, competitive
  semicarbazone formation 659–
  62
2-furanmethanol, oxidation 513–5
furfural, competitive semicarbazone
  formation 659–62
fusion
  Lassaigne fusion technique 230–3
  Middleton's method 230, 233

gas ballasting 46
gas bubblers 82–3, 95, *96*
gas chromatography **161**, 191–203, 428
  4-*t*-butylcyclohexanols 475–7
  co-injection 202
  columns 192–5, 225
  derivatization 196–7
  1,2-dimethyl-1,4-cyclohexadiene
    497–8
  flame ionization detectors 195–6
  insect pheromones 627–9
  limonene 616–9
  and mass spectrometry 191–203, 377–
    8, 380
  microscale distillation 159
  ovens 195
  purity determination 223–5
  retention time 192
  stationary phase 193–4
  temperature programming 192–3,
    224
  trace interpretation 199–202
gases
  addition to reaction mixture 102–4
  compressed 5, 64–8
  measurement 102–3
  scrubbing 103–4
gel filtration 118
gel permeation chromatography **161**
glassware 5, 15–23
  assembly 91–105
  cleaning and drying 20–3, 81, 87–8
  cracks 5, 20, 152
  greasing 16–17, 111
  ground glass joint equipment 16–20
  microscale equipment 17, 19–20, 24,
    32–3
  'O' ring compression seals 17
  separatory funnels 109–16
  stopcocks 17, 42–4, 45–6, 111–14
  tar deposits 22
  tubes for nuclear magnetic resonance
    spectroscopy *311–13*
gloves 6, 8, 45, 61, 81
gravity column chromatography
  175–80
  solvent systems 177
  wet packing 177–8
gravity filtration 74, 75–6
Grignard reagents
  carbon–carbon bond-forming
    reactions 522–33, 575–6

insect pheromone synthesis 628, 629
Guggenheim method 656–7

halides
  acid halides 269–71
  acyl halides 238, 245, 246
  crystallization solvents **134**
  derivatization procedures 260, 263–4
  mass spectrometry fragmentation
    694
  nitration 264
  qualitative analysis 230–4, 241–3
  quaternary ammonium halides 246
haloalkanes, qualitative analysis *229*
halogens, qualitative analysis 230–4,
  241–3, 246
Hammett plots 650–2
Handbuch der Organischen Chemie
  (Beilstein) 414–15
handling of hazardous chemicals 5–6,
  69–91, 669–76
hardware 23–4
harmful reagents 9, **671–6**
hazardous chemicals
  accident procedures 12–14
  disposal 10–11, 179–80, 184, 187
  first aid 13, **669–76**
  handling 5–6, 69–91, 423, **669–76**
  measuring 70–4
  properties **669–76**
  solvents **677–81**
  transferring 70–4
  unknown compounds 205, 227
  warnings 6–10, 69–70, **669–76**
heating 25–33, 95–100
  addition of reagents 98–100
  baths 27–9, 105–6
    fluids **106**
  hotplates 6, 29–30
  under inert atmosphere 100
  mantles 6, 29, *30*
  microscale reactions 32–3
  qualitative analysis 227
  refluxing 96–101, 105
  stirred reactions 98–100
helicenes, specific rotation 220
1-heptanol, oxidation 507–10
heteroatom-stabilized carbanions,
  carbon–carbon bond-forming
    reactions 560–80
hexane-1,6-diol, oxidation 513–5
hexan-2-ol, preparation 444–6
Hickman still 158, *159*
high performance liquid
  chromatography 188–91
  and mass spectrometry 190, 378
high voltage apparatus, ozonolysis
  57–8
Hinsberg's method 246, 273–4
Hirsch funnels 77–9
Hofmann rearrangement 516–8
hoods see fume hoods
Hooke's law 278
hot-air guns 30, 32
hot filtration 75, 76–7

hotplate 6
  stirrer 29–30, *31*, 92
Huang–Minlon modification 489–91
hydration, alkenes 444–6, 461–2
hydrazones, qualitative analysis 235,
  236–9
hydride transfer reagents, reduction
  472–88
hydroboration–oxidation 461–2
hydrocarbons
  crystallization solvents **134**
hydrogenation
  catalytic 54–7, 248, 250–1, 428, 490–6,
    491–6
  reaction thin layer chromatography
    alkenes **248**
    phenols **248**
hydrogen bonding
  infrared spectroscopy **290**, 292–5, 302
  proton nuclear magnetic resonance
    spectroscopy 322–3
hydrogen-evolving reagents **675–6**
hydrolysis
  acid anhydrides 269–70
  acid chlorides 269–70
  alkaline 244
  amides 266–7
  nitriles 267
hydroxamic acids, qualitative analysis
  238–9
2-hydroxyacetophenone, preparation
  589–90
hydroxylamines, qualitative analysis
  243
hygroscopic reagents **672–5**
  solvents **681**

ice–salt mixtures **107**
impurities
  boiling point 213–14
  crystallization 132, 135
  gas chromatography 200–1
  mass spectrometry 378–9, **696**
  nuclear magnetic resonance
    spectroscopy 324–5
  polymers 325
  ultraviolet spectroscopy 364–6
  see also purification
incandescence 640
indigo, preparation and use 622–4
indole, reactions 542–4
inert atmospheres
  apparatus drying 81
  balloons 83, *84*, 89, *90*, 95
  microscale reactions 89, *90*, 95
  reactions 89–91, 95, 100, 428
    alkene hydration 461–2
    t-butyl-lithium preparation
      529–33
    butyrolactone reduction 485–8
    cyclopentadiene cycloaddition
      600–2
    ethyl phenylpyruvate synthesis
      574–80
    ferrocene acetylation 586–9

lithium diisopropylamide as base
  555–7
  ylid preparation and isolation 566–
    8, 571–4
reagent transfer 84–5, 88–9
refluxing 97–8
sources 82–3
infrared spectra
  2-allylphenol 608
  benzyne furan rearrangement
    product 599
  butanal *304*
  butenal *304*
  chloroform *283*
  2-chlorophenol *294*
  cyclohexanecarboxylic acid *295*
  cyclohexanone *303*
  cyclohexylamine *296*
  cyclopentanone *303*
  7,8-dihydrocarvone 494–6
  1,5-diphenyl-(*E,E*)-1,4-pentadien-3-
    one 537–9
  ethyl cyanoacetate *301*
  flavone 624–7, *626*
  1-heptyne *299*
  hexachlorobutadiene *286*
  2-hydroxypyridine 658–9
  2-methylcyclohexanol *292*, 501–5
  2-methylcyclohexanone 501–5
  Nujol® *285*
  E-4-phenylbut-3-en-2-one 537–9
  N-phenylethanamide *297–8*
  salicylaldehyde *294*
infrared spectroscopy 234, 244,
  276–306, 428
  correlation tables 289–291, 683,
    684–6
  fingerprint region 289–91, 305–6
  Fourier transform spectroscopy 280
  hydrogen bonds **290**, 292–5, 302
  record keeping 403
  sample preparation 280–7
    hydraulic press and die *287*
    Nujol® mulls 284–6, 288
    neat liquids 280–2, 288
    potassium bromide disks 286–7,
      288
    sodium chloride plates and cells
      280–5
    solutions 282–4, 288
    solvents 282–3
  spectrum interpretation 288–306
  spectrometers 279–80, 287–8
  wavenumber 279
inhalation 6, 9
injection see syringe techniques
insects, pheromone syntheses 627–33
iodides, qualitative analysis 242
iodine-liberating reagents **675**
1-iodobutane, preparation 465–6
iodoform reaction 237–8, 239
iodomethane, handling 631
ion exchange chromatography **161**
ions
  acetylide anions 528–9

carbanions
  enolate anions 533–59
  heteroatom-stabilized 560–80
carbocation preparation and
  properties 646–8
dianion aldol condensation 557–9
molecular 384–95, **694–6**
irritant reagents 6, 10, **670–6**
  gases 103
  respiratory system 9
  solvents **677–8, 681**
Isatis tinctoria (woad plant) 622
isocyanates, infrared spectroscopy **290**,
  300
isolation, reaction products 109–18
isotopes
  1-deuterio-1-phenylethanol 654–57
  mass spectrometry 383–4

journals, primary literature **413**

Karplus Conroy curve 331–2
ketals, mass spectrometry
  fragmentation **694**
  protecting group for ketones 436–7
ketenes, infrared spectroscopy 300
ketones
  derivatization procedures 254–5
  infrared spectroscopy 302, **685**
  mass spectrometry 387, **695–6**
  nuclear magnetic resonance
    spectroscopy **689**
  protection as ethylene ketals
    436–7
  qualitative analysis 235, 236–9
  reaction thin layer chromatography
    252
  reduction to methylene 488–90
  thin layer chromatography 171
  ultraviolet spectroscopy 369–70,
    692–3
kinetics
  competitive semicarbazone
    formation 659–62
  1-deuterio-1-phenylethanol isotope
    effects 654–57
Knoevenagel reaction 535
Kofler blocks 212
Kugelrohr distillation 154, 158
Kyrides seal 34, *35*

labelling 204
laboratory equipment 5, 15–68
laboratory notebooks 398–408
  data sheets 406, *407*
  microanalytical data 404–5
  references 406, 408
  spectroscopic data 400–5
  style and layout 398–402
  yield calculation 405–6
lachrymatory reagents 10, 255, 272,
  670–6
  solvents **677–8, 681**
lactams, infrared spectroscopy **685**
lactones, infrared spectroscopy **685**

Lampyridae (firefly), bioluminescence 639
Lassaigne fusion technique 230–3
leaks, pressurized gas cylinders 68
limonene, isolation and characterization 616–9
Lindlar catalyzed reduction 54
liquefied gases
  oil immersion rotary vacuum pumps
    nitrogen 41–2, 43–4, 45
    oxygen 41–2, 43–4
  pressurized gas cylinders 66–7
liquid ammonia reactions 104–5, 428, 497–8, 553–4
liquid chromatography, high performance 188–91, 378
liquid–liquid extraction *see* solvent extraction
liquids
  measurement and transfer 72–4
  product isolation 109
  volume 72–3
literature 411–18
  compound searching 416–18
  databases 411–12
  major reference works 413–16
  primary 412, **413**
  review 412, **414**
  see also references
lithium, handling 530
lithium diisopropylamide, enolate formation 555–7
lophine, preparation 644
low temperature reactions 428, 485–8, 529–33, 555–7, 574–80
Lucas' test 239–40
lycopene, isolation 613–6

McLafferty rearrangement 387
McLeod gauge 42, 48
macrocyclic compounds, preparation 636–9
magnetic stirring 33–4, 92–4
  hotplates 29–30, *31*, 92, 98
  stirrer bars 33–4, 94, 153
manganese dioxide (active), preparation 510–13
Mannich reaction 542–4
manometers, for use with
  oil immersion rotary vacuum pumps 42, 45, 46, 48
  water aspirators 46–7
mantle, heating 6, 29, *30*
mass spectra
  benzoic acid *382–3*
  benzyl acetate 394
  clove oil *616*
  cyclohexylamine *386*
  1,4-dibromobenzene 394–5
  1,3-dichloro-5-nitrobenzene 394–5
  flavone *627*
  limonene *619*
  2-octanone 392–3
  2,4-pentanedione 392
  propanamide 393

mass spectrometry 276–8, 373–96
  bar graphs 382
  calibration 382
  chemical ionization 385
  correlation tables 683, **694–6**
  derivatizing procedures 380
  electron impact ionization 385
  fragmentation pathways 386–8, **694–6**
    McLafferty rearrangement 387
    metastable peaks 388, *390*
    retro-Diels–Alder reaction 387
    Stephenson–Audier rule 388
  and gas chromatography 191–203, 377–8, 380
  and high performance liquid chromatography 190, 378
  high resolution 389
  intermolecular self-protonation 385–6
  molecular ions 384–95, **694–6**
  nitrogen rule 385
  photographic charts 381, 388
  record keeping 404
  relative abundance 376
  sample preparation 378–80
    impurities 378–9
    sample submission 379–80
  spectrum interpretation 381–95, 390–5
    flow diagram *391*
  spectrometers 374–8, 380–1
    double focusing 376–7
    gas chromatography mass spectrometers 377–8, 380
    single focusing 375–6
  tabular data 382
mechanical stirring 34–6, 92–3
  Kyrides seals 34, *35*
medical assistance, accident procedures 12–13
medium pressure chromatography 180–4
melting point 206–13, 228–9
  calibration 213
  capillary tube method 208–11
  functional group characterization 234, 235, 246, 252–3, 259
  heated block method 211–13
  mixed melting point 208
  organic solvents **677–81**
  range 207–8, 210
menthol, oxidation 505–7
mercury arc lamps 60, 62–3
mercury vapour diffusion pumps 37
metal stands and rings 23–5
4-methoxymethylbenzoic acid, preparation 467–71
methylation, carboxylic acids, reaction thin layer chromatography **248**, 251–2
methyl benzoate, nitration 581–3
3-methyl-1-butyl ethanoate, preparation 430–4
1-methylcycloheptene, ozonolysis 632

N-methylcyclohexanecarboxamide
  preparation 434–5
  reduction 484–5
2-methylcyclohexanol, oxidation 501–5
3-methylcyclohex-2-enone, preparation 545–6
methylenecyclohexane oxide, preparation 571–7
4-methylheptan-3-ol, synthesis 627–9
4-methylheptan-3-one, synthesis 627–9
methyl 9-oxodec-2-enoate, synthesis 630–3
Michael addition 540–2
Michaelis–Arbusov reaction 568–71
microanalysis 206
  record keeping 404–5
microburner 26
micro-pipette 165–6
microscale procedures 17, 19–20, 24
  E-benzaldoxime preparation 437–9
  benzophenone reduction 473–5
  boiling point determination 216–17
  4-bromoaniline preparation 439–43
  4-bromomethylbenzoic acid preparation 470–1
  4-*t*-butylcyclohexanone reduction 476–7
  catalytic hydrogenation 57
  crystallization 137–8
  cis-cyclohex-4-ene-1,2-dicarboxylic acid Diels–Alder preparation 593–4
  3,5-diphenylisoxazoline preparation 609–11
  distillation 158–9
  drying pistols 143
  functional group characterization 247–52
  heating 32–3
  1-heptanol oxidation 509–10
  inert atmospheres 89, *90*, 95
  in liquid ammonia 105
  4-methoxymethylbenzoic acid preparation 470–1
  methyl benzoate nitration 582–3
  3-methyl-1-butyl ethanoate preparation 430–3
  2-methylcyclohexanol oxidation 503–5
  peracid epoxidation of cholesterol 455–8
  E-3-phenylpropenoic acid preparation 536–7
  photolysis 63
  product isolation 117–18
  rotary evaporators 53–4
  solution drying 131
  stirring 36
  structure determination 226–7
  4-vinylbenzoic acid preparation 565–6
Middleton's method 230, 233
moisture-sensitive reagents 70, 79–91, 95, **670–5**, 682
  handling 486, 570, 641

moisture-sensitive reagents, continued
  solvents 131, 148
molecular sieves **127**
molecular weight *see* mass spectrometry
mother liquor 132, 136
Murex brandaris (mollusc) 622

natural products
  colour 624
  isolation and identification 612–49
  physiologically active components
    612
  ultraviolet spectroscopy 359–60
neutral organic compounds, separation
    124, *125*
nitration
  aromatic halides 264
  methyl benzoate 581–3
  reaction thin layer chromatography
    248, 252
nitriles
  derivatization procedures 265–7
  hydrolysis 267
  infrared spectroscopy 300, **684**
  qualitative analysis 243–4
3-nitroacetophenone, reduction 479–81
nitro compounds
  derivatization procedures 264–5
  qualitative analysis 243
  reaction thin layer chromatography
    252
  reduction 264–5
4-nitrophenylhydrazones, qualitative
    analysis 238
6-nitrosaccharin, synthesis 633–5
nitrosamines, qualitative analysis 247
nitroso compounds, qualitative analysis
    243
nitrous-fume-liberating reagents **675**
nomographs 152–3
nuclear magnetic resonance spectra
  2-allyl phenol 608
  azines 662–5
  benzyl acetate *315, 317, 326*
  benzyne–furan cycloadduct
    rearrangement product 599
  Z-3-chloropropenoic acid *315*
  7,8-dihydrocarvone *494–6*
  N,N-dimethylacetamide *346*
  ethyl 3-ethoxypropanoate *340*
  2-methylbutane *320*
  E- and *Z*-methylbutenedioic acids
    353
  4-(1-methylpropyl)phenol *339*
  myrtenol *342, 344*
  2-phenylethanol *348*
  E-3-phenyl-2-propenal *512*
nuclear magnetic resonance
    spectroscopy 276–8, 306–56, 428
  ¹H nuclear magnetic resonance 311,
    314–41
  ¹³C nuclear magnetic resonance 312–
    13, 341–5, **689**
  ¹⁴N nuclear magnetic resonance 323
  acylation 348–9

chemical shift 314–25, 329, 334–5,
    342–3, **687–9**
  anisotropic effects 319, 321–2, 349
  chemical exchange 323, 345–8
  δ-scale 316–17, 319–25, 339–41,
    342–3, **687–9**
  hydrogen bonds 322–3
  manipulation 349–52
  mesomeric effects 320–1
  shielding 318–19, 321–2, 349
  shift reagents 350
  substituent effects 319–21, 324,
    337–8
correlation tables 683, **687–90**
coupling 315–16, 326–38, 339–40, **689**
  dihedral angles 331
  dipolar coupling 327
  first-order model 327–9, 334–8
  geminal coupling 331–2, **689**
  heteronuclear coupling 342
  homonuclear decoupling 333–4,
    352
  long-range coupling 332–3
  multiplets 327, 329, 334–8, 341
  scalar coupling 327
  valence angles 331–2
  vicinal coupling 331–2, **689**
  W coupling 333
difference spectroscopy 353
equilibrium constant determination
    662–5
Fourier transform spectroscopy
    341–2, 352–5
nuclear Overhauser effect 352–3
nuclear resonance 307–10, 326–7
nuclear spin 307–9, 332, 335–6
peak intensities 314–15, 325–6, 334–8
record keeping 403–4
referencing 350–2
sample preparation 310–12
  deuteration 310–11, 347–8, **690**
  drying agents 311–12
  filtration 311
  impurities 324–5
  solvents 310–13, 324–5, 349, 352
  vortex suppressor 313
spectrum interpretation 314–56,
    338–41
  spectrum editing 343–4
spectrometers *308*, 313–14, 351–2
spinning sidebands 312
stereochemistry 332, 477–9
two-dimensional 333, 354–5
nuclear Overhauser effect 352–3
nucleophilic substitution 465–71
Nujol®, infrared spectroscopy 284–6

octan-1-ol, preparation 461–2
oil baths 27–9, *31*, 208, 216
oil immersion rotary vacuum pump 37,
    40–6
  cold traps 41–2, 43–4, 45–6
  gas ballasting 46
  manometers 42, 45, 46, 48
  operation 44–6

pressure measurement 42
oiling out 134, 136
optical rotation measurement 428,
    437–9, 458–60, 494–6, 505–7
organolithium reagents, carbon–carbon
    bond-forming reactions 522–33
organomagnesium reagents *see*
    Grignard reagents
ovens
  gas chromatography 195
  vacuum ovens 140
oxidation
  alcohols 501–15
  aromatic hydrocarbon side chains
    261–2
  biological 501
  1-deuterio-1-phenylethanol 654–57
  functional group interconversions
    500–15
  hydroboration–oxidation 461–2
  organic supported reagents 513–5
  Pfitzner–Moffatt 501
  reaction thin layer chromatography
    248, 250, 252
  Swern 501
oxidizing reagents 8, 243, 252, 501,
    670–5
  'active' manganese dioxide
    preparation 510–13
oximes
  Beckmann rearrangement 518–21
  preparation 254–5
ozonolysis 57–9, 428
  intermediate ozonides 58–9
  1-methylcycloheptene 632

partition chromatography **161**
Pascal's triangle 329–30, 334
Pasteur pipette
  microscale extraction 117–18
  spectroscopy sample preparation
    281, 311–12, 366
pear essence, preparation 430–4
peracid epoxidation, cholesterol
    455–8
percolation *see* gravity column
    chromatography
pericyclic reactions 590–611
periodic table 697
peroxide forming reagents **671–2**
  solvents **677–8, 680**
peroxyoxalates, chemiluminescence
    640–1
Pfitzner–Moffatt oxidation 501
pH, reaction monitoring 109
phase diagrams
  boiling point 214–15
  distillation 145
  melting point 207–8
phase transfer catalysis, ylid generation
    561–3
  carbene generation 603–5
phenacyl esters, qualitative analysis
    245
phenolphthalein 266–70

phenols
    acid dissociation constants 649–52
    benzoylation 272–3
    bromination 260, 262–3
    derivatization procedures 253, 255–7,
        260, 262–3
    infrared spectroscopy 291–5, 305, **684**
    qualitative analysis 228–9, 238, 239,
        244, 245–6
    reaction thin layer chromatography
        hydrogenation **248**
        nitration 252
    separation 122, 124
    thin layer chromatography *171*
    ultraviolet spectroscopy 371, 649–52
phenyl acetate, Fries rearrangement
    589–90
N-phenyl amides, qualitative analysis
    245
1-deuterio-1-phenylethanol, kinetic
    isotope effect 654–57
phenylhydrazones, qualitative analysis
    238
E-3-phenylpropenoic acid, preparation
    535–7
E-3-phenyl-2-propenol, oxidation
    510–13
phenylthioureas, qualitative analysis
    247
pheromones, syntheses 627–33
photochromism 641–8
photolysis 60–4
    degassing 62, 63
    light sources 60–1
    microscale apparatus 63
phthalimide, Hofmann rearrangement
    516–8
phthalocyanines 636–7
physical characteristics, qualitative
    analysis 227–8
physical organic chemistry 649–65
physiologically active compounds 612
picrates
    amine–picrate complex preparation
        274
    qualitative analysis 247
piezochromism 641–8
pinacol–pinacolone rearrangement 594
Planck's constant 357
plants see natural products
plasticizers, mass spectrometry
    impurities 378–9, **696**
Pogonomyrmex barbatus (harvest ant)
    628
poisoning 13, 643
polarimeters 221–3
polarity
    solvents 652–4
    synthon 575–7
    umpolung 574–9
polymers, wax-like impurities 325
polynitrated aromatic compounds,
    explosion risks 264
polyols, mass spectrometry 385
porphyrins 638

pressure
    boiling point determination 213–8
    measurement in oil immersion rotary
        vacuum pumps 42
    regulation 48–9, 67–8
pressure liquid chromatography
    188–91, 378
pressurized gas cylinders 5
    contents identification 66
    diaphragm regulators 67–8
    safe handling 64–6
2-propenyloxy-benzene, Claisen
    rearrangement 605–9
propiophenone, Wolff–Kishner
    reduction 489–91
protective clothing 5
    gloves 6, 8, 45, 61, 81
    liquefied gases 66
    see also clothing; safety
proteins 637–9
proton nuclear magnetic resonance
    spectroscopy 311, 314–41
    spectrum interpretation 338–41
purification
    reaction products 118–203
    solvents **679–81**
    structure determination 228–9
    see also impurities
purity
    criteria 206
    qualitative analysis 204–26, 228–9
pyrophoric reagents 80, 491, **671**

qualitative analysis
    elemental composition 229–34
    functional group identification
        235–47
    general physical characteristics
        227–8
    purity 204–26, 228–9
    structure determination 227–47
    see also spectroscopic analysis
quantitative elemental microanalysis
    206
quaternary ammonium halides,
    qualitative analysis 246
queen bees, pheromone synthesis 630–3

racemic acid resolution 138
Raoult's law 144–5
Rayonet® photochemical reactors
    60–1
reactions 91–118
    kinetic versus thermodynamic control
        659–62
    in liquid ammonia 104–5, 497–8,
        553–4
    products
        isolation 109–18
        purification 118–203
    progress monitoring 108–9
    temperature
        control 105–8
        measurement 93–5
reaction thin layer chromatography

elatography 249
    functional group characterization
        247–52
    reactions **248**
    solvent systems 250
rearrangements
    Baker–Venkataraman 624
    Beckmann 518–21
    benzyne–furan cycloadduct 597–600
    Claisen 605–9
    Cope 605
    Fries 589–90
    functional group interconversions
        515–21
    Hofmann 516–8
    McLafferty 387
    pinacol–pinacolone 594
record keeping 397–418
    distillation **148**
    laboratory notebooks 398–408
    observations 108
    research reports 408–11
recrystallization 132
reduction
    Birch 497–8
    Clemmensen 489
    dissolving metal 496–500
    functional group interconversions
        472–500
    Huang–Minlon modification 489–91
    hydride transfer reagents 472–88
    nitro compounds 264–5
    reaction thin layer chromatography
        248, *249*, 252
    Wolff–Kishner 489–91
reductive alkylation, enones 553–4
references
    major reference works 413–16
    record keeping 406, 408
    research reports 409–11
    see also literature
refluxing 96–101, 105
refractive index 218–20
    chromatography eluants 190
    organic solvents **677–81**
Reichardt's dye 653
research reports 408–11
respirators 66
retro-Diels–Alder reaction 387
reverse phase chromatography **161**
rotary evaporator 5, 49–54
    microscale sample concentration
        53–4
    splash trap 51

safety 3–14, 422–3
    bottles 102
    dress 5
    face masks 8
    handling of chemicals 5–6, 69–91,
        669–76
    hazardous waste disposal 10–11,
        179–80, 184, 187
    procedures 4, 15
        accidents 12–14

safety, continued
hydrogenation 55–7
pressurized gas cylinders 64–8
spills 6, 8, 13, 71
rules 3–6
screens 8, 24, 45
unknown compounds 205, 227
see also protective clothing

salting out 117, 120–1
sample preparation
infrared spectroscopy 280–7
mass spectrometry 378–80
nuclear magnetic resonance
spectroscopy 310–12
ultraviolet spectroscopy 362–6
saponification, esters 265–6
scale, of experiments 70
Schotten–Baumann reaction 246, 247,
255, 272–3
Science Citation Index (SCI) 415
Scolytus multistriatus (European elm
beetle) 628
scrubbing (gases) 103–4
seals
Kyrides seals 34, *35*
'O' ring compression seals 17
rotary evaporators 50
seeding 136
selenium-containing compounds, thin
layer chromatography *171*
semicarbazones
formation 659–62
qualitative analysis 238
ultraviolet spectroscopy 659–62
sensitized photolysis 60
separatory funnel 109–16
septa 84–6, 95
Sharpless epoxidation 453–5, 458–60
short path distillation 146, 154–5, 428
boiling point determination 217–18
butyrolactone reduction 485–8
carvone reduction 494–6
cyclopentadiene cycloaddition 600–2
1,2-dimethylbenzene reduction
497–8
limonene isolation and
characterization 616–9
N-methylcyclohexanecarboxamide
reduction 484–5
methylenecyclohexane oxide
preparation 571–4
octan-1-ol preparation 461–2
2-(prop-2-enyl)-3-
methylcyclohexanone reductive
alkylation 553–4
Sharpless epoxidation 458–60
silicone-based grease impurities
glass equipment 16
mass spectrometry 379
proton nuclear magnetic resonance
spectroscopy 325
silver nitrate test for halides 242–3
silylation 196–7, 200
simple transformations 429–43

sintering point 210
skin contact
absorption of chemicals 6, 9, **681**
chemical spills 8, 13
corrosive reagents 8–9
reactions **671–4**
solid carbon dioxide
oil immersion rotary vacuum pumps
43–4, 45
ozonolysis 59
solids
extraction 129–30
measurement and transfer 70–2
product isolation 109
solid waste 10–11, 179–80
solubility
qualitative analysis 227–9, 244, 245
see also dissolution
solution drying 130–1
solvatochromic dyes 652–4
solvent extraction 109–30
acid–base–neutral 119, 121–9
aqueous–organic 119–21
continuous extraction 121
layer separation 113–17
microscale 117–8
partition coefficient 119–21
salting out 117, 120–1
solution drying 130–1
solvent choice 121, **122**
Soxhlet 129–30, 428, 613–5, 619–21
solvents
chromatography 163–4, 177, 181–2,
185–6, 189
crystallization 133–4
degassing 189, 191
distillation 81–2, 147–8, 682
drying 81–2
emulsion formation 113, 115–6
fires 12
flammability 5–6, 7–8, 25–6, 364,
677–81
handling 70
infrared spectroscopy 282–3
nuclear magnetic resonance
spectroscopy 310–13, 349
deuterated 310–11, 347–8, 352, **690**
impurities 324–5
polarity 652–4
properties **677–81**
purification 147–8, **679–81**, 682
qualitative analysis 227–8
reaction thin layer chromatography
250
refluxing 96–8, 100–1, 105
for solvent extraction 121, **122**
stills 148, *149*
thin layer chromatography 224
ultraviolet spectroscopy 363–6, 369,
652–4, **692–3**
cut-off points **364**
waste disposal 11
Soxhlet extractor 129–30, 428, 613–5,
619–21
spatulas 24

specific rotation 220–3
spectrometers 278
infrared spectroscopy 279–80, 287–8
mass spectrometry 374–8, 380–1
double focusing *376*
single focusing *375*
nuclear magnetic resonance
spectroscopy *308*, 313–14, 351–2
ultraviolet spectroscopy 361–2, 366–7
spectroscopic analysis 234, 276–396
correlation tables 683, **684–96**
record keeping 400–5
see also qualitative analysis
spills 6, 8, 13, 71
spinning band distillation 151–2, 214
spiranes, specific rotation 220
star-cracks 5, 20, 152
steam baths 6, 8, 27, *28*, 77
steam distillation 155–8, 428, 589–90,
613–5, 616–9
stench 10, 268, **674**
Stephenson–Audier rule 388
stereochemistry, nuclear magnetic
resonance spectroscopy 332,
353, 477–9
stereoelective reactions
Beckmann rearrangement 518–21
benzoin reduction 477–9
cyclohexane-1,2-diols 447–53
lithium diisopropylamide as base
555–7
stirring 33–6, 92–5
hotplates 29–30, *31*, 92, 98
under inert atmosphere 95, *96*, 100
magnetic 29–30, *31*, 33–4, 92–4
mechanical 34–6, 92–3
microscale 36
stopcocks 17
air-leak 43
isolation 44
oil immersion rotary vacuum pump
42–4, 45–6
rotary evaporator 50, 52–3
separatory funnel 111–14
structure determination
chemical methods 226–75
see also spectroscopic analysis
sublimation 159–60, 428, 597–600
substitution 464–71
aniline 439–43
aromatic electrophilic 580–90
free radical 467–71
nucleophilic 465–71
suction filtration 74–5, 77–9
sugars 633–5
sulfonamides
preparation 260–1
from amines 246, 273–4
qualitative analysis 241, 246, 247
sulfones, qualitative analysis 244
sulfonic acids
derivatization procedures 268–9,
274–5
qualitative analysis 228–9, 246
separation 122, 124

sulfonyl chlorides, derivatization procedures 274–5
sulfoxides, qualitative analysis 244
sulfur-containing compounds, thin layer chromatography *171*
sunlight 60
support stands 23–5
Sure/Seal® system 84–5
Swern oxidation 501
symbols, hazard warnings 7
synthon 575–7
syringe techniques 79–81, 83–9, 95, 428
   borane dimethylsulfide 461–2
   boron trifluoride 587–8
   t-butyl-lithium reactions 529–33, 555–9, 574–80
   diethyl tartrate 460
   diisobutylaluminium hydride 485–8
   gas chromatography 197–9
   high performance liquid chromatography 190
   infrared spectroscopy 282–4

tautomeric systems 658–9
tea, caffein isolation 619–21
Teflon® key 325
temperature
   control 105–8
      cold baths 106–7
      exothermic reactions 96, 105, 106
   low 428, 485–8, 529–33, 555–7, 574–80
   reaction 93–5
   see also heating
terpenoids 616–7
tetraphenylporphin, synthesis 637–9
theobromine, isolation from cocoa 619–21
thermochromism 641–2
thermodynamic control, competitive semicarbazone formation 659–62
thermometer, ethanol-based 108
thin layer chromatography 108, 165–75, 428
   developing tanks 166–8
   E-diphenylethene 561–3
   diphenylmethanol 473–5
   ferrocene acetylation 586–9
   functional group characterization, RTLC 247–52
   multiple elution 172–3
   oxidation reactions 513–5
   purity determination 223–5
   reaction 247–52
   retention factor 169–73, 182–3, 187
   solvent systems 224
   spotting 166
      double spotting 170–1
   staining systems 169, **170**
   streaks 173–5
   structure determination 226–7
   supports 225
   two-dimensional 171–2, *173*
   visualizing agents 168–70, 225
thioethers, qualitative analysis 244

thiols, qualitative analysis 244
thiophenols, qualitative analysis *229*
thiouronium salts, *S*-alkylated 242, 245–6, 263, 268, 274
titration, reaction monitoring 109
Tollen's test 237–8
toluidides, preparation 270
p-toluidine salts
   preparation 274–5
   qualitative analysis 246
tomatoes, lycopene isolation 613–4
toxic reagents 5–6, 9, 251–2, **670–6**
   gases 103
      liquefied 66
   handling 70, 423
   mass spectrometry samples 380
   ozonolysis 57–9
   solvents 364, **677–8, 681**
      extraction **122**
      for infrared spectroscopy 282–3
   unknown compounds 205, 227
   waste disposal 10–11, 179–80, 184, 187
transformations 429–43
tri-*t*-butylcarbinol (3-(1,1-dimethyl)ethyl-2,2,4,4-tetramethylpentan-3-ol, preparation 529–33
7-trichloromethyl-8-bromo-Δ¹-*p*-menthane, preparation 462–4
1,3,5-trinitrobenzene adduct, preparation 261
2,4,5-triphenylimidazole, preparation 644
triphenylmethyl fluoborate, preparation and properties 646–9
trolleys, for pressurized gas cylinders 65–6
tropylium fluoroborate, preparation and properties 646–9

ultraviolet detectors, chromatography 168–70, 190
ultraviolet spectra
   1-deuterio-1-phenylethanol 654–7
   7,8-dihydrocarvone 494–6
   5,5-dimethylcyclohexane-1,3-dione 540–2
   E,E-1,4-diphenyl-1,3-butadiene 569–71
   1,5-diphenyl-(*E,E*)-1,4-pentadien-3-one 537–9
   isophorone *364*, 367
   phenols 649–52, 650–1
   E-4-phenylbut-3-en-2-one 537–9
   semicarbazones 659–62
   tetraphenylporphin 647–40
   triphenylmethyl fluoroborate 646–9
   tropylium fluoroborate 646–9
ultraviolet-visible spectroscopy 276–8, 356–73, 428
   absorbance 367–73
   auxochromes 368–9, **691–2**
   bathochromic shifts 359, 369–71
   Beer–Lambert law 360

   calibration 366–7
   chromophores 359, 368–71
   correlation tables 683, **691–3**
   hypsochromic shifts 359, 372–3
   record keeping 404
   sample preparation 362–6
      cells 362
      concentration 362–3
      dilution 365–6
      impurities 364–6
      solvents 363–6
      end absorption 366
      solvent effect **693**
   solvent polarity 652–4
   spectrum interpretation 367–73
   spectrometers 361–2, 366–7
   ultraviolet–visible spectroscopy 356
   wavelengths 367–73, **691–3**
umpolung 574–9
urethanes
   preparation 255–5
   qualitative analysis 239

vacuum distillation *see* distillation, under reduced pressure
vacuum filtration 74–5, 77–9
vacuum pumps 5, 36–46
   oil immersion rotary 37, 40–6
vapour pressure 144, 155–6
Venturi effect 37
vibration frequencies 278–9, 289–306, **684–6**
Vilsmeier reaction 542–4
   Vilsmeier–Haack reaction 542–3
4-vinylbenzoic acid, preparation 563–6
vinyl compounds, proton magnetic resonance spectroscopy 320
visible spectroscopy *see* ultraviolet-visible spectroscopy
volatile reagents **673**

Wadsworth–Emmons reaction 560, 568–9
Wagner–Meerwien shifts 594
warnings
   hazardous chemicals 6–10, 69–70, **669–76**
   in research reports 410
waste disposal
   chromatography adsorbant 179–80, 184, 187
   hazardous chemicals 10–11
water
   continuous removal 100–4
      experiments 428, 433–4, 436–7, 510–13, 546–52
   reaction with hazardous chemicals **669–76, 673–5**
   see also moisture-sensitive reagents
water aspirator 36–40
   manometers 46–7
   pressure regulation 49
   rotary evaporator 50–2, 54
water bath 27
water-soluble waste 11

water traps *38*, 39–40, 78, 157
weighing 70–2
Wheland intermediate 580–1
Wilkinson's catalyst 494–6
wire gauze 26–7
Wittig reactions 560–8, 630–3
Wolff–Kishner reduction 489–91
Wood's metal baths 28–9, **106**
Woodward method 450–3
Woodward rules 368–70, **691–2**

Woodward–Fieser rules 368
Woodward–Hofmann rules 590, 600
work-up procedures 109–18

X-ray crystallography, crystal quality
  139–40

yeast, ethyl 3-oxobutanoate reduction
  498–500
yield calculation, record keeping 405–6

ylids
  definition 560
  generation under phase transfer
    conditions 561–3
  preparation and isolation 566–8,
    571–4
    stabilized ylids 566–8
  sulfur ylids 571–7

zirconium–alizarin red S paper 231, 232